JOHN DONNE

A LIFE

JOHN DONNE

A LIFE

R. C. BALD

1970

OXFORD UNIVERSITY PRESS

NEW YORK AND OXFORD

© Oxford University Press 1970
Library of Congress Catalogue Card Number: 71-83007
Printed in The United States of America

TO
THE MEMORY OF
MY MOTHER

PREFACE

THIS book, left unfinished by Professor Bald at the time of his sudden death, I have completed in fulfilment of a request made in his will. The first ten chapters, half of Chapter XI, and Chapter XIII were left in fair copy, though not finally checked for the printer; the rest were in fairly final form, with clear indications of certain rearrangements of the material and of how a few gaps were to be filled, so that I have been able to reach a final text of these chapters with the certainty (not complete in respect of a passage about the *Essayes in Divinity*, pp. 299–300) that Professor Bald's intentions have been carried out. Throughout I have left untouched all matters of interpretation and conjecture, and have been concerned only with consistency and accuracy in presentation and in matters of fact. The great bulk of the text, fortunately, I have been able to give in Professor Bald's own words. Appendices B and D have been compiled according to his plan from materials which he assembled; but I have added Appendices A and C on my own initiative; and I have also essayed an Index. References to works upon which Professor Bald left no opinion (almost all published shortly before, or since, his death) are made within square brackets; instead of distracting the reader by inserting such brackets in the body of the text, I have thought it safe to leave it to be inferred that material in the text to which the bracketed notes refer is also an addition of my own.

Professor Bald was the most generous of scholars in sharing with others the results of his researches, and much that might have appeared here for the first time has already been printed, with his permission, by other students of Donne. Conversely, he was scrupulous in acknowledging his own debts, and I have included in the notes every indication of such indebtedness that I have found among his papers.

I am grateful to Mrs. Bald for much help and kindness, and in particular for sending me her husband's materials (as he also requested in his will), which will eventually join those of his books which he bequeathed to his first university (the University of Melbourne). I appreciate also the assistance given to me by the Australian National University through the professors of English, Professors A. D. Hope and G. H. Russell, in preparing the typescript for the printer. In respect of the illustrations, I am indebted to the following: Her Majesty the Queen, for gracious permission to use a reproduction of the miniature of Donne by Isaac Oliver in the Royal Collection; the Trustees of the Marquis of Lothian, for kind permission to include a reproduction of the 'Lothian' portrait; the Very Revd. the Dean of St. Paul's Cathedral, for kind permission to include a reproduction of the 'Deanery' portrait; the Dean and Chapter of St. Paul's for kindly allowing me to use a photograph of the head of the effigy of Donne in St. Paul's Cathedral; and the Trustees of the Victoria and Albert Museum, for kind permission to use a reproduction of the portrait of Donne in the Dyce Collection.

I have been helped in various ways by others, who admired Professor Bald's contributions to the study of Donne and have offered their assistance as a tribute to his work. His own dedication stands at the beginning of this book. It is hoped that *John Donne—a Life* will be found to satisfy, in its completed form, his own high standards, and will be a worthy memorial of Professor Bald himself.

W. MILGATE

The Australian National University
Canberra, A.C.T.
Australia

CONTENTS

APPENDICES

REFERENCES AND ABBREVIATIONS

Quotations from Donne's works are taken from the following texts:

Gardner, *Divine Poems* — *John Donne—The Divine Poems*, ed. Helen Gardner. Oxford, 1952

Gardner, *Elegies etc.* — *John Donne—The Elegies and the Songs and Sonnets*, ed. Helen Gardner. Oxford, 1965

Milgate, *Satires etc.* — *John Donne—The Satires, Epigrams and Verse Letters*, ed. W. Milgate. Oxford, 1967

Grierson — *The Poems of John Donne*, ed. H. J. C. Grierson. 2 vols., Oxford, 1912

Sermons — *The Sermons of John Donne*, eds. G. R. Potter and Evelyn M. Simpson. 10 vols., University of California Press, 1953–62

Keynes, *Paradoxes and Problems* — *John Donne, Paradoxes and Problemes*, ed. G. Keynes. London, 1923

The Courtier's Library — *The Courtier's Library, or Catalogus Librorum Aulicorum . . .*, ed. Evelyn M. Simpson, with a translation by P. Simpson. London, 1930

Letters — *Letters to Severall Persons of Honour*. 1651

Tobie Mathew Collection — *A Collection of Letters, made by Sr Tobie Mathews K^t*. 1660

Biathanatos — *ΒΙΑΘΑΝΑΤΟΣ*. [1646]

Pseudo-Martyr — *Pseudo-Martyr*. 1610

Simpson, *Essays* — *Essays in Divinity*, ed. Evelyn M. Simpson. Oxford, 1952

Sparrow, *Devotions* — *Devotions upon Emergent Occasions*, ed. J. Sparrow. Cambridge, 1923

Hayward — *John Donne—Complete Poetry and Selected Prose.* London, 1929 (with later revisions)

Gosse — *The Life and Letters of John Donne*, by E. Gosse. 2 vols., London, 1899

Simpson, *Prose Works* — *A Study of the Prose Works of John Donne*, by Evelyn M. Simpson, 2nd ed., Oxford, 1948

Walton, *Lives* — Unless specific reference is given to a particular early edition, quotations are made from the reprint of the 1675 ed. of the *Lives* in the World's Classics series, Oxford, 1927

Other references:

Chamberlain, *Letters*	*The Letters of John Chamberlain*, ed. N. E. McClure. 2 vols., Philadelphia, 1939
Donne and the Drurys	*Donne and the Drurys*, by R. C. Bald. Cambridge, 1959
Jessopp	*John Donne, Sometime Dean of St. Paul's*, by A. Jessopp. London, 1897
Keynes	*A Bibliography of John Donne*, by G. Keynes. 3rd ed., Cambridge, 1958
Southwell, *Humble Supplication*	Robert Southwell, *An Humble Supplication to her Majestie*, ed. R. C. Bald. Cambridge, 1953
APC	*Acts of the Privy Council*
C.S.P. (*Dom.*), (*Col.*)	*Calendar of State Papers—Domestic Series, Colonial Series*
DNB	*Dictionary of National Biography*
ELH	*A Journal of English Literary History*
Eng. Stud.	*Englische Studien*
HLQ	*The Huntington Library Quarterly*
JEGP	*Journal of English and Germanic Philology*
MLR	*Modern Language Review*
MP	*Modern Philology*
NQ	*Notes and Queries*
OED	*Oxford English Dictionary*
P.C.C.	Prerogative Court of Canterbury
PMLA	*Publications of the Modern Language Association of America*
PQ	*Philological Quarterly*
P.R.O.	Public Record Office
RES	*Review of English Studies*
S.P.	State Papers
TLS	*Times Literary Supplement*

I

INTRODUCTION: ON WRITING THE LIFE OF DONNE

> Should I endeavour to deliver his exact character, I (who willingly would not doe any wrong) should do a four fold injury.
> 1. To his worthy memory, whose merit my pen is unable to express.
> 2. To my self, in undertaking what I am not sufficient to perform.
> 3. To the Reader, first in raising, then in frustrating his expectation.
> 4. To my deservedly honored friend Master *Isaac Walton*, by whom his life is so learnedly written.[1]

THE words are Thomas Fuller's, and they must necessarily haunt anyone who attempts to write a life of Donne. The brilliance and complexity of Donne's character, the range of his experience and of his learning, are enough to make one pause, while the grace and distinction of Walton's *Life* are such as to forewarn any who come after him that, by comparison, what they write must seem mere hack work. Nevertheless it is possible, even today, to learn more about Donne's life than Walton knew; and Donne's reputation, which has stood higher in the twentieth century than at any time since the seventeenth, has begotten a curiosity which can be satisfied only by the bringing together of every scrap of relevant information which has survived.

Donne must be the earliest major poet in English of whom an adequate biography is possible. The life of Chaucer can only be pieced together from fragmentary records. Records likewise are the basis of any account of Shakespeare's life; one letter addressed to him has survived, but none of those he wrote himself. A life of Shakespeare is usually filled out with copious descriptions of the age in which he lived and with an autobiographical reading of the works,

---

[1] T. Fuller, *History of the Worthies of England,* 1662, p. 221 *bis*.

especially of the *Sonnets*. Somewhat more is known of the lives of Spenser and Dryden, yet there are serious gaps in our knowledge of both. Some remnants of the private correspondence of both men have survived, but it is so fragmentary as to be relatively unilluminating. Milton's state papers are available in some bulk, and a number of other Latin letters, but of intimate communications in his native tongue to his friends there is a mere handful. After the year 1700 the bulk of such biographical materials increases enormously; the letters of Addison, Swift, Pope, and Dr. Johnson have survived in quantity to supplement their published works, not merely by telling us what passed through their minds in their less formal moments, but also by affording a guide to their daily activities and by illuminating their relations with many of their friends.

The Renaissance was prolific in guides to letter-writing, and gradually acquired the habit of reading letters in print. It was, of course, already familiar with the letters of Cicero, Seneca, and Pliny and admired them, but Donne himself, in a letter which is itself virtually an essay on letter-writing, asserts that 'The Italians . . . abound so much in this kinde of expressing, that *Michel Montaig[n]e* saies, he hath seen, (as I remember) 400 volumes of Italian Letters'.[1] Donne's memory was sadly at fault as to the number of volumes Montaigne claimed to have seen; his remark, however, draws attention to a type of literature that was becoming increasingly popular abroad, though as yet it had no representatives in English. The first English work of this kind was probably Joseph Hall's *Epistles*, which appeared between 1608 and 1611; the best known such collection in the first half of the seventeenth century was James Howell's *Epistolae Ho-Elianae*, of which the first edition appeared in 1645. Donne himself had evidently during his lifetime earned a reputation as a letter-writer, and the early editions of his *Poems* from the first contained a number of letters: eleven in 1633 and fifteen in the subsequent editions. In 1651 John Donne the younger published his father's *Letters to Severall Persons of Honour*; private letters were by now sufficiently esteemed to justify such a collection.

---

[1] *Letters*, p. 106. What Montaigne actually said was, 'The Italians are great Printers of Epistles, whereof I thinke I have a hundred severall Volumes' (I. xxxix, trans. Florio).

Then a decade later, when he was bringing out the collection of letters made by Sir Toby Mathew, he added at the end whatever of his father's correspondence had been left over from the earlier volume or had come to hand since. Thus over 150 of Donne's letters were printed within thirty years of his death, in all about three times as many as have come to light in the years since then. The only early seventeenth-century figure of literary distinction from whom more letters have survived is Frància Bacon, and it is undoubtedly on the strength of his many official letters and state papers that his total is higher.

The younger Donne has often been adversely criticized, but there is little doubt that his obstinate determination to make all he could out of the manuscripts of his father which had fallen into his hands resulted in the preservation of a mass of materials which would probably have otherwise been lost. From so substantial a body of letters the records (which are considerable in quantity, and cannot be ignored) can be supplemented by Donne's own comment and reflection during nearly all the years of his mature life. His letters, it is true, differ strikingly in kind from those familiar to the present-day writer or reader. Donne thinks of a letter as a vehicle rather for the exchange of ideas or compliments than for news. When he sends news it is often of public and not of personal affairs, and even then the news may be confined to a postscript and not to the body of the letter. Many of the longer letters are in fact brief essays, even though they tend to be discursive in a way that the tighter structure of one of Bacon's essays, say, would not have allowed.

Still, in spite of one's gratitude to the younger Donne for having salvaged a large quantity of his father's correspondence, it is difficult in trying to use it not to feel frequent exasperation. In the *Letters to Severall Persons of Honour* there was, apparently, no proof-correction by the editor, so that there are a substantial number of misprints, especially of proper names. Secondly, there was almost no attempt to arrange the letters in any useful order. By far the largest batch consisted of letters that had been written to Sir Henry Goodyer, but it was broken up into groups so as not to swamp the volume. For the sake of variety, too, the name of the addressee was sometimes changed, and certain of the letters were said to have been sent to such men as Sir George More and Sir Thomas Lucy (to whom Donne undoubtedly wrote, but not the letters addressed to them here), and to mysterious figures like 'Sir G. F.' and 'my Lord G. H.' Addresses are omitted almost always and dates very often. In the *Collection* attributed to Sir Toby Mathew addresses and dates appear even less frequently; in accordance with a plan observed throughout the volume, many of the letters are headed by captions like 'A Letter of much kindness from one friend to another'. Towards the end of the volume they become more specific and take such forms as 'A Letter from Dr. Donne to the Lord Hay', but one is conscious that in every instance the editor could have furnished more information had he chosen to do so.

A third collection of letters, which had survived in manuscript, did not come to light until the present century; they perished by fire a few years after their discovery, though fortunately not before a transcript had been made. These letters occurred in a volume which had apparently been copied out by secretaries for Sir Henry Wotton, and there is one group of thirty-four private letters apparently addressed to Wotton, but without addresses or signatures. Indeed, it is not always certain that the whole text of a letter has been preserved. Several in the collection are unquestionably from Donne; in one of them, for instance, were enclosed some of his paradoxes, which were also copied into the manuscript. Others seem indubitably to be in his style, but others are again certainly not, and of some his authorship is doubtful.[1]

It will be seen, then, that Donne's letters present many problems. In two of the three collections it is not always certain which letters are his and which are not; the question of authorship therefore has to be settled. In the two printed collections there is frequently uncertainty about the identity of the recipient. Most important of all, the majority of the letters have to be given dates. Sometimes this is not difficult, but at other times it is almost impossible. Indeed, there are a number of letters which will never be accurately dated. Close students of Donne's life will always disagree on the

---

[1] The letters from the transcript of the lost Burley MS. are printed with comments in Simpson, *Prose Works*, pp. 300–36. For a discussion of the problem of authorship, see also I. A. Shapiro, *TLS*, 12 Sept. 1952, p. 597.

order of some of the letters, and problems of interpretation will also remain.[1]

Among Donne's correspondence the biographer is justified in including the poems in that section of the poetical works entitled (in the 1635 and later editions) 'Letters to Severall Personages'. These verse letters addressed to friends and patrons differ from normal correspondence mainly because of the metrical form into which they were cast. More than one of the poems addressed to Lady Bedford were enclosed in packets sent to Sir Henry Goodyer to be handed on to her; and there also exist poems from Wotton and Thomas Woodward addressed to Donne which show clearly that such correspondence was not one-sided. Most interesting of all, perhaps, is the manuscript in the Bodleian of some verses by Sir William Cornwallis.[2] The sheet on which the lines are written has been folded and sealed like any other letter of the period, and is addressed on the outside: 'To my ever to be respeckted freand Mr John Done Secretary to my Lorde Keeper giue these.' This, therefore, is the actual document which Donne received, presumably from Cornwallis's footman, and, whatever opinion one may hold of its literary merit, there is little doubt that this poem once formed part of a correspondence between two friends.

Though there are some of Donne's poems which thus have an unquestioned biographical significance, this is by no means true in the same sense of all of them. Too many attempts have been made to extract autobiography from the love poems—from the 'Songs and Sonets' as well as the 'Elegies'. Such a reading of the love poems constitutes the most serious flaw in the interpretation of Donne in the study by H. L'A. Fausset (1924). Gosse earlier adopted the same method, and indeed, even more than Fausset, stepped out into this quagmire with his eyes fully open; none the less, he was deceived by its seeming firmness:

The dangers of such a conjectural reconstruction of biography are

---

[1] Since Gosse's *Life and Letters of John Donne* the most valuable work that has been done on the letters will be found in: I. A. Shapiro, 'The Text of Donne's *Letters to Severall Persons*', *RES*, vii (1931), 291–301; R. E. Bennett, 'Donne's Letters from the Continent in 1611–12', *PQ*, xix (1940), 66–78, and 'Donne's *Letters to Severall Persons of Honour*', *PMLA*, lvi (1941), 120–40.

[2] MS. Tanner 306, ff. 237–8; printed in Grierson's edition of the *Poems*, ii. 171–2.

obvious, yet I believe that in few cases in literary history is that method more legitimate than here. When Donne speaks of his personal experience, there is something so convincing in his accent, poignant and rude at once, that it is impossible not to believe it the accurate record of a genuine emotional event.[1]

In taking the lyrics and love elegies to be truthful accounts of actual events in Donne's life, Gosse has ignored two considerations, the first of which has been very effectively put by W. H. Auden: 'What makes it difficult for a poet not to tell lies is that, in poetry, all facts and all beliefs cease to be true or false and become interesting possibilities.'[2] Secondly, Donne had a gift, certainly unrivalled until Browning attempted the same sort of thing in the middle of the nineteenth century, for creating a situation and presenting it vividly by means of a few deftly economical touches:

> For Godsake hold your tongue, and let me love,
>   Or chide my palsie, or my gout,
>   My five gray haires, or ruin'd fortune flout, . . .

> By our first strange and fatall interview,
> By all desires which thereof did ensue,
> By our long sterving hopes, by that remorse
> Which my words masculine perswasive force
> Begot in thee, and by the memory
> Of hurts which spies and rivalls threatned mee,
>   I calmely beg; . . .

It is so skilfully done that one accepts without any questioning the illusion of a man speaking out of authentic and literal experience. It is true that as yet no one has speculated when Donne first felt twinges of gout, or when his hair began to turn grey, but the elegy of which the second quotation gives the opening words has from the seventeenth century onwards been interpreted as an address to his wife—an interpretation which, while it has something to substantiate it, has even more to contradict it.[3] If fact and fiction

---

[1] Gosse, i. 62.   [2] *The Dyer's Hand* (London, 1963), p. 19.
[3] In the Bridgewater MS. the poem is headed 'His wife would have gone as his Page'.
    Gosse (i. 151) conjectured that 'Mrs. Donne jestingly proposed to accompany her husband in the dress of a page' when he went abroad 'in 1606'. Gosse's reviewer in

are mingled here, the fiction outweighs the fact. Nor must one neglect to mention that Donne apparently suffered in his lifetime from such misinterpretation. In a letter to his father-in-law, attempting to clear himself from the aspersions that had been laid on him after his marriage and subsequent dismissal, he wrote:

as that fault wch was layd to me of having deceivd some gentlewomen before, and that of loving a corrupt religion, are vanishd and smoakd away (as I assure myself owt of theyr weaknes they are), and that as the devyll in the article of o^r death takes the advantage of o^r weaknes and fear, to aggravate o^r sinns to o^r conscience, so some uncharitable malice hath presented my debts doble at least.[1]

One can see how such a poem as the elegy 'The Perfume' would have started rumours that it would be difficult to kill. One does not claim that Donne, before his marriage, was devoid of all sexual experience, but rather that he was not the licentious figure that some of the elegies might suggest. Besides, later in life he himself remarked to a friend: 'You know my uttermost when it was best, and even then I did best when I had least truth for my subjects.'[2] He may have been referring to the *Anniversaries* alone, but the words are capable of a wider application.

An example of Donne's tendency to give a poetic heightening to a situation can be observed even in his religious poetry. Before setting out in 1619 as a member of Viscount Doncaster's train in the embassy to Germany, Donne took solemn leave of his congregation in a sermon at Lincoln's Inn:

Remember me thus, you that stay in this Kingdome of peace, where no sword is drawn, but the sword of Justice, as I shal remember you in those Kingdomes, where ambition on one side, and a necessary

the *Athenaeum* of 11 Nov. 1899 (p. 645) successfully disposed of this conjecture but substituted another of his own: 'The date would naturally be 1600 or 1601, and the journey was probably one of those which Mr. Gosse conjectures Donne to have taken in the service of Lord Keeper Egerton.' Of such journeys, actual or intended, there is, however, no shred of evidence.

For a much more extravagant piece of biographical interpretation based on a love poem, see D. Louthan's treatment of 'A Nocturnall upon S. Lucies Day', *The Poetry of John Donne*, 1951, pp. 139–53.

[1] A. J. Kempe, *The Loseley Manuscripts*, 1835, p. 334.

[2] Letter to Sir Robert Ker with 'An Hymne to the Saints, and to Marquesse Hamylton', Grierson, i. 288.

defence from unjust persecution on the other side hath drawn many swords; and Christ Jesus remember us all in his Kingdome, to which, though we must sail through a sea, it is the sea of his blood, where no soul suffers shipwrack; though we must be blown with strange winds, with sighs and groans for our sins, yet it is the Spirit of God that blows all this wind, and shall blow away all contrary winds of diffidence or distrust in Gods mercy; where we shall be all Souldiers of one Army, the Lord of Hostes, and Children of one Quire, the God of Harmony and consent. . . .[1]

In the 'Hymne to Christ, at the Authors last going into Germany', which was written at about the same time and to give utterance to some of the same feelings, it is only natural that some of the same imagery should reappear:

> In what torne ship soever I embarke,
> That ship shall be my embleme of thy Arke;
> What sea soever swallow mee, that flood
> Shall be to mee an embleme of thy blood;
> Though thou with clouds of anger do disguise
> Thy face; yet through that maske I know those eyes,
>   Which, though they turne away sometimes,
>   They never will despise.
>
> I sacrifice this Iland unto thee,
> And all whom I lov'd there, and who lov'd mee;
> When I have put our seas twixt them and mee,
> Put thou thy sea betwixt my sinnes and thee.
>
>   .   .   .   .
>
> Churches are best for Prayer, that have least light:
> To see God only, I goe out of sight:
>   And to scape stormy dayes, I chuse
>   An Everlasting night.

Admittedly, the sermon shows Donne fulfilling a pastoral function, and the poem, on the other hand, is self-centred. Nevertheless, the imagery of sea and storm in the two extracts performs quite different functions. In the sermon the sea becomes at once 'the sea of his blood, where no soul suffers shipwrack', and the wind such a one as 'shall blow away all contrary winds of diffidence or distrust in Gods

---

[1] *Sermons*, ii, no. 11, ll. 502–14, pp. 248–9.

mercy'. In the poem this imagery is much more pervasive. The ship and the sea are real ones, which can also take on an emblematic function, but their reality is envisaged so forcefully as to leave the impression that the poet actually expects death by water. Yet, in fact, Donne, who in his youth had braved two extended naval operations against the Spaniards, had in 1619 to anticipate no more than two Channel crossings, not in a ragged fishing-boat but in the most seaworthy vessel that could be provided for a royal emissary. In other words, Donne has deliberately intensified the situation in the poem for greater effect, though it thus becomes less true in a literal and factual sense to the situation from which it sprang.

Even in the 'Divine Poems', then, one must expect a certain dramatic heightening; but are the religious poems to be treated by a biographer with as much caution as the love poems? Obviously a distinction must be made. The caveat against the misuse of the love poems is directed against the assumption that a particular poem is, in the absence of all internal or external evidence, addressed to a particular woman, or that it is the transcript of a particular experience. For instance, the elegy 'His Picture' is an exploration of the feelings of a lover about to set out on an expedition such as those of 1596 and 1597 in which Donne participated. It is more than probable that the poet had felt apprehensions such as the poem describes; but that he had given his portrait to any particular woman before leaving, or that she is to be identified with anyone of Donne's acquaintance, or even with a woman referred to in any other of his poems, is a conclusion that cannot be drawn. Again, the elegy 'The Bracelet' may or may not be based on an actual event; the assumption that it was is one that cannot be made without further evidence; we simply do not know. On the other hand, the elegy 'The Autumnall' is said to have been written to Mrs. Herbert; it is, according to Walton, 'a Character of the Beauties of her body, and mind', and was written 'at his leaving *Oxford*' after Donne's first meeting with her. This is good authority, and must be respected, though normally Donne himself would have put a check on such speculation, when he exlaimed:

> Who ever guesses, thinks, or dreames he knowes
> Who is my mistris, wither by this curse.

In any case, in all these poems the states and attitudes of mind revealed are more significant than the name of any woman, and in so far as the biographer is concerned with such states of mind they are part of his material. The interpretation of the 'Divine Poems' is on a different footing; many of them partake of the mood of the confessional; the sole relationship they envisage is with God; and thus the attitudes of mind become the sole significant factor.

The poems, then, can be used only within certain defined limits; the prose works have a more precise and more easily perceived value. They too are an index to the development of Donne's mind, but their main purpose is instruction, or edification, or persuasion, or satire. Unlike some of the writings of the Romantics—Lamb or Coleridge, for instance—they are not autobiographical in the sense that they are built largely on the author's experiences; nevertheless, there are a few—a very few—anecdotes and reminiscences in the sermons, the *Devotions*, and even in *Pseudo-Martyr*. He recalls a visit to a synagogue, or to the ancient Hôpital des Quinze-Vingts for the blind in Paris, and as he lies ill listening to the tolling of bells there comes into his mind the recollection of other bells he has heard at Antwerp and Rouen.[1] But the dates and occasions of these incidents are lacking and cannot precisely be inferred, though this is not invariably true of Donne's anecdotes. Again, he tells how there was brought to him, as dean no doubt, a child prodigy for him to wonder at:

An Artificer of this Citie brought his Childe to mee, to admire (as truly there was much reason) the capacitie, the memory, especially of the child. It was but a Girle, and not above nine yeares of age, her parents said lesse, some yeares lesse; wee could scarse propose any Verse of any Booke, or Chapter of the *Bible*, but that that childe would goe forward without Booke. I began to *Catechise* this childe; and truly, shee understood nothing of the *Trinitie*, nothing of any of those fundamentall poynts which must save us; and the wonder was doubled, how she knew so much, how so little.[2]

Such anecdotes are as authentic as anything related in the letters,

---

[1] *Sermons*, vii, no. 6, ll. 184–91, p. 169, and iii, no. 4, ll. 454–5, p. 126; Sparrow, *Devotions*, p. 92.

[2] *Sermons*, iv, no. 7, ll. 893–902, pp. 203–4.

and obviously no biographer can afford to neglect them, though it is not always easy to decide where they most appropriately belong.

Anecdotes, poems, letters—all contribute information about the facts of Donne's life and help to enrich the drab official records. But Donne was also fortunate in that the story of his life was written by Izaak Walton within a few years of his death, and was elaborated in subsequent editions through thirty-five years until it became more than twice as long as the original version. Walton's account preserves a number of facts about Donne that otherwise would certainly have been irretrievably lost, and is still a prime source for any modern life of Donne. Nevertheless, the reader, who is only too ready to be enchanted by the grace and simplicity of Walton's manner, should be aware of his limitations.

The *Life of Donne* was Walton's first published writing of any extent, and is thus the work of his prentice hand. Though it was revised and expanded during thirty-five years, its essential character remained unaltered. In spite of the fact that Walton's technique as a biographer matured with the years, and his last *Life*, that of Sanderson, shows a far greater degree of precision than his first because of his dependence on records, it seems never to have occurred to him during revision to retrace his steps and incorporate into the earlier biography facts similarly ascertainable. Walton's disregard for exact chronology can be fairly briefly illustrated (from the text of 1640):

> Immediately after his returne from Cambridge [when he received his D.D.], his wife died. . . . In this retirednesse [*later* In this time or sadnesse], he was importuned by the grave Benchers of Lincolns Inne, (once the friends of his youth) to accept of their Lecture, which (by reason of M. *Gatakers* removall) was then void; of which he accepted. . . .

In fact, Donne was made a Doctor of Divinity by the University of Cambridge towards the end of March 1615; Mrs. Donne died on 15 August 1617, and Donne had previously been appointed Reader at Lincoln's Inn on 24 October 1616.[1] Yet when Walton wrote these

---

[1] It should be added further that Thomas Gataker, who was still alive in 1640, had resigned from Lincoln's Inn as long ago as 1611, and that in the interim the post had been filled by Thomas Holloway.

words he was still living in the parish of St. Dunstan-in-the-West, close to the corner of Fleet Street and Chancery Lane. The church of the neighbouring parish of St. Clement Danes stood less than 200 yards to the west; in it was the memorial tablet giving the date of her death which Donne had caused to be fixed above his wife's grave; not merely was the inscription there for all to read, but it had also been printed in the 1633 edition of Stow's *Survey of London*. About 300 yards to the north was Lincoln's Inn, whose records contained the minute of Donne's appointment, and where there must still have been members who remembered the days of his ministry there. It is true that no record now survives of Donne's Cambridge degree,[1] yet Walton in writing the life of Sanderson was to search and use the equivalent Oxford records, and if he had made inquiries in 1639 or 1640, if not later, he might well have been able to obtain the relevant information from Cambridge. There was no need for Walton to commit such errors of chronology, but he seems to have been unconscious of their existence or of the possibility of correcting them. He seems in the main to have relied on the memory of his informants, for his information often came orally or, sometimes, in the written reminiscences of some of Donne's friends. He himself had known Donne as vicar of the parish of St. Dunstan, and he had visited him in his last illness, but his own personal recollections could not have covered more than the last six or seven years of Donne's life.

The modern concern for historical accuracy and for the scrupulous presentation of documentary evidence makes it hard to accept another of Walton's practices. In describing Donne's melancholy

---

[1] Walton makes almost as many mistakes in the passage immediately before that which has just been cited, which refers to the conferring of his Cambridge degree:

'That Summer, the same month in which he was ordained Priest, (and made the Kings Chaplaine) his Majestie (going his Progresse) was intreated to receive an entertainment in the University of Cambridge, and M. *Donne* attending his Majestie there, his Majestie was pleased to recommend him to be made Doctor in Divinity, Doctor *Harsnet* (after Archbishop of York) being then their Vice-Chancellour, who knowing him to be the Author of the *Pseudo-Martyr*, did propose it to the University, and they presently granted it, expressing a gladnesse they had an occasion to entitle and write him Theirs' (1640 text). Donne was ordained on 23 Jan. 1615; James visited Cambridge on 7 Mar., not in the course of a summer progress, as Walton states. Donne received his degree before the end of the month, but, according to Chamberlain, only after the University had received a royal mandate commanding them to confer it.

during his Mitcham years he quotes what appear to be the major portions of two letters; the first is dated 'From my hospital at *Micham*, Aug. 10' and the second 'Sept. 7'. The first is part extract and part paraphrase of a much longer letter written several years after Donne had left Mitcham, the date and address being transferred from another letter. The second is actually put together of eight excerpts from five different letters; the date 'Sept. 7' seems to have been invented to make it look as if this pastiche followed closely after the previous extract. Yet Walton had no desire to deceive; he introduces the first 'letter' with the words: 'I shall present you with an extract collected out of some few of his many Letters', and links the two with 'Thus he did bemoan himself: And thus in other letters'. He has, in fact, told his readers what he has done, though they were slow to perceive the fact.[1]

Nevertheless, Walton had access to all sorts of information denied to the modern inquirer. He had probably heard Donne himself talk of some of his earlier experiences; he knew Sir Henry Wotton, Donne's lifelong friend, and had the use of his papers; he received information about Donne's most troubled years from Bishop Morton; he was well acquainted with Henry King and Thomas Mountfort, Donne's closest associates during his later years. There is no doubt that the impression he tried to convey was as truthful as he was capable of making it. And unquestionably he has traced the main outlines of Donne's life; even if the pattern has since had to be modified here and there, the essential impression remains. Furthermore, Walton's contemporaries seem to have recognized the fundamental truth of the *Life*, which was widely praised, quoted, and summarized. John Hales of Eton declared that 'He had not seen a Life written with more advantage to the Subject, or more reputation to the Writer'.[2] Indeed, the very fact that so full and so widely admired a life was readily accessible probably prevented more than

---

[1] *Lives*, pp. 36–8. The credit for discovering what Walton has done here belongs to R. E. Bennett, 'Walton's Use of Donne's Letters', *PQ*, xvi (1937), 30–4. For a fuller discussion of these aspects of Walton's *Life*, see my article, 'Historical Doubts respecting Walton's *Life of Donne*' in *Essays in English Literature from the Renaissance to the Victorian Age presented to A. S. P. Woodhouse*, 1964, pp. 69–84.

[2] 'The Copy of a Letter writ to Mr. Izaak Walton, by Doctor King', prefixed to Walton's *Lives* (p. 15).

one other writer from making any independent attempt to collect information about Donne while it was still easy to be had.

The next account of Donne's life that is of any value appeared in the English version of Bayle's dictionary, *A General Dictionary, Historical and Critical*, which came out in ten folio volumes between 1734 and 1741. The life of Donne in volume iv was almost certainly written by Thomas Birch, whose name appears on the title-page as one of the editors of the work and who, according to the *DNB*, was the author of 'most of the English lives'. Though Birch is not a great writer (Johnson is said to have remarked of him: 'Tom Birch is as brisk as a bee in conversation; but no sooner does he take a pen in his hand than it becomes a torpedo to him, and benumbs all his faculties'), he represents the best tradition of eighteenth-century antiquarianism, and the period of Donne's life was that with which he was most familiar. Inevitably, he had to rely for much on Walton, but he is always critical of him, and corrects some of his grosser errors. He had read Donne's letters, to say nothing of *Pseudo-Martyr* and the sermons, with a historian's eye, and for reference he had works like Wood's *Athenae Oxonienses* and Le Neve's *Fasti Ecclesiasticae* which had been compiled since Walton's day. Like a true scholar, he cites his authority for every statement he makes. As a sample of his method, here is part of a footnote (side-notes omitted) on what Walton says about Donne's appointment to the vicarage of St. Dunstan-in-the-West:

Mr. Walton tells us that it fell to him IMMEDIATELY *after his admission into his Deanery . . . by the death of Dr. White*. But this is a mistake; for he was admitted into his Deanery in the latter end of 1621, and the Vicarage of St. Dunstan's was not vacant till the death of Dr. White, which happened March 1st 1623/4. Dr. Donne's first Sermon at that Church, as Vicar there, was preached there April 11th 1624, and is printed in the *second volume* of his *Sermons*.

We have moved away from the hagiography of Walton to the precision of the modern historian. If some of the nineteenth-century writers on Donne had read Birch with care, they would have been saved from more than one blunder, and Walton's limitations would have been sooner recognized.

When Walton's reputation was revived at the time of the

Romantic Revival, his work became generally admired sooner than Donne's, so that readers at this period may well have turned to the poet's writings through having been stimulated to do so by the *Life*. The *Lives* were fairly well known; several different editions were available, but the best and best known was that of Thomas Zouch, which had four editions between 1796 and 1825. Zouch adorned Walton's text with ample annotations, but his main efforts were spent not in amplifying information about the subjects of the five biographies but in identifying the other men and women whom Walton mentions as having influenced their careers. Subsequent editions of the *Lives*, down to A. H. Bullen's in 1884, were heavily indebted to Zouch.

One other edition of Walton is important. In the middle years of the nineteenth century,[1] in Henry Kent Causton's 'Contemplative Man's Library for the Thinking Few', appeared an edition of *The Life of Donne*, 'with some original notes, by An Antiquary'.[2] The 'antiquary' was a man of some talent and considerable learning. He was familiar with the letters of Donne that had been printed by A. J. Kempe in his selection from the Loseley manuscripts (published in 1835), and incorporated most of them into his volume. More important, he searched various classes of records for references to Donne; in particular, he was the first, and for a century the only, person to go to the archives of the Ironmongers' Company for information about Donne's father. All subsequent lives of Donne are under a real debt to him.

It fell to the lot of Augustus Jessopp during a long lifetime to write three different accounts of Donne. The first was published in 1855 as a preface to an edition of the *Essayes in Divinity*, and is a remarkable performance for a young curate in a country parish. Jessopp at this time hoped to bring out a complete edition of Donne's works to supplant that of Alford (1839), of which he had a low opinion, but he was probably unable to find a publisher who could

[1] The book is undated; Keynes (no. 151) gives the date as 1852, but the British Museum catalogue dates it 1865. Keynes, however, is probably right, for Jessopp acknowledges his indebtedness to the book in 1855.

[2] The antiquary was apparently Thomas Edlyne Tomlins; see Keynes, loc. cit. and *NQ*, ser. 10, vi (1906), 228 and 338. Neither the book nor the series is listed in the *English Catalogue of Books 1835–62* or *1863–71*.

be convinced that Alford had not already satisfied such demand as
might have existed. Nevertheless, despite the necessities of earning
a living and despite a wide range of other literary and historical
interests, Jessopp continued to maintain his interest in Donne and
in 1888 wrote his life for the *DNB*. This is, of course, the most
factual and most closely packed of his three accounts, and has, in
accordance with the plan of the work to which it was contributed,
a valuable list of sources appended. Finally, in 1897 Jessopp brought
out a little book on Donne in the 'Leaders of Religion' series, but
the very plan of the series demanded that the main emphasis should
be on the later years of Donne's life, and on the religious rather than
the secular writings. It was also a 'popular' book in the best sense
of the term, and not a scholarly one. At the end of the Preface there
is an apology for the absence of some of the usual scholarly adjuncts:

If no authorities are cited for the new facts that have been brought
forward, that is no fault of mine. I am told—and I suspect it is true—
that the generality of readers would rather be without them. In
literature as in the ordinary affairs of life we must be content to trust
one another. If a man tries to cheat his neighbours by imposing upon
their credulity, he will not long escape being found out. Of course, to
err is human; but, for myself, I would not, for all that this world could
give, pass into that other world—the world of spirits blest—fearing
to meet my great teacher and master and friend, Dr. John Donne, as
I should fear to meet him if consciously I had borne false witness
here—against him or for him.[1]

Jessopp did a great deal of thorough and painstaking research into
the life of Donne and its background, and he shows in all his work a
fuller sense than any previous writer of the connections between
the events of Donne's life and contemporary happenings. But the
fact that in only one of his three accounts was he allowed to cite his
authorities (and then only in an incomplete and limited fashion) has
resulted in several very positive assertions about Donne's life that
still rest on Jessopp's word alone.[2]

Since Jessopp had begun even as an undergraduate to collect

---

[1] p. x.
[2] See further Chapter IX and R. C. Bald, 'Donne's Activities', *TLS*, 13 May 1949,
p. 313.

material on Donne, it must have reached considerable proportions by the 1890s. By this time Jessopp had found that his enthusiasm for Donne was shared by Edmund Gosse, and for some years they planned a joint study of his life and work. But with the publication of his little book in 1897 Jessopp turned all his materials over to Gosse, who completed what was to have been their joint task and in 1899 brought out *The Life and Letters of John Donne* in two volumes. How much of Jessopp's work is behind the book it is impossible to tell. Gosse also had been interested in Donne for many years, and as early as 1880 had considered undertaking a life. But presumably, from what Gosse says in his preface, most of the book was put into shape only in the two or three years before publication.

Gosse had an unenviable reputation for inaccuracy, and his life of Donne is by no means free from it. A striking example occurs on p. 151 of the first volume:

> On the 16th of February 1606 licence was granted to Sir James Bourchier, Sir Alexander Morrison, Sir William Chute, and John Donne to travel for three years. Whether they were to travel separately or in a party does not appear.

The licence was issued in 1605, not 1606; Morrison was Sir Charles, not Sir Alexander, and Chute was Sir Walter, not Sir William. Reference to the document cited shows that separate permits were granted to Sir James Bourchier and Sir Charles Morrison, but that the names of Chute and Donne were to appear jointly on the same licence; Chute and Donne, therefore, were travelling together. One of Gosse's failings was that he must have placed complete trust in an amanuensis who searched lists and indexes for him, and then supplied him with transcripts of the documents thus discovered. It never occurred to him that there was any need to check such transcripts for accuracy. Thus whenever Gosse prints one of Donne's letters from a manuscript the text is peppered with errors, and every statement he makes for the first time has to be checked carefully. If *The Life and Letters of Donne* impressed contemporary reviewers (as it did) as being less faulty than most of Gosse's previous books, some of the credit must probably be given to Jessopp; nevertheless, it is far from faultless.

In spite of such criticism, Gosse's services to the reputation of
Donne were many and great; his book has plenty of redeeming
qualities. It is written with some skill, even though, by now, it is
rather old-fashioned in tone. The decision to include the letters in
full was a wise one; the attempt to arrange them chronologically
and to annotate them was not, of course, executed without flaws,
but one is constantly impressed by the learning and acumen
brought to the task. Here at last was an assemblage of all the biographical facts and materials then available, together with an interpretation of the character of the man, on a scale worthy of a
writer who was at least beginning to be recognized as one of the
really significant figures in the history of English literature.

The present century has seen an enormous growth in the reputation and influence of Donne, yet in spite of a flood of critical essays,
in spite even of two fictional treatments of his life,[1] it has been left
to the present work to extend the range, and to attempt a re-exami-
nation, of the known biographical materials. Imperfect it must be,
but in the scholarly enthusiasm for Donne of the last fifty years a
good many fresh details have come to light and have been published
here and there in the learned periodicals; these must be incorporated
in any complete account. Other facts appear here for the first time,
and it is hoped that the archival resources of the Anglo-Saxon world
will have relatively little still to yield. If any quantity of new light
is to be shed on the details of Donne's life it is most likely to come
from continental sources. Walton speaks of Donne's relations with
learned men from abroad, and it is difficult not to believe that somewhere, in more than one European library, are letters of Donne,
written in Latin or French, in which he exchanges compliments and
learned gossip with scholars and statesmen. But the clues to such
writings are still to be found, and in the meantime what follows
must suffice.

---

[1] R. Ince, *Angel from a Cloud* (London, 1939); Elizabeth G. Vining, *Take Heed of
Loving Me* (Philadelphia, 1964).

II

ANCESTRY AND PARENTAGE

DONNE's England was also Shakespeare's, but with a difference. Donne was eight years the younger, and died fifteen years later than his greater contemporary, so that he lived into the reign of Charles I and, had he had the eyes to see, might have perceived the beginnings of the break-up of the social system which must still, when Shakespeare died, have shown few, if any, signs of instability. Whereas Shakespeare was born into the house of a moderately prosperous member of a smallish country community and, after a successful career in the capital, was content to return to it to spend his last years, Donne was a Londoner born and bred. His father, though a tradesman, claimed gentle birth, and his mother came from one of the most cultured households in the kingdom. The atmosphere of the city and court was in Donne's blood, and he steadfastly refused appointments that would remove him permanently from it. By birth and economic status he also had the advantage of education at the universities and at one of the Inns of Court, privileges denied to Shakespeare. Though for many years Shakespeare's career touched the fringes of the royal court as much as Donne's, Shakespeare's profession, as he well knew, set a limit to his opportunities, and in his moments of depression he felt himself the victim of 'Fortune's dearest spite'. Fortune had debarred him from 'public honour and proud titles' and thus had become

> The guilty goddess of my harmful deeds
> That did not better for my life provide
> Than public means which public manners breeds.
> Thence comes it that my name receives a brand,
> And almost thence my nature is subdu'd
> To what it works in, like the dyer's hand.

Donne at least, by virtue of his birth and upbringing, had the entrée to the court and, though some of his tribulations were more prolonged than Shakespeare's, he ended his life not perhaps quite on terms of equality but certainly on terms of genuine friendship with, as well as acceptance by, many of the greatest in the kingdom. Whether or not Donne sacrificed himself to a snobbish ideal of gentility is arguable, yet he framed his life within the restrictions of certain standards of conduct, and because of those restrictions he may be said to have belonged to his age more completely than Shakespeare, who, however keenly he may have regretted the shackles imposed by his birth and upbringing, was freer of them.

Since Donne's ancestry and position in society were of great significance to him, and helped to frame the ideals by which he lived, they cannot be disregarded. According to Walton, he was 'masculinely and lineally descended from a very antient Family in *Wales*'. His earliest portrait, made in 1591, displays a coat of arms which he also used on one of his seals and is similar to that which appears on his monument, parted per pale with the arms of St. Paul's Cathedral. These arms, azure a wolf salient, with a crest of snakes bound in a sheaf,[1] are those of the ancient family of Dwn of Kidwelly in Carmarthenshire, which traced its descent back to 'Meirick King of Dyvet, one of the four that bare golden swords before King Arthyr at his coronation'.[2] By the opening of the fifteenth century the family had emerged into authentic history, when its head, Henry Don, cast in his lot with Owen Glendower against Henry IV. A later generation of Dons provided the House of York with active adherents during the Wars of the Roses. Two sons of Griffith Donne of Kidwelly, Henry and John, aided Sir William Herbert, whom Edward IV created Earl of Pembroke, to subdue South Wales. Both the Earl of Pembroke and Henry Donne perished in 1469 at the battle of Banbury,[3] but John Donne was knighted by

---

[1] The arms are not tinctured in the engraving (prefixed to editions of the *Poems*, 1635–54) nor, of course, in the seal or on the marble monument. In the engraving the arms also bear a label for difference, the label being the sign of the eldest son; it probably signifies no more than that Donne's younger brother Henry was alive at this date.

The number of snakes in the crest seems to have been immaterial. There are five in the armorial seal, six in the engraving, and seven in the seal of the crest alone. For the seals see MS. Add. 29,598, ff. 13 and 15, in the British Museum.

[2] 'Golden Grove Book' (P.R.O., G.D. 13), ii, D777.

[3] Sir John E. Lloyd, *History of Carmarthenshire*, i (1935), 252–60.

Edward IV after the battle of Tewkesbury, lived to make his peace with Henry VII, and died in 1503. Portraits of him and of his wife, as kneeling donors, can be seen in a famous triptych by Memling at Chatsworth. He lies buried in St. George's Chapel at Windsor, close to Edward IV, whom he had served, and to William Lord Hastings, whose daughter he had married.[1] This Sir John had two sons, Sir Edward (who died in 1551) and Sir Griffith (who died in 1544), but neither left male heirs; their estates passed to their daughters, and this branch of the family became extinct. The pedigree in the 'Golden Grove Book' shows further ramifications of the family, but seems to include only those branches of it that had retained their position among the Welsh gentry.

That Donne believed himself to be descended from the Dwns of Kidwelly is further suggested by a remark of his son. In 1660 the younger Donne edited the poems of William Herbert, third Earl of Pembroke (1580–1630), and in the dedicatory epistle he stated that he was 'obliged to that Honorable Family [the Herberts] not only by descent, but . . . by many favours now bound to that Person, who is Heir to all their Virtues as well as Fortunes'. This claim to descent from the Herberts must have been through his father and not his mother, and while it cannot be fully substantiated, it is at least partially confirmed by the close association of the Dwns with the Herberts during the Wars of the Roses, and by the fact that Jane, sister of Henry and Sir John Donne, married a William Herbert.[2]

Donne's father, however, was a citizen and ironmonger of London.

[1] *Visitation of Berkshire*, Harleian Society Publications, vol. lvi, p. 2

[2] 'Golden Grove Book', loc. cit. Gosse (i. 4–5) regards Donne's claim to such descent as 'breathing no more than a pious wish', and regards it as significant that 'he never claims relationship with his prominent contemporary, Sir Daniel Donne, the Master of Requests, nor with John Donne of St. Martins-in-the-Fields, who was Gentleman of the Privy Chamber to James I'. John Donne of St. Martins-in-the-Fields was apparently descended from John Don of Hackluit in Gloucestershire, and bore argent, four bars azure, on a bend gules three arrows argent (MS. Harl. 2288, fo. 49). Daniel Dun was a Londoner by birth, the son of Robert Dun, who died in 1553 (his will, P.C.C. 5 Tashe, was proved 17 March 1552/3); and his attempts to provide himself with a coat of arms and a pedigree suggest that he knew very little about his descent (see Joseph Foster's *Grantees of Arms*, Harleian Society, 1915, and MSS. Harl. 1541, fo. 36b, and 2288, fo. 49). The pedigree in MS. Harl. 2288 is patently inaccurate; that in Harl. 1541 is more reliable, and shows that he did not know his grandfather's name. Daniel Dun's uncertainty is in striking contrast to the poet's assumption that his claim to bear arms needed no authentication from the College of Heralds.

At least one generation of tradesmen must have separated him from the Welsh forebears who had sent a younger son to London to be apprenticed. There had been a John Don of London and Kidwelly who died in 1480; he was a prosperous mercer, and though his will shows him to have been a bachelor or childless widower,[1] he may well have been the means through whom others of his kindred established themselves in London. But even of the generation immediately preceding the poet's father nothing has been discovered beyond the fact that he had an uncle, named like himself John Donne.[2]

Of Donne's ancestry on the maternal side much more is known. His mother was the youngest daughter of John Heywood, epigrammatist and writer of interludes. Heywood came of a Coventry family, and he had married the daughter of another Coventry man who had made for himself a successful career in London. His wife was Joan, daughter of John Rastell, printer and author of the *Interlude of the Four Elements*. Rastell was himself the husband of Elizabeth, daughter of Sir John More, Judge of the King's Bench, and sister of Sir Thomas More. On his mother's side, therefore, Donne was descended from a group of men remarkable for their intellectual attainments, most of whom won distinction in literature as well as in law.[3] Furthermore, his mother had grown up in a household where music and poetry were not only esteemed but also practised; Heywood

waz not only very well skylled in Muzik, and playeng on þe virʒinals but also such an english *poet*, az þe lyk, for hiz witt and invension, with þe quantite þat hee wrot, waz not az þen in England, nor befor hiz tym sinse Chawsers tym.[4]

Some of Heywood's talents and independence of mind were almost certainly inherited by his daughter and transmitted to her son.

In one of his rare references to his ancestry Donne speaks of him-

---

[1] P.C.C., 2 Logge. He was called John Don the elder because he had a younger brother of the same name.

[2] Possibly either John Dun, merchant tailor of St. Giles without Cripplegate, who died at the end of 1570 and whose will is to be found in P.C.C., 1 Daper, or John Done, armourer of London, who died intestate in 1573 (letters of administration granted 24 Oct.).

[3] See A. W. Reed, *Early Tudor Drama*, 1926, *passim*.

[4] *The Autobiography of Thomas Whythorne*, ed. James M. Osborn, 1961, p. 13.

self as 'being deriued from such a stocke and race, as, I beleeue, no family, (which is not of farre larger extent, and greater branches,) hath endured and suffered more in their persons and fortunes, for obeying the Teachers of Romane Doctrine, then it hath done'.[1] Since so little is known of his immediate ancestry on his father's side, it can only remain a matter for speculation whether he was related to any of the Donnes who suffered for the old faith. There was a John Donne who was arrested at Canterbury in 1579, on his way to take ship for the Continent, because of 'certen leude speeches by him uttered in the defence of the Romishe Relligion';[2] another, or perhaps the same, 'John Dunne of Ipswitch, gentleman' was forced, with other recusants, to make special contributions towards the cost of Elizabeth's Irish wars.[3] Finally, there was Henry Dunne, son of Christopher Dunne of Addington in Kent, who was executed in 1586 for his part in Babington's plot to kidnap Elizabeth, restore the Catholic religion, and put Mary Queen of Scots upon the throne.[4]

The records of suffering among Donne's maternal relatives are much fuller. The story of Sir Thomas More is well known, and need not be repeated here. Each successive generation of Mores for two and a half centuries supplied the Roman Church with devout servants who suffered civil disabilities or exile for their religion, and among the direct descendants of More who were contemporaries of Donne at least eight—four men and four women—were members of Roman Catholic religious orders. To what extent Donne kept in touch with the More family can only be conjectured,[5] but the passage from *Pseudo-Martyr* suggests that at least he had some knowledge of their fortunes. The Heywoods too were sufferers. John Heywood, Donne's grandfather, fled with his wife in 1564 because he was unwilling to accept Elizabeth's religious settlement, and at Louvain joined his brother-in-law William Rastell, a former Judge of the

---

[1] *Pseudo-Martyr*, 'Advertisement to the Reader', sig. ʃ 1ʳ.
[2] *APC*, (1578–80), 124.   [3] *APC* (1598–9), 131.
[4] A report of Christopher's examination concerning his son, 10 Aug. 1586, appears in S.P. Eliz., vol. 192, item 21.
[5] One of More's grandsons, another Thomas More, scandalized his family by becoming an Anglican clergyman. It would be interesting to know whether 'Thomas Moore a younge boye whome I tooke latelie', to whom Donne left £5 in his will, was one of his descendants.

Queen's Bench who, with his father-in-law Dr. John Clement, had taken refuge there in the previous year. In 1574 Thomas Heywood, a brother of John and a former monk of St. Osyth's in Essex, was executed for saying mass. Richard Heywood, the most successful of the brothers in the worldly sense, who died in 1570, managed to keep his peace with the authorities, but there can be little doubt where his sympathies lay. He had been closely associated at Lincoln's Inn with William Roper, More's son-in-law, and they had been Prothonotaries of the King's Bench together.[1] After his death Richard Heywood's widow took as her second husband William Parry. He was an unscrupulous rogue who, after having run through his own inheritance and that of his wife, now attempted to get his hands on the Heywood properties, and involved the family in a protracted lawsuit. He nearly murdered one of his creditors, and was condemned to death at Newgate for burglary, but secured the Queen's pardon. Then he went abroad, and for several years acted as a government spy on the Catholics. He returned to England in 1584 and entered Parliament, where he dumbfounded the Commons by protesting against new repressive legislation aimed at the Catholics; finally, in 1585, he was executed as a traitor for conspiring against the life of the Queen. Apparently he tried to incriminate Sir Edmund Neville by broaching treasonable proposals to him, but Neville betrayed Parry first, and he went to the scaffold.[2]

For what reasons we do not know, Richard Heywood had tried to disinherit his eldest son Christopher and left the major share of his possessions to John, his second son,[3] who stoutly opposed Parry's attempts to get control of his inheritance. The law upheld Christopher's rights, however, and John secured only his father's Lincolnshire properties. This John Heywood was a staunch Catholic who suffered severely for his recusancy; he was a friend not only of Donne's father, who remembered him in his will, but also of Donne himself.

[1] A. W. Reed, *Early Tudor Drama*, ch. 2, 'The Heywoods'.
[2] On Parry and the Heywoods, see *DNB*; *APC* (1571–5), p. 16; Katharine Lee Bates, 'A Conjecture as to Thomas Heywood's Family', *JEGP*, xii (1913), 93–109 at pp. 103–5; Hasted's *Kent*, ed. 1886, pp. 149–50; and P.R.O., C2 Eliz., H21/44. See further Conyers Read, *Mr. Secretary Walsingham*, 1925, ii. 399–405, and Southwell, *Humble Supplication*, p. 17.
[3] His will is in P.C.C., 18 Lyon.

Two other Heywoods of the generation immediately preceding Donne are even more important. Donne's grandfather had two sons who both gave up promising careers in England and eventually became members of the Jesuit order. Ellis, the elder, was born in 1530; he was educated at Oxford and in 1548 obtained a fellowship at All Souls. He left England towards the end of Edward VI's reign and found service in Italy in the household of Reginald Cardinal Pole. He returned to England, but went abroad again with his parents. He became a Jesuit and in 1573 was appointed to the Jesuit college at Antwerp, where, by a special dispensation, his aged father was allowed to join him. He died in Louvain in 1578, to which city the fathers of the Antwerp college had been expelled. Ellis's younger brother Jasper was born in 1535 and as a boy served for a time as a page to the Princess Elizabeth. He followed his brother to Oxford, was elected Fellow of Merton in 1554, and, four years later, Fellow of All Souls. He is best known for his translations of three of Seneca's plays, which were published between 1559 and 1561; he must have left England shortly afterwards, for he took his first Jesuit vows at Rome in 1562. From 1564 to 1581 he was Professor of Theology at the Jesuit college at Dillingen, where his brother Ellis spent his novitiate.

Such a brief recital of bare facts can give little understanding of the way in which the members of this group felt bound together by a sense of solidarity; they were united not only by their fidelity to the old religion and by their common exile, but also by their kinship and, above all, by their reverence for the memory of Sir Thomas More. John Heywood, we are told, had been 'Thomae Moro multis annis familiarissimus'; Ellis had spent part of his Italian exile in commemorating More's memory in *Il Moro*, which he published at Florence in 1556; and Cresacre More's *Life of More* relates an anecdote which involves both Ellis and Jasper: 'It was also credibly reported, that two of *John Haywood*'s sons, *Jasper* and *Ellis*, hauing one of the teeth of Sir THOMAS MORE betweene them, and either of them being desirous to haue it to himselfe, it suddenly, to the admiration of both, parted in two.'[1] Even more significant as an illustration of the temper of the group is the will of William

[1] Ed. 1726, p. 304.

Rastell, made at Antwerp in 1564.[1] Ellis Heywood was Rastell's principal heir; he received outright certain lands in North Mimms in Hertfordshire, and in trust part of a perpetual annuity which Rastell had purchased from the city of Antwerp; this was to be disposed of within seven years to the advancement of theology or for other pious uses. To Ellis there was also the special bequest of a gold chain and locket 'cum effigie Thomae Mori'. To Bartholomew More, one of More's grandsons, there was the bequest, later revoked, of the remainder of the annuity, but only on condition that the beneficiary should not fall into heresy or return to England until that land had been reconciled to the Catholic faith. There were other bequests to Rastell's parents-in-law, John Clement and Margaret Clement (More's adopted daughter), and their surviving children.[2] Finally, the members of the family in England were remembered; rings were bequeathed to his brother John Rastell and his wife, and to John Heywood's three married daughters: Joan Stubbes, wife of Christopher Stubbes of Lincoln's Inn, Elizabeth Marvin, and Elizabeth Donne. Such was the family from which Donne's mother came, and it is small wonder that she remained a devout Catholic until her death.

Donne's father must have been born in or before 1535. Though there is no record of the fact in the Presentment Book of the Ironmongers' Company, he was apprenticed to Thomas Lewen, a successful ironmonger and alderman of the City of London, who had been one of the sheriffs for 1537/8. Lewen died in 1555. He was buried in his parish church of St. Nicholas Olave in Bread Street, and his sumptuous funeral was described by Henry Machyn.[3] He left all his property, subject to a life interest for the benefit of his wife, to the Company of Ironmongers for various charitable uses, to be held by them 'until such time as a new monastery be erected at Sawtrey, in the county of Huntingdon, of the same order of monks

[1] W. Bang, 'Acta Anglo-Lovaniensia. John Heywood und sein Kreis', *Eng. Stud.* xxxviii (1907), 234–50.

[2] 'Two of the Clement girls, Dorothy and Margaret, became nuns at Louvain, the latter not dying until 1612, three years before Donne entered the Anglican priesthood' (B. W. Whitlock, 'The Heredity and Childhood of John Donne', *NQ*, cciv (1959), 259). These two nuns should be added to those among the family connections who gave up their native land for the Catholic faith.

[3] *The Diary of Henry Machyn*, ed. J. G. Nichols, Camden Society, 1848, p. 91.

as were then in the old monastery before its suppression'. This, as Jessopp pointed out, is 'the first and last important bequest made after the plunder of the monasteries by Henry VIII for the restoration of a suppressed religious house'.[1] Needless to say, Lewen's charities are still administered by the Ironmongers' Company.

John Donne completed his apprenticeship under Lewen's widow, Agnes, who seems to have carried on her husband's business. He became free of the Ironmongers' Company in the civic year 1556/7, probably before the end of 1556, since his name is the first on the list for the year.[2] He remained in Mrs. Lewen's service until her death, which occurred on 26 October 1562, and he must have borne the main responsibility in the management of her affairs. Her funeral is likewise chronicled by Machyn, who wrote:

The xxxj day of October was bered good mastores Luwen, wedowe, latte the wyff of master Thomas Luwen yrmonger and altherman, and she gayff a xxiiij gownes to powre women, and she gayff mony blake gownes; and ther was the compene of the Clarkes; and a ij dosen of skochyons of armes; and master Chamburlayn the shreyff and John Dune here servand was here sekturs, and master Wylliam Draper oversear; and dyre dyd pryche for here master Goodman the dene of Westmynster; and all the crafte of the Yrmongers ther; and after to here plase, for ther was a grett dener for as mony as wold cum, and after was sent spyse bred to evere howse and about the cette unto worshephulle men and women.[3]

As Machyn noted, Mrs. Lewen's executors were John Donne and Richard Chamberlain, a prosperous ironmonger, whose son John is

[1] p. 9.
[2] The earliest of the Company's Freedom Books begins with the year 1555/6, and the first entry for 1556/7 reads:

John Donne   Mr Lewen

but this part of the book is in a seventeenth-century hand. About half-way through the book, which is unpaged, is a single leaf, evidently part of the original from which the transcript was made, containing part of the entries for 1555/6 and 1556/7. Here one finds:

a° 1556. & a° 1557
John Donne   By Mrs Lewen

It has previously been stated that he served his apprenticeship under James Harvey (by T. E. Tomlins, by Jessopp, p. 8, and by Gosse, i. 9); this is an error, due to the fact that on 14 Jan. 1549/50 James Harvey took an apprentice named John Downe. A number of other Downes also appear in the records of the Ironmongers.
[3] *Diary*, pp. 294–5.

still remembered as the gossipy letter-writer who kept Sir Dudley Carleton informed of all that was happening in London during the reign of James I. Most of Mrs. Lewen's property went in charitable bequests, but there were gifts to the two executors.[1] To John Donne she left 'the lease of the house I promised hym, and xxx[li] of mouney, all promyses made vnto hym at any tyme being hereby clerely discharged', and in the codicil there was another bequest: 'if yt shall pleace god to send home my shipp safe, Then I giue one of my thre partes to M.r Richarde Chamberlen, an other to John Donne condiconally that every of them shall paye for his saide parte, the halfe of the iust value of the same.' We do not know if Mrs. Lewen's ship came safely home, but this bequest may well have been the foundation of John Donne's prosperity.

The lease which Mrs. Lewen bequeathed to John Donne was not for the house which she herself had occupied, since that had been left to the Ironmongers' Company, subject to her life interest, by her husband, and passed to them on her death; it is referred to as a 'great capitall howse' and was leased by the Company on 3 November 1572 to William Skidmore and his partner Robert East for an annual rent of £20.[2] John Donne occupied somewhat smaller premises in Bread Street close by, and this property was also owned by the Ironmongers. A subsidy roll of 5 Elizabeth (1563), shortly after Mrs. Lewen's death, for the parishes of St. Nicholas Olave, St. Mildred, and Trinity in Queenhithe Ward, shows that he was assessed at £5. 5s. 0d., and his name appears next to that of William Harrison, who was assessed for the same sum.[3] This suggests that

---

[1] Her will is in P.C.C., 33 Streat, proved by the executors on 22 Dec. 1562.

[2] An entry in the Ironmongers' Court Book I refers to the activities of Mrs. Lewen's executors in winding up her affairs and handing over the house to the Company:

'M.r Chamberleyns & M.r dounes promys towching certen ymplements in M.r Lowyns howse	Also it is agreed that we shall pay the rest of the bill of the implements w.ch we have agreed vpon w.ch did Amounte to the some of xxj[li] x[s] so that we haue paid the whole some of the Inventorie of Implements and M.r Alderman Chamberleyn and John Don doth promise to leve certein implements in the house not praysed to the valewe thereof and better' (fo. 35).

The house was thus well equipped for an ironmonger to carry on his trade, and it was only natural that the Company should lease it to members of their craft. The lease to East and Skidmore is entered in the Court Book, fo. 89.

[3] K. Rogers, *The Mermaid and Mitre Taverns in Old London*, 1928, p. 116, and 'Bread

John Donne lived next door to Harrison, who has been identified as the keeper of the famous Mitre Tavern, and the Mitre was in Bread Street almost opposite the church of St. Nicholas Olave. Not long after this date John Donne expanded his premises, for the Iron-mongers' Court ruled on 8 August 1564 that he should 'pay for the Chamber whiche the priest laye in by Mrs Lewens house .x^s. by yere'.[1] Thereafter he paid an annual rent of £5 until the year 1571/2, but on 3 November 1572 the Court granted him the lease of 'two Chambers adioyning to his howse' ('late Wydow Whittredges'), for 20s. a year, and at the next Court he was granted a new lease of the joint properties for twenty-five years at £6 a year.[2]

John Donne's name also occurs fairly frequently in the Court Book of the Ironmongers' Company in connection with other matters. When the whole Company was assessed on 4 January 1566 at £75. 10s. 0d. for a contribution to 'the Burse' (Gresham's Royal Exchange), John Donne's share was 20s.[3] Later in the same year a member of the Company, Sir Christopher Draper, was elected Lord Mayor, and there are constant references to his pageant and the other celebrations at his inauguration, which were organized and paid for by his Company. In the list of 'those wch be appointed to serve for Bachelers in the tyme of Mr. Alderman Draper lorde maior of this Cittie of London and also what they haue given towardes the charges therof', John Donne comes second and the sum of £3 is entered against his name.[4] He was appointed with three others to oversee the trimming of the foist, or barge, in which the new Lord Mayor was rowed from London to Westminster, and to provide it with banners.[5] His name also appears in a list of 'suche persons as shall haue gownes giuen vnto them to be worne & to bere torches', and opposite his name, as torchbearer, is 'John Donne his vncle'.[6] In the procession itself he was one of eight bachelors in foyn who pre-ceded the Lord Mayor,[7] and later he received payment for several hundredweight of gunpowder which he had supplied for fireworks.[8] In the following year, on 25 April 1567, he was admitted to the livery of the Company,[9] and from this date onwards his attendance

Street, its Ancient Signs and Houses', *London Topographical Record*, xvi (1932), 52–76 at pp. 70–1.
[1] Court Book I, fo. 40b. [2] fo. 89. [3] fo. 45b. [4] fo. 51a.
[5] fo. 54a and b. [6] fo. 54b. [7] fo. 55b. [8] fo. 88. [9] fo. 59b.

at the Court is frequent. As time went on, he served on various committees and filled offices in the Company; on 4 May 1569 he was appointed with four others to go to the Court of Wards 'to knowe whereof our troubles do arise there';[1] he was one of the viewers and searchers for 1571 and again for 1572,[2] one of the eight auditors of the Company's accounts for 1571, and one of the two rentors for the year 1571/2.[3] On 26 April 1574 he was elected a warden of the Company,[4] and several months later was appointed a member of a committee to oversee the buildings on some property belonging to the Company in Horsehead Alley.[5] The impression one receives is of a prosperous citizen steadily advancing in his trade and in the esteem of his fellow ironmongers.

Several other documents provide somewhat less favourable glimpses of him and his business dealings. St. Bartholomew's Hospital had a monopoly of weighing coal and iron bought and sold in London, and the Journal of the Hospital shows that John Donne was before the Court on 18 February 1570 for failing to weigh seven tons of coal which he had recently bought. Evidently this was not his first offence, for the Court ruled that, besides forfeiting the coal, 'the said Mr Dvne shall pay for the weyinge of the same Irone wch latly was forfeted as is accustomed to be paid & so from hensforth to pay & contynew in the same vpon the payne lymyted in the statute'.[6]

Nevertheless, John Donne prospered, for in the year in which his son was born he was assessed jointly with Robert East and William Skidmore (in what proportion is not known) at £100 for the subsidy that was then being collected.[7] Presumably the three men were in some sort of partnership; East and Skidmore were fellow iron-mongers, and Skidmore was a former apprentice of Thomas Lewen. It will be recalled that the two men were joint tenants of the 'great capitall howse' which Lewen had bequeathed to the Ironmongers' Company and which Mrs. Lewen had lived in until her death. The

[1] fo. 70.   [2] ff. 81b and 85.

[3] Court Book, fo. 82a; fo. 81b and Register II, fo. 217b.

[4] Court Book I, fo. 101b.   [5] fo. 103.

[6] B. W. Whitlock, 'The Heredity and Childhood of John Donne', NQ, cciv (1959), 261.

Whitlock, loc. cit.

house occupied by John Donne probably adjoined this larger house, for, it will be remembered, when Donne enlarged his premises he-rented 'the Chamber whiche the priest laye in by Mrs Lewens house'. John Donne left bequests in his will to both East and Skidmore, and the two men in their turn were among the sureties who became bound in order to secure his children's inheritance.[1]

John Donne's will also reveals the fact that he had a married sister in Oxford. She was the wife of Robert Dawson, who kept the Blue Boar Inn, on the corner of St. Aldate's and Blue Boar Lane. Dawson first leased the site from New College in 1570 and soon established a thriving business. The Blue Boar was an inn of considerable size; it was not dismantled until 1893 after the site had been purchased by the City of Oxford. The Public Library is now where the inn once stood.[2] It was probably through his brother-in-law that John Donne was persuaded to invest in Oxford real estate. On 21 June 1571 he acquired from John Ward, citizen and grocer of London, a tenement at the upper end of Catte Street which abutted on Black Hall (immediately beyond which was Hart Hall, of which his two sons were later to become members) and an orchard on the west side of St. Giles' bounded on the north and south by holdings of Robert Dawson.[3]

John Donne's efforts on behalf of John Heywood are more important. When Heywood fled in 1564 he seems to have left his affairs in his son-in-law's hands, and for some years John Donne regularly remitted at least a part of Heywood's rents to him at Louvain. After the Rising in the North, however, Parliament passed a statute (13 Eliz. c. 3) summoning all fugitives to return within six months, and

---

[1] See Appendix D, p. 560 below, and B. W. Whitlock, 'The Orphanage Accounts of John Donne, Ironmonger', *The Guildhall Miscellany*, no. 4 (Feb. 1955), 24.

[2] See H. Hurst, *Oxford Topography*, 1899, pp. 50–1; H. E. Salter, *Oxford City Properties*, 1926, pp. 152–3 (where there is a plan and elevation of the building as it was early in the nineteenth century) and *Survey of Oxford* (1960), i. 227–8 (all published by the Oxford Historical Society).

[3] 'Illud messuagium sive tenementum cum pertinentibus modo vel nuper in tenura sive occupatione Henrici Trypley Glover scituatum iacens et existens in Catts Streete in parochia Sancte Marie in villa Oxon . . . videlicet abuttans super tenementum modo in tenura Johannis Johnson Scissoris ex parte Boreali et in parte Occidentali et super Aulam ibidem vocatam Blackhall ex parte Australi et in parte Occidentali et super tenementum modo vel nuper in tenura Doctoris Bayly ex parte Orientali' (P.R.O., C54/838). I cannot make proper sense of this; the points of the compass seem wrong, as Black Hall was east of Catte Street, not west of it.

penalizing those who did not do so with forfeiture of all their lands
and goods. As a preliminary to confiscation, commissions were to
be issued out of the Exchequer for inquiries into the lands of such
fugitives, and at least seven such commissions were issued for Heywood's properties, which were widely scattered throughout England. Some of these documents are now damaged and only partly
legible, but certain facts emerge clearly enough. The findings of the
Hertfordshire commissions of 1574 and 1577 were that both Ellis
and John Heywood had been in possession of certain lands in North
Mimms. The tenants of these lands deposed that after their land-
lords had left the kingdom they had paid their rents to John Donne
until Lady Day 1571 and since then to Elizabeth Marvin, John
Heywood's daughter, who had affirmed that she was now the owner
of Hawkshead, her brother's farm, which, she said, he had given to
her for her life, and after her death to her daughter Anne.[1]

The Kent commission of 1572 reported that Heywood held a
forty-year lease of about 300 acres in Romney Marsh, in the parishes
of Blackmanstone, St. Mary Church, and Newchurch, which had
been granted to him by Queen Mary.[2] On 26 March 1563 these
leases had been conveyed to John Donne on the condition that if
£300 were paid to him according to the terms that had been agreed
upon, the conveyance should be void. In other words, the leases
were conveyed to Donne as security for the payment of a debt, and
a likely explanation is that this £300 represented his wife's dowry.
The commission found, however, that the debt had been discharged
before 1571, and that the conveyance to Donne was therefore of
no effect; nevertheless, Donne had collected the rents ever since
Heywood went overseas.[3]

As a result of the reports of the various commissions Heywood's
lands became forfeit to the Crown, and the exile soon felt the pinch
of losing all his resources. Three years later, doubtless after putting
out feelers to see if an appeal might have any success, he addressed
a letter to Lord Burleigh, from which it is clear that Lady Burleigh
had already pleaded his cause:

[1] P.R.O., E178/1019.
[2] For the grant, see *Calendar of Patent Rolls, Philip and Mary*, vol. ii (1554–5), p. 164.
[3] P.R.O., E178/1095.

Right Honorable and my verie good Lord:

I understand of late what a good earnest sewtor, it hath pleased my good honorable Ladie, your good wiffe, to be for me, nowe in my poore old age, when my frendes are in a manner all dead, and manie of them utterlie forsaken me and my wholle lyvyng detayned from me, and the chieffest parte of it, whiche was a lease for yeares, in Romney Marshe, begged, and bought away utterlie from me; And neither of that, nor of the rest, not one pennye of it, paid, or sent hither unto me, for my maintennance for these twoo yeares, and a half: And (nowe) it pleaseth you[r] good Lordshippe as I heare, to comaund my sonne Doonne, to send me over the arrerages, whiche hath bein deteyned from me.

No remittance had yet arrived and Heywood ventured to ask Burleigh 'to appoynte some one of the officers of the escheker, or whom it pleaseth your honor, that maye help my dowghter Marvin that I may have my Arrerages that is dewe, since I was procleymed, quietlie and spedelie paid, and sent unto me'. He would like, too, official leave to enjoy what was left of his estate—

except my lease, that is begged and bought away whollie frome me, whiche I dare not crave, whiche was the verie chefe of my lyvyng: and nowe I have no manner of benefit of it, whiche I thinke the quene's magestie never ment, when it was bowght frome me by Justice Manhoode and sold by him to my sonne Doonn, who never sent me one penye yet either of that lease or (of anie) of my lyvyng since the tyme he bought my lease, for he sayth he durst not.[1]

The reference to Roger Manwood, who at this stage of his career was one of the judges of the Common Pleas, is interesting, for he had been a friend of Richard Heywood and was one of the executors of his will, so John Heywood was obviously not unknown to him. But furthermore, he had been at the head of the commission which had inquired into Heywood's Kentish holdings. Manwood's later reputation as a just judge was not high, and it looks as if he took advantage of his position on the commission to benefit himself. Heywood seems to suggest that Manwood secured a conveyance of the Kentish leases to himself, and then sold them to John Donne so that they could be kept in the family and Heywood would still benefit

[1] A. W. Reed, *Early Tudor Drama*, pp. 35-6.

from them. But if any such trust was intended, it did not legally exist, and the old man had no recourse but to acquiesce in the loss of his lands. He was clearly suspicious of his son-in-law's good faith, and put more trust in his daughter Elizabeth Marvin who, it is almost certain, was either visiting him or had just visited him, and had doubtless told him her side of the story.[1] It must be added, however, that John Donne would have been liable to severe penalties for succouring fugitives abroad, and his reluctance to send money to Heywood was not without some justification. Hence, no doubt, Heywood's eagerness to secure official consent for his remittances.

Manwood appears briefly in *The Courtier's Library*, where one of the items is

A Manual for Justices of the Peace, comprising many confessions of poisoners tendered to Justice Manwood, and employed by him in his privy. . . .[2]

The exact point of the joke is lost, but it is clear that Heywood's grandson regarded the judge with a degree of contempt that may well have been based on a sense of family injury.

It is pleasant to know that Heywood's appeal to Burleigh did not go unanswered. He did not get all he asked for (he had, for instance, requested letters patent confirming his rights, and a licence to live abroad), but the authorities took a kindly view of his age and infirmities, and his obvious incapacity to do any harm. Six months later he wrote again to Burleigh:

syth the said tyme of my said writting to your honor I have here receyved fro my sonn in Law John Doon ffiftie pounds that being a part or parcell of the said arrerage: for the whiche I most humbly thanke the Quene her Majestie And also your honor & my good Ladie for your speciall favor & ffurtherance in the same.[3]

It is pleasant to know also that John Donne fulfilled at least some of his obligations towards his father-in-law.

---

[1] Whitlock, 'The Heredity and Childhood of John Donne', *N&Q*, cciv (1959), at p. 348.

[2] *The Courtier's Library*, ed. E. M. Simpson, p. 49.

[3] Reed, p. 237.

III

EARLY LIFE

JOHN DONNE and Elizabeth Heywood were certainly married by 8 August 1564, when William Rastell made his will in Antwerp and left 'Elizabethae Donne, alie sorori dicti Elizei, annulum meum aureum cum saphiro', and indeed it is reasonable to believe that Heywood would not have left England without seeing his youngest daughter safely provided for. If I am right in suggesting that the conveyance of Heywood's leases in Romney Marsh was by way of security for the payment of Elizabeth's dowry, the marriage would have occurred in March or April 1563, about six months after the death of Agnes Lewen, when the bridegroom was approaching thirty and the bride was eighteen or twenty years old. There were six children of the marriage who survived their father: Elizabeth, Anne, John, Henry, Mary, and Katherine. It has been shown, after a close examination of the sometimes conflicting evidence, that John must have been born between 24 January and 19 June 1572.[1] It is quite likely that more than one child of the marriage died in infancy. Elizabeth, the eldest, died not long after her father, and there seems to have been a gap of several years between John and his sister Anne, who was old enough to marry in 1585, when John was thirteen. Henry was younger than John by little over a year, and the births of the two younger children must have followed closely. The children were born in their father's house in Bread Street, and spent their early years in the heart of London. Their father was prospering, and though his sympathies were probably not always with the religious policies of those in power, he was, as we have seen, discreet enough

---

[1] F. P. Wilson, 'Notes on the Early Life of John Donne', *RES*, iii (1927), 272–9; H. W. Garrod, 'The Date of Donne's Birth', *TLS*, 1944, p. 636; W. Milgate, 'The Date of Donne's Birth', *NQ*, cxci (1946), 206–8; I. A. Shapiro, 'Donne's Birthdate', *NQ*, cxcvii (1952), 310–13. On 17 June 1618, Donne gave evidence in a case concerning Thomas Egerton the younger (see below, Chapter XII, p. 335), and was described as being 'aged 46 yeres or nere thereabouts'.

to avoid giving any offence. The mother, anxious though she
doubtless often was for the members of her family in exile, must
have had her time fully taken up by her household duties and the
cares of her rapidly increasing family. She and her husband took
seriously the obligations of parenthood, for her son recalled in later
years that 'My parents would not give mee over to a *Servants* correction.'[1] To the son it also seemed that these years had been the
happiest of his mother's life, but, he wrote to her, 'The happinesse
which God afforded to your first young time, which was the love
and care of my most dear and provident Father, whose soul, I hope,
hath long since enjoyed the sight of our blessed Saviour, and had
compassion of all our miseries in this world, God removed from you
quickly.'[2] John Donne died in his early forties, when his elder son
was barely four years old.

His will is dated 16 January 1575/6 and was proved on the 8th of
the following month.[3] He desired that 'according to the laudable
vse and custome of the Cittie of London' his property should be
divided into three equal parts: one for the widow, one to be divided
among the children, and the third for the payment of debts and
legacies, with the residue shared equally by his wife and children.
He left £300 to be distributed by certain friends in charities, and he
made smaller specific bequests to the poor of his parish of St.
Nicholas Olave, to the prisons, and to the hospitals. There were
also legacies to other friends, relatives, and servants. Three servants,
a 'cozen' Alice Donne, who was under twenty-one and a member of
his household, and the Dawsons of Oxford all received bequests. In
addition, there was a bequest to Mrs. Donne's elder sister Elizabeth
Marvin.[4] 'My cozen John Heywood', who received £3 'to make him

---

[1] Sparrow, *Devotions*, p. 8.
[2] *Tobie Mathew Collection*, pp. 324-5.   [3] See Appendix D, pp. 560-2.
[4] Mrs. Marvin had a house in Bartholomew Close, which she rented from the
Hospital. When she went abroad in 1574 and 1575 she evidently sub-let it, in contra-
vention of the provisions of her lease, for on 12 Feb. 1575 John Donne had to
appear before the governors of the Hospital and go surety for her to the extent of
£10. She was ordered to return before 24 July and live in her house, on pain of
forfeiture of her lease. Though she returned, she lost her lease later, on 9 Mar. 1577,
for sub-letting again; see B. W. Whitlock, 'The Heredity and Childhood of John
Donne', *NQ*, cciv (1959), at pp. 348-51. This is the last that is heard of her. It is conceivable that she went again to the Low Countries to be with her father in his
declining years, or she may have died soon after she had to give up her house.
What is important to note is that John Donne's willingness to go surety for her,

a ringe with a deathes hedd', was almost certainly Richard Heywood's son and not the aged exile. Rings or other mementoes were also left to William Skidmore, Robert East, John Eustace, Christopher Rust, Robert Harrison, Francis Sandbache, and Edmund Adamson.[1] The total value of his property must have been close to £3,500, a clear indication of John Donne's prosperity.[2]

The story of the administration of the estate can be told in detail.[3] The interests of the children were safeguarded by the Lord Mayor and Aldermen, sitting as a Court of Orphans at the Guildhall, and the widow as executrix was bound to find securities for the payment into the Chamber (or treasury of the City) of the fund belonging to the children. A certain amount was allowed to remain in the hands of recognitors, as they were called, but they too had to furnish sureties for its eventual repayment. Interest on the fund at the rate of 5 per cent was furnished by the Court for the maintenance of the children. By May 1576 the securities had been found, and £300 had been paid into the Chamber, and by July, six months after her husband's death, Elizabeth Donne married again. Her second husband was John Syminges, a doctor in physic of Oxford, who had received his training at Oxford and Bologna, and had several times been President of the Royal College of Physicians. In 1556 he and Dr. John Clement had both been Censors of the College, so it is possible that his association with the kin of Sir Thomas More was already of long standing when he married Donne's mother. Syminges was a man in his fifties, a widower with three children, and of considerable standing in his profession. (His two daughters

and his bequest to her of a gown of black cloth, do not suggest any ill feelings or strained relationships; it is therefore rendered less likely that John Donne was guilty of bad faith in his financial dealings with John Heywood, as Whitlock seems to hint (pp. 261 and 349).

[1] Skidmore, the former apprentice of Thomas Lewen, was a close neighbour, and East was his partner. John Eustace was another ironmonger, Robert Harrison a salter and perhaps a son of William Harrison, the keeper of the Mitre. Sandbache is described as esquire and Adamson as gentleman.

[2] The specific legacies total £469; the children's portion was about £1,500, and the widow's would have been the same. Walton's statement that Donne inherited £3,000 is probably due to a misunderstanding; Donne's father left something over £3,000, but, apart from the legacies, it had to be divided among his wife and children.

[3] Wilson, pp. 272–6, and Whitlock, 'The Orphanage Accounts of John Donne, Ironmonger', *Guildhall Miscellany*, no. 4, Feb. 1955, pp. 22–9.

were already married; his son died in July 1581.[1]) He was a man who
had already acquired wealth and in 1570 had been able to purchase
two manors in Monmouthshire for £1,200.[2] Other dealings in land
are also recorded, of which the most important was the purchase in
May 1561 of a messuage in Trinity Lane called Le Priors House,
with an adjoining messuage on which were two houses and a garden.[3]
He was presumably living here when he remarried, though how
soon the Donne house was vacated must remain uncertain. Mrs.
Donne paid the rent on the Bread Street house to the Ironmongers'
Company for the year 1575/6, and the accounts for the following
year show that Syminges paid the rent 'for the howse that Mr.
Donne dwelt in',[4] but thereafter the lease of the house passed into
other hands. The family was still living in the parish of Trinity the
Less when, on 25 November 1581, the register recorded the burial
of the two youngest Donne children, Mary and Katherine; but in
the autumn of 1583 Syminges moved into the parish of St. Bartholomew the Less, presumably to be near St. Bartholomew's Hospital.[5]

   The home in which most of Donne's formative years were spent
and round which most of his childish memories clustered was thus
headed by his stepfather. To Syminges's religious opinions there is
no decisive clue, but the career of Thomas Lodge shows that it was
possible to be a successful London physician while still professing
the old religion. There seem to have been no children of the second
marriage, and there is no reason to believe that Syminges's step-
children suffered any neglect. Certainly, there is no doubt that their
education was well cared for. Of the earliest stages of his training
there appears to be a reminiscence when, in a sermon, Donne remarked that 'a man can remember when he began to *spell*, but not
when he began to *reade perfectly*, when he began to joyne his letters,
but not when he began to write perfectly'.[6] Walton relates that
Donne was educated at home by a private tutor until he entered

   [1] B. W. Whitlock, 'John Syminges, a Poet's Stepfather', *NQ*, cc (1954), 421–4.
   [2] P.R.O., E178/2213.
   [3] Whitlock, op. cit., p. 423. The sale by Syminges of extensive properties in
Gloucestershire is recorded in P.R.O., C54/1150 (22 Apr. 1583).
   [4] Ironmongers' Company, Register II, ff. 261ᵛ, 271ᵛ.
   [5] Whitlock, op. cit., p. 424, and 'The Heredity and Childhood of John Donne',
NQ, cciv (1959), at pp. 351–2.
   [6] *Sermons*, iv, no. 5, ll. 160–2, p. 149.

Oxford, and that he came to the University with 'a good command both of the French and Latine Tongue'. That his tutor was a good Catholic, perhaps even a seminary priest, may be accepted without question. In writing of his eventual acceptance of the Anglican creed, Donne stated:

I had a longer work to doe then many other men; for I was first to blot out, certaine impressions of the Romane religion, and to wrastle both against the examples and against the reasons, by which some hold was taken; and some anticipations early layde vpon my conscience, both by Persons who by nature had a power and superiority ouer my will, and others who by their learning and good life, seem'd to me iustly to claime an interest for the guiding, and rectifying of mine vnderstanding in these matters.[1]

The influences and impressions of which he speaks must have gone back to his earliest childhood, and continued until he had the independence of mind to make his decisions for himself.

It has often been suggested (no doubt because two of his uncles were members of the Order) that Donne had a Jesuit education. A little reflection, however, will show that this was impossible. The first two Jesuit missionaries to land in England were Edmund Campion and Robert Persons, who arrived on 25 June 1580; Campion was captured on 16 June 1581 and suffered on the scaffold on 1 December; Persons fled to the Continent soon after Campion's arrest. It is conceivable that either or both of these men secretly visited Donne's mother to bring tidings of her brother Jasper, but their lives were too full and active for any more considerable intercourse. The next Jesuits to come to England were Jasper Heywood himself and William Holt, who arrived during the summer of 1581. Heywood now became head of the Jesuit mission, since Campion was in prison and Persons had fled. Heywood was captured and imprisoned at the beginning of December 1583, and about the same time Holt escaped to Scotland. There was no other Jesuit at large in England until William Weston arrived in September 1584, within a month of Donne's entry at Oxford. Unquestionably Jasper Heywood got in touch with the members of his family in England; he may even have taken refuge from time to time under his sister's roof.

---

[1] *Pseudo-Martyr*, 'A preface to the Priestes, and Jesuits', sig. B2ᵛ.

The children must have seen and spoken to him, and no doubt he made a deep impression on them; but that he or Holt had the time to undertake their education is unthinkable. Jasper Heywood was busy organizing, with hopelessly inadequate resources, the recon-version of all England. Besides, the official instructions to the missioners were that they should associate as much as possible with men of high rank, and avoid familiar conversation with women and boys.[1]

Donne's education, though Catholic, was not therefore Jesuit, nor was it even humanist in the best tradition of Sir Thomas More. Walton speaks only of Donne's early command of French and Latin; his youthful training seems to have included little or no Greek. Later, it is true, he acquired some Greek, but there are no signs of the influence of Greek literature in his poetry, and it has been shown, by a careful study of his sermons, that his knowledge of Greek was far less than his knowledge of Hebrew.[2] On the other hand, Donne's early knowledge of French is significant, and opens the way for an interesting speculation. There are signs in his poetry that he had read such works as *Le Roman de la Rose* and the *Testaments* of Villon, books much reprinted at the beginning of the sixteenth century, but little read, as far as can be ascertained, in England in the later part of the century. Further, the British Museum copy of a French farce, the *Dialogue du fou et du sage*, which John Heywood almost certainly knew, was once in Donne's library, since it bears his signature and motto on the title-page; this might, indeed, have been Heywood's copy, which had descended to Donne.[3] It is quite probable that Heywood owned a representative collection of French literary works printed early in the sixteenth century, and these, left behind in his daughter's house, could easily have been at hand for the youthful Donne to explore.

[1] *Letters and Memorials of Father Robert Persons, S.J.*, ed. L. Hicks, Catholic Record Society, vol. xxxix (1942), i. 316–21.

[2] D. C. Allen, 'Dean Donne sets his Text', *ELH*, x (1943), 208–29, especially pp. 220–2. Professor Allen concludes that 'his [Greek] scholarship is far below that of the average preacher of the age. It is not impossible that his knowledge of Greek was very limited.' It should be added, however, that Professor Allen's conception of the 'average' preacher seems to be based somewhat too exclusively on a study of the sermons of Bishops Andrewes and Hall.

[3] I. R. Maxwell, 'John Donne's Library', *TLS*, 11 July 1935, p. 448.

However absorbed in his studies, and whatever promise of
brilliance he may have given in pursuing them, Donne must have
been aware of many other things going on around him. The sense
of being apart from others in his family's fidelity to the old religion
would have brought with it, on the one hand, a feeling of almost
aristocratic exclusiveness as well as a specific pride in his descent
from the line of Sir Thomas More. On the other hand, there was
around him a constant sense of watchfulness, of whispered conversation and innuendo, of disguises and secret comings and goings. His
uncle Jasper Heywood's mission, which for two years kept him
constantly on the move and took him from one end of England to
the other, was succeeding beyond all expectation; the harvest was
rich, although the reapers were pitifully few. All would have been
well had not a dispute about the observance of fasts arisen between
the older priests of Queen Mary's time and the newer generation
trained abroad. Heywood's rather tactless decision in the dispute
gave widespread offence. As a result, he was recalled, and towards
the end of November 1583 he set out to cross the Channel. Within
sight of the French coast a storm arose, which drove the ship
back and forced the passengers to land in England again. There
Heywood was arrested on suspicion; his identity was soon dis-
closed, and he was hurried off to prison. He was committed
to the Clink, Southwark, on 9 December and was brought to trial
on 6 February following. A contemporary has given an account of
the proceedings:

The 6 day of February [1584] Mr Heywood and five other priests
were brought to the Kings-bench barre, indited of high treason for
conspiring at Rhemes and Rome, as it was surmised against F.
Campian. They all pleaded not guilty and so were conveyed to the
Tower. F. Haywood was in Jesuit's weed, so grave a man as ever I
sett my eyes upon, he wore a coate of black very low and upon the
same a cloke of black, downe almost to the grownde. He had in his
hand a black staff and upon his head a velvet coyfe and there upon a
broade seemly black felt.
The 9 of February the five priests were brought againe to the barre,
and arrained upon the former endightment: they pleaded and protested innocency. . . . The Jury found them out of hand Guilty, and

the Judge gave sentence of death. Whereupon the priests soung *Te Deum* and such like godly verses.[1]

Sentence was not executed on Heywood, however, and he remained a prisoner in the Tower for nearly a year. There is no question that both John and Jasper Heywood received more lenient treatment from the Queen and her ministers than many of their fellow Catholics; no doubt Elizabeth retained kindly memories of the old man's wit and gaiety in the days when he had supplied entertainment for the court and remembered affectionately Jasper's services when, as a boy, he had been her page.

Meanwhile there had been other changes and anxieties in Donne's home. Elizabeth, the eldest child, had died in 1577 or soon afterwards; Mary and Katherine, the two youngest, died in November 1581,[2] so that only Anne, one of the elder sisters, and John and Henry, the two boys, were left. The portions of the three who died went to swell those of the surviving children, since no division was made until they came of age or, in the case of the daughters, until they married. It was decided, too, that the boys were sufficiently advanced to enter a university. Accordingly John and Henry Donne, of London, 'generosi filii', matriculated from Hart Hall, Oxford, on 23 October 1584, their ages being given as eleven and ten respectively.[3] Though younger than the average undergraduate, they were not phenomenally young, and many examples can be cited of others who entered the university at similar ages.

Catholics were under disabilities at the universities as in most other spheres of English life. The Act of Supremacy required an oath acknowledging the royal supremacy in matters of religion from all supplicants for university degrees, and the Oxford Statute of Matriculation of 1581 insisted on subscription by all students over the age of sixteen not only to the Queen's supremacy but to the Thirty-nine Articles as well.[4] Boys of a less mature age were not considered

---

[1] From the letter of an unknown correspondent to Robert Southwell, S.J., printed by J. H. Pollen in *Documents relating to the English Martyrs* (Catholic Record Society, vol. v, 1908), p. 60.

[2] B. W. Whitlock, 'The Heredity and Childhood of John Donne', *NQ*, cciv (1959), at pp. 351–2.

[3] Andrew Clark, *Register of the University of Oxford*, Oxford Historical Society, vol. ii, pt. 2, p. 138.

[4] C. E. Mallet, *History of the University of Oxford*, ii. 121.

capable of comprehending the nature of the Articles or of the oath. These regulations were probably responsible, in part at least, for the fact that Donne and his brother entered Oxford so early, and also for the fact that they gave their ages as a year less than they actually were. Discipline was less strict in the halls than in the colleges, and Hart Hall, which they entered, had the reputation of being a centre for Catholics. Hart Hall had no chapel, though it had a reader in divinity, a Spanish Protestant named Antonio Corrano, who more than once had to face charges of heresy. The principal, Philip Rondell, who held office from 1549 to 1599, was, according to Anthony Wood, one who 'had weathered out several changes of religion, though in his heart he was a Papist'. Under him the Hall had certainly produced some notable Catholics: Francis Throckmorton, who was convicted of high treason and executed in 1584, Alexander Briant, executed as a seminary priest in 1581, and Richard Holtby, a former tutor who became a Jesuit and successfully evaded the pursuivants in the north of England for over forty years.[1]

Walton tells us that it was at Oxford that the lifelong friendship of Donne and Henry Wotton began. Wotton was a Wykehamist who matriculated from New College on 5 June 1584, but transferred first to Hart Hall and then to Queen's, from which he took his degree in 1588. Other Wykehamists whom Donne probably knew through Wotton were John Owen and John Hoskyns (who matriculated from New College on 22 March 1583 and 5 March 1585 respectively), and John Davies of Hereford (who matriculated from Queen's on 15 October 1585). Richard Baker, the future chronicler, matriculated from Hart Hall on the same day as the Donne brothers, and was for a time Wotton's 'chamber-fellow'. Other friends of later years who were Oxford contemporaries were Hugh Holland (at Balliol) and Richard Martin (of Broadgates Hall). This is all that is known or can be surmised of Donne's friendships at Oxford, but such a group of boys, all destined to win distinction and all possessed of literary talent, must have been capable of providing lively companionship for one another. Donne and his brother, however, were more fortunate than most of their fellow undergraduates in having relatives living in Oxford, and no doubt they visited the Blue Boar

[1] S. G. Hamilton, *Hertford College*, 1903, pp. 15–21, and Mallet, ii. 297.

Inn from time to time to see the members of the Dawson family.
Mrs. Dawson, their aunt, died a little over a year after their admission to Hart Hall.[1] She left two children, Edward and Grace, whom
Donne always remembered affectionately. Grace became the wife of
Thomas Whitfield, by whom she is known to have had five children;
Edward inherited his father's lease of the Blue Boar.[2] Edward renewed his lease in 1614, but he was not as successful as his father
had been.[3] In their old age both he and his sister fell into poverty,
and Donne as Dean of St. Paul's not only made them an allowance
but also made provision for them in his will.

Meanwhile Jasper Heywood was languishing in the Tower, and
William Weston, newly arrived from Rome, was attempting to get
in touch with his imprisoned superior. In his autobiography Weston
relates how this was achieved. The passage is a long one, but so
interesting that it deserves quotation in full:

This was the time that Father Heywood was held a prisoner in the
Tower of London. There, in addition to the ordinary discomforts of
prison life, he was suffering from a very severe illness and was in great
pain. In consideration of his age and poor health he was allowed to
receive visits from his sister, who in some measure was able to attend
to his needs and nurse him. She was a Catholic, and it was through
her that I got in touch with him by letter and received letters from
him in reply.

It was now near the opening of Parliament—the Parliament which
passed the most severe and fearful laws against Catholics and against
priests in particular, and at this time such priests as were still in
prison were ordered into exile. One of them was Father Heywood,
and I was most anxious to see and speak to him before he left. I discussed the matter, therefore, with his sister, and I understood from

---

[1] She was buried at St. Aldate's Church on 27 Nov. 1585. Her husband
married again on 11 Sept. 1588; his second wife was Agnes Drew, who was buried
on 2 June 1601. Robert Dawson himself died early in 1605 and was buried on 22 Jan.
1604/5 (Anthony Wood's *Survey of the Antiquities of the City of Oxford*, ed. A. Clark,
Oxford Historical Society, iii (1899), 201–4). His will is to be found at Somerset
House in *Archdeaconry of Oxford Wills and Administrations*, ser. 2, vol. i, fo. 66ᵛ. It
appears that there was a son, Martin, by the second marriage.

The 'John Dawson, Butler at Christ-Church' whom Bishop Corbet commemorated
in one of his poems, was a cousin of Robert, who bequeathed him the lease of a shop
between the Blue Boar and the Guildhall.

[2] These particulars about Grace and Edward are from Robert Dawson's will.

[3] H. E. Salter, *Survey of Oxford*, Oxford Historical Society, 1960, i. 227–8.

her that it could be arranged without grave risk, for in view of his imminent exile he was granted greater liberty to deal with his friends. So I accompanied her to the Tower, but with a feeling of great trepidation as I saw the vast battlements, and was led by the warder past the gates with their iron fastenings, which were closed behind me. So I came to the cell where the Father was confined. We greeted one another and then, as was natural, exchanged the information we each had about the affairs that concerned us. . . .

At last, when I had finished talking to Father Heywood—we spent almost the whole day together—I embraced him and said goodbye. Then I returned the same way that I had come; and the moment I reached safety outside the walls I felt as if I had been restored to the light of day.[1]

Weston's guide was presumably Donne's mother,[2] but he was writing many years after the event with only his memory to guide him, so he does not mention her name. The Parliament to which he refers met on 23 November 1584, and the law against the Catholic clergy was 27 Eliz. c. 2, which made it high treason for any Jesuit or seminary priest to be found in England forty days after the passing of the act. The bill had not yet passed both Houses on 21 January 1585, when Heywood and nineteen other priests were put aboard ship for France. The Government did not want to have them on its hands when the new act came into force. Heywood never saw England again, but died in Naples in 1598.

Walton gives Donne three years at Oxford, which would have been natural enough. He soon distinguished himself by his ability, which 'made one then give this censure of him; *That this age had brought forth another* Picus Mirandula; *of whom Story says, That he was rather born, than made wise by study*'. He had no intention of taking a degree, because of the Oath of Supremacy, although, as Walton says, 'time [had] made him capable,[3] and his learning expressed in

---

[1] William Weston, *The Autobiography of an Elizabethan*, translated from the Latin by Philip Caraman, 1955, pp. 10–11.

[2] She could conceivably have been Elizabeth Marvin; there are, however, no known references to Mrs. Marvin after 1577.

[3] This is inaccurate; sixteen terms, or four years, of residence were required for the B.A. degree, except from sons of peers and knights and eldest sons of esquires, who were allowed to take degrees after three years of residence. In the first edition of the *Life* Walton says that Donne entered Oxford at the age of nine; in later

publick exercises declared him worthy to receive his first degree in
the Schools'. If he had remained a fourth year, he would have reached
the age of sixteen, and would have become liable under the Matriculation Statute to subscription to the Thirty-nine Articles and the
Oath of Supremacy. Even though his age was inaccurately given
in the Matriculation Register, the risk was probably too great to
take.

Some writers have doubted Walton's further assertion that
Donne transferred from Oxford to Cambridge, because there is no
record at Cambridge of his ever having had any connection with the
University,[1] and because of some obvious errors in the statements
linking him with Cambridge.[2] But the records of the University at
this period are far from complete,[3] and there is no need to dismiss
Walton's statement. If Donne was at Cambridge, it is hardly likely
that he entered a college. There was nothing at Cambridge corresponding to the requirements of the Oxford Matriculation
Statute; religious discipline was left to the colleges, and for that very
reason it was the more strict. Daily attendance at college chapel was
enforced, and there were even fines for failure to attend the University sermons.[4] The medieval hostels of Cambridge were at this time
almost, but probably not quite, extinct; one of these, or lodgings
with some college tutor, could have satisfied Donne's wish to remain
aloof from the religious observances of the Church of England. On
the other hand, though Walton gives him three years at Cambridge,
he could not have remained at the University for twelve terms

editions, presumably after he had consulted the matriculation registers, he corrected
the age to eleven, but without altering the sentence quoted (*Lives*, pp. 23–4).

[1] Even Donne's honorary degree is not recorded.

[2] For instance, Walton refers (*Lives*, p. 29) to Samuel Brooke as Donne's 'Compupil
in *Cambridge*'. Brooke took his B.A. early in 1595, and therefore presumably matriculated when Donne was already a law student in London.

[3] See J. and J. A. Venn, *Alumni Cantabrigienses*, pt. 1, vol. i, pp. vi and vii. Two
instances of the incompleteness of the records may be cited: (1) Ben Jonson told
Drummond that he 'was Master of Arts in both the Universities, by their favour, not
his study'. The Oxford records show that the degree was conferred on 19 July 1619;
but there is no record of any degree at Cambridge. (2) Sir George Buc, James I's
Master of the Revels, in a genealogical work still surviving in manuscript, writes:
'Cadets ther wer of the Pinqueneys, for I remember that ther was a yong gentilman
of that surnam a scholler in Cambridg in my tym' (*MLR*, xx, 1935, 6). Neither Buc
himself nor any Pinkney who could be the one referred to is recorded by the Venns.

[4] J. B. Mullinger, *The University of Cambridge from the Royal Injunctions of 1535 to the
Accession of Charles the First*, 1884, pp. 392 n., and 428–9.

without matriculating, so that his stay there must have been some-what less than three years.

It is probable that certain of Donne's friendships, to which further reference will be made, were first formed at Cambridge. Beaupré Bell, son of Sir Robert Bell, Chief Baron of the Exchequer, was admitted a pensioner of Emmanuel College on 16 May 1587; Everard Guilpin was admitted to the same college a year later. In Michaelmas term 1587 Henry Goodyer matriculated as a fellow-commoner of St. John's, and John Pory matriculated from Caius in Easter term 1588.

At this time Cambridge may have been more interesting than Oxford to a young writer ambitious of contributing to English letters. Greene had left Cambridge in 1583, Marlowe in 1586, and Nashe probably in 1588. The three Harvey brothers were still at the University, and in 1592 became involved in a quarrel with Greene and then with Nashe that caused a considerable stir in educated society. Thus, though there was but the memory of Greene and Marlowe in Cambridge, Nashe and the Harveys were still to be seen in street and tavern. Literary debate was in the air as it had not been at Oxford. At Cambridge Donne is likely first to have come upon some of the writings of Marlowe, who had already translated Ovid's *Amores* (the main models of Donne's love elegies) and had written *Dido, Queen of Carthage*, probably for performance on a university stage. Marlowe, indeed, made a deeper impression on Donne than any other English contemporary. Something of Donne's feeling for Cambridge is revealed in the sonnet addressed 'To Mr. S. B.' This was young Samuel Brooke, who, probably in 1592, entered Trinity as a Westminster scholar. In spite of all temptations to absorb himself wholly in study, Donne advises him not to neglect the Muses but 'wisely take / Fresh water at the Heliconian spring'. The reference to

> those Scismatiques with you,
> Which draw all wits of good hope to their crew;

seems clearly to refer to the Harvey brothers, but whether they were schismatics because of Gabriel's advocacy of classical metres in English poetry or because Donne sided with Greene and Nashe in the Harvey–Nashe quarrel must be left in doubt.

It is difficult to assess Donne's debt to the universities. He

attended them, as did many of his contemporaries, without intending
to take a degree, and his reading was probably from the first un-
restricted by the bounds of the prescribed academic curriculum.
That curriculum was still largely based on the medieval *trivium* and
quadrivium. Grammar was, of course, the concern of the grammar
schools, and arithmetic, as too practical an art, had a comparatively
meagre place in university studies. Rhetoric and logic were therefore the main subjects of study for undergraduates, and the bachelor's degree was awarded on the basis of skill in disputation.
Donne's training in formal rhetoric is displayed much more fully in
his sermons than in his poems, but his skill in dialectic, most
obvious in his *Paradoxes and Problems*, is employed in season and out
of season through all his writings. Walton relates that at Cambridge
Donne was 'a most laborious Student, often changing his studies',
and his writings display the command of a wide range of knowledge
that is even more impressive than the evidence of his formal training. In some fields of learning he was genuinely erudite, and in
others he had a first-hand acquaintance with at least the main
authorities, both orthodox and unorthodox. Donne's mature mind,
indeed, could range over a considerable extent of human knowledge,
but how much of it was acquired during his university days it is
impossible to tell. In an age when the universities were dominated
by the spirit of theological controversy he could hardly have remained unaffected by the prevailing rage, especially as it touched
so nearly his own personal problem, that of the Catholic in a
Protestant state. Aristotelian philosophy fell within the range of
university studies, as did the civil law, and so unorthodox and
unconfined a student as Donne may well have embarked in his
university days on subjects so far beyond the undergraduate curriculum as these. Of the theory of medicine, of which he had at least
a smattering, he could have learned something from his step-father
and more from university lectures, but his knowledge of such subjects as French and Italian literature and of canon law could have
come only from more private studies. He was by habit an avid and
voracious reader, who to aid his memory formed at an early age the
habit of taking systematic notes, and almost everything in print
seems to have come under his eager scrutiny.

While Donne and his brother were away at the universities changes had been occurring in the household of the family in London. It was probably from Dr. Syminges's house in Bartholomew Close that Anne, Donne's only surviving sister, was married in the latter part of 1585. Her husband was Avery, or Alvarey, Copley, a barrister of Lincoln's Inn and second son of Avery Copley of Batley in Yorkshire.[1] He had been admitted to Lincoln's Inn from Thavies Inn in 1574, was called to the bar in 1583, and was about thirty years of age at the time of his marriage. That he was a Catholic is certain, since his name appears in a list of recusants,[2] but he had nevertheless attested his loyalty to the Queen by signing the Oath of Association at Lincoln's Inn in 1584.[3] He seems to have lived beyond his means, and there is an interesting reference to one of his debts among the State Papers.[4] Soon after his marriage, however, his wife received her portion of £500, of which £234. 6s. 8d. came from the Chamber of the City, and the rest from the recognitors.[5] Apparently Anne's dowry did not last long, for Copley not only ran through it but also through a loan of £600 which he secured from his mother-in-law.[6]

John Syminges, Donne's step-father, died in 1588 and was buried in the church of St. Bartholomew the Less on 15 July. He died intestate, and the administration of his very substantial possessions passed into the hands of his widow. Not long after his death she left the house in Bartholomew Close, and moved across the river to the parish of St. Saviour's. Here her obstinate recusancy soon got her into trouble, and the token-books of the parish show that on 28 September 1589 'mystres Symones Mr. doctor Symones wyfe lait dessesed' was presented 'for not komyng to chirche to receive

---

[1] The most accessible pedigree of the family is that in Dugdale's *Visitation of the County of York, 1665-6*, Surtees Society, vol. xxxvi (1859). It is stated there that Avery Copley died unmarried, but in Joseph Foster's privately printed *Visitation of Yorkshire Made in the Years 1584-85* (1875) it is more correctly but not very precisely stated that he married '—— da. of —— Dunn'.

[2] Printed in H. Foley, *Records of the English Province of the Society of Jesus*, 1875-83, vi. 744. The date of the list is 20 Jan. 1593, when Copley was already dead.

[3] *Egerton Papers*, ed. J. P. Collier, Camden Society, 1840, pp. 108-11.

[4] *C.S.P.* (*Dom.*), *Addenda 1580-1625*, p. 131.

[5] F. P. Wilson, *RES*, iii (1927), 275-6.

[6] Copley *v*. Copley and Rainsford, C2 Eliz., C10/41.

the communyon'.[1] Not long afterwards Mrs. Syminges married again, probably in 1590, and certainly before 7 February 1591. Her third husband was Richard Rainsford, who, in the earliest reference to him that has been found, is described as a 'gentleman, dwelling in Southwark near London'.[2]

As has been seen, Donne was probably at Oxford for three years and at Cambridge for a somewhat shorter period. If we allow him five years in all, we allow him one more year than was taken by the average undergraduate of similar social status who cared enough for his studies to stay up long enough to take a degree. This chronology would bring Donne to the summer of 1589, but from then until the spring of 1591 nothing definite can be asserted about him. Such a hiatus inevitably raises problems, even though it is no cause for surprise that nothing whatever should be known of the doings, nearly 400 years ago, of a youth between the ages of seventeen and nineteen. Was this the period of his travels abroad? He would not have been regarded as too young for a 'grand tour', or even for military service. His friend Sir Robert Drury, for instance, won his knighthood on the field of battle before he was seventeen.[3] The engraving prefixed to the *Poems* of 1635, made from a portrait dated 1591, does not suggest a scholar fresh from the university; the firmly clasped sword, transferred from its natural position at the sitter's side in order to be included in the picture, may even be meant to suggest military experience.[4]

Walton's account of Donne's travels cannot be accurate, and it has been subjected more than once to close analysis in order to ascertain what basis of fact may lie beneath it. After taking part in the expeditions of 1596 and 1597 against the Spaniards Donne, Walton asserts,

returned not back into *England*, till he had staid some years[5] first in *Italy*, and then in *Spain*, where he made many useful observations of

---

[1] B. W. Whitlock, 'The Family of John Donne, 1588–91', *NQ*, ccv (1960), 380–6 at p. 383.

[2] In the bill (dated 21 Oct. 1591) referred to on p. 49, n. 6 above.

[3] *Donne and the Drurys*, pp. 19–20.

[4] B. W. Whitlock, in 'Donne's University Years', *English Studies*, xliii (1962), 1–20, believes (like Gosse, i. 24) that this portrait shows Donne in uniform, but this is far from certain.

[5] The first edition of the *Life* reads 'staid a convenient time'.

those Countreys, their Laws and manner of Government, and returned perfect in their Languages.

The time that he spent in *Spain* was at his first going into *Italy* designed for travelling to the *Holy Land*, and for viewing *Jerusalem* and the Sepulchre of our Saviour. But at his being in the furthest parts of *Italy*, the disappointment of Company, or of a safe Convoy, or the uncertainty of returns of Money into those remote parts, denied him that happiness: which he did often occasionally mention with a deploration.[1]

On his return, Walton continues, Donne became secretary to Sir Thomas Egerton. But any lengthy travels after the Azores expedition are quite out of the question, and enough is known of Donne's movements between 1591 and the time of his marriage to preclude any but considerably briefer periods of absence from England. If he was travelling abroad for any extended period during his early life, it was almost certainly between 1589 and 1591.

Another puzzle is provided by one of his epigrams. A number of these short pieces clearly refer to the capture of Cadiz in 1596 and were presumably composed during the campaign, but one of them, 'Fall of a Wall', is without question based on an incident that occurred during the siege of the citadel, or upper town, of Corunna in the course of the expedition against Lisbon in 1589.[2] Of course, the poem could have been suggested by the recollections of old campaigners whom Donne met during the 1596 expedition, or, indeed, it could have been written at any date after 1589, but it does suggest the possibility that Donne might have cut short his studies at Cambridge and was present at the occasion it commemorates. The expedition of Drake and Norreys in 1589 was joined by just as many eager gentlemen volunteers as were those of Essex in 1596 and 1597. Furthermore, if Donne first saw service in 1589, Walton's account becomes more intelligible; confusion between the earlier and the later expeditions would make Donne set out on his European travels

---

[1] *Lives*, p. 26. The second paragraph was first added in 1658. Originally Walton believed that Donne *had* visited the Holy Land, and in his elegy on Donne wrote that he

Went to see
That blessed place of Christs nativity.

[2] R. C. Bald, 'Three Metaphysical Epigrams', *PQ*, xvi (1937), 402–5.

in 1597, which was manifestly impossible, whereas, on the other hand, he could well have gone in 1589.

This is all speculation; nevertheless, it seems that 1589–91 is the only period of Donne's early life during which he could have undertaken such extensive travels. It would have been natural for a young Elizabethan to visit Italy, after passing through France or the Low Countries and Switzerland. One might expect to find some record of him in the guest-book of the English College at Rome (which even the sturdily Protestant Milton visited some forty years later), or in the records of some of the other institutions established by the English Catholics abroad, but there is none. He would have had more inducement than most such travellers to go further south than Rome in order to visit his ailing uncle, Jasper Heywood, at Naples. The wish to visit Palestine could have been the result either of youthful piety or of mere curiosity, though Venice would have been a better place than Naples from which to secure a passage. On the other hand, it would not have been difficult to pass from southern Italy, which was virtually a Spanish dominion, to Spain. But it should not be forgotten that from 1587 to 1604 England was at war with Spain, and that Englishmen who fell into Spanish hands could usually expect short shrift. If Donne went to Spain at this period he could only have gone as a Catholic refugee. He would obviously have had to be discreet, and some of the obscurity which attaches to these early travels may be due to his having availed himself of opportunities denied to his Protestant fellow-countrymen.[1]

---

[1] [At some time, probably between 1597 and 1601, Donne presented a copy of an edition (1578) in German of Munster's *Cosmographia* to Edward Parvish. This was the brother of Henry Parvish the business magnate who, among his other activities, ran a forwarding service for mail, money, and goods, of which Henry Wotton availed himself for his first visit to Europe in 1589. Whatever the date of Donne's own travels, it is probable that he followed his friend's example. Henry Parvish kept agents in Germany at Stade (near Hamburg), at Nuremberg, and perhaps at Frankfurt; Edward Parvish was living at Nuremberg in 1583, and may have been Henry's agent there for some years (though he was definitely residing in England in January 1597). It seems possible that Donne visited Germany, or that he met Edward Parvish at one of the firm's stations elsewhere. His gift to a man so much his senior may have been an acknowledgement of kindnesses experienced during his travels abroad. See the full study by I. A. Shapiro, 'Donne, the Parvishes, and Munster's "Cosmographey" ', *N&Q*, July 1966, 243–8.]

IV

LINCOLN'S INN

FROM 1591 to 1594 and perhaps longer, Donne was at least nominally a student of the laws of England. After a minimum of a year of preliminary study at Thavies Inn, he entered Lincoln's Inn in May 1592. It was natural for one of his family to become a member of Lincoln's Inn; Sir John More, Sir Thomas More, William Roper, Christopher Stubbes (the husband of John Heywood's eldest daughter), William Rastell, Richard Heywood and his son John, had all belonged to the Society, and the bonds of family tradition were strong in the household in which Donne had grown up. Though he never attempted to practise the law, nor was ever called to the bar, Lincoln's Inn was of great importance in Donne's development, and he made friendships and formed associations there which persisted for most of the rest of his life. There he met men like Christopher Brooke, who was to be his lifelong friend, his younger brother Samuel (still at Westminster School in 1592), and their cousin John Brooke (who entered Lincoln's Inn at the same time as Donne). The Brooke brothers shared Donne's poetic tastes, as did Rowland Woodward, who was slightly his senior, and Woodward's younger brother Thomas. Much of Donne's early poetry was written during these years, at first experimentally but with a growing sense of finding the modes of expression best fitted to his talents and temperament.

Lincoln's Inn was also a gateway to the great world. Among the young men whom he first met there, for example, were Thomas and John Egerton, the sons of the Lord Keeper. Like his contemporaries at the Inn, Donne seems not wholly to have confined himself to the routine of law studies but from time to time to have presented himself at court. The satires show that he was familiar with Westminster and Whitehall. Nearer at hand were the other Inns of Court, Gray's Inn and the Temple, while to the east the City stretched beyond St. Paul's and the site of his birth to the Tower of London. All the life of the metropolis beckoned to him.

The earliest portrait of Donne to survive belongs to the beginning of this period. It bears the date 1591, and is known only from the engraving by William Marshall prefixed to the *Poems* of 1635. The original was clearly a miniature, and so authoritative an expert as Lawrence Binyon has ventured the opinion that it was in all probability painted by Nicholas Hilliard.[1] From an early age Donne possessed the instincts of a connoisseur, and esteemed Hilliard highly:

> a hand, or eye
> By *Hilliard* drawne, is worth an history,
> By a worse painter made;

and he would scarcely have been satisfied with the work of any lesser artist. The miniature probably shows Donne just before he entered Thavies Inn. The Inns of Court and of Chancery had various sumptuary regulations, such as those forbidding the wearing of long hair and of swords, and in the first Satire Donne refers to his clothing as a member of Lincoln's Inn as 'this course attire, which I now weare', but the young man of the portrait is wearing clothes which, though simple, are of a highly fashionable cut. It is true that he is wearing a falling band rather than a ruff (which was forbidden at the Inns of Court), but this may be no more than a sign that the winter was over, for ruffs must have been unbearable in hot weather, especially to the young. His hair is worn long, and there are ear-rings in his ears; a delicate hand grasps the hilt of his sword. His doublet, close buttoned down the front, is exaggeratedly wide at the shoulders and is cut to form a peak at the waist; the sleeves of the doublet are slit to reveal under-sleeves of some contrasting material. His face, though not handsome, is arresting. His forehead is broad; his eyes, set widely apart, look out intensely and eagerly; his cheek-bones are high and prominent; his nose is large, and without any pretensions to gracefulness; the beginnings of a moustache fringe his upper lip. Such was Donne in the spring of 1591.

The admission register of Lincoln's Inn shows that he was admitted from Thavies Inn on 6 May 1592 and that he paid the reduced fee of 31s. required of those who had already been members

---

[1] Mr. John Bryson, the discoverer of the portrait of Donne at Newbattle Abbey, also speaks of the earlier portrait as 'certainly based on a lost miniature by Nicholas Hilliard' (*The Times*, 13 Oct. 1959, p. 13). [Cf. Gardner, *Elegies etc.*, Appendix E.]

for at least a year of either of the two Inns of Chancery affiliated with Lincoln's Inn. Thavies Inn was in Holborn, adjoining the church of St. Andrew on the west side. The land on which it stood was owned by Lincoln's Inn, and it was usual for its junior members to pass on to Lincoln's Inn. They normally did so as soon as possible, after they had attained some knowledge of the rudiments of the common law. The Lincoln's Inn of Donne's day was a society of about 150 members who shared commons in the hall. Some thirty or forty students joined it each year, but less than a third of these were ever called to the bar; the majority were young men of good family who were completing their education by acquiring a smattering of the law and some experience of the metropolis. This fact made the Inns of Court vital centres of intellectual and even of literary activity, fulfilling a function in the national life which has since belonged to the universities but which, owing to the much lower age of the undergraduates, they had as yet scarcely begun to perform.

Two members of the Society were required to act as sureties for each new entrant to Lincoln's Inn, and this function was performed for Donne by Christopher Brooke and Edward Loftus. Both were Yorkshiremen; Loftus had been admitted on 24 November 1584,[1] and Brooke on 15 March 1587; neither had yet been called to the bar. Of other associations between Donne and Loftus nothing is known, but Christopher Brooke became one of his closest friends. The son of Robert Brooke of York, a wealthy merchant who was twice mayor of that city, Christopher Brooke was several years

---

[1] Edward Loftus was a kinsman of Adam Loftus (1533?–1605), Archbishop of Dublin, and of his nephew Adam Loftus, first Viscount Loftus, Lord Chancellor of Ireland. After being admitted to the English bar Edward Loftus went to Dublin to practise, and eventually reached the rank of sergeant.

A little over a month after Donne's admission to Lincoln's Inn, Adam Loftus 'of Ireland, gen. of Thavies Inn' was also admitted. He was perhaps one of the twenty children of the Archbishop. Donne would certainly have known him at Thavies Inn, and he furnishes the most likely link between Donne and Edward Loftus.

The entry in the Admission Register reads:

'1592 london. Joha*n*nes Donne Generosus Admiss*us* est in Societatem istius hospicij sexto die maij Anno *regni regi*ne Eliz. xxxiiij° p*er* m*anu*cap*tores* q*uorum* nom*i*na hic subsc*ri*bun*tur* p*ro*p*ria* Et soluit ad vsum hospicij p*re*dic*t*i xxxj[s] quia fuit de hospicio de Thavies Inne

manucaptores	{ Christ: Broke	[signed]
	{ Edwarde Loftus	[signed]
Admiss*us* p*er*	R. Rokeby'	[signed; apparently by the Master
of the Court of Requests]		

Donne's senior. Nothing is known of his education before he entered Lincoln's Inn, and it is useless to hazard a guess how Donne first met him. Both he and his younger brother Samuel wrote verse, and Donne was no doubt drawn to them by his interest in poetry.

The legal education of the time was protracted, since at least seven years of study were necessary before a call to the bar, and even then further subsidiary activities were required before a barrister could appear before the courts at Westminster. Instruction was given mainly by means of moots (where points of law were discussed and argued) and readings (where statutes were interpreted by senior members of the bar). These exercises were held in the vacations, that is, in the intervals between the regular sittings of the courts; there were three 'learning' vacations in the year, and students were required either to keep six vacations in their first three years, or at least four successive vacations. The two years following Donne's entrance to Lincoln's Inn were years of plague, and in consequence the life of London suffered serious disruption. In 1592 Michaelmas term was deferred and then eventually held at Hertford; in 1593 Trinity term was deferred and Michaelmas term held at St. Albans; in both years also the customary Christmas celebrations in the Inns of Court were cancelled. At Lincoln's Inn itself no commons were kept during twenty-one weeks in 1592 and twenty-six weeks in 1593; in other words, the dining-hall of the Inn was closed during two successive years for almost half of the time. The records show, however, that Donne kept the autumn vacation of 1592, the first that he could have kept after his admission. The next, the Christmas vacation of 1592, was not held, and there were no Christmas festivities. Nevertheless, Donne was appointed a Master of the Revels for the year; the office was one usually held by newly admitted members of the Inn. But the appointment was not even made this year until 6 February 1593, when the Christmas season was already over, so that in comparison with other years the office was a sinecure. The Easter vacation was held, but Donne did not keep it;[1] he seems to have been in London in the summer of 1593,

---

[1] Since there was no Christmas vacation and Donne did not keep the Easter vacation, it is just possible that he made a brief trip to Italy at this time, though his appointment as Master of the Revels on 6 Feb. may seem to make this improbable. Nevertheless it should be recorded that on 13 Feb. 1593 Father Claude

however, for on 19 June he acknowledged the receipt of part of his inheritance at the Guildhall. There are references, too, to this same plague-stricken summer in the verse letters. It is hell, he says in one of them,

> where I am, where in every street
> Infections follow, overtake, and meete:

and in another he alludes to the deserted streets and places of entertainment about London:

> Our Theaters are fill'd with emptines;
> As lancke and thin is every Street and way
> As a Woman deliver'd yesterday.

The plague did not abate and neither the autumn nor the Christmas vacation was held in 1593, and once again there were no Christmas festivities. The rate of plague deaths, however, fell off appreciably in the new year, and the Easter vacation was held. Donne was one of those who kept it. There were fears of a fresh outbreak of the plague in 1594, but happily it did not occur. This summer he stayed in or near London, as his second verse letter to Mr. I. L. seems to imply. He kept the autumn vacation, which was held, and was chosen Steward of Christmas, but declined the office and in due course paid the customary fine of 26s. 8d. for his refusal to act.[1]

Thereafter Donne appears no more in this part of the records. He is not named as having kept the Christmas or any subsequent vacation or as having failed to do so. One can only conclude that he

---

Aquaviva, the General of the Jesuits, wrote from Rome to Jasper Heywood in Naples concerning a kinsman of his:

'Non ho mancato di mostrare quell' affetto che dovevo al cognato di V[ostra] R[everenza] et insieme procurato che per quel poco che noi potevamo in servitio suo, si sia partito da noi consolato. Harei voluto poter piu per amor di V. R. et per l'opera in se pia. Prego N. S. l'accompagni sempre con sua santa Grazia et conceda a V. R. quelli doni spirituali che desidera.'

The passage is from Father Aquaviva's letter book in the Archivum Romanum Societatis Jesu, *Neap.* 4, II, fo. 450ᵛ. I owe the reference to the kindness of Fr. Edmond Lamalle of the Instituto Storico della Compagnia di Gesù at Rome, who comments: 'Les expressions du P. Aquaviva me semblent une allusion plus que transparente à une petite aide financière.' One has to decide, however regretfully, that while it is conceivable that the reference is to Donne, on the whole it is unlikely.

[1] The references to Donne in the records of Lincoln's Inn have been collected and discussed by I. A. Shapiro, 'John Donne and Lincoln's Inn', *TLS*, 16 and 23 Oct. 1930, pp. 833 and 861.

was regarded as having fulfilled the necessary requirements, or that he had severed his connection with the Inn. If credit were granted for the autumn and Christmas vacations of 1593, for which no lists survive and which were apparently not held, it will be seen that Donne could have claimed four successive vacations and have had one to spare. The conclusion that he had reached the stage at which no more vacations were required seems the natural one. The keeping of vacations, of course, marked only the preliminary stages of a legal education. In the years that followed a student was expected to participate in bolts and moots; in the former a simple case was argued between students only, and in the latter both inner barristers (those who had not yet been called) and utter barristers took part. That Donne participated in such exercises may be inferred from Walton's statement that at Lincoln's Inn 'he gave great testimonies of his Wit, his Learning, and of his Improvement in that profession'.

The death of Donne's brother Henry in 1593 must have come to him as a sobering shock. All that is known of Henry Donne is that he entered Oxford with his brother and was now presumably a student at Thavies Inn. The two had probably been together during most of the intervening years, but John, as the elder, had entered Lincoln's Inn ahead of his younger brother. Early in May 1593 a young priest of Yorkshire extraction named William Harrington was discovered and arrested in Henry Donne's chambers by Richard Young, the principal colleague of the notorious Topcliffe. Both were committed to prison, where Harrington at first denied that he was a priest, but Henry Donne broke down under cross-examination and admitted that 'hee said he was a prieste & did shriue him'. Harrington was brought to trial, and lingered in prison for some months, but on 18 February 1594 he suffered a traitor's death; as Stow tersely expresses it, he was 'drawne from Newgate to Tyborne; and there hanged, cut downe aliue, struggled with the hang-man, but was bowelled, and quartered'. But before Harrington went to the scaffold Henry Donne was dead. Like Harrington he was removed from the Clink, to which they had first been committed, to Newgate, where the plague was rampant, and he died within a few days.[1]

---

[1] Fr. John Morris, 'The Martyrdom of William Harrington', *The Month*, xx (1874), 411–23, prints all the documents bearing on the deaths of Henry Donne and William

Donne had come of age about three months before Henry's arrest, and it was probably while his brother was still in prison that he received his portion from the Chamber of the City of London. On 19 June 1593 William Skidmore, his father's old friend and neighbour, and Robert Chambers, cordwainer, appeared before the Court of Aldermen and 'deposed upon their Oaths John son and orphan of John Dunn Iremonger deceased to be of full age of xxi years and upwards'. He received from the funds of the Chamber the sum of £232. 16s. 8d.; there is no record of the exact amount of the balance of his father's estate still in the hands of recognitors, but Donne formally acknowledged himself satisfied on 19 June, when he received the money in the Chamber, and again a week later. Henry, of course, never reached his majority, and after his death his share, still in the Chamber or in the hands of recognitors, was divided between his surviving brother and sister. On 11 April 1594 John and Anne each received £149. 5s. from the Chamber, and their shares from the recognitors. In all, it has been estimated, Donne inherited about £750 from his father.[1]

When Anne received her share of her brother Henry's inheritance she was the wife of William Lyly of London, gentleman, who joined with her in signing the receipts.[2] Avery Copley had died in January 1591, heavily in debt and leaving his widow with one small child. A Chancery suit brought against her soon afterwards by the father and elder brother of her late husband reveals some interesting particulars. It is here that we learn that, besides Anne's portion of £500 Avery Copley had received a loan of £600 from Donne's mother, both of which sums had been consumed by his debts. Copley's sister had, however, recently married a wealthy Yorkshire gentleman, Francis Bosvile of Gunthwaite Hall, and Copley himself had been a party to their marriage settlement;[3] to provide for his

---

Harrington. The charge of a contemporary Catholic writer that Henry Donne was transferred to Newgate for the express purpose of exposing him to the plague and defeating him of his inheritance (p. 417) is answered by F. P. Wilson, 'Notes on the Early Life of John Donne', *RES*, iii (1927), at p. 275.

[1] F. P. Wilson, op. cit., and B. W. Whitlock, 'The Orphanage Accounts of John Donne, Ironmonger', *Guildhall Miscellany*, no. 4, Feb. 1955, pp. 22–9.

[2] See *Donne and the Drurys*, pl. iv, p. 71, for a facsimile of the signatures of Donne, his sister, and his brother-in-law on this occasion.

[3] Joseph Hunter, *South Yorkshire*, 1828–31, ii. 346–8.

wife he procured from Bosvile an annuity of £30, payable to her in the event of his death. But Anne also alleged that his father, as an expression of his satisfaction at his son's marriage, granted by deed to his son and his son's wife, for their lives, an annual rent charge of £20. 13s. 4d. on the manor of Sutton. This deed was the subject of the litigation,[1] since the elder Avery Copley now refused to acknowledge it. The deed had been deposited by the son with a certain William Stamford as security for a loan of £8, but Richard Rainsford had redeemed it, and had taken it into Yorkshire to demand payment of the rent charge. There had been an angry scene, and Copley, who had been bringing up his grandson since his son's death, not only refused to support him any longer but also declared that the deed was a forgery. Rainsford, since he had no children of his own, asserted that he would take the boy and be responsible for his welfare, but in fact he did no more than leave him with his aunt and uncle, the Bosviles, at Gunthwaite. Nothing more is heard of the child, and it can only be presumed that he died before reaching maturity.

William Lyly, Anne Donne's second husband, was a man in his early forties.[2] He had had early experience of travel in France and Italy, and probably spoke the languages of both countries with fluency when he accompanied Sir Edward Stafford, the new English ambassador, to Paris in 1583 as one of his secretaries. Except for two brief visits to England, he spent the next seven years in France. At first it had been one of his principal duties to maintain contact with English Catholics and malcontents in Paris and report on their activities; later, after 'the day of the barricades' and Henri III's flight from Paris, it became his duty to follow the court and report to Stafford in Paris. When Henri III was assassinated at St. Cloud on 1 August 1589 Lyly was waiting for an audience in an antechamber and actually spoke to the King after he had been wounded. In the new reign he followed Henri IV in the field, and was present with him at the battle of Ivry. His reports provided the English Government with authentic news of the most vital developments in the

---

[1] Copley v. Copley and Rainsford, P.R.O., C2 Eliz., C10/41; the commission is in C33/86, fo. 126ᵛ.

[2] For a fuller account of William Lyly, see *Donne and the Drurys*, ch. vi, pp. 69–84.

French civil war. Lyly returned to England with his master, when Sir Edward Stafford was recalled towards the end of 1590.

Lyly, therefore, was a man accustomed to the courts of princes. Henri III had liked 'his manner of behaviour and readiness to answer all things marvellous well'. His own queen looked on him less favourably but with full consciousness of his ability; she is reported to have said that he had 'a shrewd tongue and a shrewd head', and that 'they two met together were dangerous'. Joseph Hall, who disliked him strongly, called him 'a witty and bold Atheist', but was forced to concede that he had 'Abilities of Discourse and Behaviour'. Though his professional duties had led him to collect evidence against Catholic refugees and plotters, he had seen enough in France of the conflict between Catholic and Protestant to look with detachment on either side, nor were his religious feelings very deep. Perhaps Donne's sister found in his company some relief from the repressed and stifling Catholicism in which most of her previous life had been spent.

In the year after Anne Lyly received the last instalment of her patrimony Lionel Rolston bound himself to the amount of £600 to pay to William Lyly and Anne his wife, at the Benchers' table in Lincoln's Inn, £130 at Michaelmas and £130 at Lady Day next ensuing.[1] Francis Bosvile had died in 1592, leaving his widow (under the terms of his marriage settlement) tenant for life of his very considerable properties, and Lionel Rolston was her second husband.[2] The entry in the recognizance rolls presumably records an agreement under which Bosvile's liability to pay Anne Lyly's annuity was cancelled by a cash payment from Rolston. With this £260 from Rolston and her half share of her brother Henry's patrimony, Anne brought her second husband a dowry of over £500, roughly the same amount as she had brought her first husband.

According to Walton, Donne's general education was continued while he was studying the law in London:

His Mother and those to whose care he was committed, were

---

[1] L.C. 4/193, fo. 14ᵛ. The agreement was made on 9 July 1595. The reference is to the index of the recognizance rolls; the actual roll to which the entry refers is said to be unfit for inspection.
[2] Joseph Hunter, loc. cit.

watchful to improve his knowledge, and to that end appointed him
Tutors both in the *Mathematicks*, and in all the other *Liberal Sciences*,
to attend him. But with these Arts they were advised to instil into him
particular Principles of the *Romish Church*; of which those Tutors profest (though secretly) themselves to be members.[1]

This should doubtless be taken to refer to the year at Thavies Inn
and to the early part of his stay at Lincoln's Inn; after he had reached
his majority he would have been less under his mother's tutelage
and able to exercise greater responsibility in making his own
decisions. But the student's habits had been formed, and they never
left him. Walton's account is confirmed, too, by the opening lines
of the first Satire, which describe his 'study' in the chambers in
Lincoln's Inn which, Walton says, he shared with Christopher
Brooke. These studies were in reality small cells, which must have
been extremely cramped, partitioned off from the larger chamber
by wainscoting, and furnished with little more than a stool, a table,
and a set of shelves.[2]

> Leave mee, and in this standing woodden chest,
> Consorted with these few bookes, let me lye
> In prison, and here be coffin'd, when I dye;
> Here are Gods conduits, grave Divines; and here
> Natures Secretary, the Philosopher;
> And jolly Statesmen, which teach how to tie
> The sinewes of a cities mistique bodie;
> Here gathering Chroniclers, and by them stand
> Giddie fantastique Poëts of each land.

There were poets and historians, philosophers and theologians on
Donne's bookshelves, but no law books, or none that he thought
worth mentioning. It is clear that his interests ranged far beyond
the curriculum that he was supposedly following.

   The years as a law student were for Donne a period of rapid de-

---

   [1] *Lives*, p. 24. Walton's account of Donne's education is confused, and at first sight
appears to be a series of general statements, meant to apply to the whole of his education, but broken up rather clumsily by various insertions of specific facts. However,
that the sentences quoted are intended to refer to the years at Lincoln's Inn is made
clear in the first version of the *Life*, which reads: 'and to that end appointed him
there also [italics mine] Tutors in severall Sciences'.
   [2] *The Black Books of Lincoln's Inn*, vol. i (1897), p. iv, and vol. ii (1898), p. xv.

velopment and severe tensions. He was in the process of finding himself. He had to come to terms both with the world in which he lived and with the conflict of religious faiths into which, by virtue of his family inheritance, he was inevitably plunged. As a Catholic the gates of preferment and success were barred to him; as he knew only too well, his religion offered him nothing in this world but exile or the patient endurance of persecution. Active participation in the life of his age could only be purchased at the cost of disloyalty to all that he had been taught to revere. Besides, his restless intellectual curiosity refused to allow him to accept any creed unquestioned, and it eventually drove him to a systematic examination of the issues at stake between the conflicting faiths. His investigation brought him perilously close to complete cynicism in matters of religion, for he was not unreceptive to that Renaissance spirit of scepticism and free-thought which to many serious minds was more dangerous and deadly than heresy.

At Thavies Inn in 1591 Donne was not only a Catholic, influenced and guided by Catholic tutors, but also in contact with the most active Catholic proselytizers in England. A third Jesuit mission had followed in the wake of the preceding two, and was in the process of establishing itself. The leaders were Henry Garnet, who was arrested in the aftermath of the Gunpowder Plot and went to the scaffold after nearly twenty years of missionary activity in England, and Robert Southwell the poet. They had arrived in 1586, and by 1591 had five years of strenuous but rewarding labour to their credit. In November 1591 the Government opened a fresh campaign against priests and Jesuits with the issue of a proclamation to introduce new and stricter regulations for searching them out and exterminating them. In his indignation and distress Southwell drew up a 'humble supplication' for submission to the Queen, in which he sought justice and a measure of toleration for his oppressed co-religionists, and which was submitted for approval to a gathering of Catholics, priests and laymen. This, at least, is the most feasible explanation of a sentence embedded in *Pseudo-Martyr* in the midst of a rather prosy historical argument on the right of kings to include the term 'sacred' among their titles:

For so at a Consultation of *Jesuites* in the *Tower*, in the late Queenes time, I saw it resolued, that in a Petition to bee exhibited to her, shee might not be stiled *Sacred*.[1]

Conceivably the sentence might refer back to the winter of 1584–5, when Jasper Heywood was a prisoner in the Tower, when William Parry startled the House of Commons by protesting against the new anti-Catholic statutes, and when William Weston was desperately trying to get in touch with his imprisoned superior. On this assumption Donne would have accompanied his mother and Weston on the occasion of the latter's visit to Heywood. Yet it is much more probable that Donne was at Oxford at this time. A petition *was* presented to Elizabeth a few weeks after Heywood's expulsion, though the Jesuits are not known to have been concerned in it, but there Elizabeth is 'stiled *Sacred*' some four times, so that the Jesuit ruling, if actually made, had little effect. On the other hand, there is evidence that near the beginning of Southwell's *Humble Supplication to her Majestie* Elizabeth was originally addressed as 'sacred', but that subsequently the objectionable epithet was removed.[2] Thus, even though the reference to a consultation of Jesuits 'in the *Tower*' becomes difficult to explain, Donne seems to be alluding to a meeting, held probably between 15 December 1591 and the end of the year,[3] to consider the disabilities inflicted on the Catholics and to approve a petition to be submitted to the Queen.[4]

Even without the evidence of *Pseudo-Martyr*, it is quite possible that Donne, a brilliant young layman with Catholic antecedents, should have met Southwell and have felt his influence. Certainly, Southwell's *Humble Supplication* is a document of the first importance for an understanding of the environment in which Donne grew up. In form the work is a defence of the Catholics against the slanderous and opprobrious terms applied to them in the proclamation and

[1] p. 46.
[2] In all the surviving English texts there is a reference to 'your Maiesties goodnesse, (perfect in all Princely duties, & the only shot-anker of our iust hopes)', but a Latin version of this passage, submitted to the Pope in 1602 to illustrate the heretical tendencies of the book, reads: 'Bonitas maiestatis vestrae perfecta in omnibus officijs Principe dignis, solaque nostrae iustae spei anchora sacra.'
[3] The surviving texts of the *Humble Supplication* fall into two groups, one dated 14 Dec. and the other 31 Dec.
[4] For a fuller discussion of the problems involved in the interpretation of the sentence in *Pseudo-Martyr* see Southwell, *Humble Supplication*, Appendix III.

accepted by the popular imagination as a justification of the repressive measures against them; it relates their sufferings under persecution, and asserts their unswerving loyalty to the Queen. It is full of the ardour of martyrdom, with the meditation of which Donne's youthful imagination had 'beene euer kept awake'. The missionary priests, Southwell asserts, have come but for the sake of religion; treason and murder are far from their thoughts: 'we rather hope to make our owne Martyrdomes our steppes to a glorious eternity, then others deaths our purchase of eternall dishonour.' With almost equal ardour Southwell protests his loyalty, and that of his fellow Catholics, to the Queen; they are ready, he insists,

to defend your Realme, as the Catholique subiects of your Maiesties Auncestors, or any other Prince were, are or ever shalbe. . . . We doe assure your Maiestie, that what Army soever should come against you, we will rather yeald our brests to be broached by our Cuntrie swords, then vse our swords to th' effusion of our Cuntries bloud.[1]

The same note was sounded two years later in a letter of appeal addressed during his imprisonment by the priest William Harrington to the Lord Keeper, Sir John Puckering. Though condemned to death as a traitor he has been condemned, he protests, under 'that law too severe, and to be abrogated, or at least mitigated, which, though it make my religion, or rather my function, treason, yet can it never make me an enemy to God, my prince, nor my country'. He speaks, too, of his detestation of any form of 'treachery, which I always, even from my cradle, abhorred, in thought, word, or work, against my prince or country, for whose good and at whose appointment I am ready and willing to lease my life and liberty; yea, twenty lives, if so many God had lent'. His dedication to his calling has been made with full knowledge of what it might entail, for, he writes, 'after once I had determined this course, . . . I made no more account of life, or any worldly pleasure, but, sleeping and waking, death was the continual object of my mind, the end of my desires, and the greatest honour which in this world I expected as the reward of my long and painful labours'.[2]

---

[1] pp. 32, 35.
[2] John Morris, *The Month*, xx (1874), loc. cit.

In the *Humble Supplication* Southwell was unquestionably speaking for the majority of his fellow Catholics, and he shows a keen awareness of the dilemma in which they found themselves. They were trying to reconcile the irreconcilable. They wished to be loyal to the Catholic Church, but the law of England had established the royal supremacy, had penalized all those who refused to subscribe to the Thirty-nine Articles, or to attend Anglican services, and had branded as traitors all those in Roman orders who entered the kingdom. They wished to be loyal to the Queen, but the Pope had stigmatized her as a bastard, had excommunicated her, and had absolved her Protestant subjects from their oath of obedience to her. To stay at home meant persecution; to go abroad meant the loss of all landed possessions and all the sufferings of exile. To the logical mind there were only two courses open: either to accept the Anglican settlement and abandon the old faith, or to accept the full consequences of the papal supremacy and work with Elizabeth's enemies for her downfall. Yet the majority of Elizabethan Catholics refused to do either, and in Southwell they found a spokesman such as they had not had since the death of Edmund Campion. But Southwell was not wholly representative of his order, which had been specifically formed to uphold the papal supremacy, and those of more rigorous mentality found his position untenable. The extreme Jesuit point of view is more accurately reflected in *A Conference about the Next Succession* (1594), attributed to Robert Persons, in which the claims of the Infanta of Spain to the throne of England were advocated; and the superior intellectual force of the numerically inferior Jesuits succeeded in producing a cleavage among the English Catholics that persisted for nearly a century. Donne nowhere in his writings makes the mistake of identifying the Catholic with the Jesuit point of view; he always distinguished them carefully. The Jesuits were more than once the objects of his bitter attack, but the studied moderation of *Pseudo-Martyr*, with its appeal to 'tender and afflicted consciences' among the Catholic laity, shows that he sympathized deeply with their dilemma, for it had been his own.

The antagonism against the Jesuits felt by many of the Catholics, which did not come to a head until a few years later when the arch-priest controversy erupted, was nevertheless already beginning to be felt, and it is possible that Donne's own feelings against them were crystallized by the circumstances surrounding the death of his brother. William Harrington, the priest found in Henry Donne's rooms, was a secular priest who had been ordained at Rheims little over a year before his arrest. In his youth he had known Edmund Campion, and had for a time wished to follow him into the Jesuit order, but as priest he had speedily found himself in opposition to the Jesuits. An anonymous pamphlet written some years later during the archpriest controversy speaks bitterly of the feuds that had grown up between the Jesuits and seculars, and relates that 'Ma. *Harrington* was so oppressed with such calumnies in like sort, that hauing honest meanes for his libertie offered him, he reiected it; saying, that then he should be accounted for no honest man, and that he must be hanged to proue him selfe honest, and free from such calumniations'.[1] If Donne felt that Jesuit intrigue had any part in shaping the circumstances which led to his brother's death, the consequent bitterness could well have hardened into unflinching opposition.

Donne's own account of his spiritual progression is, however, on another plane. It is to be found in the preface to *Pseudo-Martyr*, part of which has already been quoted:

I had a longer worke to doe then many other men; for I was first to blot out, certaine impressions of the Romane religion, and to wrastle both against the examples and against the reasons, by which some hold was taken; and some anticipations early layde vpon my conscience, both by Persons who by nature had a power and superiority ouer my will, and others who by their learning and good life, seem'd to me iustly to claime an interest for the guiding, and rectifying of mine vnderstanding in these matters. And although I apprehended well enough, that this irresolution not onely retarded my fortune, but also bred some scandall, and endangered my spirituall reputation, by laying me open to many mis-interpretations; yet all these respects did not transport me to any violent and sudden determination, till I had, to the measure of my poore wit and iudgement, suruayed and digested the whole body of Diuinity, controuerted betweene ours and the Romane Church.

1 W. C., *A Replie vnto a Certaine Libell*, 1603, p. 17.

Walton, who paraphrases much of the passage from which this extract is taken, adds a few further particulars. About a year after Donne's admission to Lincoln's Inn he had as yet 'betrothed himself to no Religion that might give him any other denomination than *a Christian*'. Then, a year or so later

he, being then unresolv'd what Religion to adhere to, . . . did therefore . . . to rectifie all scruples . . . presently lay aside all study of the Law: and, of all other Sciences that might give him a denomination; and begun seriously to survey, and consider the Body of Divinity, as it was then controverted betwixt the *Reformed* and the *Roman Church*. . . . Being to undertake this search, he believed the *Cardinal Bellarmine* to be the best defender of the *Roman cause*, and therefore betook himself to the examination of his Reasons. The Cause was weighty: and wilful delays had been inexcusable both towards God and his own Conscience: he therefore proceeded in this search with all moderate haste, and about the twentieth year of his age, did shew the then *Dean* of *Gloucester* (whose name my memory hath now lost) all the Cardinals works marked with many weighty observations under his own hand; which works were bequeathed by him at his death as a Legacy to a most dear Friend.

There is considerable chronological telescoping in this part of the *Life*, for Walton sends Donne to Lincoln's Inn at the age of seventeen and assigns his service in the Cadiz expedition of 1596 to the year following the incident related in the last part of the passage just quoted. It is an over-simplification, too, to assert that early in the Lincoln's Inn period Donne 'had betrothed himself to no Religion that might give him any other denomination than *a Christian*'. Such a statement not only ignores any taint of scepticism, but also entirely overlooks the earlier influences of Donne's mother (which Walton elsewhere acknowledges) and of his whole family tradition. Donne himself, too, admits the hold on him of 'others who by their learning and good life, seem'd to me iustly to claime an interest for the guiding, and rectifying of mine vnderstanding'. These, no doubt, were his tutors and spiritual advisers, among the latter of whom Southwell may have been numbered. But Walton supplies the interesting detail that Donne undertook a systematic examination of the works of Cardinal Bellarmine, whom 'he believed . . . to be the best defender of the *Roman cause*'.[1] Bellarmine's famous *Disputationes de controversiis Christianae Fidei, adversus huius temporis haereticos* was published at Ingolstadt, the first volume in 1586, the second in 1588, and the third in 1593; their reputation spread rapidly over Europe. They were based on Bellarmine's lectures on controversial theology in the recently founded Gregorian University at Rome, and were specifically addressed to students for the priesthood who expected to return to the Protestant countries from which they had come, where they would have to face the full force of Protestant argument against the doctrines and practices of the Roman Church. The English Jesuits Garnet, Southwell, and Oldcorne had all been Bellarmine's pupils, and it is more than likely that it was from one or other of these men that Donne first heard of Bellarmine's skill in controversy. If Donne's interest was thus aroused and he had begun a study of the *Disputationes* as early as 1591, when he was nineteen, even though at first he had no specific intention of criticizing or refuting Bellarmine, such a study could, and almost inevitably would, have lasted continuously beyond 1593, when Bellarmine's third volume was published.[2]

The Dean of Gloucester to whom Donne showed his annotated copy of Bellarmine's writings, and whose name Walton had forgotten, was Antony Rudd, who became Bishop of St. David's in 1594. He had been a fellow of Trinity College, Cambridge, though he had left there before Donne became a student in that University. How Donne came into contact with him can only be surmised, but it is very probable that Donne's religious opinions had been the object of some scrutiny, perhaps because of his kinship to his recently arrested brother. It was the practice at the time to refer recusants, especially converts, to some theologian of distinction who would then hold a series of conferences with them on matters of faith and doctrine. It is significant of Rudd's interest in the conversion of Catholics that about this time the Privy Council committed

---

[1] This statement (*Lives*, pp. 25–6) has been needlessly questioned and qualified by both Jessopp (pp. 14–15) and Gosse (i. 25), who were under the erroneous impression that no part of Bellarmine's *Disputationes* appeared before 1593.

[2] There can be no doubt of the thoroughness with which Donne had studied Bellarmine's *Disputationes*. For an interesting passage illustrating Donne's later familiarity with his writings, see *Sermons*, vii, no. 7, ll. 9–58, pp. 190–1.

to his care Margaret, the daughter of Sir Thomas Throckmorton, who had 'by the perswasion of her mother . . . become a verie obstinate Recusant, to [the] no small greife of her father', and at the same time commanded him also 'to take some paine to conferre with' Lady Throckmorton 'to instructe her either by your self or suche other as you shall thinke fitt to remove her from her presente obstinacie'.[1] Donne was probably sent to Rudd in very much the same way. Yet if he had proved an obstinate Romanist, it is quite possible that he would have been expelled from Lincoln's Inn.[2] He must have been able to persuade Rudd that his attitude towards Bellarmine was by no means uncritical, and that he was far from being an unyielding Catholic.

It has been suggested that in the *Satires* Donne, though he does not state his position unequivocally, writes from the point of view of a Roman Catholic,[3] but this is not entirely true. He certainly refers to the 'mutinous Dutch'[4] and sneers at those who 'out-sweare the Letanie'; further, in the original version of the fourth Satire he gibed at Topcliffe and the Protestant historian Sleidan. But these allusions are balanced by others to the 'fires of Spaine' (surely a sideglance at the Inquisition) and to those

> Who with sinnes all kindes as familiar bee
> As Confessors;

and he scornfully exclaims

> Bastardy'abounds not in Kings titles, nor
> Symonie'and Sodomy in Churchmens lives,
> As these things do in him.

Donne may perhaps reveal a greater intimacy with Catholicism than other contemporary satirists, but his references to the Roman Church are, if anything, severer than those to Protestantism. Into the second Satire, too, there creeps a note of impatience, almost of

---

[1] *APC* (1592–3), pp. 279–80.

[2] See below, pp. 367–8, for two incidents which occurred while Donne was Reader in Divinity there.

[3] Grierson, *Poems*, ii. 117; and *Metaphysical Lyrics and Poems of the Seventeenth Century*, 1921, p. 235.

[4] [This phrase echoes the policy of the Queen and Burghley towards the rebellious Netherlands. Though others, even at Court, sympathized with the Dutch, the feeling was by no means universal. See Gardner, *Elegies etc.*, p. 129.]

cynicism, at the methods of the religious controversialists on both sides:

> he'impaires
> His writings, and (unwatch'd) leaves out, *ses heires*,
> As slily'as any Commenter goes by
> Hard words, or sense; or in Divinity
> As controverters, in vouch'd Texts, leave out
> Shrewd words, which might against them cleare the doubt.

The combined effect of such passages is to cause one to recall the words of Preserved Smith: 'The sight of several churches mutually anathematizing each other's dogmas, and giving each other the lie, suggested to the puzzled seeker for truth that possibly all of them were right in their mutual accusations, though each false in its own claims.'[1] Such perhaps was Donne's feeling, for a time at least, when the mood of the satirist was upon him.

If must not be forgotten, further, that about the same time as Donne wrote the earlier satires he composed most of the elegies and some of the love lyrics. Here there is a more explicit revolt against conventional attitudes, which extends beyond the mere celebration of sexual infidelity in such poems as 'Womans Constancy' or 'The Indifferent' to the witty justification of it in terms of a set of principles in other poems like 'Confined Love' and 'Change'. In such poems Donne reveals his familiarity with the main stream of Renaissance free-thought,[2] which supplied him with a body of ideas to play with, and which enabled him to give poetic expression to the more cynical moods of the young lover. The tone of the third Satire is, however, less cynical and more mature. There is still a sceptical balancing of the adherents of the various sects against one another so that they are all made to seem equally contemptible, along with the man who accepts all the creeds and the man who will have none of any. But the rejection of all the commonly accepted reasons for religious belief does not involve the abandonment of the search for truth. Donne may know that he

---

[1] *A History of Modern Culture*, 1930, p. 401.
[2] L. I. Bredvold, 'The Naturalism of Donne in Relation to some Renaissance Traditions', *JEGP*, xxii (1923), 471–502, and 'The Religious Thought of Donne in Relation to Medieval and Later Traditions', *Studies in Shakespeare, Milton, and Donne by members of the English Department of the University of Michigan*, 1925, pp. 191–232.

knows nothing, but this is only the beginning of the quest, the urgency of which is beyond denial:

> though truth and falshood bee
> Neare twins, yet truth a little elder is;
> Be busie to seeke her, beleeve mee this,
> Hee's not of none, nor worst, that seekes the best.
> To'adore, or scorne an image, or protest,
> May all be bad; doubt wisely; in strange way
> To stand inquiring right, is not to stray;
> To sleepe, or runne wrong, is.

The evidence of the poems, such as it is, suggests that Donne's immersion in controversial divinity resulted in a period of unsettlement during which neither Catholicism nor Protestantism could wholly satisfy him. His natural inclination to scepticism was for a time reinforced by a mood of cynicism in which he flaunted his sense of insecurity. The third Satire, probably written about 1596, marks the beginning of his emergence from this attitude, but he found no immediate solution of his problems, and for a time he sought distraction in activity of other kinds.

For Donne's life between 1591 and 1595 was not wholly one of study and religious crisis. The discrepancy between Walton's account of these years and the evidence of Donne's own writings is patent; clearly Walton attempted to describe only one side of Donne's life. It is fortunate that a brief sketch of Donne as he appeared at this time to a contemporary has survived from the pen of one who had known him since his Oxford days. At the end of the account of the reign of James I, Sir Richard Baker in his *Chronicles* 'desire[s] the Readers leave to remember two of my own old acquaintance', Donne and Wotton, of whom the first was 'Mr. *John Dunne*, who leaving *Oxford*, lived at the *Innes of Court*, not dissolute, but very neat; a great visiter of Ladies, a great frequenter of Playes, a great writer of conceited Verses'.[1] This fastidious young man about town, distinguished for the daring of his wit and for his rather startling verses, and not the earnest seeker after truth of Walton's

---

[1] First ed., 1643, Part II, p. 156. 'Dissolute' is apparently used in the obsolete sense of 'careless or negligent', and not in the current sense of 'profligate or debauched'.

early pages, is the Donne whom most of his contemporaries knew. Yet this portrait is incomplete without reference to the close of Walton's *Life*, since certain qualities he observed in the mature man must also have been characteristic of the younger one:

He was of Stature moderately tall, of a strait and equally-proportioned body, to which all his words and actions gave an unexpressible addition of Comeliness.

The melancholy and pleasant humor, were in him so contempered, that each gave advantage to the other, and made his Company one of the delights of Mankind.

To his other gifts was added the most attractive of all social accomplishments, the power to charm.

It is reassuring to learn from Baker that Donne eagerly followed the most vital of contemporary arts, the drama. This fact is confirmed by a verse letter written to him several years later by his friend Sir William Cornwallis:

> What tyme thou meanst to offir Idillnes
> Come to my den, for heer she allwayes stayes;
> If then for change, of howers you seem careles
> Agree with me to loose them at the playes.[1]

But the drama seems to have left surprisingly few traces on Donne's work; all that can be said is that of contemporary English poets Marlowe seems to have made the deepest impression on him. 'The Baite', of course, carries its own confession of its relation to Marlowe's 'Come live with me and be my love'; there are, besides, two allusions to *Tamburlaine* in his writings,[2] and it has been shown that recollections of the damnation of Faustus returned to haunt his imagination in after years.[3] Donne's regular theatre-going probably

---

[1] Bodley MS. Tanner 306, fo. 237.

[2] In 'The Calme', l. 33, and in the letter printed in Simpson, *Prose Works*, p. 332.

[3] Miss M. M. Mahood, *Poetry and Humanism*, 1950, pp. 89–90, cites three passages, viz. *Sermons*, viii, no. 7, ll. 518–70, pp. 188–9, and no. 14, ll. 748–70, pp. 332–3, and x, no. 4, ll. 556–61, p. 118. To these may perhaps be added ii, no. 11, ll. 169–72, p. 239, and vii, no. 16, ll. 742–5, p. 413.

Since the article by Victor Harris, 'John Donne and the Theatre', *Studies in English Drama presented to Baldwin Maxwell*, PQ, xli (1962), 257–69, does not succeed in collecting all the relevant passages, it should be added that item 27 in *The Courtier's Library*, 'The Brazen Head of Francis Bacon: concerning Robert the First, King of England', shows that Donne was certainly familiar with the legend of Friar Bacon

came to an end with his marriage, and when the majority of Shakespeare's great tragedies were first appearing he no longer had the
time or the inclination to spend an afternoon at the Globe or Black-
friars. But during the 1590s Donne must have been seen fairly frequently among the gallants at the theatres, and there is a strong
suggestion that, like many of the young blades of the time, he
sometimes made his way behind the stage, and from there to the
taverns where actors and playwrights congregated. Many years
later the retired actor Edward Alleyn (the original creator of the
roles of Tamburlaine, Faustus, and Barabas), in writing an angry
and reproachful letter to him, reminded him of his youth: 'you
presently being enflamed sayd twise itt was fals & a lye, wordes in
my mynd mor fitting you 30 years ago when you might be question[ed] for them then now vnder so reverent a Calling as you are'.[1]
It sounds as if Alleyn is writing from his own personal recollections
of Donne in his earlier days. It can never be proved, of course, but
if Donne knew Alleyn it is quite possible that he also knew Burbage,
and even Marlowe and Shakespeare.

Perhaps the earliest, and certainly the least mature, of Donne's
poems are to be found in a group of verse letters addressed to friends
of the Lincoln's Inn days.[2] Most of them consist of little more than
elaborate exchanges of compliment; they suggest a coterie of ingenious young men assiduously cultivating the Muse and warmly
applauding each other's efforts. The group included Christopher
Brooke and his brother Samuel, Rowland and Thomas Woodward,
Everard Guilpin, Beaupré Bell, and a certain Mr. I (or J.) L. who has
not been identified.[3] Rowland Woodward, son of John Woodward,
vintner, of the parish of St. Mary le Bow, was born in 1573 and

and suggests that he had probably seen *Friar Bacon and Friar Bungay* on the stage.
E. Le Comte (*Grace to a Witty Sinner*, 1965, p. 255) believes that the reference to
Petruccio in the letter on p. 313 of Simpson, *Prose Works*, is to the hero of *The Taming
of the Shrew* but, however much one could wish it were so, his case is not proven. [For
evidence that Donne was acquainted with *Soliman and Perseda* and *Romeo and Juliet* see
Gardner, *Elegies etc.*, pp. 112-13, 116, 140.]

[1] Dulwich College MS. III. 102; cf. Chapter XVI, p. 465 n.

[2] For a discussion of the dates of these poems, see R. C. Bald, 'Donne's Early Verse
Letters', *HLQ*, xv (1952), 283-9.

[3] I tried for some time without success to prove that his name was John Legard;
Mrs. Duncan-Jones tells me of similar efforts on her part to show that he was a
member of the Lowther family.

entered Lincoln's Inn on 21 January 1591; his younger brother Thomas, of whom practically nothing is known, was born in 1576.[1] Beaupré Bell, a son of Sir Robert Bell, formerly Chief Baron of the Exchequer, and Guilpin had both been at Cambridge at the time Donne was probably there; Guilpin was now a member of Gray's Inn,[2] and Bell, who had outstayed his contemporaries at Cambridge for more advanced studies, joined Donne at Lincoln's Inn in 1594.

That most of these early verse epistles received replies in kind can be surmised from the single example that has survived, apparently from the pen of Thomas Woodward.[3] It is what would nowadays be regarded as a sample of undergraduate wit, and is clearly written in imitation of Donne's manner. No verses by Rowland Woodward or Beaupré Bell are known to exist, and the surviving poems of the two Brookes all belong to a later period. But Guilpin in 1598 published *Skialetheia*, a collection of epigrams and satires which contains a number of echoes and imitations of Donne,[4] and confirms the impression given by Thomas Woodward's lines that Donne's was the dominant voice in the group.

The epistles to I. L. ('Blest are your North parts') and Christopher Brooke presumably mark Donne's first authentic appearance in the role of a lover. That these poems are a prentice's effort is shown by the use of the sonnet form in the letter to Brooke, and in both of the conventional language of love poetry; they are Donne's concession to the sonneteering vogue of the early nineties, and show him trying to use a mode of expression that soon proved alien to him. In the manner of the sonneteers he pays his court to a mistress who, though unidentifiable, seems nevertheless to have been a real person, since

---

[1] M. C. Deas, 'A Note on Rowland Woodward, the Friend of Donne', *RES*, vii (1931), 454–7. Donne wrote five surviving verse letters to Woodward; the copy of *Pseudo-Martyr* which Donne gave him has been preserved; [and the Westmoreland MS. of Donne's poems is in Woodward's handwriting. See Milgate, *Satires etc.*, pp. xlvi, 214–15, 222–3.]

[2] R. E. Bennett, 'John Donne and Everard Gilpin', *RES*, xv (1939), 66–72.

[3] It was printed from one of the manuscript copies by Grierson, ii. 166.

[4] Some of the indebtednesses to Donne have been pointed out, but by no means all; R. E. Bennett, in the article already cited, lists a number. Bennett also believed that Donne was satirized in Guilpin's third Satire, but the passage which he cites as having reference to Donne refers to at least three different people. See further P. J. Finkelpearl, 'Donne and Everard Gilpin: Additions, Corrections, and Conjectures', *RES*, N.S. xiv (1963), 164–7.

it is implied that she is known to both his friends, if indeed the same
lady is referred to in both poems. I. L. has married, left London, and
settled down on his estate somewhere north of the Trent, and in
August 1594 the lady to whom Donne was paying court was visiting him. She is 'that beauteous Sun', and Donne implores his friend's
aid in softening her heart. In the letter 'To Mr. C. B.' the same
image is used, and she is still unkind, but the situation is reversed,
since it is Donne who is about to journey into the north and the
lady who is remaining behind. Unfortunately it is impossible to tell
which is the earlier of the two poems, and nothing is known of
any journey Donne made 'to where sterne winter aye doth wonne'.
The imagery in both poems is conventional and unconvincing, and
their tone is altogether different from that of the love poems Donne
was soon to write.

In these verse epistles, whenever Donne mentions himself and
his verse, the lines are always 'harsh' and he is urged 'by Satirique
fyres' to write 'in skorne of all'. The first Satire may be as early as
1593, and the second soon followed; Donne seems at this time to
have regarded them as his most significant achievement. With their
combination of keen observation and savage wit, they express a
characteristically youthful attitude of impatience and contempt for
things and persons which older men have learned to endure unper-
turbed. It is not surprising that Donne carried over something of
the tone of these satires into the 'Elegies' and into such verse
letters as 'The Storme' and 'The Calme', but his sense of decorum
kept it out of all but a few of his love lyrics.

It seems to be agreed that nearly all the Elegies are early. Ben
Jonson, besides affirming 'Done to have written all his best pieces err
he was 25 years old', boasted that he had by heart 'his verses of the
Lost Chaine, . . . & that passage of the calme, that dust and feathers
doe not stirr, all was so quiet'.[1] It is perhaps pedantry to point out
that the latter piece was written after Donne had reached his
twenty-fifth birthday, but it can be taken that 'The Bracelet' at
least is typical of what Jonson admired in Donne's early work. On

---

[1] *Ben Jonson*, ed. Herford and Simpson, i. 135. [It has been argued that thirteen of
the love-elegies and the funeral elegy 'To L. C.' make up a 'book' of Elegies dating
from 1593 to 1596. See Gardner, *Elegies etc.*, pp. xxxi–xxxii.]

the other hand, there is often no evidence at all for determining when the individual poems in the 'Songs and Sonets' were written; most of those to which an approximate date can be given are relatively late, but that is no justification for saying that all the un-datable poems must be early. Above all, too much stress must not be put on theme or tone, for Donne is just as capable of writing cynically and satirically about love and women after 1600 as before it. One may take it for granted, then, that the first two Satires, nearly all the Elegies, and an uncertain number of the 'Songs and Sonets'[1] (as well as the verse letters already referred to) belong to Donne's Lincoln's Inn days. Another poem from this period is the 'Epithalamion made at Lincolnes Inn'. The piece has real charm, and shows that even Donne could not escape the all-pervasive influence of Spenser. With Spenser in mind, however, critics have been dis-turbed by the forced and tasteless conceits that occur here and there in the poem, and by what looks like uncertainty in the control of the tone. These difficulties would vanish if, as has been suggested, Donne's poem was in fact written, not for a real wedding, but for a mock-wedding included in summer revels at Lincoln's Inn; hence the jocular outrageousness of the style and the topical parody of Spenser's recently published *Epithalamion* (1595).[2] This theory of the occasion of the poem is, however, difficult to sustain, since there is no evidence that revels were ever held at Lincoln's Inn at any time other than the Christmas season.

Donne is last mentioned in this part of the Lincoln's Inn records at the end of 1594; he is next heard of on 20 July of the following year, when he took into his service 'at the speciall request and earnest intreatie' of a Yorkshire gentleman named Christopher Danby 'to instructe and bringe vpp one Thomas Danbye of the age of fifteene yeres or there about*es* naturall brother of the sayde Christopher Danbye'.[3] He was evidently mature enough, or prosperous enough, or dandified enough, to want to have a boy to attend on him. Now

---

[1] [For further discussion of the dating of the love-lyrics, see Gardner, *Elegies etc.*, pp. xlix–lxii.]

[2] D. Novarr, 'Donne's "Epithalamion made at Lincoln's Inn", Context and Date', *RES*, N.S. vii (1956), 250–63, where it is further suggested that the poem is a mock-epithalamion written for Lincoln's Inn revels in midsummer, 1595.

[3] For this document see Appendix D III below.

that he had received his patrimony he perhaps felt that such expenditure was necessary to enhance his prestige.

Another poem, 'Elegie on the L. C.' (a title first given to it in the 1635 edition of the *Poems*), has further biographical implications. There is no date to the poem, and its style is unquestionably early; indeed, before 1635 it appears, in manuscripts and (as 'Elegie VI') in the first edition of the *Poems* (1633), in association with love elegies. The problem is the identity of 'the L. C.' An early owner of the 1639 edition of the *Poems* has expanded the letters to 'Lord Carey',[1] presumably indicating William Carew, first Lord Hunsdon and Lord Chamberlain, who died in 1596. It is not a very good guess, for he does not seem to fit the man mourned by Donne, who had died by a 'strange chance' and was grieved for by his 'children', and who obviously was not a great officer of state. Lord Hunsdon died after an illness at the age of sixty-nine; his youngest son (and he had seven) was thirty-six at the time of his father's death, so that the word 'children' does not seem very appropriate. Further, Donne seems to identify himself with the bereaved family; he refers to 'this house' and uses the pronoun 'we' throughout in describing the grief of the family and the household. It has been suggested that 'on' in the title added, apparently without authority, in 1635 should be 'to', and that the poem was addressed 'To L. C.', that is to Lionel Cranfield (later Earl of Middlesex), on the death of his father Thomas Cranfield in 1595. The dead man is mourned by his family, not (as an elegist would say of a great lord) by the nation or the court, and the lines (13–18) referring to 'venturing' are much more justly applied to a merchant like Cranfield (a member of the Baltic Company).[2]

In retrospect the years at Lincoln's Inn seemed to Donne to have been largely wasted. A certain unworldliness, tinged perhaps with youthful snobbery, characterized his attitude during these years. The majority of his contemporaries, though studying the law, had

[1] For an account of this copy see J. Sampson, 'A Contemporary Light upon John Donne', *Essays and Studies by Members of the English Association*, vii (1921), 82–107. Giles Oldisworth, the annotator of the copy here described, does not deserve the respect that has been accorded to him, for some of his notes are palpably inaccurate.

[2] [See Gardner, *Elegies etc.*, pp. 145–6. We have no evidence that Donne knew Lionel Cranfield before 1611 (see pp. 191–2 below), but it is quite possible that they were acquainted as young men.]

no thought of making it their profession, and Donne accordingly was contemptuous of

> men which chuse
> Law practise for meere gaine.

He put off as long as possible the decision of how he was to employ his talents. The result was that before long he was beginning to reproach himself for his failure to 'digest / Th'immense vast volumes of our common law' and to confess that it was a grief to him

> that that which I should have begun
> In my youthes morning, now late must be done.

Yet he was not idle; he was probably living with more intensity than at any other period of his life. By his own account, he was diverted from the study of the law 'by the worst voluptuousnes, which is an Hydroptique immoderate desire of humane learning and languages',[1] and he spent his time in acquiring accomplishments which at that date were regarded as suitable only to a man of great fortune, instead of preparing himself for an active and useful place in the world. But this, of course, is not the whole story. He sought pleasure in study, in the theatre, and in friendship; he made the discovery first of sex, and then of love. The truth is rather that life was calling to him from all sides. No experience seemed alien to him, and the complexity of human life was fascinating enough for him to linger over it for a time with little thought of the future.

[1] *Letters*, p. 51.

V

MILITARY SERVICE

AT the beginning of 1596 preparations were being made for an expedition against Spain on a scale that had not been attempted since the year after the Armada. The expedition was to be ready to sail early in April; the fleet was to be commanded by Lord Howard of Effingham and the land forces by the Earl of Essex. As soon as the news of what was afoot began to spread there was much excitement among the more high-spirited young men in fashionable circles and in the Inns of Court. They were eager to participate in the adventure, the more because one of the leaders was Essex, whose warm and impetuous personality captured their imagination, and they hastened to attach themselves to the expedition as volunteers, or 'voluntaries' as the term then was. Donne, it appears, presented himself to Essex and offered his services; access to the Lord General would not have been difficult for him. His old friend of Oxford days, Henry Wotton, was now one of Essex's secretaries; and Henry Cuffe, his chief secretary, had a brother at Lincoln's Inn whom Donne must have known. Donne's services were accepted, and he was assured of a place in the expedition.[1]

[1] Walton states that Donne 'waited upon' Essex in 1596 and 1597, and this has often been interpreted to mean that he was attached to Essex's staff. But this was not so, in the 1597 expedition at least. Accordingly it seems more probable that the phrase was intended to mean only that he presented himself to Essex.

In MS. Harl. 253, item 36 (fo. 51ᵛ) is 'A liste of her Majesties Armye by Sea and Lande for the present voyage to Cades, vnder the Conducte of the Earle of Essex, 1 June 1596'. The ships are listed by squadrons, and in each squadron the first four or five are separated by a space from the rest. The first group were the Queen's ships, the others ships hired as transports or contributed by merchants; a note states that 'There are noe Souldiers placed in any of her Ma:ᵗⁱᵉˢ Shipps but such gentlemen as goe volluntarelie and the Comaunders make choyse of.' In other words only a privileged few were permitted to sail in the ships of the Royal Navy.

MS. 250 at Lambeth Palace contains 'A Journal of all the particularities that fell out in the voyage under the charge of the two Lord Generals, the Earl of Essex and the Lord Charles Howard, Lord High Admiral of England, and also the names of all the commanders and great officers with the captains and voluntary gentlemen that appertain to the army.' If this manuscript had lived up to its title it would have

Donne's motives in thus seeking foreign service were mixed. In
'The Calme' he alludes to them with a certain cynicism:

> Whether a rotten state, and hope of gaine,
> Or to disuse mee from the queasie paine
> Of being belov'd, and loving, or the thirst
> Of honour, or faire death, out pusht mee first,
> I lose my end.

No doubt he had been living extravagantly and his inheritance was
dwindling, so that hopes of booty could not be ignored; no doubt,
too, the gallantries of the past few years were beginning to wear
rather thin; restlessness and a desire for action both egged him on.
He had no romantic illusions, however, about the nature of the
enterprise in which he was engaging, and he quite clearly saw its
risks. In the elegy 'His Picture', which must have been written
about this time, he envisaged the possibility of his return after a
period of captivity in the Spanish galleys:

> weather-beaten I come backe; my hand,
> Perchance with rude oares torne, or Sun beams tann'd,
> My face and brest of hairecloth, and my head
> With cares rash sodaine hoarinesse o'rspread,
> My body'a sack of bones, broken within,
> And powders blew staines scatter'd on my skinne.

In another respect, too, his participation represented a real decision.
He was overtly identifying himself with his country's cause and,
even though his religious uncertainties may have been still unre-
solved, he was at least certain of his patriotism. The reference in
'The Storme' to 'England to whom we'owe, what we be, and have'
is evidence of a deep and genuine feeling.[1]

been possible to say definitely which ship Donne sailed in, but fo. 359 r. and v. are
blank. The writer promised a list but never filled it in.

That such lists of the gentlemen volunteers and the units to which they were
attached were once current is clear from Gervase Holles's *Memorials of the Holles
Family* (Camden Society, 3rd series, vol. lv, 1937), p. 93, where he writes of his
kinsman Sir John Holles, first Earl of Clare: 'His last military employment was with
the Earle of Essex to the Terceraes in the yeare 1597 in the company of his kinsman
Sir Francis Vere . . . as I finde in a list of gentry at the end of a discourse concerning
that voyage.'

[1] [For further evidence of Donne's patriotism—his pride in English ways, and his
acceptance of the official English attitude to the Netherlands—see Gardner, *Elegies
etc.*, pp. 114, 129.]

On 19 March 1596 the Queen signed the commissions of the two leaders, the Earl of Essex and Lord Howard of Effingham, and it was probably in the days immediately following that the volunteers flocked around them to offer their services. But the expedition was delayed by the rapid development of events on the Continent. France and Spain were at war, and on 29 March Spanish forces from the Low Countries suddenly threatened Calais. Essex hurriedly assembled at Dover such troops as were ready, and they were actually embarking for France when the news of the fall of Calais reached them. There was some talk of diverting the expedition to deal with a threat so near home, but wiser counsels prevailed and the urgency of a blow at the enemy's homeland was seen to be even greater than it had been before. By 2 May the main body of the forces had assembled at Plymouth, and while Elizabeth was still hesitating, Raleigh, the vice-admiral, brought his squadron round from Dover. A few days later sailing orders arrived. How long before this the gentlemen volunteers had been in readiness and attached to their units it is impossible to say, but there were over 'three hundred green headed youths, covered with feathers, gold and silver lace' in the expedition, and some of them had probably been fretting impatiently for at least two months before they actually embarked.

The fleet set sail on 3 June, and by the 18th was off Cadiz, although the attack on the Spanish ships in the harbour was not launched until the 21st. From dawn, when the English ships closed in and opened fire, until mid morning the Spaniards gradually fell back towards the inner harbour, where they were protected by a fort and by four great galleons, which had anchored so as to block the entrance at its narrowest point. The English ships crowded into the narrow channel to attack. For three hours the cannonading was incessant, and the target specially singled out was the largest of the galleons, the Spanish flagship *San Felipe*. What followed is best told in Raleigh's own words:

I laid out a warp by the side of the *Philip* to shake hands with her (for with the wind we could not get aboard): which when she and the rest perceived, finding also that the *Repulse* (seeing mine) began to do the like, and the Rear-Admiral, my Lord Thomas, they all let slip, and ran aground, tumbling into the sea heaps of souldiers, so thick as if coals had been powred out of a sack in many ports at once, some drowned and some sticking in the mud. The *Philip* and the *St. Thomas* burnt themselves: the *St. Matthew* and the *St. Andrew* were recovered with our boats ere they could get out to fire them. The spectacle was very lamentable on their side; for many drowned themselves; many, half burnt, leapt into the water; very many hanging by the ropes' ends by the ships' side, under the water even to the lips; many swimming with grievous wounds, strucken under water, and put out of their pain; and withal so huge a fire, and such tearing of the ordnance in the great *Philip*, and the rest, when the fire came to them, as, if any man had a desire to see Hell itself, it was there most lively figured.[1]

Donne probably commemorated the loss of the *San Felipe* in his epigram 'A Burnt Ship':

Out of a fired ship, which, by no way
But drowning, could be rescu'd from the flame,
Some men leap'd forth, and ever as they came
Neere the foes ships, did by their shot decay;
So all were lost, which in the ship were found,
They in the sea being burnt, they in the burnt ship drown'd.

It is not too much to assume that he was well within sight of this action, either in one of the ships in the squadron led by Raleigh, or perhaps in one of those carrying the other high officers which had forced a way into the forefront of the battle, such as the *Repulse* with Essex or the *Nonpareil* with Lord Thomas Howard on board.

Cadiz was taken on the same afternoon. About 800 of the troops were landed at once on the sandy neck of the peninsula at whose extremity the city stood, but as they approached the walls they found a body of Spaniards drawn up awaiting them. A plan of action was quickly arranged. A force of two hundred, under Sir John Wingfield, was to launch a frontal attack and then, in order to lure the enemy away from the gates, to fall back in apparent disorder. The ruse succeeded perfectly. As soon as the fleeing English had reached

[1] Edward Edwards, *Life of Ralegh*, 1868, ii. 152-3.

the main body they turned, and all charged together. Wingfield himself ran through one of the Spanish leaders with his pike, and soon there was a mad rush for the city gates. Half the Spaniards were nearly shut out lest the English should get there first, but the gates were hurriedly reopened and most of the Spaniards got safely in. A fierce assault was begun on the gates, and at the same time two other small bodies of men scaled the walls at different points, so that in barely half an hour an entrance was forced, though Wingfield was wounded in the thigh. Meanwhile fresh troops from the ships were coming up, and although sporadic street fighting continued till well into the night, Essex and Vere with an intrepid band had already secured the plaza. Wingfield, though unable to walk, was unwilling to be left behind and mounted a captured horse. He reached the plaza while fighting was still in progress, but as he was the only mounted Englishman there he presented an easy target, and fell with a bullet in his head just before the plaza was won. His exploits had made him the hero of the day, and five days later he was buried in the Cathedral of Cadiz

with all the funerall solemnities of warre, the Drums and Trumpets sounding dolefully, the shot bearing the noses of their pieces downe-ward, the pikes trayled, his body was borne by six Knights, the Generals threw their handkerchiefs wet from their eyes into the graue, and at the instant the most part of all the shot great and small, aboord and a shoare were discharged.[1]

Such was the man to whose memory Donne wrote these lines:

> Beyond th'old Pillers many'have travailed
> Towards the Suns cradle, and his throne, and bed.
> A fitter Piller our Earle did bestow
> In that late Iland; for he well did know
> Farther then Wingefield no man dares to go.

On the day after Wingfield's funeral the victory was celebrated by the dubbing of no fewer than sixty-four knights, 'even all almost that did deserve it or affect it or not neglect or refuse it (as some did)'. Among these knights were Sir Maurice Berkeley, a friend

[1] From the account by Sir George Buc incorporated in Stow's *Annals*, ed. 1631, p. 775.

whom Donne always regarded with affection and whose acquaintance he may first have made about this time, and Sir Edward Conway, whom Donne certainly knew in later days and who became one of the principal Secretaries of State. As for Donne himself, his experiences in the capture of the city were doubtless similar to those of many others who did not happen to get into the thick of the fighting. One officer, not among those who achieved the honour of knighthood, wrote sardonically of those who did that most of them 'deserved as I did, and that was to march into the market place with an armour on my back and a pike on my neck in an extreme hot day'.[1] Such, in all probability, was Donne's experience too.

Indiscriminate looting had begun on the night on which Cadiz was entered, but on the following day more orderly arrangements were made. Each of the military officers was assigned a house from which he could take everything he could get by ransom or plunder, and certain districts were similarly put at the disposal of the troops. Only the Queen could complain that the expedition had not paid for itself, since the West Indian fleet, which was still aground or sheltering some miles away, was fired by the Spanish authorities while negotiations for a ransom were still in progress with the merchants who owned the cargoes.

Looting, ransoming and celebrating the victory all took time, and it was not until 4 July that the English re-embarked, leaving the city in flames. A few days later the troops were put ashore again near Faro, which they sacked and burnt, although they found the town deserted and empty. Among the plunder was the Bishop's library, which Essex brought home to present to the Bodleian.

The concluding stages of the expedition were marked by disunion and irresolution amongst the leaders. Corunna and Ferrol were found to be empty of shipping, and so not worth attacking. Ever since leaving Cadiz Essex had been pressing for a descent on the Azores so as to intercept the Spanish fleet coming home from the West Indies, but the winds proved unfavourable, and most of the captains were satisfied with the plunder they had already won. By the beginning of August the fleet was straggling back into Plymouth, whence it was brought round to Chatham to be disbanded.

[1] John Stanhope, quoted by J. S. Corbett, *The Successors of Drake*, 1900, p. 108.

Donne, his fortunes somewhat repaired, doubtless went back to his old life. His interest in the common law, never very strong, was, if anything, weaker than before, and he turned again to verse-making. The fourth of the *Satires* is, however, the only poem that can certainly be assigned to the months after the Cadiz expedition. It is the longest and most brilliant of them all; the reference at line 114 to 'the losse of Amyens' (which occurred on 1 March 1597) as a recent event dates it fairly precisely. Another allusion in the Satire to 'Guianaes rarities' shows that Donne had followed with interest Raleigh's explorations there. Raleigh first visited Guiana in 1595, and early in 1596 he published his glowing account of what he had seen there in *A Discoverie of the large, rich, and bewtiful Empire of Guiana*. After his return he sent out an expedition under Lawrence Keymis, who was exploring part of the Amazon delta at the very time that Raleigh was in action at Cadiz. Keymis published his *True Relation of the Second Voyage to Guiana* in October 1596. Raleigh, still unable to return to Guiana, despatched a pinnace, the *Wat*, on a third voyage of exploration, and himself turned to the vigorous prosecution of the war against Spain.

When 1597 opened, plans were already afoot for an attaçk on Ferrol, where a new Armada was being fitted out, but it was not until May that an expedition, with Essex as commander-in-chief, Lord Thomas Howard as vice-admiral, and Raleigh as rear-admiral, was definitely decided upon. The success of the previous year's campaign attracted an even greater number of adventurers; many who had fought then, including Donne, offered their services again, and they were joined by a crowd of newcomers. There were 'of Knights and Gentlemen voluntaries, to the number of 500. or better, very gallant persons, and as brauely furnished of all things necessary (besides superfluitie in gold lace, plumes of Feathers, and such like)'.[1] The fleet was not completely assembled at Plymouth until 8 July, and this year there was certainly a tedious period of waiting for the volunteers, since Donne specifically mentions

> How in the port, our fleet deare time did leese,
> Withering like prisoners, which lye but for fees.

[1] Stow, op. cit., p. 783.

But even the restless volunteers must have had their moments of interest and excitement, for on 2 July Raleigh's ship, the *Wat*, entered the harbour with fresh news of Guiana, and three days later one of the famous Shirley brothers, Sir Anthony, who promptly joined the expedition, returned from a freebooting voyage in the West Indies.

On 10 July Essex's fleet of over a hundred ships set sail, but almost at once the weather changed for the worse. The storm continued to grow in violence, and the fleet was scattered. Before the end of a week the ships were limping back into port. Raleigh was the first to return to Plymouth, but Essex's flagship had sprung a dangerous leak and two days later she put into Falmouth.

> Many of our Gentlemen and Knights [wrote Raleigh's captain], with this boysterous and bitter entertainment on the seas, returned extreame weake and lay dangerously sicke long after. . . . This violent and dangerous tempest had so cooled and battered the courages of a great many of our young Gentlemen (who seeing that the boysterous winds and mercilesse Seas, had neither affinitie with London delicacie, nor Court bravery) as that discharging their high Plumes, and imbroydered Cassockes, they secretly retired themselves home, forgetting either to bid their friends farewell, or to take leave of their Generall.[1]

Only the squadron commanded by that veteran seaman Lord Thomas Howard succeeded in riding out the gale, and when the storm abated he proceeded to the rendezvous off Corunna, where he cruised for five days before returning to England. In Plymouth, meanwhile, the battered ships were being refitted, and they were almost ready to set out again on 31 July when Lord Thomas Howard's squadron re-entered the port.

The tempest that delayed the expedition was commemorated by Donne in 'The Storme', with its vivid description of the distressed ship in a raging sea and the misery of its human cargo. But the prose letter which he wrote soon after his return to Plymouth[2] is even

---

[1] Gorges, *A Larger Relation of the said Iland Voyage*, in *Purchas his Pilgrimes*, 1905–7, xx. 43–4.

[2] Simpson, *Prose Works*, pp. 303–4. Donne's authorship of this letter has been questioned by B. W. Whitlock ('Donne's "First Letter" ', *TLS*, 22 Aug. 1952, p. 556) on the grounds that Donne would have been aboard Essex's flagship, as the

more valuable for the additional personal details which it contains. The army carried by the fleet had been organized into ten regiments each of five companies a hundred strong, and each transport in the fleet carried either one company or a company and a half. Donne's statement that he had been 'troubled with *th*e stinke of 150 land soldiers' makes it clear that he had been in one of the larger transports. He had also endured '20 dayes of so very very bad wether', and had 'seene *th*e land of promise Spaine', so his ship was one of those that had borne the full brunt of the storm and had proceeded with Lord Thomas Howard's squadron to Corunna.

When Donne returned to Plymouth the town was swarming with men from the fleet; money and provisions were scarce; many of the gallants, too, had run out of both money and credit. Donne writes amusingly of their dejection, and with something of the contempt of an old campaigner:

Never was extreame beggery so extreamely braue except when a company of mum*m*ers had lost theire box. I do not think that 77 Kelleys could distill 10*l* out of all *th*e towne⟨;⟩ he *th*at hath supt and hath 2 or 3*s*. is a king; . . . and but for *th*e much gay cloathes (w*h*ich yet are much melted) I should thinke wee were in vtopia: all are so vtterly coyneles, in one bad bare word *th*e want is so generall that *th*e lo: generall wants & till this day wee wanted *th*e lo: generall.

The last sentence helps to date the letter. Essex and Raleigh had ridden to the court the day after Howard's squadron returned, and reached Plymouth again on 8 or 9 August.[1] Their purpose had been to persuade Elizabeth to allow them to abandon the attack on Ferrol and make a descent on the West Indies, but the Queen would not be persuaded, and held them to their instructions. Two of Donne's poems belong to this period, when the hopes of the fleet, stimulated by the stories brought back by Raleigh's men in the *Wat* and by Sir Anthony Shirley, were first set on an attack on the Spanish

author of this letter clearly was not. But, as Mr. I. A. Shapiro was quick to point out, Walton's statement that Donne 'waited upon his Lordship' does not necessarily imply that Donne sailed aboard the same ship (*TLS*, 12 Sept. 1952, p. 597). Nevertheless, Mr. Shapiro is still doubtful of Donne's authorship of the letter, though he hesitates to 'reject it outright'. I have taken the risk of accepting it as Donne's (see *TLS*, 24 Oct. 1952, p. 700).

[1] *The Naval Tracts of Sir William Monson*, ed. M. Oppenheim (Navy Records Society, 1902), ii. 54-5.

Main, and were then dashed. The hopes are reflected in the epigram 'Cales and Guyana', addressed to the leaders of the expedition:

> If you from spoyle of th'old worlds farthest end
> To the new world your kindled valors bend,
> What brave Examples then do prove it trew
> That one things end doth still beginne a new.[1]

The disappointment is reflected in a verse letter to Rowland Woodward:

> Guyanaes harvest is nip'd in the spring,
> I feare; And with us (me thinkes) Fate deales so
> As with the Jewes guide God did; he did show
> Him the rich land, but bar'd his entry in:
> Oh, slownes is our punishment and sinne.
> Perchance, these Spanish businesse being done,
> Which as the Earth betweene the Moone and Sun
> Eclipse the light which Guyana would give,
> Our discontinu'd hopes we shall retrive.[2]

On 15 August the fleet set out again from Plymouth, though it was no longer as large as it had been before. Essex had dismissed 5,000 of the 6,000 troops which the fleet had originally carried, and a number of the transports had also been left behind. It is possible that in the consequent reshuffling Donne was assigned to another ship, as his subsequent adventures suggest that he was in a different part of the fleet. Once again the expedition encountered bad weather in the Bay of Biscay, and the various units of the fleet were scattered. Raleigh's ship lost its mainyard; Essex's flagship again sprang a leak, and he was forced to drop behind. Raleigh proceeded down the Portuguese coast to Lisbon, and some of the other vessels, not finding Essex at the first rendezvous, followed after Raleigh. The fleet was thus split in two, and although contact was re-established, Essex decided, partly because the fleet was scattered and partly because accidents had befallen the vessels he had intended to use as fire-ships, to abandon the attack on Ferrol. Just then news

---

[1] Gosse (i. 46–7) assigns the composition of these lines to circumstances during the Cadiz expedition which are largely the figment of his imagination.

[2] For a fuller discussion of the allusions in this poem see 'Donne's Early Verse Letters', *HLQ*, xv (1952), 283–9.

came from Raleigh that the armada at Ferrol was reported to have slipped out of the harbour and had sailed for the Azores. Without hesitation, and without staying to verify the truth of the report (which was false), Essex set out in pursuit, sending orders to Raleigh and his thirty-odd ships to follow at once. On reaching the Azores Essex cruised among the islands without finding any sign of the enemy, and then waited off Flores, the westernmost island, where he cruised until Raleigh joined him on 15 September.

Donne's poem 'The Calme' belongs to the period just before the two parts of the fleet made contact again. Raleigh's captain, Sir Arthur Gorges, says that they sighted the Azores on 8 September, and sent two of their smaller vessels out as scouts to see if Essex's ships were close at hand. He continues:

> Whilest we were before Saint Georges, we were very much be-calmed for a day or two, and the weather extreamely hot, insomuch as the winde could not beare the sailes from the mastes, but were faine to hull in the Sea, to our great discontentment, that before had used such great diligence and haste to meete with our Admirall, and the rest of the Fleete.[1]

This dead calm, which kept the ships stationary on 9 and 10 September, is the one which Donne describes, when the ships stood motionless, their tackling draped with the sailors' washing instead of sails, and the men were stretched out indolently on the decks and hatches or vainly sought to cool off by diving into the sea. So still and breathless was it by night as well as day that there was

> No use of lanthornes; and in one place lay
> Feathers and dust, to day and yesterday.

That Donne was in Raleigh's squadron is strongly suggested by the reference to 'the Iles which wee seeke' and the line 'We can nor left friends, nor sought foes recover'; Raleigh was still endeavouring to overtake Essex, whereas by 10 September, the day on which Donne's poem was most probably written (or to which it refers), Essex was already off Flores, and knew that Raleigh could not have reached the Azores ahead of him.

After Raleigh rejoined Essex, he was allowed to remain behind at

[1] Purchas, xx, 65–6.

Flores to take on fresh water, but before he was able to do so he received orders to proceed at once to Fayal, where Essex was said to be waiting for him. When he arrived the roadstead was empty, and after four days of waiting he decided to land on the island. If Donne was in one of the ships under Raleigh's command he would have been present at the capture of Fayal, the one real achievement of the expedition. After a dangerous landing on the coast four miles away, a little army of five hundred men advanced towards the town. Raleigh and his staff officers led the march, with forty gentlemen behind them and the regular troops following in the rear. As they came within reach of the fortifications the enemy opened fire; the vanguard continued its steady march in the direction of shelter, but the troops broke and ran for cover. The fire was so hot that none of the troops would volunteer to reconnoitre; Raleigh and a few officers had to brave the fire and do it themselves. But when the orders to advance again were given the Spaniards had had enough, and Fayal was entered without further opposition. Essex arrived the day after its capture, and the fleet was regrouped.

There is no need to describe the rest of the campaign in detail. Through bad organization and ill-laid plans the Spanish West Indian fleet slipped into the harbour at Angra under what have been described as 'the strongest fortifications outside Europe' a bare three hours after the English fleet had been off the island. Nor, when its presence was discovered, was there any plan of attack that could be devised with the remotest chance of success. Three richly laden stragglers were captured, though this booty was meagre compensation in comparison with what had been lost. A few days later, when Raleigh's squadron was anchored off the island of San Miguel, another straggler, 'a mightie huge Carack', rounded a point, and taking the ships ahead of it to be Spanish was about to anchor among them. But an indiscreet shot from one of the smaller ships gave her warning just in time; she turned and ran aground under a Spanish fort near by, and was a blazing mass of flames before the English could reach her. Meanwhile Essex had taken the town of Villa Franca; most of the men enjoyed themselves ashore for a few days, and Essex created some knights, among whom was the Lord Keeper's son, Thomas Egerton. But by now it was clear that nothing more could be won in the Azores. On 9 October the fleet sailed from Villa Franca for home, and by the end of the month the ships, dogged once more by bad weather, had straggled back to England.

After the failure of 1597 there was no immediate opportunity for further service of the sort which Donne had seen in this and the previous campaign. The next such opportunity came in 1599 when Essex, his prestige still undiminished, was sent to Ireland, and it was eagerly embraced by a number of Donne's friends. By this time, however, Donne had found a career, and his days of military service were over.[1]

[1] It has sometimes been thought that Donne was engaged early in 1598 in bringing letters and two Spanish prisoners over to England from France. Sir Edmund Chambers found records of the payment to 'Capten John Donne' of two sums for such services ('John Donne, Diplomatist and Soldier', *MLR*, v (1910), 492–3) and Grierson accepted his suggestion (ii. 141). But this Captain Donne can be distinguished from the poet. In S.P. 12, Eliz., vol. 264, no. 3 is a 'Note of the ffleete' in the 1597 expedition written by someone in authority, and no. 4 is a copy of the list in a secretary's hand. The last section of the list contains 'The Names of the Dutche which followe the Fleete' and among them is 'Captain Dome in the Drake' in no. 3. That the writer omitted a minim is clear from no. 4, where the name appears as 'Captaine Donne'. This man is more likely to have been employed to carry letters and transport prisoners than the twenty-six-year-old poet.

VI

SECRETARY TO THE LORD KEEPER

BY the beginning of November 1597 Donne was back in London, feeling that his years of preparation were ended and that it was time to settle down. Among his companions on the Islands expedition had been young Thomas Egerton, the elder son of the Lord Keeper, who was among the few whose services had signalized him as being worthy of the honour of knighthood. Since both Thomas Egerton and his younger brother John were members of Lincoln's Inn, Donne had probably been acquainted with them both before the expedition took place. Their father, who had only recently been appointed Lord Keeper, was the most distinguished living member of the Inn, and it is possible that Donne had already been introduced to him, so that when the younger Sir Thomas communicated to his father Donne's wish to find service with him, he may well have already had sufficient knowledge of Donne's abilities to regard him with favour. 'I had a desire to be yor Lordships servant, by the favor wch yor good sonn's love to me obtein'd',[1] Donne wrote subsequently. Walton adds that Egerton 'took him to be his chief Secretary; supposing and intending it to be an Introduction to some more weighty Employment in the State; for which, his Lordship did often protest, he thought him very fit'. As Walton's words show, such an appointment was recognized as an avenue to high public service just as a secretaryship to a Cabinet minister would be at the present time. Besides, Egerton soon acquired a reputation for picking out young men of talent and advancing their interests. One of his secretaries, George Carew, was knighted, served for a time as ambassador to France, and succeeded the Earl of Salisbury in the lucrative office of Master of the Court of Wards. John King, who was Egerton's chaplain when Donne joined the household, became successively Dean of Christ Church, Oxford, and Bishop of London.

[1] *Loseley Manuscripts*, ed. A. J. Kempe, p. 341.

A later chaplain, John Williams, attained still higher distinction by becoming first Dean of Westminster, then Lord Keeper and Bishop of Lincoln, and finally Archbishop of York. Donne therefore had every expectation of rising as high in the service of the state as his abilities could take him, and he could congratulate himself that he, the son of a London ironmonger, had secured his initial appointment without any advantages of birth, family influence, or wealth. He may not at this time have seemed as advantageously situated as his friend Henry Wotton was in the service of the Earl of Essex, but he could console himself with the reflection that the fortunes of favourites were notoriously insecure.

The elder Sir Thomas Egerton was himself a striking example of the success attainable in Elizabeth's reign by sheer ability. He was the illegitimate son of a Cheshire squire who had been acknowledged by his father and sent first to Oxford and then to Lincoln's Inn. Only once did he jeopardize his future, when he and four other members of the Inn were summoned before the Court of Star Chamber for 'not cominge to devine service, nor Receavinge the Communyon, and for usinge unlawfull rightes & serimonies'. All five were excluded from the practice of the law 'untill they shoulde reconcile them selues'. Soon afterwards Lincoln's Inn was able to report that Egerton and two of the others 'are sins reconcyled into our howse'.[1] Egerton's own early recusancy doubtless gave him sympathy and understanding for Donne's religious predicament, though one imagines that he had to be assured that his new secretary was no longer a secret Romanist. Egerton himself certainly never had reason to regret his decision to throw in his lot with the established religion. He acquired a large chancery practice, and it is said that the Queen, hearing him on one occasion plead in court in a case in which some of the rights of the Crown were involved, swore that he should never appear against her again. He was appointed Solicitor General in 1581, Attorney General in 1592, and was knighted in the following year. He took a leading part in presenting the case for the prosecution in the trials of such important figures as Edmund Campion the Jesuit, Mary Queen of Scots, the Earl of Arundel, and Sir Francis Davison. He became Master of

---

[1] *Publications of the Catholic Record Society*, vol. xxii, Miscellanea xii (1921), p. 101.

the Rolls in 1594, and in 1596 the Queen appointed him to the office of Lord Keeper of the Great Seal immediately it fell vacant. Anthony Bacon wrote that

the late Lord Keeper, Sir John Puckering, was dead of an apoplexy, very suddenly; into whose place, with an extraordinary speed, Her Majesty hath *ex proprio motu et speciali gratia*, advanced Sir Thomas Egerton, with a general applause, both of court, city, and country, for the reputation he hath of integrity, law, knowledge, and courage. It was his good hap to come to the place freely, without competitor or mediator, yea, against the desire and endeavour of the omnipotent couple.[1]

As a further sign of the Queen's favour, Egerton was allowed to keep the Mastership of the Rolls along with his new office.

Soon after his appointment as Lord Keeper, Egerton moved to York House. This house, which stood in the Strand, was the London residence of the Archbishops of York, but it was customarily leased to the Lord Keeper on condition that he found suitable accommodation for the Archbishop whenever he visited London. All that now remains of it is the water gate, added by Inigo Jones for Buckingham in 1626, in the present Embankment Gardens. When Egerton took up his residence there it was a rambling old mansion, with an extensive garden stretching down to the river. Egerton was at this time a widower with three children, but feeling the need for a wife to do the honours in his new establishment he entered into a second marriage. His choice fell on Elizabeth, the widow of Sir John Wolley, the Queen's former Latin Secretary. Wolley had succeeded Roger Ascham in 1568, and in due course had been knighted by the Queen and appointed to the Privy Council; he had acquired a very considerable fortune, consisting largely of estates in Surrey. His widow was the daughter of Sir William More of Loseley, near Guildford, and had been one of the Queen's favourite maids of honour. Her only son, Francis Wolley (born in 1583), was being brought up with the children of her brother, Sir George More, at Loseley,[2] since her regular attendances at court prevented her from overseeing his education. Though the marriage with Egerton

---

[1] Francis Henry Egerton, Earl of Bridgewater, *Life of Thomas Egerton*, Paris, 1828, p. 166. The 'omnipotent couple' were, of course, Lord Burleigh and his son, Sir Robert Cecil.　　　　　　　　　　　　　　　　　　　　[2] Kempe, p. 318.

was a carefully calculated marriage of convenience on both sides, it was a successful one, and Egerton soon became devotedly attached to his second wife. The marriage took place early in October 1597, and was celebrated quietly by the household chaplain, with the result that the Lord Keeper had to secure absolution from the Bishop of London for marrying without a special licence or the calling of the banns.[1]

Egerton's only daughter married Francis Leigh of Cheshire about three months before her father married again,[2] but there was no lack of young people in the household to which Donne was now familiarly admitted. The younger Sir Thomas Egerton had a wife and three small daughters; his brother John, as yet unmarried, was still a student at Lincoln's Inn. Young Francis Wolley, now almost fifteen and an undergraduate at Oxford, also joined the household. He was married not long afterwards to Mary, the eldest daughter of Sir William Hawtrey. Sir John Wolley and Sir William Hawtrey had been close friends, and this marriage had apparently been arranged as early as 1594, when both fathers were still alive. Hawtrey had no son, and Mary was his principal heiress, so by the terms of the settlement of 1594 the family manor of Chequers in Buckinghamshire passed to her.[3] When the marriage took place she was already an orphan, and apparently she came to live at York House with her mother-in-law, who was now her guardian,[4] while her youthful husband was sent back to Oxford to complete his studies. Another member of the household was Ann More, daughter of Sir George More, a girl of about fourteen, whom Lady Egerton was bringing up and introducing to the great world in return for her brother's kindness to her son.

The staff in such an establishment was a large one.[5] There were two 'ushers', Thomas Marbury and Arthur Mainwaring, who remained in Egerton's service until his death; Mainwaring was a

---

[1] Typewritten 'Calendar of the Bridgewater and Ellesmere Manuscripts' in the Huntington Library, vol. i, item 517.

[2] Op. cit., item 1000.   [3] *Victoria County History of Buckinghamshire*, ii. 336.

[4] P.R.O., C3, James I, 392/32.

[5] Several lists of the household officers exist, although they are all of a period slightly later than that of Donne's service. They are not in the Huntington Library, but in the possession of the present Earl of Ellesmere, and have not been available for consultation.

particularly trusted servant, and was connected by marriage with Lady Egerton.[1] He had literary friends, too, for John Davies of Hereford addressed a poem 'To my deare and much respected friend, Arthur Maynwarring, Esquire, bearer of the purse before the Lo: Chancellor'. Such men as Henry Jones and John Panton, whom Donne had probably known as a student at Lincoln's Inn, were often in and out, concerned with the management of Egerton's private transactions, for the Lord Keeper was busy building up a heritage to pass on to his sons. The chaplain, John King, had recently come from the north; he had formerly been chaplain to the Archbishop of York, but the deaths of the Archbishop and his other patron, Henry, Earl of Huntingdon, Lord President of the Council of the North, had forced him to seek other patronage. King's stay in Egerton's household was relatively brief, for he was obviously destined for promotion, and by 1600 he had been succeeded by another chaplain, Nathaniel Harris. Though Walton says that Egerton made Donne his chief secretary, this is hardly likely, since there were two other secretaries, George Carew and Gregory Downhall, or Donhault, men considerably senior to Donne, whom the Lord Keeper had inherited from his predecessor. Before he left Egerton's service to go as ambassador to France, Carew managed to combine his duties as secretary with a mastership in Chancery, and in 1598 he was sent on a diplomatic mission to Poland. Downhall also became a master in Chancery, but remained in Egerton's service until his death.[2] Thus Egerton's secretaries could expect

---

[1] Her sister had married Sir George Mainwaring, Arthur Mainwaring's cousin. Sir George had a son Arthur, knighted in 1603, who is not to be confused with Egerton's servant.

[2] There is a brief account of Downhall in R. Willis's *Mount Tabor*, 1639. Willis, who was a pupil of Downhall at Christ's School, Gloucester, says: 'Hee came thither but Batchelour of Arts, a good scholler, and who wrote both the secretary and the Italian hands exquisitely well. But after a few yeares that hee had proceeded Master of Arts, finding the schooles entertainment not worthy of him, hee left it, and betook himselfe to another course of being Secretary to some noble man, and at last became Secretary to the worthy Lord Chancellour *Ellesmere*, and in that service (as I think) dyed' (p. 98). Willis says that Downhale (as he spells the name) was 'of *Pembrook Hal* in *Cambridge*', but he is not included in the Venns' *Alumni Cantabrigienses*, as there is apparently no record of him at Cambridge. On the other hand, he is recorded as having been admitted *ad eundem gradum* at Oxford in 1577/8 on the strength of his Cambridge degree. He provides another example of the fallibility of the Cambridge records of this period.

promotion either in the service of the state or in the courts of law.

Egerton was a kind and liberal master, and he enjoyed the conversation of those who worked under him. John Williams's only legal training before he became Lord Keeper had been in Egerton's household, where the ageing Chancellor had gone over with his chaplain the famous cases in Chancery in which he had been concerned either as advocate or judge. Walton relates that Egerton did not account Donne 'so much his Servant, as to forget he was his Friend; and to testifie it, did alwayes use him with much courtesie, appointing him a place at his own Table, to which he esteemed his Company and Discourse to be a great Ornament'. Thus Donne had the opportunity not only of acquiring intimacy with Egerton's family and enjoying the Lord Keeper's familiar conversation, but also of becoming acquainted with many of the guests who were entertained at meals.

Egerton's official duties were many and varied. As Lord Keeper he not only presided over the Upper House of Parliament from the Woolsack, but also acted as an intermediary between the Crown and Parliament. He was responsible for passing on all documents which by their nature required the Great Seal. As Lord Keeper and Master of the Rolls the whole weight of the work of the Court of Chancery fell on his shoulders. As a Privy Councillor he attended the almost daily meetings of the Council, and could exert his influence on almost any decision of national importance. When the Council sat as the Court of Star Chamber he became its presiding officer and handed down its decisions. In addition to all this, he was a member of the Court of High Commission, and served on numerous other special commissions. His load was one to tax the stoutest heart and the highest ability.

Until late in life, when his energies began to wane, Egerton fulfilled his offices with the greatest distinction. He was a handsome and dignified man, and Fuller relates that all '*Christendome* afforded not a *Person* which carried *more Gravity in his Countenance* and *Behaviour*, . . . in so much that many have gone to the *Chancery* on purpose only to see his *Venerable Garb*, (happy they who had no other business) and were highly pleased at so acceptable a *Spectacle*'.

Yet, Fuller continues, 'was his *Outward Case nothing* in comparison of his *Inward Abilities, Quick Wit, Solid Judgment, Ready Utterance*'.[1] His integrity was unquestioned, and Ben Jonson voiced the general opinion when he wrote:

> Whil'st I behold thee liue with purest hands;
>   That no affection in thy voyce commands; . . .
> Whil'st thou art certaine to thy words, once gone,
>   As is thy conscience, which is alwayes one: . . .
> The *Virgin*, long-since fled from earth, I see,
>   T'our times return'd, hath made her heauen in thee.[2]

Much of Egerton's reputation as a judge is due to his work in reforming and regularizing the procedure of the courts over which he presided. One of his principal aims was to eliminate redundancy and unnecessary complexity. A certain Richard Mylward submitted on behalf of a client a replication of 126 pages when sixteen would have sufficed. The Lord Keeper ordered that a hole should be cut in the offending document; Mylward's head was thrust through the hole, and for punishment he was led through Westminster Hall from the bar of one court to another.[3] Soon after his appointment, too, Egerton began an investigation into the fees charged by the Clerk of the Star Chamber in order to 'purge [the office] of the exactions newly imposed'. The reversion of the clerkship was held by Francis Bacon; it was, in fact, the sole official grant he had as yet been able to secure; and the letters on the subject which he wrote to Egerton[4] provide a valuable insight into the relations of the two men. After defending some of the fees charged by the Clerk, Bacon eventually decided for the side of discretion, and 'determined not to meddle' in the matter, but not before he had written a long and confidential letter to Egerton on his present difficulties and his hopes for the future. He gratefully acknowledged 'your loving courses held towards me; specially in your nomination and enablement of me long sithence to the Solicitor's place', and, more recently, 'your countenance and favour in my practice'; and he then went on 'as freely to communicate of my poor state with

---

[1] *Worthies*, 1662, p. 176. [2] *Epigrams*, no. lxxiv.
[3] W. S. Holdsworth, *History of English Law*, v. 231–8.
[4] J. Spedding, *Life and Letters of Bacon*, ii (1862), 57–67.

your Lordship, as I could have done to my honourable father, if he had lived'. It is clear that, after Essex, Bacon placed his main hopes of advancement in Egerton, and regarded him with affection and respect. In view of the close relations existing between Bacon and his master, it is almost inevitable that Donne should have made Bacon's acquaintance at this time, even if he had not known him earlier.[1]

Egerton's new secretary must from the first have been occupied with a large share of the legal business that passed through the Lord Keeper's hands,[2] and it is clear that he was employed in investigating the ruinous fees exacted from suitors by the officers of the Chancery and Council. The fifth Satire records some of Donne's impressions of these new experiences, and it differs from the earlier Satires in that the poet is no longer a mere spectator, but a participant in the issues of which he writes. Contempt and scorn have given way to indignation, and in the place of witty observation of individual affectations there is a strong, even a shocked, perception of moral corruption. The poem is concerned with the exactions levied on suitors by the lawyers and officials of the courts, not merely in

[1] Grierson, in 'Bacon's Poem "The World": its Date and Relation to Certain other Poems', *MLR*, vi (1911), 145–56, argues that Donne's verse letter to Wotton beginning 'Sir, more then kisses, letters mingle Soules' was 'called forth' by Bacon's poem, and is to be dated 1597–8. It may be taken as established that Bacon and Wotton were acquainted with one another at this time, if only through their common association with Essex; that Wotton had received a copy of Bacon's verses from him; and that Donne's verse letter takes up the same themes as those handled by Bacon. But that Thomas Bastard's epigram to Wotton is a contribution to the same *débat* is by no means as certain as Grierson believes. This is unfortunate, for the epigram, which was published in Bastard's *Chrestoleros* in 1598, is the only one of the three pieces which can be dated even approximately. On the other hand, Donne's poem certainly shows acquaintance with Bacon's; it is also early, and was written before Wotton went abroad at the end of 1600 since it is addressed in some of the manuscripts to 'Mr.' and not 'Sir' H. W.

Fairly early in the next reign Donne was introduced to James Hay (afterwards Earl of Carlisle) by Bacon, as he recalled in a letter to Sir Robert Ker: 'So, when I reckon all the favours that I have received from my Lord Chancellor I return to that, that he was the first man that ever presented my name to my Lord *Carlile*, and entred me into his service' (*Tobie Mathew Collection*, p. 308). If Donne knew Bacon well enough to rely on him for such favours, it is more than likely that their acquaintanceship went back into the previous reign.

[2] It is disappointing that there is no clue to Donne's secretarial activities among the Ellesmere manuscripts in the Huntington Library. At any rate it can safely be said that his duties did not include the more routine ones of transcribing documents, endorsing and filing letters, etc.

the Star Chamber and in the law courts generally, but also in the
Chancery and other offices to which those who had obtained royal
grants had to go to get their grants validated.[1] The Queen does not
know, and cannot be expected to know, of the abuses committed in
her name, and Egerton is only beginning to learn of their extent:

> Greatest and fairest Empresse, know you this?
> Alas, no more then Thames calme head doth know
> Whose meades her armes drowne, or whose corne o'rflow:
> You Sir, whose righteousnes she loves, whom I
> By having leave to serve, am most richly
> For service paid, authoriz'd, now beginne
> To know and weed out this enormous sinne.

Yet the suitors, though their misery is an object for pity, are not
blameless:

> a wastfull warre
> Is fought against you, and you fight it; they
> Adulterate lawe, and you prepare their way
> Like wittals; th'issue your owne ruine is.

Donne's disillusionment with the administration of the law did

---

[1] A letter among the Ellesmere MSS. (no. 1556) illustrates the troubles of the
last class of suitors:

'Right honorable my good Lo: It is almost seaven yeares since I compounded at a
deare Rate, for the Warrant by which I was to haue passed my troublesome booke of
Concealmentes, afterward I spent three yeares, in seeking, and sending, into many
partes of the Realme, to compound with the Tenantes, before I could procure the
late Lo: Thesorer to allowe of my particulers, which was no small charge vnto me,
After that Mr. Sollicytor for penning the booke, had xx li. of me, Mr. Attorney
generall for penning the Tenure had xx li. of me, Theire Clarks had xij li. of me. The
Mr. of Requestes to gett her Maiestie to signe it, had xl li. of me, and after to gett
it passd the Signet and pryvie Seale, and to make itt ready for the great Seale, cost
me at Least xl li. more, All which done yt pleased your Lordship vppon iust cause of
dislike of the generalleties to make staye thereof, to the ende yt might be reformed
but not vtterlye overthrowne, whereof I haue had good proofe bothe before the booke
[was] cansalled and synce assuring me of your honorable favoure yf I could gett her
Maiestie moved thereof in your presence, which Mr. Chauncellor hath often promised
but by his greater affaires I haue beene Longe delayed, So as now I am almost in
dispayre, and that the Rather, because I heare of a generall Warrant likely to be
graunted, which will carry away all my particulers, and frustrate my booke, for
ever/ My humble sute therfore is, that your Lo: will vouchesaffe me the contynuance
of your woonted favoure, that I may be releived by some suche meanes as your Lo:
in your honorable wisdome shall thinke fitt/ And so with my most humble duty I rest
Your Lordshipps most humbly bovnden
Edw: Wymarke   vj⁰ Maij 1599'

not, however, prevent him from initiating a Chancery suit in the early days of his secretaryship. The employment of the boy, Tom Danby, had not been a success. He had remained with Donne for some eighteen months (and hence may have gone with him on the Cadiz expedition), but about January 1597 he had decamped, taking with him from his master's wardrobe 'one blacke Cloake of the valewe of xx^{tie} ^{s} one laced satten suite of the valewe of iij^{li} one payer of blacke velvet laced hose of the valewe of iiij^{li} x^{s} & as much gold lace as came to the valewe of v^{li}'. Donne was indignant at the loss he suffered, and tried without success to obtain recompense from Christopher Danby. At last, on 10 May 1598, he filed a bill of complaint. The bill was drawn up and signed by his friend Christopher Brooke, and its economy of wording bears eloquent witness to the Lord Keeper's dislike of unnecessary verbiage. It cites the oral agreement with Christopher Danby, itemizes the stolen articles, and estimates Donne's losses at £30. 10s. Since 'the wittnesses which were by at the tyme when the sayd Christopher did make the sayde promise in maner aboue sayde are dead, and soe your sayd orator remedilesse by the stricte Course of the common lawe', Donne prays for the issue of a subpoena to cause Danby to appear in the Court of Chancery and answer the claim against him.[1] Fortunately no protracted litigation ensued; the subpoena was duly served, but Danby did not appear, and on 29 May judgement was given for Donne.[2]

Donne did not give his whole time to the legal side of Egerton's duties; public affairs must have occupied him constantly. Egerton frequently needed the attendance of a secretary when he went to Whitehall, and there were often urgent messages to be conveyed between the Lords of the Council. Sometimes, when the Queen was on progress or at one of the palaces outside London—Nonsuch, Greenwich, or Richmond—the Council remained at Westminster to transact business, but kept in daily touch with her; at other times it accompanied her. Donne's verse letter to Henry Wotton, beginning 'Here's no more newes, then vertue', is dated in some manuscripts '20 July 1598 at Court', and was probably written from

---

[1] Donne v. Danby, C3 Eliz. 266/93; see Appendix D, p. 568.
[2] Chancery Decrees and Orders, C33/94, fo. 812^{v}.

Greenwich.[1] At that time old Lord Burleigh was slowly dying and
the Earl of Essex was in deep disgrace. Three weeks before at a
Council meeting the Queen had boxed Essex's ears; with his sword
half drawn the angry Earl had stalked from the chamber declaring
that not even from Henry VIII would he have endured such treatment, and had taken his followers with him into retirement in the
country. Donne writes with unsparing contempt for the court and
its intrigues:

> here no one is from the'extremitie
> Of vice, by any other reason free,
> But that the next to'him, still, is worse then hee . . .

> Suspitious boldnesse to this place belongs,
> And to'have as many eares as all have tongues;
> Tender to know, tough to acknowledge wrongs . . .

> Then let us at these mimicke antiques jeast,
> Whose deepest projects, and egregious gests
> Are but dull Moralls of a game at Chests.

The letter is, in effect, a consolatory epistle, designed to raise
Wotton's mind above the pleasures of the court in which he cannot
share.

The quarrel between Essex and the Queen did not inspire the
same philosophical detachment in other minds. However pleased
Essex's enemies might be at his disgrace, his absence from the
Council was a serious embarrassment to the transaction of public
business, and Egerton wrote him a widely circulated letter urging
him to make his submission to the Queen. There was a real friendship between the two men, in spite of the difference in their ages,
and Egerton believed that he could bring about a reconcilement;
but the quarrel dragged on, and it was not until 10 September that
Essex returned to the court.

The quarrel between Essex and the Queen had been about the
appointment of a commander in Ireland. The situation there was
rapidly deteriorating, but the deadlock in the Council continued.

---

[1] E. K. Chambers, *The Elizabethan Stage*, iv. 111. [It has been suggested that the
poem addressed to Rowland Woodward ('Like one who'in her third widdowhood')
also belongs to this period, when Donne was settling into a secure position as
Egerton's secretary; see Milgate, *Satires etc.*, pp. 222–3.]

In the end Essex offered his own services, and by the beginning of
1599 it was decided that he should go. His reputation in the country
at large had lost none of its glamour, and more than ever before the
swarm of young men eager to serve under him pressed about him.
He crossed the Irish Channel with his forces in April, and accompanying him were many of Donne's friends and acquaintances.
There is no need to relate the events of the next five months; Donne
was not directly concerned with them, though no doubt he followed
them with the closest attention. Some fragments of his correspondence during this period have survived, preserved by Wotton, who
had accompanied Essex as one of his secretaries. Both men wrote
frequently, but both complained of the loss of their letters. Wotton,
who had entrusted Donne with some of his business affairs during
his absence, wrote as soon as he landed on Irish soil. 'May I after
these', he concluded, 'kiss that fair and learned hand of your mistress, than whom the world doth possess nothing more virtuous',
and in the postscript he adds: 'You must not forget *septies in hebdo-
mada* to visit my best and dearest.' Later Wotton sent with letters
of introduction to Donne a German whom he had met in Ireland and
had helped there; for the rest, his tone is carefully guarded, and one
can sense his growing awareness that the campaign was not going
well.[1] From Donne's side there survive only a verse letter, 'To
H. W. in Hiber. Belligeranti', and perhaps a letter to a common
friend enclosed in another to Wotton.[2] Donne laments that death
'gleanes . . . many of our frends away', though some, like Wotton
himself, remained safe, and others, like Sir William Cornwallis and
Sir Henry Goodyer, returned with knighthoods conferred by Essex
that the Queen so much resented that for a time she thought
seriously of degrading the recipients.

Of the friends Donne lost in Ireland the name of only one is
known. The younger Sir Thomas Egerton was wounded in a skirmish, was brought to Dublin, and died in Dublin Castle on 23
August 1599 at the age of twenty-five. Essex himself wrote a letter
of condolence to the bereaved father. The body was brought by sea
to Chester, and before it was buried in the parish church of Doddle-

---

[1] L. Pearsall Smith, *The Life and Letters of Sir Henry Wotton*, 1907, i. 306–10.
[2] Simpson, *Prose Works*, p. 306.

ston a splendid funeral ceremony was held in Chester Cathedral. A full account of the procession has survived in the notebook of a post-Restoration Lancaster Herald, who transcribed it for use as a precedent. The document is worth transcribing in full:

The funerall of Sir Tho Egerton sonne & heyre to Th[e] Lo Chancelor who dyed in Dublyn Castell   his body was brought ouer & buried in Dodleston church   his funerall was solemnised in ⟨the⟩ cathedrall church in Chester 26 Sept 1599   his funerall diner kept in bushopps pallas:

first 2 Conducters with black staues
the bellman
24 poore in gownes
seruingmen in cotes
2 dromes & fife
Souldiers trayling pikes
the Ensigne trayled by Capt phillips
the seruants of the defunct in clokes
The Trumpitt sounding dolfully
The Standard borne by dauid Holand gent
The Horse led by Antho Rauenscroft gent
    then theis Esquires in clokes

Mr birkenhead	Mr goodman
Mr Tho pulston	Mr ch goodman
Mr Tho bumbury	Mr peirs moston
Mr Hen mainwaringe	Mr Leuersage sen^r
Mr Tho Aston	Mr Brooke
Mr Tho smyth	Mr Roger pulston
Mr Leigh of Adlington	Mr Tho Wilbram
Mr Worberton of Arley	Mr Venables

    then the knightes in clokes

Sir Geo booth	Sir Geo Leicester
Sir Jo Lloyd	Sir Jo Sauage
Sir Tho Moston	Sir Jo Egerton
Sir peter Leige	Sir Rich Treuor
Sir Geo mainwaringe	Sir Wm brereton
Sir Hugh Cholmley	Sir Ed ffitton

    Mr Tho Holcroft sheriff of Cheshier
      betwene the 2 last Knights
The penon borne by Mr Tho Rauenscroft

the spurrs by Captaine Salisbury
The gauntletts by Mr Rich brereton
The helme & Crest by Mr Hope
The Target borne by Mr Marbury
The sword borne by Mr Jo done
The cote borne by Mr Norroy Kinge of Armes
  the bushopp of chester who
    preached
  The Corpes borne by theis 4
    Mr Roger brereton
    Mr Robert dauis
    Mr Wm liuersage
    Mr Grosuenor
The cheife mourner Mr Jo Egerton
  4 Assistants
  Mr Sargant Worberton
  Mr Rafe Egerton
  Mr francis Leigh
  Mr Rafe Rauenscroft
then the Mair Knightes & Esquires
& Aldermen & frends hauinge no
blackes.[1]

Donne, it will be seen, occupied a position of considerable honour, preceding only the Norroy King of Arms and the Bishop of Chester (Richard Vaughan) before the bier, and bearing the sword of his dead friend.

The Lord Keeper did not attend his son's funeral; the opening of Michaelmas term was at hand, and he was kept in London by the pressure of public business. Indeed, before the members of his household who had represented him at Chester had returned to

---

[1] MS. Harl. 2129, fo. 67. Not all the participants can be identified nor, perhaps, is the attempt worth making, but it may be remarked that the Breretons were of the family into which the Lord Keeper's half-sister (and only legitimate child of their father) had married; the Ravenscrofts were of the kindred of Egerton's first wife, and the Leighs belonged to the family into which his daughter had married. Mr. John Egerton was, of course, the Lord Keeper's second son, Mr. Francis Leigh his son-in-law, and Mr. Marbury his usher. Sir George Booth, Sir Peter Leigh, and Sir Richard Trevor had all been companions-in-arms in Ireland of the younger Sir Thomas Egerton, and Mr. Brooke was perhaps Christopher Brooke. For an episode immediately after the funeral which involved some of the others present, see the *Calendar of the Salisbury Papers*, Hist. MSS. Com., ix. 393.

London he was fully occupied with even more urgent affairs. While the funeral service was taking place in the cathedral, Essex himself with only a few retainers passed hurriedly through the town,[1] on his flight from Ireland in defiance of the Queen's orders. On his arrival at Nonsuch Palace he forced his way into her presence before she was dressed. The Council was hastily summoned to meet at Nonsuch on the following morning to consider Essex's misdemeanours, and the meeting lasted all day. In the evening a report was made to the Queen, who remained undecided for thirty-six hours, and then announced her decision. Essex was to be banished from court, and was to remain a prisoner in the Lord Keeper's charge until her further pleasure should be known. Egerton returned to London with his prisoner in the Earl of Worcester's coach, and Essex remained in captivity for nearly six months.

Essex may have been installed at York House by the time that Donne returned from Chester. His presence was a source of discomfort to the whole household since, though a prisoner, he had to receive the attention due to his rank. Soon after his imprisonment he fell ill, and for a time his condition was so serious that one November evening the Queen came secretly in her barge with only two attendants and paid him a brief visit. But the next day, when the Court of Star Chamber assembled for the last session of the term, there was a public recital of Essex's offences, and a few days later his household was dismissed. Only a few personal servants and one or two more influential attendants such as Henry Cuffe were retained. Wotton seems to have left Essex's service at this time and to have retired to the country. A letter from Donne almost certainly belongs to the Christmas season of 1599–1600.[2] The Court was at Greenwich; there were plays during the holidays; and the Queen was active and eager for amusement, coming almost every night into 'the presence, to see the ladies dawnce the old and new country dawnces, with the taber and pipe'.[3] The Admiral's Men played Dekker's *Old Fortunatus* and *The Shoemaker's Holiday*; the Chamberlain's Men gave three other plays,[4] one of which may have been

[1] Daniel King, *The Vale-Royall of England*, 1656, p. 208.
[2] Simpson, *Prose Works*, p. 310.
[3] Chambers, *The Elizabethan Stage*, iv. 112, n. 14.   [4] Ibid., 112.

Twelfth Night, for Virginio Orsino, Duke of Bracciano, was visiting the Court from Italy, and the festivities were gayer than usual.[1] Donne writes from the Court, which was 'not great but full of iollyty & revells & playes and as merry as if it were not sick'. 'My lo: of Essex & his trayne', he continues, 'are no more mist here then the Aungells *which* were cast downe from heaven nor (for anything I see) likelyer to retourne.' Then he gives some news of Essex himself:

He withers still in his sicknes & plods on to his end in the same pace where yo*u* left vs. the worst accidents of his sicknes are *tha*t he conspires w*i*th it & *tha*t it is not here beleeved. that *whi*ch was sayd of Cato *tha*t his age vnderstood him not I feare may be averted of yo*ur* lor*d* that he vnderstood not his age: for it is a naturall weaknes of innocency. That such men want lockes for themselues and keyse for others.[2]

Donne shrewdly perceived that Essex's despondency had prolonged his illness, and that his innate romanticism had not only disabled him from making a true appraisal of his situation but had also laid him open to every kind of self-deception. Like so many of his contemporaries, Donne had been attracted by the charm of Essex's personality, but closer acquaintance with him in misfortune was bringing a measure of disillusionment. Two other letters to Wotton, not certainly from Donne, must belong to the succeeding weeks,[3] and are more guarded. The writer has recovered from an 'ague', and is delighted at the arrival in town of Sir Maurice Berkeley, Donne's friend and Wotton's since at least the days of the Cadiz expedition.[4]

[1] J. L. Hotson, *The First Night of 'Twelfth Night'*, 1954.
[2] Simpson, p. 310. Though Mr. I. A. Shapiro (*TLS*, 12 Sept. 1952) will only concede that this letter is 'possibly' by Donne, the writer shows the kind of knowledge of Essex's condition that one would expect from an inmate of York House, and more perhaps than the current gossip would furnish him with.
[3] Simpson, pp. 308–9.
[4] The second letter (numbered 5 by Mrs. Simpson) might have been written by Wotton. There is a good deal of information about Sir Maurice Berkeley in Leslie Hotson's *I, William Shakespeare*, 1937, *passim*, but nothing that throws any further light on his relations with Donne or Wotton. Berkeley was half-brother to Thomas Russell, one of the overseers of Shakespeare's will. While it does not seem possible to trace any connection between Donne and Shakespeare via Berkeley and Russell, one can nevertheless see that Russell could have had opportunities such as would have been possible to very few others for compiling a commonplace book from the poems of Donne and Shakespeare that could conceivably have served as copy for the book of verses entered in the Stationers' Register on 3 Jan. 1600 by Eleazar Edgar,

As Essex gradually recovered his health the Lord Keeper's household was troubled by a fresh anxiety, the illness of Lady Egerton. She died on 20 January 1600, to the great grief of her husband. 'The Lord Keeper doth sorrow more, then the Wisdom of soe great a Man ought to doe. He keapes priuat, hath desired Judge *Gawdy*, to sitt in *Chancery*, and yt is thought he will not come Abroade this Terme', wrote a contemporary, and the Queen was forced to disturb his grief and remind him that 'the publiq Service must be preferred before priuat Passions'.[1] Lady Egerton's death inevitably brought about changes in the household. The Wolley estate of Pyrford in Surrey, which the Lord Keeper had used as a country home, now reverted to her son Francis, who had just taken his degree at Oxford, and he, though a minor, probably began to live there with his wife. Her niece, Ann More, left London and the Court to return to the quiet life of the country at her father's house.

When Donne fell in love with Ann More and what first attracted him to her are now beyond conjecture, but, although she was not yet sixteen, there had been opportunities for intimacy to ripen, and she had responded to his admiration. 'So long since as her being at York House', Donne wrote later to her father, 'this had foundation, and so much then of promise and contract built upon yt as without violence to conscience might not be shaken.' Donne knew that, whatever his prospects might be, he could not hope to offer himself to her father as a suitor, since his own dwindling resources could never make him a match for the daughter of one so secure in his landed possessions as Sir George More. Hence the affair was kept secret, and though Ann and he pledged themselves to one another and made resolutions to remain faithful, they parted with no assurance that they would ever meet again, and only a vague hope that Sir George would not provide a husband for his daughter before they could prevent it.

Meanwhile Essex's health steadily improved, and towards the end of March he exchanged his imprisonment at York House for confinement no less rigorous in his own London residence, Essex

'Amours by J. D. with certen other sonnetes by W. S.'—supposing, that is (for, if the book was ever printed, no copies are known to survive), that Donne and Shakespeare are the poets intended by the initials.

[1] A. Collins, *Letters and Memorials of State* (Sidney Papers), 1746, ii. 164.

House. Sir Thomas Egerton, too, as his sorrow for his wife's death waned, began to think of remarrying. His third marriage, which took place in October 1600, was by worldly standards the most successful of all. His bride was Alice, daughter of Sir John Spencer of Althorp and widow of Ferdinando Stanley, Earl of Derby, a lady whom Spenser had hymned and for whom in later days Milton was to write *Arcades*. The marriage took place quietly in the presence of a few friends at Russell House, with Egerton's chaplain officiating. The Countess was embroiled in a succession of lawsuits with the new Earl of Derby, the brother of her former husband, and she doubtless felt that Egerton's position would safeguard her interests and those of her daughters. Egerton, on his side, became allied to some of the most powerful families in England.

The marriage was not a happy one. The Countess was twenty years her husband's junior; she was wilful, hot-tempered, and used to having her own way; in spite of her grace and charm, she vexed her husband sorely. At the end of his life he penned for the benefit of his son 'An vnpleasant declaration of thinges passed betwene the Co[u]ntesse of Derby and me since our mariage' in which he told of her extravagance and greed, and her 'cursed railing and bytter tongue'. He wrote sadly, 'I thanke God I neuer desired longe lyfe nor neuer had lesse cause to desire it then synce this my last mariage, for before I was neuer acquaynted with such tempests and stormes', but he had borne them all in silence so as not to become 'fabula vulgi'.[1] But this was still in the future, and at the time of his marriage Egerton must have looked forward happily enough to a repetition of the harmonious relations that had existed between himself and his second wife.

Egerton's new marriage meant a very large increase in the household at York House. With the Countess came her three daughters. Anne, the eldest, married Lord Chandos in 1608; Frances, the second, married John Egerton, with her mother's connivance though, oddly enough, without the Lord Keeper's knowledge, in 1601 or 1602;[2] Elizabeth, the youngest, married Henry, Lord Hastings, who

---

[1] Calendar of the Ellesmere Manuscripts, Huntington Library, vol. i, no. 213.

[2] On the other hand, the possibility of the marriage was rumoured at the time of the marriage of Egerton and Lady Derby (Collins, op. cit., ii. 219).

became Earl of Huntingdon in 1604. The last-named was a boy of fifteen at the time of his marriage on 15 January 1601, and immediately after the ceremony was sent back to his tutors, while the bride continued to live with her mother until 1604.[1] With the Countess and her daughters came a large train of servants, amounting to forty in all, and their coming raised the household expenses by no less than £650 a year, though this was offset by the value of the properties which Egerton through his marriage now controlled. Donne was soon on cordial terms with the Countess's daughters, and the two younger ones remained his friends for the rest of his life.

Essex had been set at liberty towards the end of August 1600 and had spent the rest of the summer in the country, but when the Lord Keeper's third marriage occurred he was back in London, living quietly at Essex House, and anxiously waiting for the Queen to make what was, for him, a momentous decision. He held the

[1] Donne's verse letter to the Countess of Huntingdon beginning 'That unripe side of earth' (assuming that it *is* Donne's) presents some almost insoluble problems. The concluding lines of Donne's other epistle to the Countess suggest that he had addressed verses to her at the time that she was living at York House:

> And if I flatter any, 'tis not you
> But my owne judgement, who did long agoe
> Pronounce, that all these praises should be true,
> And vertue should your beauty,'and birth outgrow.

This view is confirmed by a letter to Goodyer in which Donne seems to have enclosed the later verses and in which he admits having addressed her before, but only once:

'For the other part of your Letter, spent in the praise of the Countesse, I am always very apt to beleeve it of her, and can never beleeve it so well, and so reasonably, as now, when it is averred by you; but for the expressing it to her, in that sort as you seem to counsaile, I have these two reasons to decline it. That that knowledge which she hath of me, was in the beginning of a graver course, then of a Poet, into which (that I may also keep my dignity) I would not seem to relapse. The Spanish proverb informes me, that he is a fool which cannot make one Sonnet, and he is mad which makes two. The other stronger reason, is my integrity to the other Countesse ... But because I hope she will not disdain, that I should write well of her Picture, I have obeyed you thus far, as to write' (*Letters*, pp. 103–4).

If, however, the verses beginning 'That unripe side of earth' were addressed to the Countess soon after her marriage, as it seems we must assume after J. Yoklavich's article, 'Donne and the Countess of Huntingdon', *PQ*, xliii (1964), 283–8, it would be hard to find a better example to justify Dryden's criticism that Donne 'perplexes the minds of the fair sex with nice speculations of philosophy, when he should engage their hearts, and entertain them with the softnesses of love'. It is scarcely credible that these verses were addressed to a girl of thirteen, her age at the time of her marriage. [See further, Milgate, *Satires etc.*, pp. 242–3, 293–4.]

grant of the farm of sweet wines, and it was due shortly to expire. This was his principal source of income, and if the Queen refused to renew it he faced financial ruin. On 30 October Elizabeth announced that for the present the grant would not be renewed, but that she would keep it in her own hands. Essex was in despair, and his animus turned against those whom he regarded as his enemies and who, he believed, had influenced the Queen to procure his ruin. His easily inflamed imagination began to cherish wild schemes for winning back his position by force. Early in the new year Essex House began to fill with all kinds of ill-assorted characters, some of them devoted and faithful followers, others notorious malcontents. By Saturday, 17 February, it was obvious that something was brewing, and an emergency meeting of the Council was called. Twice Essex was summoned to attend, but each time refused. He realized that the moment had come for open action, and he called his adherents to assemble at his house on the following morning. Meanwhile the Council was not idle, and at ten o'clock on the Sunday morning the Lord Keeper, the Lord Chief Justice, the Earl of Worcester, and Sir William Knollys knocked on the gate of Essex House demanding entrance in the Queen's name. After a parley they were admitted, but their retinues were forced to remain outside. An angry exchange of words took place in the courtyard, after which the councillors were led upstairs to Essex's study, from which he presently emerged, locking the door behind him. Essex and his followers then set out for the City to raise a force for a march on Whitehall, while the councillors were left behind as prisoners. They remained locked up until late in the afternoon, when they were released by Sir Ferdinando Gorges only a quarter of an hour before Essex returned with the bitter consciousness of the utter failure of all his hopes. Soon afterwards the house was surrounded by the Queen's forces. Essex surrendered that night, and was led away to prison, to be tried and then executed.

Of Donne's part in the happenings of that eventful Sunday nothing is known, though he may have been one of the Lord Keeper's attendants who waited outside the gates of Essex House when only the councillors were admitted. Whatever feelings he may still have cherished towards Essex, he obviously had no hesitation in following the path of duty, and the ill-fated rebellion can have been for him no more than a further symptom of the degeneracy of the age. Meanwhile there was much to be done, and Donne was no doubt busily employed in assisting the Lord Keeper in examining the more important witnesses and in the other preparations for the trials of the rebels. After justice had been done life resumed its more normal routine. But by now Wotton was abroad and Ann More was at Loseley, and his life seemed more savourless than it had at any time before.

It may be assumed, however, that Donne was profoundly disturbed by Essex's fall. He had doubtless been conscious for some time of the weaknesses of the one-time hero, but he watched with something like horror the behaviour of those who had formerly surrounded him. Some, like Henry Cuffe, whom he had probably known, perished on the scaffold.[1] Others, like the Revd. Abdy Ashton, his chaplain, unctuously co-operated with the authorities, gave evidence against his former patron, and urged him to make a full confession of his sins. But he was perhaps most shocked for a time by the conduct of Francis Bacon, who had placed all his hopes in Essex, and now appeared for the prosecution at his trial. Donne owned a copy of the official account of Essex's misdemeanours, the *Declaration of the Practises and Treasons committed by Robert late Earle of Essex* (1601) which had been drawn up by Bacon, then corrected by the Council, and finally revised by the Queen herself.[2] On the title-page Donne has written part of 2 Samuel 16 : 10, 'Sinite eum Maledicere na*m* Dominus iussit', which is best rendered by combining the words of the Bishops' Bible and the Authorized Version: 'Let him curse even because the Lord hath bidden him.' This seems to refer, with bitter irony, to the vehemence of Bacon's denunciation of his former patron, and the charge of hypocrisy it entailed. The same criticism is implicit in two of the titles of imaginary books in *The Courtier's Library*:

27. The Brazen Head of Francis Bacon: concerning Robert the First, King of England.

[1] It is worth noting that Donne owned a copy of Cuffe's book, published in 1607, *The Differences of the Ages of Mans Life*. This copy has been in the Harvard library since 1767 (Keynes, pp. 212–13).

[2] It is in a bound volume of pamphlets in the Cambridge University Library, press-mark Syn. 7. 60. 26.

28. The Lawyer's Onion; or, the Art of Lamenting in Courts of Law, by the same.[1]

Donne was later to express his admiration for Bacon and to accept his friendship again, but several years must have elapsed before he could regard him once more with equanimity.

The summoning of Parliament in the autumn of 1601 provided the occasion for a fresh experience for Donne. As the Lord Keeper's secretary it would be convenient that he should be in the House of Commons; it would provide him with a chance to show his quality and also give him an additional insight into the conduct of public affairs. Accordingly he was returned as one of the members for Brackley, Northants.[2] The manor and borough of Brackley had formerly belonged to the Earls of Derby, and in the partition of the Derby estates it passed to Frances, the second daughter who married John Egerton. The borough was thus in the control of the Lord Keeper, and as John Egerton was returned as one of the members for Shropshire, Brackley was available for other nominees of York House. The other member for Brackley was the son of one of the more important gentlemen of the county: Edward Montagu, afterwards Lord Montagu of Boughton, and a cousin of Lucy, Countess of Bedford. Among the members of this Parliament were many with whom Donne was to be on terms of friendship, though whether he was yet acquainted with them all is uncertain. Sir George More was a member for Surrey and his son Robert for the borough of Guildford. Young Edward Herbert was a member for Montgomeryshire, in which his principal estates lay; Francis Wolley was also a member, as were two other men who both married daughters of Sir George More, Thomas Grymes and Nicholas Throckmorton. Robert Cotton and Sir Maurice Berkeley were unquestionably already among Donne's friends, and members from the Inns of Court whom Donne knew or was soon to know included such men as Francis Bacon, Dr. Julius Caesar, William Hakewill, John Davies, Richard Martin, and Toby Mathew, the son of the Archbishop of York.

Parliament met on 27 October and sat until its dissolution on 19 December. It had been called principally to grant fresh supplies

[1] Ed. E. M. Simpson, p. 51.
[2] I. A. Shapiro, 'John Donne and Parliament', *TLS*, 10 Mar. 1932, p. 172.

for the war in Ireland, and the Lord Keeper in his opening speech emphasized that it was the Queen's wish that Parliament should not waste time over unnecessary legislation. Nevertheless proceedings were stormy from the very beginning, when the officiousness of an usher shut the doors too soon and excluded the majority of the Commons from the House of Lords where the Lord Keeper was delivering his speech. Then, when the question of voting supplies came up, the Commons almost at once began to voice their discontent with the number of monopolies that had been granted, and the protests became so vociferous that the Queen was forced to send for the Speaker and announce her intention of revoking the monopolies. The Commons expressed their gratitude in the warmest terms, and went back to the business of voting supplies. This done, the Parliament was dissolved. As far as is known, Donne neither took part in any of the debates, nor served on any committees.[1] He was probably busy on the Lord Keeper's behalf, probing opinions and sensing the feeling of the House for his master, and had neither the time nor the inclination to participate actively in parliamentary business as an independent member. Such activities he left to men like Sir George More, an eager parliamentarian who was constantly on his feet, or to others who, like Bacon or Sir Robert Cecil, brought the weight of their authority to the guidance of the House.

Donne's membership of the Parliament of 1601 was the last significant development in his public career as Egerton's secretary. Of other events that affected his private life during this period there is comparatively little to relate. Before 10 September 1595 his mother and her third husband, Richard Rainsford, had gone abroad and settled at Antwerp in search of freedom in the exercise of their religion. This is proved by an inquisition, held in 1598 under an Exchequer commission to investigate the possessions of fugitive Catholics, into a statute staple for £2,000 which had been granted to John Syminges by Charles Somerset and had since passed to Rainsford by his marriage to Syminges's widow.[2] His mother's

---

[1] So Shapiro, op. cit. This is probably, though not necessarily, true. D'Ewes briefly reports a speech by 'Mr. Dunn' against a bill to prevent pluralities of benefices, but Heywood Townshend gives the speaker as 'Dr. Dunn', i.e. Daniel Dun the civilian.

[2] P.R.O., E178/1383. A statute staple was a bond so binding that the person bound

departure had removed Donne from the last vestiges of parental control, and however little she may have approved of the life he had chosen for himself, she at least had the assurance that he was well launched in the world. Another document relating to Donne reveals, however, that he had by no means cut himself off from his Catholic connections. In recalling his services to Egerton after his marriage Donne wrote: 'I was four years your Lordship's secretary, not dishonest nor greedy', and it is doubtless true that he did not use his position, as others in similar situations did, to secure for himself gratuities from suitors, or royal grants obtainable through his master's favour. Nevertheless, in July 1601 there issued from the Chancery a patent for a lease 'to John Dunne of ij part*es* of the Manor of Uphall in Carleton in the County of Lincoln, p*a*rcell of the possess*ions* of John Heyward Recusant for xx^{tie}j yeares if it soe longe remaine in her M*a*iesti*es* hand*es*; rent p*er* an*n*um xl *li*, fine xx *s*'.[1] John Heywood's recusancy had been so stubborn that it could not be ignored; his name first appears in a list of recusants in 1584, and in 1599 John Lilly, the Jesuit lay brother, was captured in his house.[2] Under the penalties imposed by the Act of 1587 two-thirds of his lands became forfeited to the Crown as a result of the findings of a commission on recusancy held at Lincoln on 3 April 1601. The confiscated two-thirds of his lands were leased to Donne shortly afterwards, and he had clearly made use of his official position to obtain the lease. That he held lands directly from the Crown now enabled Donne to write 'esquire' after his name, but whether he derived any further benefit from the grant is doubtful. The arrangement to which he had become a party is explained by a recent writer:

In theory, it was possible for the King to seize the forfeited lands,

was estopped from denying it or avoiding it by alleging fraud or any other deficiency in it. (Somerset had sold Syminges the two manors in Monmouthshire mentioned above, p. 38.) In a Privy Seal Docket Book (P.R.O. Index 6744) occurs, 29 May 1606, 'A remittall of a Statute staple of 2000*l*. made by one Charles Somersett esquier to John Syming docto^r of Phisicke which came to Richard Rainsford esquier in right of his wife being Administratrix of the said doctor Symyng and forfeited to the late Queene by the said Rainsford by reason he wente beyond Seas and remayned there wthout licence, as of his Mat^{es} free gift & favo^r to the said Rainsford.'

[1] The quotation is from the same Privy Seal Office Docket Book (P.R.O., Index 6744); the full text of the lease is enrolled in C66/1566, no. 37. The lands had been inherited by Heywood from his father Richard (see above, Chapter II, p. 24).

[2] H. Foley, *Records of the English Province of the Society of Jesus*, i. 449 n. and vi. 718.

and to sell them, but this was rarely, if ever, done. It was a far better proposition to let the lands to a tenant, and to replenish the Exchequer with the annual rentals. Moreover, in this way, the Recusant was encouraged to conform, for, upon conformity, he recovered his lands; if his lands had been sold, this would have been impossible, and he could not have recovered his property. Thus it was that Recusants' lands were commonly let, the rents being payable to the Crown. In practice, the tenant was frequently the Recusant himself, though this was illegal. In many cases, also, the lands were commonly let to a friend or relative of the Recusant, who thus in practice remained in possession of his lands.[1]

Donne did not hold the lease for its full term; John Heywood died in 1605, leaving his property to his widow and after her death to his sons.[2] His eldest son, who had no conviction for recusancy against him, was able to recover the lands, and the lease accordingly came to an end.[3]

Donne's circle of acquaintances must have been steadily widening during the years of his secretaryship, though it is no longer possible to trace all his friendships. But he was certainly by now well acquainted with men like Sir Henry Goodyer and Robert Cotton, and Sir William Cornwallis the essayist was among his friends. Cornwallis addressed the verse letter[4] already noticed to his 'ever to be respeckted freand Mr. John Done Secretary to my Lorde Keeper' inviting him to be his companion in idleness when he had an afternoon or evening to spare; and

> If then for change, of howers you seem careles
> Agree with me to loose them at the playes.

Cornwallis also dedicated to Donne a paradoxical 'Encomium or Richard the Third' (not composed by Cornwallis himself), or, perhaps one should say, prefixed a letter to a presentation copy intended for Donne which eventually became the basis of the manuscript

[1] B. Magee, *The English Recusants*, 1938, p. 63. The terms of Donne's lease are entered annually into the Recusant Rolls, P.R.O., E377/11 (44 Eliz.) sub *Lincoln*, E377/12 (1 Jas.) sheet 13, E377/13 (2 Jas.) sheet 18, and E377/14 (3 Jas.) sheet 27; one of his payments of rent (1 May 1602) is recorded in E401/1870, fo. 58.

[2] His will, which is in P.C.C., 59 Hayes, was proved on 5 Aug. 1605.

[3] P.R.O., E368/521.

[4] MS. Tanner 306, printed by Grierson, ii. 171–2.

now at Chatsworth.[1] The letter is a tribute to the warmth of Cornwallis's feelings towards Donne:

To his worthey frende Mr. John Donne.

It is the leaste, and leaste assured parte of Loue, to say ⟨we⟩ Loue, Loue beinge soe deuine a truth as it lookes for more t⟨hen⟩ a bare affirmation: often I haue toulde thee I loue thee and a⟨s⟩ often hath my Conscience related thy Deserts; our loue is now o⟨f⟩ some Continuance, so that to goe still in that longe worne Liuery (I loue thee) would show me to harde a master to soe worthie a Seruan⟨t:⟩ Noe let Courtiers haue Loue still in their mouthes, and none in their hartes. It is not, It cannot be soe in me, beinge of a nature more fflexible and inioyinge a ffrende able to make softe the most obdurate, and moste disembled nature. Receue then as a marke of my loue my Charitye of this defamed Prince, . . .

. . . like it (I pray thee) because thou louest me, And soe vertuous worthie ffrende, ffarewell./

> Thy euer most affectionate ffreende
> William Cornewaleys.

The little that is known of the friendship between Donne and Cornwallis all comes from Cornwallis's side, since none of Donne's letters to him has survived, nor, indeed, is there any reference to him in any of Donne's other letters.

It was probably during these years too that Donne first became acquainted with the Herbert family. Walton, in the *Life of Mr. George Herbert*, relates how Magdalen Herbert lived for a time in Oxford to oversee the education of her sons, and says that her sojourn there

gain'd her an acquaintance and friendship with most of any eminent worth or learning, that were at that time in or near that University; and particularly, with Mr. *John Donne*, who then came accidentally to that place, in this time of her being there: . . . and he at his leaving *Oxford*, writ and left there in verse a Character of the Beauties of her

---

[1] The dedication survives in a single copy only, although there are several manuscripts and printed texts. See W. G. Zeeveld, 'A Tudor Defense of Richard III', *PMLA*, lv (1940), 946–57. Professor Zeeveld very generously lent me his photostats of the Chatsworth MS. and allowed me to transcribe the dedication. See also R. E. Bennett, 'Four Paradoxes by Sir William Cornwallis, the Younger', in *Harvard Studies and Notes in Philology and Literature*, xiii (1931).

body, and mind; . . . in that Elegy which bears the name of the *Autumnal Beauty*.[1]

Mrs. Herbert could not have resided in Oxford for much longer than a year, from about the early spring of 1599 until the summer of 1600, but Edward, her eldest son, was the ward of Sir George More, and Francis Wolley, who took his degree in December 1599, was still in residence at Oxford. It is therefore quite possible that Donne visited Oxford with messages to deliver to the two young men, perhaps even on his way to or from Chester when he attended the funeral of the younger Sir Thomas Egerton, and thus met Mrs. Herbert. But Walton is certainly wrong in saying, as he does in connection with 'The Autumnall', that both Donne and Mrs. Herbert 'were then past the meridian of mans life', for Donne was then twenty-seven and Mrs. Herbert scarcely five years older. 'The Autumnall' may have been written at this time, though the acquaintance could so far only have been a casual one, for it did not ripen fully until some years later.[2]

The friend of the period of Donne's secretaryship with whom his relations are most fully documented, is, of course, Henry Wotton. If the verse letter beginning 'Sir, more then kisses, letters mingle Soules' is rightly assigned to 1597–8,[3] it set the tone for the whole of their subsequent correspondence. The lives of men in the city, the country, and the court, says Donne in this poem, are all equally bad:

> The Country is a desert, where no good,
> Gain'd (as habits, not borne,) is understood.
> There men become beasts, and prone to more evils;
> In cities blockes, and in a lewd court, devills.

The only advice he can give to a friend is, accordingly, to be 'thine owne home, and in thy selfe dwell'. At the conclusion, however, he

[1] *Lives*, pp. 264–5.
[2] Mario M. Rossi, *La vita, le opere, i tempi di Edoardo Herbert di Cherbury*, 1947, i. 39–43, and iii. 380. H. W. Garrod, 'Donne and Mrs. Herbert', *RES*, xxi (1945), 161–73, argues that Mrs. Herbert was in Oxford again in 1607–8, to oversee the education of her younger son William, and that the 'amity' between them began at this time. But Donne's letters show that the acquaintance had been consolidated in the previous year. [See also Gardner, *Elegies etc.*, pp. 251–4.]
[3] Cf. p. 100, n. 1 above.

passes from moralizing to compliment, and with exquisite grace he apologizes for presuming to give advice to one who does not need it:

> But, Sir, I'advise not you, I rather doe
> Say o'er those lessons, which I learn'd of you:
> Whom, free from German schismes, and lightnesse
> Of France, and faire Italies faithlesnesse,
> Having from these suck'd all they had of worth,
> And brought home that faith, which you carried forth,
> I throughly love. But if my selfe I'have wonne
> To know my rules, I have, and you have
>
> DONNE.

Wotton's reply to these lines is extant; in his graver and simpler pastoral manner he elaborates on the theme that 'The mind is its own place':

> Worthie Sir:
> 'Tis not a coate of gray or Shepheards life,
>   'Tis not in feilds or woods remote to live,
> That adds or takes from one that peace or strife
>   Which to our dayes such good or ill doth give:
> It is the mind that makes the mans estate
> For ever happy or unfortunate,

and with no less grace he achieves a complimentary close in the same manner as Donne's:

> But this I doe not dedicate to thee,
>   As one that holds himself fitt to advise,
> Or that my lines to him should precepts be
>   That is less ill then I, and much more wise:
> Yet 'tis no harme mortality to preach,
> For men doe often learne when they do teach.

Wotton seems to have preserved a number of the letters he received from Donne after he had returned from Ireland. In one of them Donne (if indeed Donne is the writer) apologizes for being unable to make a journey into the country to see his friend because he has been 'overtaken, & mett & inwrapd in businesses which I could nether suspect nor avoyd'; on another occasion, when Wotton was in town, he was unable to meet him as soon as he wished because he had been taking physic.[1] Otherwise there is little news of the ordinary sort in the correspondence. On the other hand, there is some interesting comment on Donne's reading—in Rabelais, Aretino, and perhaps Dante—though it is difficult to be convinced if it is Donne who claims in another of these letters to be 'no great voyager in other mens works: no swallower nor devowrer of volumes nor pursuant of authors'.[2] Such a statement might perhaps be valid for this particular period of Donne's life, and it may refer only to works of the more purely literary sort, but it is not easy to reconcile with Walton's reference to 'the resultance of 1400 Authors, most of them abridged and analysed with his own hand', which he left at his death.[3]

Most interesting of all is a letter which accompanied the *Paradoxes*,[4] for which Donne found it necessary to apologize at some length. Donne's insistence that no copies should be made from them was not without some justification; as he wrote, 'to my satyrs there belongs some feare & to some elegies & these perhaps shame'. Ever since Drayton had rather petulantly referred, in an Epistle to Henry Reynolds, 'Of Poets and Poesie', to

> such whose poems, be they nere so rare,
> In priuate chambers, that incloistered are,
> And by transcription daintyly must goe;
> As though the world vnworthy were to know
> Their rich composures,

there has been a tendency to criticize Donne for his reluctance to publish his verses. Yet, as the letter to Wotton makes clear, he was aware that there was a real danger in doing so, not merely to his reputation and his prospects but even to his person. In the previous year the Archbishop and the Bishop of London had been spurred into action, by the scandal caused by the dedication to Essex in Hayward's *History of Henry the Fourth*, to make fresh regulations for

---

[1] Simpson, *Prose Works*, pp. 312, 315. Mr. Shapiro (*TLS*, 12 Sept. 1952) includes the first of these letters among those 'possibly' by Donne, and the second among those 'doubtfully' by him. It is possible that a word has dropped out of the last sentence of the second letter, and that it should read 'I shalbee strong enough to find you att Essex Ho: or rather then not at all at Court'.

[2] Simpson, p. 313.   [3] *Lives*, p. 67.   [4] Simpson, p. 316.

the press and, besides ordering 'That noe Englishe historyes be printed excepte they bee allowed by some of her maiesties privie Counsell', had forbidden any satires or epigrams to be printed hereafter. As a result of these orders, books had been collected and burnt in Stationers' Hall, among them Marston's *Pygmalion's Image*, Davies's *Epigrams*, Marlowe's translation of Ovid's *Elegies*, and Guilpin's *Skialetheia*.[1] Had Donne's satires and elegies been in print they would inevitably have met a similar fate, and his future career would have been jeopardized.

For the rest, the letters that Wotton chose to preserve are so full of contempt for the ways of the court and of a sense of the depravity of the age that one is inclined to wonder how Donne could have been satisfied with the way of life he had chosen. 'It was an excellent brag of Livies', he writes, '*that* th*e* R*o*man state (whose actions he entended to deliv*er*) was of all other in *the* world most fertill of good examples. I call it a brag & so think it. For certaynly all tymes are of owne nature & all courts produce *the* same effects of envie & detraction of ielousy & other humane weakneses.' And again: 'These tymes . . . are ariued to *that* height of illnes *that* no man dares accuse them bycause every one contributes much himself to *that* accesse.'[2] Even the apparently eccentric judgement of Dante as 'a man pert enough to bee beloved & to much to bee beeleeued'[3] is consistent with this attitude. Irritation at Dante's treatment of Pope Celestine springs from his contempt of court life, and Dante's failure to sympathize with Celestine's desire to escape from the seat of power to a life of retirement angers him. Donne's attitude, however, is not so much one of disillusionment as the product of his sense of that conflict which agitated so many men of his age, from Essex and Raleigh downwards, between the life of action and the life of contemplation. Another symptom of this conflict can be found in the motto which Donne chose to inscribe, along with his name, on the title-pages of the books he owned: 'Per Rachel ho servito, e non per Lea.' The actual words are from a canzone of Petrarch, but according to the symbolical interpretation current in the Middle Ages Leah

---

[1] E. Arber, *Transcript of the Stationers' Register*, iii (1876), 677–8.
[2] Simpson, p. 308 (no. 4), and p. 311.
[3] Ibid., p. 314.

came to stand for the active life and Rachel for the contemplative one. 'This pairing off of Leah and Rachel runs through mediaeval literature from Gregory the Great to Dante, who developed it in a beautiful passage of the *Purgatorio* (xxvii. 97–108).'[1] But in Renaissance England the conflict between active and contemplative life is most often expressed in terms of Senecan stoicism. Egerton had quoted Seneca in his letter to Essex, and Donne and Wotton constantly expressed themselves in the terms and phraseology of Senecan ideals. The temper of the Court in the closing years of the century had to wait for nearly a decade before it found full literary expression on the stage in the tragedies of Chapman.

The central theme of Donne's correspondence with Wotton also runs through his most ambitious and most disappointing poem, 'The Progresse of the Soule'. The poem, which has a preface dated 16 August 1601, was never completed, and all that was written is the first canto of a satirical epic, brought to an end by an abrupt concluding stanza which was added, perhaps, after Donne knew that he would never carry out his original plan. Even the plan itself seems not to have been clearly realized; different accounts of it appear in the Epistle and in the poem itself. The preface promises to 'deliver you by her relation all her [the soul's] passages from her first making, when shee was that apple which Eve eate, to this time when shee is hee, whose life you shall finde in the end of this booke', but in the sixth and seventh stanzas Donne writes:

> For though through many streights, and lands I roame,
> I launch at paradise, and saile toward home;
> The course I there began, shall here be staid,
> Sailes hoised there, stroke here, and anchors laid
>   In Thames, which were at Tigrys, and Euphrates waide.

> For this great soule which here amongst us now
> Doth dwell, and moves that hand, and tongue, and brow,
> Which, as the Moone the sea, moves us; to heare
> Whose story, with long patience you will long;
> (For 'tis the crowne, and last straine of my song)
> This soule to whom *Luther*, and *Mahomet* were

[1] See Percy Simpson, 'A Book from the Library of John Donne', *Oriel Record*, Jan. 1935.

Prisons of flesh; this soule which oft did teare,
And mend the wracks of th'Empire, and late Rome,
And liv'd where every great change did come,
    Had first in paradise a low, but fatall roome.

The account of the poem which Ben Jonson gave Drummond of Hawthornden accords more closely with the first of Donne's two statements: 'the Conceit of Dones transformation or Μετεμψύχωσις was that he sought the soule of that Aple which Eva pulled, and therafter made it the soule of a Bitch, then of a sheewolf & so of a woman. his generall purpose was to have brought in all the bodies of the Hereticks from the soule of Caine & at last left it in the body of Calvin.' It is to Jonson that we owe the idea that the main theme of the poem was to be heresy. The 'great soule which here amongst us now Doth dwell' and 'as the Moone the sea, moves us' (ll. 61–3) has not, however, been satisfactorily identified.[1]

The poem was conceived in the epic tradition of the Renaissance. By temperament Donne leaned more to Ariosto than to Spenser, and needed the variety of tone and attitude with which Ariosto had endowed the form, but Spenser was his only available English model, and so his influence is there. The stanza form is an adaptation of Spenser's, and the final alexandrine quite frequently recalls Spenser's characteristic rhythms. The first seven stanzas have strength and dignity, and a masculine force beyond Spenser's range; but after the introduction the poem changes, and Donne relates the soul's progress up the steps of the scale of creation, from plants (the apple, the mandrake) to a bird (the sparrow), through several fish to the whale, from one mammal to another (the mouse, the wolves, the ape), and finally to the woman Themech, sister and wife of Cain. The poem is thus a rapid succession of brief episodes, and the life of each creature provides an opportunity, not, as in a medieval bestiary, for moralizing of a naïvely serious kind, but for terse and savage satire directed at court and public life through parallels with the activities of the beasts. The essential moral seems to be one which is stated in the earliest verse letter to Wotton:

Onely perchance beasts sinne not; wretched wee
Are beasts in all, but white integritie,

[1] [See the discussion in Milgate, *Satires etc.*, pp. xxv–xxxiii.]

and when the soul achieves its human habitation it brings with it its full heritage of bestiality.

The *Paradoxes* are lighter in tone and intention. Only an occasional touch, such as the description of the fop in 'That a wise man is knowne by much laughing', recalls Donne's contempt for the court:

A *foole* if he come into a *Princes Court*, and see a *gay* man leaning at the wall, so *glistering*, and so *painted* in many *colours* that he is hardly discerned from one of the *pictures* in the *Arras*, hanging his *body* like an *Iron-bound-chest*, girt in and thicke ribb'd with *broad gold laces*, may (and commonly doth) envy him. But alas! shall a *wiseman*, which may not onely not *envy*, but not *pitty* this *monster*, doe nothing? Yes, let him *laugh*.

The *Paradoxes* were, as Donne wrote, 'but swaggerers', made 'rather to deceaue tyme then her daughter truth'.[1] Nevertheless he added far more vitality and wit to the form than his Italian predecessors had given it, and some of his most striking effects were gained not through the denial of a commonly accepted truth but by treating commonplaces, such as 'That good is more common then evil' or 'That Virginity is a Vertue', as if they were paradoxes in which no one had any belief. They are brilliant trifles, learned as well as ingenious, but it would be a mistake to regard them as anything more than *jeux d'esprit*.

The years of service under Egerton were crucial years for Donne in several respects. In the first place, they familiarized him with the ways of the court, and taught him how favours were won and dispensed. In the second place, they caused him to identify himself with the then numerically small class of gentlemen who were finding a career in the service of the state. Until he took holy orders Donne continued to hope that by courting the favour of the great he could win a way to a life of public service such as his friend Henry Wotton actually achieved. Any other life than this he regarded only as a temporary stop-gap, so ingrained had the habits of mind engendered by his service under Egerton become. But even before this service came to an end there were dangers in his situation which he failed to perceive, for there is little question that he had become

[1] Simpson, p. 316.

over-confident of himself and of his position. Among the letters of this period is one to an unidentified friend who was in prison and whose pardon Donne had exerted himself to see through its various stages until it had safely passed the Great Seal. Beneath the formal courtesies there is a vein of scarcely concealed irony and contempt, as if the writer were incapable of conceiving himself in such a situation or of behaving in such a fashion:

> Sir,
> The little businesse which you left in my hands is now dispatched; if it have hung longer then you thought, it might serve for just excuse, that these small things make as many steps to their end, and need as many motions for the warrant, as much writing of the Clerks, as long expectation of a Seal, as greater. It comes now to you sealed, and with it as strong and assured seals of my service and love to you, if it be good enough for you. I owe you a continuall tribute of Letters. But Sir, even in Princes and Parents, and all States that have in them a naturall Soveraignty, there is a sort of reciprocation, and a descent to doe some offices due to them that serve them: which makes me look for Letters from you, because I have another as valuable a pawn therefore, as your friendship, which is your promise; lest by the Jailors fault this Letter stick long, I must tell you, that I writ and sent it 12° *Decemb.* 1600.
>
>

Your friend and servant and lover

J. Donne.[1]

The impression made by this letter is confirmed by a piece of gossip, not recorded until after Donne's death but from a fairly reliable source, in Francis Osborne's *Advice to a Son* (1656):

> It is not safe for a *Secretary* to mend the copy his Master hath set him, unlesse own'd as from his former inspirations; Least he should grow jealous, that you valued your conceptions before his; who measures his sufficiency by the length of his Employment, not the breadth of his naturall Parts: This made the Lord Chancelour *Egerton* the willinger to exchange incomparable Dr. *D.* for the lesse sufficient, though in this more modest, Mr. *T. B.*[2]

---

[1] *Letters*, pp. 206–7.

[2] p. 12. The reference was pointed out in *NQ*, 9th ser. vii (1901), 183–4, and by L. I. Bredvold, 'Sir Thomas Egerton and Donne', *TLS*, 13 Mar. 1924. T. B. was Thomas Bond, who succeeded Donne; see *Middle Temple Records*, ii. 447. There is an

The upshot of both pieces of evidence is the same, that Donne was too sure of himself, and such over-confidence is traditionally the forerunner of a fall.

interesting letter from him to the first Earl of Bridgewater describing the trial of the Overbury murderers among the Ellesmere manuscripts; and there also survives a friendly letter to him from Jonson, printed in Herford and Simpson's *Ben Jonson*, i. 201.

VII

MARRIAGE

WHEN Parliament was assembling in October 1601 Ann More came up to town with her father. Donne soon learnt that she was near at hand, and it was not long before they met secretly. Several other meetings followed. They were both very much in love, and they knew that they had no hope of obtaining the consent of Sir George, who was, indeed, busying himself to find a suitable husband for his daughter. Their situation was thus desperate, and the lovers plainly saw that they must either take their destiny into their own hands or resolve to part for ever. Accordingly, 'about three weeks before Christmas', they were married. 'At the doing there were not used above five persons', Donne later wrote. Christopher Brooke was there to give away the bride, and his brother Samuel, now in holy orders, performed the ceremony. A fortnight later Parliament was dissolved, and Ann presumably returned to Loseley with her father.

Neither the exact date nor the place of Donne's marriage is known, although a conjecture as to the place is worth hazarding. At the time of his marriage Donne was living in lodgings. After his appointment as secretary to Egerton he had probably been assigned quarters in York House, but at a later date, owing to the congestion caused either by the imprisonment of Essex or by the arrival of the Countess of Derby and her retinue, he had apparently been obliged to move. He now lodged in the house of a Mr. Haines beside the Savoy. Originally a hospital, the Savoy at the end of the sixteenth century was leased out by the masters as tenements, and was much frequented by people of fashion who had no town houses of their own.[1] The precincts of the hospital were also a 'liberty', free from the ordinary civil and ecclesiastical jurisdiction, and the chapel was

---

[1] E. B. Chancellor, *Annals of the Strand*, 1912, pp. 172–3.

notorious later in the century for its clandestine marriages. Here, within easy distance of Donne's lodgings, the marriage was most likely to have taken place.

Both Donne and his wife judged it inopportune to break the news to her father immediately, and Donne resolved to wait for a favourable occasion, when his wrath might be tempered. Sir George More was given to violent outbreaks of rage, and those who knew him on such occasions dreaded the consequences.

Sir George was no mere country squire. He had been born in 1553 and, after taking his degree at Oxford, had in 1574 entered the Inner Temple. He then took service with the Earl of Leicester, and 'travelled with Sir Philip Sidney as his kinsman and companion all over France, Italy and Germany'.[1] Elizabeth knighted him in 1597, and on the death of his father in 1600 he succeeded to the family estate of Loseley Park, near Guildford. He lived there on an almost princely scale, and was, according to one of his sons-in-law, 'a great housekeeper, for, when I first married his daughter, he kept 50 liveries, spent every week an ox and 12 sheep, kept his steward's table and had all things proportionable to it'. His household also included a chaplain, a certain Mr. Holney, as we learn from a letter of Donne's many years later.[2] Sir George was active in local affairs, and in addition was a member of every Parliament during his lifetime from 1584 onwards; 'the King, and also Queen Elizabeth', we are told, 'often employed him in commissions and for to work the Parliament House to such things as they desired to have effected'. Nor was Sir George without an interest in literature and learning. He was a friend of Sir Thomas Bodley and contributed generously to Bodley's new library at Oxford, and in 1597 he published a little 'treatise against atheism' entitled *A Demonstration of God in His Workes*. The book is written with fervour, and gives proof of its author's wide reading, which ranged from Manilius to St. Bernard, but it is inclined to be verbose; it is unquestionably the work of a humourless and orthodox mind. Sir George, for all his energy and public spirit, was, in fact, rather a bore. It is easy to see why he was not

---

[1] Sir John Oglander has probably exaggerated the extent of Sir George More's acquaintance with Sidney, for, as my colleague Professor W. A. Ringler points out, no one of the name of More is mentioned by Sidney's early biographers, nor in Sidney's or Languet's correspondence.   [2] See p. 487 below.

favourably impressed by Donne, and why he was suspicious of his intellectual brilliance.

By his wife, who had died in 1590, Sir George had nine children. Of the four boys only one, Robert, survived to marry and beget children. Ann was the third of the five girls. All the others in due course married country gentlemen of wealth and assured position. Mary, the eldest, was already the wife of Nicholas Throckmorton, the brother of Lady Raleigh, who took the name of Carey in 1607 when he inherited the estate of Beddington in Surrey from a maternal uncle. Margaret, the second, became the wife of Sir Thomas Grymes of Peckham. Elizabeth More married Sir John Mills of Camois Court in Sussex, but died not long afterwards in child-birth, and Frances, the youngest, married Sir John Oglander of Nunwell in the Isle of Wight. It is easy to see why Donne was regarded as no fit match for one of Sir George More's daughters.

Sir John Oglander, who greatly admired his father-in-law, left a brief account of him which has already been quoted from.[1] Sir George, he relates, enjoyed the confidence of both Elizabeth and James, but

He was only unfortunate in that the favourites never affected him, for Somerset would often tell him, being his prisoner in the Tower, that he had often heard King James nominate him for great places when they fell vacant, and that he had still crossed him and moved the King for others, and that Sir George would have had divers of the best places if he had not hindered him. The like did Buckingham do when the King had sworn to Sir George that he should be Master of the Wards when he went out of Town, yet the Duke of Buckingham would have it for another of his creatures.

Sir George was generous too, and always willing to busy himself to do good offices for others, even at the cost of neglecting his own interests. He was 'by nature very passionate', though eventually he learnt to control his anger in public. 'He was little and good', Sir John Oglander quaintly concludes.

Donne must have realized that he was taking a serious risk in marrying without her father's consent a girl of wealthy family who was still a minor. Not only did it involve a specific offence against

[1] *A Royalist's Notebook*, ed. F. Bamford, 1936, pp. 164–9.

the canon law, but it was a serious breach of the social code. Walton's comments on Donne's marriage sum up the feeling of the age:

love is a flattering mischief, . . . a passion! that carries us to commit *Errors* with as much ease as whirlwinds remove feathers, and begets in us an unwearied industry to the attainment of what we desire. And such an Industry did . . . bring them secretly together . . . and at last to a marriage too, without the allowance of those friends, whose approbation always was, and ever will be necessary, to make even a vertuous love become lawful.

Arthur Brooke in the preface to his *Tragicall Historye of Romeus and Iuliet* had in 1562 drawn essentially the same moral:

to this end, good Reader, is this tragicall matter written, to describe unto thee a couple of unfortunate lovers, thralling themselves to un-honest desire; neglecting the authority and advice of parents and friends; conferring their principal counsels with drunken gossips and superstitious friars. . . .

The same attitude is also expressed by Polixenes at the sheep-shearing festival in *The Winter's Tale*, when Perdita and Florizel are about to plight their troths:

Reason my son
Should choose himself a wife; but as good reason
The father—all whose joy is nothing else
But fair posterity—should hold some counsel
In such a business.   (IV. iv. 398-402)

It was a deeply held social principle that families were participants in the arranging of marriages.

There were contemporary examples, of which Donne must have known, both to encourage and to deter him in the course he had taken. Egerton's second and third marriages, for instance, were celebrated privately by the household chaplain without any asking of the banns or special licence. But both the ladies had been widows of mature age, and Egerton had relied on his high position in the state to secure an episcopal dispensation after the ceremony. A similar dispensation had been granted by the Archbishop of Canterbury on 8 February 1599/1600 for the marriage without banns or licence of Thomas Coningsby, one of the Clerks of the Petty Bag, and Frances

Haughton. It took place at the house of Henry Jones in the parish of St. Martin-in-the-Fields, and was celebrated by Nathaniel Harris, Egerton's chaplain. Among those present were John Egerton, his sister and brother-in-law, Mary and Francis Leigh, and his cousin William Ravenscroft,[1] with all of whom Donne was almost certainly acquainted. On the other hand, among the Lord Keeper's papers has been preserved the summary of a case before the Court of High Commission which had occurred just a year before and which must have attracted a good deal of attention at the time:

> The breife of the Cause betwene Walter Aston,
>
> An°. 1600   Warde to Mr. Edward Coke Attorney generall to the Qu: Matie, and Anne Barnes.

Vpon reporte of the mariage betwene *Mr. Aston* and *Mris. Barnes,* the *Comissioners* are mooved to call before them such Persons as were present thereat: *Mr. Atturney* mooveth this, and giveth direction vnder his hand to the *Register* what *Persons* shold be sent for, vizt, *William Harte, John King, Wm. Foster, Mris. Dominico &c.*

Ex⟨c⟩omunication is denounced against all present at the clandestine mariage, according to the *Canon,* and thereby they are disabled to give witnesse./

One *Lloyde* was by the Comissioners comitted *Prisoner* to the *Gatehouse* about that mariage./

John Gill, and *Ambrose Dakin,* two witnesses in the *Cause,* were comitted to the *Clincke* for their misdemeanor touching that mariage, and for being present at it./

Anne Barnes who was clandestinely maried to *Mr. Aston,* was comitted to the *Fleete,* where she remayned almoste a twelue-month.

On *Thursday,* the 12th of *Marche* An°. 1600. there sate in Comission at Lambeth, *John Lo: Arch Bp. of Cant: Richard Lo: Bishop of London, Sr John Popham Lo:* cheef *Justice* of the *Kings* Benche, *Mr. Edward Coke Attorney generall, Do^r. Dun, Do^r. Stanhope, Do^r. Swale, Do^r. Ferrand,* And there *Sentence* is pronounced whereby *Mr. Aston* is freed from that mariage.

This *Sentence* is subscribed by all the Comissioners saving *Mr. Attorney,* who sate with the rest, but praied that hee might be excused from subscribing, because the Cause concerned himself./[2]

[1] Reg. Whitgift, pt. iii, fo. 113 at Lambeth Palace.
[2] MS. Ellesmere 5920 in the Huntington Library.

Presumably the John King mentioned here was Egerton's former
chaplain and the celebrant of the marriage, though this does not
necessarily follow. Walter Aston, afterwards Lord Aston of Forfar,
was one of the wealthiest heirs in England, reputedly worth
£10,000 a year; the right of disposing of him in marriage was worth
much money to his guardian, for, as Donne was well aware,

> Wards still
> Take such wives as their Guardians offer, or
> Pay valewes.

Donne's offence was heavier than that of Thomas Coningsby and
Frances Haughton, but not so heavy as that of Walter Aston and
Anne Barnes. Donne's real problem was, in fact, to break the news
to Sir George More in such a way as to prevent him from going
to extremes, as Coke had obviously done on learning of Walter
Aston's marriage. It would be a ticklish business, for Donne knew
that his father-in-law did not like him.

The right moment showed no sign of coming, and Donne remained in a pitiful state of indecision for almost two months. He
tried to break the news gently, for, says Walton, 'that preappre-
hensions might make it the less enormous, when it was known: it
was purposely whispered into the ears of many that it was so, yet by
none that could affirm it'. Donne's anxiety probably helped to make
him ill, for when at last he confessed to Sir George what he had done
he did not do so in person, but in a letter written from his sick-bed.
His messenger was Henry Percy, ninth Earl of Northumberland,
and obviously the most influential messenger he could find. How
Donne had become sufficiently familiar with him to ask him to perform such an office is not known, though the Earl was active in the
political manœuvrings of this period, and was also well known for
his patronage of poets and men of science. He had at first been an
active friend and partisan of Essex, whose sister he had married, but
their friendship had cooled and Northumberland was serving in the
Low Countries at the time of Essex's rebellion and execution. On his
return he allied himself with Raleigh and Cobham against the Cecil
faction. He dabbled in science and alchemy, became known as the
'Wizard Earl', and patronized such men as Hariot the mathematician

and George Chapman the poet.[1] Northumberland was on friendly
terms with Sir George More, as some letters among the Loseley
manuscripts testify,[2] and probably visited Loseley frequently on his
journeys between London and his house at Petworth.

The letter from Donne which the Earl of Northumberland delivered was dated 2 February 1601/2. It clearly betrays the writer's
nervousness. Donne attempted to be at once respectful and firm,
but succeeded only in achieving a certain jauntiness. He excused
himself for sending his news through a third party on the ground
that he was too unwell to present himself in person, briefly told of
the marriage, and insisted that he had not gained his purpose by
suborning any of Sir George's domestics. His justification, which
can have given Sir George small satisfaction, was that he and Ann
were already contracted:

I knew my present estate lesse then fitt for her, I knew (yet I knew not
why) that I stood not right in yor opinion. I knew that to have given
any intimation of yt had been to impossibilitate the whole matter.
And then having these honest purposes in o^r harts, and those fetters
in o^r consciences, me thinks we should be pardoned, of o^r fault be but
this, that wee did not, by fore-revealinge of yt, consent to o^r hindrance
and torment.

Though they had both 'adventurd equally', Donne implored the
irate father that Ann might not feel 'the terror of yor sodaine anger'.
He then told him, in effect, that what was done was done, and that
therefore Sir George had best swallow his anger and accept the *fait
accompli*:

I know this letter shall find yo^w full of passion; but I know no passion
can alter yor reason and wisdome, to wch I adventure to commend
these particulers; that yt is irremediably donne; that if yo^w incense
my *Lord* yo^w destroy her and me; that yt is easye to give us happines,
and that my endevors and industrie, if it please yo^w to prosper them,
may soone make me somewhat worthyer of her.[3]

---

[1] J. Sampson, 'A Contemporary Light upon John Donne', *Essays and Studies by
Members of the English Association*, vii (1921), 82–107 at pp. 94–5, suggests that the link
between Donne and the Earl was Donne's friend George Garrard, but Garrard's
relations with the Percy family belong to a later period and were almost entirely with
the tenth Earl. Donne was subsequently acquainted with Edmund Whitelocke, a
pensioner of the ninth Earl, but when this acquaintance began is also uncertain.

[2] Kempe, pp. 496–7.   [3] Ibid., pp. 328–9.

All in all, the letter was scarcely calculated to assuage the anger that Donne had every reason to anticipate.

Donne's worst fears were abundantly justified, for Sir George, says Walton, in a 'passion of anger and inconsideration', hastened at once to the Lord Keeper. There was no doubt that there had been an offence against the canon law, and Donne and the two Brookes were arrested and committed to prison, Donne to the Fleet and Christopher Brooke to the Marshalsea. Sir George insisted that the culprits should be brought before the High Commission, and pressed in addition for Donne's dismissal from Egerton's service. The Lord Keeper hesitated for a while, reminding the angry father-in-law (says Walton) that 'Errors might be overpunished, and desired ⟨him⟩ therefore to forbear till second considerations might clear some scruples'. Donne being out of favour, however, busy tongues were urging everything they could to his discredit—his Catholic upbringing, his earlier amours, his debts—and Sir George, only too willing to believe everything he heard, redoubled his petitions for Donne's dismissal until at last Egerton consented. Meanwhile Donne, after remaining silent as long as he dared, but now thoroughly alarmed by the reports brought to him by friendly visitors, wrote to Sir George More on 11 February in a much more abject and penitential tone than that of his earlier letter. His illness, exacerbated by the distress of mind he was enduring and by his imprisonment, was now serious, and his suffering was acute. He asked for an opportunity to clear his name of slander and protested that 'all my endevors, and the whole course of my lyfe shal be bent, to make my selfe worthy of yor favor and her love, whose peace of conscience and quiett I know must be much wounded and violenced if yor displeasure sever us'.[1] Sir George apparently returned a message intimating coldly that Donne's fate was now in the Lord Keeper's hands, and on the following day Donne addressed him a letter, couched in the same humble terms, in which he made full submission and prayed for relief of his imprisonment. Egerton, who was genuinely fond of Donne, was touched, and since Sir George More did not object, Donne was immediately allowed to return to his lodgings, though he was still nominally under restraint. As soon

[1] Ibid., pp. 331–2.

as he was back in familiar surroundings his spirits began to revive, and he wrote again at once (13 February) to both Egerton and More. Sir George had been persuaded that Donne's character was not as bad as he had at first been inclined to believe and was beginning to relent a little, so that Donne ventured to ask for his help in bringing about a reconciliation with Egerton and for permission to write to Ann. To Egerton he appealed in more general terms for pardon. A few days later he wrote to Egerton again, asking to be allowed to complete his convalescence by taking exercise, and was at once granted 'the liberty to take the ayre about the towne'. His confinement was now purely nominal, though the two Brookes were still imprisoned. Christopher Brooke, in particular, was seriously embarrassed; the York assizes were about to begin and clients were waiting for him there. His absence would be a blow to a rapidly growing practice.

Immediately after learning of his daughter's marriage Sir George More had initiated proceedings before the High Commission, presumably in the hope of getting the marriage annulled, and the case now came up for hearing. In a letter to his friend Sir Henry Goodyer dated 23 February Donne briefly reported that 'The Commissioners by Imprisoning the wittnesses and Excommunicating all vs have implicit[l]ie iustified our Marriage'.[1] A letter from Christopher Brooke to the Lord Keeper gives a little more information about the actions of the Court:

My Lord [he writes], it was injoyned *tha*t I should make some submission. I have drawen one out of my hart, and writt it wth myne owne hande, and sent it to his Grace, and the rest of the Commissioners for those causes, wherein I have confessed myne offence against the canon lawes, and constitu*ti*ons provinciall of this realme, and have testified my sorrowe for the whole fact.[2]

Walton affirms that Donne 'neither gave rest to his body or brain, nor to any friend in whom he might hope to have an interest, until he had procured an enlargement for his two imprisoned friends'.

---

[1] Anderdon MS., a copy in a seventeenth-century hand, in the possession of Miss Mary Donne of Chester. Donne wrote over-optimistically; the Aston case cited above shows that such a presumption at this stage of the case was far from being justified. The reader will notice the similarities in the procedure of the Court in the two cases.

[2] Kempe, p. 337.

Probably they were released at, or soon after, the end of term. The
final sitting of the High Commission in each term was known as the
Day of Mitigations; on that day, upon evidence submitted of com-
pliance with the decrees of the Court, sentences were lightened or
remitted, and on 1 March Donne wrote to the Lord Keeper: 'That
offence wch was to God in this matter, his mercy hath assurd my
conscience is pardoned. The comissioners who minister his anger
and mercy, incline also to remitt yt.'[1]

After his return to his lodgings Donne's health and spirits had
rapidly improved. He had written to Robert Cotton on 20 February
to borrow a book to lighten the tedium of his confinement; and
after telling Sir Henry Goodyer of the decree of the High Commission, he had gone on to speak of his hope that Ann would gradually
mollify her father's anger. He then added, with a return of his earlier
jauntiness: 'I have Liberty to ride abrode and feele not much of an
Imprisonment. For my retorne to my L: and Sir George his pacifi-
cacion, you know my meanes, and therefore my hopes.' Sir George
More, no doubt, was beginning to yield to his daughter's importunities; besides, it was also becoming apparent to him that, as
Donne shrewdly perceived, the Commissioners were not going to
question the validity of the marriage. Should its legality be upheld,
his part in procuring Donne's dismissal was, as the latter had only
too clearly pointed out to him, an action for which his daughter
would inevitably suffer along with her husband. A phrase in a further letter of Donne's to Sir George on 1 March suggests that there
had been a meeting of the two after the High Commission had
delivered its decree, and that Donne had succeeded in making an
impression on his father-in-law, for, as Walton well knew, his
behaviour, 'when it would intice, had a strange kind of elegant
irresistible art'. Thus, when Donne applied to him on 1 March with
more candour and directness than he had previously shown and

---

[1] Ibid., p. 341. The full Court, presided over by the Archbishop of Canterbury,
normally sat only on Thursdays in Jan., Feb., May, June, Oct., and Nov. (R. G.
Usher, *The Rise and Fall of the High Commission*, 1913, p. 259). Donne's letter to Goodyer
of 23 Feb. was written on a Tuesday, so the previous Thursday, when the Court
delivered its decree, would have been 18 Feb. Mitigation Day would have been the
following Thursday, the 25th, and Christopher Brooke's letter to Egerton, which
bears that date, was presumably written early in the day and was intended to be
delivered before the sitting of the Court.

besought his aid in procuring his reinstatement with Sir Thomas Egerton, More was inclined to consent. Other friends too were doing what they could for him; even Christopher Brooke in writing to Egerton from the Marshalsea had put in a good word for Donne: 'Pardon me a word for him, my Lord [he had written]; were it not now best, *tha*t every one whome he any way concerns should become his favourer or his frind, whoe wants (my good Lord) but fortune's hands and tonge to reare him upp, and sett him out?'[1] Donne added his own plea to Egerton on the same day on which he wrote to Sir George More. He first reviewed his past life:

I was carefully and honestly bred: enjoyd an indifferent fortune; I had (and I had understandinge enough to valew yt) the sweetnes and security of a freedome and independency; withowt markinge owt to my hopes any place of profitt. I had a desire to be yo[r] Lord*shi*ps servant, by the favor w[ch] yo[r] good sonn's love to me obtein'd. I was 4 years yo[r] Lord*shi*ps secretary, not dishonest nor gredy. The sicknes of w[ch] I dyed ys, that I begonne in yo[r] Lord*shi*ps house this love. Wher I shal be buried I know not.

Then he went on to state his predicament as forcibly as he dared:

To seek prefer*men*t here wth any but yo[r] Lord*shi*p were a madnes. Every great man to whom I shall address any such suite, wyll silently ·dispute the case, and say, would my Lord Keeper so disgraciously have imprisond him, and flung him away, if he had not donne some other great fault, of w[ch] we hear not. So that to the burden of my true weaknesses, I shall have this addi*ti*on of a very pre*ju*diciall suspic*i*on, that I ame worse then I hope yo[r] Lord*shi*p dothe think me, or would that the world should thinke. I have therfore no way before me; but must turn back to yo[r] Lord*shi*p who knowes that redemtion was no less worke than creation.[2]

But neither Donne's appeal nor Sir George's seconding was of any avail. Egerton admitted (according to Walton) that in losing him 'He parted with a Friend; and such a Secretary as was fitter to serve a King then a Subject', but he remained obdurate. He told Sir George, in words reported by Walton, that 'though he was unfeignedly sorry for what he had done, yet it was inconsistent with his place and credit, to discharge and readmit servants at the

---

[1] Kempe, pp. 337–8.   [2] Ibid., pp. 341–2.

request of passionate petitioners'. It must have been after receiving
this decisive answer that Donne wrote to his wife. In his letter of
I March to her father he had asked a second time for permission to
write to her, stating specifically that 'Though I understand ther
upon, that after the Thursday[1] yo^w were not displeased that I
should, yet I have not, nor wyll not withowt yor knowledge do yt'.
Permission was at last forthcoming, and it was presumably then (if
ever) that he wrote the famous 'sad Letter to his Wife, . . . and, after
the subscription of his name, writ,

John Donne,   Anne Donne,   Vn-done.'

This, the most famous of the many puns on Donne's name, is probably not his at all.[2]

In the meantime Donne had launched a suit to test the validity
of the marriage. The case was heard by Dr. Richard Swale in the
Court of Audience of Canterbury, a court which exercised the Archbishop's personal jurisdiction and which came to an end with the
Civil War.[3] Final judgement was delivered on 27 April 1602, and a
certified copy of the decree has been preserved among the Loseley
manuscripts.[4] It is not a very informative document, though its
purport is clear. It declares that in January 1601/2 John Donne and
Ann Donne alias More were free from all marital contracts or obligations except those into which they had entered with one another,
and that their marriage, duly celebrated by a priest, was good and
sufficient, and that they were therefore lawful man and wife. Sir

---

[1] On which the High Commission had sat.

[2] Walton, *Lives*, p. 29. The earliest version of this anecdote occurs about a year
after Donne's marriage in the *Diary* of John Manningham (Camden Society, 1868,
p. 99): 'Dunne is undonne; he was lately secretary to the Lord Keeper, and cast of
because he would match him selfe to a gentlewoman against his Lords pleasure.'
Manningham is evidently repeating a witticism that was still current; there is no
hint that it was derived from Donne himself. The anecdote did not appear in
Walton's *Lives* until the 1675 edition, but before then it had appeared in print in two
other places. The version in William Winstanley's *Englands Worthies* (1660), p. 379,
is somewhat garbled; the version Walton probably knew was that related by Charles
I, and printed in *Witty Apophthegms delivered at severall times . . . by King James, King
Charles*, etc., 1658, p. 26. See further the article 'Historical Doubts respecting
Walton's *Life of Donne*', *Essays in English Literature from the Renaissance to the Victorian
Age presented to A. S. P. Woodhouse*, pp. 69–84, at 76–8.

[3] None of its records are known to be extant.

[4] Folger Shakespeare Library. [See E. Le Comte, 'The Date of Donne's Marriage'
and the 'Reply' to his note, *Etudes Anglaises*, xxi (1968), xxii (1969).]

George More no longer had any motive for withholding his daughter, but he surrendered her to her husband with bad grace. Donne might have her, but he refused to contribute a penny to her support.

Donne was thus at the age of thirty without employment and with a young wife to care for. The fees connected with his imprisonment and that of his friends (as he said in his letter of 1 March to Sir George) had amounted to £40, and the suit in the Court of Audience had also proved expensive. His patrimony was nearly exhausted; he was in debt; and he knew the ways of the world sufficiently well to feel that it was hopeless for the present to seek a post such as he was qualified for. There seemed to be no alternative but to live quietly until the scandal had been forgotten. His plight was not entirely desperate, for his wife had still to receive a legacy of £100 left her by her aunt, and Egerton, realizing how useful the money would be to the young couple, gave orders for its payment. Donne's receipt is still extant:

6° Julij 1602/

Received the Day and year aboue written, of the right ho: Sir Thomas Egerton Knight L: Keeper of the great Seale of England, my ho: L: and Master, by the hands of hys seruant Mʳ John Panton, the summ of one hundred pounds of Lawfull Money of England: which sayd hundred pounds was given by the right ho: the Lady Egerton Late wyfe to the sayd L: Keeper, to her Neece, Anne the Daughter of Sir George More, now my wyfe, and ys now for her received by me

J. Donne[1]

Other friends also came to their aid, especially Francis Wolley, who offered Donne and his wife an asylum in his home at Pyrford. There the Donnes spent the early years of their married life.

Pyrford is about eight miles to the north-east of Guildford, and within easy distance of Loseley Park. The old manor house has long since been pulled down, but Evelyn, who visited it on 24 August 1681, wrote that 'The seate stands on a flat, the ground pastures, rarely watred, & exceedingly improved; . . . The house is Timber, but commodious, & with one ample dining roome, & the hale adorned with paintings of fowle, & huntings &c'. Here Donne lived

[1] Loseley MS. 2013/31 (see Plate VIIIa).

placidly, no doubt helping Wolley with his accounts and with the management of his estates, but devoting himself in the main to an intensive study of the civil and canon law. His first child, a daughter christened Constance, was born about the beginning of 1603, and his son John some time in the spring of the following year.[1]

Before Donne had been a year at Pyrford the old Queen died, and with her death an era came to an end. The new King, James I, was everywhere received with acclamation. The fact that he had a wife and three children meant a very considerable increase in the royal establishment, and the consequent scramble for places was met with an equally lavish bestowal of honours in the spring and summer of 1603. Egerton was raised to the chancellorship and became Baron Ellesmere; Sir George More became Treasurer of the Household to the Prince of Wales, and Sir Henry Goodyer became a Gentleman of the Privy Chamber to the King. The Knights of the Bath created in honour of the coronation on 25 July included John Egerton, Fulke Greville, Edward Herbert, Francis Leigh (Egerton's son-in-law), and Edward Montagu, Donne's fellow member for Brackley in 1601. Among those knighted were Francis Wolley and his cousin, Arthur Mainwaring, Sir George More's son, Robert More, and his two sons-in-law, Nicholas Throckmorton and Thomas Grymes; other friends and acquaintances of Donne such as Francis Bacon, Robert Cotton, Thomas Roe, Richard Baker, and Walter Chute received similar honours. On 10 August 1603 the new Court had set out on its first progress; the first night was spent at Pyrford with Sir Francis Wolley and the two following nights at Loseley with Sir George More. Of these visits no record remains except a bad sonnet 'Uppon a Horologe of the Clock at Sr George More's, at his Place of Loseley, 1603' by the new Queen's secretary, William Fowler, whose acquaintance Donne almost certainly made during these visits.[2] Donne must have had the opportunity of being presented to the King at either or both of the houses, and of renewing many old friendships among those who followed the Court. James at this time

[1] The parish registers of Pyrford for this period are not extant. John Donne the younger was born before the middle of May 1604, since his recent birth is referred to in a letter to his father of this date which is printed in the *Tobie Mathew Collection*, p. 294.

[2] J. Nichols, *Progresses of James I* (1828), i. 250–1.

probably first heard the story of Donne's marriage and his dismissal
from Egerton's service; certainly he knew of it, and referred to it
seven years later when Donne's claims for an appointment were
urged on him by Lord Hay.[1] The aura of opprobrium that still hung
around him would have made Donne feel in 1603 that as yet it was
too early to hope for any sign of royal favour.

Of Donne's studies during this period of retirement only the
slightest indications remain, apart from Walton's statement that he
occupied himself principally with the civil and canon law. But one
or two of the books that Donne read at this period have survived.
One is a copy of a Latin poem, *Diarium Historicopoeticum*, by Robert
More, Fellow of New College, Oxford,[2] who published his book in
1595 and dedicated it to Sir John and Lady Wolley. It is a strange
mixture of history and astrology, divided into twelve books, one
for each month of the year and each celebrating important historical
anniversaries. The copy that Donne used[3] was the dedication copy,
since it bears Sir John Wolley's signature on the title-page as well
as Donne's name and motto. Another is a copy of *De dignitate regum
regnorum Hispaniae et honoratiori loco eis, seu eorum legatis, a conciliis
ac Romana sede jure debito* (1602) by Jacobus Valdesius, or Diego de
Valdes, now in the Cottonian Library with a letter from Donne
bound in. French and Spanish ambassadors had disturbed the peace
of most of the courts of Europe with their quarrels for precedence;
England, owing to the long war with Spain, had been free of such
disturbances for many years, but now that a treaty was imminent
there was a representative of Spain in England again, and such
wrangles were inevitably breaking out.[4] Cotton had evidently been
consulted on the matter, and had sent Donne the latest work on the
subject with a request for his opinion, which Donne gave in a
lengthy letter.[5]

---

[1] *Tobie Mathew Collection*, p. 330.

[2] Not Donne's brother-in-law, who entered Corpus Christi College, Oxford, in the
year in which his namesake's book was published.

[3] Keynes, no. L126, formerly in the possession of Philip Bliss and of Sir Leicester
Harmsworth, now in the Folger Shakespeare Library.

[4] See *C.S.P., Venetian, 1603–07*, pp. 143, 149, 152.

[5] Cotton MS. Cleop. F. vii. The question was of interest to Cotton, who wrote a
brief treatise on a closely related topic. The fifth tract in *Cottoni Posthuma* (1651) is
entitled 'A breife abstract of the question of Precedencie between England and

Nevertheless, Donne's life at Pyrford was not that of a recluse. Friends came to visit him as well as the Wolleys, and he was always an active correspondent. In the *Collection of Letters, made by Sr Tobie Mathews K^t.*, edited in 1660 by the younger John Donne, there is a group of letters addressed to Donne at Pyrford by an unnamed correspondent, who may well have been Mathew himself.[1] Toby Mathew was the son of the Bishop of Durham; he had matriculated at Oxford from Christ Church in 1590, and in 1599 he entered Gray's Inn, where he formed a lasting friendship with Francis Bacon. He was a member of Elizabeth's last Parliament, where, if he had not done so already, he probably met Donne, and was a member also of James's first Parliament. In the first of the letters to Donne the writer complains that business has kept him at Chertsey, and that he cannot return to Pyrford as he had anticipated. The next, written from Winchester, to which the Court and the law term had removed on account of the plague in London, contains a lengthy narrative of the trial of Sir Walter Raleigh for treason, and goes on to promise another visit to Pyrford: 'When I see you next, you cannot shake me off in a senight. Tell *S. F. W.* I will scarce thank him for his entertainment of me then, when I shall bring the particulars with me: which I do not forbear to deliver now, out of any reason I have yet alleadged *sed quia literae sunt loqua[c]es*, and may lose their way.' The letter concludes with some gossip of the Court, and contains a reference to two young men who were already beginning to bask in the

Spaine; Occasioned by Sir *Henry Nevill* the Queen of *Englands* Ambassador, and the ambassador of *Spaine*, at *Calais*. . . .'

[1] The letters to Donne at Pyrford begin on pp. 272 (misnumbered 262), 279, 288, 290. The first letter cannot be dated precisely; the others were written about 17 Nov. 1603, 12 Mar. 1603/4, and 19 May 1604 respectively.

The *Collection of Letters* falls into two parts. Pp. 1–271 seem to represent the collection originally made by Mathew, and pp. 272–356 were added by the younger Donne, who edited the volume, from his father's unpublished correspondence. Pp. 272–95 contain a series of letters to, not from, Donne, and (except for the last, which is headed 'A Letter from a Lord') may be from the same person. Two of these letters (pp. 273 and 276) are clearly from Mathew to Donne and were written to him while he was a member of Viscount Doncaster's embassy; a third seems to have been written to Donne while he was in Amiens with the Drurys. Professor J. P. Feil, author of an unpublished Chicago dissertation on 'Sir Tobie Mathew and his *Collection of Letters*', therefore argued that the whole group of letters was from Mathew to Donne, and that the younger Donne placed them at the beginning of his extracts from his father's correspondence as a tribute to Mathew, whose name appeared on the title-page as the maker of the *Collection*.

royal favour: '*Philip Herbert*, and *James Hayes*, joyned in a Suit for Transportation, of I know not how many cloaths, and have obtained it, to the value of 10000*l*.' The next letter, which was written several months later, makes it clear that the visit promised in the previous one had been paid. The letter itself, however, is briefer and more urgent:

> Your friends are sorry, that you make your self so great a stranger; but, you best know your own occasions. Howbeit, if you have any designe towards the Court, it were good you did prevent the losse of any more time. For, Experience and Reason are at odds in this, that the places of Attendance, such as may deserve you, grow dailie dearer, and so are like to do. Notwithstanding that, the King's hand is neither so full, nor so open, as it hath been. You have not a poor friend, that would be gladder of your good fortunes; and out of that conscience, I challenge to my self this liberty.

The appeal to come to London was repeated at the end, intermingled with other news and messages. But Donne was content for the time being to spend most of his time quietly in the country, and deemed it wisest to postpone any appeals for preferment at court. Among other news and gossip in the letter, there is a reference to Sir Henry Goodyer—'Sir *Henry Goodyere* is well, but no better then when you saw him'—and the writer continues: 'When I was at *Purford*, I left behind me Mr. *Bacon*'s Discourse of matters Ecclesiasticall; I pray you return it by this Bearer.' The writer, even if not Mathew, was at least intimate with the circle which Donne had frequented before his marriage, and may have been near enough to Bacon to obtain a copy of his unpublished 'Discourse'.[1]

The fourth and last letter is full of news of James's first Parliament and of the coming of the ambassadors to treat for peace with Spain. It regrets Donne's failure to follow the advice of the previous letter, but is written with a special eye for news that will interest him. In Parliament, declares the writer,

The vild Speakers are, *Hoskins*, *Fuller*, with an *&* *caetera* of an hundred

[1] Presumably *Certain Considerations touching the better Pacification and Edification of the Church of England*, which was published not long afterwards (its publishing history is a complicated and still unravelled problem), but which at the time the letter was written almost certainly existed only in manuscript.

men. And surely, saving that Sir *George Moor* is your father in law, and not in conscience, he speaks as ill as ever he did, saving that he speaks not so much.[1] . . . The choise and usuall Speakers are, *Bacon, Edwin Sands, Yelverton, Martin,* with some few more. I am content to tell you, that Sir *Maurice Barkley* hath done exceeding well, and, so that you believe me, you shall have good leave to wonder at it with me.

Then follows some news about the cases of parliamentary privilege, which occupied so much of the attention of the opening session of this Parliament, and which produced from Donne the satirical title in *The Courtier's Library*: 'Tarltonus de privilegiis Parliamenti'. Next come some comments on the slow progress of the proposed union of England and Scotland:

Sir *William Cornwally[s]* hath taken upon him to answer the Objections against the Union, but they are done so lamely; and, although it seem scarce possible, so much worse than his Book, as (if he were not a kind friend of yours) I would expresse that wonder which I have in my heart, how he keeps himself from the Coat with the long sleevs. It is incredible to think, if it were not true, that such simplicity of conceit could not be joyned in him, with so impudent utterance.[2]

The letter just quoted from opens with the remark: 'It is long since you were in *London*, and long since I was at Purford; but not so long.' Nevertheless Donne visited London shortly afterwards to see another old friend. Wotton, who had been abroad since he left the service of Essex, returned to England at the end of 1603, and to the surprise of the court was received by the King with great warmth. It had happened that in the autumn of 1601 Wotton was sent to Scotland by the Grand Duke of Florence to warn James of an attempt on his life, and he had spent the winter at the Scottish court as an Italian gentleman named Ottavio Baldi, his true identity being known only to the King. Having thus had experience of Wotton's diplomatic skill, James decided to send him as ambassador to Venice. Just before he set out the King knighted him, and by

---

[1] Sir George More, we learn from another source, had the annoying habit of rising up in Parliament 'about Eleven of the Clock, . . . [to] make Repetition of all that had been spoken that Day' (W. Knowler, *The Earl of Strafforde's Letters and Dispatches,* 1739, i. 178).

[2] Sir William Cornwallis's book was *The Miraculous and Happie Union of England and Scotland,* 1604, S.T.C. 5782.

19 July 1604 he was at Dover waiting to cross the Channel with his
suite, which included another close friend of Donne, Rowland
Woodward, who accompanied the ambassador as one of his secretaries. Donne's lines, 'To Sir Henry Wotton at his going Ambassador to Venice', were sent to him shortly before he left London,
accompanied by a postscript in prose urgently inquiring 'whether
you haue your last despatches at court or whether you make many
dayes stay there or at London ⟨so that⟩ such a one as I may yett
kisse your hand'.[1] Donne's affection for Wotton was such that he
could not face another separation as long as this promised to be
without taking leave of him in person.

    When compared with the earlier verse letters, that to Wotton
reveals an interesting change in Donne. It suggests an inner content
which marriage had brought, even in spite of his dependent position
in Wolley's household. The satirical impulse and the mood of stoicism are both gone; in their place is a new sense of religion which he
does not hesitate to reveal to Wotton, for whom more than anyone
else he had formerly assumed the role of stoic, and the closing lines
of the epistle to him breathe a spirit of quiet resignation:

> For mee, (if there be such a thing as I)
>   Fortune (if there be such a thing as shee)
> Spies that I beare so well her tyranny,
>   That she thinks nothing else so fit for mee;
>
> But though she part us, to heare my oft prayers
>   For your increase, God is as neere mee here;
> And to send you what I shall begge, his staires
>   In length and ease are alike every where.

Though Donne's restlessness was soon to drive him on to fresh
unhappiness, this mood while it lasted was none the less deeply felt.
    At least two of the most famous of the 'Songs and Sonets' must
belong to the early years of Donne's married life, and the possibility
that some of the others come from the same period is strong. Both
'The Sunne Rising' and 'The Canonization' must from internal
evidence have been written in the reign of James. In the one, 'Goe
tell Court-huntsmen, that the King will ride' alludes, of course, to

---

[1] Simpson, *Prose Works*, p. 320.

James's well-known love of the chase; in the other, the advice, 'the Kings reall, or his stamped face / Contemplate', would have been pointless in the reign of Elizabeth.[1] In 'The Canonization' too the allusion to his 'ruin'd fortune' is surely a reference to his plight after his marriage, and the further reference in the same poem to 'the plaguie Bill' would come naturally in the plague years of 1603 and 1604. It is possible, then, that these two poems express some of the moods of the early years of his marriage.[2]

One victim of the plague was Donne's brother-in-law, William Lyly. About three years after his marriage to Anne, Lyly was appointed (in October 1596) 'Comisserie of the Musters' in Picardy, and sent frequent reports on matters of interest to Burghley, to Sir Robert Cecil, and to Essex. Early in 1598 he returned from abroad to settle at Hawstead under the patronage of Sir Robert Drury. Here in some way he aroused the anger of Drury's other protégé Joseph Hall, who wrote that 'this malicious man going hastily up to *London*, to exasperate my Patron against me, was then and there swept away by the Pestilence, and never returned to do any farther Mischief'. In fact Lyly had gone to London in 1603 to try to obtain an office under the new King; but the plague carried him off before 16 August, when Anne, his widow, was granted letters of administration of his goods.[3]

The need to get some employment beset his brother-in-law also. It was impossible for Donne to regard his sojourn at Pyrford as permanent, and it is likely, too, that he began to feel a growing uneasiness at the conduct of Sir Francis Wolley. On coming of age Wolley had embarked on a spendthrift career at the court. His marriage was unsatisfactory; his wife bore him no children, and he had taken a mistress, a certain Joan Harris. He had a daughter by her, whom he forced his wife to acknowledge by acting as godmother

---

[1] Gosse, i. 65 n., in noticing 'The Sunne Rising', refuses to accept the obvious implications of the allusion to the King, and comments, more ingeniously than convincingly, 'If, as I think likely, this was written about 1595, the "clime" was probably France, and "the King" Henry IV, a mighty hunter, our ally, and very popular in England.'

[2] [For arguments that, because of the sources on which Donne drew, 'The Undertaking' was written after 1599 and 'A Valediction: of the Booke' after 1602, see Gardner, *Elegies etc.*, pp. lix–lx.]

[3] *Donne and the Drurys*, pp. 81–3.

and by giving her name to the infant.[1] But there was no breach between the Donnes and the Wolleys, and the fact that Donne's fourth child was christened Francis in January 1607 not only suggests that Wolley was his godfather, but also implies that friendly relations persisted after the Donnes had left Pyrford.

On 16 February 1604/5 a licence was granted to 'Sir Walter Chute knight & John donne gent to travaile for three yeares with two servantes four nagges & iiij^{xx} ^{li} in money'.[2] Donne evidently felt that the time would soon be ripe to sue for public employment once more and that a journey to the Continent would put him in touch with current developments abroad; the chance of going as travelling companion with Sir Walter Chute gave him the opportunity he sought. Sir Walter was a young Kentishman slightly Donne's junior; he was the son of George Chute of Bethersden, had been at Hart Hall and Gray's Inn, and had served with some distinction in the Islands expedition of 1597. Though practically nothing is known of the travels of Chute and Donne, some conjectures must perforce be made.

Donne seems to have left his wife and children in the care of her sister Lady Grymes, since their third child, George, was born at Peckham and baptized in the parish church of Camberwell on 9 May 1605.[3] The next child, Francis, was baptized at Mitcham on 8 January 1607; therefore Donne must have been at home again by at least the beginning of April 1606. Thus, if he left with Chute soon after the issue on 16 February 1605 of their licence to travel, he could have been absent from England for just over a year. If this was so, he was away from home at the time of the Gunpowder Plot. He

---

[1] *Victoria County History of Surrey*, iii. 5 and 393. In his will P.C.C., 118 Dorset, Wolley left some lands to this child, Mary, which, if she were to die without issue, should pass to his cousin, Sir Arthur Mainwaring (Egerton's steward), or failing his issue to Sir George More and his issue. In *C.S.P. (Dom.)*, *Jas. I, 1619–23*, p. 85 (14 Oct. 1619), is noted a letter to the Lord Chancellor to hear a cause of Henry Wroth against Mainwaring and a Mr. Wintern concerning a legacy left by Wolley to his child.

[2] S.P. 38/8. *C.S.P. (Dom.)*, *1603–10*, combines into one entry (p. 196) three separate items in the original docket book, thus: 'Feb. 16. License to Sir Jas. Bourchier, Sir Charles Morrison, Sir Walter Chute, and John Donne to travel for 3 years.' The form of this entry led Gosse into inaccuracies already commented upon; see above, p. 17.

[3] W. H. Blanch, *Y^e Parish of Camerwell*, 1875, p. 172. The form of the entry in the parish register suggests that Donne himself was not present.

missed the horror and excitement that gripped the nation when the news of the plot was revealed, but returned to England while the news of the trial of Henry Garnet the Jesuit was still on everyone's lips. Garnet was executed on 3 May 1606, and in the next month the Earl of Northumberland was tried in the Star Chamber for complicity in the plot. There is little doubt that he was innocent, but he was found guilty, and sentenced to imprisonment during the King's pleasure. He joined Sir Walter Raleigh in the Tower, and remained a prisoner there for fifteen years.

To return, however, to Donne's travels in 1605 and 1606. That Donne and Chute went to Paris may be taken as certain. In a letter written in January 1612, when Donne was again in France, he wrote:

That which was much observed in the Kings more childish age, when I was last here, by those whom his father appointed to judge, by an assiduous observation, his naturall inclination, is more and more confirmed, that his inclinations are cruell, and tyrannous; and when he is any way affected, his stammering is so extreme, as he can utter nothing.[1]

To explain this passage Gosse posits an unrecorded visit to Paris between 1608 and 1610, on the ground that such a disposition 'would not be observable in a child of less than seven or eight years'.[2] But at the beginning of 1606 the future Louis XIII, not yet five years old, was keeping his own court and receiving distinguished foreign visitors, who observed and reported on him. Sir George Carew, the English ambassador, wrote in his first dispatch from Paris, dated 14 January 1606:

Some five days after our first audience wee visited Monsieur le Dauphin, at St. Germains, where wee were vsed with honor and good respect, and entertained at dinner. . . . The child, I find to be of a very strong, and vigorous Constitution, and of a hardy, and ready spirite. . . . His maiestie at (my next) audience . . . asked me what I thought of Monsieur le Dauphin, I sayd his Countenance promised, he would prove a sonne worthy of so greate a ffather.[3]

Sir George Carew was Egerton's former secretary, then newly

---

[1] *Letters*, pp. 124–5. Interestingly enough, Sir Walter Chute also visited Paris in 1611 or 1612, when he fought a duel with William Becher (J. W. Stoye, *English Travellers Abroad, 1604–1667*, 1952, p. 72).

[2] i. 294.   [3] S.P. Foreign (French), vol. 53, p. 6.

arrived in France, and Donne would almost certainly have called on him if he were in Paris at this time. It is even conceivable that he and Chute were in his train on the occasion described in the dispatch, though if they were not they could easily have heard, soon afterwards, his impressions of the young prince as well as those of others. By this time, however, they would probably have been on their way back to England, and were returning from Italy, and perhaps from Spain as well.

If Donne and Chute visited Venice in 1605,[1] they would have done so not merely because of the attractions of the famous city-state, but also because of the presence there of such friends of Donne as Wotton and Woodward, through whose aid they could hope for opportunities and privileges superior to those granted to most English travellers. Three clues suggest rather than prove that they went there. Henry King, in a letter to Walton (eventually prefixed to the *Life* of Donne), remarked that between Donne and Wotton 'there was a Friendship begun in *Oxford*, continued in their various Travels, and more confirmed in the religious Friendship of Age'. It sounds as if King meant that the two men met abroad as well as at home. Certainly Donne was in touch with Wotton when he was travelling with the Drurys, and it is only natural that he should also have been in contact with him and have visited him in 1605. A second clue is furnished by Walton: commenting on the bequest in Donne's will of the 'twoe Pictures of *Padre Paolo* and *Fulgentio* which hange in the Parlour at my howse at Pauls',[2] he interposes a

---

[1] Somewhat slender evidence survives to suggest that Donne had crossed the Alps by the Mont Cenis pass and had passed through Turin, though whether in 1605 or earlier one cannot say. In one of the sermons there is a reference to a famous relic still preserved in the cathedral at Turin: 'if that be the true winding sheet of Christ which is kept in Savoy, it appeares, that that sheet stuck so close to his body, as that it did, and does still retaine the dimensions of his body, and the impressions and signatures of every wound that he had received in his body. So that it would have beene no easie matter for those women to have pulled off that sheet, if it had had no other glue, no other gumme, but his own precious blood to hold it' (*Sermons*, ix, no. 8, ll. 307–13, p. 197). It does sound as if Donne had actually seen the relic. Nevertheless, Mr. John Sparrow has drawn attention to the fact that Donne was familiar with Archbishop Alfonso Paleotti's treatise on the shroud, *Jesu Christi Crucifixi stigmata sacrae Sindoni impressa*, Venice, 1606 ('More Donne', *TLS*, 13 Mar. 1953, p. 169), and one cannot, therefore, put much stress on the words of the sermon.

[2] On these portraits see L. Pearsall Smith, *The Life and Letters of Sir Henry Wotton*, ii. 478–9; that of Sarpi is reproduced opposite ii. 370.

statement that the two Servite friars were 'men of his [Donne's] acquaintance when he travelled *Italy*'.[1] There is nothing whatever to suggest that Donne was in Italy after 1605 and 1606, so he could not have made Father Paul's acquaintance after those years; he must have done so earlier. Paolo Sarpi and Fulgenzio Micanzio were, of course, both in Italy in 1590, or whenever it may have been that Donne first travelled there, and it is conceivable that Donne could have met them then, though they were comparatively young and obscure, and such a meeting could in all likelihood have been only a chance occurrence. By 1605, however, Sarpi, though not yet Theological Counsellor to the Republic of Venice, was famous for his learning, was already a man of influence in affairs of state, and was in contact with many learned Protestants throughout Europe. He was such a man, in other words, as a visitor to Venice like Donne would be eager to meet. It is true that the close relations between Wotton and Sarpi which existed later are not known to have begun as early as 1605, since the conflict between Venice and the papacy did not come out into the open until the following year. Several years previously, however, Sarpi had been in close touch with an Englishman with whom Donne was in all probability acquainted, Sir Edwin Sandys, and had aided him in the composition of *Europae Speculum*, with its temperate but penetrating analysis of the influence of the Church of Rome in Europe. It seems safe to assume, therefore, that if, as Walton asserted, Donne met Sarpi and Micanzio in Italy, he did so in 1605.

There is a third argument in favour of Donne's having visited Italy in 1605/6. If the conjecture is well founded that the group of letters in the *Tobie Mathew Collection* are letters from Mathew to Donne,[2] then one of them[3] assumes a new significance. Mathew had left England, and in defiance of a promise made to his parents was now in Italy, on the edge of a decision to join the Roman Church. He had been residing for some time in Florence and had in addition

---

[1] *Lives*, p. 68. In the Preface to the Reader in *The Letters of the Renowned Father Paul*, *translated out of the Italian* by Edward Brown, 1693, Brown refers to 'a very excellent Person, and a very good Friend of Father Paul's', glossing this passage with 'Dr. *Donne*' in a side-note (p. ix). Whether this is independent evidence for Donne's friendship with Sarpi is uncertain; Brown may have possessed information since lost, but, on the other hand, he may merely be relying on Walton.

[2] See p. 143, n. 1.   [3] pp. 274–5.

visited Rome. The date of his letter can be fixed fairly precisely as the summer of 1606, and the relevant passages which seem to throw light on Donne's movements are as follows:

SIR,

Your Train takes not fire. I received a young Letter from you, dated as out of *England*; but I will not believe, but that you were as far as *Venice*, upon your way to *Florence*, when you wrote it: And that, after these heates, we shall have you here; Or if, indeed, you be in *England*, what wind, or water could drive you back so soon? I am not so glad of any thing I got to day (except my dinner,) as I am of having lost my place, this Parliament: and, next the not exercising of it my self, I am most glad, you had it not. It is an hard choice, when a man must either be undone or damn'd.

Mathew, it seems, knew that Donne was to visit Venice and was expected to go on to Florence, but the travellers had moved more rapidly than he had anticipated, and were now back in England.[1]

It is tempting also to suggest that these travels may have been the occasion of Donne's visit to Spain, and that Walton is in error in placing it earlier in Donne's career. Peace with Spain had been concluded in 1604, and in the following year a number of young Englishmen flocked there, just as they flocked to France after the end of the Napoleonic wars. The newly appointed ambassador to Spain was Sir Charles Cornwallis, father of Donne's friend Sir William. The younger Cornwallis was in Spain with his father for most of 1605, and once again the presence of influential friends at a

---

[1] The date of the letter can be determined as the summer of 1606 by means of the references to Bacon's recent marriage and to the two Shirley brothers. Furthermore, there is a striking parallel with a letter written by Toby Mathew to Dudley Carleton from Florence on 8 Aug. 1606, which not only confirms the date but also goes a long way towards proving the authorship of the letter.

'The Venetian business is *in statu quo prius*, and although they speak bigg, yet the matter is likely to come to a quiet end. Sr Thomas Shirley hath longe since shaken off his fetters and lives in Naples like a gallant, his brother is in Barbary, and in greater show than he was in Persia' (A. H. Mathew and A. Calthrop, *Life of Sir Tobie Mathew*, 1907, p. 57).

'*Sr. Thomas Shirley* is come to *Naples*, is gallant, but came not thither So; *Sr. Anthony* is in *Barbary*, as brave as the Sun, and I think as hot as the Sun can make him. We think that the *Venetians* business will accommodate a friend of yours and mine [Wotton], they say, hath been an enemy to his own reputation, in changing his occupation to be a blower of coals' (*Tobie Mathew Collection*, p. 275). [Some of the foregoing evidence for Donne's visit to the Continent has been independently discussed by Mr. I. A. Shapiro, 'Donne in 1605–6', *TLS*, 26 Jan. 1967.]

foreign court may have been an added inducement to Donne and Chute.[1] Yet this is mere speculation; all that is reasonably probable is that they visited Paris and Venice in 1605 and early 1606, and that Donne was back in England by the beginning of April 1606.

Whether Donne took his family back to Pyrford for a short time after his return to England cannot now be determined. Walton inaccurately states that 'Mr. *Donne* and his wife continued with Sir *Francis Wolly* till his death',[2] but continues:

a little before which time, Sir *Francis* was so happy as to make a perfect reconciliation betwixt Sir *George* and his forsaken son and daughter; Sir *George* conditioning by bond, to pay to Mr. *Donne* 800 *l.* at a certain day, as a portion with his wife, or 20 *l.* quarterly for their maintenance: as the interest for it, till the said portion was paid.[3]

It is more likely that the reconciliation was brought about near the time that Donne left Pyrford than just before Wolley died, since the assurance of a small but regular income probably justified Donne in deciding to take a house for himself and his family.

The evidence that suggests that Donne may have gone back to Pyrford for a short time after his return from the Continent is to be found in an undated letter written from there to Sir Henry Goodyer. The concluding sentences show how seriously Donne treated the obligations of friendship:

SIR,

I live so farre removed, that even the ill news of your great losse (which is ever swiftest and loudest) found me not till now, your letter speaks it not plain enough but I am so accustomed to the worst, that I am sure it is so in this. I am almost glad that I knew her so little: for I would have no more additions to sorrow. If I should comfort you, it were an almes acceptable in no other title, then when poor give to poor; for I am more needy of it then you. And I know you well provided of Christian, and learned, and brave defences against all humane

---

[1] The Earl of Nottingham went on an embassy to Spain in 1605; among his companions were Sir Robert Drury and Sir Walter Cope (J. W. Stoye, *English Travellers Abroad, 1604–1667*, 1952, pp. 331–2).

[2] Wolley died in 1609 at the age of twenty-six.

[3] Arrangements of this sort for the payment of a dowry seem to have been fairly common; see L. Stone, 'The Anatomy of the Elizabethan Aristocracy', *Economic History Review*, xviii (1948), 1–41 at p. 11. Ten per cent was the normal rate of interest on debts at this period.

accidents. I will make my best haste after your messenger: and if my self and the place had not been ill provided of horses, I had been the messenger, for you have taught me by granting more to deny no request.

Pyrford 3 a clock   *Your honest unprofitable friend*
just as yours came.   J. Donne.[1]

This letter has been taken to refer to the death of Goodyer's wife, which is now known to have taken place in 1606.[2] Yet the lady is not named in Donne's letter, nor is it even absolutely certain that she had died. Nevertheless, it is likeliest that the reference is to Lady Goodyer, and if so it follows that Donne was back at Pyrford for a while after returning from his travels with Chute. Before the year 1606 was out, however, Donne had moved his family to a small house nearer London at Mitcham, which became his home for the next five years.

---

[1] *Letters*, pp. 212–13.
[2] John Owen addressed an epigram 'Ad D. Henricum Goodyer Equitem, optima conjuga orbatum 1606' (*Epigrammatum ad Arabellam Stuart liber singularis*, no. 74).

VIII

MITCHAM AND LONDON

FROM 1606 to 1611 are 'the most difficult years of Donne's life to describe in a connected narrative. His life seems more complex during these years than at any other period, though this may be to some extent only because a much wider range of materials suddenly becomes available to the biographer. In particular, the number of surviving letters increases very considerably, yet, instead of adding precision to the narrative, the letters, owing to the circumstances of their publication, raise more problems than they solve. A number of them still defy all the efforts of modern scholarship to assign them accurate dates, and the identities of the correspondents addressed are sometimes far from certain. Even apart from such problems, however, the sense of complexity remains. Donne was in London as often as with his wife and family at Mitcham; he followed the Court and cultivated patrons and patronesses; he devoted laborious hours of study and research to problems of divinity and canon law; and while he addressed poems to great ladies and theological pamphlets to the King, he also cultivated a certain Bohemianism in his leisure hours and liked to relax in the company of wits and writers. His friends and acquaintances were to be found in every rank of society, and he moved from one group to another with surprising ease. The very lack of regular employment and of a sense of definite direction contributes to the sense of complexity in Donne's life at this period, though doubtless no one regretted it more than he or wished more fervently that his varied endeavours could be reduced and domi-nated by singleness of purpose.

If Mitcham was his home, it was also a place of retirement where he could pursue his studies, not without interruptions, it is true (for what father of a growing family could ever so seclude himself as to be free from interruptions?), but free at least from those calls on his time and company which he expected when in London. The house in Mitcham stood in Whitford Lane,[1] on a site which is now covered with workmen's dwellings. It survived, however, until after 1840, and a sketch of it was made by Richard Simpson, the biographer of Edmund Campion. Simpson's father owned the house, and he him-self spent the early years of his life there. The sketch[2] shows a two-storied cottage, with two projecting gables in front and a wing stretching to the left; from the door to the lane stretched a row of yews, said to have been planted in Donne's time, with other trees and shrubs on the opposite side of a garden path. Here Donne found adequate quarters for his rapidly increasing family and, doubtless, one or two servants to aid his wife. The Donnes brought three children with them to Mitcham; four others were born during the five years they were there. Francis, the third son, was baptized in the parish church of St. Peter and St. Paul on 8 January 1607; then followed three girls: Lucy, baptized on 8 August 1608, Bridget, baptized on 12 December 1609, and Mary, baptized on 31 January 1611.[3]

Donne's letters give various glimpses of his life at Mitcham. Probably the pleasantest and most intimate are given in a letter to Goodyer:

I write from the fire side in my Parler, and in the noise of three gamesome children; and by the side of her, whom because I have transplanted into a wretched fortune, I must labour to disguise that from her by all such honest devices, as giving her my company, and discourse, therefore I steal from her, all the time which I give this Letter, and it is therefore that I take so short a list, and gallop so fast over it, I have not been out of my house since I received your pacquet.[4]

There are references, too, to his study with its book-lined walls, 'where to cast mine eye upon good Authors kindles or refreshes sometimes meditations not unfit to communicate to near friends'; nevertheless, the room had a cellar underneath it, and was cold and damp. Donne frequently refers to the house as his 'hospital', and sometimes as his 'prison' or 'dungeon'; for there was often illness in

---

[1] *Victoria County History of Surrey*, iv. 229.
[2] Reproduced by Jessopp, p. 58. The original is now in the possession of Miss Mary Donne of Chester.
[3] Parish register.   [4] *Letters*, pp. 137–8.

the household. The older children were of an age to be most suscep-tible to childish ailments, and a letter of a slightly later period mentions that the harassed father had had to forgo attendance at court because of measles at home. The strain of child-bearing, too, was beginning to tell on his wife, and in a letter which must refer to the birth of Francis at the begining of 1607 Donne says that he writes

only to convey to you this paper opposed to those, with which you trusted me. It is (I cannot say the waightyest, but truly) the saddest lucubration and nights passage that I ever had. For it exercised those hours, which, with extreme danger of her, whom I should hardly have abstained from recompensing for her company in this world, with ac-companying her out of it, encreased my poor family with a son. Though her anguish, and my fears, and hopes, seem divers and wild distractions from this small businesse of your papers, yet because they all narrowed themselves, and met in *Via regia*, which is the con-sideration of our selves, and God, I thought it time not unfit for this dispatch.[1]

It is characteristic of Donne that, as he sat huddled over his study fire through the long winter's night with his wife in prolonged and audible suffering overhead, he should have striven in his helpless-ness to stifle his anxiety, and to distract his mind by concentrating it on the expression of some elaborate and intricate train of thought.

To Donne himself physical illness never brought any slackening of mental activity. It is impossible to date all the references to ill-health in Donne's letters, but one of the severest attacks seems to have been in the winter of 1608/9, when he suffered from prolonged neuritis. He was forced to take to his bed, and was in such agony of pain that he feared his life was in danger; nevertheless, in this state he composed his 'Litanie', a poem of over 250 lines.[2] Yet, though such ill-health accelerated rather than slowed down the activity of his mind, it profoundly depressed his spirits. Many of the Mitcham letters are thus full of melancholy and show that at such times Donne's mind could not help turning to thoughts of suicide. His

[1] Ibid., pp. 146–7. Unfortunately there is no means of identifying the writing with which Donne says he occupied himself.
[2] Ibid., pp. 32–3.

Biathanatos was in some degree the product of such moods. Donne's motive in writing this treatise was, like that of Burton in composing *The Anatomy of Melancholy*, to overcome a temptation, not by trying to banish it altogether from the mind, but by giving it full place there and at the same time rendering it innocuous by transferring it from the plane of action to that of learned investigation and contemplation.

For the rest, though Donne complained, and no doubt justly, of 'the incommodity of a little thin house', it was certainly less uncomfortable during the summer months. Nor were his quarters so mean or restricted that he had any need to be ashamed of them, or fear to ask his great or wealthy friends to visit him there. Lady Bedford consented to be godmother to his daughter Lucy, baptized on 8 August 1608, and presumably attended the ceremony and the christening party that would normally follow it. A letter addressed to 'Sir I. H.', possibly her brother Sir John Harrington, invites him too.[1] Furthermore, it was undeniable that the Mitcham house was conveniently situated. Two of Mrs. Donne's sisters were close at hand, the one near by at Beddington and another only a little further off at Peckham. Donne himself could reach London Bridge with less than two hours' riding in any weather. He rode back and forth so often that the journey lost all novelty for him; it became his habit to give the horse its head and withdraw his mind altogether from his surroundings. 'The high way, where I am contracted, and inverted into my self' was, he told Goodyer, one of 'my two ordinary forges of Letters to you', and in a verse epistle he expresses the same thought more gracefully and poetically:

> Riding I had you, though you still staid there,
> And in these thoughts, although you never stirre,
> You came with mee to Micham, and are here.

In London Donne seems to have had lodgings, at least from early in 1607 until the latter part of 1611, in the Strand at the house of a

---

[1] *Letters*, p. 118. R. E. Bennett, *PMLA*, lvi (1941), 121, maintains that this letter was actually addressed to Goodyer, but this is very far from certain. Donne asks his correspondent to visit his house on his way to London, which suggests that he lived in Surrey or Sussex. Goodyer, of course, did not live thereabouts, nor was the Court south of the Thames during the summer progress of 1608.

man named Tincomb.[1] Walton says that Donne's lodgings were near Whitehall, but they must actually have been further east than such a statement would suggest. Tincomb apparently had a number of lodgers, one of whom was George Garrard, second son of Sir William Garrard of Dorney, Bucks., and member of a wealthy mercantile family which gave London two Lord Mayors during the reign of Elizabeth. George Garrard's mother was Elizabeth, daughter of another Lord Mayor, Sir Thomas Roe, grandfather of a more famous Sir Thomas who went to India and Constantinople as ambassador of James I. Donne was already acquainted with the younger Sir Thomas Roe; now he and Garrard became firm friends.[2] In a letter to Garrard from France in the spring of 1612 Donne offered 'my service to all the company at our lodging; in which house, if I cannot get room for a pallat, at my return, my comfort is, that I can ever hope to be so near them as the Spittle in the *Savoy*, where they receive Travellers'.[3] Garrard in the summer of 1616 addressed a letter from the 'Strand ouer agaynst Salisbury House',[4] and this address fits in very well with Donne's reference to the proximity of the Savoy. Thus it would seem that Donne's lodgings, which he did not give up until he left for France at the end of 1611, were between the present Bedford and Southampton Streets. Thither 'his friends and occasions', says Walton, 'drew him very often'. Here, too, 'he was as often visited by many of the Nobility and others of this Nation, who used him in their Counsels of greatest

---

[1] The letter to Goodyer written early in Jan. 1607 (*Letters*, pp. 146–7) was written 'whilest my fire was lighting at Tricombs', but the spelling of the name here is the result of a misreading. The correct form is established by Donne's Latin letter to Goodyer, written in 1611, in which he alludes to himself as 'commoranti apud Rabbinum Tincombum'. It has not been possible to discover anything further about Tincomb, or Tinkham, or to explain why he was called, jestingly, no doubt, 'rabbi'. Was he, like Rabbi Busy in *Bartholomew Fair*, a puritan? The *OED* offers no illustration of the slang use of 'rabbi'.

[2] Garrard was an admirer of Donne's poetry. Writing to Viscount Wentworth several years after Donne's death, Garrard says that he encloses 'Verses made in the Progress. I that never had Patience in all my Life to transcribe Poems, except they were very transcendent, such as Dean *Donn* writ in his younger Days, did these with some Pain' (*The Earl of Strafforde's Letters and Dispatches*, i. 338).

[3] *Letters*, p. 248.

[4] S.P. 14, James I, vol. 87, no. 57. A letter of 9 May 1617 (vol. 92, no. 15), which refers to 'Mr. Beecher my Camerario', makes it clear that he was then still in lodgings, but he had apparently been at least since 1614 in the service of the Earl of Salisbury, and subsequent letters are dated from Hatfield and Salisbury House.

consideration: and with some rewards for his better subsistence'. Donne's purpose in spending so much of his time in London was unquestionably to secure some employment for himself, and, as a means to that end, to make or renew as many desirable social contacts as possible.

Of his attempts to secure an appointment it is probable that only comparatively few traces remain. The earliest is a letter dated 13 June 1607 to Sir Henry Goodyer, who is asked to approach William Fowler, the Queen's secretary,[1] on Donne's behalf. A vacancy had arisen in the Queen's household; some time previously Fowler had promised to help and, Donne writes, 'if my means may make me acceptable to the Queen and him, I should be very sorry, he should make so farre steps therein with any other, that I should fail in it, onely for not having spoke to him soon enough'.[2] But Donne also admits to 'the wide distance in which I have lived from Court', and it is clear from the start that this appeal was doomed to failure.

The next time that Donne is known to have sought office was in November 1608. Clearly, however, there had been numerous intermediate disappointments, since, in telling Goodyer of his new hopes, he wrote: 'I am content to go forward a little more in the madnesse of missing rather then not pretend; and rather wear out, then rust.'[3] There is already a note of hopelessness in his voice. The death of Sir Geoffrey Fenton had created a vacant secretaryship in Ireland, and this Donne now sought. In his younger days Fenton had cherished literary ambitions, and he is best remembered as the translator of Bandello; he and Spenser had gone to Ireland together as secretaries to Lord Grey, and Fenton had remained there until his death. His position was one, therefore, which might seem to be the natural reward for a literary man, and Donne could conceivably feel justified in applying for it; certainly, in urging his claims he used far more skill than he had done earlier towards Fowler. He succeeded in having his name presented directly to the King by one of the royal favourites. This intermediary was James Hay, now Lord Hay, a handsome young Scot who had come south with the King. His good

---

[1] Fowler had come from Scotland with the Queen; he was an uncle of William Drummond of Hawthornden.   [2] *Letters*, pp. 81–2.   [3] Ibid., p. 146.

looks and graceful manners were accompanied by an indolent and easy-going nature; he never aspired to the heights of power seized by the later favourites, Somerset and Buckingham. He was the greatest dandy of the court; an anecdote relates that 'the Earl of Southampton told that my Lord Carleil had answered him, when hee had asked the cause of his melancholye, How can I be but melancholye, my Lord; they have spoiled the fashion of my band!'[1] Hay was an extravagant spender, and ran through vast sums of money, though James seemed always willing to grant him more. One would scarcely think of him as the sort of man to form a friendship with Donne, but there was a warmth of feeling between them from the time of their first meeting, and they remained friends for the rest of Donne's life. It was Sir Francis Bacon who first introduced Donne to Hay,[2] but Goodyer also did his part, and 'begot, or nursed these good impressions of me in him'. The result astonished Donne:

as I have had occasion to imploy all my friends, so I have not found in them all (except *Bedford*) more hast and words (for when those two are together, there is much comfort even in the least) then in the L[ord] *Hay*. In good faith he promised so roundly, so abundantly, so profusely, as I suspected him, but performed what ever he undertook, (and my requests were the measures of his undertakings) so readily and truly, that his complements became obligations, and having spoke like a Courtier, did like a friend.[3]

Nevertheless Hay was unsuccessful; he urged the King to appoint Donne, but the King was familiar with Donne's story and felt that the circumstances of his marriage counted against him. As soon as he learnt of this, Donne wrote to Hay: 'I have been told', he began, 'that when your Lordship did me that extream favour, of presenting my name, his Majestie remembred me, by the worst part of my historie, which was my disorderlie proceedings, seaven years since, in my nonage',[4] and he begged Hay

not to be too apprehensive of any suspition, that there lies upon me anie dishonourable staine, or can make my King have anie prejudice against me, for that intemperate and hastie act of mine: for the Lord Chancellor and his brother in law, *Sr. G. M.* whose daughter I

[1] *Archaeologia Scotica*, iv (1857), 79.　　[2] *Tobie Mathew Collection*, p. 308.
[3] *Letters*, p. 145.　　[4] *Sic*; read '. . . my marriage'?

married, would both be likelie, and will be readie to declare it, for his Majestie's satisfaction, or your Lordships, that their displeasure, commenced so long since, should ⟨not⟩ be thought to continue still, or interrupt any of my fortunes.[1]

That he should be so confident of the recommendations of Lord Ellesmere and Sir George More is evidence that the two men most closely concerned had forgiven him for the presumption of his marriage, but the whole incident shows how right Donne had been at the time in asserting that if he were dismissed any efforts to secure similar employment elsewhere would be sure to fail. Even the King, who had not yet come to England when Donne's marriage occurred, was unwilling seven years later to consider him seriously for responsible public service.

Donne's third attempt to secure a position was made about two months later; there is no reference to it in his surviving correspondence, but on 14 February 1608/9 Chamberlain wrote to Dudley Carleton: 'Newes here is none at all but that John Dun seekes to be preferred to be secretarie of Virginia.'[2] At this time the affairs of the Virginia Company were being thoroughly reorganized. A new charter, said to have been drawn up by Sir Edwin Sandys, was being prepared, and a very considerable expedition was being fitted out to sail to the assistance of the languishing colony. Since Sir Francis Bacon, Sir Maurice Berkeley, Sir Edwin Sandys, Sir Thomas Roe, and Christopher Brooke were all members of the newly constituted Council of the Company, Donne must have felt that he had good reason to hope for the post; but it was not given to him. Had he sailed for Virginia in June 1609 with Sir Thomas Gates he would have suffered shipwreck on the Bermudas and have participated in those events, the report of which stimulated Shakespeare's imagination and helped to determine the pattern of *The Tempest*.

Far more fully documented than his failures to obtain employment are Donne's relations during this period with some of his

---

[1] *Tobie Mathew Collection*, pp. 330–1.

[2] Chamberlain, *Letters*, i. 284, and *C.S.P.* (*Dom.*), *1603–10*, p. 492; see also S. Johnson, 'John Donne and the Virginia Company', *ELH*, xiv (1947), 127–38. [It is possible, as I. A. Shapiro suggests, *RES*, N.S. i (1950), 263, that Donne applied for the secretaryship of the Council of the Company in London, and had no intention of going abroad.]

friends. Despite the problems of dating letters and sometimes of determining to whom a particular letter was addressed, Donne's correspondence now begins to illuminate certain aspects of his life in considerable detail. The great majority of the surviving letters were written to Sir Henry Goodyer. He was Donne's closest friend, and the two had made a compact, which Donne kept with remarkable fidelity, to write to one another once a week whenever they were not in town together.

Sir Henry Goodyer was about the same age as Donne, though the exact year of his birth is unknown.[1] He was the only son of William Goodyer of Monks Kirby and the nephew of an earlier Sir Henry, of Polesworth in Warwickshire. The elder Sir Henry had been a friend and companion of Sir Philip Sidney—he was with him at Zutphen when he died—but he had also been too ardent a supporter of Mary Queen of Scots, and having thus lost Elizabeth's favour could never regain it. 'For the zeale hee bare to his Ma*jes*tyes house and family [wrote his nephew] ranne all his fortunes a grounde in the time of our late Queene, having suffered much both in estate and person.'[2] In his later years he lived a comparatively retired life at Polesworth, the former abbey which his father had secured during the distribution of plunder after the dissolution of the monasteries. Here Michael Drayton spent his early years in the service of the household, and here he fell in love with Anne, Sir Henry's younger daughter, who afterwards married Sir Henry Rainsford of Clifford Chambers, near Stratford-upon-Avon. Frances, the elder daughter and only other child of Sir Henry, married her cousin Henry Goodyer, Donne's friend, and the Polesworth estates were settled upon them. The elder Sir Henry had previously made a settlement in favour of his younger brother Thomas, but on Thomas's death he revoked it. Nevertheless he provided Thomas's son with the basis for a claim which he attempted to establish in a series of suits at law which lasted for nearly ten years after Sir Henry's death in 1595.[3]

The younger Henry Goodyer was educated at Cambridge and

[1] [Professor Bald was evidently unable to confirm Gosse's statement (i. 153) that Goodyer was baptized on 21 Aug. 1571.]

[2] Sir Henry Goodyer to Lord Cecil, in F. C. Cass, *Monken Hadley* (1880), p. 149; cf. *Calendar of Salisbury Manuscripts*, Hist. MSS. Com., xvi. 240.

[3] B. H. Newdigate, *Michael Drayton and his Circle*, 1941, chap. 3, 'The Gooderes of Polesworth'.

Gray's Inn, and was knighted by Essex in Ireland. When, after the accession of James I, he secured a post in the King's household as Gentleman of the Privy Chamber, he threw himself for a while with ardour into the frivolities of the new court. He took part in the masque on New Year's Day, 1604, and two years later performed at the barriers in Jonson's *Hymenaei*, in honour of the ill-starred marriage of the Earl of Essex and Lady Frances Howard; in 1605 he went to Brussels with the Earl of Hertford's embassy to ratify the peace treaty with Spain. Even though the suits brought by his cousin to decide the ownership of Polesworth were finally dismissed in 1606, Goodyer soon fell into financial difficulties; the estates had been heavily encumbered when he inherited them, the legal battle that ensued had been costly, and his style of living was scarcely calculated to restore the family fortunes. Hence he sent a number of urgent appeals to Secretary Cecil, a distant family connection, for grants and other royal favours with which to repair his 'decayed estate'. Such grants as he obtained fell far short of his hopes, and soon his creditors were beginning to press hard upon him. He was driven to the necessity of obtaining from the King protections which secured him and his sureties from arrest for the space of a year, and these grants were renewed annually upon their expiration up till and even beyond his death.

Goodyer was pleasure-loving and easy-going. He was also hospitable and generous to the point of extravagance, though it must be said in extenuation that he not only made loans of money to Donne with very small hope of repayment, but that he went surety for him as well. He was also a keen sportsman, passionately devoted to hawking. One of Jonson's two epigrams addressed to him begins:

> Goodyere, I'am glad, and gratefull to report,
>   My selfe a witnesse of thy few dayes sport;

but the other stresses that side of Goodyer's personality which was more capable of winning him the friendship of men like Donne and Jonson:

> When I would know thee GOODYERE, my thought lookes
>   Vpon thy wel-made choise of friends, and bookes;
> Then doe I loue thee, and behold thy ends

> In making thy friends bookes, and thy bookes friends:
> Now, I must giue thy life, and deed, the voice
>   Attending such a studie, such a choice.
> Where, though't be loue, that to thy praise doth moue,
>   It was a knowledge, that begat that loue.[1]

Goodyer was thus not only sensitive and well-read, but he was also a warm-hearted and sympathetic friend. He succeeded in engaging and keeping Donne's warmest affections, and for years Donne confided in him as in no one else. Donne was aware of certain faults in his character, and tried often as gently as he could to suggest remedies, but there was never any loss of affection between them. In one letter Donne, though he specifically disclaims the intention of making any such suggestion, shows clearly that he thought Goodyer negligent in attending to his affairs:

> Not that I can fear any slacknesse in that business which drew you down, because your fortune and honour are a paire of good spurs to it; but here also you have both true businesse and many *Quasi negotia*, which go two and two to a businesse; which are visitations, and such, as though they be not full businesses, yet are so near them that they serve as for excuses, in omissions of the other.

Then, to soften the implied criticism, he passes quickly and tactfully from such remarks to the confession that

> only the observation of others upon me, is my preservation from extream idlenesse, else I professe, that I hate businesse so much, as I am sometimes glad to remember, that the *Roman Church* reads that verse *A negotio perambulante in tenebris,* which we reade from the pestilence walking by night, so equall to me do the plague and businesse deserve avoiding.[2]

Donne's fears for his friend find their fullest expression in the verse letter he addressed to Goodyer. The letter was a New Year (or a birthday) gift, couched in a style of grave and graceful compliment; nevertheless Donne does not hesitate to express his opinion that nothing would be better for Goodyer than a complete amendment of his way of living, and advises him to make the break by going abroad for a time:

---

[1] *Epigrams*, lxxxv and lxxxvi.   [2] *Letters*, pp. 141–2.

Provide you manlyer dyet; you have seene
　　All libraries, which are Schools, Camps, and Courts;
But aske your Garners if you have not beene
　　In harvests, too indulgent to your sports.

Would you redeeme it? then your selfe transplant
　　A while from hence. . . .

Goe; whither? Hence; you get, if you forget;
　　New faults, till they prescribe in us, are smoake.

Our soule, whose country'is heaven, and God her father,
　　Into this world, corruptions sinke, is sent,
Yet, so much in her travaile she doth gather,
　　That she returnes home, wiser then she went;

It payes you well, if it teach you to spare,
　　And make you'asham'd, to make your hawks praise,
　　　　yours,
Which when herselfe she lessens in the aire,
　　You then first say, that high enough she toures.

It is uncertain how far Donne's advice was heeded. Goodyer was apparently abroad for a time in 1609,[1] but it may be doubted if this journey did anything to extricate him from his financial difficulties, and from 1610 onwards he must have been continually hounded by creditors.

Goodyer did not scruple to make use of Donne's talents in his rather half-hearted efforts to recoup his fortunes. The younger Donne included among the *Letters to Severall Persons of Honour* one addressed to Goodyer which is oddly misassigned, since the letter consistently addresses 'your Lordship'. This same letter is also found among the Salisbury manuscripts in Goodyer's handwriting, signed by him and addressed to the Earl of Salisbury.[2] The draft must have been found among Goodyer's papers in Donne's handwriting and accordingly sent to the younger Donne for inclusion among the *Letters*. Actually, it was probably one of several such letters which Donne composed for Goodyer, and which he described in the covering letter sent with them as written 'drowsily, and

[1] See I. A. Shapiro in *MLR*, xlv (1950), 7, n. 3.
[2] S. Johnson, 'Sir Henry Goodere and Donne's Letters', *MLN*, lxiii (1948), 38–43.

coldly, as the night and my indisposition commanded: yet perchance', he continued, 'those hinderances have done good, for so
your Letters are the lesse curious, in which, men of much leasure
may soon exceed, when they write of businesse, they having but a
little'. Donne was perfectly content to be made use of in this fashion
by such a friend as Goodyer: 'I am always glad', he wrote, 'when I
have any way to expresse my love; for in these commandments you
feed my desires, and you give me means to pay some of my debts
to you.'[1]

Goodyer also purloined Donne's letters to him for material he could
use over again as his own. Some sentences in what is perhaps Donne's
most remarkable letter to him were applied by Goodyer to himself
in a letter written years afterwards to the Duke of Buckingham:

This I made account I did early when by my parents care I vnder-
tooke the study of our lawes but was diverted by a voluptuous desire
of humaner learning and languadges, good ornaments to greate fortunes but mine needed an occupation and a course: That I considered
againe, and thought I entred well into when in active times I looked
into the warres: But there I stumbled too, first by the death of my Lo:
of Essex: and after by the Queenes.[2]

Even when Goodyer tried to attract notice by versifying he did not
hesitate to paraphrase what Donne had communicated to him
privately, as when he addressed a congratulatory poem to Prince
Charles on his journey to Spain in 1623:

> Who seeke t'imprison, fetter and immure
> Religion (that is onely good and pure)
> In Wittenbergh, Geneua, and in Rome,
> Transported by their zeale, too farr presume,
> Into those Churches virtuall beames doe runne
> I hope in different lines from the same sunne,
> Which finding dry clay hearts, their heate needs must
> First harden, and then moulder into dust;
> But waxen hearts with pure and feruent zeale
> They soften, and then fitt them for heauens seale.[3]

---

[1] *Letters*, pp. 192–4.
[2] Johnson, loc. cit., where other examples can also be seen. Donne's original of
this passage is in *Letters*, p. 51.
[3] S.P. (Dom.), James I, S.P. 14/145, no. 12a.

More than a dozen years previously Donne had written to Goodyer:

You know I never fettered nor imprisoned the word Religion; not straightning it Frierly, *ad Religiones factitias*, (as the *Romans* call well their orders of Religion) nor immuring it in a *Rome*, or a *Wittemberg*, or a *Geneva*; they are all virtuall beams of one Sun, and wheresoever they finde clay hearts, they harden them, and moulder them into dust; and they entender and mollifie waxen.[1]

In another letter Donne had specifically warned Goodyer against expressing such sentiments,[2] which were so liberal at the period in which they were written as to be unorthodox, but Goodyer did not hesitate to ventilate them when there was every prospect that the Prince would marry a Spanish princess and wider toleration would be granted to Catholics. Nor is there anywhere sharper proof of the difference in the quality of the minds of the two men than in the contrast between the rather dull prosiness of Goodyer's lines and the vitality of the sentences of Donne which he versified. Doubtless Donne never knew the full extent of borrowings such as this last one, but even if he did he would not for a moment have grudged Goodyer the use of his words. Goodyer's devotion to Donne's superior ability is, indeed, a little touching.

In addition to Donne's verse letter to Goodyer, Goodyer is known to have written one, now lost, to Donne, and once when Donne was staying at Polesworth the two joined together in addressing a poem, which they composed in alternate stanzas,[3] to two ladies whose

---

[1] *Letters*, p. 29. When he was thinking of publishing his poems in 1614, Donne asked Goodyer (ibid., p. 197) whether he had 'ever made any such use of the letter in verse, *A nostre Countesse chez vous*, as that I may not put it in, amongst the rest to persons of that rank'.

[2] Ibid., pp. 100–3.

[3] [Milgate, *Satires etc.*, pp. 76–8], 'A Letter written by Sir H. G. and J. D. *alternis vicibus*'. This poem received the tribute of some verses by Thomas Pestell, who seems to have thought it was written in alternate lines, not alternate stanzas, by the two poets:

On the Interlinearie poëme begott twixt Sr H. Goo:
        & Dr Donne
Here two rich rauisht spirrits kisse & twyne;
Advanc'd, & weddlockt in each others lyne.
Gooderes rare match with only him was blest,
Who haes out donne, & quite vndonne the rest.

(MS. Malone 14, Bodleian Library, p. 28; *Poems of Thomas Pestell*, ed. Hannah Buchan, 1940, p. 28.) Cf. p. 270 below. Goodyer's verse letter is mentioned in *Letters*, p. 87.

names are no longer known. They also exchanged problems, and Donne usually communicated anything he had written to his friend. In his weekly letters (written on Tuesdays) Donne is at pains to present himself as the gentleman of leisure, with all the time in the world for the cultivation of his 'second religion', friendship. 'The memory of friends, (I mean onely for Letters)', he wrote, 'neither enters ordinarily into busied men, because they are ever emploied within, nor into men of pleasure, because they are never at home'; but he who had no fixed occupation could meet all the obligations owed to a friend.[1] And indeed Donne wrote to Goodyer with remarkable regularity, so that these letters were often brief essays on some topic that had engaged his attention, with little or no attempt to communicate news or information. Donne began one such letter by remarking:

I make account that this writing of letters, when it is with any seriousness, is a kind of extasie, and a departure and secession and suspension of the soul, which doth then communicate it self to two bodies: And as I would every day provide for my souls last convoy, though I know not when I shall die, and perchance I shall never die; so for these extasies in letters, I oftentimes deliver my self over in writing when I know not when those letters shall be sent to you, and many times they never are, for I have a little satisfaction in seeing a letter written to you upon my table, though I meet no opportunity of sending it.[2]

Many of these letters, then, were written with full deliberation, but even those which Donne himself admits had to be written in haste were able to draw upon a reservoir of thought and feeling associated in his mind with Goodyer that had the power to raise the letter far above the level of a perfunctory communication merely about matters that could not be neglected.

Goodyer must have been aware just as often as Donne of the gap between their fortunes, but this consciousness was never allowed to affect their relations. When it flooded Donne's mind, it was not (as it might have been) matter for envy; rather, it was

[1] Ibid., pp. 86-7.
[2] Ibid., p. 11. This letter is headed 'To my honoured friend Sr T. Lucey', but seems actually to be for Goodyer.

cause for self-reproach, and it was objectified by more than normal intellectual elaboration:

> Though I know you have many worthy friends of all rankes, yet I adde something, since I which am of none, would fain be your friend too. There is some of the honour and some of the degrees of a Creation, to make a friendship of nothing. Yet, not to annihilate my self utterly (for though it seem humblenesse, yet it is a work of as much almightinesse, to bring a thing to nothing, as from nothing) though I be not of the best stuffe for friendship, which men of warm and durable fortunes only are, I cannot say, that I am not of the best fashion, if truth and honesty be that; which I must ever exercise, towards you, because I learned it of you: for the conversation with worthy men, and of good example, though it sow not vertue in us, yet produceth and ripeneth it.[1]

In another letter, with perhaps a little more detachment, he contrasts their respective ways of life in a passage from which only a few lines can be quoted: 'you living at Court without ambition, which would burn you, or envy, which would devest others, live in the Sun, not in the fire: And I which live in the Country without stupefying, am not in darknesse, but in shadow, which is not no light, but a pallid, waterish, and diluted one.'[2] If Donne was sensitive to the humiliations inherent in his situation, Goodyer on his side was careful not to arouse them, and there is probably no surer proof of the tact which was united to his warmth of heart than the endurance of his friendship with Donne.

Donne's sense of obligation to Goodyer was strong, and was frequently acknowledged. 'I owe you what ever Court friends do for me,' he once wrote, 'yea, whatsoever I do for my self, because you almost importune me, to awake and stare the Court in the face.'[3] Among such debts Donne almost certainly owed to Goodyer his introduction to Lucy, Countess of Bedford, since the Goodyers had long been intimate with the Harrington family, from which Lady Bedford sprang. Born in 1581, she was the daughter of Sir John Harrington of Coombe and Exton. This Sir John was a close friend of the elder Sir Henry Goodyer, and was named by him one of the overseers of his will. The talent and vitality of Lucy Harrington

---

[1] *Letters*, pp. 65–6.   [2] Ibid., pp. 62–3.   [3] Ibid., p. 146.

were sufficiently well known at Polesworth for Michael Drayton to dedicate a poem to her in 1594 and for 'H. G. Esquire' to contribute to the volume a commendatory sonnet which is as much addressed to Lucy Harrington as to the young poet of *Matilda*. Drayton's dedication best suggests the relationships within the group:

Your rarest vertues, (honourable Mistres LUCIE,) have made me, amongst many other competent Judges of your worth, both to love and admire you; but the exceeding kinde affection (which I knowe) the House of POWLESWORTH doe beare you, (a Family where-unto I must confesse, I am both in love and dutie more devote then to any other) hath mooved mee, for a more particuler proofe of that honor which both they and I are willing to doe you, to dedicate my Poeme to your protection.

At the end of this same year, on 12 December 1594, Lucy Harrington, still only thirteen years of age, married Edward Russell, Earl of Bedford, then a young man of twenty-two. Two years later Drayton dedicated his *Mortimeriados* to her, invoking her as 'thou my hope, my Lady, and my Muse', and in *Englands Heroicall Epistles*, which he published in 1597, he dedicated one epistle to her and another to her husband. In the letter to the Earl of Bedford Drayton stated that his patron, the elder Sir Henry Goodyer, had 'bequeathed' him to the Countess's service, although other dedicatory epistles in the same volume to the younger Goodyer and his wife show that he was still on terms of close friendship with the remaining members of the Goodyer family.

The Earl of Bedford indiscreetly permitted himself to become involved in Essex's rebellion and was for a time imprisoned in the Tower. On his release he was confined to his estate of Chenies until after the death of Queen Elizabeth. His wife, however, set out northwards with her parents immediately after Elizabeth's death was known and met the new King and Queen on their journey southwards. Her father was created Lord Harrington, and to him and his wife was entrusted the upbringing of the new King's only daughter, the Princess Elizabeth. Lady Bedford succeeded at once in winning the favour of the new Queen and was appointed one of the Ladies of the Bedchamber. She became, in fact, the closest friend of James I's consort, and from the first took a prominent place in his court. Her husband, on the other hand, though he regained his freedom, never took the position in public life to which by his rank he was entitled, and a fall from his horse in 1612 afflicted him with partial paralysis so that he was not only lame, but stammered badly as well.

From 1603 until about 1620 Lady Bedford was one of the most influential women in England. Twenty-two years of age at the accession of James I, she was at the height of her charm and vivacity. She was, with the Queen, one of the most prominent performers in the brilliant series of masques which Ben Jonson and Inigo Jones designed for the Court during the early years of the reign, and her house was the meeting-place for poets and wits. Goodyer, besides his appointment at Court, seems also to have been attached to the Bedford household: when, it is impossible to say, but certainly by 1605.[1] In 1607, acting for Lady Bedford, he helped to acquire the reversionary lease of Twickenham Park, an estate bordering the Thames which had formerly been occupied by Francis Bacon, but which straitened circumstances obliged him to give up. In the following year both the current and the reversionary leases were transferred to trustees for Lady Bedford,[2] with the result that from 1607 for the next ten years it became her principal home.

It is unknown when Donne was first introduced to Lady Bedford. His earliest reference to the family is in a letter which he wrote while confined to his lodgings after he had confessed to his marriage with Ann More: 'I hope somebody else hath had the ill luck to tell you first that the young Bedford is dead', he wrote on 23 February 1601/2,[3] with reference to the death of Lady Bedford's infant son. This sentence does not, of course, imply that Donne was then acquainted with the Bedfords, but merely that he was aware of Goodyer's friendship with them. The next reference is in a letter from Peckham, perhaps written soon after his return from the Continent with Sir Walter Chute; in it he presents his humble thanks to 'that good Lady' and to Sir John Harrington, Lady Bedford's brother.[4] It

[1] Each Gentleman of the Privy Chamber was in actual attendance on the King for only one-quarter of the year, so that he was free of his duties at Court for the other three-quarters. That Goodyer was also attached to the Bedford household seems clearly implied by Lady Bedford's letter to Cecil, June 1605, *Calendar of the Salisbury MSS.*, xvii. 291.

[2] D. Lysons, *The Environs of London*, iii. 565.

[3] Gosse, i. 109 (Anderdon MS.).   [4] *Letters*, p. 151.

is probable that close relations between Donne and Lady Bedford did not develop until 1607, the year in which she acquired Twickenham Park. From then on she figures constantly in his letters to Goodyer, as it was usually through him that Donne sent messages and enclosures to her, although she was also addressed directly in letters and poems. A number of pieces sent to her by Donne are undoubtedly missing, and the chronology of those which survive is uncertain, but the attempt must be made to trace the probable growth of their relations.

The friendship with Lady Bedford developed with rapidity and fervour. There was a strong element of mutual attraction between them. She possessed, besides rank and wealth, youth and charm as well as wit and an unusual share of intellectual capacity, and all those qualities attracted Donne to her. She, on her side, found something intoxicating in the brilliance of his mind and in the quality of his flattery. The first reference in Donne's correspondence to his tributes to her seems to be in a note written on 31 December 1607 which enclosed a letter to be presented to her 'now, or when the rage of the Mask is past'.[1] The enclosure was possibly the verse letter beginning 'This twilight of two yeares', since it is clearly intended as a New Year's gift for his patroness, and has in it something of the feeling of excitement that accompanies a discovery:

since these times shew'd mee you.

In recompence I would show future times
    What you were, and teach them to'urge towards such.
Verse embalmes vertue;'and Tombs, or Thrones of rimes,
    Preserve fraile transitory fame, as much
    As spice doth bodies from corrupt aires touch.

Lady Bedford was just as eager as Donne to explore all the possibilities of her new friendship, and as anxious to find out all she could about him as he was to celebrate her beauty and virtue. She was at pains, perhaps without his knowledge,[2] to secure a manuscript of his satires, and it came to her accompanied by some verses of Ben Jonson, whose aid she had evidently enlisted to procure the poems:

---

[1] Ibid., p. 204.
[2] [More recently it has been suggested that Donne revised his satires to send to her; see Milgate, *Satires etc.*, pp. lix–lx.]

> LUCY, you brightnesse of our spheare, who are
>   Life of the *Muses* day, their morning-starre!
> If workes (not th'authors) their owne grace should looke,
>   Whose poemes would not wish to be your booke?
> But these, desir'd by you, the makers ends
>   Crowne with their owne. Rare poemes aske rare friends.
> Yet, *Satyres*, since the most of mankind bee
>   Their vn-auoided subject, fewest see:
> For none ere tooke that pleasure in sinnes sense,
>   But, when they heard it tax'd, tooke more offence.
> They, then, that liuing where the matter is bred,
>   Dare for these poemes, yet, both aske, and read,
> And like them too; must needfully, though few,
>   Be of the best: and 'mongst those, best are you.
> LUCY, you brightnesse of our spheare, who are
>   The *Muses* euening, as their morning-starre.

Donne responded to her admiration of the satires by telling her that her influence and example had caused him to renounce satire for religious verse:

> Temples were not demolish'd, though prophane:
> Here *Peter*, *Joves*; there *Paul* hath *Dian's* Fane.
> So whether my hymnes you admit or chuse,
> In me you'have hallowed a Pagan Muse,
> And denizend a stranger, who mistaught
> By blamers of the times they mard, hath sought
> Vertues in corners, which now bravely doe
> Shine in the worlds best part, or all It; You.

Despite her apparent worldliness there was a pietistical strain in Lady Bedford which, as she grew older, became more and more tinged with Puritanism.

Further stages in the ripening of the intimacy can be observed. With a curiosity bordering on jealousy Donne scanned Lady Bedford's actions, observed her household, and delighted in the warmth with which he was received:

> Therefore I study you first in your Saints,
>   Those friends, whom your election glorifies,
> Then in your deeds, accesses, and restraints,
>   And what you reade, and what your selfe devize.

But soone, the reasons why you'are lov'd by all,
  Grow infinite, and so passe reasons reach,
Then backe againe to'implicite faith I fall,
  And rest on what the Catholique voice doth teach;

That you are good: and not one Heretique
  Denies it: if he did, yet you are so;
For, rockes, which high top'd and deep rooted sticke,
  Waves wash, not undermine, nor overthrow.

Lady Bedford sometimes wrote verses herself, and on one occasion in the garden at Twickenham she hesitantly showed some of them to Donne. He was enchanted with them, and on his return home wrote earnestly begging for copies of these poems, promising likewise to keep them secret. About the same time, probably,[1] he sent her the most beautiful of all his verses to her, the epistle beginning 'Madam, You have refin' dmee', which describes her arrival at Twickenham from court, and begs for permission to visit her and pay his respects.

The verses entitled 'Twicknam Garden' which are included among the 'Songs and Sonets' are also probably connected with Lady Bedford. This is a poem of spring. Though the time of year brought him in his soberer moments only melancholy reflections upon his own situation, as when he wrote to Goodyer, 'Because I am in a place and season where I see every thing bud forth, I must do so too . . . [yet] the pleasantnesse of the season displeases me. Every thing refreshes, and I wither, and I grow older and not better, my strength diminishes, and my load growes',[2] yet in writing 'Twicknam Garden' he depicted the dejection of a lover whose love is

---

[1] The letter asking for copies of her poems (*Letters*, p. 67) begins: 'I do not remember that ever I have seen a petition in verse, I would not therefore be singular, nor adde these to your other papers. I have yet adventured so near as to make a petition for verse, it is for those your Ladiship did me the honour to see in *Twicknam* garden, except you repent your making.' Donne's letter is ambiguous; it is itself probably the petition for Lady Bedford's verses, not the 'petition in verse' which accompanied it. This interpretation is borne out by the letter written at the same time to Goodyer, in which he says (ibid., p. 64): 'I send you, with this, a Letter which I sent to the Countesse . . . I also writ to her *Ladiship* for the verses she shewed in the garden.'

That the verses Donne sent were probably those beginning 'Madam, You have refin'd mee,' is suggested by line 33: 'These are *Petitions*, and not *Hymnes*; they sue.'

[2] Ibid., p. 78.

hopeless, using a Petrarchan theme—the contrast of the miserable lover and the life and beauty of the spring. The lady of the poem is referred to throughout in the third person; and the thought of the poem develops consistently until it achieves the climax of the concluding paradox:

> O perverse sexe, where none is true but shee,
> Who's therefore true, because her truth kills mee.

But the incidental references to the garden, the 'True Paradise' with its laughing trees and 'stone fountaine weeping out my yeare', show how profoundly it too had touched Donne's sensibility. The suggestion that he should write upon this theme might, indeed, have come from Lady Bedford herself.[1]

Donne's correspondence shows that during the summer and autumn he was seeing her frequently. As we have seen, she consented to be godmother on 8 August to a newly born daughter of the Donnes and gave the infant her name. It was probably at the time of this visit to Mitcham that Donne happened to refer to some verses he had translated years ago 'at Sea', perhaps during the Islands voyage; Lady Bedford was immediately interested, so he promised that she should see them. But the translation had been long since lost, and he was forced to do the work all over again before he could send it to her.[2] Next month, pausing in London for a few days on his return from a visit to Edward Jones in Essex, he wrote that 'this Tuesday all the Court came to a Christening at *Arondell* house, and stay in town so that I will sup with the good Lady'. Back at Mitcham Donne reported in his next letter that Lady Bedford had returned from Twickenham, and that he had also had a letter from her waiting-woman, Jane Meautys, who a few months later became the bride of Sir William Cornwallis, uncle of Donne's friend. In the November, when the capital was once more thronged with fashionable society, Donne wrote again of going to sup with Lady Bedford. In all these references there is just as much warmth of feeling as in the poems addressed to her; she 'only hath power to cast the fetters of verse upon my free meditations', and 'I would

---

[1] [See the discussion in Gardner, *Elegies etc.*, pp. 249–51.]
[2] *Letters*, pp. 207–8.

write apace to her, whilest it is possible to expresse that which I yet know of her, for by this growth I see how soon she will be ineffable'.[1]

Donne's illness during the winter of 1608/9 probably prevented him from seeing as much of Lady Bedford as he would have wished, but after his recovery the intimacy was renewed on an even closer footing. During 1609 he acted almost as if he were Lady Bedford's officially appointed laureate. On 4 May there died at Twickenham at the age of thirty Bridget, Lady Markham. She was daughter of Sir James Harrington, and therefore Lady Bedford's cousin. She had married Sir Anthony Markham and was one of the Ladies of the Queen's Bedchamber; and, as her epitaph puts it, she was 'inclytae Luciae Comitissae de Bedford sanguine (quod satis) sed et amicitia propinquissima'. Donne supplied an elegy, probably in time for her funeral, which took place on 19 May; frigid and artificial as his lines are, they are not so tortured as those which Francis Beaumont provided for the same occasion. Another of Lady Bedford's close friends died at Twickenham just three months later, on 4 August. This was Cecilia Bulstrode, also one of the Queen's ladies-in-waiting. A few days previously Donne had reported to Goodyer:

I fear earnestly that Mistresse *Bolstrod* will not escape that sicknesse in which she labours at this time. I sent this morning to aske of her passage of this night; and the return is, that she is as I left her yester-night, and then by the strength of her understanding, and voyce, (proportionally to her fashion, which was ever remisse) by the eavennesse and life of her pulse, and by her temper, I could allow her long life, and impute all her sicknesse to her minde. But the History of her sicknesse, makes me justly fear, that she will scarce last so long, as that you when you receive this letter, may do her any good office, in praying for her; for she hath not for many days received so much as a preserved Barbery, but it returnes, and all accompanied with a Fever, the mother, and an extream ill spleen.[2]

At the time of her death Sir Thomas Roe was probably her lover.[3]

---

[1] Ibid., pp. 53–4, 139, 143, 117, 64.   [2] Ibid., pp. 215–16.

[3] Donne wrote in an undated letter to George Garrard:

'I came from thence [London] upon *Thursday*, where I left Sir *Tho. Roe* so indulgent to his sorrow, as it had been an injury to have interrupted it with my unusefull company. I have done nothing of that kinde as your Letter intimates, in the memory of that good Gentlewoman; if I had, I should not finde any better use of it, then to

George Garrard busied himself going about to secure memorial verses; Ben Jonson composed a set while Garrard's servant waited at his door, proclaiming that her name was sufficient to call

> Vp so much truth, as could I it pursue
> Might make the Fable of *Good Women* true.

Yet it was she with whom he had earlier fallen out, and in revenge had written his 'Epigram on the Court Pucell' (*Underwood*, xlix). There, over and above charges of vanity and licentiousness, we learn that Miss Bulstrode had been twice engaged to be married, but had broken off both engagements, and that she versified and passed her verses about among the court wits. Garrard, it seems, also approached Donne for an elegy, which he promised, and then wrote. It is, if anything, even more unfeeling than his lines in memory of Lady Markham. Donne may well have been conscious of this fact, for another elegy has survived, beginning 'Language thou art too narrow', which in most of the early texts is said to have been written on the occasion of Miss Bulstrode's death. Some

put it into your hands. You teach me what I owe her memory; and if I pay that debt so, you have a part and interest in it, by doing me the honour of remembring it: and therefore it must come quickly to you' (*Letters*, p. 39).

Gosse believes that the lady who was mourned by Roe and on whom Donne was asked to write was Lady Markham (i. 232), but it was Garrard who had written to Ben Jonson for an epitaph on Cecilia Bulstrode, and he is likely to have written to Donne for the same purpose. Sir Edward Herbert also supplied memorial verses: 'Epitaph. *Caecil. Boulstr.* quæ post languescentem morbum non sine inquietudine spiritus & conscientiæ obiit.'

If Roe was Miss Bulstrode's lover, light is thrown on an incident that occurred years later during his embassy to India. He had promised to show the Great Mogul some European pictures (miniatures, no doubt) and on 2 Sept. 1616 had an interview with him:

'I showed him two [pictures]. He seemed astonished at one of them; and demanded whose it was. I answered a frend of myne that was dead. Hee asked mee if I would give it to him. I replied that I esteemed it more then any thing I possessed, because it was the image of one that I loved dearly and could never recover: . . . hee confessed hee neuer sawe so much arte, so much bewty, and conjured mee to tell him truly whither ever such a woeman lived. I assuered him ther did one live that this did resemble in all things but perfection, and was now dead' (*The Embassy of Sir Thomas Roe to India, 1615–1619*, ed. Sir William Foster, 1926, pp. 222–3).

Roe's editor rather lamely argues that the picture must have been of Roe's wife, whom he secretly married in 1614, just before leaving England for India, but this is a contradiction of Roe's own statement that the lady represented was dead. [It has also been suggested, on the strength of Sir John Roe's 'Elegie to Mris Boulstred: 1602' (Grierson, i. 410–11), that Miss Bulstrode and Sir John had been lovers. See B. N. De Luna, *Jonson's Romish Plot*, Oxford, 1967, pp. 157 ff.]

further lines also exist, beginning 'Death be not proud'; they are said in some manuscripts to be in memory of Lady Markham, but in others the name of Miss Bulstrode is given, and in two the author-ship is assigned to Lady Bedford herself. They seem to be intended to follow on from Donne's lines on Miss Bulstrode, beginning 'Death I recant',[1] and may be referred to in a letter to Goodyer dated 14 August (1609), where Donne writes: 'in stead of a Letter to you, I send you one to another, to the best Lady, who did me the honour to acknowledge the receit of one of mine, by one of hers.'[2] On the assumption (probably hazardous) that the elegies were enclosed in letters exchanged with Lady Bedford, Donne would here refer to his 'Death I recant', to which Lady Bedford had replied with 'Death be not proud'. However that may be, the exchange of verse letters between Donne and Lady Bedford about this time is suggested by one addressed to her, which begins 'T'have written then, when you writ'. The opening line of this last poem clearly acknowledges a communication of the same kind as the one which Donne is return-ing, and the reference in his poem at lines 67-8 to the 'Two new starres' sent 'lately to the firmament' almost certainly alludes to the deaths of Lady Markham and Cecilia Bulstrode.

In the same year, however, Donne's devotion to Lady Bedford was put to the test. Goodyer was paying a visit to the Countess of Huntingdon (whose husband was a cousin of Lady Bedford), and was to bring her back to London with him. Donne had not seen her since he had left York House after his marriage, but when Goodyer mentioned him to her, her lively interest caused him to write at once to Donne, suggesting that he should address some poetic tribute to her. Donne's response is interesting. He does not refuse to write it, although he protests that Lady Bedford has all his allegiance; he is not even sure that Lady Huntingdon is sufficiently intelligent to appreciate his verses:

For the other part of your Letter, spent in the praise of the Countesse, I am always very apt to beleeve it of her, and can never beleeve it so well, and so reasonably, as now, when it is averred by you; but for the expressing it to her, in that sort as you seem to coun-saile, I have these two reasons to decline it. That that knowledge

---

[1] Cf. Grierson, ii, pp. cxliii–cxlv, 209.   [2] *Letters*, p. 117.

which she hath of me, was in the beginning of a graver course, then of a Poet, into which (that I may also keep my dignity) I would not seem to relapse. The Spanish proverb informes me, that he is a fool which cannot make one Sonnet, and he is mad which makes two. The other stronger reason, is my integrity to the other Countesse, of whose worthinesse though I swallowed your opinion at first upon your words, yet I have had since an explicit faith, and now a knowledge: and for her delight (since she descends to them) I had reserved not only all the verses, which I should make, but all the thoughts of womens worthinesse. But because I hope she will not disdain, that I should write well of her Picture, I have obeyed you thus far, as to write: but intreat you by your friendship, that by this occasion of versifying, I be not traduced, nor esteemed light in that Tribe, and that house where I have lived. If those reasons which moved you to bid me write be not constant in you still, or if you meant not that I should write verses; or if these verses be too bad, or too good, over or under her understanding, and not fit; I pray receive them, as a companion and supplement of this Letter to you.[1]

Donne's verse letter was no doubt presented; it may have been that beginning 'Man to Gods image', which pretty certainly dates from this time. There are, however, no further references in his surviving correspondence to Lady Huntingdon for several years.

Donne had clearly been embarrassed at the thought that if he wrote too effusively to the Countess of Huntingdon he might compromise himself in the eyes of Lady Bedford and lose her friendship. Nevertheless it is to be feared that from time to time he addressed himself to other ladies with equal fervour. Shortly before the growth of his intimacy with Lady Bedford he had made or (more probably) renewed his acquaintance with Mrs. Herbert, and soon became a frequent visitor at her town house near Charing Cross. By the time

[1] In *Letters*, p. 225, Donne refers to Goodyer's projected trip to escort Lady Huntingdon; the passage quoted is from ibid., pp. 103–5. Neither letter is dated, but the two letters are clearly close together in time, and the second refers to 'a Christning at *Peckam*'. Anne, daughter of Sir Thomas Grymes, was baptized on 30 Dec. 1615; Mrs. Donne was presumably the godmother. This fact seems to have caused Gosse to date the letter 1615, but it is most unlikely, from its contents, that it should have been written after Donne's ordination. Other Grymes children were baptized as follows: Martha, on 4 Oct. 1607; Arthur, on 29 Jan. 1609; and Thomas, on 28 June 1610 (W. H. Blanch, *Y^e Parish of Camerwell*, 1875, pp. 54–5). 1607 seems too early for the letter, and 1610 too late, so that 1609 is the likeliest year.

the fashionable world left London for the summer of 1607, Donne
had promised to keep in touch with her by letter. Walton claimed
to possess a considerable number of the letters they exchanged, but
he printed only four, all of which belong to the early stages of the
friendship.[1] In the three letters that belong unquestionably to the
summer of 1607 the reader is disconcerted to discover that Donne's
tone is playfully arch: 'By my troth, as desperate and perplexed men,
grow from thence bold; so must I take the boldness of accusing you,
who would draw so dark a Curtain betwixt me and your purposes,
as that I had no glimmering, neither of your goings, nor the way
which my Letters might haunt', he wrote in the first. As a result,
his flattery seems intended to appear deliberately exaggerated:
'you, who are not only a World alone, but the Monarchy of the
World', and 'the greatest vertue in the World, which is you'. Mrs.
Herbert was no doubt intended to take it all with a grain of salt if
she was as intelligent a woman as Donne believed her to be. In the
fourth letter, however (which Walton inserted in the body of the
Life of George Herbert), Donne's tone is much more genuine; he had
just returned to Mitcham from London, where he had been the
recipient of Mrs. Herbert's favours, to find further gifts for himself
and his wife awaiting his return. As Walton observed, 'in this time
she prov'd one of his most bountiful Benefactors'.

Madam,

Your Favours to me are every where; I use them, and have them. I
enjoy them at *London*, and leave them there; and yet find them at
Micham: such Riddles as these become things unexpressible; and such
is your goodness. I was almost sorry to find your Servant here this
day, because I was loth to have any witness of my not coming home
last Night, and indeed of my coming this Morning: But my not
coming was excusable, because earnest business detein'd me; and my
coming this day, is by the example of your St. *Mary Magdalen*, who

[1] One is given in the text of, and the other three in an appendix to *The Life of George
Herbert*. The three in the appendix form a clear sequence, and are dated 11 July,
23 July, and 2 Aug. 1607. The letter in the text is dated, like the first of the other
group, 11 July 1607, but this date must be incorrect, since the letter states that it
was written on a Sunday and 11 July 1607 was not a Sunday. H. W. Garrod, in 'Donne
and Mrs. Herbert', *RES*, xxi (1945), 161–73, attempted without much success to
amend the date. The likeliest explanation is that, as in *The Life of Donne*, Walton
simply clapped a date on the end of the letter where there was originally none. [See,
however, Gardner, *Elegies etc.*, p. 252.]

rose early upon *Sunday*, to seek that which she lov'd most; and so did
I. And from her and my self, I return such thanks as are due to one
to whom we owe all the good opinion, that they whom we need most,
have of us—by this Messenger, and on this good day, I commit the
inclosed *Holy Hymns* and *Sonnets* (which for the matter, not the workmanship, have yet escap'd the fire) to your judgment, and to your
protection too, if you think them worthy of it; and I have appointed
this inclosed *Sonnet* to usher them to your happy hand.

Micham,   *Your unworthiest Servant,*
    July 11.   *unless your accepting him to be so,*
    1607.   *have mended him.*
                                            JO. DONNE.

'These *Hymns*', Walton adds, 'are now lost to us; but doubtless they
were such, as they two now sing in *Heaven*.' Nevertheless, the sonnet enclosed, which Walton printed, seems clearly to refer to the
group of sonnets entitled 'La Corona', and is now always printed
with them.

Walton was at pains to insist that the friendship between Donne
and Mrs. Herbert 'was not an *Amity* that polluted their Souls'. His
first acquaintance with her was probably made (as Walton says) at
Oxford, perhaps in 1599, and the Elegy 'The Autumnall' may well
have been a complimentary poem inspired by their first meeting. It
has been suggested that some of the 'Songs and Sonets' were also
addressed to her;[1] they occur together in the edition of the *Poems*
in 1633 and in some groups of manuscripts, and may therefore
have been associated with the same person. These lyrics are 'The
Funerall', 'The Blossome', 'The Primrose', and 'The Relique', and
their connection with Magdalen Herbert may be indicated by a
line (17) in 'The Relique', 'Thou shalt be'a Mary Magdalen'. Such
an interpretation is suggested by the letter just quoted, in which
Donne refers to 'the example of your St. Mary Magdalen', and by
the accompanying sonnet with its advice:

> so much good there is
> Deliver'd of her, that some Fathers be
> Loth to believe one Woman could do this;
> But, think these *Magdalens* were two or three.

---

[1] See Grierson, ii, pp. xxii–xxv, 9–10, 48.

Increase their number, *Lady*, and their fame:
To their *Devotion*, add your *Innocence*;
Take so much of th'example, as of the name;
The latter half.

That 'The Primrose' is associated with Mrs. Herbert is also suggested by its title in some versions: 'The Primrose, being at Montgomery Castle, upon the hill, on which it is situate'; and Montgomery Castle was the seat of Sir Edward Herbert.[1] The case for linking the four lyrics with his mother is, however, too tenuous to be sustained. Their occurrence together in the texts can be explained more plausibly on other grounds; and no one has supposed that a fifth lyric, 'The Dampe', often grouped with these four, could possibly have been addressed to, or could have any connection with, Mrs. Herbert. 'The Primrose', furthermore, seems much more likely to have been written for the benefit of Sir Edward Herbert than as a complimentary address to his mother.[2] There can be little doubt, however, that the verse letter 'To Mrs M. H.' was sent to her. Donne had learnt that Mrs. Herbert had resolved to remarry, though as yet, apparently, no public announcement had been made. His concluding lines show his wish that the friendship may not be broken, but that it may include Mrs. Herbert's new husband as well as herself:

so much I doe love her choyce, that I
Would faine love him that shall be lov'd of her.

This poem therefore belongs to the winter of 1608/9, since Magdalen Herbert married young Sir John Danvers in February 1609.[3]

[1] Sidney Lee, in his edition of Herbert's *Autobiography*, pointed out that on 9 Feb. 1606/7 Montgomery Castle, which the Herberts had held as constables for the Crown, was granted by James I to the newly created Earl of Montgomery, who on 11 July 1613 sold it back to Sir Edward Herbert for the comparatively small sum of £500. It is doubtful, however, if the castle was ever out of Sir Edward Herbert's occupancy; after the grant to the Earl of Montgomery he presumably stayed on as tenant until he bought it. Both Lord Salisbury and a certain John Bright expected to find him there in 1608 (Garrod, loc. cit., p. 168), and on 7 Apr. 1613, two months before Sir Edward Herbert bought it, Donne was staying there as his guest and wrote from the Castle to Sir Robert Harley.

[2] [See the discussion in Gardner, *Elegies etc.*, pp. 255–8.]

[3] 'Young Davers is likewise wedded to the widow Herbert (mother to Sir Edward) of more then twise his age' (Chamberlain to Carleton, 3 Mar. 1608/9, *Letters*, i. 288). The marriage had presumably occurred since Chamberlain's previous letter to Carleton, which is dated 21 Feb.

The friendship survived Mrs. Herbert's second marriage, and lasted until her death, but Walton's parsimony in printing Donne's letters to her makes it impossible to follow it through all its stages.

A little more, though only a little more, is known about Donne's relations with her eldest son, Sir Edward Herbert, afterwards Lord Herbert of Cherbury, who merits the title of Donne's first poetic disciple. There is a very interesting passage in Herbert's earliest surviving letter, written from the country, shortly before he attained his majority, to his guardian, Sir George More:

Least you should think this countrey ruder then it is, I have sent you some of our bread, which I am sure wilbe dainty, howsoever it be not pleasinge: it is a kinde of cake which our countrey people use and made in no place in England, but in Shrewsbury, yf you vouch safe the tast of them, you enworthy the countrey and sender. Measure not my love by substance of it, which is brittle; but by the forme of it, which is circular, and *circulus* you knowe is *capacissima figura*, to which that mind ought to bee like, that can most worthily love you. Yet I would not have you to understand forme so as though it were hereby *formall*: but, as *forma dat esse*, so my love and observance to be essential.[1]

Here, if anywhere, was a mind that moved and thought as Donne's did, and it is unfortunate that we do not know whether Donne and Herbert were acquainted by 17 August 1602, the date of this letter. Is Herbert affecting a mannerism picked up from Donne, or is he expressing a turn of mind as individual to him as to Donne? Or was it something in the air to which Donne, as writers of genius often do, had been the first to give literary expression? Either Herbert had already felt Donne's influence, or was ready in an exceptional degree to receive it.

From about 1606 onwards[2] Edward Herbert began to mix in literary as well as social circles in London. When in town he still resided with his mother at her house near Charing Cross, and when Donne began to visit her frequently the two men had every opportunity of becoming well acquainted. By 1608 Herbert was also on familiar terms with Ben Jonson. In that year he made his first

[1] Kempe, p. 355.

[2] M. M. Rossi, *La vita, le opere, i tempi di Edoardo Herbert di Cherbury* (Florence, 1947), i. 74 and n.

sojourn in France, and towards the end of the summer he wrote two Donnian satires at the Duc de Montmorency's château of Mello, where he was on a visit. The second is addressed to Ben Jonson; the first, on 'The State Progress of Ill', was probably sent to Donne.[1] Certainly Donne recalled these verses two years later, when Herbert had gone abroad again to take part as a volunteer in the siege of Juliers. Herbert had concluded his satire with the couplet:

> The World, as in the Ark of *Noah*, rests,
> Compos'd as then, few Men, and many Beasts;

in his lines 'To Sir Edward Herbert, at Julyers' Donne transfers the image from the greater world to the microcosm and develops it during the first eighteen lines of the poem. In his fantastic elaboration of the idea of man as a Noah's ark Donne is almost certainly only half serious. If, as he told Ben Jonson, 'he wrott that Epitaph on Prince Henry Look to me Fath to match Sir Ed: Herbert in obscurenesse', he can be expected to have made fun occasionally of Herbert elsewhere, and it is difficult not to believe that he is doing so here. Donne was sufficiently fond of Herbert to write to him on the day of his ordination to tell him the news, but there was in Herbert, as his *Autobiography* reveals, the same combination of the sober and the fantastical as Shakespeare's two Welshmen, Glendower and Fluellen, both possessed, and Donne, for all his Welsh ancestry, could not resist the temptation sometimes to laugh at it.

Herbert in his *Autobiography* relates how on his return from Juliers the Earl of Dorset introduced himself to him. This hero-worshipping young nobleman was apparently also an admirer of Donne, but had made his acquaintance somewhat earlier, since a dedicatory poem survives which accompanied six of the 'Holy Sonnets' sent to him by the poet. Donne, however, was probably indebted to Herbert for his acquaintance with Sir Robert Harley, whose wife was a cousin of Herbert, and through Herbert began or renewed an acquaintance with Sir Thomas Lucy of Charlecote. A number of the *Letters to Severall Persons* are addressed to Lucy, though recent scholarship has deprived him of almost all of them and declared that they were

---

[1] D. A. Keister, 'Donne and Herbert of Cherbury: an Exchange of Verses', *MLQ*, viii (1947), 430–4.

actually addressed to Goodyer. The use of Lucy's name in the volume can probably be taken as evidence that the younger Donne, who edited it, was aware of his father's friendship with Lucy and knew that letters had passed between them, even though he was unable to include them in the book.[1]

Another acquaintance Donne perhaps made through the Herberts was Bridget White, daughter of John White of Southwick, Hampshire, who spent the spring of 1610 in London. She returned home about midsummer, and before the end of the year married Sir Henry Kingsmill, the son and heir of a neighbouring squire. Four letters to her occupy a place of honour at the beginning of the *Letters to Severall Persons*. Two, written on 29 June soon after her departure, refer to earlier letters which had evidently gone astray; the third was written a little later but lay on Donne's table for months, awaiting a bearer. Meanwhile Donne's mind was otherwise occupied, and not until 8 November did he find time to scribble a note to accompany the neglected letter to its destination. The second letter of the series is the most charming, and illustrates the heights of ingenious flattery to which Donne could be stimulated by a pretty and lively girl:

Madame,

I could make some guesse whether souls that go to heaven, retain any memory of us that stay behinde, if I knew whether you ever thought of us, since you enjoyed your heaven, which is your self, at home. Your going away hath made *London* a dead carkasse. A Tearm, and a Court do a little spice and embalme it, and keep it from putrefaction, but the soul went away in you: and I think the onely reason why the plague is somewhat slackned, is, because the place is dead already, and no body left worth the killing. Wheresoever you are, there is *London* enough: and it is a diminishing of you to say so, since you are more then the rest of the world. When you have a desire to work a miracle, you will return hither, and raise the place from the dead, and the dead that are in it; of which I am one, but that a hope that I have a room in your favour keeps me alive; which you shall

---

[1] Note also that Mistress Bridget Dunch, to whom *Letters to Severall Persons* was dedicated, was a grand-daughter of Donne's Sir Thomas Lucy, and it was especially appropriate that her grandfather should be represented among Donne's correspondents.

abundantly confirme to me, if by one letter you tell me, that you have received my six; for now my letters are grown to that bulk, that I may divide them like *Amadis* the *Gaules* book, and tell you, that this is the first letter of the second part of the first book.

Strand S. Peters   *Your humblest, and affectionate*
  day at nine.   *servant* J. D.

We learn from a letter from France belonging to the early part of 1612[1] that Donne continued to write to her after her marriage, but nothing further is known of their relations until 1624, when Donne wrote her a long letter of consolation on the death of her husband.[2]

Another group of friends, whom Donne shared with Goodyer, is mentioned in the autobiography of Sir Toby Mathew. In 1606 Mathew had become converted to Catholicism at Florence. That a bishop's son should thus desert his father's faith was cause for grave scandal; yet Mathew, on his return to England in 1607, openly admitted his conversion. The Archbishop of Canterbury himself reasoned with him and, when he proved obdurate, committed him to the Fleet. He remained in prison for about six months, but was eventually given his freedom to put his affairs in order and depart from the kingdom, which he did in April 1608. During his imprisonment, he relates,

I had very many friends, who, out of courtesy, and much acquaintance, and some others also, who, out of curiosity, came to visit me

---

[1] *Letters*, p. 263.

[2] Ibid., pp. 7–10. Rossi, i. 169–73, believes that Bridget White was the lady, 'the fairest of her time', with whom Sir Edward Herbert confesses he was in love (*Autobiography*, ed. Lee, p. 70). This is no more than a guess, based no doubt on the fact that Donne informs her in the first of his four letters (*Letters*, p. 3) that Herbert has just recovered from a fever. Since Herbert also states that after his return from Juliers he suffered from a fever that almost proved fatal, Rossi would date this letter, and the one quoted in full above (which was written later on the same day) 1611. But by St. Peter's day (29 June) 1611 Bridget White was Lady Kingsmill, and the reference to the plague in the letter would be appropriate enough in 1609 or 1610, but much less so in 1611.

Rossi seems unwilling to consider 1610 as a possible date because he apparently believes (i. 147) that Herbert left for Juliers in April of that year, or very soon afterwards. But the siege did not begin until 17 July, and Herbert states in the *Autobiography* that when he arrived the siege had already begun. Donne's reference on 29 June to his recent recovery, presumably in London, from a fever is therefore not inconsistent with the year 1610. That the third letter was written a short time afterwards is clear from the reference to the fact that the lady's brother has departed for Cleves (in which Juliers lay), possibly in the company of Herbert.

very often; and particularly Sir Maurice Barkley, Sir Edwin Sands, Sir Henry Goodyear, Mr. Richard Martin, and Mr. John Dunne, besides a thousand others. I lived with them all in great love; and ordinarily there was no set discourse of religion. . . .

Sir Henry Goodyear was ever pleasant and kind, and gave me much of his sweet conversation; and he would ingenuously confess whensoever in discourse he thought I had the better reason of the two. But if his constancy had been as great as his nature was good, he had been much happier in both worlds. Both Dunne and Martin were very full of kindness to me at that time, though it continued not to be hearty afterward. By their discourses with me, when I was in prison, I found that they were mere libertines in themselves; and that the thing for which they could not long endure me was because they thought me too saucy, for presuming to show them the right way, in which they liked not then to go, and wherein they would disdain to follow any other. . . .

Captain Whitlock came also often to see me, and would be talking to me like a madman, as he was, both profanely against piety, and licentiously against modesty; though he did it after so jolly and witty a manner that he would tempt a man almost to forgive him even in spite of his heart. I answered as I thought fit, and asked him once withal what security he could have that the earth would not shrink under him, that so he might be swallowed up into hell, as he went drolling, and fooling, and blaspheming, up and down the world, both against the Catholic faith, from which he was not wholly a stranger, as having been long bred in France, as also against the modesty of virtuous minds. . . .

But now, before I passed the sea, I was delivered out of the Fleet, and committed for some two months to the house of a most noble, civil friend of mine, Mr. Edward Jones, for the more easy despatch of my domestical affairs. I was visited there daily by a multitude of persons, and, now and then, I was vexed a little (and it was but a little) by men who would be talking to me of religion.[1]

Most of the members of this group are mentioned in Donne's correspondence with Goodyer. In one letter, dated 14 March 1607/8, he conjectured, when he 'knew how near M. *Mathews* day of

---

[1] *A True Historical Relation of the Conversion of Sir Tobie Matthew to the Holy Catholic Faith; with the Antecedents and Consequences Thereof*, ed. A. H. Mathew, 1904, pp. 85, 86, 90–1, 121.

departing this kingdome was', that Goodyer would soon be back in town; in another, written about six months later, he describes the sudden death of Edmund Whitelocke and mentions a number of their common friends:

I came this evening from M. *Jones* his house in *Essex*, where M. *Martin* hath been, and left a relation of Captain *Whitcocks* [*sic*] death, perchance it is no news to you, but it was to me; without doubt want broke him; for when M. *Hollands* company by reason of the plague broke, the Captain sought to be at M^ris. *Jones* house, who in her husbands absence declining it, he went in the night, his boy carrying his cloakbag, on foot to the Lord of *Sussex*, who going next day to hunt, the Captain not then sick, told him he would see him no more. A Chaplain came up to him, to whom he delivered an account of his understanding, and I hope, of his beliefe, and soon after dyed; and my Lord hath buryed him with his own Ancestors. Perchance his life needed a longer sicknesse, but a man may go faster and safer, when he enjoyes that day light of a clear and sound understanding, then in the night or twilight of an ague or other disease. And the grace of Almighty God doth every thing suddenly and hastily, but depart from us, it inlightens us, warms us, heats us, ravishes us, at once. Such a medicin, I fear, his inconsideration needed; and I hope as confidently that he had it. As our soul is infused when it is created, and created when it is infused, so at her going out, Gods mercy is had by asking, and that is asked by having.[1]

The tone of Donne's comments should be compared with Mathew's; Donne, it is true, tells less about Whitelocke, but in human tolerance and in essential seriousness he is greatly superior to Mathew. Nothing could more effectively refute the charge that he was at this time a 'mere libertine'.

Of the group that visited Toby Mathew in the Fleet, two need further comment. Sir Edwin Sandys was the son of a former Archbishop of York; in his youth he was a devoted pupil of Richard Hooker at Oxford; in his later years he was one of the most active and far-sighted of the group of adventurers who established the

---

[1] *Letters*, pp. 140, 52–3. Another account of Whitelocke's death occurs in a letter of Carleton to Chamberlain, dated 8 Sept. 1608, among the State Papers. There is also a fairly full account of Whitelocke by his brother in the *Liber Famelicus of Sir James Whitelocke*, Camden Society, 1858, pp. 7–11.

colony of Virginia. Richard Martin was a somewhat more frivolous character. Though he had a fairly successful career at the bar and eventually became Recorder of London, his principal renown among his contemporaries was as a wit. A member of the Middle Temple, he was the victim of the assault at dinner in the hall which led to the expulsion of John Davies and the composition of *Nosce Teipsum*; he was also the acknowledged leader in all revels within the Temple. Sandys was the older of the two men, immersed in public affairs, but Martin never lost an opportunity for convivial gaiety.

A number of the same names occur again in rather unexpected company. Even after his imprisonment in the Tower, the Earl of Northumberland's alleged complicity in the Gunpowder Plot was not allowed to drop. As late as 1611 a certain Timothy Elkes was asserting that Captain Whitelocke, the Earl's retainer now dead, had had special knowledge of the Earl's actions on that famous 5 November, and that his most intimate friends and associates should be examined to substantiate the writer's charges against the Earl. Among those who were 'much conversant with Whitlocke' are mentioned 'Henego Jhones', 'Mr. Martin of the temple', Sir Henry Goodyer, Mr. Ingram 'of the custome house', and Thomas Hariot the mathematician.[1] Apparently nothing came of Elkes's accusations, but all those whose names were mentioned were friends of Donne, even Arthur Ingram the financier, and nearly all of them belonged to a convivial group of which Donne was also a member.

These men, and others, are presented in a Latin poem which survives in several manuscripts and is entitled 'Convivium philosophicum tentum in clauso termini Sti. Michaelis in crastino festi Sancti Egidii in Campis, authore Domino Radolpho Colfabio Aeneonasensi'.[2] The authorship of the piece is uncertain, though an English version was made by John Reynolds, Fellow of New College. The

[1] S.P. 14, James I, vol. 66, no. 28.
[2] The text and translation are printed in Aubrey's *Brief Lives*, ed. A. Clark, ii. 50–3, and in John Hoskyns's *Life, Letters and Writings*, ed. Louise B. Osborn, pp. 196–9 and 288–91. Radolphus Colfabius of Brasenose College is unidentifiable. The manuscript of the poem in the handwriting of John Chamberlain among the State Papers is endorsed 'Latin Rimes of Tom Coryat', but 'of' means *about* and not *by* Coryate. Two other manuscripts name Hoskyns as the author, but he was of New College and not of Brasenose.

poem celebrates a gathering held at the Mitre Tavern,[1] probably in
the latter part of 1611.[2] In boisterous dog-Latin rhymes the author
puns on the names of the feasters, and then launches into a long
comic eulogy of Thomas Coryate, which occupies more than half
of the poem. Besides Coryate, the guests, in the order in which they
are mentioned, were Christopher Brooke, Donne, Lionel Cranfield
(afterwards Earl of Middlesex), Arthur Ingram (financier and Secretary of the Council of the North),[3] Sir Robert Phelips (son of the
Master of the Rolls), Sir Henry Neville (later Lord Abergavenny),
Richard Connock (a member of the household of Prince Henry),
John Hoskyns, Richard Martin (both of the Middle Temple), Sir
Henry Goodyer, John West (secondary to the King's Remem-
brancer in the Exchequer), Hugh Holland (recusant and poet), and
Inigo Jones. The group were presumably members of a club, since a
fine of forty pence was levied for non-attendance at the feast. As has

[1] There were several taverns of this name in London, but the Mitre in Fleet Street
is specified in the Duke of Rutland's manuscript; see Hist. MSS. Com. Rep., ii. 318.
This is as one would expect, since the Mitre in Fleet Street is in the heart of the legal
district of London; the celebration took place at the end of term, and a number of the
feasters were barristers.

[2] See I. A. Shapiro, 'The "Mermaid" Club', *MLR*, xlv (1950), 6–17, at p. 7, n. 3.
The month and day of the gathering are uncertain. 'The feast of St. Giles in the
Fields' is a jest, the point of which is now lost. Michaelmas Term usually
extended from 6 Oct. to 28 Nov.

[3] The most important stanza reads:

> Veniet, sed lente currens
> Christopherus vocatus Torrens
>   Et Johannes Factus,
> Gruicampus et Arthurus,
> Ante coenam non pransurus
>   Veniet primo exactus.

This was Englished as

> There will come, though scarcely current
> Christopherus surnamed Torrent,
>   And John ycleped Made,
> And Arthur Meadow-pigmies-foe,
> To sup, his dinner will foregoe,
>   Will come as soon as bade.

Gruicampus is, of course, Cranfield, but the translator does not seem to have realized
that 'Arthurus' was a separate person, Arthur Ingram (Cranfield's Christian name
was Lionel). Cranfield and Ingram were frequently involved together in business
transactions, and from time to time were aided in a subordinate capacity by Sir
Robert Phelips, Christopher Brooke, William Hakewill, and Richard Martin (see,
for instance, Hist. MSS. Com., *Calendar of MSS. of Lord Sackville at Knole*, i. 100 and
271).

been pointed out,[1] the group was not primarily literary in its interests; the majority of the members belonged to the Inns of Court, and a number of them had links with Prince Henry's household. Since Coryate, as the poem shows, was the member who provided most mirth for the others, it is not surprising that they rallied to his aid in commending the *Crudities*. Only three of them (Ingram, Connock, and West) did not supply Coryate with verses. Coryate relates that Prince Henry on hearing the poems commanded their publication; accordingly Coryate published them in *The Odcombian Banquet* (1611) as a sort of preliminary puff, and again in the *Crudities* itself. The members of the club were not, of course, the only contributors; their verses were intermingled with those of Coryate's other contributing friends, the order being that of social precedence. Other friends of Donne occur here too. John Davies of Hereford (who addressed Donne in an epigram and paid him the compliment of imitation) must have made his acquaintance not long before this time.[2] Richard Baddeley, secretary of Dean Morton and subsequently his biographer, appears here too, as does the French Protestant Jean L'Oiseau de Tourval, who afterwards became an Anglican clergyman and received a legacy in Donne's will.[3]

Through all the verses addressed to Coryate runs a note of extravagant chaffing. Donne, for example, showered mock-praises upon the *Crudities*. The book, he alleged, was an

> Infinite worke, which doth so farre extend,
> That none can study it to any end.
> 'Tis no one thing; it is not fruite, nor roote;
> Nor poorely limited with head or foote.
> In man be therefore man, because he can
> Reason, and laugh, thy booke doth halfe make man.
> One halfe being made, thy modesty was such,
> That thou on th'other halfe wouldst never touch.

---

[1] Shapiro, loc. cit.

[2] Davies, though of humbler station (he was a writing master by profession), was on the edge of this circle. Besides Coryate he addresses poems in his *Scourge of Folly* to Martin, Donne, Sir Edward Herbert, Sir Thomas Lucy, Ben Jonson, Inigo Jones, Hoskyns, and William Hakewill.

[3] On de Tourval see below, pp. 488–9.

Even when dismembered by shopkeepers for wrapping-paper, the book will still do good:

> Some shall wrap pils, and save a friends life so,
> Some shall stop muskets, and so kill a foe.

Not since the period of the fourth Satire had Donne given such a brilliant display of wit and high spirits.[1]

Before the end of 1612 Coryate set off on another journey from which he never returned. He sent home various letters from India, however, which found their way into print not long afterwards. In 1616 four of these (all written in the previous year) were published as *Thomas Coriate Traveller for the English wits: Greeting*. The first letter is to Sir Edward Phelips, father of Sir Robert and himself the son of Coryate's godfather; its conclusion is interesting for the list of friends to whom Coryate would be remembered. He recommends himself to

your Honour, and vertuous Lady, your well-beloued Sonne and Heir-apparant, Sir *Robert*, (to whom I haue written a few times also) & his sweet Lady; M. *Martin* also, M. *Christopher Brooke*, whom I thanke still for his no lesse elegant then serious verses: M. *Equinoctiall Pasticrust* [Hoskyns] of the middle Temple, M. *William Hackwell*, and the rest of the worthy gentlemen frequenting your Honourable table.

The second letter is addressed to Sir Edward Phelips's secretary, Lawrence Whitaker, one of Coryate's closest friends, and the leading spirit in collecting the verses that formed *The Odcombian Banquet*; in it Coryate sends remembrances to Richard Martin, Hugh Holland, Inigo Jones, and, in a postscript, to Ben Jonson. The third letter is the most important; it is addressed 'To the High Seneschall of the right Worshipfull Fraternitie of Sireniacal Gentlemen, that meet the first Fridaie of euery Moneth, at the signe of the Mere-Maide in Bread-streete in London', and in its postscript contains the fullest list of friends to whom Coryate sent his greetings. Lawrence Whitaker, it is clear, was the 'seneschal' of the 'Sireniacal Gentle-men' (apparently so named because of their association with the

---

[1] Another set of verses signed 'John Dones' has sometimes been attributed to Donne, but the orthography is against such an ascription. Donne is remarkably consistent (even though others were not) in the spelling of his name.

Mermaid), but to what extent those in the list at the end were members of this group is uncertain; some certainly were not, others probably were. Those mentioned who may have been include Sir Robert Cotton, Donne, Martin, Christopher Brooke, Hoskyns, George Garrard, William Hakewill, Ben Jonson, Inigo Jones, Hugh Holland, and possibly Thomas Bond.[1] Of Donne, 'the author of two most elegant Latine Bookes, *Pseudo-Martyr*, and *Ignatij Conclaue*' (it is clear that Coryate had not read the first of these), it is related that he is to be found at 'his abode either in the Strand, or elsewhere in London; I thinke you shall bee easily informed by the meanes of my friend, M. *L. W.*', while of George Garrard's whereabouts 'you shal vnderstand by Master *Donne* aforesaide'.[2]

These lists of names, so similar to one another, unquestionably give information about Donne's associates in his more convivial moments. Some of them, of course, like Christopher Brooke, were friends of long standing; others, such as Arthur Ingram, were perhaps more recent acquaintances. What is less certain is whether the group that dined at the Mitre is identical with the 'Worshipfull Fraternitie of Sireniacal Gentlemen, that meet the first Fridaie of euery Moneth, at the signe of the Mere-Maide'. Since so many of the feasters at the Mitre supplied encomiums for Coryate's *Crudities*, and since the 'Sireniacal Gentlemen' banded together to furnish Coryate with a magnificent safe-conduct when he set out again on his travels in 1612, it is quite likely that they were one and the same. Nevertheless Lawrence Whitaker, seneschal of the sireniacal gentlemen, was not one of the Mitre feasters, so it is possible that, in spite of the overlapping membership, these are the records of not one but two convivial clubs. In any case it by no means follows that these were the gatherings of poets at the Mermaid immortalized first by Beaumont and later by Keats, or that Donne was present at the wit-combats between Shakespeare and Ben Jonson of which Fuller makes mention. Various dining clubs doubtless met at the Mermaid, and Coryate's sireniacal friends were only one such group. That so clubbable a man as Ben Jonson belonged only to a single one would

---

[1] The last is misnamed John Bond, but Donne's successor as secretary to the Lord Chancellor is probably intended. This letter appears also in *Purchas his Pilgrimes*, 1625, p. 597.
[2] pp. 44–5.

be surprising; it would be equally surprising if Donne's social relations had followed a pattern identical with Ben's.

A letter of Donne to Sir Henry Goodyer, written from France
early in 1612, is in the same vein of fooling as the Mitre feasters
amused themselves with, and may well have been intended for the
amusement of the sireniacal gentlemen. Donne sends 'the first
knowledge, of two millions confiscated to the Crown of England';
his friends will be able to share the percentage granted by way of
reward. William Fowler, Martin, Brooke, Hakewill, George Garrard, Inigo Jones, and Sir Robert Cotton are all mentioned by name.[1]
But the letter is a heavy-handed piece of work, altogether lacking
the verve of the lines to Coryate.

Most of the members of the Mitre and Mermaid circles were
capable of occasional verses, such as those they contributed to
Coryate's *Crudities*, and several of them, such as Christopher Brooke
and John Hoskyns, were minor poets of some quality. But they were
not professional men of letters. Besides Donne, the only literary
figure of major importance whom Coryate mentions was Ben Jonson, and that the friendship between Donne and Jonson was of long
standing is attested by several pieces of evidence. In 1607 Donne
supplied commendatory verses for *Volpone* addressed 'Amicissimo et
meritissimo Ben. Jonson', and in pointed hendecasyllabics he told
Ben such things as his friend most wanted to hear:

> Priscis, ingenium facit, laborque
> Te parem; hos superes, ut et futuros,
> Ex nostra vitiositate sumas,
> Qua priscos superamus, et futuros.

Donne's poetical tribute was generously answered by Ben, who
expressed his admiration of Donne several times in his Epigrams.
Donne is like himself, he feels, in seeking the praises of the select
few; this is part of the theme of the Epigram 'To John Donne', and of
that already quoted, 'To Lucy, Countesse of Bedford, with Mr.
Donnes *Satyres*'. In Epigram 23 his admiration finds fullest expression:

> DONNE, the delight of PHŒBVS, and each *Muse*,
> 'Who, to thy one, all other braines refuse;

<hr>

[1] *Letters*, pp. 54–6.

Whose euery worke, of thy most earely wit,
　　Came forth example, and remaines so, yet:
Longer a knowing, then most wits doe liue.
　　And which no'affection praise enough can giue!
To it, thy language, letters, arts, best life,
　　Which might with halfe mankind maintayne a strife.
All which I meant to praise, and, yet, I would;
　　But leaue, because I cannot as I should!

The other epigram to Donne shows that in addition Jonson esteemed him highly as a critic, and submitted epigrams to him for his approval or correction. He paid him a still higher compliment in the preface, in dialogue form, to his translation of Horace's *Ars Poetica*. Though the dialogue is lost—for it was doubtless destroyed in one of those fires which ravaged Jonson's library—he told Drummond of Hawthornden that by Criticus, one of the principal interlocutors, he intended Donne. The dialogue also contained an apology for *Bartholomew Fair*, so it was presumably written after 31 October 1614, when the play was first performed. As Donne was probably in orders by the time the dialogue was complete, he can scarcely have been much concerned over the fortunes of the play, and the portrait of him in the dialogue must obviously have been based on recollections of earlier years.

A letter written by Jonson to Donne has also happened to survive.[1] It shows that on one occasion Donne intervened to soothe Ben's ruffled feelings when he felt that he had been misrepresented to the Countess of Bedford; Jonson had sufficient respect for Donne to allow himself to be persuaded even against his better judgement to hold his peace and repress his resentment. Another passage, this time in one of Donne's letters, shows that some of Ben's friends were just as touchy as he, and that once again Donne had to act as mediator:

I did your Commandement with Mr. Johnson; both our interests in him needed not to have been ymployed in it. There was nothing obnoxious, but the very name, and he hath Chaunged that. If vpon haveing red it before to diverse, it should be spoken that the person

---

[1] *Tobie Mathew Collection*, p. 328. [See also B. N. De Luna, *Jonson's Romish Plot*, pp. 155–6.]

was concerned in it, he sees not how Mr. Holland wilbe excused in it, for he protesteth, that no hearer but Mr. Holland ever apprehended it soe.[1]

This somewhat cryptic passage in a letter of 17 July 1613 to Goodyer admits of a readier explanation than might have been thought possible. The key is to be found in a passage in Selden's *Table Talk*: '*Ben Jonson* Satirically expressed the vain Disputes of Divines by *Inigo Lanthorn*, disputing with his Puppet in a *Bartholomew Fair*. It is so; It is not so; It is so; It is not so; crying thus one to another a quarter of an Hour together.'[2] Selden's reference is to the dispute between the puppet, manipulated by Lantern Leatherhead, and Zeal-of-the-land Busy in Act V, scene v of *Bartholomew Fair*. Selden, who was a close friend of Jonson, had no doubt heard the play read in its original form, and has recalled the name originally given to the character. Inigo Jones's friends were the ones who had taken offence; Donne and Goodyer both intervened on his behalf. But Donne remarked, 'There was nothing obnoxious, but the very name, and he hath Chaunged that', indicating that he saw no cause for offence in the play as it has come down to us.

Of Donne's relations with other literary contemporaries more must be surmised than can be known. It is inconceivable, for instance, that he was unacquainted with Michael Drayton. Drayton had spent his boyhood and early manhood at Polesworth; he was intimate with the members of the Goodyer family, and he enjoyed their fullest confidence until his death; yet Donne never mentions him, nor does Drayton overtly mention Donne. Sir John Davies had been first the friend, then the foe, and then the friend again of Richard Martin; he had sought the patronage of Egerton and had presented a manuscript of *Nosce Teipsum* to the Earl of Northumberland before departing for Ireland; Donne might be expected to know him, and doubtless did. He paid him a compliment he paid to no other English contemporary, that of borrowing with approval one

---

[1] Anderdon MS.

[2] Ed. 1860, p. 243. This edition is a reprint of the original edition of 1689. The Oxford edition of 1892, p. 164, reads at this point 'Rabbi Busy disputing with a puppet . . .' after MS. Harl. 1315. Though the editor says that this 'is the only reading which is not obviously incorrect', he would have seen, had he read the play, that either makes perfectly good sense.

of his images, which was in turn borrowed by later metaphysical poets.[1] George Chapman, too, may have moved on the edge of Donne's circle; Chapman's elegy on the death of Prince Henry was dedicated in terms of warmest friendship to Edward Jones, perhaps a kinsman of the Edward Jones (dead by 1613) who had been Toby Mathew's host in the period just before his banishment, and the Huntington Library's copy of this book is inscribed by the author to Inigo Jones. One can only say that if Donne did not know Chapman he could easily have done so.

Jonson's conversations with William Drummond testify not only to Jonson's high estimate of Donne but also to Drummond's deep interest in him and his works. When the shy young Scot was in London he had apparently met Donne, probably through the intermediary of his uncle William Fowler, secretary to Queen Anne. Among the Hawthornden manuscripts is a slim quarto of 69 pages in Drummond's handwriting, and on the title-page he has written 'Thirre Poems belonginge to Jhon Don Transcribed by William Drummond'. Some of the poems, though by no means all, are by Donne. If the title means what it says, as there is no reason to doubt, Drummond must have had access to Donne's own commonplace book (or to a copy of it) and was able to transcribe from it such poems as he wished to keep. The two had probably met, and the meeting would have occurred before Donne entered holy orders. The only occasions when Drummond is known to have been in London before then were in 1606, when he was on his way to France, and in 1610, shortly after his father's death. But since the manuscript contains the elegy on the death of Cecilia Bulstrode,

---

[1] In *Nosce Teipsum* Davies had written:

> For though the Soule doe seeme her grave to beare,
> And in this world is almost buried quick;
> We have no cause the bodie's death to feare,
> For when the shell is broke, out comes the chick.

This becomes in *The Second Anniversary* (ll. 183–4):

> This to thy Soule allow,
> Thinke thy Shell broke, thinke thy Soule hatch'd but now.

The image was picked up again by Thomas Carew, who wrote in his memorial lines on Lady Mary Wentworth:

> the soule grew so fast within,
> It broke the outward shell of sinne,
> And so was hatch'd a Cherubin.

who died in 1609, Drummond must have made his transcriptions on his second visit. He may also have met some of the other members of Donne's circle, for his transcript of the second Satire has alongside its title 'Satyre 2 after C. B. coppy'. Christopher Brooke also, apparently, gave him access to a transcript of some of Donne's poems.[1]

An attempt has been made in the preceding pages to enumerate as many as possible of Donne's friends in the years 1606 to 1611. Such an attempt cannot, of course, even approach completeness, and as one moves into the succeeding period of his life one finds in his correspondence casual reference to many other men and women with whom he was on terms of greater or less familiarity, and obviously had been for some time. Among those referred to in this way are: the Earl of Arundel, famous as a connoisseur; Lord Chandos, husband of one of the Lord Chancellor's step-daughters; Sir Robert Rich, afterwards Earl of Warwick; Sir Edward Conway, a future Secretary of State; and Sir John Brooke, a cousin of Christopher.[2] Yet what part any of these played in Donne's life, or how he felt towards them, it is impossible to say.

The life that has been described in this chapter might appear to be sufficiently full for most men of the period, but in fact it was probably the smaller part of Donne's life during these years. Besides dividing his life between Mitcham and London, besides finding many friends in extremely varied circles in London itself, besides following the court and seeking an appointment that would furnish adequate provision for his wife and family, Donne was leading another life as well: a life of intense study and meditation, a life which found expression in poems, satires, and works of learning and of religious controversy. To this we must now turn.

[1] The manuscript is in the National Library of Scotland. [It contains two epigrams not accepted as Donne's by Grierson, one of which ('Manliness') was first included in an edition of the *Poems* by R. E. Bennett (1942), the other being included, with less reason, in the *Complete Poetry*, ed. J. T. Shawcross (1967). That Drummond's transcript depends very closely on copies of poems in Donne's possession is made rather less likely by the recently discovered Wedderburn MS., described by A. MacColl, 'A New Manuscript of Donne's Poems', *RES*, N.S. xix (1968), 293–5.]

[2] *Letters*, pp. 92, 149, 187, 256.

IX

CONTROVERSY AND CONFLICT

DURING the Mitcham years Donne was nearer to being a professional author than at any other period of his life, and certainly busier with his pen than at any other time, except perhaps during the months later in life when he revised and rewrote a large number of his sermons. The principal products of these years were the three prose pieces, *Biathanatos*, *Pseudo-Martyr*, and *Ignatius his Conclave*, but he also wrote, in addition to the poems mentioned in the last chapter, the majority of the 'Divine Poems' and most of the prose Problems. Of the three books, *Biathanatos* may be thought of as an outgrowth of the study of civil and canon law with which Donne had occupied himself at Pyrford, the other two as the result of his 'constant study of some points of Controversie betwixt the *English* and *Roman Church*; and especially those of *Supremacy* and *Allegiance*', to which Walton says he gave much of his time in his study at Mitcham.

That the Problems belong to the earlier years of this period needs to be insisted upon, because the fact that they and the Paradoxes constituted the volume entitled *Iuvenilia* suggests that they were all very early pieces, written, say, during the Lincoln's Inn years. But, while most of the Paradoxes may belong to the period before Donne's marriage, the Problems seem to have been written in James I's reign, and some of them certainly in 1607, when several of the letters to Goodyer refer to individual problems, of recent composition, which Donne was sending to his friend.[1] Though the medical student at Leyden who translated Donne's Problems into Latin in 1616 thought of the author as reluctant at this date to acknowledge such frivolous pieces,[2] some of them at least seem to have been composed in the same year as 'A Litanie' and 'La Corona'.

[1] Simpson, *Prose Works*, pp. 146–8.
[2] R. C. Bald, 'A Latin Version of Donne's Problems', *MP*, lxi (1963–4), 198–203, at pp. 200–1.

Certainly Donne was conscious that *Biathanatos*, also written about 1607 or 1608, was a work of his unregenerate days. In presenting a manuscript of the book in 1619 to his friend Sir Robert Ker he wrote: 'Let any that your discretion admits to the sight of it, know the date of it; and that it is a Book written by *Jack Donne*, and not by D. *Donne*.'[1] It is first heard of in a letter usually thought to have been written in 1607 or 1608; it is the same letter in which Donne describes the composition of 'A Litanie'. He wrote:

The day before I lay down, I was at *London*, where I delivered your Letter for Sr *Ed. Conway*, and received another for you, with the copy of my Book, of which it is impossible for me to give you a copy so soon, for it is not of much lesse then 300 pages. . . . At this time I onely assure you, that I have not appointed it upon any person, nor ever purposed to print it.[2]

This cannot possibly be *Pseudo-Martyr*, which consists of 216 leaves, or 432 pages of print; *Biathanatos*, on the other hand, consists of 120 leaves or 240 pages, and might also seem to be disqualified. But the manuscript which Donne presented to Sir Edward Herbert (now MS. e Musaeo 131 in the Bodleian) contains 286 pages; 'not of much lesse then 300 pages' is therefore an accurate description of its length, and corroborates the identification.

It was not until 1646 that *Biathanatos* was published by the younger Donne, but both *Pseudo-Martyr* and *Ignatius his Conclave* came out soon after they were written, the first in 1610 and the second in the following year. There was a topicality in them both which demanded prompt publication. They were contributions to a controversy that was being fiercely waged at the time, and Donne's intervention was a calculated act. He not only came to the defence

[1] *Letters*, p. 22.
[2] Ibid., pp. 34–5. The supposed apostasy of Hugh Broughton, referred to in the same letter, cannot, unfortunately, be dated. The reference to the increase of the plague is appropriate to 1607, but would be equally appropriate to 1608 or 1609 (see F. P. Wilson, *The Plague in Shakespeare's London*, 1927, pp. 117–21). On the other hand, Professor S. E. Sprott seems to favour 1608 as the date for *Biathanatos* when he remarks: 'Though the majority of Donne's most important sources were published or republished on the Continent between 1601 and 1608 (Azpilcueta, Azorius, Salon, Sayr, Soto), he did not make use of the third tome of Azorius (in which suicide was specifically treated), first published in 1612, or of Molina's fourth tome (in which suicide was discussed), first published in 1609 and soon widely influential' (*The English Debate on Suicide from Donne to Hume*, 1961, p. 25 n.).

of the official policy of the state; he also sought to distinguish himself by a display of his learning and controversial skill, and he even hoped to catch the favour of the King. It has been suggested that he had already for some time been participating in the controversy in a subsidiary capacity, but that he now for the first time came out into the open as an antagonist. How far this is true, or even likely, must now be examined.

The opinion of Valdesius's *De Dignitate Regum Regnorumque Hispaniae* which Donne submitted to Sir Robert Cotton in 1603 or 1604 makes it clear that his skill as a civilian was already respected among a select circle of friends. As his knowledge of the canon law also increased, it was natural that he should be drawn towards some of the more learned divines of the age, and especially those who were interested, as Donne himself was interested, in the issues disputed by Catholic and Protestant. Nevertheless, any such relations with members of the clergy at this period of his life would be largely matter for conjecture, were it not for the fact that in 1658, while the second edition of the *Life of Donne* was being prepared for the press, Izaak Walton received a lengthy communication from Thomas Morton, the ejected Bishop of Durham. Morton, who was then ninety-four years of age and who died a few months later, had been persuaded just in time to send Walton his recollections of Donne. His narration, no doubt, had had some colouring added to it during the years, but in the principal details, and especially in the dating of the central incident, it can scarcely be wrong.

Morton is so important for an understanding of this period of Donne's life that some account of his own earlier life and activities is necessary.[1] He was born in 1564, the son of a substantial citizen and alderman of York. As a boy he was a schoolfellow of Guy Fawkes, but unlike Fawkes he went from school to Cambridge, and took holy orders in the established Church. Morton left Cambridge and a Fellowship at St. John's in 1598 for the rectory of Long Marston, just outside his native city, which had been procured for him

---

[1] The principal authorities for Morton's biography are *'IEPONIKHΣ, or The Fight, Victory, and Triumph of S. Paul. Accommodated to the Right Reverend Father in God Thomas late L. Bishop of Duresme, In a Sermon Preached at his Funeral*, 1660, by John Barwick, his chaplain, and *The Life of Dr. Thomas Morton, Late Bishop of Duresme*, 1669, by R[ichard] B[addeley], formerly Morton's secretary.

by the influence of his father. There he soon distinguished himself
for his skill in disputation against the Romanists. In 1602 he accepted a chaplaincy in the household of Lord Eure, who had just
been appointed ambassador to the Emperor and to the King of Denmark. Owing to Elizabeth's death the embassy terminated abruptly
and Morton was abroad for less than a year, but he made good use
of his time. Obtaining leave from the ambassador to travel by himself, he visited the annual book fair at Frankfurt, where he laid out
every penny he could afford on works of theology from all parts of
Europe. He also visited a number of seats of learning in the Catholic
states, and made the acquaintance of such distinguished Jesuit theologians as Mulhusinus and Serarius at Mainz, and Becanus at
Cologne. On his return to England Morton became chaplain to the
Earl of Rutland, an appointment which he welcomed because it
brought him fairly frequently to London with the Earl and, by
removing him from pastoral duties, gave him opportunities for
concentrated study. These studies bore fruit in 1605 with the
publication of the first part of his *Apologia Catholica*, dedicated to
Archbishop Bancroft. The book was, according to its title-page, 'ex
meris Jesuitorum contradictionibus conflata, in qua Paradoxa,
Hæreses, Blasphemiæ, Scelera, quæ a Pontificiis objici Protestantibus
solent, ex ipsorum Pontificiorum testimoniis diluuntur omnia'.
Morton's preface makes it clear that he envisaged Catholic as well
as Protestant readers, and his temperance in controversy, as well as
his learning, were such as could scarcely be treated with anything
but respect.

   Morton was busy working on a second part of his *Apologia* when
the Gunpowder Plot was discovered. His notes were full of passages
carefully extracted and arranged from the writings of the more
extreme and violent contemporary Jesuit theologians, and it was a
comparatively simple task to select and codify some of these. This
Morton did in his *Exact Discoverie of Romish Doctrine in the case of
Conspiracie and Rebellion*, which is dated 1605 on the title-page and
was probably rushed out with all possible speed at the end of the
year. It is a brief and telling piece of propaganda consisting of a
series of propositions stated in terse and logical terms, presenting
the Roman doctrine on one side of the opening and, on the opposite

page, the passages from the works of contemporary theologians from which they were deduced. Morton's tract proved far too influential to go unanswered, and an anonymous reply from a loyal Catholic was published in 1606, *A Iust and Moderate Answer to a Most Iniurious and Seditious Pamphlet*. The dedication to the King contains a naïve complaint against Morton: 'this discouerer, by so many not vsuall Catholike Authors alleaged in his booke, discloseth his inueterate malice against vs.' This unconscious tribute to Morton's learning shows that his reading was not only wide in range but also up to date in its scope.

Morton must have worked very hard in 1606. The second part of his *Apologia Catholica* appeared during the year, as well as a considerably enlarged edition of the first part. The *Iust and Moderate Answer* demanded a reply, and this Morton furnished in *A Full Satisfaction concerning a Double Romish Iniquitie; Hainous Rebellion, and more then Heathenish Æquiuocation*. This is essentially a continuation and elaboration of the *Exact Discoverie*. But Morton was by now also engaged on a much larger task, that of refuting John Brerely's *Apologie of the Romane Church*, published in 1604. 'John Brerely' was the pseudonym of Lawrence Anderton, a seminary priest who later became a Jesuit, and in his *Apologie* he not only anticipated the method, but also probably suggested the title, of Morton's *Apologia Catholica*. Anderton's title-page asserted that his book consisted of

three severall Tractes whereof

1. *The first*, Concerneth the Antiquitie and continuance of the Catholike Romane Religion ever since the Apostles time.
2. *The second* That the Protestantes Religion was not so much as in being, at or before *Luthers* first appearing.
3. *The thirde* That Catholickes are no less Loyall and dutifull to their Soveraigne, then Protestantes.

All which are vndertaken and proved by testimonies of the learned Protestantes themselves.[1]

Though this book was not a very large one (191 pages in all) and was neither as thorough nor as erudite as Morton's *Apologia*, its

[1] A facsimile of this title-page may be found as an illustration to the article by A. J. Hawkes, 'The Birchley Hall Secret Press', *The Library*, vii (1926–7), 136–83, plate vi.

examination went right to the heart of the Anglican claims. It was not only learned and acute but also sufficiently damaging not to be left unopposed. Bancroft summoned a group of divines to plan a reply, but they were scattered by the plague and Morton was left to carry out the design single-handed. For the next three years it was the centre of his most strenuous activities.

There is no clue as to when Donne first met Morton; it could have been at Cambridge, or in any of the years that followed, for there can be little doubt that Christopher Brooke's father knew Morton's father well, and that the two families were acquainted. Again, John King must have known Morton when both men were in the north, and King could have introduced Donne to Morton. In any case, by 1607 Morton regarded his friendship with Donne as of some length, so he had probably known him at least since the time of his appointment as chaplain to the Earl of Rutland, and during the period of the composition of his controversial works. Morton's labours were suitably rewarded on 22 June 1607, when the King presented him to the Deanery of Gloucester. Almost immediately, Walton says,

He sent to Mr. *Donne*, and intreated to borrow an hour of his time for a Conference the next day. After their meeting, there was not many minutes passed before he spake to Mr. *Donne* to this purpose;

'Mr. *Donne*, The occasion of sending for you is to propose to you what I have often revolv'd in my own thought since I last saw you: which nevertheless, I will not declare but upon this condition, that you shall not return me a present answer, but forbear three days, and bestow some part of that time in Fasting and Prayer; and after a serious consideration of what I shall propose; then return to me with your answer. Deny me not, Mr. *Donne*; for, it is the effect of a true love, which I would gladly pay as a debt due for yours to me.'

This request being granted, the Doctor exprest himself thus:

'Mr. *Donne*, I know your Education and Abilities; I know your expectation of a State-employment; and I know your fitness for it; and I know too, the many delays and contingencies that attend Court-promises; and let me tell you that, my love begot by our long friendship, and your merits, hath prompted me to such an inquisition after your present temporal estate, as makes me no stranger to your necessities; which I know to be such as your generous spirit could not bear, if it were not supported with a pious Patience: you know I have formerly perswaded you to wave your Court-hopes, and enter into holy Orders; which I now again perswade you to embrace, with this reason added to my former request: The King hath yesterday made me Dean of *Gloucester*, and I am also possessed of a Benefice, the profits of which are equal to those of my Deanry; I will think my Deanry enough for my maintenance (who am and resolve to dye a single man) and will quit my Benefice, and estate you in it, (which the Patron is willing I shall do) if God shall incline your heart to embrace this motion. *Remember*, Mr. *Donne*, no mans Education or Parts make him too good for this employment, *which is to be an Ambassadour for the God of glory, that God who by a vile death opened the gates of life to mankind.* Make me no present answer; but remember your promise, and return to me the third day with your Resolution.'

At the hearing of this, Mr. *Donne*'s faint breath and perplext countenance gave a visible testimony of an inward conflict; but he performed his promise and departed without returning an answer till the third day, and then his answer was to this effect;

'My most worthy and most dear friend, since I saw you, I have been faithful to my promise, and have also meditated much of your great kindness, which hath been such as would exceed even my gratitude; but that it cannot do; and more I cannot return you; and I do that with an heart full of Humility and Thanks, though I may not accept of your offer; but, Sir, my refusal is not for that I think my self too good for that calling, for which Kings, if they think so, are not good enough: nor for that my Education and Learning, though not eminent, may not, being assisted with God's Grace and Humility, render me in some measure fit for it: but, I dare make so dear a friend as you are my Confessor; some irregularities of my life have been so visible to some men, that though I have, I thank God, made my peace with him by penitential resolutions against them, and by the assistance of his Grace banish'd them my affections; yet this, which God knows to be so, is not so visible to man, as to free me from their censures, and it may be that sacred calling from a dishonour. And besides, whereas it is determined by the best of *Casuists*, that *Gods Glory should be the first end, and a maintenance the second motive to embrace that calling*; and though each man may propose to himself both together; yet the first may not be put last without a violation of Conscience, which he that searches the heart will judge. And truly my present condition is such, that if I ask my own Conscience, whether it be reconcileable to that rule, it is at this time so perplexed about it, that I can neither give my self nor you an answer. You know, Sir, who says, *Happy is that man whose Conscience doth not accuse him for that thing which he does.* To these I might add other reasons that disswade me; but I crave your favour that I may forbear to express them, and, thankfully decline your offer.'[1]

This account, of course, emphasizes most strongly Donne's high conception of the ministry and his refusal to enter it until he was convinced that he had a genuine call to do so.[2] But there are other points of great interest. Donne was, for instance, still conscious of sins in his past life (and there is little doubt that he referred to more than the mere circumstances of his marriage) that in the eyes of some were sufficient to stand in the way of his performing the holy offices of priesthood. Nevertheless, Morton had already urged him more than once to enter the Church. It is certain, too, that this was not his sole attempt to relieve Donne's needs; Richard Baddeley, for many years Morton's secretary, relates an instance of Donne's 'ripe and sudden wit'. On one occasion Morton gave Donne 'a good quantity of Gold', saying, '*Here Mr.* Donne, *take this, Gold is restorative*', to which he replied, '*Sir, I doubt I shall never restore it back again*'; and, adds Baddeley, 'I am assured that he never did'.[3] In spite of his necessities, however, Donne refused to be driven into the Church by them. Even admitting that hopes of worldly success still drew him away, one cannot but respect his scruples.

Morton did not allow his deanery to interfere with his controversial activities. It is clear from the accounts of his biographers that he still spent a large portion of his time in London, and Baddeley specifically states that his refutation of Brerely was 'finished in his private Library in the Deanery house of St. *Pauls London*, where he then resided, *Dr. Overall* his reverend friend being Deane there'.[4] But he was not able to proceed uninterruptedly with his book. His skirmish with the Moderate Answerer had not gone unobserved in Rome, and in 1607 he was attacked by the veteran Jesuit controversialist Robert Persons in his *Treatise tending to Mitigation*

[1] *Lives*, pp. 32–5.
[2] It should be remarked, however, that here Walton is to some extent drawing on Donne's later poem 'To Mr. Tilman'; see Gardner, *Divine Poems*, pp. 100, 129.
[3] Baddeley, *Life of Morton*, pp. 103–4.
[4] pp. 35–6; cf. Barwick, p. 73.

towardes Catholicke-Subiectes in England. Wherin is declared, That it is not impossible for Subiects of different Religion, (especially Catholickes and Protestants) to liue together in dutifull obedience and subiection, vnder the gouernment of his Maiesty of Great Britany. Against the seditious wrytings of Thomas Morton Minister. Such a plea for toleration from Persons represented a quite startling about-face from his earlier works, although the tone of this book, especially towards his opponents, is the reverse of tolerant. Actually, the book is as vituperative as anything he ever wrote. He made the further mistake of defending the doctrine of equivocation at length, and then concluded that, notwithstanding the Catholic acknowledgement of papal supremacy and the legitimacy of equivocation, 'these two pretended obstacles do not let, but that *Catholicke* and *Protestant* English Subiectes may liue togeather in vnion of dutifull obedience vnder his Maiesty'. It is easy to see how, in an England where memories of Gunpowder Treason and the trial of Henry Garnet were still fresh, an argument on such lines would evoke not sympathy but indignation.

Morton replied to Persons in *A Preamble vnto an Incounter with P. R. the Author of the deceitfull Treatise of Mitigation,* 1608. This was a relatively brief pamphlet of 128 pages, and a mere foretaste of what was to come. Meanwhile another interruption had also to be reckoned with. Theophilus Higgons, a popular young preacher at St. Dunstan's-in-the-West, went over to Rome, and spent a couple of years in French seminaries, from which he published the reasons for his conversion. His book was entitled *The First Motive of T. H. Maister of Arts and lately minister, to suspect the integrity of his religion . . . [with] an appendix intituled, Try before you trust, wherein some notable vntruths of D. Field, and D. Morton are discouered.* Higgons accused Morton of falsifying his authorities, and this Morton could not suffer. He replied briefly but forcibly in *A Direct Answer vnto the scandalous exceptions, which Theophilus Higgons hath lately obiected,* 1609.[1]

---

[1] Higgons, it should be added, returned to England in the latter part of 1610, was seized, and lodged in the Deanery of St. Paul's, where the combined efforts of Overall and Morton succeeded in reconverting him to the Anglican Church. The King granted him a special pardon, and he proclaimed his penitence in a highly edifying sermon preached at Paul's Cross on 3 Mar. 1611.

At last, towards the end of 1609, the reply to Brerely appeared, a folio of 680 pages, entitled *A Catholike Appeale for Protestants, out of the confessions of the Romane Doctors, particularly answering the mis-named Catholike Apologie for the Romane Faith*. It was duly presented by its author to the King, to whom it was dedicated, on 27 October. On the following day, however, Morton received a rude shock. Brerely too had not been idle in the intervening years. The *Protestants Apologie* came out in a revised edition, enlarged to about four times its original size. It was dated 1608 on the title-page, but its appearance was probably delayed, since it has not one but several lists of errata and addenda at the end. Certainly Morton had not seen a copy before his *Catholike Appeale* came out. He had, however, been so indiscreet as to forewarn his adversary of his intentions, since in the dedication of the *Preamble vnto an Incounter with P. R.* he had promised to write a more forcible '*Incounter*, after that I haue discharged my part in another taske of more importance, namely, in *The Answer* vnto the misconceived Catholike *Apologie*: which by this calumnious *Treatise* of *P. R.* his *Mitigation*, as by an aduerse tempest, hath receiued some interruption'. Hence, on the morning after he had presented *A Catholike Appeale* to the King, Morton received a copy of the enlarged *Protestants Apologie*, accompanied by an ironical challenge inserted on a cancel in the preliminaries:

To the worshipfull M. Doctor Morton, Deane of Glocester, these be deliuered with all speed possible.

Worshipfull Maister Doctor, I haue met by good chance with this booke, which I send you here inclosed: I take it to be another Edition of that booke, which I vnderstand you are in answering, which is the cause that I make so much speed to send you it, lest that you should haue committed some ouersights, which are discouered in this, and may tend to your great disgrace, if you vse not due preuention. It seemeth to me not to be an easie matter to satisfie any iudicious Reader, for this Author is very exact, and quoteth your owne Authors, which are extant, and cannot be denied: and if you should not answer very directly, but runne to other not so pertinent discourses, I feare your credite will not be a little stained. I wish you well, but my chiefe desire is that truth may be discouered in such important affaires as these are. Wherefore be sure to helpe to set forward this, or else

suppresse your bookes, and impose silence to your selfe. And I will
be glad to heare of your best resolutions, and euer rest

> Your louing friend,
> Roger Brerely.

A similar insertion in the preliminaries of the *Catholike Appeale* contains Morton's righteously indignant reply to his unscrupulous
adversary. There, fortunately, the controversy came to an end.
Barwick claimed that Morton 'gave such a deadly blow to his
Romish Adversaries, as none of them hitherto (and yet it is above 50.
years since it was written) have ever been so hardy as to attempt
any *Answer* to it';[1] it is more likely that sheer exhaustion brought
the argument to an end. Anderton was glad to retire from the conflict, and Morton went on to publish his promised *Encounter against
M. Parsons* in 1610. Persons's death soon afterwards put an end to
this controversy also, and Morton was able to turn from authorship
to ecclesiastical administration for the next decade or so.

Morton's activity as a controversialist has been related at such
length because it has been asserted by all writers on Donne since
Jessopp that Donne was an assistant in the composition of many of
these works. Gosse, in particular, declares: 'I believe that from 1605
to the summer of 1607 Donne was mainly employed in revising,
collecting, and even perhaps composing, for Morton',[2] and then
proceeds on the assumption that Morton's appointment to his
deanery brought this employment to an end; this, as we have seen,
cannot be maintained. If Donne was absent from England for a full
year in 1605 and 1606, such work would either have suffered a
lengthy interruption or, as is perhaps more likely, would not even
have had a beginning until after his return and the removal to
Mitcham. If, however, Morton did employ Donne, he would undoubtedly have been able to provide him with continuous employment until the completion of the *Encounter against M. Parsons*, which
was entered in the Stationers' Register on 27 April 1610. The span
of such employment is thus much more likely to have been 1606–10
than 1605–7.

That Donne was ever systematically employed by Morton is,

---

[1] Barwick, p. 132.   [2] Gosse, i. 149.

however, far from certain, and in fact rests solely on the unsupported
assertion of Jessopp. There is nothing inherently unlikely in the
supposition, and such objections as can be raised against it are none
of them so strong that they would not immediately collapse in the
face of a single piece of decisive evidence. Such evidence Jessopp
may have possessed, but he never stated it,[1] and it has successfully
eluded all inquiry, unless, as is possible, his assertion was based on
an inference from a sentence in one of Donne's letters. In the postscript to a letter to Goodyer, which fortunately happens to be dated
'*First Saturday* in March. 1607' (i.e. 5 March 1607/8), Donne wrote:
'You forget to send me the Apology; and many times, I think it an
injury to remember one of a promise, lest it confesse a distrust. But
of the book, by occasion of reading the Deans answer to it, I have

[1] There is no suggestion of any such relations between Donne and Morton in
Jessopp's earliest account of Donne, prefixed to the *Essays in Divinity* in 1855. In the
DNB (1888) Jessopp suggests rather than asserts it; no one, he remarks, who has
compared the list of authorities cited by Morton with those cited in *Pseudo-Martyr*
and *Biathanatos* 'could have much doubt that Morton and Donne must for years have
worked in close relations with each other, or could avoid a strong suspicion that
Morton owed to Donne's learning very much more than it was advisable, or at that
time necessary, to acknowledge in print'. By 1897, however, in the book on Donne,
there is no uncertainty: '*Even if we had not been told* [italics mine] that [Donne] gave
Morton constant and valuable help, a comparison of the authorities quoted and
referred to in Morton's *Catholic Appeal*, with those set down in Donne's *Pseudo-Martyr*,
would have convinced a careful reader of the fact. The curious and out-of-the-way
books cited in both works are very numerous, and not to be found elsewhere' (p. 57).
But the argument from the similarity of the two lists is not convincing. Those prefixed to Morton's two books, *Apologia Catholica* and *A Catholike Appeale*, are certainly
remarkably similar and are obviously closely related; but no such close relationship
exists between either of them and Donne's list of authorities in *Biathanatos* or the
lists of additional authors cited in *Pseudo-Martyr* set out by Miss M. P. Ramsay in
the second appendix of her *Doctrines Médiévales chez Donne*. Fewer than 25 per cent
of the authors cited by Donne are also in Morton's list. It was natural enough that
both writers should refer to some extent to the same works. Many of those referred
to in *Pseudo-Martyr* seem not so much out-of-the-way books as books which Donne
would cite because of the nature of his topic and because they were the recognized
authorities on the subject. Nor is it fair to Morton to ascribe to Donne alone the
erudition required for the citation of abstruse or unusual works. It is clear from contemporary accounts that Morton collected a very considerable library, and one which
Donne, at this period of his life, would hardly have been able to afford. Thus, if Donne
and Morton both cite an unusual work, Donne could well have read it in Morton's
copy without necessarily having been employed by him. Finally, it is worth noting
that Barwick admits (p. 132) that Morton had some help with *A Catholike Appeale*,
though not from Donne, when he states that 'Doctor *James* took the pains to examine
some of his *Quotations* in the *University Library* of *Oxford*'. [On the relations of Donne
and Morton see further an appendix in Fr. T. Healy's edition of *Ignatius his Conclave*,
Oxford, 1969.]

sometimes some want.'[1] It is thus clear that Donne was reading portions of the manuscript of *A Catholike Appeale* a full eighteen months before that work was published. Morton clearly had sufficient confidence in Donne's learning and acumen to submit the manuscript to him for criticism and possible correction, but there is no suggestion in Donne's postscript that he was doing more than performing a friendly office. As the evidence stands at present, further inferences are unwarranted.

Of Donne's interest in the controversies then raging between Catholic and Protestant there cannot, however, be any doubt, and the controversy which owed its origin to the Gunpowder Plot especially engaged his attention. When the Parliament which had originally been summoned for 5 November 1605 eventually met, one of its first actions was to impose fresh penalties on the Catholics and exact from them the Oath of Allegiance. By this Oath the Catholics were to acknowledge James as their lawful sovereign, and to deny that the Pope had any power to depose him, to authorize any foreign sovereign to invade his dominions, or to free his subjects from their allegiance; the Oath was taken without any equivocation or mental reservation, and no one, not even the Pope, had any power to grant absolution from it. Thus stated, there was nothing in the Oath to which the vast majority of the English Catholics could not adhere; indeed, James himself protested that it was 'ordained onely for making of a trew distinction betweene Papists of quiet disposition, and in all other things good subiects, and such other Papists as in their hearts maintained the like violent bloody *Maximes*, that the Powder-Traitours did'.[2] Nevertheless, there can be small doubt that one clause, by which the Catholic was compelled to swear that he did 'from his heart abhor, detest, and abjure, as impious and heretical, this damnable doctrine and position, that princes which be excommunicated or deprived by the Pope may be deposed or murdered by their subjects', was couched in deliberately offensive terms; and this clause more than anything else helped to crystallize a solid body of opposition to the Oath.

---

[1] *Letters*, p. 66. Gosse, i. 182, states inaccurately that the 'Apology' was Persons's *Treatise tending to Mitigation* and that 'the Deans answer to it' was Morton's *Preamble unto an Incounter with P. R.*

[2] *The Political Works of James I*, ed. C. H. McIlwain, 1918, p. 113.

ANNO DNI. 1591
ÆTATIS SVÆ 18

ANTES MVDADO
MVERTO QVE

This was for youth, Strength, Mirth, and wit that Time
Most count their golden Age; but t'was not thine.
Thine was thy later yeares, so much refin'd
From youths Drosse, Mirth, & wit; as thy pure mind
Thought (like the Angels) nothing but the Praise
Of thy Creator, in those last, best Dayes.
    Witnes this Booke, (thy Embleme) which begins
    With Love; but endes, with Sighes, & Teares for sins.

Will: Marshall sculpsit.   IZ: WA:

1. Donne in 1591; from an engraving by William
Marshall (? after an original by Nicholas Hilliard)
prefixed to *Poems*, 1635

11. Donne in the pose of a Melancholy Lover; from the portrait (*c.* 1595?) at Newbattle Abbey; by kind permission of the Trustees of the Marquis of Lothian

III. Donne in 1616; from the miniature by Isaac Oliver at Windsor Castle; by gracious permission of Her Majesty the Queen

IV. Donne as shown in the portrait in the Deanery of
St. Paul's Cathedral, inscribed 'Aetatis Suae 49
1620'; by kind permission of the Very Revd. the
Dean

v. Donne; from the portrait in the Dyce Collection at
the Victoria and Albert Museum; presumably a
copy of the portrait in the Deanery of St. Paul's,
? from the school of Cornelius Janssen

VI. Donne; from the engraving by Martin Droeshout
used as frontispiece in *Deaths Duell*, 1632

VII. Donne's head, from the effigy by Nicholas Stone in St. Paul's Cathedral; by kind permission of the Dean and Chapter

VIII. (a) Donne's receipt to Sir Thomas Egerton; from
Losely MS. 2013/31, in the Folger Shakespeare
Library

(b) Donne's letter to Bishop John Williams; from
Lincolnshire Archives, L.T. and D. 1626/11

Yet this opposition did not take shape at once, and in the months immediately after its imposition the Oath was taken by large numbers of Catholics, priests and laymen, including the head of their clergy, the archpriest George Blackwell.

The English Catholics were far more willing to make concessions that would placate James than was the papacy; on 22 September 1606 the Pope issued a breve condemning the Oath. Blackwell, who had taken it and was being kept under surveillance by the Government, not only suppressed the breve but also yielded to political pressure so far as to issue a letter exhorting Catholics to follow his example and swear allegiance to James. The Pope was compelled to issue a second breve, repeating more emphatically what he had previously said, and a few weeks later Cardinal Bellarmine sent Blackwell a letter, which was made public, in which he expostulated with him for his disobedience and further condemned the Oath as contrary to the Catholic faith. To these three documents—the two papal breves and the letter of Bellarmine—James himself composed a reply, which appeared anonymously before the end of 1607 in both English and Latin as *Triplici Nodo Triplex Cuneus or an Apologie for the Oath of Allegiance*. James's authorship was, of course, no secret, and Bellarmine had no scruples about replying; this he did in *Responsio ad Librum inscriptum Triplici Nodo Triplex Cuneus*, published in 1608 as by one of his almoners, Matthaeus Tortus. In the next year James retaliated by reissuing his book in an enlarged form, with an elaborate new preface entitled 'A Premonition . . . to all most Mightie Monarches, Kings, free Princes and States of Christendome', and at the same time commissioned Lancelot Andrewes to prepare a more detailed reply to Bellarmine. This appeared later in the same year as *Tortura Torti*. Thereafter the controversy became general, and raged vigorously from one end of Europe to the other for more than a decade.[1]

One of the effects of the Oath of Allegiance and the controversy that followed its imposition was an intensification of the divisions among the English Catholics. The intrusion of Bellarmine into the controversy on the heels of the second papal breve was looked at

---

[1] By far the best account of the controversy is to be found in McIlwain's introduction to *The Political Works of James I*, pp. xlix–lxxx.

askance as yet one more example of the Jesuits' assertion of the more extreme papal claims, and while Jesuit writers in all parts of Europe sprang to the Cardinal's defence, a number of other Catholics ranged themselves on the side of the Protestant King. Of these the two most important were William Barclay, an exiled Scot living in France, whose *De Potestate Papae*, published posthumously in 1609, is one of the most learned works on its subject, and Thomas Preston, an English Benedictine who wrote prolifically under the name of Roger Widdrington. This new cleavage in the ranks of the English Catholics was comparable to that of the last years of Elizabeth's reign when the archpriest controversy was at its height, and a renewed sense of bitterness against the Jesuits among the more moderate Catholics was inevitable.

The situation facing intelligent and thoughtful Catholics was thoroughly intelligible to Donne, who had formerly shared many of their difficulties. His attitude was further complicated not only by the fact that some of his friends were still Catholics but also by the return of his mother and her husband to England. In May 1606 the King had granted to Richard Rainsford, 'as of his Maiesties free gift and favor', a remittal of the statute staple of £2,000 formerly made by Charles Somerset to John Syminges, which had come to Rainsford through his wife, and which had been forfeited to the Crown 'by reason he wente beyond Seas and remayned there without licence'.[1] It is possible that Donne had not merely visited the Rainsfords while he was abroad with Chute, but had also succeeded in persuading them to return to England. When they returned they soon found that they had done so only to be plunged into difficulties which they had not anticipated, and it was not long before Rainsford found himself in trouble with the authorities.

Meanwhile the great controversy was rapidly spreading from kings and cardinals to men of humbler rank. Persons, who kept a watchful eye on everything that happened in England, was actually in it from the beginning. He had sprung at once to the defence of the Gunpowder plotters against their prosecutor Sir Edward Coke, the Attorney General. His defence of Garnet in the preface to *An Answere to the Fifth Part of Reportes lately set forth by Syr Edward Cooke* is masterly

[1] P.R.O., Privy Seal Docket Book, Index 6744. Cf. pp. 115–16 n. above.

for its control and its ironic restraint. As might be expected, Persons was ready to express himself as soon as James's defence of the Oath appeared, and this he did in his *Judgment of a Catholicke English-man living in banishment for his religion . . . concerning a late booke set forth, and entituled, Triplici nodo, triplex cuneus,* 1608. In the following year he assisted Henry Leech in writing a reply to James's 'Premonition', which was entitled *Dutifull and Respective Considerations vpon foure seuerall Heads of Proofe and Triall in matters of Religion.* Persons is at his best as a controversialist in these pamphlets. In the *Judgment of a Catholicke English-man* he affects not to know the author of *Triplici Nodo*, and scores more than one hit by means of his pretended ignorance. In *Dutifull and Respective Considerations* he and Leech take as their point of departure James's indignant denial that he was a heretic, then proceed to examine his writings, and finally conclude, with every appearance of anxious solicitude, that he is in imminent danger of hell-fire. These three works justify Swift's linking together the names of Persons and Hooker as the only two prose writers of the Elizabethan age who, in his opinion, 'would not offend any present Reader';[1] and it may well have been from Persons that Swift learned the elements of his irony.

James could scarcely be expected to reply to Persons's impertinences, but a reply was clearly in order, and the task of preparing it was entrusted to William Barlow, who had recently been appointed Bishop of Lincoln. Barlow had successfully won the confidence of both Elizabeth and James. He had attended the Earl of Essex from his condemnation to his execution, and had preached on his treason at Paul's Cross on the Sunday after his death; he had likewise preached at Paul's Cross on the Sunday after the discovery of the Gunpowder Plot. Nevertheless, in an age when sycophancy and flattery were cultivated with a skill almost inconceivable today, Barlow owed his rapid promotion to his exceptional command of these arts. His florid rhetoric, his wide and pleasing command of literary allusion, and his assiduous boot-licking were the chief articles of his stock-in-trade. His unction was that of a Collins or a Pumblechook, but neither of those characters commanded that strain of self-assurance which success had added to Barlow's natural arrogance. His

[1] *The Tatler*, no. 230.

opponents were treated to a show of vituperative contempt for which even he had qualms,[1] and which was assumed to hide his lack of learning in theology and canon law. He was not made for the rough and tumble of controversy, but he had no alternative when the King commanded. His *Answer to a Catholike English-man* was entered in the Stationers' Register on 14 April 1609, and appeared not long afterwards.

Donne had no very high opinion of Barlow, and had already expressed resentment at his behaviour towards Essex by including as item 31 in *The Courtier's Library* 'An Encomium on Dr. Shaw, chaplain to Richard III, by Dr. Barlow'.[2] The *Answer to a Catholike English-man*, when it appeared, confirmed all his worst fears. Soon after reading it, he wrote to Goodyer a long letter about the book:

To you that are not easily scandalized, and in whom, I hope, neither my Religion nor Morality can suffer, I dare write my opinion of that Book in whose bowels you left me. It hath refreshed, and given new justice to my ordinary complaint, That the Divines of these times, are become meer Advocates, as though Religion were a temporall inheritance; they plead for it with all sophistications, and illusions, and forgeries: And herein are they likest Advocates, that though they be feed by the way, with Dignities, and other recompenses, yet that for which they plead is none of theirs. They write for Religion, without it. In the main point in question, I think truly there is a perplexity (as farre as I see yet) and both sides may be in justice, and innocence; and the wounds which they inflict upon the adverse part, are all *se defendendo*: for, clearly, our State cannot be safe without the Oath; since they professe, that Clergie-men, though Traitors, are no Subjects, and that all the rest may be none to morrow. And, as clearly, the Supremacy which the Ro. Church pretend, were diminished, if it were limited; and will as ill abide that, or disputation, as the Prerogative of temporall Kings, who being the onely judges of their prerogative, why may not Roman Bishops, (so enlightned as they are presumed by them) be good witnesses of their own suprem-

---

[1] 'Some tearmes haue passed, not fully *Episcopall*, or not so fitting (perhaps) the calling and place, which . . . I hold in the Church' (*Answer to a Catholike English-man*, A1ᵛ).

[2] Shaw, at Richard III's instigation, preached a sermon at Paul's Cross challenging the legality of Edward IV's marriage to Elizabeth Woodville, and so questioned the legitimacy of the two Princes, afterwards murdered in the Tower.

acie, which is now so much impugned? But for this particular Author, I looked for more prudence, and humane wisdome in him, in avoiding all miscitings, or mis-interpretings, because at this time, the watch is set, and every bodies hammer is upon that anvill; and to dare offend in that kinde now, is, for a theef to leave the covert, and meet a strong hue and cry in the teeth: and yet truly this man is extremely obnoxious in that kinde; for, though he have answered many things fully, (as no book ever gave more advantage then that which he undertook) and abound in delicate applications, and ornaments, from the divine and prophane authors, yet being chiefly conversant about two points, he prevaricates in both. For, for the matter, which is the first, he referres it intirely, and namely, to that which D. *Morton* hath said therein before, and so leaves it roundly: And for the person (which is the second) upon whom he amasses as many opprobies, as any other could deserve, he pronounceth, that he will account any answer from his adversary, slaunder, except he do (as he hath done) draw whatsoever he saith of him, from Authors of the same Religion, and in print: And so, he having made use of all the Quodlibetaries, imputations against the other, cannot be obnoxious himself in that kinde, and so hath provided safely. It were no service to you, to send you my notes upon the Book, because they are sandy, and incoherent ragges, for my memory, not for your judgement; and to extend them to an easinesse, and perspicuity, would make them a Pamphlet, not a Letter. I will therefore deferre them till I see you; and in the mean time, I will adventure to say to you, without inserting one unnecessary word, that the Book is full of falsifications in words, and in sense, and of falshoods in matter of fact, and of inconsequent and unscholarlike arguings, and of relinquishing the King, in many points of defence, and of contradiction of himself, and of dangerous and suspected Doctrine in Divinitie, and of silly ridiculous triflings, and of extreme flatteries, and of neglecting better and more obvious answers, and of letting slip some enormous advantages which the other gave, and he spies not.[1]

Donne's harsh judgement was abundantly justified by the eagerness with which the Jesuits fell on Barlow. Persons, Fitzherbert, and Coffin all attacked him with gusto, and only the death of Barlow in 1613 put an end to this phase of the controversy.

---

[1] *Letters*, pp. 160–3. It is interesting to notice the discretion with which Donne names neither the book nor the author; he shows on more than one occasion his fear that his letters might go astray, and be seen by those for whom they were not intended.

Donne's letter about Barlow, which belongs, presumably, to the late spring or early summer of 1609, shows that he had not yet entirely made up his mind about the issues involved in the controversy about the Oath.[1] But his detachment is quite impressive; he perceives that both sides could be 'in justice, and innocence; and the wounds which they inflict upon the adverse part, are all *se defendendo*'. This impartiality did not, however, persist. Barlow's *Answer* seems to have had a twofold effect on Donne: it stimulated him to make a more systematic examination of the issues at stake, and it made him feel that, since Barlow had failed so miserably, the need for a firm statement of every aspect of James's case against Persons was all the greater. Both these motives are stressed in the dedication of *Pseudo-Martyr*:

> For, since in prouiding for your Maiesties securitie, the Oath defends vs, it is reason, that wee defend it. The strongest Castle that is, cannot defend the Inhabitants, if they sleepe, or neglect the defence of that, which defends them; No more can this Oath, though framed with all aduantagious Christianly wisedome, secure your Maiestie, and vs in you, if by our negligence, wee should open it, either to the aduersaries Batteries, or to his vnderminings.[2]

To this extent, then, Barlow was responsible for Donne's entering the controversy, with *Pseudo-Martyr*.

The earliest stages of *Pseudo-Martyr* seem to be recorded in two brief letters to Goodyer (undated except for 'Wednesday' and 'Friday morning'), which were probably written not very long after the criticism of Barlow.[3] In the first Donne recalls that 'about this time you purposed a journey to fetch, or meet the Lad. *Huntington*', and continues:

If you justly doubt any long absence, I pray send to my lodging my written Books: and if you may stay very long, I pray send that Letter in which I sent you certain heads which I purposed to enlarge, for I have them not in any other paper: and I may finde time in your absence to do it, because I know no stronger argument to move you to love me.

---

[1] This is a further fact that makes it unlikely that he had been assisting Morton for three or more years previously; if he had been, one would expect him to be more sure of himself.

[2] A2ᵛ–A3.   [3] *Letters*, pp. 225–6 and 68–9.

Two days later his need for his notes had become more urgent, and he wrote again:

If you have laid my papers and books by, I pray let this messenger have them, I have determined upon them. If you have not, be content to do it, in the next three or four days.

This request was followed by a postscript:

When you are sometimes at M. *Sackvills*, I pray aske if he have this book, *Baldvinus de officio pii hominis in controversiis*; it was written at the conference at *Poissy*, where *Beza* was, and he answered it; I long for it.[1]

Edward Sackville, from whom he hoped to borrow a book on the conduct of controversies, was the younger brother of the Earl of Dorset and succeeded to the title in 1624. It looks as if Donne was getting ready to enter the controversy. But he had entrusted the first rough sketch of an outline to Goodyer, and now he wanted to pass it around among his other friends. Apparently it even circulated among some of the Catholics, since in the 'Aduertisement to the Reader' prefixed to his book Donne refers to 'these Heads hauing beene carried about, many moneths', and mentions that 'some of the Romane profession, hauing onely seene the Heads and Grounds handled in this Booke, haue traduced me, as an impious and profane vnder-valewer of Martyrdome'. Thus, one may surmise, all through the summer of 1609 the outline of Donne's argument was available to his friends and acquaintances, and he himself was assiduously extending his reading, collecting facts and opinions to support his case.

Walton's account of the origins and composition of *Pseudo-Martyr* has been received with caution by all modern writers on Donne, and cannot be correct in all its details. Walton begins by remarking that 'The *King* had formerly both known and put a value upon his Company: and had also given him some hopes of a State-imployment; being always much pleas'd when Mr. *Donne* attended him,

---

[1] Donne was misinformed; the true author of the book was Georges Cassandre; the true title was *De Officiis pii ac publicae tranquillitatis vere amantis viri in hoc religionis dissidio*, and it was an appeal by a moderate Catholic for compromise and reconciliation with the Protestants. The authorship was ascribed to Baldvinus (François Bauduin) because he arranged for the printing of the book in Paris at the time of the opening of the Colloquy of Poissy.

especially at his meals.'[1] After describing how it was James I's habit at dinner to sit eating at table, surrounded by a group of standing courtiers and divines, to whom he broached all sorts of arguments, Walton goes on to remark that on one such occasion

his Majesty discoursing with Mr. *Donne*, concerning many of the reasons which are usually urged against the taking of those Oaths; apprehended, such a validity and clearness in his stating the Questions, and his Answers to them, that his Majesty commanded him to bestow some time in drawing the Arguments into a method, and then to write his Answers to them: and, having done that, not to send, but be his own messenger and bring them to him. To this he presently and diligently applied himself, and, within six weeks brought them to him under his own handwriting, as they be now printed; the Book bearing the name of *Pseudo-martyr*, printed *anno* 1610.

In the dedication addressed to the King, however, there is no suggestion that the book was written by royal command, or that a manuscript in the author's own hand had already been presented and accepted; Donne merely declares that James's example had 'wrought vppon me, and drawen vp, and exhaled from my poore Meditations, these discourses'. Nevertheless, this is not a conclusive argument against Walton's accuracy. A more serious objection has, however, been raised:

There is little reason to doubt that Walton consciously misinterpreted a passage in the dedicatory epistle to the King of Donne's *Pseudo-Martyr*. . . . [In the epistle] Donne had spoken of the King's vouchsafing to descend to a conversation with his subjects and of his own conceiving an ambition to ascend to the King's presence, and the phrase 'by your Majesties permission' did occur. But Donne had said that the King's *books* had influenced him to write his book, that the King had conversed with his subjects *by way of his books*, and that he desired to ascend to the King's presence in the same way, that is, by way of his book. . . . By turning a figure of speech into a personal interview, Walton did not bind himself superstitiously to Donne's words, but even made Donne's words speak not Donne's sense but his own.[2]

This goes too far. We know from Donne's later conduct that when he

[1] *Lives*, p. 44.   [2] D. Novarr, *The Making of Walton's 'Lives'*, 1958, pp. 57–8.

dedicated to the Prince of Wales or the Duke of Buckingham he was careful to find out first that such a dedication would be acceptable; thus James would certainly have known that Donne was at work on *Pseudo-Martyr* and have given his consent to the dedication. But Donne's own words seem to imply more: 'in this, I make account, that I haue performed a duetie, by expressing in an exterior, and (by your Maiesties permission) a publicke Act, the same desire, which God heares in my daily prayers, That your Maiestie may very long gouerne vs. . . .'[1] The public act, performed with the King's permission, does not, I think, refer solely to the dedication but rather to the publication of the book. If Donne had had an opportunity of presenting the 'heads which [he] purposed to enlarge', the King's encouragement to make them into a book and the consequent permission to dedicate it would have followed naturally.

Some will perhaps question Walton's statement that the book was written in six weeks, but this would not have been impossible, provided that Donne had already organized his notes and references.[2] It was always his habit to work in furious bursts of energy. Not only had 'these Heads . . . beene carried about, many moneths', but during that period they had also been 'quarrelled by some, and desired by others', so that in the intervening months he would have had every reason to marshal his arguments and buttress them with authorities. The book was finished by 2 December, when it was entered in the Stationers' Register, and on 24 January 1610 the author journeyed to Royston, where the King was hunting, to present him with a copy as he was relaxing after the day's sport.[3]

---

[1] Sig. A3ᵛ.

[2] In the 'Aduertisement to the Reader' Donne says that he had been 'willing to giue the Booke a hasty dispatch, that it might cost no man much time, either in expecting before it came, or in reading, when it was come'.

[3] See Donne's letter to Sir Robert Cotton, reproduced in facsimile in Gosse, i, facing p. 108. This letter accompanied a copy of *Pseudo-Martyr* which Cotton was asked to deliver to 'my Lord' (almost certainly the Earl of Northampton) as soon as the royal copy had been presented.

Donne doubtless interested Cotton in *Pseudo-Martyr*, and probably consulted him during its composition, seeking his aid on historical and antiquarian points. Cotton's interest in the topic of Donne's book is testified by his authorship several years later of a tract, included in *Cottoni Posthuma*, entitled 'Twenty Foure Arguments, whether it be more expedient to suppress popish practices against the due allegeance of his Maiesty'.

Presentation copies of *Pseudo-Martyr* went to other important people as well as to

The heads of the argument which had been in circulation before the book was actually written are presumably the chapter summaries which constitute the table of contents of the book. At least, they seem to antedate the book itself, for, though they present the main steps in the argument, they are far from being complete outlines of the chapters. Donne ranges far more widely than the table of contents suggests; an excursus on the quarrels of the popes and the medieval emperors (chapter iii) or an inquiry into the nature and authority of precedents (chapter xi) were all felt to be germane to his purpose. But if in some respects he exceeds the limits set by his outline, in other respects he failed to fulfil the expectations that he had raised. The book consists of twelve chapters; the table of contents summarizes fourteen. Chapter xiii was to have proved that James was asking no more of his Catholic subjects than was already exacted by the King of France, and chapter xiv that no events in English history had given the pope any greater rights in England than he possessed in France. The reason for the omission of these two chapters was explained in the 'Aduertisement to the Reader'. The position to be taken up in chapter xiv was essentially that which had been upheld in Cawdrey's case, reported in the fifth part of Coke's Reports and attacked by Persons. Coke had indeed noticed the *Answere to the Fifth Part of Reportes*, briefly and with dignity, in the preface to the sixth part, but this hardly constituted a reply. The right of defence, Donne felt, belonged to Coke, or to someone authorized by him, so for the present he had resolved to refrain from discussing the topic, or the closely allied one of the extent of the papal authority in France. Nevertheless it is interesting to see that he still believed that the future of English Catholicism depended on its adopting a policy closely allied to the Gallicism developed and fostered by the Sorbonne. Here at least his views had scarcely changed from those he had held while still a Catholic.

Donne's book is based on the two mutually dependent propositions: that Catholics ought to take the Oath of Allegiance, and that

---

some of Donne's close friends. The letter accompanying a presentation copy to the Prince of Wales has survived; Lord Ellesmere's copy, accompanied by a letter, turned up not many years ago; and the copy Donne gave Rowland Woodward is in the collection of Mr. John Sparrow. J. Beaulieu sent William Trumbull a copy on 31 Jan. 1609/10 (Hist. MSS. Com., *MSS. of the Marquess of Downshire*, ii (1936), p. 227).

those who suffered for not doing so were not entitled to the dignity of martyrdom. The emphasis on the second proposition as of almost equal importance to the first is a tribute to the continuing influence of Donne's early training, for, as he had admitted, he had 'beene euer kept awake in a meditation of Martyrdome', so that for him and for many Catholics it wás the highest glory to be sought and attained by Christians. It is symptomatic, too, of the Donne who had written *Biathanatos* that he based his discussion of martyrdom on what he regarded as the innate and universal urge in human beings towards self-destruction. But God, who turns all things to good, and 'disposes all things sweetly, hath beene so indulgent to our nature, and the frailty thereof, that he hath afforded vs the meanes, how wee may giue away our life, and make him, in a pious interpretation, beholden to vs for it; which is by deliuering ourselues to Martyredome, for the testimony of his name, and aduancing his glorie'.[1]

Such an attitude towards martyrdom was perhaps inevitable in an age of faith and religious persecution, and it was natural too that what exactly constituted martyrdom should already have been discussed on various occasions. Donne owned a copy of Nicholas Harpsfield's *Dialogi Sex*, in the sixth and longest dialogue of which, 'contra Pseudo-martyres', the claims of Protestants to martyrdom were denied and Fox's *Actes and Monuments* was fiercely assailed. The other early attack on Fox, Persons's *Treatise of Three Conversions of England* (1603–4), together with Matthew Sutcliffe's reply to it, *The Subversion of Robert Parsons* (1606), seem to have left few traces in Donne's book, although a copy of Sutcliffe's pamphlet which once belonged to Donne is at Harvard.[2] Persons, though the term 'pseudo-martyr' occurs casually in his book, is more concerned with historical facts and their interpretation than with the nature of martyrdom, and Sutcliffe's refutation closely follows the pattern of Persons's book. Donne was certainly aware of the attacks on Fox, however, and even endorsed them for satirical purposes, since item 5 in *The Courtier's Library* is 'The art of copying out within the compass of a Penny all the truthful statements made to that end by John Foxe, *by Peter Bales*'.[3]

[1] Ch. 1, sec. 7, p. 4.   [2] Keynes, nos. L49 and L174.
[3] Peter Bales was the famous writing master. There is probably an allusion here

Donne's discussion of martyrdom culminates in the seventh chapter, with the assertion 'That if the meere execution of the function of Priests in this Kingdome, and of giuing to the Catholiques in this land, spiritual sustentation, did assure their consciences, that to dye for that were martyrdome: yet the refusall of the Oath of Alleageance doth corrupt and vitiate the integrity of the whole act, and dispoile them of their former interest and Title to Martyrdome.' The second half of the book is concerned with the topics, and uses the method, which, according to Walton, had originally captured the King's interest and caused him to command Donne to set them down on paper. Donne goes on to a searching examination of the reasons urged against the taking of the Oath, showing that the priests have no justification for advising their flocks to refuse it, since by canon law the authority of the pope to forbid it is doubtful and the legality of the breves is uncertain; in fact, Bellarmine's opinion, based on his famous doctrine of indirect power, is the sole source of the more extreme point of view. Finally, Donne declares that 'nothing requir'd in this Oath, violates the Popes spirituall Iurisdiction; And that the clauses of swearing that Doctrine to bee Hereticall, is no vsurping vpon his spirituall right, either by preiudicating his future definition, or offending any former Decree'.

Since one of Donne's principal aims in writing the book was to clarify the doubts and uncertainties of wavering Catholics and persuade them to accept the Oath, he was naturally careful to avoid antagonizing them. His tone is therefore one of sympathy and understanding, and, whenever possible, he identifies himself with their feelings. On the other hand, he loses no opportunity of attacking the Jesuits. In the 'Aduertisement to the Reader' Persons is referred to as 'an ordinary Instrument of [the devil], (whose continuall libels, and Incitatorie bookes, haue occasioned more afflictions and drawne more of that bloud, which they call Catholique, in this Kingdome, then all our Acts of Parliament haue done)';[1] and there are three more references to him in the preface, besides other satirical

also to the fact that he had transcribed some incriminating letters of Essex for a certain John Daniel, who used them to blackmail the Countess of Essex after her husband's death.

allusions to the Jesuits. Donne made the Jesuits his target right from the outset, and his attacks reach a climax in chapter iv, which is much wider in its scope than the summary suggests; it is no mere criticism of the order for begetting and cherishing 'this corrupt desire of false-Martyrdome', but a survey of every principle or practice of the order to which Donne can take exception.

It is clear that Donne expected to be attacked by Persons, but Persons died in April 1610, shortly after the publication of *Pseudo-Martyr*, and it is doubtful if he ever saw the book. At the time of his death, however, he had written part of a reply to Barlow's *Answer*. Barlow, Persons's friends asserted, would ordinarily have been beneath his notice, but he undertook this reply at the command of the Holy Inquisition, the members of which, being unable to read English, regarded Barlow's book as of some consequence. Persons's unfinished *Discussion of the Answere of M. D. Barlow* eventually appeared in 1612 with a long preface by Edward Coffin, and was completed in 1613 by *A Supplement to the Discussion of M. D. Barlowes Answere*, written by Thomas Fitzherbert, who succeeded some years later to Persons's post of rector of the English College at Rome. In the course of this last book Fitzherbert refers to some objections raised by Donne against the Canons of the Lateran Council, and spends some twenty pages in refuting him. On the whole he has the better of the argument, and convicts Donne of over-ingenuity. But this was no excuse for a spate of vituperation. Fitzherbert, it is clear, was aware of Donne's early career as a satirist, and tried to discredit him, in the manner of the controversialists of the time, by aspersions of atheism and by mere abuse:

he sheweth such a venemous malignity towards Catholickes, that it may serue for a Simptome to discouer another more malignant, and dangerous disease bred in his hart, from whence he hath belched out so many Lucianicall, impious, blasphemous, and Atheisticall iests against Gods Saints and Seruants, that he may well be thought to be one of those, of whom the Royall Prophet sayd: *Posuerunt in caelum os suum: They haue put, or set theyr mouth against heauen*, whose impunity in their impiety amazed the sayd Prophet (as he testifieth) and made him stagger, vntill he entred into the consideration of Gods secret iudgments, & of the payment that they shall receiue *in nouissimis eorum*, which I pray God M. *Dunne* may haue grace to foresee and avoyd.[1]

In 1619 Edward Coffin, Persons's other defender, derisively referred in passing to *Pseudo-Martyr* as 'a meere bundle of rotten rags ill fauouredly bound togeather',[2] but it never achieved a full-scale refutation, though Donne for some time continued to expect one. He had a sight of Fitzherbert's book, but no more: 'For that book which you command me to send,' he wrote to Garrard, 'I held it but half an hour: which served me to read those few leafes, which were directed upon some few lines of my book.'[3] At the same time he wrote to the Earl of Somerset: 'This day and not before I came to the sight of the book, which your Lordship mentioned to me; but because I know that the Jesuites at *Louaine* are in hand with an answer expreslie to my whole book, I forbear yet to take knowledge of this.'[4] Nothing ever came from Louvain, and Donne can be taken as having had the last word in this phase of the controversy.

Pseudo-Martyr considerably enhanced Donne's reputation in England. The Dean of Canterbury, John Boys, in a work published in the same year as *Pseudo-Martyr*, cited Donne alongside Bacon for his share in discrediting the learning of the Middle Ages: 'I will not meddle with the cobwebs of learning in the Schoole,[5] which have more wit then Art, yet more Art then vse; nor with the distorted and idle glosses of the Canonists: he that list may burthen his memory with a shipfull of their fooleries, accurately collected by the penner of Pseudomartyr, cap. 10.'[6] The King was pleased with the

---

[1] Pp. 105–6. Cf. Simpson, *Prose Works*, pp. 190–1. It is difficult to believe that Fitzherbert is referring only to *Pseudo-Martyr* in this passage; the description simply does not fit. The 'many Lucianicall, impious, blasphemous, and Atheisticall iests' seem to be a reference to *Ignatius his Conclave*; Fitzherbert, apparently, had not merely seen the latter book but also knew that Donne was its author.

Nevertheless, it is also worth noting in connection with Fitzherbert's attitude towards Donne, that the 'wit' of Andrewes and Donne seems merely to have baffled their ultramontane adversaries—an attitude which persists in some quarters to the present day; see, for example, J. Brodrick, *Life and Works of Blessed Robert Francis, Cardinal Bellarmine*, 1925, ii. 208.

[2] *A Refutation of M. Joseph Hall . . . by C.E., a Catholike Priest*, p. 240, side note.

[3] *Letters*, p. 284.   [4] *Tobie Mathew Collection*, p. 317.

[5] Side-note: 'Aduancement of learning, *lib.* 1, *pag.* 20.'

[6] *An Exposition of the Dominicall Epistles and Gospels vsed in our English Liturgie*, in Boys's *Works*, 1629, p. 277.

book but, instead of giving Donne the reward for which he hoped, was apparently so impressed with his learning in theology and canon law as to insist on the Church as the proper place for his particular talents. 'When the King had read and considered that Book,' wrote Walton, 'he perswaded Mr. *Donne* to enter into the Ministery.'[1] James's attitude must have been a bitter disappointment to Donne, though he continued to press for secular employment. Another consequence of the book, however, was an honorary M.A. from Oxford, for which Donne was probably in some measure indebted to his friend John King, now Dean of Christ Church and Vice-Chancellor of the University. On 17 April 1610 Convocation permitted John Donne, 'armiger, olim ex Aula Cervina', to proceed to the degree of M.A. without exercises and without a B.A.: 'Causa est quod huic Academiae maxime ornamento sit ut ejusmodi viri, optime de republica et ecclesia meriti, gradibus Academicis insigniantur.' On the following day the degree was conferred, and at the same time an acquaintance, John Pory, was incorporated from Cambridge.[2] A couple of years later Donne was to deny haughtily that he had any intention of going on to a degree in civil law so as to practise at Doctors' Commons, though Richard Baddeley, Morton's secretary, distinctly remembered that Donne wrote from France a letter 'wherein he requested his advice, Whether taking the Degree of a *Doctor* in that Profession of the Laws, it might not be conducible and advantagious unto him to Practice at home in the *Arches London*'. The degree of master would have been an essential preliminary to the higher one; indeed, it would have made such a career possible for Donne, and it may be taken for granted that he seriously considered it for a couple of years, in default of any court promotion or other encouragement from the King.

Donne's next controversial work was probably written during the later part of 1610, since the Latin *Conclave Ignati* was entered in the Stationers' Register on 24 January 1610/11. It was entered 'vnder thandes of Doctor Moreton, Doctor Mokett and master Adames warden'. Richard Mocket, D.D., was one of the Archbishop's

---

[1] *Lives*, p. 45. 'Perswaded', i.e. tried to convince; see *OED*, persuade, *v*. I. 3.
[2] A. Clark, *Register of the University of Oxford*, vol. ii, pt. i, pp. 237 and 358, and J. Sparrow in *A Garland for John Donne*, ed. T. Spencer, at pp. 136–7.

chaplains and a regular licencer of books at this period, but Morton did not normally act in this capacity. Donne had evidently shown the manuscript to him before seeking a publisher or taking it to the regular licencer, and Morton had signified his approval of the contents of the manuscript in order, no doubt, to make it easier for Donne to secure official approval. The book must have appeared soon afterwards, both in London and on the Continent,[1] and Donne almost at once set to work to turn it into English. Another translator, who has remained anonymous, was also attracted by the pamphlet, and he must barely have completed his English version when Donne's own translation, entered in the Stationers' Register on 18 May 1611, came off the press. The anonymous version has accordingly lain unnoticed among the Harleian manuscripts for 200 years, under the title 'Ignatius his Closet, or his late Installinge in the Highe Courte of Parlament, summoned by generall consent of the chiefe gouerninge Furyes of the deepest Hell'.[2]

During the seventeenth century there were, in all, three Latin and four English editions of *Ignatius*, so that clearly the work was more widely read than *Pseudo-Martyr*, which never achieved a second edition. Its comparative popularity was obviously due to its satiric verve. It was as though Donne in *Pseudo-Martyr* had been unable to use a whole sheaf of the more extreme and ridiculous utterances of his opponents, and in *Ignatius* he found a setting in which to display them to best advantage. To the modern critic the pamphlet has the additional attraction of illustrating the range of Donne's reading, and especially of drawing attention to the keenness with which he followed developments in contemporary science. Furthermore, Donne was probably indebted to Kepler's most recent work, his *Somnium*, for even the framework of the cosmic voyage and the fiction of the moon as a habitable region. At least, Kepler himself thought

[1] Probably at Hanau; see Keynes, pp. 10 and 14.;

[2] MS. Harl. 1019. To the transcript of the title in the printed catalogue Wanley has added: 'The Book is fitted for the Press; and at the beginning is a Preface under the printers Name, containing an Apology for the Authors way of Writing. (Qu. if the Author was not Dr. Donne?)'; but in saying that the book is 'fitted for the Press' Wanley has been misled by the fact that the translator has, of course, translated Donne's preface, 'The Printer to the Reader'. [Donne's attitude to Loyola persisted unchanged; see the recently discovered Latin epigram, occasioned by Loyola's canonization in 1622, first printed by P. G. Stanwood, 'A Donne Discovery', *TLS*, 19 Oct. 1967, p. 984.]

so some years later when he came across *Conclave Ignati* and read it.[1] Yet the *Somnium* was not published until after Donne's death, though it had previously enjoyed a circulation in manuscript, and the problem arises of how Donne could have seen it. The most natural link between Donne and Kepler would have been the mathematician Thomas Hariot, a protégé of Sir Walter Raleigh and pensioner of the Earl of Northumberland, who was at this time living in a house specially built for him in the grounds of Sion House. Hariot, moreover, was a frequent visitor to the Tower of London, where the Earl was deep in his alchemical studies and Raleigh was busying himself with the composition of the *History of the World*, with the help of Ben Jonson and various other learned writers. It is thus not unlikely that Donne was in touch with the two famous prisoners in the Tower during these years, and that he was also acquainted with Hariot, the trusted friend of both. Hariot is known to have been in regular correspondence with Kepler at this time through a certain John Eriksen, who travelled frequently between London and Prague, and could well have brought Hariot a manuscript of the *Somnium*. Another possible link between Donne and Hariot was Hariot's pupil and correspondent Sir William Lower, who is twice mentioned in Donne's letters.[2] A letter from Lower to Hariot at this very period[3] shows something of the excitement felt by those who followed the new astronomy. Lower had been observing the moon through his own telescope; he was familiar with the latest theories of Galileo

---

[1] See Marjorie Nicolson, *Science and Imagination*, 'Kepler, the *Somnium*, and John Donne', pp. 58–79, especially pp. 63 and 67. It must not be forgotten—as, indeed, Miss Nicolson points out—that the idea of a moon-world is to be found as far back as Plutarch and Lucian; and the concept of the journey of the soul to the otherworld is equally ancient (see, for example, M. W. Bloomfield, *The Seven Deadly Sins*, pp. 12–26, 47–53). Indeed, Donne was to use another variant of the soul-journey only a few months later in *The Second Anniversary*. None of this, however, is to suggest for a moment that he might not have read Kepler's *Somnium*.

Kepler's note is as follows: 'Fallor an author Satyrae procacis, cui nomen Conclave Ignatianum, exemplar nactus erat hujus opusculi; pungit enim me nominatim etian in ipso principio. Nam in progressu miserum Copernicum adducit ad Plutonis tribunal, ad quod, ni fallor, aditus est per Hecla voragines.' ('I suspect that the author of that impudent satire, the *Conclave of Ignatius*, had got hold of this little work, for he pricks me by name in the very beginning. Further on, he brings up poor Copernicus to the judgment seat of Pluto—if I don't mistake, the approach to that is through the yawning chasms of Hecla.') Quoted and translated by Miss Nicolson, pp. 63 and 67.

[2] *Letters*, pp. 152 and 195.   [3] H. Stevens, *Thomas Hariot*, 1900, pp. 116–18.

and Kepler; and he was eager for any scrap of new knowledge. If Donne felt but half his enthusiasm, the ardour with which he would have borrowed and read the *Somnium* is easily understood.

Yet, in spite of all these activities and interests Donne seems, throughout the Mitcham years, to have been deeply despondent at the lack of direction in his life:

I would fain do something; but that I cannot tell what, is no wonder. For to chuse, is to do: but to be no part of any body, is to be nothing. At most, the greatest persons, are but great wens, and excrescences; men of wit and delightfull conversation, but as moales for ornament, except they be so incorporated into the body of the world, that they contribute something to the sustentation of the whole.

. . . such as I am, rather a sicknesse and disease of the world then any part of it. . .

If I aske my self what I have done in the last watch, or would do in the next, I can say nothing; if I say that I have passed it without hurting any, so may the Spider in my window.[1]

He watched his fits of melancholy and tried to diagnose his alternations of mood, but they seemed only to emphasize the uncertainties by which he was beset. In the passage that follows one can see his feeling of responsibility at odds with his consciousness that nothing has been accomplished, and both of these opposed by his urge for companionship and conviviality:

sometimes when I finde my self transported with jollity, and love of company, I hang Leads at my heels; and reduce to my thoughts my fortunes, my years, the duties of a man, of a friend, of a husband, of a Father, and all the incumbencies of a family: when sadnesse dejects me, either I countermine it with another sadnesse, or I kindle squibs about me again, and flie into sportfulnesse and company: and I finde ever after all, that I am like an exorcist, which had long laboured about one, which at last appears to have the Mother, that I still mistake my disease.[2]

His sense of not 'belonging' made him feel a cipher, a nothing, and this feeling is the base for the conceit not merely of one of the poems to Lady Bedford, but also of one of his letters to Goodyer:

[1] *Letters*, pp. 50–1, 59, 48.　　　　[2] Ibid., p. 71.

Though I know you have many worthy friends of all rankes, yet I adde something, since I which am of none, would fain be your friend too. There is some of the honour and some of the degrees of a Creation, to make a friendship of nothing.[1]

Only occasionally in the letters are there glimpses of the mood out of which *Biathanatos* grew:

With the first of these [temptations] I have often suspected my self to be overtaken; which is, with a desire of the next life: which though I know it is not meerly out of a wearinesse of this, because I had the same desires when I went with the tyde, and enjoyed fairer hopes then now: yet I doubt worldly encombrances have encreased it.[2]

Though it is well that we should be reminded that *Biathanatos* 'treated a subject of emerging public, not perversely personal, interest', and that it is 'not to be viewed as an elaborate whim, or reduced to the sublimation of a private death-wish',[3] none the less it is Donne himself who links its theme to his own predicament:

I have often such a sickely inclination. And, whether it be, because I had my first breeding and conversation with men of a suppressed and afflicted Religion, accustomed to the despite of death, and hungry of an imagin'd Martyrdome; Or that the common Enemie find that doore worst locked against him in mee; Or that there bee a perplexitie and flexibility in the doctrine it selfe; Or because my Conscience ever assures me, that no rebellious grudging at Gods gifts, nor other sinfull concurrence accompanies these thoughts in me, or that a brave scorn, or that a faint cowardlinesse beget it, whensoever any affliction assailes me, mee thinks I have the keyes of my prison in mine owne hand, and no remedy presents it selfe so soone to my heart, as mine own sword.[4]

Yet, in the main, Donne seems to have kept such thoughts to himself, though *Biathanatos* itself is proof of their persistence and of the need to find some such way of exorcizing them.

In the letters of this period we can also trace something of the course of Donne's theological studies. One passage makes use of the schoolmen's classification of conscience into *errantem, opinantem,*

[1] Ibid., p. 65.　　　　　　　　　　　　　　　　　　[2] Ibid., p. 50.
[3] S. E. Sprott, *The English Debate on Suicide from Donne to Hume*, p. 25.
[4] Preface to *Biathanatos.*

dubiam, and *scrupulosam,* which is of interest not only because it indicates Donne's interest in casuistry but also because it was used again years later in a sermon.[1] Similarly, another letter shows his concern with the efficacy of prayers for the dead, which was to be the theme of an important sermon,[2] and with a further problem to which he often recurs, the time at which the soul enters the infant's body, and the manner by which original sin is transmitted to us by our parents.[3] These are problems with which the subtle soul can vex itself, yet Donne would hardly have maintained that the proper answers to such questions were essential to salvation. While it is possible to think of *Biathanatos* and *Pseudo-Martyr* as primarily works of scholarship (as in a sense they are) in which only the intellect was engaged, it is clear that Donne's emotions as well as his thinking, and indeed his whole way of life, were insensibly becoming involved in the solution of such theological problems. This the letters to Goodyer show. His religious sense was steadily deepening. 'If at any time I seem to studie you more inquisitively,' he wrote to his friend, 'it is for no other end but to know how to present you to God in my prayers, and what to ask of him for you.'[4] About the same time he was also asserting that 'Two of the most precious things which God hath afforded us here . . . are a thirst and inhiation after the next life, and a frequency of prayer and meditation in this.'[5] Such sentences would never have come from Donne when he married Ann More seven or eight years previously. This deepening seriousness even led him to question his earlier writings: '. . . even at this time; when I humbly thank God, I ask & have, his comfort of sadder meditations; I doe not condemn in my self, that I have given my wit such evaporations, as those, if they be free from prophaneness, or obscene provocations.'[6] It is inconceivable that Donne should have written in this strain even a few years earlier.

Nevertheless he rejected the persuasions of the King and of Thomas Morton that he should enter the Church. He probably felt

---

[1] *Letters,* pp. 85–6; *Sermons,* iv. 222 [see A. E. Malloch, 'John Donne and the Casuists', *St. in Eng. Lit.* ii (1962), 57–76].

[2] *Sermons,* vii, no. 3.

[3] e.g. ibid. v, no. 8, ll. 137–46, p. 172, and no. 17, ll. 388–408, pp. 348–9. Cf. *Letters,* pp. 15–18.

[4] Ibid., p. 110.   [5] Ibid., p. 49.   [6] Ibid., p. 36.

that his support of the Anglican position was intellectual rather than spiritual, for he still retained some of the scepticism against the sects which he had expressed in the third Satire, and could write to Goodyer: 'You know I never fettered nor imprisoned the word Religion; not straightning it Frierly, *ad Religiones factitias*, (as the *Romans* call well their orders of Religion) nor immuring it in a *Rome*, or a *Wittemberg*, or a *Geneva*; they are all virtuall beams of one Sun.'[1] Ultimately, however, this was no obstacle, for even after his ordination he could write the sonnet beginning 'Show me deare Christ, thy spouse, so bright and cleare'. Again, he probably felt that the tone of a work like *Ignatius his Conclave* was unsuitable for a minister of the gospel to acknowledge; nevertheless he made no attempt to disown the book, as he might have done after he became Dean of St. Paul's. The essential cause was his lack of conviction of his own salvation, without which no man was qualified to preach the gospel of Christ.

In the same letter in which Donne related that God had given him the 'comfort of sadder meditations' he also told Goodyer that he had composed 'A Litanie'. The poem, unquestionably, was an example of the more serious meditations to which he had referred. It is now recognized that not only 'A Litanie' and 'La Corona' were composed during the Mitcham years, but the majority of the 'Holy Sonnets' as well.[2] In 'La Corona' and 'A Litanie' there is a ritual element that gives them a certain restraint and formalism which are much less strongly marked in the 'Holy Sonnets'.[3] Even so, Donne confesses that 'La Corona' was 'Weav'd in my low devout melancholie' and in 'A Litanie' that 'My heart is by dejection, clay, / And by selfe-murder, red'. He was one in whom

> want, sent but to tame, [did] warre
> And worke despaire a breach to enter in.

In the more personal 'Holy Sonnets' a far greater sense of urgency is revealed. Despair has entered in at the breach it had made.

---

[1] Ibid., p. 29.

[2] Gardner, *Divine Poems*, pp. xliii–xlix. D. Novarr, 'The Dating of Donne's "La Corona"', *PQ*, xxvi (1957), 259–65, argues that 'La Corona' does not necessarily belong to 1607, but is more likely to have been written in 1608 or early 1609.

[3] Gardner, *Divine Poems*, pp. xxii–xxix.

Despair, it should be recalled, was in the seventeenth century sin as well as suffering, for it implied distrust in God and His mercy; and Donne was afflicted by this distrust.

> Oh I shall soone despaire, when I doe see
> That thou lov'st mankind well, yet wilt'not chuse me.

> I dare not move my dimme eyes any way,
> Despaire behind, and death before doth cast
> Such terrour.

He was in doubt of his salvation, and therefore terrified at the thought of death. He was also haunted by recollections of sin, so that he seemed the chief of sinners and his sins abounded above those of all the 'numberlesse infinities Of soules' who would arise to go to the Last Judgement. He felt like a traitor to his King, or like a condemned criminal being led to the scaffold, so that it was too late to repent. He looked with envy on the dumb animals, and even on the tree that bore the forbidden fruit, because none of them could ever suffer damnation:

> Why doe the prodigall elements supply
> Life and food to mee, being more pure then I,
> Simple, and further from corruption?
> Why brook'st thou, ignorant horse, subjection?
> Why dost thou bull, and bore so seelily
> Dissemble weaknesse, and by'one mans stroke die,
> Whose whole kinde, you might swallow and feed upon?
> Weaker I am, woe is mee, and worse then you,
> You have not sinn'd, nor need be timorous.

Here are all the classic symptoms of what William James calls 'the sick soul', even to the envy of the dumb animals which, says James, 'seems to be a very widespread affection in this type of sadness'.[1]

[1] *The Varieties of Religious Experience*, p. 156. On this whole topic see especially Lectures VI and VII.

Donne's spiritual state as portrayed in the 'Holy Sonnets' finds some remarkable parallels in Bunyan's narrative of his conversion in *Grace Abounding* (ed. R. Sharrock, 1962):

After this, that other doubt did come with strength upon me, *But how if the day of grace should be past and gone*? how if you have over-stood the time of mercy? (sec. 66; cf. sonnet IV, 'Oh my blacke Soule!', ll. 9–10).

Further, in these days I should find my heart to shut itself up against the Lord, and against his holy Word; I have found my unbelief to set as it were the shoulder

Thus the years 1607–10 were probably the most disturbed and anxious years of Donne's life. He passed through a spiritual crisis which was in large measure concealed from those closest to him. He tried consciously, no doubt, to hide it from his wife, and Sir Henry Goodyer, as his closest friend, was permitted to see only occasional glimpses of it. But it is revealed clearly enough in the 'Holy Sonnets', and in the sermons of later years he looked back with a particular sense of poignancy to the despair and suffering through which he had passed.[1] That Donne was able to diagnose his own complaint is not surprising, for he was doubtless well read in the literature of penitence and conversion from the *Confessions* of St. Augustine down to his own time.

But as melancholy in the body is the hardest humour to be purged, so is the melancholy in the soule, the distrust of thy salvation too. Flashes of presumption a calamity will quench, but clouds of desperation calamities thicken upon us; But even in this inordinate dejection

to the door to keep him out, and that too, even then when I have with many a bitter sigh cried, Good Lord, break it open; *Lord, break these gates of brass, and cut these bars of iron asunder* (sec. 81; cf. sonnet XIV, 'Batter my heart').

I saw that I wanted a perfect righteousness to present me without fault before God and this righteousness was nowhere to be found but in the Person of Jesus Christ. But my Original and inward pollution, that, that was my plague and my affliction; that I saw at a dreadful rate always putting forth it selfe within me, that I had the guilt of to amazement; by reason of that, I was more loathsom in mine own eyes then was a toad, and I thought I was so in God's eyes too: . . . I thought, none but the Devil himself could equalize me for inward wickednes and pollution of minde. I fell therfore at the sight of my own vileness, deeply into dispair, for I concluded that this condition that I was in, Could not stand with a state of Grace, sure, thought I, I am forsaken of God, sure I am given up, to the Devil, and to a reprobate mind: and thus I continued a long while, even for some years together (secs. 83 and 84; cf. sonnets II, 'As due by many titles', ll. 9–14, and VI, 'This is my playes last scene', ll. 13–14).

Man Indeed is the most noble, by creation, of all the creatures in the visible World; but by sin he had made himself the most ignoble. The beasts, birds, fishes, &c., I blessed their condition, for they had not a sinful nature, obnoxious in the sight of God; they were not to go to Hell fire after death; I could therefore a rejoyced had my condition been as any of theirs (sec. 88; cf. sonnets IX, 'If poysonous mineralls', ll. 1–6, and XII, 'Why are wee by all creatures waited on?').

[1] Compare Helen Gardner (*Divine Poems*, p. xliii): 'Anyone who reads Donne's sermons in the folios, going steadily through them in their formidable bulk, must be struck by the persistence with which he recurs to certain themes. As a moral theologian he is much concerned with the sin of diffidence, or its extremer form, despair. This subject occurs again and again, frequently in not very obvious contexts, as if it were of great personal importance to him. We know from his letters and poems that it was. He was deeply infected with melancholy, which, like Dr. Johnson, he regarded as a sin.'

thou exaltest thy self above God, and makest thy worst better then his best, thy sins larger then his mercy.

And again:

I make my selfe worse then Christ found me, and in an inordinate dejection of spirit, conceive a jealousie and suspition, that his merit concernes not me, that his blood extends not to my sin; And in this last and worst state, the Holy Ghost finds me, the Spirit of Consolation, And he sends a *Barnabas* . . . to my sick bed side, A Physitian that comforts with hopes, and meanes of health. . . .[1]

The frequent outcome of such crises is conversion, either sudden or gradual, but Donne still had some years to wait before he was secure in the conviction of God's ever-present mercy. As yet there is no sense of release, or that his prayers have been fully answered. When the true date of most of the 'Holy Sonnets' is recognized, however, a host of difficulties vanishes. One is no longer startled by the utter absence of inward peace, nor puzzled by the lack of any sense of priestly vocation. These sonnets were not written, as was earlier supposed, by a man in holy orders, but during a period of Donne's life when he had no vocation and felt keenly that he had no place in the divinely ordered scheme. His integrity, too, is vindicated, and one understands far better his prolonged hesitation to enter the Church.

[1] *Sermons*, iii, no. 14, ll. 394–400, pp. 302–3, and vii, no. 4, ll. 659–66, p. 136.

X

ABROAD WITH SIR ROBERT DRURY

EARLY in 1611 Donne found a new patron and one who, directly or indirectly, exercised a deeper influence on his life and work than any of the others. This was Sir Robert Drury of Hawstead in Suffolk. The fortunes of the family had been founded a century earlier by another Sir Robert, a lawyer who had been one of Henry VII's privy councillors. Not only had he greatly increased the family estates in Suffolk but he had also acquired a large town house at the southern end of what came in due course to be known as Drury Lane. The great-grandson of the first Sir Robert, Sir William Drury, was a courtier and soldier who was killed in France early in 1590, not on the field of battle but in a duel with a fellow officer. Sir William was succeeded by his eldest son Robert, a lad who reached his fifteenth birthday a few weeks after his father's death. He was clearly anxious to emulate his father's military career, and in the next year he joined the English forces still fighting in France under the command of Henri IV against the League. In the same summer the young Earl of Essex became Lord General of the English forces, and in September he dubbed twenty-four knights in the fields outside Rouen, which was then being besieged. One of these was young Robert Drury, who thus became a knight while still only sixteen. He returned to England towards the end of the year, and on his seventeenth birthday he married the daughter of his guardian. His bride was Anne, the eldest daughter of Sir Nicholas Bacon, son and heir of Elizabeth's former Lord Keeper and half-brother of Francis Bacon.

For some years Sir Robert Drury was much away at the wars. For instance, he took part in the 1596 expedition against Cadiz, was in the fighting at Ostend in 1596–7, and in 1599 he saw service in Ireland under Essex. In 1600 he was in the Low Countries again and distinguished himself by his gallantry at the battle of Nieuport.

Two years later he made a tour of Italy, and was still abroad when Queen Elizabeth died, but early in the next reign he secured an appointment as Gentleman of the Chamber. He visited Spain in 1605, with the embassy sent to confirm the recently made treaty of peace, and was a member of James's first two parliaments. From this time onwards Sir Robert actively sought state employment, preferably an ambassadorship. By temperament, however, he was scarcely fitted for such a post, in spite of his experience abroad. He seems to have been a warm-hearted but quick-tempered and rather domineering man who never hesitated to speak his mind freely; he lacked any considerable intellectual interests and had little subtlety of mind. Hence he never obtained the appointments which he sought, or succeeded in achieving the recognition to which he felt he was entitled. Though he was not as wealthy as has sometimes been alleged, his properties in Suffolk and London brought him an income of between £2,000 and £3,000 a year, so that his wealth was ample for the indulgence of all but the most extravagant tastes.[1]

Sir Robert and Lady Drury had had two daughters. Dorothy, the elder, died at the age of four in 1597 and Elizabeth, the younger, died in London during the earlier part of December 1610 when she was within a few weeks of her fifteenth birthday. Her body was buried in the church at Hawstead on 17 December. Her portrait, which has survived, shows a delicate and rather childish figure, dressed in all the stiff elegance of the age and stretched out at full length in a reclining posture. The effigy on her tomb is copied from this picture, though it is much less skilfully executed.

It is impossible to be sure when Donne first became acquainted with Sir Robert Drury. Drury had been at Corpus Christi College, Cambridge, between 1588 and 1590 and had been in the expedition against Cadiz in 1596. His brother-in-law Sir Edmund Bacon was an intimate friend of Sir Henry Wotton, and Drury himself, like Sir Henry Goodyer, was in personal attendance on the King. Hence it is possible that he and Donne had known one another slightly for years. But there was a further link that is more significant. Donne's brother-in-law William Lyly had served in France under Sir Edward Stafford, who was Sir Robert Drury's uncle, and when Lyly

---

[1] *Donne and the Drurys*, pp. 64–6.

returned to England at the conclusion of Stafford's embassy he eventually found a house at Hawstead, where, as we have seen, he enjoyed the patronage of the Drurys. His signature appears as that of a witness to a document signed by Sir Robert Drury in 1598, and a letter written by Drury while he was on service in Ireland in the following year refers to an enclosure (long since lost) for 'M^r. Lylley'.[1] A further glimpse of Lyly at Hawstead comes from the pen of the man who was then the rector there. Joseph Hall was a promising young man from Emmanuel College, Cambridge, who had recently been presented to Hawstead Rectory; in later years when, as a bishop, he came to write his autobiography, he recalled:

Having then fixed my foot at *Halsted*, I found there a dangerous Opposite to the Success of my Ministry, a witty and bold Atheist, one Mr. *Lilly*, who by reason of his Travails, and Abilities of Discourse and Behaviour, had so deeply insinuated himself into my Patron, Sir *Robert Drury*, that there was small hopes (during his entireness) for me to work any good upon that Noble Patron of mine; who by the suggestion of this wicked Detractor was set off from me before he knew me; Hereupon (I confess) finding the obduredness and hopeless condition of that man, I bent my prayers against him, beseeching God daily, that he would be pleased to remove by some means or other, that apparent hindrance of my faithful Labours, who gave me an answer accordingly: For this malicious man going hastily up to *London*, to exasperate my Patron against me, was then and there swept away by the Pestilence, and never returned to do any farther Mischief.[2]

A letter among the Salisbury papers[3] shows that actually Lyly had gone to London to see what chance he had of securing a post under the new regime. He died intestate, but on 16 August 1603, not long after his death, the Prerogative Court of Canterbury granted letters of administration of his goods to Anne Lyly, 'relict of William Lilly, formerly of Hawstead in the county of Suffolk, deceased'.

Of Anne Lyly's subsequent history nothing whatever is known except that she died about 1616, so one can only guess whether she continued to live at Hawstead or moved away. Yet, in spite of the

[1] Hist. MSS. Com., *MSS. of the Marquis of Salisbury*, xiv. 118.
[2] *The Shaking of the Olive-Tree*, 1660, pp. 13–14.
[3] Vol. 103, 23/3.

antagonism between Hall and his brother-in-law, Donne probably met Hall during the latter's Hawstead days. Walton mentions Hall as one of those to whom Donne gave one of his cross and anchor seals, suggesting that their friendship had been of long duration; but, more important, the earliest relations between Donne and Hall of which there is definite knowledge are not such as to suggest recent acquaintance. They belong to the latter part of 1611, and are the less likely to have been brought about by Sir Robert and Lady Drury, since Hall had resigned from Hawstead in 1607 and was now at Waltham Holy Cross, near St. Albans.[1] If, then, as this rather tenuous argument suggests, Donne first met Hall at Hawstead between 1601 and 1607, he is also likely to have met Sir Robert Drury then if he had not met him already.

Nevertheless, it was not until after the death of Elizabeth Drury that a closer intimacy developed between Donne and the parents of the dead girl. Donne afterwards wrote that he had never seen Elizabeth, though his sister must have known her during most of her childhood, and it was perhaps at his sister's suggestion that Donne was persuaded to present the sorrowing parents with an elegy on their daughter's death. This was a consolatory poem of the same sort as those he had written for Lady Bedford in 1609 on the deaths of Lady Markham and Cecilia Bulstrode; it appeared in print as an appendix to *An Anatomy of the World* under the title 'A Funerall Elegie', and contains the germ of some of the motifs subsequently developed in the two *Anniversaries*.

There is no doubt that Donne's poem made a deep impression on the bereaved parents, and that both Sir Robert and Lady Drury were attracted to him. As the two men became better acquainted, they realized that they had more in common than they had at first supposed. Donne, like Drury, had been unsuccessfully seeking public employment overseas. Both men were widely travelled, though

---

[1] In his autobiography (*The Shaking of the Olive-Tree*) Hall relates how he left Hawstead for Waltham at the invitation of Lord Denny and just at the same time became a chaplain to Prince Henry. Thereafter Hall would have been in London at regular intervals to preach before the Prince, and would soon have become acquainted with some of the members of the Prince's household who were also friends of Donne. Furthermore, his patron, Lord Denny, was the father-in-law of Lord Hay, whom Hall in 1616 accompanied to France as chaplain; thus Donne would be likely to have seen Hall from time to time through his association with Lord Hay.

Donne was by far the better linguist. Drury seems to have perceived that they might be able to combine forces, and that Donne's talents could be of real service to him. He had been abroad with his wife and daughter for some months in 1610, and in the following year he proposed a more extended journey. Accordingly he invited Donne to accompany him.

On 2 July 1611 'A licence to travell ⟨was⟩ graunted vnto Sir Roberte drury of Halsted in the County of Suff., Kt., with his wife and familie, for three yeares, with Twelve Horses, Coach and Fifty poundes in money',[1] but they did not set out immediately, for Sir Robert 'was by many businesses held in England some months after my purpose of a present cominge away'.[2] The first reference to the invitation in Donne's correspondence occurs in a Latin letter, unfortunately undated, which he sent to Goodyer.[3] There has arisen, he writes, a new opportunity of visiting foreign lands, although it may involve leaving his wife and children for several years. He wishes to discuss the matter with Goodyer, but is reluctant to do so at the Bartlett's house (where Goodyer lodged),[4] since he fears that his friendship with that house is wearing thin. He waits at his lodging ('apud Rabbinum Tincombum') for word of a time at which Goodyer can meet him. Then follows a most interesting passage only indirectly connected with his proposed travels abroad which suggests that Donne was in the course of revising some of his writings for the press. He requests Goodyer to set aside for him some of his papers, which had been lent only on promise of their speedy return. He hopes that his Latin epigrams and his satirical Catalogue of Books will be there, though of this he is uncertain. His writings are to undergo their Last Judgement. Some will pass through purgatory, to emerge corrected; others will be consigned to hell and

---

[1] S.P. 38, vol. 10, *sub* date.   [2] *Donne and the Drurys*, p. 91.

[3] *Works of John Donne*, ed. H. Alford, 1839, vi. 440–1; the letter was first printed in the 1633 edition of Donne's *Poems*, pp. 351–2.

[4] The phrase in the printed text is 'in aedibus Barlotianis', but in view of other references in Donne's letters Sir Thomas and Lady Bartlett must be meant. Sir Thomas Bartlett had been knighted at James's coronation; he came of an old Gloucestershire family, and married Mary, daughter of Sir John Dauntsey. Bartlett was appointed Carver to Queen Anne. In February 1611 he got into serious trouble for using 'unseemly and desperate language in preferring petitions to the King for protection and relief'. He was sent to the Tower and remained there until Dec. 1614, although immediately on his release he secured a patent for making pins.

consumed by fire, so that the state of such copies of these originals as have escaped into the world proclaims their damnation. The rest, which have not been multiplied, can collapse of their own lack of inner substance. But if Donne had any intention in 1611 of publishing a selection of his poems and shorter prose pieces the plan was postponed, perhaps because of his travels with the Drurys, though it was taken up again several years later.

The letter to Goodyer seems to have been written almost immediately after Donne had received Sir Robert Drury's invitation, and before he had had an opportunity to mention the proposal to his wife. When he did so her distress was at once manifest. She was then, according to Walton,

with Child, and otherways under so dangerous a habit of body, as to her health, that she profest an unwillingness to allow him any absence from her; saying, *her divining soul boded her some ill in his absence*; and therefore, desired him not to leave her. This made Mr. *Donne* lay aside all thoughts of the Journey, and really to resolve against it. But Sir *Robert* became restless in his perswasions for it; and Mr. *Donne* was so generous, as to think he had sold his liberty when he received so many Charitable kindnesses from him: and, told his wife so; who did therefore with an unwilling-willingness give a faint Consent to the Journey.

Walton here implies that the song beginning 'Sweetest love, I do not goe, / For wearinesse of thee' was written and addressed by Donne to his wife at this time; and elsewhere he says this explicitly of the famous 'Valediction: forbidding Mourning'. If so, these two poems are probably the latest in date of all the 'Songs and Sonets'.[1]

After reaching the decision to accompany Sir Robert and Lady Drury Donne apparently gave up the house at Mitcham and made arrangements to send his wife and children to the Isle of Wight, where they stayed during his absence with her younger sister Frances, the wife of John Oglander (later Sir John) of Nunwell. Donne himself seems to have remained in his London lodgings until the time came to set out. It was probably during this period of

[1] Cf. Walton, *Lives*, pp. 39, 42–44. It should be noted, however, that the passage quoted was added in the 1675 edition of the *Lives*. [For arguments against Walton's association of the 'Song' ('Sweetest Love') and the 'Valediction' with Ann Donne in 1611, see Gardner, *Elegies etc.*, pp. xxviii–xxix, 155.]

waiting that he wrote *An Anatomy of the World*, 'wherein, by occasion of the vntimely death of Mistris Elizabeth Drury the frailty and
the decay of this whole world is represented'. The poem must not
only have been presented at once to Sir Robert and Lady Drury, but
must also have been shown either by them or by Donne himself to
Joseph Hall. Immediately pressure was put on Donne to publish
the piece, together with the 'Funerall Elegie', and with some reluctance he consented. To the poem were prefixed some lines 'To the
praise of the Dead, and the Anatomy', and there is little doubt that
Hall was their author. Ben Jonson told Drummond that Hall was
'the Harbenger to Dones Anniversarie', and though the reference
is to the lines headed 'The Harbinger to the Progres' prefixed to *Of
the Progres of the Soule*, they are so similar in style and purpose to those
prefixed to the earlier poem that the conclusion that they are the
work of the same author seems inescapable. Though in 1611 Donne's
friendship with Hall may scarcely have ripened, Hall had none the
less more than one reason for wishing to associate himself with the
Anniversaries. While Donne had never seen Elizabeth Drury, Hall had
watched her grow from her sixth to her thirteenth year, and thus
could share some of her parents' sorrow for her premature death. He
also wished, no doubt, to show his former patrons that his warmth
of feeling for them still persisted in spite of his removal elsewhere.
Indeed, in the letter he wrote on leaving Hawstead he had promised
that it would not put an end to his relations with the Drurys:
'What if God had called mee to Heauen? would you haue grudged
my departure? Imagine that I am there, where I shall be; altho the
case be not to you altogether so hopelesse: for, now I may heare of
you, visit you, renue my holy counsels, and be mutually comforted
from you.'[1] Above all, the theme of *The First Anniversary* appealed
to him deeply, for he had been 'noted in the University, for his
ingenuous maintaining, (be it *Truth*, or *Paradox*) that *Mundus
senescit, The World groweth old*'.[2] The publisher, moreover, was
Samuel Macham who was, like Hall, a native of Ashby-de-la-Zouche
and had already published several books for Hall.[3] It is therefore

[1] Hall, *Epistles, the First Volume*, 1608, pp. 103–4.
[2] Fuller, *Worthies*, 1662, Leicestershire, p. 129.
[3] John Donne, *An Anatomy of the World, a Facsimile of the First Edition*, Roxburghe
Club, 1951, ed. G. L. Keynes, 'Postscript', p. 6.

clear that Hall had some share, perhaps a fairly considerable share, in seeing the little book into print. Nevertheless, it is highly probable that Donne saw and passed the proofs, since the book was almost certainly in print before he left England with the Drurys.[1]

Meanwhile Sir Robert Drury was being delayed by one hindrance after another, and it must have been early November before the party embarked for France. Donne's farewell letter to Goodyer has survived. It is a gloomy letter, and Donne was clearly disturbed at not being able to discharge his financial obligations, for Goodyer had not only lent him money, but had also gone surety for some of his other debts:

I am near the execution of that purpose for *France*; though I may have other ends, yet if it do but keep me awake, it recompenses me well. I am now in the afternoon of my life, and then it is unwholesome to sleep. It is ill to look back, or give over in a course; but worse never to set out. I speake to you at this time of departing, as I should do at my last upon my death-bed; and I desire to deliver into your hands a heart and affections, as innocent towards you, as I shall to deliver my soul into Gods hands then. I say not this out of diffidence, as though you doubted it, or that this should look like such an excuse, as implyed an accusation; but because my fortune hath burdened you so, as I could not rectifie it before my going, my conscience and interpretation (severer I hope then yours towards my self) calls that a kinde of demerit, but God who hath not only afforded us a way to be delivered from our great many debts, contracted by our Executorship to *Adam*, but also another for our particular debts after, hath not left poor men unprovided, for discharge of morall and civill debts; in which, acknowledgement, and thankfulnesse is the same, as repentance and contrition is in spiritual debts.[2]

The party was bound for Amiens, where Drury proposed to spend the winter. He had written earlier to a French nobleman of his acquaintance, the Comte de St. Paul, who lived in Amiens, asking him if he could find him a house for the winter. He proposed to

---

[1] Sir Arthur Throckmorton's diary shows that he received a copy on 21 Nov., when Robert Pound brought him several books recently published in London. See A. L. Rowse, *Ralegh and the Throckmortons* (London, 1962), p. 288.

[2] *Letters*, pp. 93–5. This letter is headed '*To my Lord* G. H.', but Donne addresses his correspondent as 'Sir', and the reference in the letter to Lady Bedford makes it almost certain that it was addressed to Goodyer.

bring with him not only the horses mentioned in his permit to travel (among which must have been included several hunters) but also a pack of hounds and two or three hawks.[1] Here, clearly, was plenty of occupation for Sir Robert, but less for his wife or for Donne. Donne, however, had brought a collection of books to which he was prepared to devote himself if time hung heavy on his hands.

Once landed in France, the party would have constituted a small cavalcade, with the coach and horses, the accompanying riders and servants, the pack of hounds, and the hawks. Travel must have been slow; there were various delays, and they were held up until the house in Amiens was ready for occupancy. They must have moved into it by the end of November, for on 4 December Chamberlain was able to report from London that Sir Robert and Lady Drury were 'already settled at Amiens, and with them John Dun'.[2] Before long they began writing to their friends in England. Donne's letters to George Garrard and Sir Thomas Roe have survived,[3] as well as two he drafted for Sir Robert Drury to send to Viscount Rochester, the reigning favourite, and to Sir David Murray, a member of the household of the Prince of Wales.[4] All four letters are complimentary in tone; Donne hoped that his two friends would write to him, and Drury that he would not be forgotten by the two courtiers. And all four letters confess that as yet there is no news worth sending.

Yet Donne must already have been at work on the second of his *Anniversaries, Of the Progres of the Soule*, which certainly belongs to the early part of his stay at Amiens. The concluding lines refer to the fact that the writer is in France:

> Here in a place, where mis-devotion frames
> A thousand Prayers to Saints, whose very names
> The ancient Church knew not, Heaven knows not yet:
> And where, what lawes of Poetry admit,

---

[1] *Donne and the Drurys*, p. 86.
[2] *Letters*, i. 322. Similarly, on 9 Jan. 1611/12, J. Beaulieu wrote from Paris to William Trumbull: 'Sir Robert Drury hath been this month with his lady to Amiens and proposes to stay there longer' (Hist. MSS. Com., *MSS. of the Marquess of Downshire*, iii. 217).
[3] *Letters*, pp. 41 and 264.
[4] *Donne and the Drurys*, pp. 90–1.

> Lawes of Religion have at least the same,
> Immortall Maide, I might invoke thy name.
> Could any Saint provoke that appetite,
> Thou here should'st make me a French convertite.
> But thou would'st not; . . .

and in the opening lines he had stated that

> a yeare is runne,
> Since both this lower world's, and the Sunnes Sunne,
> The Lustre, and the vigor of this All,
> Did set.

The poem was probably begun on the very anniversary of Elizabeth Drury's death. It was sent to England as soon as it was completed; Hall wrote a second set of preliminary verses, and it was published by Macham early in 1612[1] along with the second edition of *An Anatomy of the World* as *The First and Second Anniversaries*. It is probable that Hall, as part author and because of his relations with Macham and the Drurys, saw the book through the press.

Donne soon found that his life in Amiens settled into a dull routine, and he began before long to allude in his letters to 'this barren place', or 'the dullness of this place'. He found, too, that he had plenty of time to himself, and perforce he turned to his books. Richard Baddeley, Morton's secretary, recalled in after years that Donne

passed over into *France*, where he gave himself to the Study of the Laws: And from *Amiens*, (as I remember) he writ a Letter to his always true friend *Deane Morton*, wherein he requested his advice, Whether taking the Degree of a *Doctor* in that Profession of the Laws, it might not be conducible and advantagious unto him to Practice at home in the *Arches London*. Unto whom the *Deane* then returned him answer, That in his Judgement, he thought the Ministry in the Church of God would be safer, and fitter for him: Whereupon he desisted from further prosecution of those Studies.[2]

Certainly, any serious notions of practising as an advocate at

---

[1] Sir Arthur Throckmorton received his copy on 10 May (Rowse, op. cit., p. 289 n.), but this date is of small help since Donne had already replied to criticisms of the *Anniversaries* from Paris on 14 April.

[2] *Life of . . . Morton*, pp. 100–1.

Doctors' Commons had been abandoned by the time Donne reached Paris. When rumours that he intended to do so reached him from England, he haughtily pretended that he had never entertained them, and wrote to George Garrard on 14 April: 'For my purpose of proceeding in the profession of the Law, so far as to a Title, you may be pleased to correct that imagination where you finde it. I ever thought the study of it my best entertainment and pastime, but I have no ambition, nor design upon the Stile.'[1]

Donne's letters are, as one would expect, the principal source of information about his activities while travelling with the Drurys,[2] in spite of the fact that his correspondence suffered numerous delays and interruptions. Donne wrote weekly, as he had been in the habit of doing for years, to Goodyer, and attempted to write with similar regularity to Garrard. Yet comparatively few of these letters reached their destinations, and still fewer came to him from England. All the time he was at Amiens he received but one letter from Goodyer, which was written on 10 December and reached him on 7/17 January. It was brought by John Pory, who was on his way to Paris on a semi-diplomatic mission, carrying to Cardinal du Perron the latest controversial works of Bishop Andrewes and Isaac Casaubon as a gift from King James. Goodyer's was the first letter from England to reach Donne, and he did not hesitate to express his disappointment in his next letter to Garrard:

All your other Letters, which came to me by more hazardous waies, had therefore much merit in them; but for your Letter by M. *Pory*, it was but a little degree of favour, because the messenger was so obvious, and so certain, that you could not chuse but write by him. But since he brought me as much Letter as all the rest, I must accept that, as well as the rest. By this time, M. *Garret*, when you know in your conscience that you have sent no Letter, you beginne to look upon the superscription, and doubt that you have broken up some other

---

[1] *Letters*, pp. 254–5.

[2] For a discussion of this group of letters, see R. E. Bennett, 'Donne's Letters from the Continent in 1611–12', *PQ*, xix (1940), 66–78. Bennett's arrangement and dating of these letters are followed here, with two exceptions: (1) the letter to Garrard in *Letters*, p. 259, and Gosse, i. 294–5, belongs not to this period but to 1614, and (2) the letter to Goodyer in *Letters*, p. 54, and Gosse, i. 239–41, was written not doubtfully but certainly from Paris, since it can scarcely be questioned that the illness described in the postscript occurred there.

bodies Letter: but whose so ever it were it must speak the same language, for I have heard from no body. Sir, if there be a Proclamation in *England* against writing to me, yet since it is thereby become a matter of State, you might have told M. *Pory* so. And you might have told him, what became of Sir *Tho. Lucies* Letter, in my first pacquet, (for any Letter to him makes any paper a pacquet, and any peece of single money a Medall) and what became of my Lady *Kingsmels* in my second, and of hers in my third, whom I will not name to you in hope that it is perished, and you lost the honour of giving it.[1]

In spite of Donne's irritation at his friends, Pory left Amiens with letters to take back to England, even though he was going to Paris first. Sir Robert Rich passed through soon afterwards and was warmly welcomed by the exiles, though once again Donne was disappointed by the lack of letters. Rich, afterwards the second Earl of Warwick and Admiral under the Parliament, was at this time a young man gleaning his first experience of the world; he was expecting shortly to join Sir Henry Wotton as he passed through France on an embassy to Savoy,[2] and promised on his way homewards to meet Donne and the Drurys at Frankfurt at the end of May, when the imperial election was to take place. Rich must have spent several days in Amiens, for while there he persuaded Donne to address some verses to his sisters, Lady Carey and Miss Essex Rich. As he acknowledges in the poem, Donne had never met them; but he has had an 'Extasie And revelation' of them both, and so speaks of 'things which by faith alone I see'. Hence he was not forced to restrict his praises; or, as he said not long afterwards when criticism of his excessive praise of Elizabeth Drury came to his ears: 'since I never saw the Gentlewoman, I cannot be understood to have bound my selfe to have spoken just Truth: but I would not be thought to have gone about to praise any bodie in rime, except I tooke such a Person, as might be capable of all that I could say.'[3] Elizabeth Drury, however, was dead; Rich's sisters were alive, and scandal still had time to besmirch their names. They were the daughters of Penelope Devereux, Sidney's Stella, who deserted her husband, Lord Rich,

---

[1] *Letters*, pp. 262–3.
[2] L. Pearsall Smith, *Life and Letters of Sir Henry Wotton*, ii. 2.
[3] *Letters*, p. 255.

for Charles Blount, Lord Mountjoy and later Earl of Devonshire.[1] Lettice, her eldest daughter, married first Sir George Carey of Cockington in Devon and second Sir Arthur Lake, son of Sir Thomas Lake, the Secretary of State. Donne's friend Richard Martin was apparently her lover for a time.[2] Of Essex Rich, who married Sir Thomas Cheke of Pirgo, less is known; but it may be doubted whether the beauty and virtue of Donne's vision were equally balanced in the two daughters of so notorious a mother. If some of Donne's contemporaries felt that Donne had overstepped the bounds of propriety in the *Anniversaries*, they must have felt that he had done so even more recklessly in his praise of these two living ladies.

Eventually Donne received a letter from Garrard on 1 February, and on 7 February, when an opportunity occurred of sending letters to England, he must have spent a large part of the day writing. He had to act again as his patron's secretary, and composed for him an elegant epistle to Sir Robert Cotton. The style of this letter is clearly Donne's (and one can scarcely doubt that Cotton recognized it), the body of the letter is in Lady Drury's handwriting, and the signature alone is Sir Robert's; the letter is a significant example of the way in which all three collaborated when a chance arose to send off letters. Donne also wrote on his own behalf to Garrard, to Garrard's sister Martha, and to Sir Robert More at Loseley. Enclosed in the letter to his brother-in-law was one to his wife, and he did not hesitate to reveal to him his anxiety for her:

When there is any way open to you to send unto Wight, I pray give this letter a passage. If one could not get to that isle but by the north-west discovery, I could not think the returns so difficult and dilatory, for yet I have had no return from thence of any letter since my coming out of England, and this silence, especially at this time

---

[1] M. S. Rawson, *Penelope Rich and her Circle*, 1911, pp. 299–306, is uncertain of the paternity of Penelope's various children, but G. E. C., *Complete Peerage, sub* Mountjoy, lists those whom Mountjoy in his will acknowledged to be his. Neither Lettice nor Essex is included in this list.

[2] After her death Chamberlain reported to Carleton that 'Since the death of Sir Arthur Lakes Lady there is a daughter of hers come to light (thought to be Dicke Martins, or rather a greater mans) that by the helpe of goode frends layes claime to Sir George Caries land because she was borne in wedlocke' (Chamberlain, *Letters*, ii. 247).

when I make account that your sister is near her painful and dangerous passage, doth somewhat more affect me than I had thought anything of this world could have done.[1]

The inactivity at Amiens and the continued lack of news from home preyed seriously on Donne's spirits.

About a month after the date of these letters the party moved on to Paris, and almost immediately after their arrival Donne fell ill. He suffered from 'such storms of a stomach colick as kept me in a continuall vomiting, so that I know not what I should have been able to doe to dispatch this winde, but that an honest fever came and was my physick'.[2] He was apparently attended by an English physician, Richard Andrews, with whom he was soon on terms of familiarity. Andrews was a scholar and a wit as well as a doctor; 'he had improved himself much in his faculty in his travels beyond the seas, which afterwards made him highly esteemed among learned men and others', wrote Anthony à Wood of him.[3] Andrews was known for his Latin verses; he had completed a Latin poem by one of the wits of his college, Richard Latewar, who was killed in Ireland while serving as chaplain to the Lord Deputy, and he had addressed some verses to Camden. Donne allowed Andrews to borrow from his books, but one of them came back not as he had lent it; the volume had been badly mauled by Andrews's children, and had had to be transcribed by hand for Donne. So handsome a reparation received in reply some Latin verses from Donne, carefully planned to flatter him and his literary interests.[4]

---

[1] Loseley MS., printed by Gosse, i. 289, who reads 'I may' for 'I pray'.

[2] *Letters*, p. 57; compare 'such a distemper as travelled me at *Paris*; a Fever, and dysentery: in which, that which is physick to one infirmity, nourishes the other' (ibid., p. 42). Donne's illness was perhaps a form of gastric influenza. Later in the same year (1612) one of the early influenza epidemics reached England, and it became known not long afterwards as the 'new disease' (C. Creighton, *History of Epidemics in Britain*, 1891, ii. 312–13).

[3] *Fasti Oxonienses*, ed. Bliss, part i (1815), p. 326.

[4] The interpretation accepted here was first suggested by H. W. Garrod in *RES*, xxi (1945), 38–42. The poem is addressed merely to Dr. Andrews, but Richard Andrews of St. John's College, Oxford, is the only Andrews who was M.D. of either university at this period. Of course, another Andrews who had gained his medical degree at one of the great continental schools is possible, but there seems to be no record of such a man. M. J. Simmonds, in *Merchant Taylor Fellows of St. John's College, Oxford*, 1930, p. 7, states that Richard Andrews 'travelled in France before taking his D. Med.', which he did on 1 June 1608. If Donne's poem is correctly dated (internal

It was while he was in Paris that Donne learned of the effect upon some of his friends in England of the *Anniversaries* and of the praises there lavished on Elizabeth Drury. He replied to these criticisms in letters to both Goodyer and Garrard, but the degree to which he was disturbed by them is best shown by his epistle 'To the Countesse of Bedford. Begun in France but never perfected', which clearly betrayed his uneasiness lest he should be in danger of losing Lady Bedford's favour:

> First I confesse I have to others lent
> Your stock, and over prodigally spent
> Your treasure, for since I had never knowne
> Vertue or beautie, but as they are growne
> In you, I should not thinke or say they shine,
> (So as I have) in any other Mine.
> Next I confesse this my confession,
> For, 'tis some fault thus much to touch upon
> Your praise to you, where half rights seeme too much,
> And make your minds sincere complexion blush.
> Next I confesse my'impenitence, for I
> Can scarce repent my first fault, since thereby
> Remote low Spirits, which shall ne'er read you,
> May in lesse lessons finde enough to doe,
> By studying copies, not Originals, . . .

It is more ingenious than convincing, and Donne was probably wise to leave the poem unfinished.

In the very letter to Goodyer from Paris, written about mid April, in which Donne replied to the criticisms of the *Anniversaries*, Donne also stated that he was 'yet in the same perplexity, which I mentioned before; which is, that I have received no syllable, neither from her self, nor by any other, how my wife hath passed her danger, nor do I know whether I be increased by a childe, or diminished by the losse of a wife'.[1] It must have been about this time that he

evidence shows it to have been written in Paris, and it acknowledges a debt to Andrews's medical skill), Andrews must have been in France again in 1612, and have had his family with him. Perhaps he was attached to the household of the English ambassador, Sir Thomas Edmundes. [Richard Andrews acted as deputy for William Harvey in 1633; see G. L. Keynes, *The Life of William Harvey*, 1966, pp. 69, 196–7, 202–3.]

[1] *Letters*, p. 74.

saw the apparition of his wife, of which Walton writes at such
length. Donne, he relates, was left alone after dinner one day, and
when Sir Robert Drury rejoined him half an hour later he was astonished at the change in Donne's appearance. In reply to his startled
questionings, Donne,

after a long and perplext pause, did at last say, *I have seen a dreadful
Vision since I saw you: I have seen my dear wife pass twice by me through this
room, with her hair hanging about her shoulders, and a dead child in her arms:
this, I have seen since I saw you.* To which, Sir *Robert* reply'd; *Sure Sir, you
have slept since I saw you; and, this is the result of some melancholy dream,
which I desire you to forget, for you are now awake.* To which Mr. *Donnes*
reply was: *I cannot be surer that I now live, then that I have not slept since I
saw you: and am, as sure, that at her second appearing, she stopt, and look'd me
in the face, and vanisht.*

The following day a messenger set out for London, who returned
twelve days later with the news that Mrs. Donne had been delivered
of a still-born child on 'the same day, and about the very hour that
Mr. *Donne* affirm'd he saw her pass by him in his Chamber'.

This episode first appeared in the 1675 edition of Walton's *Life*,
more than forty years after Donne's death, though Walton declared
that it was

told me (*now long since*) by a Person of Honour, and of such intimacy
with him, that he knew more of the secrets of his soul, then any person then living: and I think they [?he] told me the truth; for, it was
told with such circumstances, and such asseveration, that (to say
nothing of my own thoughts) I verily believe he that told it me, did
himself believe it to be true.

Nevertheless, Walton's account is riddled with inaccuracies. He says
that Donne crossed from London to Paris with the Drurys in twelve
days, and that the vision occurred two days later; the servant sent
to London to make inquiries found Mrs. Donne still confined to her
bed in Drury House. Actually, of course, Donne did not arrive in
Paris until more than three months after he left England, and his
wife was not in London but in the Isle of Wight. The still-born child
was buried on 24 January, for an entry in the church register at
Brading in Sir John Oglander's hand records the burial of 'the

abortive of Mtris. Dunne, wife of Doctor Dunne, Deane of Paules, and syster to ye Lady Oglander. At Sir John's she was brought a bedde, the best of women.'[1] Yet as late as 14 April Donne in Paris was still ignorant of his wife's ordeal. Attempts have been made to dismiss the whole story as completely unreliable,[2] and perhaps it is. Any reader of Aubrey knows how much the seventeenth century cherished such tales of apparitions and supernatural appearances. Even so, it is not inconceivable that some such hallucination occurred, and that it was related to Donne's ill-health while he was in Paris. Not only had he suffered prolonged anxiety on behalf of his wife, but he was also for a time feverish and debilitated; such a combination of circumstances might well have combined to bring about the 'vision'. In the course of telling and retelling, the story, no doubt, became more and more circumstantial and therefore less accurate, but the substratum of truth may well be there.

The Paris to which Donne had come with the Drurys was that of the regency of Marie de Medicis. It was less than two years after the assassination of Henri IV; France was still restless and apprehensive. The internal stability which Henri had given the kingdom was showing signs of crumbling, and there were constant stirrings of uneasiness beneath the brilliance and extravagance of the court. The Protestants in particular did not know how long the Edict of Nantes might endure, and were fearful lest a new war of religion might break out at any time. The foreign policy of France was also shifting, and her old allies, England and Holland, were greatly disturbed by prospect of an alliance between France and Spain, to be consummated by the double marriage of the youthful Louis XIII with an Infanta of Spain and of his sister with the heir to the Spanish throne. The public announcement of these betrothals was to be made on 25 March and Sir Robert Drury had hastened to Paris to witness the celebrations that were to accompany the event. The Queen's brother had recently died, so the celebrations were postponed until 5, 6, and 7 April. In a letter written to Sir Henry

---

[1] F. Bamford, *A Royalist's Notebook*, 1936, p. 168, n. 3. Bamford reads 'At St. John's', but the original surely read 'Sr Johns'. Part of the passage at least must be a later insertion, for in 1612 Donne was not Dean of St. Paul's nor was Oglander yet Sir John.

[2] See Bennett, 'Donne's Letters from the Continent', at p. 78.

Goodyer when they were barely over, Donne gave an account of recent events in Paris:

That which was done here the 25 of *March*, and which was so long called a publication of the marriages, was no otherwise publique then that the Spa[nish] Ambassador, having that day an audience delivered to the Queen that his Master was well pleased with all those particulars which had been formerly treated. And the French Ambassador in *Spain* is said to have had instruction, to do the same office in that Court, the same day. Since that, that is to say, these 4 last days, it hath been solemnized with more outward bravery then this Court is remembred to have appeared in. The main bravery was the number of horses which were above 800 Caparazond. Before the daies, the town was full of the 5 Challengers cartells, full of Rodomontades: but in the execution, there were no personall reencounters, nor other triall of any ability, then running at the Quintain, and the Ring. Other particulars of this, you cannot chuse but hear too much, since at this time there come to you so many French men. But lest you should beleeve too much, I present you these 2 precautions, that for their Gendarmery, there was no other trial then I told you; & for their bravery, no true stuffe.[1]

Donne's illness probably caused him to look on all these celebrations with a somewhat jaundiced eye, for the pageantry was on a scale of magnificence that was not surpassed until the most splendid shows of the reign of Louis XIV. Stands had been erected all around the Place Royale and an estimated 200,000 had been crammed into them. Even so, there were many thousands who did not succeed in getting places, and gorgeous cavalcades paraded through the city in the evenings so that all might see their splendour.[2] Donne's severest criticism was based on the fact that there were no trials of skill between combatants as there were at the English court; evidently he did not know that since Henri II had received his death wound in a tournament such encounters were forbidden at the court of France, and only riding at the ring was permitted.

One can see from Donne's letters that, in spite of ill health and

---

[1] *Letters*, pp. 127–9.

[2] There is a modern account of these celebrations in J. Vanuxem, 'Le Carrousel de 1612 sur la Place Royale et ses devises', in Jean Jacquot (ed.), *Les Fêtes de la Renaissance*, i (1956), 191–200; there were also several contemporary accounts. Vanuxem reproduces a contemporary engraving to illustrate the extent of the pageantry.

anxiety, he was exhilarated at being in a great city again, and in touch with the march of events. The same letter to Goodyer that recounts the celebrations in honour of the Spanish marriages also recounts the activities of the Huguenot synod, then divided on points of doctrine. But between the two passages another topic intervenes. During the months that followed the assassination of Henri IV, the Sorbonne had publicly condemned a number of the more extreme Jesuit writings upholding the papal power at the expense of the authority of kings, and in 1611 Edmond Richer, syndic of the faculty of theology and thus virtual head of the University, published his *Libellus de Ecclesiastica et Politica Potestate*. The book contained a bare thirty pages, but stated in highly condensed form the limitations of the pope's power. It created an immediate sensation; though the Parlement of Paris took Richer's side, an assembly of the bishops of the province under Cardinal du Perron condemned the work. Many of Richer's colleagues, lacking his hardihood, deserted him, and added their voices to those of the superior clergy. In the end Richer was removed from his office and silenced, but when Donne wrote the tide was only beginning to run strongly against him. He was said to be preparing a reply not only to the censure of the bishops but also to the pamphlets against him which had already appeared.

Before it should come forth I desired to speak with him, for I had said to some of the Sorbonist⟨s⟩ of his party, that there was no proposition in his Book, which I could not shew in Catholique authors of 300 years: I had from him an assignation to meet, and at the hour he sent me his excuse, which was, that he had been traduced to have had conference with the Ambassadors of *England*, and the States, and with the D[uke] of *Bo[u]illon*, and that he had accepted a pension of the King of *England*; and withall, that it had been very well testified to him that day, that the Jesuits had offered to corrupt men with rewards to kill him. Which I doubt not but he apprehended for true, because a messenger whom I sent to fixe another time of meeting with him, found him in an extreme trembling, and irresolutions: so that I had no more, but an intreaty to forbear comming to his house, or drawing him out of it, till it might be without danger or observation.[1]

---

[1] *Letters*, pp. 130-1.

Donne's eagerness to throw himself into the struggle against the ultramontanists shows how headstrong he could be, and Richer was surely wise to dissociate himself from any Protestant aid. It must be admitted, too, that there was a certain *naïveté* in Donne's belief that he could instruct a leading member of the theological faculty of the Sorbonne, and one, moreover, who had edited the works of Gerson, than whom there had been in his day no more determined opponent of the papal claims. Richer eventually composed his reply, but was forbidden to publish it in his lifetime, and it was not until 1702 that it saw the light. Nevertheless, Donne's confidence that he could supply Richer with abundant authority for every assertion in the *Libellus* is evidence of the thoroughness of his study of the Gallican position, and of the fact that he had fully prepared himself to write the unwritten thirteenth chapter of *Pseudo-Martyr*.

While still at Amiens Donne had been welcomed to France by a letter from Toby Mathew,[1] and when he reached Paris Mathew was not slow to call on him. He had been wandering rather aimlessly from one European capital to another in the five years since his expulsion from England, and his greatest wish was to secure permission to return. Hence he sedulously cultivated anyone from England who might conceivably have any influence that could be exercised on his behalf. Donne, however, was guarded in his attitude: 'When I came to this Town', he wrote to Goodyer, 'I found Mr *Matthew*, diligent to finde a means to write to you; so that at this time, when there go so many, I cannot doubt but he provides himself, therefore I did not ask his commandement, nor offer him the service of this Pacquet.'[2] Goodyer was evidently still looking after some of Mathew's affairs in England; hence his eagerness to write. Donne, on the other hand, was clearly reluctant to involve himself with him in any way. Another friend whom Donne would much rather have seen, but whom he missed, was Sir Henry Wotton. Wotton had returned from Venice in March 1611; after a year at home he set out again on a special mission to the Duke of Savoy. He passed through Amiens early in April 1612, with letters for Donne and his party which he sent on from there, but went himself directly to Lyons and thence to Turin.

---

[1] *Tobie Mathew Collection*, p. 278.   [2] *Letters*, p. 133.

Meanwhile Sir Robert and Lady Drury were renewing their acquaintance with some of the nobles of the French Court. In particular, Sir Robert was in constant attendance on the Duc de Bouillon, the leading Protestant nobleman of France, with whom he had been acquainted since at least 1600. The Duc de Bouillon was on the point of setting out for England as Ambassador Extraordinary to bear the formal announcement of the betrothals which had just been celebrated in Paris, and at the same time to explore the possibility of a marriage between Prince Henry and a French princess. His wife was a daughter of William of Orange, and one of her sisters was the widow of the Elector Palatine. He therefore warmly supported the proposed alliance between the Princess Elizabeth and the young Elector as a curb on the growing power of the house of Austria. The Duc de Bouillon left Paris about the middle of April and reached England on the 26th of the month.

Donne's last letter from Paris is dated 14 April, though he promised to write more than one subsequent letter before leaving it. In a letter to Goodyer already quoted from he outlined the plans of his patrons: 'Presently after Easter we shall (I think) go to *Frankford* to be there at the election, where we shall meet Sir *H. Wotton* and Sir *Ro. Rich*, and after that we are determined to passe some time, in the Palatinate.'[1] It had been intended that Wotton should go on from Turin to Frankfurt so as to congratulate the new emperor on behalf of King James, but the Duke of Savoy detained him so long that this proved impossible, and the meeting Donne hoped for did not take place. By this time the arrangements for the Princess Elizabeth's marriage to the young Elector were almost concluded, and the English travellers were therefore eager to visit the land that was to be her home. Easter day in 1612 was on 22 April (N.S.), so it is to be presumed that Donne set out with the Drurys for Frankfurt during the succeeding week. It is not clear whether they went directly to Frankfurt and then to Heidelberg, the Elector's capital or, as is more likely, went first to Heidelberg and thence to Frankfurt. The imperial election, which they hoped to witness, was to take place on 25 May, so they had plenty of time.

---

[1] Ibid., pp. 75–6.

That they went to Heidelberg is certain, and they carried letters from the Duchesse de Bouillon to the Dowager Electress. Sir Robert Drury was subsequently, it appears, rather critical of the reception that he received, 'because he was not intertained perhaps by him or his, as in his vanitie he expected'.[1] Nevertheless Lady Drury wrote the Duchesse de Bouillon a warm letter of thanks for her introductions; the letter was composed for her by Donne and has survived in his handwriting.

Madame

Come vos vertus sont douées des autres qualités de nostre bon dieu qui vous les a données, ainsy participent elles de son infinité. Tellement, qu'estant esloigné de uostre presence, je sens encore vos influences, et tro[u]ue en touts lieus des belles impressions de uostre bonté. Je les ay trouué, Madame, en l'accueil, et autres faueurs, dont sont Alteze, et Madamoiselle d'Aurange vos tres-dignes soeurs ont esté contentes, par uostre Mediation, honorer leur pauure servante et la vostre. Je les ay trouué dans vos lettres lesquelles iay eu l'honneur auoir de la maine de madamoiselle vostre soeur; Ainsy que par tout je trouue des representations et images de vostre bonté et presence. Mais, quand rien de cela ne m'eust arriué, ma memoire m'en fourniroit abondamment. Car encore que je ⟨ne⟩ suis pas capable d'estre imitatrice de uos vertus sy suis je neantmoins de les admirer, et de conserver vne perpetuelle memoire de leur fruicts et effects par de uers moj, par lesquels vous aves obligé a vne servitude eternelle

vostre tres humble et
tres obeissante servante

Madame, Je vous remercie tres humblement de m'avo[i]r faict l'honneur de me communiquer les bonnes nouuelles de l'auenement de Monseigneur de Bouillon, et de la santé de vos enfans; car je participeray tousiours de vos affections, et auray ma part en tout ce que vous est a coeur ou a regret.[2]

The reference in the postscript to the Duc de Bouillon is to his return from his English embassy early in June.

The imperial electors duly met at Frankfurt, and chose Matthias to succeed his elder brother, Rudolf II. The election did not actually

---

[1] Chamberlain, *Letters*, i. 384.

[2] *Donne and the Drurys*, p. 101, with facing facsimile. Some accents have been added in the transcription.

take place until 13 June (N.S.), and the electors dispersed on the 18th. Drury and his party were still in Frankfurt on the 27th, when Donne composed another letter for him to send to Sir Robert Cotton. 'All the princes of Germany,' he wrote, 'when after they had declared an Emperor, and crowned him, and drunke with him, and slepte, they disposed them selues to goe home agayne.'[1] At Frankfurt the travellers received news from England of the recent death of the Earl of Salisbury, and the prospective reshuffle of high offices at Court was a matter of great interest to them. Only a few days earlier Sir Robert Drury had received a letter from his friend Sir Walter Cope[2] giving an account of the illness of Salisbury (whom he had accompanied to Bath) and expressing high hopes of his speedy recovery. The letter concluded with some interesting remarks about the travels of Drury and Donne:

I marvell, that my Lord Treasurer never receaues any letters from you, although Mr. Dun, and you haue noe place of Ambassadors yet I trust you haue, that canne and doe obserue as much as the best that haue imploiement from the State, and it will be noe ill Introduction towards the setting such idle persons on worke; But I presume your silence hath growne rather from my Lords long Sicknes, which in me (I must confesse) hath bredd such a dulnes, as I haue been carelesse of all writing or complement; And this I assure you hath been the cause that my Lord Treasurer wrote not according to his appointement his letters unto my noble freind Sir *Robert Druerie*, vnto whom with his noble Ladie, I commend my seruice; not forgetting my best commendation to Mr. Donne, who is inriching his Treasury, for his Countries better service, towards the which, if I be not able to add a mite, yet I shall be euer ready to cry Amen.[3]

From this letter it appears that both Donne and Drury had a kind of roving commission to report anything of particular interest that

---

[1] Bennett, 'Donne's Letters from the Continent', p. 75.

[2] Sir Walter Cope had already made an appearance in Donne's satirical catalogue of books, *The Courtier's Library*, in conjunction with John Pory '11. *Believe in thy havings, and thou hast them.* A test for antiquities, being a great book on very small things, dictated by Walter Cope, copied out by his wife, and given a Latin dress by his amanuensis John Pory.' As might be guessed, Cope was a member of the Elizabethan Society of Antiquaries. He was also Chamberlain of the Exchequer from 1609, and in 1613 became Master of the Court of Wards and Liveries; he was the original builder of Holland House. He died in 1614.

[3] *Donne and the Drurys*, p. 100.

occurred while they were abroad, though neither of them seems to have exercised it.

The letter to Sir Robert Cotton also reported Drury's intention of going on to Spa, and Donne's next surviving letter was written from there on 16/26 July. The watering-place where they now found themselves was already a popular resort for aristocratic English travellers, and in his remaining letters from abroad Donne makes constant references to his fellow country-men. He mentions having met Lady Worcester, Sir Edward Conway, and a Captain Peter. Otherwise life in Spa was uneventful, and after a stay of several weeks the travellers pushed on, intending to take a barge down the Maas in order to pass through Holland on their way home. They just missed Lord Chandos, who reached Spa with letters for them a couple of hours after they left, but their letters overtook them at Maastricht. They had had thoughts of going from there to the Hague, 'where we think to finde again the young Palatine' who was visiting his uncle, Maurice of Nassau. But the river at Maastricht was so low as to make questionable the wisdom of trying to sail down it, so plans were changed and the party made for Brussels. At Louvain they met the Earl of Arundel, bound for Spa, and reached Brussels not long afterwards. Here, on 16 August, Donne wrote to Goodyer, and at about the same time to Garrard and his sister. His principal wish now was to reach home, though there was still the possibility that they would go 'through *Antwerpe*, and some parts of *Holland*' before taking ship; still he hoped (and a note of impatience creeps into his voice), 'if we should by miracle hold any resolution', to 'sneake into *London*, about the end of *August*'. Donne had given up his lodgings before going abroad, but Goodyer would be in the country, so he planned to spend a few nights in his rooms, and he besought Garrard 'to think mee at *Constantinople*, and write one large Letter to be left at my Ladie *Bartlets*, my lodging; for I shall come in extreame darkneṣse and ignorance, except you give me light'.[1] By the beginning of September the party was back in England, the Drurys going first to Hawstead and Donne hastening ahead to London. On 15 September Sir Robert was in London and in trouble. His reception in the Palatinate still rankled, and he spoke

[1] *Letters*, pp. 187–8 and 251–2.

out too freely; he received a reprimand from the Council for 'some derogat[orie] speech against the state, and person, whereof he had lately taken some view'.[1] Meanwhile Donne had missed Garrard and his sister, who happened to be in town, and had already hastened to join his wife and family on the Isle of Wight.[2]

The conclusion of this chapter is perhaps the place to bring together several reminiscences of his travels that are scattered through Donne's works, though it is not always possible to specify the particular journey to which each refers. For instance, in the *Devotions* the tolling of the bell reminds him that 'I have heard both *Bells* and *Ordnance*, but never been so much affected with those, as with these *Bells*. I have *lien* near a *Steeple*, in which there are said to be more than *thirty Bels*; And neere another, where there is one so bigge, as that the *Clapper* is said to weigh more than *six hundred pound*, yet never so affected as here.'[3] The steeple, the sidenotes inform us, was at Antwerp, and the great bell at Rouen. Donne was probably at Antwerp in 1612, but when he was at Rouen is quite uncertain, though he might easily have visited it from Amiens. At Paris he noted that 'there is a whole *Hospitall* of *three hundred* blinde men together';[4] this is a reference to the Hospice de Quinze-Vingts, originally founded by St. Louis, and Donne had no doubt seen or visited it. But Donne visited Paris more than once, and he was probably familiar already with most of the sights there. It is less easy to date a visit of some length to Aix-la-Chapelle. He passed through the town in 1619, but probably did not stay there; a visit in 1612 would have been natural, but it is not easy to fit into what is known of his itinerary. Nevertheless, Donne carried away a vivid recollection of the house there in which he had lodged:

Lying at *Aix*, at *Aquisgrane*, a well known Town in *Germany*, and fixing there some time, for the benefit of those *Baths*, I found my self in a house, which was divided into many families, and indeed so large as it might have been a little Parish, or, at least, a great lim of a great one; But it was of no Parish: for when I ask'd who lay over my head, they told me a family of *Anabaptists*; And who over theirs? Another

[1] Hist. MSS. Com., *MSS. of the Duke of Buccleuch*, i. 114; cf. Chamberlain, *Letters*, i. 381.

[2] *Letters*, p. 258. [3] Sparrow, *Devotions*, p. 92.

[4] *Sermons*, iii, no. 4, ll. 454–5, p. 126.

family of *Anabaptists*; and another family of *Anabaptists* over theirs; and the whole house, was a nest of these boxes; severall artificers; all *Anabaptists*; I ask'd in what room they met, for the exercise of their Religion; I was told they never met: for, though they were all *Anabaptists*, yet for some collaterall differences, they detested one another, and, though many of them, were near in bloud, and alliance to one another, yet the son would excommunicate the father, in the room above him, and the Nephew the Uncle.[1]

Another passage in a sermon indicates that Donne had attended worship in a Jewish synagogue; he is speaking of the practice of offering up prayers for the dead:

That is true that I have read, that after Christs time, the Rabbins laid hold upon it, and brought it into custome; And that is true which I have seene, that the Jewes at this day continue it in practise; For when one dies, for some certaine time after, appointed by them, his sonne or some other neere in blood or alliance, comes to the Altar, and there saith and doth some thing in the behalfe of his dead father, or grandfather respectively.[2]

It is possible that Donne is here referring to a visit paid while he was abroad with Doncaster in 1619, for Taylor the Water Poet, who was abroad a very short time afterwards, was much interested by the number of Jews in Prague, and confessed that he went to a service at a synagogue out of curiosity.[3] But Donne is perhaps more likely to have attended Jewish worship as a layman than as an ordained Christian minister, and may well have done so in Holland when he was with the Drurys, if indeed the party crossed the border into the United Provinces.

[1] *Sermons*, ii, no. 3, ll. 635–49, p. 112. This is from a Lincoln's Inn sermon, and may be earlier than 1619, when Donne went abroad with Lord Doncaster.

[2] Ibid., vii, no. 6, ll. 184–91, p. 169.

[3] *Taylor his Travels*, 1620, C4.

XI

STEPS TO THE TEMPLE

BEFORE Donne parted from the Drurys it had been agreed that
he was to bring his family back to London and occupy a house
belonging to Sir Robert Drury close to his house in Drury Lane. In
the original version of the *Life* Walton wrote that Drury assigned
him 'a very convenient house rent-free, next his own in Drury-
lane', but in later editions this was altered to 'an useful apartment
in his own large house in *Drewry lane*'. The earlier statement is the
correct one, and thanks to some documents among the Drury
papers it is possible to give some account of the London house in
which Donne lived for a number of years.[1]

Soon after his return from the Continent Sir Robert's steward
presented him with a list of his tenants in Drury Lane and the
quarterly rents which they paid. Sir Robert used the blank space on
the sheet to work out the annual value of his property, and in doing
so jotted down two additional items which had not been included
in the steward's list:

> More   The brick stable
> may be lett for 12^{li}
> Mr. Dunns lodginge   16

Other records show that building operations went on from time to
time on the Drury properties, and it looks as if these were two new
buildings, probably completed while Sir Robert had been abroad.
Walton says that Donne received his quarters rent free, but this is
more than doubtful. No detailed rental similar to the one just cited
survives for a later period during Donne's occupancy, but there
are accounts for two consecutive quarters which give the total of
the rents from the Drury Lane properties, and show that Drury was
receiving £19. 16s. 8d. more per annum than is shown in the rent

---

[1] See *Donne and the Drurys*, ch. viii.

roll of 1612. The £16 noted by Sir Robert against 'Mr. Dunns lodginge' shows, I think, the amount the house was capable of bringing in rather than the rent he was actually charging, but the £19. 16s. 8d. unaccounted for makes it fairly certain that Donne paid *some* rent, though the actual amount is unknown. Besides, in the document next to be cited Donne is referred to as the 'tenant' of the house he occupied, and not the 'occupant', as he would have been had he held it rent-free.

The mansion house of Drury House consisted of two parts, or wings, which were regarded as separate dwellings. They fronted on a paved courtyard, and had their gardens behind them. The courtyard, which was entered through an arched gatehouse, was cut off from Drury Lane by a row of houses which faced the street. The area of the courtyard was further curtailed by additional houses and stables which had been built within the enclosed space. It was in one of these houses that Donne lived. In an indenture of 1615 listing the tenements into which Sir Robert Drury's property had been divided there is included

one bricke howse in the tenure of Mr. Doctor Dunn with a little passage and a smale Court to the same belonginge, which howse extendeth towardes the north east vnto the yard and kitchin of the said Lord Cheife Baron and adioyneth vnto the howse nowe in the tenure of Mr. Harborne towardes the south, and on the garden and yard of the said Mr. Harborne towardes the East and abbutteth on the Court Called Drury yard towardes the west.

The 'said Lord Cheife Baron' was Sir Lawrence Tanfield, chief judge of the Court of Exchequer, who gave his name to one of the courts of the Inner Temple and who occupied the wing of Drury House which the Drurys did not use. A narrow passage would have run from Drury Lane to a small court which gave access to the front entrance of Donne's house; behind it was the much larger court of Drury House. Apparently a gate gave Donne access to this court, for some other accounts show that a shilling was paid to 'the carpinder for takine of ⟨f⟩ the dore in Mr. Dunnes yarde and makine of it broder and hangine', and twopence to the smith 'for mendine the Laches and sneches of the same dore'.[1] One cannot help wondering

[1] See *Donne and the Drurys*, ch. viii, p. 133.

if Donne's children had broken it. The site on which Donne's house stood is, as nearly as one can estimate, on the south side of Aldwych, directly opposite the western side of Kingsway.

Donne's tenancy could have begun at any time between Michaelmas 1612 and Lady Day 1613. His name first appears in the parish accounts of St. Clement Danes for the year 1613–14, the first full year of his residence in the parish, as paying a pew rent of 2s. Thereafter his name appears every year until 1621–2. When these last accounts were made up he was 'The deane of powles', though he had doubtless paid his pew rent before promotion came. These accounts thus show that Donne lived in the house just off Drury Lane until he left it for the Deanery of St. Paul's. During this period the address he put on his letters varied: some of them are dated simply from Drury House, and it was probably because of this habit that Walton altered his statement that Donne lived in a 'house' to the one that he had an 'apartment' in Drury House; one letter, however, is dated 'from my house at Drury House', and this, though it much puzzled Gosse, is the most precise address that Donne could have given during this period.[1] The house itself was furnished with some help from Lady Drury, who lent the Donnes some furnishings for what was evidently their best bedroom, since in an inventory of 16 April 1615,[2] after a list of the contents of Drury House, these items appear:

> At Doctor Dunns
> Item one Stammell furniture for a bedd with
>   gold buttons and Copper lace   ·   ·   · iij^{li}
> Item one fether bedd one boulster twoe
>   blancketts a Coveringe and twoe ould
>   Redd Chayres ·   ·   ·   ·   ·   · iij^{li}

Drury Lane was a street which had been built up comparatively recently. Without being actually fashionable, it was inhabited by prosperous men of affairs: members of the legal profession and those

---

[1] Letters dated from Drury House are those of 23 Sept.—no year given, but almost certainly 1613—(*Letters*, p. 304) and 22 Dec. 1617 (erroneously dated 1607, *Letters*, p. 210). The letter subscribed 'At my house at Drury house', Gosse, ii. 210, has no year, and may be as late as 1620; see the facsimile from the manuscript in the British Museum in Keynes, p. 123.

[2] *Donne and the Drurys*, p. 137.

who had connections with the Court and Government. It was a good address, and Donne was in every way fortunate to be living there, even though the neighbourhood was soon to acquire a bad reputation as a refuge for Catholics. Early in the reign of Charles I Coryate's friend Lawrence Whitaker asserted in the House of Commons that 'in Drury-lane there are 3 families of papists there residing, for one of protestants; insomuch as it may well be called Little Rome'.[1] This was probably an exaggeration; certainly the reputation of the neighbourhood did not drive desirable tenants away. Not long after Donne moved to Drury Lane Christopher Brooke became a near neighbour; he took a new house on the other side of the street (and therefore in the parish of St. Martin-in-the-Fields), the lease of which he acquired from Lady Drury. At the same time he leased from her one of the coach-houses in Drury Court. Brooke had married Mary, widow of Sir Robert Jacob, the former Solicitor General of Ireland, and after the manner of the time she continued to be known as Lady Jacob. Arthur Wilson tells an anecdote about her rather unmannerly behaviour towards Count Gondomar, whose passage to Whitehall usually led him through Drury Lane:

the *Ladies* as he went, knowing his times, would not be wanting to appear in their Balconies, or Windows, to present him their *Civilities*, and he would watch for it; and as he was carried in his *Litter* or *bottomless Chair* (the easiest seat for his *Fistula*) he would strain himself as much as an old man could do to the humblest posture of *Respect*. One day passing by the Lady *Jacobs* house in *Drury-lane*, she exposing her self for a *Salutation*, he was not wanting to her, but she moved nothing but her *mouth*, gaping wide open upon him. He wondred at the *Ladies incivility*, but thought that it might be happily a yawning fit took her at that time; for triall whereof, the next day he finds her in the same place, and his *Courtesies* were again accosted with no better expressions than an *extended mouth*. Whereupon he sent a Gentleman to her, to let her know, that the *Ladies* of *England* were more gracious to him, than to incounter his *Respects* with such *Affronts*. She answered, it was true that he had purchased some of their *favours* at a *dear rate*, *And she had a mouth to be stopt as well as others*. Gondemar finding the cause

---

[1] Cobbett's *Parliamentary History*, ii. 405.

of the emotion of her mouth, sent her a *Present*, as an *Antidote*, which cured her of that distemper.[1]

There must have been definite advantages for Donne and his family in being in London. The damp and draughty cottage at Mitcham was beginning to be overcrowded; in Drury Lane there was not only more room, but there was a very real increase in comfort. Donne brought seven children to the new house, and an eighth, Nicholas, was born there some time after the move. He was baptized in the church of St. Clement Danes on 3 August 1613. The move to London must have had a beneficial effect on the education of the elder boys. John was certainly sent to Westminster School, which Camden had made the best school in the kingdom. John, and probably George as well, would have been entered as town boys. George seems to have inherited his father's precocity, for he probably entered Broadgates Hall in Oxford in 1615, at the age of ten. John, though the elder, stayed on at Westminster, in due course became a King's Scholar (1619), and then passed on to Christ Church, Oxford.

Pseudo-Martyr proved unavailing where Donne probably hoped most that it would have some effect, for when he returned from the Continent it was to find his stepfather Richard Rainsford a prisoner in Newgate. He had been convicted for refusal to take the Oath of Allegiance, and conviction for this offence entailed the penalties of praemunire: loss of the King's protection, loss of property, and imprisonment during the King's pleasure. The relevant records for the period are incomplete, so the date of Rainsford's conviction is not known. His name appears in a list of Catholic prisoners in Newgate for February 1611/12, and occurs also in others for May 1612 and February 1612/13. He must have been released soon after the last of these lists, but his freedom was brief. On 6 August 1613 'Ricardus Ransford nuper de parochia sancti Bartholomei magni in warde de Farringdon extra London, pred*ictis* generos*us*' was one of twenty-three persons indicted for recusancy or, more specifically, for having failed to attend their parish churches for the space of two

---

[1] *The History of Great Britain*, 1653, p. 146. Brooke makes several appearances in the records of the parish of St. Martin's: in the Churchwardens' accounts annually 1619–22 and in the Overseers' accounts for the same years.

months.[1] The consequences of this indictment are unknown, but it may be presumed that he was convicted and sent back to Newgate for some time. Donne seems to have visited him there just about the time of his indictment, since in a letter to Goodyer he first mentions the birth of Nicholas ('The newest thing that I know in the world, is my new son'), and then goes on to report: 'I hear in *Newgate*, that M. *Mathew* is dead. The Catholiques beleeve it there: perchance out of a custome of credulity. But the report, is close prisoner; for I never met it abroad.'[2] A visit to Rainsford might have been the occasion of his hearing the false rumour of Toby Mathew's death. The same letter reveals that Mrs. Donne, though she had just been through the pangs of childbirth, was in good health and was enjoying a visit to the country, doubtless either to Loseley or to one or other of her sisters at Beddington or Peckham. Her 'being well', Donne writes, 'takes off from me any new weight upon my fortune', and he goes on to announce: 'I have now two of the best happinesses which could befall me, upon me; which are, to be a widower and my wife alive.'[3]

Nearly all the poems of the years after the journey to the Continent with the Drurys are occasional pieces. The young Elector Palatine had followed them to England very closely; he came to press his suit in person and to make preparations for his marriage. The wedding was, however, delayed, and the whole nation plunged into gloom, by the death of Prince Henry, which occurred on 6 November 1612. The Prince's death produced a remarkable outpouring of elegiac verse, considerably greater in quantity, indeed, than that which followed the death of Elizabeth. Some of the poets rushed into print with surprising speed; for instance, Joshua Sylvester, well known for his translation of du Bartas and a Groom of the Chamber of the Prince, managed to get his *Lachrymae Lachrymarum* entered in the Stationers' Register on 27 November, well in

---

[1] *London Sessions Records, 1605–85*, ed. Dom H. Bowler (*Publications of the Catholic Record Society*, xxxiv, 1934), pp. 68, 73, 86, 88.

[2] Viscount Conway wrote to his nephew, 10 June 1651, of 'The happynes which Doctor Donne found out when his wife lay inne, to be a widower and his wife alive' (Hist. MSS. Com., *Portland MSS.*, iii. 195).

[3] *Letters*, pp. 178–9; cf. also a letter probably written shortly after this one, Gosse, i. 309 (Anderdon MS.).

advance of the funeral.[1] Sylvester's lugubrious pamphlet, with interspersed pages of solid black and sombre marginal decorations, was successful enough to go into a second edition before the end of the year. A third edition, dated 1613, contained a considerable body of supplementary material. Joseph Hall (one of the Prince's chaplains) contributed three sets of verses not included in the earlier editions, and a separate title-page introduced a further group of *Sundry Funerall Elegies . . . Composed by seueral Authors*. These authors were Sir P[eter] O[sborne],[2] G[eorge] G[arrard], Hugh Holland, Donne, Sir William Cornwallis, Sir Edward Herbert, Sir Henry Goodyer, and one Henry Burton, another member of the Prince's household. Christopher Brooke was not included only because he joined with William Browne of Tavistock in publishing separately *Two Elegies*. It seems clear that Donne's circle made a concerted effort to celebrate the Prince's memory. Ben Jonson related that Donne told him that 'he wrott that Epitaph on Prince Henry Look to me Fath to match Sir Ed: Herbert in obscurenesse'. This may well be so; Herbert's elegy on the Prince is involved enough, though it seems to be animated by a degree of real emotion; Donne's, on the other hand, is almost entirely lacking in depth of feeling and manifests an aridity that is the product of mere intellectual ingenuity. Donne's next official poem, however, was in a much happier vein. The postponed marriage of the Princess Elizabeth and the Elector Palatine took place on 14 February 1614, and Donne celebrated the event in a charming epithalamion. Whether he hoped for, or received, a reward from either of the royal pair, we do not know.

Soon after the celebration of the royal wedding Donne left London on a visit to Polesworth, Goodyer's Warwickshire home. How frequently he was a visitor there cannot be known; at least

[1] An entry in Princess Elizabeth's household accounts, Michaelmas 1612–Lady Day 1613, P.R.O., E 407/57, reads:

> Geven by her gr[aces] Comaund to Mr.
> Josua Sylvester that pr[e]sented   } V^{li}
> verses to her gr[ace] vpon the
> death of the late Prince ————

[2] Osborne was knighted by James I at Whitehall on 7 Jan. 1610/11 and married a sister of Sir John Danvers. He was, of course, the father of the celebrated Dorothy Osborne.

one later visit is recorded, and it is probably an earlier one that is commemorated in the verse 'Letter written by Sir H. G. and J. D. *alternis vicibus*', a charming poem addressed to two unnamed ladies, which has survived in a single manuscript:

> Heere in our Nightingales, wee heere you singe,
> Who soe doe make the whole yeare through a springe,
> And save us from the feare of Autumns stinge.
>
> In Ancors calme face wee your smoothnes see,
> Your mindes unmingled, and as cleare as shee
> That keepes untouch't her first virginitie.
>
> Did all St. Edith Nunns descend againe
> To honor Polesworth with their cloystred traine,
> Compar'd with you each would confesse some stayne.[1]

The reference to the singing of the nightingales makes it unlikely that these lines would have been written on a visit which terminated so early in the spring as 2 April, as did the visit of 1613. The visit of that year is attested by a variant title of one of the manuscript versions of the poem 'Goodfriday, 1613. Riding Westward'. In the same manuscript that contains the poem written by Donne and Goodyer together (which may thus have been compiled by someone with access to Goodyer's papers) the poem is headed 'Mr. J. Dun*n* goeinge from Sir H. G. on good fryday sent him back this meditation, on the Waye'. Donne's visit in 1613 therefore lasted until 2 April, which was the date of Good Friday in that year. Another manuscript version of the poem describes it as composed while Donne was 'Riding to Sr Edward Harbert in Wales'. Montgomery is about sixty-five miles due west of Polesworth, so Donne may be presumed to have arrived there on 3 April. Arrive he certainly did, for on 7 April he wrote a letter from Montgomery Castle to Sir Robert Harley, Herbert's kinsman, to express his regret at not being able to see him.[2] Visits in the seventeenth century lasted

---

[1] [Milgate, *Satires etc.*, p. 77.] The first and third of the stanzas quoted are by Donne. Before the Reformation Polesworth had been a convent dedicated to St. Edith, and the river Anker, to which Drayton addressed several sonnets, flowed beneath it.

[2] Among the Portland MSS.; Hayward, p. 464.

for weeks rather than days, and it was probably May before Donne returned to London.

During his stay in the country a resolution had been gradually maturing in Donne's mind. His future was as uncertain as ever; if anything, his prospects were worse than they had been before. His alliance with Sir Robert Drury had done him no good. Drury thought himself fit for high state employment, but his indiscretions only revealed his unfitness for it; thus, whoever held the reins of power, it was unlikely that he would ever find himself anything but a member of a dissident minority. Donne's dependence on him was therefore a disadvantage. Furthermore, during the past six years Morton had twice urged a career in the Church upon him as the solution of his difficulties, and it was doubly disconcerting that the King, after reading *Pseudo-Martyr*, had again added his voice to Morton's. Though scarcely willing as yet to follow their advice wholeheartedly, however, Donne was more inclined than he had formerly been to yield to such pressure. Nevertheless he hesitated long before taking an irrevocable step. If it must be taken, then it must; but first he determined to place himself at the disposal of a man whose power and influence were second only to the King's. If he could win his favour a brilliant future might still be ahead of him, whether in the Church or out of it.

The last twelve months had seen a great change in the administration of the government. The Earl of Salisbury's death had brought to an end the rule of the Cecils, father and son, which had been continuous for nearly half a century. After his death James made no immediate attempt to fill the vacant office; for the time being he would act as his own secretary. He therefore threw himself with ardour into the task, but, as the daily accumulation of business went inexorably on, it became steadily more irksome. There were plenty of candidates, of course, for the vacant office, and both Sir Henry Wotton and Sir Henry Neville were regarded as having strong claims upon it. If either of these had secured it, doubtless Donne's future would have been assured, but in fact more and more of the conduct of public business fell into the hands of the reigning favourite, who felt that it was to his interest either to leave the secretaryship vacant or secure the appointment of a man who would be

content with only a vestige of the power which the Cecils had
wielded. Robert Ker, who in 1611 had been raised to the English
peerage as Viscount Rochester, was now at the apex of his power.
While Salisbury was alive there had always been at least two ways
to the King's ear, either through the favourite or through the man
who was, in effect, the head of the executive government; now there
was only one. Donne therefore determined to make a direct appeal
to Rochester. Among the Scots at Court Donne had two influential
friends whom Rochester could not ignore: James, Lord Hay, and the
other Sir Robert Ker, a second cousin of the favourite and a member
of the household of Prince Charles. Rochester had first come to
Court as a member of Hay's household, and Donne had already
found that he could rely on Hay's good nature and warmth of feeling towards him; accordingly he resolved to make his approach
through Hay. This is the letter which Hay presented to Rochester
on Donne's behalf:

My Lord,
   I may justly fear, that your Lordship hath never heard of the name,
which lies at the bottom of this Letter: nor could I come to the boldnesse of presenting it now, without another boldnesse, of putting his
Lordship, who now delivers it, to that office. Yet I have (or flatter my
self to have) just excuses of this, and just ground of that ambition.
For, having obeyed at last, after much debatement within me, the
Inspirations (as I hope) of the Spirit of God, and resolved to make my
Profession Divinitie: I make account, that I do but tell your Lordship,
what God hath told me, which is, That it is in this course, if in any,
that my service may be of use to this Church and State. Since then
your Lordship's vertues have made you so near the head in the one,
and so religious a Member of the other, I came to this courage, of
thrusting my self thus into your Lordship's presence, both in respect
that I was an independent, and disobliged man, towards any other
person in this State; and delivered over now, (in my resolution) to be
a houshold-servant of God. I humbly beseech your Lordship, that
since these my purposes are likelie, to meet quicklie a false and unprofitable dignitie, which is, the envie of others, you will vouchsafe to
undertake, or prevent, or disable that, by affording them the true
dignitie of your just interpretations, and favourable assistance. And
to receive into your knowledge so much of the History, and into your

protection so much of the endeavours, of your Lordships most humble and devoted servant.[1]

Donne had chosen his moment carefully. Rochester had fallen in love with the Countess of Essex, and his suit had been abetted by his friend Sir Thomas Overbury until the lovers began to devise a means of breaking the Countess's marriage so that they themselves could marry. Overbury was prepared to see the lady his friend's mistress, but not his wife, and soon earned the resentment of the lovers by his opposition to their plans. Accordingly, on 26 April 1613 he was committed to the Tower on a trumped-up charge. Overbury had always been much abler than Rochester and had helped him to handle the quantities of business that had come into his hands. He had a much readier pen than the favourite, and is said even to have helped him compose his love-letters. With Overbury removed, Rochester badly needed someone of similar ability on whom he could lean. Hence Donne's letter was even more successful in producing immediate results than he had dared to hope. Shortly afterwards he was presented to Rochester by Hay, and he created so favourable an impression that Rochester not only felt sure of being able to make use of his talents but also urged him to put aside all thoughts of entering the Church. Subsequent letters make it clear that Rochester contributed generously to Donne's support for the next year or so. 'After I was grown to be your Lordship's, by all the Titles that I could think upon,' he wrote in one of them, 'it hath pleased your Lordship to make an other Title to me, by buying me'; 'ever since I had the happinesse to be in your Lordship's sight,' he wrote in another, 'I have lived upon your bread.'[2] One cannot help asking exactly what services Donne rendered in return for such generosity. Gosse thought that he had found the answer when he discovered the record among the Ashburnham manuscripts of a document[3] entitled 'Dr. Donne's compendium of the whole course of proceedings in the nullity of the marriage of the Earl of Essex and the Lady Frances Howard, 1613', but this paper is in fact identical with the account of the case in MS. Harleian 39, attributed to Sir

---

[1] *Tobie Mathew Collection*, pp. 319–20. The letter was enclosed with one to Hay, ibid., p. 321.
[2] Ibid., pp. 318 and 311.   [3] Now MS. Stowe 423 in the British Museum.

Daniel Dun, D.C.L., who was one of the commissioners before whom the case was tried. But even if Donne can be thus exonerated from any actual share in the efforts to procure a divorce for Lady Essex so that she could marry Rochester, it is of little avail to his reputation. The fact is that he felt himself so indebted to his patron that he had no hesitation in defending the divorce, and was perfectly prepared to place his pen at Rochester's service. Sentence of nullity was pronounced on 27 September 1613, and the King himself hastened the preparations for the new marriage, which took place on 26 December, Rochester in the meantime having been created Earl of Somerset so that the bride might suffer no loss of rank. Writing a few weeks after the wedding Donne professed his ardour to write not merely an epithalamion but also a defence of the divorce:

> Some appearances have been here, of some treatise concerning this Nullity, which are said to proceed from *Geneva*, but are beleeved to have been done within doors, by encouragements of some whose names I will not commit to this letter. My poor study having lyen that way, it may prove possible, that my weak assistance may be of use in this matter, in a more serious fashion, then an Epithalamion. This made me therefore abstinent in that kinde; yet by my troth, I think I shall not scape. I deprehend in my self more then an alacrity, a vehemency to do service to that company; and so, I may finde reason to make rime.[1]

The epithalamion was written and presented, with a prefatory eclogue to excuse its not being proffered until some time after the occasion it celebrated. The epithalamion lacks the fervour of Donne's two earlier pieces in the same form, while the eclogue is an extravagant admission of the extremes to which court flattery obliged Donne to stoop. The best that can be said for him is that he unquestionably felt a lively sense of gratitude to Somerset for his favours. Fortunately the prose defence of the nullity was never needed, since the attack on it seems not to have been published.

Another of the poems certainly belonging to these years was written at the request of Lady Bedford. Donne's acceptance of Sir Robert Drury's bounty must have created rival obligations, and

---

[1] *Letters*, pp. 180–1; cf. also a letter to Sir Robert Ker, ibid., p. 270.

could scarcely have been regarded as anything but a breach of his allegiance to Lady Bedford; inevitably, therefore, the ties that had for a time held them so closely together were gradually loosened; but they were never broken. As we have seen, Donne had begun a verse letter to Lady Bedford on the Continent, but had never finished it, and in a letter from Spa he had written: 'I can glory of nothing in this voyage, but that I have afflicted my Lady *Bedford* with few Letters. I protest earnestly to you, it troubles me much more to dispatch a pacquet into *England*, without a Letter to her, then it would to put in three. But I have been heretofore too immodest towards her, and I suffer this Purgatory for it.'[1] After his return Donne scarcely had opportunity to resume relations with Lady Bedford before she fell seriously ill. She barely recovered sufficiently to attend the Princess Elizabeth's wedding, and when she returned to court it was apparent that she was a much-changed woman. She was said to have vowed in her sickness never to frequent the court again and, though she did not keep her vow, she was 'somewhat reformed in her attire, and forbeares painting, which they say makes her looke somewhat straungely among so many visards'.[2] In her illness she had had the ministrations of Dr. John Burgess, a Puritan preacher who had been silenced and imprisoned for a sermon that had offended the King. On his release he went abroad and studied medicine at Leyden; he returned to England in 1612 and with surprising rapidity built up a fashionable practice in the neighbourhood of Isleworth and Twickenham. Burgess, wrote Chamberlain to Carleton, was much with Lady Bedford during her illness, 'and did her more goode with his spirituall counsaile then with naturall phisicke'.[3] During the twelve months that followed Lady Bedford continued to need spiritual consolation, for she endured one misfortune after another. The Earl of Bedford was thrown from his horse while hunting; as a consequence he was partially paralysed and his speech was affected. After the Princess Elizabeth's marriage, Lord and Lady Harrington, in whose care she had been for so many years, left England with her to escort her to her husband's Court,

---

[1] Ibid., pp. 92–3. [2] Chamberlain, *Letters*, i. 470.
[3] Ibid. On Burgess and Lady Bedford, see P. Thomson, 'John Donne and the Countess of Bedford', *MLR*, xliv (1949), 329–40, at pp. 331–5.

but on 23 August 1613 Lord Harrington died at Worms on his way home. Finally, on 27 February 1613/14, the second Lord Harrington, Lady Bedford's brother, 'the most compleat yong gentleman of his age that this kingdom could afford for religion, learning, and courteous behaviour',[1] died of smallpox shortly before his twenty-second birthday. Donne, who had been on friendly terms with him for some years,[2] felt a keen sense of personal loss as well as a wish to honour his memory. The 'Obsequies to the Lord Harrington' are, apart from the *Anniversaries*, his longest and most elaborate set of memorial verses. They were sent (some considerable time after Harrington's death) to Lady Bedford accompanied with a begging letter that was scarcely in the best of taste. There was no actual breach between Donne and Lady Bedford; Donne still felt a strong sense of obligation towards her, but their relations can have been neither so close nor so cordial as formerly.

Sir Henry Goodyer's relations with Lady Bedford had also changed. He seems to have given up his position of semi-dependence in her household, and to have attached himself instead to the Countess of Huntingdon. In 1609 Donne had hesitated to address himself to Lady Huntingdon; in 1613 and 1614, however, he frequently sent her his respects through Goodyer. She has become 'that noble Lady at *Ashby*', 'in whose protection I am, since I have, nor desire other station, then a place in her good opinion'.[3] Clearly the day was over when Donne could profess that he reserved for Lady Bedford 'not only all the verses, which I should make, but all the thoughts of womens worthinesse'.[4] It would not be fair to say that his praises were at the disposal of any great lady who could be persuaded to take an interest in him and open her purse-strings, but his friends had less difficulty than might have been anticipated in persuading him to accede to their requests for such complimentary verses. After Prince Henry's death, George Garrard had found service with the young Earl of Salisbury, who had recently succeeded his father at the age of twenty-one. The Earl's wife was a Howard, daughter of the Earl of Suffolk, and Garrard had evidently sung

---

[1] J. Whitelocke, *Liber Famelicus*, p. 39.
[2] See *Letters*, p. 153, where Donne expresses relief at news of Harrington's recovery from an earlier bout of his illness.
[3] Ibid., pp. 181, 172.   [4] Ibid., p. 104.

Donne's praises to her with such warmth that he was assured that some verses would be graciously accepted. They are dated August 1614, and they were heralded by a letter written on the 4th of the same month.[1] The criticisms to which the *Anniversaries* had exposed him still rankled in Donne's mind, and he was at pains to discourage any comparison of what he might write to a new patroness with what he had previously addressed to other ladies; and he states the consequent dilemma rather neatly:

I should be loath that in any thing of mine, composed of her, she should not appear much better then some of those of whom I have written. And yet I cannot hope for better expressings then I have given of them. So you see how much I should wrong her, by making her but equall to others. I would I could be beleeved, when I say that all that is written of them, is but prophecy of her.

In the end, this became the theme of the greater part of the lines to the Countess:

> If in this sacrifice of mine, be showne
> Any small sparke of these, call it your owne.
> And if things like these, have been said by mee
> Of others; call not that Idolatrie.
> For had God made man first, and man had seene
> The third daies fruits, and flowers, and various greene,
> He might have said the best that he could say
> Of those faire creatures, which were made that day;
> And when next day he had admir'd the birth
> Of Sun, Moone, Stars, fairer then late-prais'd earth,
> Hee might have said the best that he could say,
> And not be chid for praising yesterday.

This, however, was the last of the pieces addressed to great ladies. Donne now declared in the 'Obsequies to the Lord Harrington' that his Muse had 'spoke her last', and he was soon to be freed from the need to seek patronage by such means.

Donne's correspondence with George Garrard spans the years from 1609 to the end of 1630, and like all Donne's close friendships this one was life-long. Two letters also survive that were written

---

[1] Ibid., pp. 259–61. Gosse (i. 294–5) dates the letter 4 Mar. 1611/12, but this is clearly wrong.

to Garrard's 'fair sister', Martha—one from Spa in 1612, the other, acknowledging a visit which she made to Donne with her brother, belonging probably to 1613.[1] If one feels that in 1613–14 Donne was cutting rather a poor figure, it is just to remember the charming courtliness of these notes to Martha Garrard. To his friends and acquaintances he was still, as he was remembered later, a man who had been Egerton's secretary, 'a Laureat Wit; neither was it possible that a vulgar Soul should dwell in such promising Features'.[2] However desperate his circumstances, he seems never to have strained the friendship and respect of those who knew him. And desperate his circumstances must often have appeared to him at this period. For besides the loss of children, the uncertainty of his future and the constant anxiety for his large family, Donne was beset by sickness.

Indeed, one reason why he did not have an epithalamion ready for Somerset's marriage, but had to write it after the event, may have been that he was ill. He and his family suffered severely during the winter of 1613–14 and the following spring. As far back as September 1613 Donne had had eye-trouble, and had written to Garrard: 'If I doe mine eyes a little more injurie, I shall lose the honour of seeing you at Michaelmas; for by my troth I am almost blinde.'[3] As Christmas approached and the decorations were being erected in celebration of Somerset's approaching marriage, Donne was still afflicted, and wrote somewhat sardonically: 'It is one of my blinde Meditations to think what a miserable defeat it would be to all these preparations of braverie, if my infirmity should overtake others: for, I am at least half blinde, my windows are all as full of glasses of Waters, as any Mountebanks stall.'[4] Four weeks later, his eyes still needed care, but were slowly improving.[5] These troubles were, however, but a prelude to what was to come. By February 1614 Donne was in reasonably good health again, but he was the only one in the house who was. The children were all in the grip of

---

[1] *Letters*, pp. 266–7, 40–1.

[2] J. Hacket, *Scrinia Reserata*, 1693, p. 63.

[3] *Letters*, pp. 280–1. The illness was doubtless also the cause of Donne's delay in sending the 'Obsequies to the Lord Harrington', which, with its concluding statement that his Muse had 'spoke her last', is hardly likely to have ante-dated the verse letter to the Countess of Salisbury.

[4] Ibid., p. 201.   [5] Ibid., p. 180.

some epidemic, and, to make matters worse, his wife had suffered a miscarriage: 'I have already lost half a child, and with that mischance of hers, my wife ⟨has⟩ fallen into an indisposition, which would afflict her much, but that the sicknesse of her children stupefies her.'[1] Gradually the children recovered, but at the beginning of March Donne fell ill again, and his wife could bear up no longer. On 14 March he wrote to Goodyer:

> It hath pleased God to adde thus much to my affliction, that my wife hath now confessed her self to be extremely sick; she hath held out thus long to assist me, but is now overturn'd, & here we be in two beds, or graves; so that God hath marked out a great many of us, but taken none yet. I have passed ten daies without taking any thing; so that I think no man can live more thriftily. I have purged and vexed my body much since I writ to you, and this day I have missed my fit: and this is the first time, that I could discern any intermission.[2]

By the end of March he was slowly recovering,[3] yet it was not until mid May that he could assure his friends that he was 'relapsed into good degrees of health'; yet even such health, he felt, had been bought at a price since, he wrote, 'I have scaped no better cheap, then that I have paid death one of my Children for my Ransome.'[4] 'Because I loved it well,' he continued, 'I make account that I dignifie the memorie of it, by mentioning of it to you, else I should not be so homely.' The child thus lost was Mary (then just over three years old), whose burial is recorded in the register of St. Clement Danes on 18 May 1614. The Churchwardens' Accounts contain the further items:

for the buryall of Mary Dun
    for the grave in the church ·   ·   · iij[s]
    for the knell   ·   ·   ·   ·   · ij[s] vj[d].

In the letter in which Donne reported the illness of his children he had continued: 'This meets a fortune so ill provided for physique and such relief, that if God should ease us with burialls, I know not well how to performe even that.'[5] This note of financial stringency is heard more often in the letters of this period than in any of the

[1] Ibid., p. 152.   [2] Ibid., p. 168.
[3] Ibid., pp. 299, 297; *Tobie Mathew Collection*, p. 311.
[4] *Letters*, p. 273.   [5] Ibid., p. 152.

earlier ones. Almost all Donne's expenses must have increased. The children were growing up, and they were more numerous; they were all in London, where expenses were inevitably higher than they had been in the country. Furthermore, Donne had to make a show of keeping an establishment if he was to cut any sort of figure with those through whose aid he hoped to climb. Thus, on the one hand, he kept a French manservant ('my Monsieur'), whom he had probably brought back from the Continent with him; on the other hand, he had to economize by giving up his horse, and was obliged to borrow one from his brother-in-law when he had to go on a journey into the country.[1] There is, too, a note of urgency in his begging letters that had not been there before. In fact, he is at pains to remind his patrons that they are under no obligations to him whatsoever, in order to make sure that they will not overlook him. 'I do rest my selfe', he wrote to Somerset, 'upon your gracious inclinations towards me, and think my selfe much safer in that, then in the possession of any place';[2] and when Lord Harrington died and Lady Bedford inherited the bulk of his property, he presented to her the poem in his memory with these words:

I have learn'd by those lawes wherein I am a little conversant, that hee which bestowes any cost upon the dead, obliges him which is dead, but not the heire; I do not therefore send this paper to your Ladyship, that you should thanke mee for it, or thinke that I thanke you in it; your favours and benefits to mee are so much above my merits, that they are even above my gratitude, if that were to be judged by words which must expresse it.[3]

It may be true that such letters reveal the least pleasant side of Donne, but they also suggest the straits to which his need had reduced him.

In spite of illness, in spite of financial worries, he never ceased to be a student. Walton says that during the years immediately preceding his entry into the Church 'he applied himself to an incessant study of Textual Divinity, and to the attainment of a greater perfection in the learned Languages, *Greek* and *Hebrew*'.[4] In a letter written

---

[1] *Letters*, p. 201; Gosse, ii. 47 (Loseley MS.).
[2] *Tobie Mathew Collection*, p. 316.   [3] Grierson, i. 270.
[4] *Lives*, p. 46.

in July 1613[1] Donne mentions that he has been 'busying [him]self a little in the search of the Eastern tongues', and the titles of some of the books from his library bear out this statement.[2] Such studies may have resulted in the completion of the *Essayes in Divinity*, which were written, according to his son John (who published them in 1651), 'Before he entred into Holy Orders'. Here we have, as in Donne's previous prose works, the intimate knowledge of the Bible and of commentaries upon it, of the Fathers and of the writings of European theologians past and contemporary, and the fairly wide knowledge of the ancient Latin classics, which mark him as a learned man even by the standards of that age; but now, instead of to casuists and controversialists, whose works were necessarily more relevant in *Biathanatos* and *Pseudo-Martyr*, we find him referring to more esoteric sources—the books of Christian Cabbalists (Pico della Mirandola, Franciscus Georgius, and Reuchlin). Even if, as seems probable, parts of the *Essayes* had been written some years before, they may have reached their final form in 1614.[3]

Donne's interest in these studies suggests that he must have kept in touch with the learned ecclesiastics of his acquaintance, and confirmation is to be found in some slight but none the less highly significant references in the letters. For instance, writing to Goodyer on 14 March 1614, while still unwell, Donne concludes somewhat abruptly, and in so doing excuses himself by asking 'leave to make this which I am fain to call my good day, so much truly good, as to spend the rest of it with D. *Layfield*, who is, upon my summons, at this hour come to me'.[4] This was John Layfield, D.D., rector of St. Clement Danes. He was an excellent Hebraist, and had been one of the group of divines who sat at Westminster to revise the Pentateuch for the Authorized Version. The fact that he was prepared to come and spend a large portion of the day with Donne on being told that Donne was sufficiently recovered makes it likely that they were studying together. Layfield may well have been reading Hebrew with Donne, and his concern with the translation of the early books

---

[1] Gosse, ii. 16 (Anderdon MS.).
[2] e.g. the works by Helvicus in the Library of the Middle Temple, published in 1611 and 1612; Keynes, L97–100.
[3] See below, pp. 298–9.
[4] *Letters*, p. 171.

of the Bible may also have helped to determine some of the topics with which Donne dealt in the *Essayes in Divinity.*

The same letter reports the delivery to St. Paul's of an enclosure that Goodyer had requested Donne to forward. Then it continues: 'In the History of that remove, this onely perchance may be news to you, that Mr *Alabaster* hath got of the King the Deans best Living worth above 300^l, which the Dean had good hope to have held a while.' 'That remove' was the appointment of John Overall, Dean of St. Paul's, to the see of Coventry and Lichfield, which had just been announced. William Alabaster, who succeeded him as rector of Tharfield, Herts., is now remembered only for his poems[1] and for his Latin comedy *Roxana*, but he had been a Fellow of Trinity, Cambridge, with Dr. Layfield, and was sufficient of an Orientalist to publish some years later a pentaglot dictionary. Donne could have known him ever since 1596, when he had been Essex's chaplain on the Cadiz expedition. John Overall, it will be recalled, had been the friend and host of Thomas Morton, whom Donne had been accustomed to visit at the Deanery of St. Paul's.[2] In this way Donne, and perhaps Goodyer too, had become acquainted with Morton's host. The deanery stood on the south side of the cathedral, not far from its present site; in the corresponding position on the north side was the ancient palace of the bishops, and with this too Donne was familiar as a guest. Another letter to Goodyer, written on 17 July 1613, speaks of a visit there to see John King, who had been Bishop of London since 1611:

I dined yesterday on the King's side at Paul's, but where there came in so many of the Queen's kindred that the house was more troubled with them than this kingdom was with the Queen's kindred, when your ancestress the Lady Gray conquered Edward IV. There was father, mother, two brothers, four sisters, and miserable I; yet there was found time to ask me where you were, and to protest that she did not know you were gone out of town because you were so equal a stranger there, in and out of town.[3]

---

[1] See *The Sonnets of William Alabaster*, ed. G. M. Story and Helen Gardner, Oxford, 1959.

[2] See p. 207 above.

[3] Gosse, ii. 16 (Anderdon MS.). The interpretation of this passage was first put forward by R. E. Bennett, 'Donne and the Queen', *TLS*, 29 Aug. 1936, p. 697.

'The Queen', of course, was the Bishop's lady, Mrs. King, and the letter indicates clearly that Donne was on terms of considerable intimacy with the family.

To many Londoners not closely of his acquaintance Donne was, at this time, still the witty poet of the *Satires*, as the earliest references to his poetry show. Thomas Freeman's tribute is fairly typical:

To John Dunne.

The *Storme* describ'd, hath set thy name afloate,
Thy *Calme*, a gale of famous winde hath got:
Thy *Satyres* short, too soone we them o'relooke,
I prethee *Persius* write a bigger booke.[1]

To his friends, however, it had long been evident that Donne's main concerns had been with graver matters. It would seem that this was also known abroad. Walton, writing of the middle years of Donne's life, says: 'Nor did our own Nobility only value and favour him, but his acquaintance and friendship was sought for by most Ambassadours of forraign Nations, and by many other strangers, whose learning or business occasioned their stay in this Nation.'[2] No specific evidence has been discovered to confirm this assertion, though there may be unknown references to Donne in the learned or diplomatic correspondence of the period still to be discovered in European archives. Nevertheless, Walton's statement invites a measure of speculation. Donne's interest in Pierre du Moulin's visit to England in 1615–16, shortly after his ordination, is known,[3] so that one may infer with some degree of probability that he knew Isaac Casaubon. Lady Bedford's brother, the youthful Sir John Harrington, early in 1610 sent Casaubon, whom he had visited in Paris a few months previously, a copy of *Pseudo-Martyr*, hoping that, in spite of its being written in English, it would interest the Frenchman.[4] Casaubon came to England at the King's invitation in October of the same year, and spent his first year there as Overall's

---

[1] *Rubbe, and a great Cast*, 1614, part ii, epigram 84.
[2] *Lives*, pp. 35–6.   [3] *Letters*, p. 296.
[4] A. L. Soens, 'Casaubon and Donne', *TLS*, 2 May 1958, p. 241. Dr. Soens also points out that in *Pseudo-Martyr* Donne twice cites Casaubon's *De Libertate Ecclesiastica*, a work still unpublished, though Casaubon had sent an incomplete copy to England.

guest at the deanery of St. Paul's. Morton was living there too, and formed so deep an attachment for Casaubon that he erected at his own cost the memorial to Casaubon in Westminster Abbey. The last year of Casaubon's life (1613–14) was spent in a house in the 'new rents' in Drury Lane, so that he must have been living not very far from Donne. Others of Donne's friends, including both Sir Henry Wotton and Sir Edward Herbert, had formerly been intimate with Casaubon, and for this reason also it would have been strange if Donne had not met him.[1] Another distinguished foreigner who visited London for a short time in 1613, was Hugo Grotius. He came ostensibly as a member of a mission to treat of maritime affairs, but he is said also to have been acting as the secret agent of the Arminian faction in Holland, his aim being to win for them the support of James I. 'It is certain', writes a modern biographer of Grotius, 'that, aided by Casaubon, he was endeavouring secretly to influence the King . . . and, at the same time, to secure the support in those efforts of the ecclesiastics of the school of Andrewes and Overall.'[2] Thus Grotius while in London moved on the fringe of some of the same circles as Donne, and while there is no evidence to show whether they became acquainted one can at least say that Grotius was such a man as Donne would have been eager to meet.

Donne's interest in public affairs at this period is further manifested by the alacrity with which he seized the opportunity of again becoming a Member of Parliament.[3] The King had dissolved his previous Parliament in 1611 because of its firm insistence on the redress of grievances before it would grant supplies, but James's financial difficulties had become so great by 1613 that the calling of a new Parliament was under consideration before the end of the year. Finally, on 16 February 1614, the Privy Council advised the King to issue writs for an election. A few days previously Donne had written:

The King at his going away left the debatements of the Parliament to his Council, who have resolved nothing therein as yet, so that the

---

[1] Wotton had lodged in Casaubon's home in Geneva in 1593–4, Herbert in his house in Paris in 1608.

[2] W. S. M. Knight, *Life and Works of Hugo Grotius* (Grotius Society Publications, no. 4, 1925), p. 143.

[3] See I. A. Shapiro, 'John Donne and Parliament', *TLS*, 10 Mar. 1932, p. 172.

assurance thereof is not so vehement as it was. It is taken ill, though it be but mistaken that certain men (whom they call undertakers) should presume either to understand the house before it sit, or to incline it then, and this rumour beforehand, which must impeach, if it do not defeat their purposes at last.[1]

As this shows, rumours of a packed House, favourable to the King, were current even before the decision to call Parliament had been made. Sir Henry Neville, one of the sireniacal gentlemen of Donne's acquaintance and a strong candidate for the vacant Secretaryship of State, was already trying to work out compromise proposals which would, he hoped, be equally acceptable to King and Commons. Others, more sanguine still, were 'undertaking' to use their influence to secure the election of members who would vote in accordance with the wishes of the King. As Donne had already perceived, the outcome was disastrous to the hopes of the undertakers. 'Constituencies which had never before raised an objection to the persons who had been pointed out to them, now declared their determination to send to Westminster men of their own selection';[2] and some heated contests ensued.

A number of Donne's influential friends were willing to recommend him to constituencies in which they had interests. On 14 March he wrote to Goodyer: 'You made me offer so long since of a place (it was when you writ into the west) [that] I could think it no merit to have offered you one since, otherwise it hath been since in my power, for since the M^r. of the Rolls provided me one, Sir *Ed. Herbert*, who makes haste away, made me a present of his; and I have had a third offer.'[3] Sir Edward Herbert went off in the spring of 1614 to fight against the Spaniards in the Low Countries, so the borough of Montgomery, which he had previously represented, in default of Donne sent Sir John Danvers (Herbert's stepfather) to Parliament. Donne says that he had accepted a seat in the gift of Sir Edward Phelips, Master of the Rolls. There is no suggestion earlier than this of Donne's acquaintance with him, but Coryate, addressing Phelips from India, had, as we have seen, sent remembrances

---

[1] Gosse, ii. 34 (Anderdon MS.).
[2] S. R. Gardiner, *History of England, 1603–42*, ii. (1889) 230.
[3] *Letters*, pp. 170–1.

through him to his son Sir Robert, to Richard Martin, Christopher Brooke, John Hoskyns, William Hakewill, 'and the rest of the worthy gentlemen frequenting your Honourable table, that fauour vertue, and the sacred Muses'.[1] All those here named were friends of Donne and all of them, except Martin, were members of the 1614 Parliament, in nearly every case for constituencies they had previously represented. Since Donne was offered, and accepted, the borough of Taunton, it may safely be presumed that he was one of the 'worthy gentlemen' who frequented Sir Edward Phelips's table. But besides the friends already mentioned Donne would have found plenty of other friends and acquaintances among the members when Parliament met. His wife's family was represented by Sir George and Sir Robert More and Sir Thomas Grymes; there were such old friends as Sir Henry Wotton, Sir Thomas Roe, Sir William Cornwallis, Sir Thomas Lucy, Sir Walter Chute, and Richard Connock; on a slightly more exalted level of rank or wealth, perhaps, were such patrons and friends as Sir John Egerton, Sir Robert Drury, Sir Francis Bacon, Sir Lionel Cranfield, and Sir Arthur Ingram.

The Master of the Rolls had great influence in Somerset, and besides recommending Donne for Taunton nominated his son as one of the knights of the shire for the county. But all did not go as smoothly as he had hoped. Chamberlain wrote to Carleton: 'I have not heard of so much contestation for places in parlement, as falles out this time. . . . The greatest incounter is like to be in Somersetshire twixt Sir Maurice Barkly, Master Paulet and Sir Rob: Phillips for whom his father sayes he will set up his rest and followes the matter with might and main.'[2] Sir Robert Phelips was defeated, much to his father's chagrin, and had to be content with a Cornish borough.

The 'Addled Parliament', as it was called, met on 5 April 1614 and was dissolved on 7 June. It is remarkable as the only recorded parliament which passed no legislation whatsoever; nearly all its time was spent on vehement discussions of questions of parliamentary privilege and on attempts to put an end to such grievances as

[1] *Thomas Coriate Traveller for the English Wits: Greeting*, 1616, pp. 8–9; cf. p. 193 above.
[2] Chamberlain, *Letters*, i. 518.

impositions and monopolies. 'Impositions', or customs duties levied solely by virtue of the royal authority, became the principal issue in Parliament. In the debate on the second reading of a bill to abolish them it was resolved to seek a conference with the Lords so that both Houses could present a joint petition to the King on the subject, and, on 5 May, Donne was appointed a member of the committee to 'prepare the manner of this Conference'. The committee's report was presented by Sir Edwin Sandys a week later, and it was decided that the case against impositions should be presented to the Lords by nine members, all learned in the law, among whom were William Hakewill and John Hoskyns. The Lords, however, refused a conference, and in the debate Neile, Bishop of Lincoln, declared that they would hear nothing but matters of mutiny and sedition from the Commons if they granted a conference. The next day the House of Commons was full of indignation at the report of Neile's speech, and a select committee, again with Donne as a member, was appointed to consider what course of action should be taken. On receiving the committee's report the Commons eventually decided to demand satisfaction of the Lords and to refuse to proceed with any further business until satisfaction had been obtained. The Lords replied evasively and on 30 May and 1 June other select committees, in which Donne was included, were appointed to consider the Lords' answer and what further action should be taken against the Bishop of Lincoln.

Meanwhile the King's patience was wearing thin, and he was especially irked by the refusal of the Commons to proceed with business until the dispute with the Lords was settled. A royal message of 3 June brought things to a head; in the debate which followed its reception, those who wished to proceed to grant supplies to the King were hotly opposed by those who sought to curb his extravagance. The debate was remarkable for its attack on the Scottish favourites:

Hereupon divers motions were made, among the rest the example of Canutus was alleged for sending hom his Danes, that these who consumed the King had no freehold among us; they paid no subsidies, they consumed both the King and kingdom in prodigality, in all riot and dissolution of apparel and other superfluities, no mean contented them, that the pensions forth of the Exchequer came to 70,000*l*. and above, that the King had given to one man 1000*l*. per annum old rent which was more than Queen Elizabeth had given to all her servants in 44 years.[1]

After this debate the King felt that further patience would be useless, and dissolved Parliament at once. On the day after the dissolution four members were sent to the Tower, and two of them were friends of Donne. In the debate against the Scots Hoskyns had adduced the historical parallel of 'the *Sicilianae Vesperae*[2] to the Scots who consumed both king and kingdom in insolvency and all kind of riot'. Sir Walter Chute's offence was a rather different one; he had been, like Donne, a member of the committee to consider Bishop Neile's indiscreet speech, and, Chamberlain reported, he had offered the committee

his service to the King, which might stand them in stead in regard that he is so neere the King that he cuts all the meat he eates, and hath much entercourse of speach with him which he commonly setts downe when he comes home for feare of forgetting, and therin hath don the house many goode offices, which he will continue so long as he continues his place, which by this course me thincks shold not be very long.[3]

In the debate of 3 June Chute also spoke against the Scots; his dismissal and imprisonment were almost inevitable. He spent four months in the Tower. Hoskyns, however, was there for a full year. In addition, the members of the select committee who were to have put the case against impositions to the Lords were summoned before the Council and the notes they had collected for their speeches were burnt in the Council chamber. Shortly after all this, the Master of the Rolls fell ill and died; it was thought, reported Whitelocke, 'that greef he toke in the king's displeasure toward him, for his son's roughenesse in the parliament, hastned his deathe. But', adds Whitelocke, 'I cannot think a man can be sutche a mope.'[4]

---

[1] Sir John Holles's report of the debate, Hist. MSS. Com., *MSS. of the Duke of Portland*, ix. 136.

[2] The spontaneous uprising at Easter 1282 against the French in Sicily, which led to the massacre of over 9,000 Frenchmen.

[3] Chamberlain, *Letters*, i. 534. But cf. *Journals of the House of Commons*, i. 497.

[4] *Liber Famelicus* (Camden Society), p. 43.

Donne is not recorded as having taken part in any of the debates of the Addled Parliament, in spite of his membership of several of its most important committees. Hence it is not easy to determine what position he took on the issues with which he was called upon to deal. He owed his place in the House to the influence of a man whose sympathies were all for confining the royal prerogative, and a number of his closest friends took the lead in upholding the privileges of the Commons. On the other hand, Donne was being supported by Somerset, and owed much to the friendship of men like Hay and Sir Robert Ker; and he was relying on them to incline the King's favour towards him. No doubt he judged it the part of discretion not to run the risk of expressing himself too openly or of giving offence. He seems to have been a good committee-man, but he probably kept out of the debates quite deliberately, lest he should spoil his chances with the King or the leading members of the Government.

Soon after the dissolution of Parliament, Donne made his supreme and final effort to secure state employment. Walton relates an incident which shows that Somerset was induced to make a confident appeal on Donne's behalf to the King:

Many persons of worth mediated with his Majesty for some secular employment for him (to which his Education had apted him) and particularly the Earl of *Somerset*, when in his greatest height of favour; who being then at *Theobalds* with the King, where one of the Clerks of the Council died that night, the Earl posted a messenger for Mr. *Donne* to come to him immediately, and at Mr. *Donne*'s coming, said, Mr. *Donne*, *To testifie the reality of my Affection, and my purpose to prefer you, Stay in this Garden till I go up to the King, and bring you word that you are Clark of the Council: doubt not my doing this, for I know the King loves you, and know the King will not deny me.* But the King gave a positive denial to all requests, and having a discerning spirit, replied, *I know* Mr. Donne *is a learned man, has the abilities of a learned Divine; and will prove a powerful Preacher, and my desire is to prefer him that way, and in that way, I will deny you nothing for him.*[1]

Like Walton's account of Donne's visit to the Continent with the Drurys, this story will not stand up to close examination. Walton tells it as having happened shortly after Donne had presented

[1] *Lives*, pp. 45–6.

Pseudo-Martyr to the King, but at that time Donne was unknown to Viscount Rochester (as he then was). During the period of Donne's dependence on Somerset there is no record of the death of any Clerk of the Council. At the beginning of 1613 there were three clerks: Clement Edmondes, George Calvert (afterwards first Lord Baltimore), and Sir William Waad, who was also Lieutenant of the Tower. Waad fell into disfavour because of the way in which he guarded (or failed to guard) Sir Thomas Overbury and the Lady Arabella Stuart, and retired into private life. Francis Cottington and Dudley Norton were sworn in as Clerks of the Council extraordinary on 22 July 1613, and two months later Cottington succeeded Waad as Clerk-in-Ordinary. At the beginning of 1614 William Trumbull was appointed a fourth Clerk-in-Ordinary[1] to cope with the increase in Council business, and on 20 December 1614 Albertus Morton, Sir Henry Wotton's nephew, was sworn in as an additional extraordinary Clerk. Thus, though several additional officers of the Council were appointed, no vacancies occurred by death. On the other hand, such a post was exactly what Donne would be expected to aspire to. Cottington, Trumbull, and Morton had all had diplomatic experience, and seem to have regarded a Clerkship of the Privy Council as the next step up the ladder. Donne had for years been striving to secure a post abroad, and now, confident in the favour of Somerset, might well have aspired to the higher post at home. Nevertheless, Walton has either made a mistake about the office which Somerset attempted to secure for Donne, or has coloured his story too vividly.

Donne's letters, however, show that he was trying hard to gain an appointment of some sort. About 20 March 1614[2] he wrote to Somerset asking explicitly for the ambassadorship to Venice:

I received [from your Lordship] a commandment, so much to assist my selfe, as to present to your Lordship whatsoever [d]o appear to me likelie to advantage me, and ease your Lordship. I am now bold, in obedience of that commandment, to tell your Lordship, that that

---

[1] He is said to have paid Sir Thomas Edmundes £300 for the place; Edmundes presumably having a grant in reversion.

[2] *Tobie Mathew Collection*, pp. 311–12. The letter is undated, but is later than one to Goodyer (*Letters*, p. 167) dated 14 Mar., and was probably enclosed in one to Sir Robert Ker (ibid., p. 299, also in the *Tobie Mathew Collection*) dated 20 Mar.

is told me, That Sir [*D.*] *C.* is likelie to be removed, from [*Ven:*] to the States. If your Lordship have no particular determination upon that place, nor upon me, I humbly beseech your Lordship to pardon me the boldness of asking you, Whether I may not be sent thither.[1]

Sir Henry Wotton was now living quietly at home, cultivating his hopes of the vacant Secretaryship, and the post he had so long filled with distinction at Venice was occupied by Sir Dudley Carleton, who would much rather have been back to his old place at The Hague. Rumours of his recall were current during February and March 1614, although he did not actually return until late in the following year, when Wotton replaced him. Meanwhile there were suitors for the office in plenty. Chamberlain wrote to Carleton that it was being sought by 'Sir Dudley Digges, Sir R[obert] Dru[ry], Lesieur, Fitzwilliams (and I know not who els)',[2] and in another letter he reported that Sir Robert Drury 'wold part with 2000li for the purchase, but yt were pitie things shold passe that way, for then we might well say *omnia Romae venalia*'.[3] Donne's candidacy could not have been very seriously pressed, since Chamberlain did not hear of it, and indeed it might have been embarrassing for him to have found himself in competition with Sir Robert Drury.

After the dissolution of Parliament Donne again put forward his claims for an appointment. He wrote to Somerset reminding him that more than a year had gone by since he had announced his intention of entering the Church; he had set it aside at Somerset's behest, but he was still without preferment:

I humbly therefore beg of your Lordship, that after you shall have been pleased, to admit into your memorie, that I am now a year older, broken with some sicknesse, and in the same degrees of honestie as I was, your Lordship will afford me one commandement, and bid me either hope for this businesse in your Lordship's hand, or else pursue my first purpose, [and] abandon all.[4]

'This businesse in your Lordship's hand' is obviously a reference to some specific grant or office, but there is no clue to its nature. The

---

[1] The text of this letter is corrupt; the original reads: 'to appear . . . Sir *P. C.* . . . . from you to the States . . .'. The second and third emendations were made without comment by Gosse (ii. 41), but there is little doubt that he was right.

[2] Chamberlain, *Letters*, i. 551.

[3] Ibid. i. 548.   [4] *Tobie Mathew Collection*, p. 315.

Court set out on the annual progress on 17 July 1614, but not before
Donne had received every encouragement to petition for a favour.
He had borrowed a horse from Loseley so that he could set out after
the Court at any time, and apparently he went through some of the
preliminary steps of having his patent drawn up for signature.
Then suddenly, without warning, his hopes were dashed by the
unexpected arrival of the King of Denmark in the Thames on
22 July. James hastily returned to London to act as host to his
brother-in-law, and all Court business was pushed aside in the
efforts to arrange suitable entertainment for the visiting monarch.
Donne did not disguise his disappointment.

Our predecessors were never so conquered by the Danes as I am at
this time, for their coming have put my little court business out of the
way and dispossessed me of so near hopes as lacked little of possession.
I must confess my weakness in this behalf; no man attends court
fortunes with more impatience than I do. I esteem nothing more
inexcusable, than to attend them chargeably, nor any expense so
chargeable, as that of time. I am so angry at their coming, that I have
not so much as enquired why they came. But they are even with me;
for, in truth, they came for nothing. . . . Therefore, Sir, I send back
your horse. . . .[1]

As the King of Denmark's brief visit drew to an end, however,
Donne's hopes revived, and he wrote to Lord Hay begging him 'to
take some time to move his Majestie before he go out of Town, that
I may be his servant'.[2] On 1 August James said farewell to his
brother-in-law and returned to Theobalds for several days before
resuming the interrupted progress. Donne, uncertain whether to
follow the Court or to go into the country with Sir Henry Goodyer,
sent to Loseley again for a horse, but did not use it.[3] In the end he
decided to stay in London, and to 'forbear to make any further tryall
in that businesse till the King come into these quarters'.[4] He did
not, however, neglect any opportunity of smoothing his path in

[1] To Sir Robert More, 28 July 1614; Gosse, ii. 46–7 (Loseley MS.).
[2] *Tobie Mathew Collection*, p. 335. Gosse thought that this letter, which is undated,
was written after Donne's ordination, and referred to his 'wish to be the King's
chaplain' (ii. 85); but it seems to contain a reference to the illness of Hay's first wife
in July 1614, which shortly afterwards led to her death.
[3] Loseley MSS., ed. Kempe, pp. 344–5; Gosse, ii. 47–8.
[4] To Goodyer, *Letters*, p. 173.

London, and to make sure that there was no danger that the Lord Chancellor might hold up the sealing of his expected patent he secured an interview with his old master. It was some years since Donne had spoken to Egerton, and he was overwhelmed by the kindness with which he was received: 'my L. Chancellor gave me so noble and so ready a dispatch; accompanied with so fatherly advise, and remorse for my fortunes, that I am now, like an Alchymist, delighted with discoveries by the way, though I attain not mine end.'[1] Secure in the knowledge that he had the backing of the Earl of Somerset, Lord Hay, and Egerton (now Lord Ellesmere), Donne must have felt justified in believing that when the King returned to London in September the appointment which he had sought for so long would be his at last. But these hopes too were destined to disappointment, for apparently the King was reluctant to sign the grant. This much at least is suggested by Walton's story of Somerset's unsuccessful appeal to the King on Donne's behalf. Nevertheless it is not confirmed by Donne himself, who says of James: 'when I asked a temporall *office*, he denied not, refused not that, but let mee see, that hee had rather I took this.'[2] Instead, that is, of the promise of financial security in state employment, which was almost within his grasp, he received the advice once more to enter the Church.

This had been Donne's last throw, and he was now finally convinced of the futility of seeking secular preferment. Before he had approached Somerset he had been ready to seek a profession in the Church, and now, with the King urging him more strongly than ever, it was his final resource. By the end of November his mind was made up, and he deliberately set about making an end to his old way of life. First, however, he sought assurances that the King would be as good as his word to provide for him in the Church, and journeyed to Newmarket especially to announce his intention. On his return he reported to his father-in-law that he had 'received from the King as good allowance and encouragement to pursue my purpose as I could desire'; but he had been alarmed to discover that Somerset was at odds with the Archbishop of Canterbury. Accordingly he was much concerned lest his relations with Somerset should

---

[1] From the same letter, ibid., p. 172.   [2] Sparrow, *Devotions*, p. 46.

reach the Archbishop's ears and stand as a barrier to his preferment in the Church. Finally, he referred to the unsigned grant on which all his hopes had been for so long fixed:

My Lord Chamberlain hath laid his commandment upon the Master of Requests to forbear to move the King in the other business, for any man; though I saw the bill for the King's hand, and saw it was still earnestly pursued out of York House. His Lordship hath assured me that it shall sleep till I move him to set it afoot hereafter, when my son or any for me may have profit thereby, with which purpose I will acquaint my Lord Chancellor, and humbly entreat him that it may be so.[1]

The fall of Somerset (the Lord Chamberlain) a year later no doubt put an end to Donne's hopes of making some profit out of the place that had been promised him and had been so nearly his.

Three more letters, all addressed to Goodyer, supply further information about Donne's activities in the last days of 1614. Goodyer was at this time being pressed by his creditors, and was deliberately avoiding the Court to curb his expenditure. In one of the letters Donne hastens to let him know that he had heard 'in *Yorkhouse* that my L. Chancellor hath been moved, and incensed against' Goodyer because of 'some refusing to appear upon processe which hath been taken out' against him. He further warns Goodyer that 'The great danger, obliquely likely to fall, is that when it comes to light, how you stand towards M. *Mathew*, you may lose the ease which you have by colour of that extent, and he may lose the benefit, of having had so much of his estate concealed.'[2] The letters also show that both Donne and Goodyer were shrewdly watching the fortunes of young George Villiers, the handsome youth recently introduced into the Court by the Earl of Pembroke and the Countess of Bedford in the hope that he would catch the King's eye and gradually undermine the influence of Somerset. Goodyer, apparently, still maintained relations with Lady Bedford, though he had also formed a connection with Lady Huntingdon. Donne would have

---

[1] Gosse, ii. 60–1 (Loseley MS.); the letter is dated 3 Dec. 1614.

[2] *Letters*, p. 195 (20 Dec.). Mathew had a rent charge in England of £80 a year, defeasible on payment of £800, which was in Goodyer's hands (but not paid for). In addition, by June 1614 Goodyer was £120 in arrears with the rents. See A. H. Mathew and A. Calthrop, *Life of Sir Tobie Mathew*, 1907, pp. 129–30.

learned from him of Lady Bedford's hostility to Somerset, and it must have needed some agility not to lose her favour altogether and at the same time to be, as Donne was, almost completely dependent upon Somerset. Lady Bedford seems to have been deeply touched by the 'Obsequies to the Lord Harrington', and nine months later was still so warm in her appreciation that impulsively she offered to pay off Donne's debts when she heard of his intention to enter the Church. He proposed immediately to take her at her word:

since one that meant but to flatter, told an Emperour, that his benefits were to be reckoned from the day of the promise, because he never failed, it were an injury from me to the constancy of that noble Lady, if I should not, as soon as she promises, do some act of assurance of the performance; which I have done, as I say, in fixing times to my creditors; for by the end of next terme, I will make an end with the world, by Gods grace.[1]

Donne further hints that if Goodyer were in town he might be able to induce the Earl of Dorset, who had been lavish in promises but slow in performance, to help as well. Nevertheless he felt confident that he would shortly reach a settlement with his creditors, and was a little startled when he began discussing terms of payment with them:

I confesse, the going about to pay debts, hastens importunity. I finde in my self, that where I was not asked money before, yet when I offered to pay next Terme, they seem loth to afford me that time, which might justly have been desperate before: but that which you told me out of the Countrey, with the assistance which I hope to finde here, (especially if your indevour may advance it at *Dorset* house) I hope will inable me to escape clamor, and an ill conscience, in that behalf.[2]

Obviously, the continuance of Lady Bedford's favour at this point was of vital importance to Donne; yet he was proposing at this very time an action of which he knew she would disapprove, and which

[1] *Letters*, pp. 148–9 (13 Dec.).
[2] Ibid., pp. 196–7 (20 Dec.). In the letter of 13 Dec. just quoted Donne also refers to his hope of help from the Earl of Dorset, to whom Goodyer was apparently making an appeal on his friend's behalf: 'I lack you here, for my L. of *Dorset*, he might make a cheap bargain with me now, and disingage his honour, which in good faith, is a little bound, because he admitted so many witnesses of his large disposition towards me' (ibid., p. 149).

Goodyer was at all costs to keep from her. He proposed not merely to print a collection of his poems, but also to dedicate the volume to Somerset, and to include a selection of verses addressed to other patrons and patronesses as well as to Lady Bedford herself. He was, he asserted, 'under an unescapable necessity' to do this, and he intended to see the volume through the press at once 'not for much publique view, but at mine own cost, a few Copies'; 'for I must do this, as a valediction to the world, before I take Orders'. Apparently the book was never printed, but there is evidence in a group of the surviving manuscript copies that Donne assembled a collection of his verse at about this time.[1] Though he did not offend her by going through with this plan, in the upshot Lady Bedford gave Donne only £30 towards the payment of his debts. Doubtless her intentions were of the best, but she was simply forced to curb her generosity. Early in the winter she wrote to a friend:

my terme businesses, which daylie are multiplied upon me, . . . make me heavil⟨i⟩e feel the burden of a broken estate; yett doe I not doubt but by the assistance of Almighty God I shall ear long overcum all those difficulties which at the present contest with me. Though yesterday Sir John Haryngton hath begunne a course in the Chaunsery against my mother, but indeed most conserning me, wherby he will gett nothing but lost labor, nor will itt cost me more then som few lawyers' fees, and a little troble, which I am borne to, and therfore imbrace it as part of my portion.[2]

The Countess's extravagances had led to the inevitable result. Nevertheless Donne was bitterly disappointed, and, ignoring the questionable loyalty of his own intentions, attributed her behaviour to the malice of Dr. Burgess. He wrote an angry letter to Goodyer in which his disappointment is only too clear:

[1] The publication of his poems is proposed in the same letter to Goodyer of 20 Dec. (*Letters*, pp. 196–7). For detailed discussion of the manuscripts which reveal the nature of the collection he assembled, see Gardner, *Divine Poems*, pp. lxiii–lxvi. In the letter Donne asks Goodyer to secure for the intended volume a copy of the verse letter that had been sent through him to the Countess of Huntingdon, provided that Goodyer had not appropriated it to his own uses; see above, pp. 167–8.

[2] *The Private Correspondence of Jane, Lady Cornwallis, 1613–44*, 1842, ed. Lord Braybrooke, pp. 28–9. See also P. Thompson, 'John Donne and the Countess of Bedford', *MLR*, xliv (1949), 329–40 at pp. 335–40.

Of my Lady *Bedford*, I must say so much as must importune you to burn the Letter; for I would say nothing of her upon record, that should not testifie my thankfulnesse for all her graces. But upon this motion, which I made to her by letter, and by Sʳ *Tho. Roes* assistance, if any scruple should arise in her, she was somewhat more startling, then I looked for from her: she had more suspicion of my calling, a better memory of my past life, then I had thought her nobility could have admitted: all of which, though I humbly thank God, I can make good use, as one that needs as many remembrances in that kinde, as not only friends but enemies can present, yet I am afraid, they proceed in her rather from some ill impression taken from D. *Burges*, then that they grow in her self. But whosoever be the conduit, the water is the holy Ghosts, and in that acceptation I take it. For her other way of expressing her favour to me, I must say, it is not with that cheerfulnesse, as heretofore she hath delivered her self towards me. I am almost sorry, that an Elegy should have been able to move her to so much compassion heretofore, as to offer to pay my debts; and my greater wants now, and for so good a purpose, as to come disingaged into that profession, being plainly laid open to her, should work no farther but that she sent me 30*l.* which in good faith she excused with that, which is in both parts true, that her present debts were burdensome, and that I could not doubt of her inclination, upon all future emergent occasions, to assist me. I confesse to you, her former fashion towards me, had given a better confidence; and this diminution in her makes me see, that I must use more friends, then I thought I should have needed. I would you could burn this letter, before you read it, at least do when you have read it. For, I am afraid out of a Contemplation of mine own unworthinesse, and fortune, that the example of this Lady, should work upon the Lady where you are [the Countess of Huntingdon]: for though goodnesse be originally in her, and she do good, for the deeds sake, yet, perchance, she may think it a little wisdome, to make such measure of me, as they who know no better, do.[1]

Further comment is needless, except to say that Donne apparently succeeded in making use of 'more friends, then I thought I should have needed', since he seems to have begun his new life free of many of the encumbrances of the old.

Of Donne's inner life during the last eighteen months before he

[1] *Letters*, pp. 218–20.

entered the Church we know almost nothing. The younger John Donne, in printing the *Essayes in Divinity*, was emphatic that they were written while his father was a layman: they were 'writ when the Author was obliged in Civill business, and had no ingagement in that of the Church', and 'they were the voluntary sacrifices of severall hours, when he had many debates betwixt God and himself, whether he were worthy, and competently learned to enter into Holy Orders'.[1] We do not know why John Donne Junior was so positive, but he tells us that the *Essayes* were 'printed from an exact Copy, under the Authors own hand'. It is possible that the manuscript bore a date, or some other clue to the time of composition, but as they stand the *Essayes* can tell us little that is certain about the frame of mind in which Donne prepared for ordination. They are learned, and highly technical, discussions of the opening verses of each of the first two books of the Bible. Donne often referred in his sermons to the topics he treats here, but in the *Essayes* there are few passages as interesting and as beautifully wrought as those that occur frequently in the *Sermons*. Chief among them are the prayers which properly form part of the *Essayes*. Each of the two sections of the book is concluded by a prayer intimately related to the subjects just treated; that at the end of Book I uses imagery of the Creation, and that at the end of Book II uses the imagery of Exodus. Two other passages of meditation and prayer are embedded in the main text, and similarly rise out of the discursive consideration of the words of the Bible.[2] While Donne's studies in 1614 may have led him to complete the *Essayes* as we have them, however, it is likely that at least some portions of the book had been written earlier. Though his treatment of the texts from Genesis and Exodus involves comparisons of the translations of the Bible, Donne nowhere refers to the Authorized Version of 1611, as he would presumably have felt obliged to do if he were actively preparing to enter the Church; and a passage in the prayer at the end of Book II seems rather to refer to the years at Mitcham than to those spent with the Drurys—God, he

[1] Simpson, *Essays*, pp. 3, 4.

[2] Ibid., pp. 36–8, 96–7; 22–3, 75–6. Three further prayers added at the end of the book are not linked to the content of the essays, and seem to be public prayers. Izaak Walton recognized their nature when in his copy of the *Essayes* he noted alongside the first of them '3 prayrs vsed before his Sermons' (see Keynes, p. 98).

says, has removed him from 'frequented and populous, glorious places, to a more solitary and desart retiredness' where he can more safely feed on God in the Communion, and in the contemplation of Him.[1]

There is an undated and fragmentary letter to Goodyer which, though it may not refer to the writing of the *Essayes*, at least seems to indicate the kind of occasion out of which they arose:

I can scarce doe any more this week then send you word why I writ not last. I had then seposed a few daies for my preparation to the Communion of our B. Saviours body; and in that solitarinesse and arraignment of my self, digested some meditations of mine, and apparelled them (as I use) in the form of a Sermon: for since I have not yet utterly delivered my self from this intemperance of scribling (though I thank God my accesses are lesse and lesse vehement) I make account that to spend all my little stock of knowledge upon matter of delight, were the same error, as to spend a fortune upon Masks and Banqueting houses: I chose rather to build in this poor fashion, some Spittles, and Hospitals, where the poor and impotent sinner may finde some relief, or at least understanding of his infirmity. And if they be too weak to serve posterity, yet for the present by contemplation of them, &c.[2]

Certainly Donne speaks of the *Essayes* as 'sermons' ('Upon this confidence, and conscience of purposing good, I proceed in these Sermons . . . Though these lack thus much of Sermons, that they have no Auditory'[3]), and he 'divides' his texts from Genesis and Exodus in the approved manner. Further, it was clearly out of an 'arraignment' of himself that the prayers in the *Essayes* arose:

Thou hast set up many candlesticks, and kindled many lamps in mee; but I have either blown them out, or carried them to guide me in by and forbidden ways. Thou hast given mee a desire of knowledg, and some meanes to it, and some possession of it; and I have arm'd my self with thy weapons against thee. Yet, O God, have mercy upon me, for thine own sake have mercy upon me. Let not sin and me be able to exceed thee, nor to defraud thee, nor to frustrate thy purposes: But let me, in despite of Me, be of so much use to thy glory, that by thy

---

[1] [See the note by Helen Gardner in *John Donne—Selected Prose*, chosen by Evelyn Simpson, and ed. Helen Gardner and T. Healy, Oxford, 1967, p. 69.]

[2] *Letters*, p. 228.

[3] Simpson, *Essays*, p. 41.

mercy to my sin, other sinners may see how much sin thou canst pardon. Thus show mercy to many in one. . . .[1]

The *Essayes*, therefore, seem to be typical of the method, before (probably some years before), as well no doubt as after his ordination, by which Donne was accustomed to prepare himself for worship and communion; the practice of meditation, the interpretation of the scriptures in the traditional four 'senses' (to which he refers in the *Essayes*[2]) and the rhetorical method of the sermon, were means to the disciplining of his spiritual life. It is perhaps not building too much on the evidence of the letter just quoted to suggest that the preparation of his sermons, when ordained, was essentially a continuation of the spiritual exercises in which he had earlier engaged. His sermons, however great the occasion or however much required by clerical routine, were not mere 'preaching engagements' but formed part of a continuing regimen of spiritual endeavour. It is fair also to say that to Donne (at least at times) before his ordination, as Walton is at pains to suggest in his general account of Donne's entry into the Church, the hand of God could be seen working through circumstance and through His representative and instrument the King, and leading him into his proper vocation as a priest of the Church. This is, at any rate, the implication of statements he later made—for example, in the inscription he wrote in the Bible which he presented to the Benchers of Lincoln's Inn and in his own epitaph.

On one subject Donne's letters and other writings are silent: the death of his son Francis, of whom he was particularly fond. The boy was buried in St. Clement Danes, according to the parish register, on 10 November 1614. The Churchwardens' Accounts record the fees for the grave and the knell in the same form as those for Mary Donne only six months earlier. This new bereavement may well have confirmed Donne's resolution to enter the Church and have hastened his preparations for ordination.

Yet, when the best has been said that can be said, it must be confessed that Donne's life during his last eighteen months as a layman does not present a particularly edifying spectacle. It is true that we

---

[1] Simpson, *Essays*, p. 97.   [2] Ibid., p. 40.

cannot expect to document the innermost workings of the human spirit. It may be that the letters from this period that have chanced to survive emphasize unfairly the vein of worldliness in Donne. Yet this is doubtful. Men like Goodyer and Garrard were friends of long standing, and this worldliness is just as apparent in the letters he wrote to them as in those he wrote to Somerset and to Sir Robert Ker. From the time of his first letter to Somerset he had known that he would be forced into the Church unless some secular employment was forthcoming, yet at no period since his marriage do his letters show so little sense of spiritual issues. In spite of his disclaimers, he appears as one who had mastered at last the arts of the courtier, and it is clear, even when he finally turned to the Church, that he did not intend to abandon those arts, but to rise by them. At no period in his life does he appear less unselfish, more self-seeking. The truth seems to be that these qualities in him were not essential and permanent traits of his character; rather, they were symptoms of his despair—not the despair of one who feels that he has been denied salvation, but that of one whom success eludes in spite of all his efforts.

XII

FIRST YEARS IN THE CHURCH

DONNE was ordained on 23 January 1614/15. The ceremony was a special one, and took place in the large chapel in the bishop's palace on the north side of St. Paul's. John King, Bishop of London, officiated, and there were only two ordinands, Donne and a certain William Trussell, gentleman, of Middlesex and New College, Oxford, who, like Donne, was taking orders at a more mature age than the usual candidate for the ministry. Both men were ordained deacons and priests on the same day.[1] And now, exclaims Walton,[2]

the *English Church* had gain'd a second St. *Austine*, for, I think, none was so like him before his Conversion: none so like St. *Ambrose* after it: and if his youth had the infirmities of the one, his age had the excellencies of the other; the learning and holiness of both.

And now all his studies which had been occasionally diffused, were all concentred in Divinity. Now he had a new calling, new thoughts, and a new imployment for his wit and eloquence: Now all his earthly affections were changed into divine love; and all the faculties of his own soul, were ingaged in the Conversion of others: In preaching the glad tidings of Remission to repenting Sinners, and peace to each troubled soul.

But Walton is inclined to exaggerate and to anticipate; for some time yet the taint of worldliness lingers about many of Donne's actions.

In the poem 'To Mr. Tilman after he had taken orders', written several years later, Donne reveals a good deal about his own feelings at this particular time. Edward Tilman was a Fellow of Pembroke College, Cambridge, who took his B.A. and won his fellowship in 1613, before taking his M.A. in 1616; he was ordained deacon in London on 20 December 1618 and priest on 12 March 1619/20. He had written a poem headed, in one manuscript, 'Mr Tilman of

---

[1] 'Liber Ordinationum 1578–1628', Bishop of London's Registry, fo. 196ʳ.
[2] *Lives*, pp. 47–8.

Pembroke Hall in Cambridge his motives not to take orders';
Donne's poem was written after Tilman had reversed his earlier
decision. Whether Donne knew him cannot be proved, but it is
worth mentioning that a Mr. Tilman or Tyllman appears in the
Surveyors' Accounts and Churchwardens' Accounts of the parish of
St. Clement Danes from at least 1610 until 1618. If this man were
a kinsman of Edward Tilman it is easy to see how Donne would not
only have taken an interest in him but also have become acquainted
with his verses. In his poem Tilman refers to his sense of unworthiness, his fear that his mind might change, his reluctance to surrender himself, his sensuality, and his capacity for such emotions as
anger, revenge, envy, and ambition.[1] Donne's reply, though obviously written with Tilman's poem in mind, nevertheless speaks
of him as overcoming certain obstacles which Tilman himself had
not mentioned. Tilman, Donne avers, has braved 'Lay-scornings of
the Ministry', and he goes on to ask

> if thy gayning doe surmount expression,
> Why doth the foolish world scorne that profession,
> Whose joyes passe speech? Why do they think unfit
> That Gentry should joyne familes with it?
> Would they thinke it well if the day were spent
> In dressing, Mistressing and complement? . . .
> Let then the world thy calling disrespect,
> But goe thou on, and pitty their neglect.

Does Tilman also feel, Donne asks further, that ordination has made
a new creature of him:

> Dost thou finde
> New thoughts and stirrings in thee? and as Steele
> Toucht with a Loadstone, dost new motions feele?

But for these questions he suggests an answer:

> Art thou the same materials, as before,
> Onely the stampe is changed; but no more?
> And as new crowned Kings alter the face,

---

[1] The poem was first printed from the manuscript referred to (Welbeck MS.) by
H. Harvey Wood, 'A Seventeenth-Century Manuscript of Poems by Donne and
Others', *Essays and Studies by Members of the English Association*, xvi (1930), 179–90 at
pp. 184–6.

But not the monies substance; so hath grace
Chang'd onely Gods old Image by Creation,
To Christs new stampe, at this thy Coronation?

In these passages Donne seems to be reflecting his own feelings rather than those of Tilman; he himself was only too conscious of the meagre social prestige which attached to his new profession, and it was he who had been disappointed to find that, in spite of his new calling, he was still the same sinner he had always been. Nevertheless, Donne 'is to be honoured because, having received his vocation thus indirectly, he tried to fulfil it worthily and set himself an exacting standard of duty'.[1]

Immediately after his ordination, Donne received a congratulatory letter and gift from Lord Hay, who, it is interesting to note, claimed some of the credit for persuading him to enter the Church. Whether Hay felt that Donne had a real talent for his new vocation, or was merely seconding the King's persuasions, cannot now be known.

SIR,

I think my perswasion first begat in you the purpose to employ your extraordinarie excellent parts in the affairs of another world, since this hath thought it self unworthie of your service. At least, I was helping, amongst others, to bring you well abed of that resolution, whereof I hope you shall never have cause to repent you. If on this day I present you with a vesture of that profession, and a token from my office, Take it as an argument of my faithfull well-wishing all the year long, of your more substantiall good fortune, To the which I shall ever contribute my best service as

Your faithfull friend,
and servant,
James Hay.[2]

Hay was Master of the Great Wardrobe, so that a gift of ecclesiastical vestments came particularly aptly from him.

After the ordination service and his return home, Donne sat down to communicate the news to various friends. A letter to Sir Edward Herbert, written 'the very day wherein I took orders', has survived,[3]

---

[1] See Helen Gardner's discussion of the two poems in Appendix D, 'Donne and Tilman: their Reluctance to take Holy Orders', *Divine Poems*, pp. 127-32.
[2] *Tobie Mathew Collection*, p. 334.   [3] First printed in Hayward, pp. 465-6.

which Herbert, then travelling in Italy, received in Venice. Donne also wrote to Sir Henry Wotton, now temporarily at The Hague. Sir Thomas Roe, who had just set out on his embassy to the Great Mogul, had already heard of Donne's intentions from his own lips, and received news of their fulfilment in a letter that reached him a year later from George Lord Carew.[1] Wotton wrote understandingly to Donne, who replied gratefully:

I haue the honor of a letter from y^r Lp: and a testimony that though better then any other you know my infirmity yet you are not scandalized with my chang of habitt. I haue S^r. besides many other internal advantages this also by itt, that besides the obligations of friendship and services towards you wch binde mee alwayes to commend y^r fortunes to God in my prayers (having never had any other way of expressing myself) I am come now to doe itt by my office.[2]

In both this letter and in the one to Sir Edward Herbert, beneath the customary graces of 'complement', there is a genuine humility of tone which contrasts quite sharply with the worldliness of some of the letters he had written a short time previously. Though he may not have felt any supernatural change in himself, ordination did at least bring to Donne a sense of his unworthiness for his new calling, and it is interesting to see that he was well aware that his taking orders might seem rather shocking to some of those who had known him formerly.

To symbolize his new life, Donne had a new seal made. This was his famous device of Christ crucified to an anchor, and the earliest known example of its use is on the letter written on the day of his ordination to Sir Edward Herbert. About the same time he sent some verses to George Herbert upon his new seal, which have survived in both Latin and English:

A sheafe of Snakes used heretofore to be
My Seal, The Crest of our poore Family.

[1] *Letters from George Lord Carew to Sir Thomas Roe*, Camden Society, 1860, p. 2. Roe left London before 20 Jan., but did not lose sight of the Lizard until 19 Mar., and hence he probably knew that Donne was in orders before he set sail. Carew's first news-letter is dated 18 Apr. 1615, but under the month of February he writes 'Mr. John Dvn is a Minister, the King's Chaplaine, and a Doctor of Divinitie'. Actually Donne became a minister in January and a D.D. in March, so that Carew was clearly writing up his letter from notes made earlier.

[2] Simpson, *Prose Works*, pp. 333–4.

Adopted in Gods Family, and so
Our old Coat lost, unto new armes I go.

Donne seems to have used this seal (though not consistently[1]) for the rest of his life, and in due course he gave copies of it to a number of friends. Walton says[2] that it was not long before his death that he had the emblem drawn and then engraved in miniature 'in *Helitropian* Stones', but this is belied by the impression on the letter to Sir Edward Herbert as well as by the lines to George Herbert, which show that Donne began using the new seal immediately after his ordination.[3]

A few days later he set out again for Newmarket to present himself to the King as a priest in the Church of which James was the temporal head. In the earlier interview in which Donne had announced his intentions, the King had evidently told him a little of what he proposed to do for him, since in a letter of 27 January to Sir Robert Ker, in which he speaks of his 'meaning to come to *Newmarket* in this weather', he also refers to his hope of procuring 'the Kings Letters to *Cambridge*'.[4] Early in March James was to pay an official visit, promised some months previously, to the University, and he had evidently told Donne that he would be made a Doctor of

---

[1] He used two other seals, one of the crest of snakes to which he refers in the poem, and the other of his coat of arms (of a wolf salient) surmounted by the crest (see above, p. 20).

[2] *Lives*, p. 63.

[3] Whether the gifts to his friends were made with his approaching death in mind is uncertain. Donne's will leaves £5 each to Robert Christmas and Thomas Roper 'to make them Seale ringes engrav'd with that Figure which I vsuallye sealle withall Of which sorte they knowe I haue given many to my particuler Frendes'. The gifts had therefore been made before the day on which Donne made his will (13 Dec. 1630) and presumably before he went to stay with his daughter at Aldborough Hatch. On the other hand, since Christmas and Roper knew of the gifts, it sounds as if they must have been made after Donne became Dean, since it is unlikely that he knew Christmas and Roper before then.

Several of these presentation seals were reported as still being in existence in the last century by correspondents to *The Gentleman's Magazine* and *Notes and Queries* (cf. Grierson, ii. 261, and also *NQ*, 6th Series, x (1884), 526; 8th Series, ix (1896), 41–3). One of these, which descended from Bishop Ken (whose half-sister was Walton's second wife) to the Merewether family is now in the Library of Salisbury Cathedral (see Gardner, *Divine Poems*, pp. 138–47, especially p. 139, n. 3). Another seal, still in existence, was bequeathed in perpetuity to the vicars of Warminster. Copies of Walton's *Life* of Donne bearing impressions of the seal have also been reported. The motto on the seal was 'Sit fides sic fixa Deo'.

[4] *Letters*, pp. 288–9.

Divinity as soon as he was in orders. Nevertheless, Donne wrote to Wotton shortly afterwards in a more detached strain than to Ker, mentioning that he had as yet no benefice, and continuing: 'I do not so much as enquire of myne owne hopes what the K. will do with me: Hee forbad me at first and I obey him still, and forbeare so much as to remember him that hee forbadd mee.'[1] In spite of this reticence Donne was almost at once appointed Chaplain-in-Ordinary to the King.[2] It is possible that he went to Cambridge in this capacity.

The royal Chaplaincy had two important consequences for Donne's career in the Church. In the first place, since it required regular periods of attendance on the King, it kept him in touch with the Court, so that there was no danger of his dropping completely out of sight and being forgotten. Secondly, Chaplains to the King were permitted to hold, in addition to their regular cures, two parsonages or benefices with cure of souls, and to purchase licence or dispensation to do so.[3] Thus they were enabled to enjoy some of the advantages of pluralism, and were assured an income on a scale higher than that of many of their less fortunate brethren.

Donne also received orders to attend the King on his visit to Cambridge. On 7 March, over foul roads and on a blustery day, the royal party, headed by the King and the Prince, entered the town. Among those who accompanied it were nobles like Lord Hay and ecclesiastics like Bishop Andrewes; at a somewhat humbler level, nearer to that of Donne, was John Chamberlain, who sent his friend Sir Dudley Carleton a full account of all that happened. There were

---

[1] Simpson, *Prose Works*, p. 334.

[2] There seems to be no record of Donne's appointment as royal Chaplain. The Dean and the Sub-dean of the Chapel Royal know of no records from Donne's period. Nor has anyone been able to describe to me the formal processes by which royal Chaplains were appointed. The only evidence on the subject is the letter of George Lord Carew to Sir Thomas Roe (see p. 305, n. 1 above), which shows that Donne was certainly a royal Chaplain by at least 18 Apr. and, if the order of events is correctly reported, before the King's visit to Cambridge. Tentatively, the evidence may be said to point to February as the time of his appointment. Jessopp (p. 91) says: 'In February it was rumoured that he had been appointed chaplain to the King. In point of fact, he did not actually receive this appointment till nearly a year later.' The source of either rumour or 'fact' is unknown to me.

[3] Stat. 21 Hen. VIII, c. 13, provided that Chaplains to the King should have 'letters under the sign and seal of the King' testifying that they *were* his Chaplains; otherwise they could not enjoy plurality of benefices. See R. Phillimore, *The Ecclesiastical Law of the Church of England*, 2nd ed. (1895), i. 452–7; cf. J. Ecton, *Thesaurus Rerum Ecclesiasticarum*, 2nd ed., 1754, p. 611.

disputations by day and plays by night, with feasting in the college halls in between. The play on the second night was the famous *Ignoramus*, by George Ruggle; that on the third night *Albumazar*, by Tomkis; and that on the last night a Latin pastoral, *Melanthe*, by Donne's old friend Samuel Brooke (himself a royal Chaplain, and also chaplain of Trinity College; he became a Doctor of Divinity in the following July). The most successful of the disputations was the Philosophy Act where, when the question was put whether dogs could make syllogisms, the King interrupted in order to relate an anecdote about one of his hounds. The proceedings ended with the conferring of honorary degrees. For what happened then Chamberlain is the chief authority:

I had almost forgotten that almost all the courtiers went foorth masters of art at the Kings beeing there, but few or no Doctors. . . . The vice chauncellor and universitie were exceding strict in that point, and refused many importunities of great men, . . . neither the Kings intreatie for John Dun wold prevayle, yet they are threatned with a mandat which yf yt come yt is like they will obey but they are resolved to geve him such a blow withall that he were better be without yt.[1]

When the royal party left, Donne was still without his degree; but, as his letter to Ker shows, he was not unprepared for such a contingency. He remained behind at Cambridge and a few days later, thanks to the efforts of his friends in high places, the University received the royal mandate commanding them to confer a doctor's degree upon him. On 26 March Chamberlain wrote again: 'John Dun and one Cheeke went out doctors at Cambridge with much ado after our comming away, by the Kinges expresse mandat, though the vice chauncellor and some other of the heades called them openly *filios noctis et tenebriones* that sought thus to come in at the windowe, when there was a fayre gate open.'[2] Chamberlain then goes on to

---

[1] Chamberlain, *Letters*, i. 588–9.

[2] Ibid., p. 591. Neither the 'Kings Letters' nor any records of the conferring of the degree have survived. It was said that the University later degraded some of those who had received honorary masters' degrees. S. G. Bolton suggested that Donne's doctorate might similarly have been removed from the registers; see his edition of Samuel Brooke's *Melanthe*, Yale Studies in English, lxxix (1928), pp. 13–14, and the references there given. Jessopp (p. 91) says that Donne's degree was conferred on 14 Mar., and adds: 'It was on this occasion that his friend Lord Hay presented him

report as fact what can only have been a piece of very unreliable gossip: 'the worst is that Dun had gotten a reversion of the Deanrie of Caunterburie, yf such graunts could be lawful, wherby he hath purchased himself a great deale of envie, that a man of his sort shold seeke *per saltem* to intercept such a place from so many more worthie and auncient divines.' No such grant was, or could ever have been, made, but Chamberlain's credulity reflects the suspicion with which Donne was regarded when he first took orders, and the feeling of some of his contemporaries that he was attempting by every device of the courtier to 'Creep, and intrude, and climb into the fold'.

Shortly after Donne's return from Cambridge Sir Robert Drury died at Hawstead—according to his epitaph, of a fever. He was but forty years old, and his death must have been sudden. Donne had abandoned the hopes which he and his patron had formerly shared, and Sir Robert's death probably made little difference to him in the worldly sense. To what extent the two men were bound together by other ties, such as those of friendship and congeniality, curiously little is known, for even when they were travelling together each seems to have pursued his own interests, and after their return to England, in spite of the proximity of their London dwellings, their ways seem to have diverged still further. In his surviving letters Donne mentions Sir Robert by name only twice, and then merely to name his house in Amiens as an address to which letters might be sent and to deny a report that Drury had been attending mass in Paris.[1] Yet he seems to have kept in close touch with the Drurys when they were out of London and he was still in town, for a Redgrave inventory of Drury papers made in 1658 recorded '25 old Letters sowed together of Mr. Jo. Donne' (now lost) which Lady Drury had evidently preserved with some care. Donne had also agreed to act as a trustee under a settlement of Sir Robert's estates made on 19 May 1613; although the duties under the settlement

---

with his doctor's robes'—but Hay's letter quoted above (p. 304) seems rather to refer to ecclesiastical vestments. Fuller, in his *Church History of Britain* (1655), x. viii. 16, says that Donne was 'made Doctor of Divinity (of *Trinity* Colledge in Cambridge)'. Fuller's whole university career (entered at Queens', 1621—M.A., 1628) occurred during Donne's lifetime, and in 1630 he became curate of St. Benet's in Cambridge, so that he had every opportunity of ascertaining the facts. There is, however, no record of Donne at Trinity.

[1] *Letters*, pp. 265, 256.

were purely nominal, Drury's choice of Donne nevertheless bespoke his confidence in him.[1] Again, Donne had composed a Latin epitaph for Elizabeth Drury's monument in Hawstead Church, and now (assuredly at Lady Drury's request) he composed another for the more elegant monument by Nicholas Stone which was erected to commemorate Sir Robert's father, Sir William Drury, and Sir Robert himself, and which was destined to cover the remains of Lady Drury as well, although the inscription was never completed to record the date of her death.[2]

Sir Robert Drury bequeathed his London properties to his cousin, Sir Henry Drury, but expressly provided that his wife 'in the partage of her thirde in drury lane . . . should haue the house I nowe dwell in allotted vnto her'. Thus, though Sir Henry Drury became Donne's landlord, Drury House remained in the possession of Lady Drury. As the years went by she seems to have come less and less often to London, so that Drury House was usually occupied by tenants. But she was in London during part of the summer and again in the autumn of 1615 on business connected with the winding up of her husband's affairs. That Donne had put his services at her disposal at this time is clear from a letter to her from the Revd. Richard Brabon of Whipstead, who had been Sir Robert's tutor and had been in London helping her, but had returned to the country ahead of her. 'Good madam', he concludes, 'remember my servic to that good Lady Gaudy and my loue to Mr. Coldby [Lady Drury's sister and brother-in-law], I pray doe not forgett me to doctor Dune and my most necessary thankes for ther kindnes.'[3] Lady Drury was again in London in the spring of 1617, when she signed some documents which marked the final settlement of her husband's estates. A few weeks earlier she also sold to Christopher Brooke two leases, one of the house on the other side of Drury Lane which he was to occupy for some years, the other of the stables in Drury Yard for his coach and horses. Donne was involved in this transaction, for he witnessed the two indentures by which the agreements were made, and it looks very much as if he had acted as intermediary between

---

[1] See *Donne and the Drurys*, pp. 3, 142–4.
[2] J. Sparrow, 'Two Epitaphs by John Donne', *TLS*, 26 Mar. 1949, p. 208.
[3] *Donne and the Drurys*, p. 150.

the two parties. Lady Drury is known to have been in town again in the spring of 1621 or 1622, by which time Donne was, or was soon to be, Dean of St. Paul's. She died in 1624, and so Donne's connection with these patrons came to an end.[1]

In speaking of the early stages of Donne's ministry, Walton remarks that his familiarity with scholars and with those in high places was 'such as might have given some men boldness enough to have preached to any eminent Auditory; yet', he continues,

his modesty in this imployment was such, that he could not be perswaded to it, but went usually accompanied with some one friend, to preach privately in some village, not far from *London*: his first Sermon being preached at *Paddington*. This he did, till His Majesty sent and appointed him a day to preach to him at *White-hall*, and, though much were expected from him, both by His Majesty and others, yet he was so happy (which few are) as to satisfie and exceed their expectations.[2]

The parish church of St. Catherine at Paddington was a donative or curacy in the gift of the Bishops of London, with a stipend of £28 a year. The last pre-Restoration curate of whom any record survives was Griffin Edwards, A.B., appointed in 1598. 'The Church was but small, and being very old and ruinous, was about the Year 1678. pull'd down and new-built.'[3] The earliest reference in Donne's correspondence to his preaching occurs in a letter to Sir Robert Ker of about June 1615, in which he refuses an invitation to hear Pierre du Moulin preach at Court because of a prior engagement:

I have always your leave to use my liberty, but now I must use my bondage. Which is my necessity of obeying a pre-contract laid upon me. I go to morrow to *Camberwell* a mile beyond *Southwark*. But from this town goes with me my brother Sir *Tho. Grimes* and his Lady, and I with them. There we dine well enough I warrant you, with his father-in-law [step-father], Sir *Tho. Hunt*. If I keep my whole promise, I shall Preach both forenoon and afternoon.[4]

Donne's relations with the Grymes family were closer than with any other kin of his wife, and he often preached at Camberwell in subsequent years; it is pleasant to know that they also encouraged

---

[1] Ibid., pp. 152–6. [2] *Lives*, pp. 48–9.
[3] R. Newcourt, *Repertorium Ecclesiasticum Parochiale Londinense*, i (1708), 703–4.
[4] *Letters*, pp. 295–6.

his early efforts. A week or two later he seems to have had his first experience of preaching before a congregation at the Inns of Court, for in a letter dated Midsummer Day 1615 Richard Prythergh of the Inner Temple wrote to Sir Edward Herbert in Paris: 'this day M^r donn preached att our temple; he had to much learninge in his sermon for ignoramus.'[1] Donne, it is clear, did not find it easy to pitch his sermon at the right level for such a congregation, though he was soon to learn how to appeal successfully to the members of Lincoln's Inn.

His first surviving sermon is, however, of earlier date than the visit to Camberwell just mentioned; it was preached, according to the heading, 'at Greenwich, Aprill 30. 1615'. Jessopp assumed that it was preached at Greenwich Palace before Queen Anne, but more probably it was preached in the parish church while Donne was still striving to accustom himself to his new tasks.[2] The style of the sermon is uneven; parts of it approach the bareness of Andrewes, though in other parts a tendency to more elaborate rhetoric begins to manifest itself. In one place Donne repeats some of the material of *Essayes in Divinity* (as he does, indeed, throughout his career as a preacher[3]), and in this way as in others there was maintained a continuity between the meditations and actions of Donne the divine and those of Donne the courtier and parliamentarian. In this sermon he keeps strictly to his primary concern, that of interpreting Scripture, and offers little in the way of advice or exhortation to his congregation. He was evidently too unsure of himself as yet to attempt much in this line.

The next surviving sermon is just a year later, and was preached at Whitehall on 21 April 1616. Whether it was Donne's first sermon at Court we do not know, but it may well have been. Of the forty-eight royal Chaplains-in-Ordinary four attended at Court each month, and April seems from the first to have been Donne's month of attendance; of the thirty-one dated sermons which he preached

---

[1] Powis MSS., P.R.O., 30/53/7/11; cf. *Sermons*, v. 15. Richard Prythergh, or Prytherych, was of Mobigian, Anglesey. He was entered in the Inner Temple in November 1596, was admitted to the Bar in 1604, became a Bencher in 1622, and a second judge of Chester in 1627 (*Students Admitted to the Inner Temple, 1547–1660*, 1877, p. 145).

[2] *Sermons*, i. 115–17.   [3] See ibid., v. 26–30.

at Court, sixteen belong to Sundays in April. He seems quite early to have gained James's favour as a preacher, and in many years he preached two sermons at Court during his month (1618, 1620, 1621, 1625, 1626). In addition he became a regular preacher at Court during Lent. Edward Chamberlayne, writing in the reign of Charles II, stated that during Lent the preacher in the Chapel Royal was 'every Friday the Dean of some Cathedral or Collegiate-Church';[1] but Donne was preaching there on the first Friday in Lent four years before he became Dean and continued to preach then until the occasion of his last, and most famous, sermon. Twelve of his Lenten sermons have survived. Thus twenty-eight out of the thirty-one datable sermons at Court can be definitely associated with his regular appearances there at the beginning of Lent and in the month of April.

In describing Donne's life from surviving sources during 1615 and 1616, one has little consciousness of what was going on in the great world; yet Donne must have followed the course of events with a kind of stunned incredulity and even, perhaps, with feelings of relief that he had detached himself from them. Sir Thomas Overbury had died in the Tower on 14 September 1613, before Lady Essex secured her divorce, and more than three months before she married Somerset. Two years elapsed before there was any inquiry into the circumstances of Overbury's death, but early in September 1615 Sir Ralph Winwood, one of the Secretaries of State, brought the King a statement he had obtained from Sir Gervase Elwes, Lieutenant of the Tower, in which he clearly stated his belief that Overbury had been poisoned. Richard Weston and Mrs. Turner as the agents, and Elwes himself as accessory, were arrested, tried, and executed. Even before their trials the Earl and Countess of Somerset were under house arrest, as principals, though it was some time before they were removed to the Tower. The new Lieutenant of the Tower was Donne's father-in-law, Sir George More, whose unswerving loyalty the King knew he could trust. His prisoners were difficult ones to handle, but before long the Countess broke down and confessed her guilt. Her husband, however, refused to make any admission, and placed his faith in his ability to secure the King's pardon. But James

---

[1] *Angliae Notitia*, 6th ed. (1672), p. 162.

insisted on a trial, and Somerset angrily threatened all kinds of dis-
closures if he were brought to the bar. Sir George More became
thoroughly alarmed, and secret emissaries came from the King to
persuade Somerset to behave rationally and with dignity. The
emissaries were Donne's friends, Lord Hay and Sir Robert Ker. The
Somersets were tried on 24 and 25 May 1616; the Countess pleaded
guilty and was sentenced, her husband was tried and found guilty
on the following day. Though the King spared their lives, they
remained in the Tower until 1621, and even after they were released
they were confined to a country estate. From the moment of his
arrest Somerset's fall was complete, and many of the courtiers hastened to attach themselves to the rising fortunes of Sir George
Villiers.

Donne must have followed these events with horror and with
shocked disbelief. He was in a position to get access, not immediately perhaps, to much confidential information. He had himself been
a dependant of Somerset at the time of the murder of Overbury; his
father-in-law had had surveillance of the prisoners; and two of his
closest friends at Court had carried messages back and forth between the King and Somerset. He must have been morally as well
as prudentially relieved that he had not unwittingly become involved in the criminal activities of his former patron and the ruth-
less Countess. As for the new favourite, letters written only a month
or so before Donne took orders show that he was watching closely
the rise of Villiers,[1] but when he first began to pay court to him is
not known.

That Donne maintained an interest in, and had a connection with,
foreign affairs also, is proved from an unexpected quarter. His name
occurs in an official cipher of the period. He seems to have been one
of eleven men to whom the cipher was entrusted; among the others
were the Archbishop of Canterbury, Secretary Winwood, and Sir
Isaac Wake.[2] The cipher can be closely dated, since one of the names

---

[1] *Letters*, pp. 149, 191, 198.

[2] P.R.O., S.P. 106/4/75, brought to my notice by Professor J. P. Feil; it is printed
in Appendix D. The other seven names besides Donne's own, are those of 'William
Parckhurst', 'William Wise', 'M*r*. Hackwell', 'Nicholas Paye', 'S*r*. Biondi', 'Fitzwilliams', 'M*r*. Trumbal', and (added) 'Isaake Wake'. On Parkhurst and Biondi see
the brief biographies appended to L. Pearsall Smith's *Life and Letters of Sir Henry
Wotton*, ii. 463-4, 467-8, and for Pey see Smith's index; on Biondi, Wake, and

represented by a number is 'Sr George Villiers', who was knighted
on 24 April 1615 and raised to the peerage on 27 August 1616. There
are also combinations for the Earl and Countess of Somerset, so that
the cipher clearly belongs to the period of their trials. Ten names,
including the three last mentioned and Donne's own, are marked
as 'Added to the Zypher of Will. Wise and Doc^r Donne'. The cipher
seems to have been in use for some years, since Sir Isaac Wake's
name has been added in two places, and a number has been added
representing the King of Bohemia, which points to a date of 1617 or
later. What Donne's connection with such secret correspondence
may have been can only be conjectural, but it looks as if he was
employed to correspond with agents abroad on affairs affecting the
welfare of the Church. It looks, too, as if he worked more closely
with Archbishop Abbot than has usually been assumed. These
activities of Donne must have continued for a good many years,
since in January 1623 Wotton sent from Venice to Sir Albertus
Morton in London 'a larger cipher, whereof I must entreat you to
consign a fair copy to the Dean of Paules'.[1]

One gets the impression both from Walton's anecdote about
Donne's first ventures in the pulpit and from his own letter to Ker
about his engagement at Camberwell that from the first he took his
preaching very seriously, and worked hard to acquire fluency of
delivery and ease of manner. His later reputation as one of the great
preachers of his age was not won effortlessly, or by his learning and
literary ability alone. Though he had twice been in Parliament, he
does not seem to have addressed the House, and it is quite possible
that when he was ordained he had had very little practice in
speaking in public. Hence the need to overcome his nervousness
and acquire first the ease and then the fervour of the accomplished
orator.

Surprisingly few of Donne's letters have survived from the early
years of his ministry, and of these some are mere notes, while others
are formal letters of compliment. A letter of 17 April 1615 to Sir

Trumbull see *DNB*. It is uncertain whether the reference is to George Hakewill or
to Donne's friend William Hakewill. It seems impossible to identify William Wise;
there is a letter from a man of this name to Carleton (*C.S.P. Dom.*, *James I, 1619–23*,
p. 10), so that it is possible that he was for a time a member of Carleton's staff.

[1] Pearsall Smith, *Life and Letters of Sir Henry Wotton*, ii. 265.

Robert Ker, however, informs him of the birth of a daughter to Donne, and asks him to stand godfather at the baptism on the following Thursday afternoon.[1] This daughter, who was christened Margaret at St. Clement Danes on 20 April, afterwards married Sir William Bowles of Chislehurst. It was probably about this time, too, that Donne wrote what is by far the most moving of all his letters—that which he addressed to his mother on learning of his sister's death.[2] The date of the letter is uncertain, but it was written while his wife was still alive, and seems from its tone to belong to the period after he had taken holy orders. Of Anne Lyly's fate from 1603 until the time of her death nothing whatever is known; in the course of the letter, however, Donne mentions that his 'father Rainsford' had been to see him, and 'as I perceive in him a loving and industrious care to give you contentment; so, I see in his businesse, a happie and considerable forwardnesse'. Richard Rainsford, apparently, was free again and was trying to build something out of the wreck of his former prosperity. Donne reviews the whole course of his mother's life as he himself had been able to observe it; it had been 'a Sea, under a continuall Tempest, where one wave hath ever overtaken another'. All the prosperity which Donne's father had achieved, and all the children of her first happy marriage, except Donne himself, had now gone.

For my part, which am onely left now, to do the office of a child; though the poornesse of my fortune, and the greatnesse of my charge, hath not suffered me to expresse my duty towards you, as became me; yet, I protest to you before Almighty God, and his Angells and Saints in Heaven, that I do, and ever shall, esteem my self, to be as stronglie bound to look to you, and provide for your relief, as for my own poor wife and children.

'And', he concludes, 'for God's sake, pardon those negligences, which I have heretofore used towards you.' Donne was not forgetful of these pledges; in later years he fulfilled them in all sincerity. Though his mother persisted in her recusancy, there is no trace of reproach or embarrassment on either side despite the fact that Donne was often moved to criticize the beliefs of her Church.

---

[1] *Letters*, pp. 271–2.
[2] *Tobie Mathew Collection*, pp. 323–7.

Walton narrates that 'within the first year of his entring into sacred Orders' Donne 'had fourteen Advowsons of several Benefices presented to him: But they were in the Countrey, and he could not leave his beloved *London*, to which place he had a natural inclination.'[1] Certainly Donne was not beneficed until he had been in orders for a full year. Though he did eventually accept two country rectories, it was evidently on the understanding that residence would not be insisted upon; he was to be free to remain in London and arrange for the parish to be served by a curate, whom he paid out of the revenue he received. His first benefice, the rectory of Keyston in Huntingdon, was bestowed on him by the King, and the patent for the grant is dated 16 January 1615/16.[2] Donne's second benefice was conferred upon him a few months later, and was the gift of his old master, Lord Ellesmere. Benefices in the King's gift valued in the King's Book at less than £20 a year were actually bestowed not by the King but by the Lord Chancellor.[3] Owing to the promotion of Richard Milborne to the bishopric of St. David's, the rectory of Sevenoaks in Kent had come into the King's gift,[4] but, being valued at only £13. 13s. 4d., was therefore at the disposal of the Lord Chancellor. The entry of the presentation of Sevenoaks to Donne on 7 July 1616 in the Chancellor's Presentation Book[5] bears the unusual notation 'This was graunted by my Lord without anie petition in Writing.' The warm kindliness of the old man, for which

[1] *Lives*, p. 50.

[2] P.R.O., Patent Roll, 13 James I, pt. 29, no. 3 (C66/2084). The presentation is listed in Signet Office Dockets (Index 6805) as 'Procured by Mr Secretary *Winwood*'. Donne appears in Foster's 'List of Incumbents since the Reformation', s.v. 'Keystone', MS. Add. 6728, Cambridge University Library. It is somewhat disconcerting to find that there is also a sign manual for the presentation of Keyston to John Scott, dated 8 Mar. 1615/16 (see *C.S.P. Dom.*, *1611–18*, p. 353), but, as we shall see, the grant went no further. Scott did eventually become rector of Keyston after Donne had resigned the living.

[3] R. Phillimore, *The Ecclesiastical Law of the Church of England*, 2nd ed. (1895), i. 296–7.

[4] J. Godolphin, *Repertorium Canonicum*, 1678, p. 263.

[5] MS. Tanner 179 in the Bodleian Library. The volume is entitled 'Beneficia sive Ecclesiae promotiones concessae per Thomam Egerton . . . a Sexto die Maij . . . 1596'; there is no pagination, but the entries are in chronological order. Donne's patent is enrolled in P.R.O., C66/2125, no. 47, and bears the annotation 'per Dominum Cancellarium Angliae'; his institution by the Archbishop of Canterbury, dated 12 July, is recorded in the archiepiscopal register at Lambeth Palace, Reg. Abbot, i. 419r. (His successor at Sevenoaks, Nicholas Gibbon, M.A., was appointed in similar terms on 1 Apr. 1631; Reg. Abbot, iii. 194.)

Donne had felt a glow of gratitude two years previously, had not changed, and he was happy to make this unsolicited contribution to Donne's prosperity in his new calling. The rectory of Sevenoaks was a sinecure; before the Reformation it had been in the gift of the Archbishops of Canterbury and had been so habitually held by a non-resident that an endowed vicarage had also been established.[1] The vicar was responsible for the care of the parishioners, and the rector had no obligations at all. A more suitable benefice for a non-resident clergyman it would not have been easy to find, though Sevenoaks was close to Knole, the seat of the Earl of Dorset, and Donne had consequently some excuse for visiting the parish of which he was rector.

The Composition Books and the Receiver's Accounts of the Office of First Fruits and Tenths show that Donne paid the taxes on his two benefices in the normal way.[2] What is of most interest in these records is the fact that the two sureties who signed bonds to guarantee the payment of the required amounts were Christopher Brooke and Walter Bailey, tailor. Bailey is not otherwise heard of in connection with Donne, but he was a neighbour and evidently a friend. He is described as of the parish of St. Dunstan's-in-the-West in the entry for Keyston and of St. Clement Danes in the one for Sevenoaks.[3]

In the autumn of 1616 Donne received another preferment, and one which justified his determination to stay in London. The minutes of the Masters of the Bench of Lincoln's Inn for 24 October declare that

Mr. Docto^r Dune is at this Councell chosen to be the diuinitye Reader of this house, and is to haue the like entertaynem*ent* that Mr Docto^r Holloway had, whoe is to preach everye sabboth daye in the tearme both fore noone and after noone, and once the sabboth dayes

---

[1] See J. Rooker, *Notes on the Parish Church of St. Nicholas, Sevenoaks*, 1910, pp. 3–4, 96–8; cf. also E. Hasted, *History of Kent*, ed. 1778, i. 357. William Turner was appointed to the vicarage of Sevenoaks on 28 Apr. 1614 (Lambeth Palace, Reg. Abbot, i. 405ᵛ), and remained vicar till 1644.

[2] P.R.O., E334/15 and E341/12. Professor Leslie Hotson drew my attention to these records.

[3] In his will (P.C.C. 25 Goare) he is 'of the parish of St. Dunstan in the West'. The will was proved on 3 Feb. 1636/7, so he survived Donne and was presumably one of his parishioners from 1625 to 1631. It is tempting to imagine that he might have been a friend also of Walton, and perhaps a source of information for the *Life* of Donne.

next before and after everie tearme and on the grand dayes everie fornoone and in the Readinge tymes Whoe is to take place next the double Readers that nowe haue Read or hereafter shall Read or hereafter shall fyne for their double Readinges.[1]

The salary was £60 per annum, besides 'diet for himself at the Bench table, and for one servant with the Benchers' clarkes, and such chamber in the House as the Masters of the Benche shall hereafter bee pleased to assigne unto him'.[2] The office had recently fallen vacant owing to the resignation of the previous occupant.[3] Donne must have been known personally to all the Benchers of the Inn, who were probably only too glad to appoint a member of their own Society. Nevertheless, the office was an important one, and Donne must have given convincing evidence of more than average competence as a preacher before the appointment was made. Though, as Jessopp pointed out,[4] the office involved the preaching of about fifty sermons a year, it allowed a certain degree of freedom and leisure. The pastoral duties were slight, and the Reader (or Preacher, as he is often called) had the assistance of a chaplain, who read the services and acted as vacation preacher. At the time of Donne's appointment the chaplain was Edward May, who had held office for little more than six months. He had been appointed on 3 February 1615/16 at a salary of £30 and a chamber, but on the day on which Donne was appointed the Benchers voted to increase his stipend by

---

[1] Black Book VI, fo. 630ᵛ; cf. *The Black Books of Lincoln's Inn*, ii. 187.

[2] *The Black Books*, ii. 235.

[3] This was Thomas Holloway, D.D., vicar of St. Lawrence Jewry, and not Thomas Gataker, as Walton states (*Lives*, p. 52). Gataker had held the office before Holloway, from 1602 to 1613. It is worth noting that on Gataker's resignation overtures were made by the Inn to William Bedell, then recently returned from his period of service in Venice as Sir Henry Wotton's chaplain, but such a post did not appeal to him. 'There is a motion made to me by Mr. Nath. Rich about Lincolnes Inne, but the stipend is little better then this here, and the place being in London I haue no great inclination to it. Yet I pray signifie to me what you thinck of it.' (*Two Biographies of William Bedell*, ed. E. S. Shuckburgh (1902), p. 258. The letter from which this is taken is dated merely 17 Feb., and the editor assigns it to 1618/19. But Bedell suggests that his correspondent should try to get a book 'by Casaubons meanes out of France', and Isaac Casaubon died on 1 July 1614; Dr. Holloway was appointed Reader at Lincoln's Inn in February 1612/13, so that the letter clearly belongs to this year. On Nathaniel Rich see *DNB*; Donne knew him and refers to him in a letter from the Continent, *Letters*, p. 74.) Bedell's attitude towards the post at Lincoln's Inn is in striking contrast to that of the town-bred Donne four years later.

[4] p. 113.

£10 a year on account of 'the good opinyon [that] is generallye con-
ceved of his good carrage and paynes in his place'.[1]

Donne must have welcomed the opportunity to renew associations with many old friends, though with some, such as Christopher
Brooke, the continuity of his friendship had suffered no break.[2]
Drury Lane is within easy walking distance of Lincoln's Inn, and
Donne, no doubt, dined regularly with the Benchers in the hall. He
had his chambers too; 'The love of that noble society', as Walton
observes,[3] 'was expressed to him many ways: . . . fair lodgings
. . . were set apart and newly furnished for him, with all necessaries.'
For the first six months Donne apparently had to be satisfied with
what chambers happened to be vacant, but on 29 May 1617 the
Benchers ordered that 'Mr Doctor Dune shall have Mr Skinners
Chamber yf he shewe not cause to the Contrarye the first Councell
of the next Terme'.[4] Mr. Skinner had recently been causing the
Benchers much trouble; he was, however, a master of delaying
tactics for, when Michaelmas term opened, he had not 'shown
cause' and was still in possession of his rooms.[5] At last, on 6 November, the Benchers lost all patience and ordered that 'Mr Skynner one
of the fellowes of this howse is to dispose of his Chamber payenge to
the Tresuror of the howse xxli. and to paye all dutyes which hee
oweth to the howse, and to dispose of the said Chambers vnto two
of the fellowes of this howse this Terme.'[6] The Treasurer's accounts
for the ensuing year show that Edward Coleman and Edward Dacres
each paid £5 for shares of 'Camere nuper dicte Mri Skinner', so that
Donne must have been accommodated somewhere else in the Inn,
especially as the same accounts acknowledge the receipt of £17. 5s.
each from James Donnelland and Adam Usher 'pro admissione sua
in partem Camere nuper Johannis Dunne sacre Theologie Professoris'.[7]

In all, twenty-one of Donne's sermons preached at Lincoln's Inn
have survived. The congregation in the chapel was a restricted,

[1] *The Black Books*, ii. 179, 188.
[2] Samuel Brooke, another friend, was admitted to the Society at the request of all
the Masters of the Bench in 1618; in June that year he became Rector of St. Margaret's, Lothbury.
[3] *Lives*, p. 53.   [4] Black Book VI, fo. 644ᵛ; cf. *The Black Books*, ii. 195.
[5] Black Book VI, ff. 647ʳ, ᵛ, 648.   [6] Red Book I, fo. 71ᵛ.
[7] Black Book VII, fo. 14.

almost a collegiate, one; its members were all men of education, and all members, present or future, of the legal profession. Donne was therefore able to take for granted a degree of learning and a professional solidarity that few preachers, even in that day, could expect; further, he was personally acquainted with many, if not most, of his auditors: hence the ease and familiarity of address in these sermons. They contain many legal images, just as the Whitehall sermons abound in references to the courtier's life. Donne obviously tried to connect what he had to say with the occupations of the congregation. He also attempted to develop a theme or a topic into a series of sermons whenever he was occupying the same pulpit at regular intervals during the year, as at Lincoln's Inn and, later, at St. Paul's. In one place he refers to a series he had delivered at the Inn, and proposed, now that it was finished, to go on to another:

as heretofore I found it a usefull and acceptable labour, to employ our Evening exercises, upon the vindicating of some such places of Scripture, as our adversaries of the Roman Church had detorted in some point of controversie between them and us, and restoring those places to their true sense, (which course I held constantly for one whole year) so I think it a usefull and acceptable labour, now to employ for a time those Evening exercises to reconcile some such places of Scripture, as may at first sight seem to differ from one another; In the morning we saw how Christ judged all; now we are to see how he judges none; *I judge no man.*[1]

The anti-Catholic sermons probably belonged to the legal year 1617–18, but none of them has survived. The second series came somewhat later, after Donne's return from Doncaster's German embassy, and two pairs of sermons belonging to it can be recognized. Of yet another course of sermons delivered at the Inn, upon Psalm 38, and probably belonging to 1618, six remain.[2] But the interest for Donne's hearers was by no means confined to the systematic exposition of Scripture or of points in dispute. Earnest and eloquent his treatment of these certainly was; but his discourses were now and then touched by personal reminiscence, by wit, and by

[1] *Sermons*, ii, no. 16, ll. 6–15, p. 325.
[2] For the two pairs of sermons reconciling apparently contradictory texts, see ibid., nos. 15 and 16; iii, nos. 3 and 4; for the earlier sermons on Ps. 38, see ibid., ii, nos. 1–6.

expressions of the individual tastes of the preacher, relished by those who knew him so well. The anecdote about the Anabaptists at Aix, already quoted, is one example. It was to members of the Inn that he explained his reasons for preaching so frequently from the Psalms and St. Paul's Epistles (for instance: 'I may have another more particular reason, because they are Scriptures, written in such forms, as I have been most accustomed to; Saint *Pauls* being Letters, and *Davids* being Poems').[1] His more sensitive hearers might also have been aware that the powers which he had exhibited in his earlier prose writings as well as in his verse were still in evidence, transformed, as occasion served, to new uses. The whole man was obviously present in his preaching; he made no attempt to conceal his past, and it was no doubt a recognition of the courage and candour in these references to himself, as well as his devotion to his new calling and his personal charm, that led the members of the Society to hold him in increasing respect and affection.

While Donne was still making his reputation as a preacher at Lincoln's Inn, he received his first invitation to preach the open-air sermon at St. Paul's Cross. The audience that assembled there on Sunday mornings and on week-days of great celebration was always a large one, made up of people from every walk of life, from the greatest noblemen to the humblest journeymen and their wives. The sermons preached often had some official function, for example the interpreting of royal or ecclesiastical policy, and such sermons were not only listened to with eagerness, but also became topics for discussion afterwards. Often, too, they were published in order to have the widest possible circulation. Donne's first sermon at Paul's Cross was preached on 24 March 1617 and was a commemorative one; the occasion was the anniversary of the death of Queen Elizabeth and of the accession of James. Fortunately Chamberlain was present to report on its reception, and he wrote to Carleton:

I had almost forgotten that on Monday the 24th of this moneth beeing the Kings day, the archbishop of Caunterburie, the Lord Keper, Lord Privie-seale, the earle of Arundell, the earle of Southampton, the Lord Hayes, the controller, Secretarie Winwood, the Master of the

---

[1] *Sermons*, ii, no. 1, ll. 6–24, p. 49. For further discussion of the Lincoln's Inn sermons, see ibid., pp. 8–12.

Rolles, with divers other great men were at Paules Crosse, and heard Dr. Donne who made there a daintie sermon, upon the eleventh verse of the 22th of Proverbes; and was excedingly well liked generally, the rather for that he did Quene Elizabeth great right, and held himself close to the text without flattering the time too much.[1]

Donne's text was: 'He that loveth pureness of heart, for the grace of his lips, the King shall be his friend'; and the words clearly had a contemporary reference. James had just left on a journey to Scotland, but before leaving he had created Sir Francis Bacon Lord Keeper. In attending Donne's sermon Bacon was probably making his first public appearance since his new appointment, and it is obvious that many eyes must have been turned in his direction[2] as Donne dilated on the pureness of heart and grace of lips of him whose friend the King would be. Then he passed on to the consideration of the anniversary he was celebrating, and to the praise of the Queen, unmatchable, inimitable, of her sex; he spoke of the apprehensions that followed her death, when London merchants 'were running up and down like Ants with their eggs bigger then themselves, every man with his bags, to seek where to hide them safely'. He recalled, too, that it was at this very place, Paul's Cross, that the new King was proclaimed, and went on to praise James for his courage and firmness in religion, and to take satisfaction in the Union of the two kingdoms. The earlier part of the sermon may be long drawn out, as Paul's Cross sermons often were, but the latter part, with its allusions to Bacon, Queen Elizabeth, and the King, is full of interest and worthy of the praise given to the sermon by Donne's contemporaries. Carleton (at The Hague) was moved by Chamberlain's account of it to write back to him (26 April 1617, O.S.): 'I would gladly see a copie (yf it were possible) of Do^r Donnes sermon wherof you make mention; wch being in so great an audience, and so generally well liked, me thincks should be hearkned after.'[3]

There is another record of Donne's preaching during 1617, and that at a place where it might least have been expected. Donne took

[1] Chamberlain, *Letters*, ii. 67.
[2] I owe this point to Dr. John Sessions. Cf. *Sermons*, i, pp. 213–17, especially at ll. 1242–5.
[3] P.R.O., S.P. 84/77/63.

his incumbency at Sevenoaks seriously enough to visit the town during the summer and preach there. He stayed for a week at Knole with the Earl and Countess of Dorset, and his visit is recorded in the Countess's diary. She notes that on 20 July 'Dr *Donne* came hither', and that on the 27th 'I went to Church (being Sunday) forenoon and afternoon, Dr *Donne* Preaching and he and the other strangers dining with me in the great Chamber'.[1] The Countess evidently valued Donne and his writings, for his poems and sermons are represented among her books in the background of her portrait, at Appleby, which was painted in her old age. Donne on his side thought highly of her and esteemed her conversation; he is said to have remarked 'That she knew well how to discourse of all things, from Predestination, to Slea-silk'.[2]

Almost immediately after his return from Kent to London, Donne had to meet one of the major crises of his life. On 10 August his wife gave birth to a still-born child, and her prolonged labours left her utterly exhausted. She lingered for nearly a week, but on 15 August she died. The circumstances were related by Jean l'Oiseau de Tourval, a French refugee living in London, to Francis Windebank:

> Helas, Monsieur, il faut bien changer le note, car a l'heure mesme que ie fay ces mots, voicy mon hom*me* que J'avois envoyé chez le Dr Dun, *pour* savoir combien luy & sa fem*me* se portoy*ent*, elle accouchee, Dimanche matin, d'vne fille qui a peyne vesquit autant de minutes, que la pauure Mere a fist de iour[?], Dieu l'ayant apelee cette nuist, & le pauure Mary restant luy mesme fort malade & affligé. Cecy est ecrit Samedy matin.[3]

The Parish Register shows that she was buried on the following day in the Church of St. Clement Danes, and the Churchwardens' Accounts record the expenses of the funerals of the infant and the mother:

> ffor the buryall of a styll borne
> chyld of Dockter Dunes
> for the grave in the church - - - - - -   iiij^s
> for the knell - - - - - - - - - - - - - - -   viij^d

---

[1] *The Diary of Lady Anne Clifford*, ed. V. Sackville West, 1923, p. 74.
[2] *Sermons*, i, p. 130 n., and Edward Rainbowe, *A Sermon Preached at the Funeral of* . . . *Anne Countess of Pembroke, Dorset, and Montgomery*, 1677, p. 38.
[3] P.R.O., S.P. 14, vol. 92, no. 107.

ffor the buryall of Mrs Dun
    for the knell - - - - - - - - - - - - - - -   v^s
    for the passing bell - - - - - - - - - -   iiij^{d1}

Evidently mother and child were buried in the same grave. The grief-stricken husband erected a monument to her memory, carved by Nicholas Stone and inscribed with an epitaph of Donne's own composition. A copy in his own handwriting has survived among the Loseley papers; it was apparently sent to Sir George More for his approval. It reads:

Annae

Georgij	⎧ More de	⎧ Filiae
Robertj	⎨ Lothesley	⎨ Soror:
Willelmj	⎬ Equit:	⎬ Nept:
Christophorj	⎩ Aurat:	⎩ Pronept:

Foeminae lectissimae dilectissimae*que*;
Coniugi charissimae, castissimæ*que*;
Matri piissimae, indulgentissimae*que*;
xv annis in coniugio transactis,
vii post xii^m partum (quorum vii superstant) dies
Inmani febre correptae,
(Quod hoc saxum farj iussit
Jpse, prae dolore Jnfans)
Maritus (miserrimum dictu) olim charae charus
Cineribus cineres spondet suos
Nouo matrimonio (annuat Deus) hoc loco sociandos
Johannes Donne
Sacr: Theolog: profess:
Secessit
A° xxxiii° Ætat: suae et sui Jesu
CIↃ DC xvii°
Avg: xv.

The monument was erected 'in the Chancel, on the North side, at the upper end',[2] and was described by Stone as 'a letell tombe in a wall', for which he had '15 peces'. It was certainly not the 'elaborate composition' envisaged by Gosse, 'with coloured figures of the lady,

---

[1] Churchwardens' Accounts, 1617–18, p. 214.
[2] Stow's *Survey of London,* ed. Strype (1720), ii, bk. iv, p. 113, col. 2.

her husband, and her children in a vanishing perspective';[1] it was much more likely to have been similar to the wall monument which Stone executed about the same time in Enfield Church to the memory of Martha Garrard, which cost £16 and consisted of a panel to contain the inscription surrounded by a cartouche.[2]

Ann Donne was thirty-three when she died, and her fate was that of many women of her time—to die worn out by child-bearing while still scarcely past her youth. Twelve times, her epitaph recorded, she had been brought to bed. Two of her children, the last, and one born in 1612 on the Isle of Wight, were still-born; of the other ten, seven survived her. Three—Francis, Mary, and Nicholas—had already died. Of the survivors Constance, the eldest, was now about fourteen and the youngest, Elizabeth, baptized on 14 June 1616, was a little over a year old.

There can be little doubt that Donne's marriage had so far been the deepest experience of his life. The personality of his wife inevitably remains elusive, although to Sir John Oglander, her brother-in-law, she was 'the best of women', and all Donne's references reveal his devotion to her. However much he had suffered during the years of his married life, his marriage itself had been a source of sustenance and comfort to him. Ann Donne must have had the perception and intelligence to be a real companion to him and to share, in some degree at least, in his interests; above all, by her steadiness and dependability, she compensated for his mercurial temperament and helped to give him a sense of stability. He repaid her love not only with his own but with gratitude as well; 'we had not one another at so cheap a rate', he wrote in 1614, 'as that we should ever be weary of one another'.[3] After her death, Walton relates, Donne solemnly promised his children 'never to bring them under the subjection of a step-mother', although he might have had

---

[1] Gosse, ii. 93.

[2] *The Notebook and Account Book of Nicholas Stone*, Publications of the Walpole Society, vii (1919), pp. 50–1. Martha Garrard, according to her monument, died 1 July 1617 of her fourth child. She had married Sir James Palmer, who was, like the Garrards, of Dorney, Bucks., and was a Groom of the Bedchamber. He later succeeded Sir Thomas Roe (first cousin of George and Martha Garrard) as Chancellor of the Garter. Cf. *Miscellanea Genealogica et Heraldica*, ed. J. J. Howard, i (1868), 109, and Chamberlain, *Letters*, ii. 86 n.

[3] To Sir Robert More, Gosse, ii. 48 (Loseley MS.).

every inducement to re-marry, if only that the children might be properly cared for. Nor could he have been blamed very severely if, after the manner of the times, he had chosen a second wife whose fortunes or influence could have helped his worldly advancement. But his marriage to Ann had forged for him the strongest emotional ties he had yet known, and a second marriage would have seemed a profanation of the first.

Walton gives a vivid picture of Donne's grief for his wife: of his shutting himself in seclusion to indulge his sorrow, and of his being recalled to himself by the recollection of 'his new ingagements to God, and St. *Pauls Wo is me, if I preach not the Gospel*'. Hence

His first motion from his house was to preach, where his beloved wife lay buried (in St. *Clements* Church, near Temple-Bar *London*) and his Text was a part of the Prophet *Jeremy*'s Lamentation: *Lo, I am the man that have seen affliction.*

And indeed, his very words and looks testified him to be truly such a man; and they, with the addition of his sighs and tears, exprest in his Sermon, did so work upon the affections of his hearers, as melted and moulded them into a companionable sadness; and so they left the Congregation; but then their houses presented them with objects of diversion: and his, presented him with nothing but fresh objects of sorrow, in beholding many helpless children, a narrow fortune, and a consideration of the many cares and casualties that attend their education.[1]

One may well inquire how Donne, the Reader at Lincoln's Inn, came to be preaching at St. Clement Danes. Was he given a special opportunity to do so? The answer is to be found in the fact that Dr. Layfield, the rector, had died on the previous 23 March, and his successor was not appointed until November.[2] It was the long vacation when Mrs. Donne died, and Donne was temporarily free from

---

[1] *Lives*, p. 52. Grierson suggested (ii. 225–6) that the verse paraphrase of *The Lamentations of Jeremy* was made about this time, since Donne would have been likely in his grief to turn to that particular book of the Bible. There is no other indication of date, but Grierson's argument is not one that carries immediate conviction, and the question is better left an open one.

A sermon on the text 'Lo, I am the man that hath seen affliction' has survived (*Sermons*, x, no. 9), but there is no indication that it was preached at St. Clement Danes, and nothing in it to suggest that it was intended to commemorate Mrs. Donne. It seems to be a sermon preached on the same text at another time.

[2] G. Hennessy, *Novum Repertorium Parochiale Londinense*, 1898, p. 128.

his obligations at Lincoln's Inn; it looks as if he was preaching whenever he could in his parish church to fill the vacant pulpit.

The death of his wife marked a turning-point in Donne's life; it deepened his sense of religious vocation, and produced something much closer to a conversion than the feelings which had prompted him to enter the Church. Until her death all Donne's deepest emotional experiences seem to have been associated with her; after her loss, his emotions concentrated themselves on the divine image and the activities connected with his sacred calling. Commentators have long been aware of the increased intensity of religious feeling expressed by Donne after 1617, and he himself was conscious of the change. It was shown in the enrichment of his preaching and in his deepened sense of Christian truth.

Donne lacked at first a full conviction of the *positive* elements in Christianity, though he was keenly alive to the negative ones, the dangers of sin, the need for divine grace to conquer sin, and so on. Then, as he continued to preach, and as his personal experience impinged on his mind, he came to feel certain things more deeply that he had before accepted intellectually. He became more perceptive of the nature of man's love for God and the glory of God's love to man. He awakened to an emotional as well as an intellectual conviction that Christ has redeemed mankind. Both of these developments appear first in sermons preached shortly after the death of his wife Ann, in 1617.[1]

For the eighteen months following Mrs. Donne's death very little is known of Donne's activities. He stayed on at Drury House, and the children were doubtless left largely to the care of servants, though Sir Thomas and Lady Grymes at Peckham showed a warm and unceasing interest in the motherless family. Donne probably made a pretence during those months of carrying on his life much as before, but it soon became clear that his health was suffering, and that much of his zest had gone; 'his friends of *Lincolns Inne*', says Walton, '. . . feared that his immoderate study, and sadness for his wives death, would, as *Jacob* said, *make his days few*, and respecting his bodily health, *evil* too: and of this there were many visible

---

[1] G. R. Potter, 'John Donne: Poet to Priest', in *Five Gayley Lectures, 1947–54* (University of California Publications, English Studies, 10), at pp. 117–18.

signs'.[1] Nevertheless, Donne preached at Whitehall on 2 November 1617, the first Sunday after the Court had come to London for the winter, and at Denmark House before Queen Anne on 14 December. Both of these sermons were specially commissioned, and in addition to his regular engagements at Court. In 1618 he preached his usual Lenten and April sermons there, and in the first of these (20 February 1617/18), with some courage, he ventured a sardonic glance at the taking of his doctorate by a means, to some even of his hearers, questionable ('If the favour of a Prince can make a man a Doctor, *per saltum* . . .').[2] Some of the Lincoln's Inn sermons besides those already mentioned doubtless belong also to this period, but as the majority of them are undated it is difficult to be certain.

One of them, however, very probably followed close on the two Court sermons just referred to—that 'Preached at Lincolns Inne, preparing them to build their Chappell'.[3] As long before as 1609, the Benchers of the Inn, realizing that their chapel was falling into disrepair and that it was by then too small to hold their full number, decided that a new and larger one would have to be built. There had followed an appeal for funds, and some desultory collecting. Towards the end of 1617 the whole matter was taken up afresh, and much more energetic measures were soon under way. A special meeting of the Council was held to consider the new chapel, and a committee was appointed to get estimates on the cost of materials. In January 1617/18 it was decided to ask Inigo Jones to prepare the plans, and Christopher Brooke was delegated to persuade him to undertake the commission.

During February the Council was considering a 'model' of the new chapel, and the collecting of funds began again. Finally, in May, a committee was appointed which recommended a levy on all members of the Inn, and it was decided that the levy was to be imposed during the following term.[4] It was no doubt at this point that Donne, who was obviously very much concerned with any of the arrangements for public worship in the Society, came forward to

---

[1] *Lives*, p. 54.
[2] *Sermons*, i, no. 6, ll. 298–9, p. 260; cf. E. Le Comte, *Grace to a Witty Sinner*, p. 165.
[3] *Sermons*, ii, no. 10.
[4] *The Black Books*, ii. 199–209.

'prepare' them to build their chapel. Characteristically, this preparation had little to do directly with the members' pockets, but
much with their hearts and minds, and with the Word of God that
would be preached in the new building. During the year there was
a good deal of discussion of its site, and it was at least November
before it was decided to erect the chapel where it still stands.[1]

Among the contacts which Donne renewed at this period with
old acquaintances was included, rather surprisingly, that with Sir
Toby Mathew. Mathew, after many prolonged efforts, had received
permission to return to England again, and was in his native
country from the middle of 1617 until the end of 1618. He and
Donne seem to have had an odd attraction for each other; neither
could unreservedly accept the other's friendship, yet, when the
opportunity came, they found that they were drawn irresistibly
towards one another. Mathew probably made no attempt to intrude upon Donne's sorrow in the days shortly after his return to
England, but before long he was seeking to renew their association;
Donne, on his side, in spite of the fact that after the false news in
1613 of Mathew's death he had been told that Mathew 'loved not
me',[2] was writing to him to 'do somewhat towards the breeding and
cherishing of such degrees of friendship, as formerly I had the
honour to hold with you'. But, he nevertheless insisted, any intercourse between them was now possible only if each fully respected
the other's religion:

That we differ in our wayes [to Heaven], I hope we pardon one
another. Men go to *China*, both by the Straights, and by the *Cape*. I
never mis-interpreted your way; nor suffered it to be so, wheresoever
I found it in discourse. For I was sure, you took not up your Religion
upon trust, but payed ready money for it, and at a high Rate. And this
taste of mine towards you, makes me hope for, and claime the same
disposition in you towards me.[3]

In no friendship does Donne appear quite so advantageously as in

[1] Cf. *Sermons*, ii. 29–31.   [2] Gosse, i. 309 (Anderdon MS.).
[3] *Tobie Mathew Collection*, pp. 67–9. This letter is undated and is headed 'Doctor
Dunne, with a kind of labour'd Complement, to a Friend of his'. The suggestion that
it was addressed to Mathew in 1617 or 1618 was made in Mathew and Calthrop, *The
Life of Sir Tobie Matthew*, p. 157. [Mr. I. A. Shapiro tells me, however, that the letter
was pretty certainly written in Nov. or Dec. 1611.]

his relation with Mathew. His openness and tolerance make Mathew seem both more bigoted and more worldly by comparison.

Though Donne could state his religious position to Mathew with a firmness that precluded any risk of interference, the same was not true of Sir Henry Goodyer. He had been unsettled ten years previously by Mathew's arguments for Roman Catholicism, and now he was once again beset by religious doubts. A letter of Donne, dated 22 December 1617, shows that the rigour of his analysis of Goodyer's difficulties had intensified rather than allayed his scruples:

God loves your soul, if he be loth to let it go inch-meale, and not by swallowings; and he loves it too, if he build it up again stone after stone; his will is not done except his way, and his leasure be observed. In my particular, I am sorry, if my ingenuity and candor in delivering my self in those points, of which you speak to me, have defaced those impressions which were in you before: if my freedome have occasioned your captivity, I am miserably sorry. . . . But I was as confident in your strength, as in mine own, so am I still, in him, who strengthens al our infirmities and will, I doubt not, bring you and me together, in all those particulars, so as we shall not part in this world, nor the next. Sir, your own soul cannot be more zealous of your peace, then I am: and God, who loves that zeale in me, will not suffer you to suspect it.[1]

The same letter contains information of other kinds. Goodyer's children were now growing up: two of Donne's letters of December 1614 had contained references to Goodyer's son, and this one refers to his eldest daughter Lucy, a godchild of the Countess of Bedford, who was now a member of the Countess's household. Goodyer himself, as we have seen, seems to have been living more and more at Polesworth in a rather futile effort to cut down his expenses and pay some of his debts. Donne proposed to visit him there in the spring of 1618, when other business was to take him into that part of the country. Toby Mathew was visiting his parents at York in March 1618, and he may have visited Goodyer at about the same time.

Another event of 1617 which must have been of interest to Donne was the marriage of Lord Hay to Lady Lucy Percy, daughter of the

[1] *Letters*, pp. 209–10. The letter is headed 'To the gallant Knight Sir *Tho. Lucy*.' and dated 'Drury house the 22 of Decemb. 1607'. The year is clearly wrong and I have taken it as a misprint for '1617'; it is almost certain that the letter was, in fact, addressed to Goodyer.

Earl of Northumberland. Hay's first wife, Lady Honora Denny,[1] had been assaulted and robbed of her jewels as she was coming home late one night; her ordeal brought on a miscarriage, and she died soon afterwards. Two years later, Hay fell in love again. He had taken a house near Sion House in Middlesex in order to be close to the lady; but then her father heard of the affair, and had the Lady Lucy brought to the Tower to share in his imprisonment, hoping in this way to put an end to her infatuation. But Hay had many friends, including Lady Bedford outside the Tower and Lady Somerset within it, and he was able to meet Lady Lucy in Lady Somerset's apartments. Eventually, though the Earl of Northumberland still disapproved, the marriage was celebrated in the King's presence on 6 November 1617. In the following year the bridegroom was created Viscount Doncaster in order to raise his rank nearer to that of his father-in-law; he, on his side, interceded with the King for the Earl of Northumberland so successfully that a reconciliation was effected, and the Earl's long imprisonment in the Tower came at last to an end.

The sole reference to Donne's activities during 1618 in addition to those already noticed shows that during that year he found himself involved, doubtless against his will, in a dispute that had broken out among members of the Egerton family. Its head, Thomas Egerton, Lord Ellesmere and Lord Chancellor, had died on 15 March 1617. For several years before his death he had been anxious to retire, but the King had refused to consent, and in November 1616 had created him Viscount Brackley. Early in the following year, when his health was visibly failing, he again petitioned to be allowed to retire, and the King reluctantly agreed, at the same time promising him an earldom. But it was too late, either for further honours or for any relief, and a few days later the old man died. His only surviving son, John, obtained the promised earldom only after paying an enormous bribe to Buckingham, and became Earl of

---

[1] She was the daughter of Lord Denny, who became patron of Joseph Hall when he left Hawstead for Waltham Abbey. Hall seems to have met Lord Hay through his patron, for in 1616 Hall went as Hay's chaplain on an embassy to France. For the courtship of Lady Percy see letters of George Garrard to Carleton, S.P. (Dom.) 14, vol. 87, no. 101; vol. 90, no. 135; and S. R. Gardiner, *History of England, 1603–1642*, iii (1890), 200–2.

Bridgewater. But his troubles were by no means over. The widow and daughters of his elder brother, Sir Thomas Egerton Junior, who had died nearly twenty years before while serving with Essex in Ireland,[1] immediately began a series of suits in Chancery. Lady Egerton laid claim to certain properties as being hers under the terms of her marriage settlement, though this settlement had, in fact, been invalidated when her husband predeceased his father the Lord Chancellor.[2] Her two children, Mary, wife of Sir Thomas Leigh, and Vere, wife of William Booth, joined with their husbands in another suit to recover the profits of a wardship, the lease of which had now been inherited by the Earl of Bridgewater, but which, they alleged, had been held by the Lord Chancellor in trust for them.[3] But the most important suit was one brought by Sir Thomas and Lady Leigh against the Earl of Bridgewater, relating to the parsonage of Gresford in Denbigh.[4] This valuable property had had, as the Earl of Bridgewater was able to show, a complicated history. It belonged to the Dean and Chapter of Winchester, but had been leased by them. The lessee was a certain Ellis Wynn, but a reversionary lease for fifty years, to take effect on the expiry of the current one, had been granted to the Queen. Ellis Wynn had leased his tythes to George Bellott (who in turn leased them to John ap Howell Tegin), and then mortgaged the lease of the parsonage to Thomas Middleton, the wealthy London merchant who became Lord Mayor in 1613. Meanwhile the Queen had bestowed her reversionary lease on Lancelot Bostock, who mortgaged it to Ralph Calveley, who then assigned his mortgage to his son John. This was the situation in 1598. Thereafter Ellis Wynn and Thomas Middleton assigned their rights in the current lease to Sir Thomas Egerton Junior; and Bostock and the Calveleys joined in assigning their rights in the reversionary lease to Robert Davies and Richard Cartwright. Next, Sir Thomas Egerton assigned his rights to John Panton[5] and Richard Cartwright; and finally, by one document

[1] Cf. pp. 104–6 above.

[2] P.R.O., C24/451, and Huntington Library, MS. Ellesmere 635 b/I.

[3] P.R.O., C2, James I, L16/38, and Huntington Library, MS. Ellesmere 7930.

[4] P.R.O., C24/448, pt. i, and C33/135, ff. 284ᵛ, 843ʳ; Huntington Library, MSS. Ellesmere 1837–61.

[5] Incidentally, John Panton was a cousin of Ellis Wynn. Panton was a Lincoln's Inn man, who became a secretary of the Lord Keeper. From 1609, as the Surveyors' and

Robert Davies and Richard Cartwright assigned the lease in being, and by another document John Panton and Richard Cartwright assigned the reversionary lease, to the elder Sir Thomas Egerton. Such is the story the documents tell, but the facts were even more complicated, since Thomas Ravenscroft, Egertòn's brother-in-law, took an active part in several of these transactions although his name did not appear at any stage as an assignee. The younger Sir Thomas Egerton was likewise an active participant in the negotiations with Bostock and the Calveleys, as well as with Bostock and Sir Thomas Middleton. Sir Thomas Leigh and his wife argued that Sir Thomas Egerton Junior was the real purchaser, and that first Davies, Panton, and Cartwright (who were joined to the suit as defendants), and then Thomas Egerton Senior, the Lord Keeper, were trustees for him and his heirs. The Earl of Bridgewater replied that it had been his father's habit to buy up lands in this fashion, and that his brother had been far too deeply in debt to make such purchases in his own behalf. Ravenscroft and the younger Sir Thomas Egerton, as well as Davies, Panton, and Cartwright, had all been acting on behalf of the Lord Keeper.

There are many gaps in the records of the case. The most important of those surviving in the Public Record Office is the set of depositions made in answer to fifty-seven questions submitted by the plaintiffs to no fewer than twenty-eight witnesses, of whom one was Donne. On 17 June 1618 he was asked solemnly to reply to the last of the fifty-seven interrogatories:

whether doe yo^u knowe of yor owne knowledge that there was a faleing out & disagreement betweene S^r: Thomas Egerton the sonne & John Panton the def*endant*: yf soe then howe doe yo^u knowe the same, & vpon what occasion did they fall out, and aboute what tyme was yt, and whether doe yo^u knowe or have hearde that they were afterward*es* ffriend*es* & reconciled againe, And whether were the said S^r: Thomas Egerton & M^r: Panton good ffreind*es* at or neare aboute S^r: Tho: Egertons goeing into Ireland as yo^u knowe or haue

the Churchwardens' Accounts show, he lived in the parish of St. Clement Danes, so that he and Donne must have seen one another from time to time after Donne moved to Drury Lane. How intimate their relations were is another matter! On Panton and the Wynns see *Calendar of Wynn Papers in the National Library of Wales*, 1926, and J. Neale, *The Elizabethan House of Commons* (1949), pp. 297–8.

heard, howe doe yo^u knowe they were not then ffreind*es*. speak the truth herein!

Donne's reply was brief and guarded:

xvij° Junij Ao. xvj° Jacobi R*egis* 1618

John Donne docto^r in dyvinitý aged 46. yeres or nere thereabout*es* sworne & ex*amin*ed &c.

57. That he knoweth not of any falling out or dysagreem^t betweene Sr Thomas Egerton the sonne & John Panton in the Interro*gatorie* named, And therefore can depose nothing to the former p*arte* of the Interro*gatorie* And as touching whether the said Sr Thomas and Mr. Panton were good friend*es* at or neere about Sr Tho: Egertons goyng into Ireland ye or no he sayth that he knoweth it to be true that the said Sr Thomas at his goyng into Ireland had a hard opinion of Mr Panton, but how Mr Panton stood affected to Sr Thomas this depon*ent* cannot declare nor more can say to any the questions of this Interro*gatorie* otherwise then what he hath alredy deposed in his ex*amin*ation taken in this cause on the deff*endantes* behalf to wch for more full answere to the questions of this Interro*gatorie* the depon*ent* referreth hymself

To the rest not ex*amin*ed

[signed] J: Donne[1]

The fuller deposition made on behalf of the Earl of Bridgewater has apparently not survived.

The case was argued before Francis Bacon for three days in the ensuing Michaelmas term, and on 21 November Bacon delivered an interim judgement. He spoke at length, with that weight and elegance for which he was so justly famous. First he freed 'the Late Lord Chaun,cello^r from any imputa*t*ion or as*pers*ion of dishono^r', declaring that 'he brake noe trust nor wrested the said Lease . . . by his great power and authority nor vsed any hard dealing in his owne family'. He then ordered briefs to be drawn upon both sides,[2]

---

[1] P.R.O., C24/448, pt. i. [Professor Bald notes that he searched C24/444–57 for depositions on the defendant's behalf without success.]

[2] What are either drafts of one of these briefs, or drafts of the barrister's brief, are to be found in MSS. Ellesmere 1855 and 1856; the latter contains frequent corrections in the handwriting of the Earl of Bridgewater. The two documents contain summaries

containing only acknowledged facts, which were to be submitted to him for his further consideration. Then, finally,

> because his Lordshipp had buried the remembrance of the late Lord Chancellor his worthy predecessor with honor, beinge desirous like-wise to bury all dissentions in the family amongst parties soe neere of blood, his Lordship wisheth and desireth that the parties in the meane tyme shall attend the Lord Bishop of London [John King] and the Lord cheife Justice of the Kinges bench [Sir Henry Montague][1] whom his lordshipp nominated and selected as two that allwaies loued and honored the late Lord Chancellor, To the end they may mediate and quiett all differences betweene them if they canne.[2]

The case came before Bacon once again, on 19 April 1619, when he of the evidence, with marginal references either to the original documents relied on or to the transcripts of the depositions. Donne's evidence is cited in both:

'7. That Sir Thomas Egerton had greate dislike with Panton at the tyme when the assign-ment was made to Panton and Cartwright ——— } John Phillipps lib. A, fo. 322 Int. 57 / Sir Raffe Bingley lib. C, fo. 267 / John Dun lib. C, fo. 124. / Antho: Rauenscrofte lib^r C, fo. 254 / Sir Richard Trevor lib. C, fo. 237 / Thomas Cowley lib. C, fo. 50 / Sir Richard Younge lib. C, fo. 240 } 31'

(MS. Ellesmere 1856, fo. 10)

'Sir Thomas Middleton beinge interessed of Gresford Lease in possession by mort-gage from Wynn the auncient tenant he assigned his interest to Sir Thomas Egerton 23° Decembris 1598: whoe before his goeinge into Ireland by the lord Chancellors direction 10 Marcij after assigned his interest to Cartwright and Panton, Sir Thomas beinge then in great dislyke[3] with Panton against whome he had conceaved great displeasure, but Panton was much imployed and often trusted by the lord Chaun-cellor in manye affaires and busynesses and his name often vsed in trust in passinge estates of his lordships land and possessions.

3   Jo. Phillips L. A. fol. 322 1:57 / Sir Raffe Bingley L. C. fol. 267 / Dr. Donne L. C. fol. 124 / Anthony Ravenscrofte L. C. fol. 254 / Thomas Cowley L. C. fol. 287 / Sir Richard Yong L. C. fol. 240 } Int. 31.'

(MS. Ellesmere 1855, ff. 1–2; I have omitted side-notes 1, 2, and 4)

It is clear from these references that liber A and liber B contained depositions on behalf of the plaintiffs, liber C and liber D those on behalf of the defendant, and that these documents relied on Donne's evidence on behalf of the Earl of Bridgewater rather than on the deposition which has survived.

1   He was apparently the Sir Henry Montagu who deposed for the defendant! Montagu had passed sentence of execution on Sir Walter Raleigh less than three weeks previously. Whether Donne had any contact with the events of Raleigh's last days is not known, but there is a long and moving letter from Raleigh to Sir Nicholas Carey, his (and Donne's) brother-in-law, describing the disasters of the last Guiana expedition among the Carey papers in the British Museum.

2   P.R.O., C33/135 (Chancery Decrees and Orders, A book, 1618–19), fo. 284^v.

closed it by ordering that 'the plaintiffs bill and all the matters therein conteyned are cleerely and absolutely dismissed out of the Courte'.[1]

For the rest, the case is interesting in that the long lists of deponents on both sides give the names of a number of members of Lincoln's Inn who had been friends of both the young Egertons during the 1590s and were now either country squires or successful members of the Bar. The most senior of these was Sir Raynulph Crewe, sergeant-at-law and one of the more famous advocates of the day.[2] Sir Thomas Leigh, the plaintiff, was a Lincoln's Inn man, as was his brother, Sir Urian, who also gave evidence. Among the lawyers were Thomas Foster (who was admitted to Lincoln's Inn from Thavies Inn along with Avery Copley on 11 March 1574), John Jeffreys of Denbighshire (admitted on 24 June 1587), John and William Phillips of Yorkshire (admitted 2 February 1586 and 9 October 1587), George Hope of Flintshire (admitted 3 June 1595), John Parkinson of Lancashire (admitted 7 August 1604), William Johnson of London (admitted 21 August 1621) and, finally, Egerton's cousin William Ravenscroft (admitted 29 October 1580). Other legal officials involved in the case beside the Lord Chief Justice were Ellis Wynn, a Clerk of the Petty Bag and a son of the original lessee of Gresford, and Valentine Saunders, a Six Clerk who had been on familiar terms with the Egerton family for twenty years. The list is all the more interesting because it mentions men whose names never occur elsewhere in connection with Donne; yet most of them were men whom Donne must have known in his youth and with whom he was thrown into close contact when he returned to Lincoln's Inn as Reader in Divinity. Of equal interest, too, is the fact that this case renewed associations between Donne and the family of his old master, cementing a connection which remained constant for the rest of Donne's life.

[1] Ibid., fo. 843^r.
[2] It is interesting to observe that he was retained as senior counsel by the Earl of Bridgewater in the parallel case of Leigh v. Bridgewater, P.R.O., C2, James I, L16/38, and signed the Earl's answer in that capacity.

XIII

IN GERMANY WITH DONCASTER

IN the spring of 1618 the tension which had held most of Europe in an uneasy peace for the last six years was increased by a sudden eruption in Bohemia. In 1617 the Emperor Matthias had presented his cousin, Ferdinand of Styria, to the Bohemian Diet as his successor to the crown of Bohemia. Ferdinand promised to accept the religious settlement that had been established by his predecessors, but it was not long before Protestant rights began to be curtailed, and in May 1618 an angry gathering of Protestant deputies met in Prague. Two days later, on the 23rd, a group of their leaders forced their way into the castle from which the deputy-governors appointed by the Emperor exercised their authority; the two officials whom they found there, together with a secretary, were flung from a window 80 feet above the level of the ground, and a Protestant government was formed to replace them. This act of defenestration, with which the revolt in Bohemia began, is also regarded by historians as the opening of the Thirty Years War, although more than a year elapsed before the conflict spread. At first it was regarded as no more than the rebellion of Protestant subjects against their Catholic sovereign, although its explosive potentialities were recognized from the first. 'The stirrs in Bohemia were speedily advertised hither, and with it they are here nott a little trobled', wrote Sir Francis Cottington, the English envoy in Madrid,[1] taking it for granted that Spain as the head of the Hapsburg confederation would have to meet some of the expenses of suppressing the rebellion. The new government of Bohemia, on the other hand, appealed for aid not only to the Protestant states of Germany but also to the stronger powers of England and the Netherlands. James I, indeed, had to

[1] *Letters and other Documents illustrating the Relations between England and Germany at the Commencement of the Thirty Years' War*, ed. S. R. Gardiner, First Series, Camden Society, xc (1865), p. 3.

receive not merely the pleas of the Bohemians but the further appeals of his son-in-law the Elector Palatine, who felt, not without
reason, that the whole future of Protestantism in Germany was at
stake.

James, however, did not reply to the letters from Bohemia;
instead, he advised his son-in-law not to be too precipitate. James
was reluctant to take sides against the King of Spain, for he had set
his mind on a Spanish princess as a bride for his son. Besides, he was
anxious to see whether it might not be possible to make peace
between the Emperor and the Bohemians, and in a message to the
King of Spain hinted at his willingness to mediate. On receiving
this communication the Spanish Council sought the advice of the
ex-ambassador to England, Don Diego de Sarmiento, better known
by his later title of Conde de Gondomar. He replied that 'the vanity
of the present King of England is so great that he will always think
it of great importance that peace should be made by his means, so
that his authority may be increased;' and he went on to recommend
that

upon the basis of the offer made to his Majesty by the King of England, it is possible and fitting to accept his mediation, since it can not
do any harm, or make things worse than they would be without it;
but that it is more likely that good will come of it, and that he will be
brought under an obligation by what he does, so as to be ashamed of
himself, and really and truly to do good offices towards the reduction
of the Bohemians to the obedience of His Imperial Majesty and the
King Ferdinand. And . . . it would not be a bad way to obtain this
object, that the King of England should send immediately to Germany
an ambassador to treat about it. . . .[1]

Gondomar's advice was followed, and James's offer of mediation was
accepted with every show of enthusiasm. For the next four years it
was one of the principal aims of Spanish diplomacy to keep England
neutral, and Gondomar was called out of retirement and sent back
to London to implement the policy which he had initiated. A
situation grew up very similar to that which existed during the
Spanish Civil War of the 1930s. Then Germany and Italy, though
nominally neutral, poured men and arms into Spain, while England

---

[1] Ibid., p. 30.

maintained a rigorous neutrality by refusing aid to the Republican cause; in the opening phase of the Thirty Years War the King of Spain and the Archduke aided Ferdinand with men, money, and supplies while James was showing a strict impartiality by studying both sides of the question and considering the reports of his ambassadors.

It was on 28 January 1619 that Cottington wrote to inform James that his offer to mediate had been accepted; on 19 February it was announced in London that 'My Lord of Doncaster is to goe Embassador to the princes of Germany, and soe to Bohemia'.[1] The King, besides appointing an ambassador, selected his chaplain as well, for on 9 March Donne wrote to Sir Henry Goodyer: 'It is true that M. *Gherard* told you, I had that commandment from the King signified to me by L. and am still under it, and we are within fourteen days of our time for going.'[2] Yet it was more than two months before the embassy actually set out, and nearly a year had passed since the first outbreak of violence in Prague had occurred.

It is ironical that this appointment came as the culmination of all Donne's earlier attempts to secure a position abroad in the service of the Government. Ireland, Virginia, Venice—for each he had applied in turn. He had gone abroad with Sir Robert Drury to keep in touch with developments on the Continent, and, while Drury had concerned himself with political events, Donne's eye had been fixed on the situation of Protestants abroad. Even since his ordination he may have been engaged in secret correspondence with agents in Europe. It is no wonder that James thought of him as a suitable person to accompany Doncaster's embassy. Yet now that the opportunity had come, Donne was far from sure that he wanted it. 'I leave a scattered flock of wretched children,' he wrote to Goodyer, 'and I carry an infirme and valetudinary body, and I goe into the mouth of such adversaries, as I cannot blame for hating me, the Jesuits, and yet I go.'[2] There is no eagerness here, and Walton declares that at this time Donne believed 'himself to be in a Consumption', and says that his friends of Lincoln's Inn feared for his poor health, of which 'there were many visible signs'.[3]

The departure of the embassy, which had seemed so near when

[1] *Letters and other Documents &c.*, p. 45.   [2] *Letters*, p. 174.   [3] *Lives*, p. 54.

Donne wrote to Sir Henry Goodyer, was postponed for various reasons. The Queen had died on 2 March, and almost immediately afterwards the King, who was at Newmarket when the news of his wife's death reached him, was taken ill. For a while it was thought that he was dying, and it was not until the middle of April that he had recovered sufficiently to be removed to Theobalds in a litter. Meanwhile news had come from Germany of the death of the Emperor Matthias; an imperial election would be held, and it was almost certain that the new emperor would be Ferdinand, who, however unsure his hold on Bohemia might be at the moment, would probably before long be able to bring against it not only the resources but the authority of the Empire as well. The situation needed reassessing, especially as the Protestant states were quick to take alarm at the new turn of events, and the Elector Palatine was trying to organize an effective opposition to the dynastic hopes of the Hapsburgs. There was, however, no thought of giving up the embassy: it now seemed more urgent than ever.

As in 1611, Donne had plenty of time to make his farewells, but his regular life did not, as then, come to a standstill; there were obligations to be met that followed one another almost till the last moment. Donne preached what was now becoming his regular sermon to the Court at the beginning of Lent, and preached again on 28 March. Perhaps, in view of his impending departure with Doncaster, he had arranged to be in attendance at Whitehall during March instead of April. At any rate, he preached 'to the Lords upon Easter-day, at the Communion, The King being then dangerously sick at New-Market'.[1] The sermon is charged with emotion, though the King is nowhere mentioned in it, and, though preached on Easter Day, it is a sermon on death rather than resurrection. It is, however, by far the most powerful sermon Donne had yet preached, and by implication betrays his deep concern for James in his illness.

Meanwhile, Donne, in preparing for his departure, was putting his affairs in order. He transcribed and sent to Lady Montgomery a sermon for which she had asked,[2] and he sent to Sir Robert Ker not

[1] *Sermons*, ii, no. 9.

[2] Ibid., no. 8. It was preached at The Cockpit, a group of apartments adjacent to Whitehall, occupied by the Earl and Countess of Montgomery, very probably on 21 Feb. 1618/19; cf. ibid., pp. 23-36.

merely some of his poems but also his own copy of *Biathanatos*, with this account of the book:

It was written by me many years since; and because it is upon a misinterpretable subject, I have always gone so near suppressing it, as that it is onely not burnt: no hand hath passed upon it to copy it, nor many eyes to read it: onely to some particular friends in both Universities, then when I writ it, I did communicate it: And I remember, I had this answer, That certainly, there was a false thread in it, but not easily found: Keep it, I pray, with the same jealousie; let any that your discretion admits to the sight of it, know the date of it; and that it is a Book written by *Jack Donne*, and not by D. *Donne*: Reserve it for me, if I live, and if I die, I only forbid it the Presse, and the Fire: publish it not, but yet burn it not; and between those, do what you will with it.[1]

He tells also of spending a morning 'surveying and emptying my Cabinet of Letters'.[2] On 4 April he was taking leave of Sir Henry Goodyer, expecting to be gone in less than a week, but it was not until the 18th that he was preaching his sermon of valediction at Lincoln's Inn. Only at the end of the sermon did he refer to his imminent departure:

In my long absence, and far distance from hence, remember me, as I shall do you in the ears of ... God, ... remember me, not my abilities; ... but remember my labors, and endeavors, at least my desire, to make sure your salvation. And I shall remember your religious cheerfulness in hearing the word, and your christianly respect towards all them that bring that word unto you, and towards myself in particular far above my merit.

In a further sentence he referred to the contrast between England and the lands to which the embassy was going:

Remember me thus, you that stay in this Kingdome of peace, where no sword is drawn, but the sword of Justice, as I shal remember you in those Kingdomes, where ambition on one side, and a necessary defence from unjust persecution on the other side hath drawn many swords.[3]

In this last sentence Donne reveals his sympathies and those of his

---

[1] *Letters*, pp. 21–2. [2] Ibid., p. 224.
[3] *Sermons*, ii, no. 11, ll. 477–89, 502–6, pp. 248–9; see also pp. 31–6.

auditors; although the ambassador was being sent as an impartial arbitrator, nearly all England and most of those close to him in his entourage were whole-heartedly on the side of the Bohemians.

In preparing to set out Donne was sorely beset by apprehensions. It was true enough that his children were ill provided for, and that their future was uncertain, but he seems to have been haunted by fears that he would not return. He told Lady Montgomery that he was 'going out of the Kingdom, and perchance out of the world'; Sir Robert Ker was to keep *Biathanatos* for him 'if I live', and he told the Benchers of Lincoln's Inn that he would pray 'That if I never meet you again till we have all passed the gate of death, yet in the gates of heaven, I may meet you all'. 'I goe into the mouth of such adversaries, as I cannot blame for hating me, the Jesuits, and yet I go', he wrote to Goodyer; and in the 'Hymne to Christ, at the Authors last going into Germany' he seems to be weighed down by fears of shipwreck or drowning. Yet in his more sober moments he can hardly have thought that he was in danger of becoming a prisoner in the hands of the Inquisition, and the storm and shipwreck of the 'Hymne' may be there as much for their effectiveness as an image of his submission to the will of God as because he really feared them. Even so, in all this it is difficult not to see the sick fancies of a troubled mind. It fully confirms Walton's account of Donne's bad health and low spirits in the years immediately succeeding the death of his wife.

When Doncaster had gone as ambassador to France in 1616 he had taken with him an immense train and, it was said, 'twenty speciall suits of apparell for so many dayes abode'.[1] Much of this sort of display was curbed in 1619, since the embassy had to wear mourning for the Queen. Its size, however, can scarcely have been any smaller, since its mission was at least as important and, in the words of a contemporary, Doncaster had with him 'a great many Noblemens Sons, and other Personages of *quality*, that the *Germans* might admire the *glory* of the *English*, as wel as the *French* did in his last *Ambassage*'.[2] No list of its members appears to have survived, though Doncaster refers in one place to 'the Lordes and Knightes . . .

[1] Chamberlain, *Letters*, ii. 13.
[2] Arthur Wilson, *History of Great Britain*, p. 154.

that honor me with their company', and in another to the physician and cooks who were there in a humbler capacity.[1] The one lord specifically mentioned is Lord Lisle, the eldest son of the Earl of Leicester and Doncaster's brother-in-law; his name is mentioned because he had to return before the conclusion of the embassy. Among the knights were Sir Robert Killigrew, Sir Robert Knollys (more than once entrusted with important messages), and Sir Charles Rich, the last two of whom were knighted by James at Theobalds just before the embassy left. Francis Nethersole, one of Doncaster's secretaries who travelled to and fro with dispatches, was knighted during the course of the embassy. Among the gentlemen were William Norreys (included for his special knowledge of Bohemia) and Peter Killigrew, a young kinsman of Sir Robert, who also carried dispatches. But there were many others, and twenty-five to thirty carriages were needed to convey them all into Brussels when they made their ceremonial entry. Thus it can be taken for granted that the embassy, with all its attendants and servants, was large enough to warrant the inclusion of a chaplain not only to minister to the spiritual needs of this company of Englishmen abroad, but also to establish relations with some of the main Protestant divines on the Continent and to advise the ambassador on problems of religion.

Certainly the embassy was a costly one. Doncaster was to receive an allowance of £6 a day as against the £4 a day allowed to Sir Edward Herbert, who went as ambassador to France at the same time. Doncaster received an advance of £500 on his allowance, and an additional £2,000 in March towards his expenses; in April a further £12,000 was granted to him. Of this, it may be added, £2,333. 6s. 8d. was still owing to him two years later.[2] In spite of the generosity of his allowances Doncaster subsequently protested that 'My last yeirs servise in Germany, though it werre chargeable to his Majesty, and that I housbanded matters with all possible frugality, yet it imployed of my owne poore meanes above his Majesties allouance at the least ten thousand pounds.'[3] At least we

---

[1] *Letters and other Documents &c.*, ed. Gardiner, First Series, pp. 174 and 96.

[2] Privy Seal Docket Books, P.R.O., Index 6744.

[3] *Letters and other Documents &c.*, ed. Gardiner, Second Series, Camden Society, xcviii (1868), p. 191.

can say that on this journey Donne must have enjoyed not merely every comfort but every luxury that was available to travellers in the early part of the seventeenth century.

Another symptom of his low spirits can perhaps be seen in the fact that, after making his farewells, he served notice on some of his friends that he did not intend to write: 'If I write no letters into *England* out of these parts, I cannot be without your pardon, if I write not to you, but if I write to any and leave you out, lay all the faults which you have ever pardoned in me, to my charge again. I foresee some reasons, which may make me forbeare; but no slacknesse of mine own, shall.'[1] Practically none of Donne's letters from this journey survive, in contrast to the quite considerable number from the journey of 1611–12 with the Drurys, so it is probable that very few were written. Certainly, news of the progress of the embassy would have circulated rapidly in London, so that his family and friends would soon have been informed had anything serious happened to him; hence perhaps letters were unnecessary. Still, almost nothing is known of Donne's feelings and reactions during the eight months for which he was absent from England. Fortunately, however, the progress of the embassy can be traced in detail partly from the State Papers, and partly from Doncaster's own papers, which are pre-served in the British Museum.[2]

Apparently it was not until 4 May that Doncaster was ready to set out. 'Yf you be not already departed foorth of London,' wrote Mr. Secretary Calvert to him on that day, 'you should sett forward to morrow morning betymes without fayle, or else blame your self.' But he had already left, and the letter overtook him at Gravesend. It was intended that he should go first to Brussels and present himself at the Archduke's court, and then go on to The Hague, where Sir Dudley Carleton had already taken a house for his staff. But winds were unfavourable and shipping was not available; Doncaster was soon complaining of 'lying idly here [at Gravesend], as I feare I shall doe yet some dayes'.[3]

---

[1] *Letters*, p. 223. The addressee is given as Sir Thomas Lucy, but was pretty certainly Goodyer. The 'reasons' may also have included diplomatic protocol.

[2] i.e. in *Letters and other Documents &c.*, ed. Gardiner, First and Second Series, and Egerton MSS. 2592–3.

[3] MS. Egerton 2592, ff. 40, 42. Joseph Hall refers to the route originally proposed

Meanwhile an incident occurred which curiously illuminates the conduct of state business in the reign of James I. William Trumbull, the English envoy in Brussels, had written for certain instructions which were to be conveyed to him not on paper but by word of mouth from Doncaster. The subject had been discussed during Doncaster's final audience with the King—and then it was discovered that Trumbull's letter had disappeared. The King, apparently, was angry and upset, and Doncaster took his leave in an atmosphere of somewhat less than the usual cordiality he was wont to expect from his sovereign. At Gravesend, however, he was relieved by a sentence at the end of one of Sir George Calvert's letters:

As I was concluding this long letter, his Majesty sent for me againe, and shewing me Mr Trumbuls letter, willed me to write vnto your Lordshipp that the Prince seeking for other papers this morning in his Majestys Bedchamber found that very letter in one of the wyndowes behind a cushion, which you thought you had putt vp in your pockett.

This letter stimulated Doncaster's memory, and he replied:

The place where that vnlucky letter of Mr Trumbulls was found, hath now put me in remembrance, that on Saterday when I presented my selfe to receyue his Majesties directions to the contents, I tooke the wicked paper out of my pocket in a readines and his Majesty commanding me at the instant to fetch him a drinke I layd it downe on the table, and by reason of his Majesties sudden going abroad forgot it then there and euer since.

The incident was not immediately forgotten, and several days later Buckingham wrote:

his Majesty was as glad as your selfe could a bene when the prince found troumbles letter notwithstanding of all his chafing before for thereby he saue [saw] it was not your falt of care but onely confusion in being imployed in another of his seruises in the meane time.

After this episode it will be no surprise that Doncaster had been allowed to set out without the cipher he was to use in his secret correspondence, and had to write back urgently for a copy of it.

for the embassy in a letter to Dr. Ward, Master of Sidney Sussex College, at the Synod of Dort: 'My Lo. of Doncaster will shortly see you in his way to Germanye, whither he goes Ambass. D^r. Dun goes his Chaplaine' (Bodleian Library, MS. Tanner 74, fo. 113).

The letter of Buckingham which has just been quoted from continued: 'his Majesty allso prayeth you to hast you now away since hee hath giuen direction that if the wind will serue not other-waye yee may go through the Archduckes contrie at the nerest to heidelberge'. In the meantime Doncaster had moved from Graves-end to Canterbury, from which he hoped to take ship at Margate; then, under the urging of this letter, he went to Dover, where he found that the Venetian ambassador had taken all the convenient shipping. At last, on 12 May, he was able to embark with only a portion of his staff on a ship which landed him at Calais the next day. The irksome delay had made it even clearer than before that he could not afford to lose any more time, and he had had to write to Carleton regretting his inability to visit The Hague, though he was still expecting to pay his respects to the Archduke at Brussels.

At Dover Doncaster and his party met Lady Bedford, who had come there to meet Lady Harrington, and at Calais they found Lady Harrington, on her way home from the Palatinate. She and her husband had accompanied Princess Elizabeth to Heidelberg after her marriage, and had remained in her service; now the widowed Lady Harrington was returning home. At Calais, too, they received an official visit of welcome from the governor who, Doncaster reported, treated them 'with all sort of humanity, and some very extraordinary by leading me, and the most of my Company into the Cittadell, which is here an vnusuall curtesy to strangers of what quality soever'.[1]

Arthur Wilson relates an incident which probably suggests very well the flavour of travelling with the ambassador, and something of the interest, and the diversion, which Donne found in the ex-perience. The story may be true enough, though clearly Wilson did not know, or had forgotten, that the embassy had changed its intended route. He adds a character sketch of the man with whom Donne was to spend most of the year in close association:

The King was modest, and allmost ashamed to tell the Parliament, how much money the Viscount *Doncasters* Journey cost, therefore he minces it into a small proportion. But this we know, when he landed at *Roterdam*, the first night and morning, before he went to the *Hague*,

[1] MS. Egerton 2592, ff. 39, 43, 55, 44, 70.

his Expences [for] those two meals, in the Inn where he lay, came to above a thousand Gilders, which is a hundred pounds sterling. And the Innkeeper at the *Peacock* at *Dort* (hoping he would make that his way into *Germany*) made great Provisions for him, upon no other Order, but a bare Fancy; and the *Ambassadour* taking his way by *Utricht*, the Innkeeper of *Dort* followed him, complaining that he was much prejudiced by his baulking that Town: For hearing of a great *Ambassadours* coming, and what he had expended at *Roterdam*, I made (saith he) Preparations suitable, and now they will lye on my hands: Which coming to *Doncasters* ear, he commanded his *Steward* to give him thirty pounds sterling, and never tasted of his Cup. And we have been assured by some of his Train, that his very Carriages could not cost so little as threescore pounds a day. . . .

But truly (set those vanities of *Grandure* aside, for the honor, though not profit of his Master) He was a Gentleman every way compleat. His Bounty was adorned with Courtesie, his Courtesie, not affected, but resulting from a naturall Civility in him. His Humbleness set him below the Envy of most, and his Bounty brought him into esteem with many. A true Courtier for complying, and one that had Language enough to be *reall* as well as *formall*; for he could personate both to the height of *expression*. So that he was very fit for his imployment, though it were purchased at a dear rate.[1]

From Calais the ambassador and his train went on to Antwerp, where Doncaster had to wait two days for the baggage to arrive. They were now, of course, within the territories of the Archduke, and intended to go directly from there to Brussels. It appeared, however, that the Archduke was unwell, and that an audience would not be possible until his health had improved. Nevertheless the embassy was received into Brussels with a great display of honour; a group of high officials 'accompanied with a good number of the principall nobility in towne' met them on the outskirts of the city 'with some 25 or 30 coaches to accommodate my trayne at my entrance'. A house had been got ready for the embassy but, as the Archduke's special representative had not been similarly lodged in England, Doncaster deemed it wisest to decline, 'pretending the promise I had long since made to put myselfe under my master's agent's roofe, where I had accordingly already bestowed my bag-

[1] *History of Great Britain*, pp. 153–4.

gage'.[1] Doncaster was, in fact, much plagued by matters of protocol during the embassy; an ambassador had to be extremely sensitive of his master's credit and reputation, and to maintain it abroad with all the finesse which a fine gentleman was expected to show in defending his own honour.

The audience with the Archduke took place on 26 May not at Brussels but at Mariemont, about fifty miles to the south, where the Archduke had been confined by his illness. After first paying his respects to the Infanta, Doncaster went next to see the Archduke, who received him sitting in a chair. Doncaster was disconcerted to find that there was no chair provided for him but that he had to remain standing throughout the interview; he was, in fact, receiving the identical treatment that had recently (during James's illness) been accorded to the Archduke's envoy in England. The first audience was a purely formal one, but it was followed by a second on the next day. In it Doncaster represented James's interests as coinciding with the Archduke's, since he 'was desirous to re-establish King Ferdinand in his kingdome, though he were of a divers religion'; accordingly he besought from the Archduke letters to Ferdinand endorsing the embassy and its aims. These the Archduke readily promised, and Doncaster came away feeling that he had secured a real diplomatic advantage. It is to be feared that he overestimated the Archduke's cordiality, and put far too much weight on the polite speeches of the courtiers, who told him only what they thought he would like to hear, as when they reported that at Brussels Ferdinand was 'valued to be but a silly Jesuited soule, and the Archduke hath absolutely refused to transfer his estate in Austria upon him, but hath made him governor for his Highnes'.[2]

From Brussels the embassy moved on to Cologne, where they took boat up the Rhine to Frankfurt. The boatman had promised to complete the journey in four days and was almost as good as his word, for he took only half a day longer. They arrived at Frankfurt on 8/18 June, and there Doncaster learned that the Elector was not at Heidelberg but at Heilbronn attending a meeting of the Princes

[1] *Letters and other Documents &c.*, First Series, pp. 94–6.
[2] Ibid., pp. 103, 107.

of the Evangelical Union, a defensive alliance of the Protestant states, in which Frederick had from the first taken a leading role. Two days later Doncaster entered the Elector's dominions; at once the Princess Elizabeth sent coaches to bring the embassy to Heidelberg, and informed Doncaster that lodgings had been made ready for him in the castle. Doncaster was reluctant to accept, lest 'by kissing her Highnes' handes first (as the manner at Bruxelles is) I should seeme as in his Ma*jes*ties name to declare her right of precedence', and so asked permission to lodge in the town until the Elector's return. But Elizabeth overrode all such scruples by the simple expedient of forbidding markets and innkeepers to sell him any provisions, so he had no recourse but to yield.

Doncaster stayed in Heidelberg for nine days. The Elector posted over from Heilbronn to see him on Saturday 12/22 June and gave him a special audience the next morning 'early before [the] sermon'. Doncaster was much attracted by the young Prince, whom he described as 'muche beyond his yeirs, religious, wise, active, and valiant', and responded warmly to the Elector's account of the dangers which threatened the Union. He was learning, too, 'that it was the common judgement of all wise men here, my mediation to perswade them to hearken to a treaty would prove a tough piece of worke, and no way likely to take effect'; hence he foresaw the need of a firm and energetic policy of aid to the Protestant cause if his overtures for peace proved unsuccessful. In forwarding to James an appeal from the Princes of the Union for money and men, he ventured to add his own plea on their behalf, and on the same day he wrote to Buckingham urging their claims, adding, 'to tell your Lordship the plaine trewth, the reason of his Ma*jes*ties tenderness in respect of the mediation he interposeth is not satisfactory heare, seinge the King of Spayne, who hath the same reason, doth not spare notwithstandinge to assist King Ferdinand'. Nevertheless, he was still determined to carry out his mission to the best of his ability, and high-spiritedly declared that 'the world hath not so much hope of the effect of my negotiation as I have'.[1]

During the embassy's stay at Heidelberg letters as well as dispatches reached them from home. Among Doncaster's letters was

---

[1] *Letters and other Documents &c.*, First Series, pp. 130–1, 118, 133, 120, 137.

one written just over a week after his departure by the Earl of Pembroke, full of Court news and gossip: 'my Lord of Lenox made a great supper to the french Embassador this night here, & even now all the company are at the play, which I being tender harted could not endure to see so soone after the loss of my old acquaintance Burbadg', and by way of postscript he added: 'I beseech your Lordship commend my best loue to Mr Doctor Dunn.'[1] The Earl of Pembroke was, according to Aubrey, 'a most magnificent and brave Peer'; to Clarendon he was 'the most universally loved and esteemed of any man of that age'. He was also 'a good Scholar, and delighted in Poetrie: and did sometimes (for his Diversion) write some Sonnets and Epigrammes, which deserve Commendation: . . . He was of an Heroiq, and publick Spirit, Bountiful to his Friends, and Servants, and a great Encourager of Learned Men '[2] His friendship with Donne is therefore not surprising, though this warm message is the only surviving evidence of it. Donne, on his side, is known to have possessed a number of Pembroke's poems in manuscript,[3] and the Earl's verses were edited by Donne's son. The claim to kinship made by the younger Donne was doubtless acknowledged by the Earl to Donne himself, and in spite of differences of rank and fortune relations between the two families may well have been closer than has been suspected.

At Heidelberg Donne also received a packet of letters, for a communication from Abraham Williams, Doncaster's steward, to one of his master's secretaries, requests his correspondent to do him the favour of 'delyvering the inclosed to Mr. Doctor Donne togeather with my love and service'. Even though Donne was a poor correspondent during his absence, his friends evidently did not forget him altogether. Donne also preached a sermon to the Elector and Electress and the English-speaking members of the household, as well, no doubt, as to the members of the embassy, on Wednesday 16/26 June. The sermon does not seem to have survived, in spite of the caption at the beginning of Sermon 20 in *XXVI Sermons*: 'Two Sermons, to the Prince and Princess *Palatine*, the Lady *Elizabeth* at

---

[1] MS. Egerton 2592, fo. 81. Burbage had died as long before as 13 March.

[2] John Aubrey, *Brief Lives*, ed. O. L. Dick (1949), pp. 145–6.

[3] The Hawthornden MS. of Donne's poems (cf. pp. 198–9 above) also contains several of Pembroke's.

Heydelberg, when I was commanded by the King to wait upon my
L. of *Doncaster* in his Embassage to *Germany*. *First Sermon as we went
out*, June 16. 1619.'[1] It is a pity it is not extant, for Donne can hardly
have been able to refer to the books he usually had in his study, so
that the sermon probably had less patristic learning than those he
preached in England.

When Doncaster and his train left Heidelberg three days later
the Elector had already returned to the conference at Heilbronn.
Doncaster's next task was to present himself to Ferdinand and, if
possible, obtain from him terms which would serve as a basis for
negotiation. The Count Mansfeld, however, had just been defeated
near Budweis, so that the tide seemed to be turning against the
Bohemians, and Ferdinand would be likely to be less willing to
negotiate than he might have been a little earlier. Besides, Ferdinand was preparing to leave Vienna to come to Frankfurt for the
imperial election, and the embassy's best hope was to meet him on
the way. Accordingly, Doncaster set out eastwards, realizing that
he would probably have time to pay his respects on the way to the
Duke of Bavaria at Munich. The Duke Maximilian was a Catholic,
but his family was closely allied to that of the Elector. His power and
influence were considerable, and he had always looked with a jealous
eye on the ambitions of the Hapsburgs. Besides, he was talked of as
a possible imperial candidate in opposition to Ferdinand. Clearly
he was worth sounding out.

Within a day or so of leaving Heidelberg Doncaster must have

---

[1] *Sermons*, ii, no. 12, at p. 250. Potter and Simpson point out in their introduction
that only one of the two sermons can have survived, but raise further doubts (pp.
36–7) as to whether this one can be the sermon to which the caption refers. They
note that it contains no reference to the occasion on which, or the persons before
whom, it was preached, and that Donne himself mentions in the sermon that the text
was one appropriated by the Church to the celebration of Advent. But, they continue, 'since the burden of proof rests on any editor who believes the heading to be
wrongly placed, and since the present editors have no such proof and have no suggestion as to any other more probable date or occasion, the heading and sermon are
in our edition accepted as they stand, though with some misgivings'. There is, however, one decisive piece of evidence in the sermon itself. Lines 535–53 (p. 265) contain
a direct confutation of Calvinistic doctrine, and it is incredible that Donne as an
official member of an embassy would have been so tactless as to assail in this manner
beliefs to which the Palatinate was still strongly sympathetic. It is therefore almost
certain that the label or title-leaf of the two sermons preached at Heidelberg became
detached and in the printed edition was prefixed to the wrong sermon.

passed through Stuttgart. The sole surviving memento of his visit there is the unique copy (now in the Huntington Library) of a quarto pamphlet in verse, consisting of a single sheet, entitled *A Panegyricke to the most honourable and renowned Lord, the Lord Hays Vicount of Doncaster, His Maiesties of Great-Brittaine Ambassadour in Germanie. Sung by the Rhine, Interpreted by George Rodolfe Weckherlin Secr[etarie] to his High[nesse] of Wirtemberg.*[1] Weckherlin had spent several years in England, and had married an English wife. He returned to England some years later, and put his knowledge of languages at the service of the state by becoming an under-secretary of the Council. He survived the changes of government and died in 1653; his death created a vacancy that was filled, through Milton's influence, by Andrew Marvell. But in 1619 he was thirty-five years old, and eager to show his command of the English tongue. The *Panegyricke* consists of fourteen stanzas in *ottava rima*; the manner is Spenserian. The lines do not always scan very readily, and Weckherlin's English syntax is sometimes uncertain. He (or rather, the Rhine, which seems to be envisaged in the manner of one of Drayton's river deities) praises Doncaster's attitude towards wealth; this was perhaps risky, since Doncaster must have been aware of the charges of extravagance levelled against him. The peroration rises to heights that probably provoked the mirth of the English courtiers:

> Thus now my Nymfs, nay all the peoples stout
> Of Germanie, which your presence doeth grace,
> Joyfully runne and sing you round about
> (Glad with their armes and harts you to embrace)
> With minds and mouths all with mee crying out:
> Ay-during bee the happie health and grace!
> Still florishing may bee the praise and bays
> (As the desarts bee great) of Mylord HAYS!

No doubt Doncaster accepted this with well-bred urbanity, and (in spite of the Rhine's avowal that she had no ulterior motives) suitably rewarded the author. Despite this slightly ridiculous effort, Weckherlin has an established place in the history of German poetry. It is not known to what extent he was acquainted

[1] The colophon states that the pamphlet was 'Printet at Stutgart by John-Wyrich Rösslin, Anno M.DC.XIX'.

with Donne, but he rendered several of Donne's epigrams into German.[1]

From Stuttgart the embassy moved on at an easy pace to Ulm, and from there to Augsburg, where they stayed two days. Here Doncaster received confirmation of the news that Ferdinand had already left Vienna. There was still, however, plenty of time to consult with the Duke of Bavaria, as Munich, his capital, lay midway between Augsburg and Salzburg, where he proposed to meet Frederick. The Duke of Bavaria was not one of the potentates to whom he had letters of credence but he had been supplied with several blanks for use in emergencies, and it was not difficult for a secretary to fill in one of them suitably. The embassy was received with all honour; they were met outside the city by Count Tilly and a large cavalry escort and were lodged in the Duke's palace, 'which', wrote Doncaster, 'I thinke is second to none in Europe'. He was not able to see the Duke at once 'because his Highnes, being in a course of phisicke, could not come from his countrey house', but he returned the following day and gave Doncaster audience. In the meanwhile Doncaster had learned from the officers of the court that Maximilian had no ambitions for the imperial crown, so he did not feel that there was anything to be gained by raising that topic. The audience therefore consisted mainly of an exchange of compliments, though Maximilian readily promised to use any influence he had with Ferdinand to incline him towards peace. He also told Doncaster that Ferdinand was travelling by a roundabout route because of the disturbed state of the country, and cordially invited the English embassy to remain in Munich until more certain news of his approach had arrived. But Doncaster refused, 'because the least lingring bringeth me more vexation of minde then any travell can give my body', and so by the advice of Tilly he determined on a route which would make it reasonably certain that he could not miss Ferdinand. So he set out eastwards again, leaving Lord Lisle to return home with a verbal report of his activities to date.[2]

It had been Doncaster's intention to go from Munich to Wasser-

[1] In *Gaistliche und weltliche Gedichte*, Amsterdam, 1641. One of the epigrams translated is 'A licentious person', and Weckherlin's rendering of the title 'An den Pfarrern Schandflecken' suggests that he interpreted 'person' as 'parson'.

[2] *Letters and other Documents &c.*, First Series, pp. 144–8.

burg, on the Inn, and from there to go downstream by boat to the Danube and then down the Danube as far as Vienna if necessary. At Wasserburg, however, he learned from three separate sources that Ferdinand was expected in Salzburg in a few days' time, so he altered his plans and arrived in Salzburg on 5/15 July to find that the King was to arrive there by noon on the following day. Ferdinand was riding post with an escort of about fifty men; his movements were rapid and unannounced because of the disturbed state of his dominions. It must have given Doncaster great relief that he had really managed to intercept the object of his journey, and that the interview which was to determine the success or failure of the whole embassy was at hand. He sent one of his staff to meet the King and to request an audience, which was granted within only a few hours of Ferdinand's arrival. Doncaster knew that the fortunes of war had turned against the Bohemians and that this was not the most favourable time to try to persuade Ferdinand into making peace, but, he wrote: 'Supposing, and I doubt too truly, this to be the face of the affayres in Bohemia, and that the King will certainly be Emperor in a short space, and he assured of it in shorter, there needed no long deliberation to resolve me that unless I could make a good step into the treaty at the first, it was likely afterward to goe slowly on.' So, as soon as the courtesies were over, he begged permission to pass on to business, and plunged at once into the objects of his mission. As he continued the King, though still cordial, became more and more unwilling to give any specific replies, and said that the issues raised by Doncaster could not be settled without the consent of his council. He said that he thought that 'his Majesty of Great Brittayne was not well informed how the Bohemians his subjects had behaved themselves toward him', and promised to supply Doncaster with a full account of the facts, but he refused to commit himself to any acceptance of James's offer to negotiate a peace. All he would do was to refer Doncaster to a member of his council and to promise another audience on the following day.[1]

When the councillor came, Doncaster had to listen to a long recital of the events in Bohemia, and was then told that the King

[1] Op. cit., pp. 158–9.

had submitted the arbitration of the whole issue to the four secular imperial electors and so could not accept the intervention of the King of England. To this Doncaster was able to reply that, though the matter might have been referred to the four princes of the Empire, it had never been undertaken by them, and that he knew at first hand from two of them at least that they would gladly accept James's mediation. Doncaster then took the offensive, and asked for terms for a cessation of hostilities which he might present to the representatives of Bohemia who were expected to come to Frankfurt for the imperial election. He even offered, if authorized to do so, to hasten to Prague to secure minimum terms from the Bohemians if Ferdinand would consider them at Frankfurt. The councillor was nonplussed; Doncaster clearly won a verbal victory, but succeeded in getting no more by way of reply from the councillor than that he would make a full report to the King, who would give his answer at the next day's audience. The following day Doncaster restated his requests to the King himself, backed 'by all the niew arguments a nightes meditation could suggest to me'. But his words had no effect; nothing that he said 'could move his Majesty one hayres breadth out of the circle wherein it seemes both he and his Counsellor were charmed to keepe, which is a generall assurance that at Francfurt, when the Spanish Ambassador and the Princes nominated to be arbitrators shall meete, his Ma*jesty* will harken further to our Master's intervention and then give him satisfaction'. Doncaster clearly realized that he was being fobbed off with fine phrases, and in his dispatch reporting the interviews he asked for instructions as to what he should do if he could obtain neither treaty nor truce at Frankfurt. As in duty bound, however, he proposed to make every effort to achieve the object of his mission.[1]

Though Doncaster can have had few illusions left after his interviews with Ferdinand, he continued to act with speed and resolution. He immediately sent a member of his staff to Prague to urge the Bohemian government to send representatives to Frankfurt with refutation of Ferdinand's allegations against them and 'such modest conditions for the making of a peace as may render the King inexcusable if he refuse to grant them'.[2] It was essential that he

----

[1] Op. cit., pp. 162–3.   [2] Op. cit., p. 167.

should be in or near Frankfurt as soon as possible so that nothing concerning him should be done in his absence, and in 'seven dayes, at twelve houres travelling the day' he reached Nuremberg ahead of Ferdinand, in spite of the latter's twenty-four hour start. From there he sent 'the greater part of [his] trayne' to Hanau, about twelve miles east of Frankfurt, where arrangements had been made for them during the period of the imperial election. He himself, 'with the Lordes and Knightes only that honor me with their company', went first to Heidelberg to report on the result of his interviews with Ferdinand to the Elector Palatine.[1]

The imperial electors, the diplomatic representatives, all with their crowds of attendants, as well as a multitude of curious travellers, were beginning to converge on Frankfurt. Ferdinand arrived on 18 July, Doncaster on the 20th, and the Spanish ambassador on the 23rd. Doncaster immediately applied to Ferdinand's councillors for the answers he had been promised and wrote to the Spanish ambassador to ask for an interview. He saw the ambassador on the 26th, and after much pressing extorted from him a promise that he would urge Ferdinand to a cessation of hostilities after the election, but, as Doncaster afterwards opined, more 'out of shame to eate his owne wordes so hott, then out of any good affection to satisfye me'. Then more than a week went by without any further communications, and at last, on 3/13 August, Doncaster received Ferdinand's promised reply together with a long statement of the offences of the Bohemians. The answer was, as Doncaster put it, 'in stuffe the very same with that I had at Saltzburg, and surely not much mended in fashion'. As a last resort he saw the Spanish ambassador once more, with far less satisfaction than before. Then, finally, Norreys returned from a mission even less successful than had been feared. He had been dismissed after a long stay at Prague 'without any manner of answere, or so much as thankes for my advertising them so carefully what had passed betweene the King and me'; indeed, there were many 'that sayd the mighty Monarch of Great Britayne might have done better to have assisted them with men or money then with an Ambassage which would prove in the end of no benefitt to them'. If Doncaster had kept any shreds of hope that he might

[1] Op. cit., p. 174.

accomplish anything they were now finally dissipated, and in his dispatch of 7/17 August he spoke as downrightly as he dared. The King of Spain had 'never intended to make other use of our master's interposition then by that meanes to diverte his royall intentions to assist the Bohemians', and even if the imperial side had formerly felt that James's efforts at peacemaking could be of use, the situation had changed, and they now intended 'to governe their counsells by their present advantages, not their past engagements'. There was, in fact, nothing further that he could do, and he proposed, after paying his respects at Heidelberg, to retire to the Spa during the imperial election, and there await further instructions from England, though he left behind him the bulk of his train as a pledge of his return. Doncaster's next dispatch was written on the way to the Spa at Cologne on 16/26 August and completed at Aix-la-Chapelle on the 18/28th.[1] On the first of these two days the Elector Frederick was chosen King of Bohemia and on the second Ferdinand became Emperor, and both sides were committed to a struggle from which there was no withdrawal.

Donne seems to have been in attendance on Doncaster both when he paid a brief visit to Heidelberg after his return from Salzburg and when he retired to the Spa. Though apparently neither has survived, Donne's note makes it clear that he preached two sermons before the Prince and Princess Palatine, 'the First Sermon as we went out'. The second, presumably (though not necessarily), was preached on the way back, and the only possible date for it was 18 July, which was a Sunday and a day on which Doncaster was at Heidelberg.[2] He must also have gone with Doncaster towards the Spa, for he wrote a letter to Toby Mathew from Cologne on the way.

Mathew had written to Doncaster early in July offering his services and suggesting that he could be of help in gathering valu-

---

[1] Op. cit., pp. 192, 197, 201, 208–9.

[2] The Elector left the following day to join his army in the Upper Palatinate, and when Doncaster went to Heidelberg on the way to Spa it was expressly for the purpose of 'kissing her Highnes handes', since Frederick was still with the army. Doncaster made one other visit to the Elector at Heidelberg, in mid September, but this was a secret visit, on a single day and 'with one onely servant of my chamber'. There would have been no opportunity for a sermon at Heidelberg on the way back from Graz because by this time Frederick and Elizabeth were in Prague and Donne would surely have referred to them now as King and Queen of Bohemia.

able news for the ambassador; apparently he also wrote to Donne about the same time. Doncaster, however, had received a letter from William Trumbull in Brussels reporting that Mathew had recently offered himself as a candidate for the prefecture of the sodality of the English Jesuits at Louvain, and in replying Doncaster had clearly suggested that this was an activity which disqualified Mathew from the society of loyal Englishmen. To this Mathew answered at once, enclosing a copy of the rules of the sodality and insisting that such activity was in no way political. 'I craue leaue', he wrote, 'to putt my selfe vpon *the* ingenuity and prudence of Doctour Dunne, whether in beinge of *th*is Sodality, I deserue to be any otherwise obnoxious, then for *the* exercise of my relligion.' Donne must have received Mathew's letter about 14/24 July, but he delayed answering for a full month; presumably both he and Doncaster had made further inquiries in the meantime and had decided that it would not be indiscreet to resume relations with the exile.[1] Donne's letter was a very skilful one; he made it quite clear that he was aware that Mathew had more than once spoken contemptuously of him behind his back, but that he still felt affectionately enough towards him to ignore their religious differences and pick up the broken friendship:

SIR,

At *Ratisbone* I had your Letter from *Brussel's*; and, in it, you. For, my former knowledge of your ingenuitie, and mine own conscience of having demerited in nothing toward you, are assurances to me, that your professions are in earnest. I dare put my selfe upon the testimony of very many very good Companies in *England*, where your Person, and your Historie, have been the discourse, that I have never forsaken your honour and reputation. And you may be pleased to make this some argument of my disposition toward you, that when I have been told, that you have not been so carefull of me abroad, I have not been easie in beleeving it; and when at some times, the authoritie of the reporter, hath brought me to a half-belief of it, I have found other excuses in your behalfe, than a meer dis-affection to me: and now I am safelie returned to my first station again, not to beleeve it. If it could be possible that any occasion of doing you a reall service, might be presented me, you should see, that that Tree which was rooted in

---

[1] MS. Egerton 2592, ff. 200, 127, 237, 238.

love, and alwaies bore leaves, readie to shadow and defend from others malice, would bear fruit also. You know, we say in the Schools, that Grace destroys not Nature: we may say too, that forms of Religion destroy not moralitie, nor civill offices. That which I add, I am farre from applying to you, but it is true, That we are fallen into so slack and negligent times, that I have been sometimes glad to hear, that some of my friends have differed from me in Religion. It is some degree of an union to be united in a serious meditation of God, and to make any Religion the rule of our actions. Our sweet and blessed Saviour bring us by his way, to his end! And be you pleased to be assured, that no man desires to renew, or continue, or encrease a friendship with you more than [I].[1]

Mathew's principal motive, no doubt, was to win Doncaster's favour in order to get his banishment repealed, and he was accordingly content to accept Donne's letter at its face value. He next sent his friend and co-religionist George Gage to Doncaster to plead his case. His letter acknowledging Donne's and at the same time introducing Gage has survived, as has also a later one sending thanks to Donne both from himself and Gage.[2] It is possible that Mathew saw Doncaster (and Donne too) at Spa; in any case, the relations thus established with Doncaster stood him in good stead, and he corresponded fairly frequently with Doncaster from this time until he returned to England.

After spending about ten days at the Spa Doncaster moved on to Maastricht. It shows how short-staffed he was that he was obliged to ask Donne to help him with his correspondence. On 31 August/10 September Donne wrote to Sir Dudley Carleton at The Hague;[3] the main concern of the letter is the remittance of Doncaster's funds, which were now being sent to Holland through Carleton's hands. A week later they were still in Maastricht, where they were awaiting the return from England of Doncaster's secretary, Francis Nethersole; Doncaster was on the point of setting out on a new mission, that of congratulating the new emperor on his election, and Donne now knew that his return to England would be delayed for some months. The long vacation was coming to an end; Michaelmas

[1] *Tobie Mathew Collection*, pp. 336–7.
[2] Ibid., pp. 273, 276.
[3] *Letters and other Documents &c.*, Second Series, pp. 5–6.

term would soon begin; and Lincoln's Inn would be expecting its preacher. On 9/19 September Doncaster wrote to Secretary Calvert:

I beseeche you be pleased to do Dr Donne this favour for my sake. At the beginninge of the terme he will be expected at Lincoln's Inne, with some impatience, except you write a letter to the Masters of the Bench there, that his coming being by his Ma*jes*ties command, he cannot returne till I do, which they may justly beleeve will be shortly. Mr. Brooke, a person (I thincke) knowne to you, will wayte upon you for such a letter.[1]

At the same time Doncaster himself wrote to the Benchers of Lincoln's Inn, of which he had recently become an honorary member, assuring them that Donne was

not alltogether absent from that Society, now whilest he is with me, who by your fauor, haue the honour of being a member of your Society. Neither is he absent from the Seruice of Gods Church, and is jn obedience to his Ma*iesti*es Commandement. In my particular I shall receyue it for a Singular fauor from you, that you would so long spare to me from yourselues, a person so necessary to you, and so aggreable to me. I hope to restore him to you, by the middest of Michelmas terme.[2]

As the sequel was to show, Doncaster was unduly hopeful of the date of his return, for he looked forward eagerly to the end of a mission that had now become irksome to him. His letter was duly read out at the first council meeting at Lincoln's Inn in Michaelmas Term (on 14 October), and with the letter 'the whole Benche stood well satisfied the rather for that good hope was giuen that his place should bee from tyme to tyme supplied till his returne'.[3] There is no record, however, to indicate what temporary arrangements were made to fill the pulpit at Lincoln's Inn.

Doncaster left Maastricht on 9/19 September, went directly to Cologne, where he stayed only two hours, and embarked on a five-day boat trip up the Rhine to Frankfurt. At Frankfurt he learned that there was no chance of overtaking Ferdinand and discharging his mission quickly; furthermore, the departing princes and other notables had hired all the carriages within some miles radius, and

---

[1] Op. cit., p. 10. [2] MS. Egerton 2593, fo. 21.
[3] Black Book No. 7, fo. 5^v; *Black Books*, ii. 212.

they had not yet been returned, so the embassy was compelled to wait until it could obtain conveyance. During this delay Doncaster ordered his staff to put aside their mourning and, as most of them had come outfitted for a much briefer journey than this had proved to be, they all had to buy new clothes. Since most of them were also unprovided to meet such an expense Doncaster had to draw on his own resources and lend them money. 'If it had bene his Ma*jes*ties pleasure to have drawne me directly into Holland, and so home', he observed ruefully, 'the moneys assigned at first would have brought us neere to our journeyes end, yet now it will be otherwise.' But his greatest difficulty was that Ferdinand, travelling quickly and secretly, seemed to have disappeared altogether. Doncaster was uncertain where to look for him: 'Now after Holyrood day we are to beginne our hunting, [he wrote] and that name which his Ma*jes*tie hath sometime given me of Master Hunter appeares now to have been ominously and prophetically given me, who am now to hunt and to search for an Emperor, which seems to have no will to be found.' There seemed to be no better plan than to make all possible haste to Vienna and there try to learn where to go next. Such a journey, however, might well be dangerous, for Bethlen Gabor, at the head of a rebellious Hungarian army, was said to be closing in on the capital.[1]

For the remainder of the embassy the documentary evidence is much more scanty. Doncaster seems to have received his final instructions at Frankfurt. Besides congratulating the Emperor, he was to remind him that the Bohemians were in a stronger position than they had been three months previously; they now had a king whom they had elected (though without James's knowledge or consent) and peace would be far harder to make. The King of England, however, might still be persuaded to act as mediator. Doncaster acted with his usual promptitude. He managed to leave Frankfurt (though he had to leave part of his train behind) before the end of September; he is next heard of as being at Nuremberg (where he expected to find remittances) on the way to Ratisbon, where he proposed to take boat down the Danube to Vienna. At Vienna he made his appearance 'con pompa grande', and was received by the

[1] *Letters and other Documents &c.*, Second Series, pp. 50-1, 55.

Emperor's brother, the Archduke of Austria, who provided him with lodgings and received him with every honour. On 21/31 October he left Vienna for Graz, where the Emperor was said to be.[1]

Ferdinand was indeed at Graz, and here Doncaster fulfilled his mission. The only record of his audience that has survived comes from Donne, who recalled an incident from it in a sermon several years later. 'I have known', he related, 'the greatest Christian Prince, (in Style and Title) even at the Audience of an Ambassador, at the sound of a Bell, kneele downe in our presence and pray; and God forbid, he should be blamed for doing so.'[2] The audience over, Doncaster took his leave with a sense of exhilaration. He felt like a schoolboy released for a well-earned holiday. He was in the southernmost parts of the Emperor's dominions, with northern Italy not far away; he had never been to Italy, so why not at least make a brief visit to Venice? Accordingly he turned southwards with a light heart. But at Pontebba, just inside Venetian territory, a difficulty arose. The Venetians had imposed a quarantine on all foreigners coming from infected territories, and the English party would have to spend several precious days waiting until they could be cleared. Doncaster did not have that much time to spare, so he regretfully turned back. This was on 7/17 November, and two days later he wrote to his old friend Zorzi Giustiniani, Venetian ambassador to the Emperor, begging that the officer who had barred his way should not suffer for doing his duty. In an earlier letter Doncaster spoke of returning by way of Salzburg,[3] but he evidently found that

---

[1] Op. cit., pp. 72–3, 79.

[2] *Sermons*, ix, no. 14, ll. 417–21, p. 325. This has been interpreted as a reference to both Philip II of Spain (T. E. Terrill, 'Spanish Influence on John Donne', unpublished Harvard dissertation, and 'Notes on John Donne's Early Reading', *MLN*, xliii (1928), 318–19) and Henri IV of France (L. Pearsall Smith, *Donne's Sermons—Selected Passages*, 1919, p. 253 n.). But 'the greatest Christian Prince, (in Style and Title)' cannot be anyone but the Emperor of the Holy Roman Empire. The King of Spain was the 'most Catholic King' and the King of France 'the most Christian King' (as Donne well knew; see 'The Bracelet', ll. 27–30), and Donne specifically refers to the superior claims of the Hapsburg monarchy: 'The first of that royall Family, which thinks it selfe the greatest in Christendome at this day, The House of Austrich, had the first marks of their Greatnesse, The Empire, brought into that House, for a particular reverence done to the holy and blessed Sacrament' (*Sermons*, vii, no. 12, ll. 752–5, p. 320). It is reasonable to believe that Donne's reference to 'the greatest Christian Prince' is to an incident that occurred after, and not before, Ferdinand became Emperor.

[3] *Letters and other Documents &c.*, Second Series, pp. 91–3.

it was too late in the season to try to cross the Tyrolean Alps in that direction and had to go back on the road by which he had come. He was reported as having passed through Vienna on his way back from Graz. While there he received a call from the Spanish ambassador, who remarked that the Elector had taken a rash step ('faict un pas chaud') in accepting the crown of Bohemia; to which Doncaster replied that it was not so surprising since Ferdinand, a prudent prince of mature years, had ridden post haste to Frankfurt to be elected emperor. After leaving Vienna Doncaster arrived at Nuremberg on 20/30 November, and six days later was hourly expected at Worms on his way to Heidelberg. The last part of the journey seems to have been made by boat down the Rhine as far as Arnhem, from which Doncaster set forward by slow stages with the intention of paying a courtesy call at The Hague that he had been unable to pay on the journey outwards. On 14 December he was at Haarlem, on the 15th at Leyden, and on the 16th he made his ceremonial entry into The Hague.[1]

There is no report on the result of his conversations with Prince Maurice and the States General; presumably he made an oral report after his return to England. But he was received with great honour, and the respect shown him extended so far as to include his chaplain, who was presented with a gold medal depicting the Synod of Dort, which was struck to be given as a memento to the divines who attended it.[2] Donne also preached a sermon at The Hague on the following Sunday which has survived in an expanded form. Sermons 71 and 72 in *LXXX Sermons* bear the title: 'At the *Haghe* Decemb. 19. 1619. I Preached upon this Text. Since in my sicknesse at *Abrey-hatche* in Essex, 1630, revising my short notes of that Sermon, I digested them into these two.'[3] Presumably Donne preached in the chapel attached to the ambassador's house and in English; if it had been given to a learned Dutch auditory he would be likely to have preached in Latin and not to have used short notes, but to have written out his sermon in full.

---

[1] *Letters and other Documents &c.*, Second Series, pp. 98–9, 97–8, 101–2.

[2] In his will Donne bequeathed 'that Medall of gold of the Synod of Dort ,which the States presented me withall at the *Hague*' to Henry King. A similar medal was bequeathed by Joseph Hall to Emmanuel College, Cambridge, where it is still preserved.   [3] *Sermons*, ii, nos. 13 and 14.

Doncaster and his company reached London on 1 January.[1] On the 8th, wrote Francis Nethersole, he was feasting at his house 'an honourable company', who 'after supper are to be entertayned with a running ballet which the two Marquises [of Buckingham and Hamilton], with other Lords and gentlemen, have at severall nightes dansed at the French Ambassadors, my Lady Hattons, my Lord of Exeter, and my Lord of Warwickes, and are now pleased to doe my Lord the honor to end at Essex house'. The King himself was present, but because of the Christmastide festivities Doncaster had as yet been unable to make a full report. Nevertheless the Spaniards had already charged him with being a principal agent in procuring the crown of Bohemia for the Elector. The King seemed to blow hot and cold, and not to be able to make up his mind what policy to follow. And then Nethersole, reporting these developments to Doncaster's recent host, Sir Dudley Carleton, allows himself a sudden shaft of savage irony, tinged with despair. These, he writes, 'are the inscrutable depths of his Ma*jes*tys incomparable wisedome, to amuse his sonnes enemyes, and I trust will at last appeare such to his friends as all good patriots wishe and pray'.[2] Doncaster's mission had accomplished nothing, and James himself had done nothing, under the delusion that he was trying to restore the peace during nine of the most fateful months in the history of Europe.

---

[1] Chamberlain, *Letters*, ii. 280.
[2] *Letters and other Documents &c.*, Second Series, pp. 132, 134.

XIV

PROMOTION

DONNE returned from Germany to Lincoln's Inn, according to Walton, 'with his sorrows moderated, and his health improved; and there betook himself to his constant course of Preaching'.[1] He would have been back in good time to resume his duties for the Hilary Term, though the earliest sermons for January 1619/20 come at the end of the month. There is a pair of them, for the morning and evening of 30 January.[2] In the evening he announced the beginning of the series of sermons to reconcile such places of Scripture 'as may at first sight seem to differ from one another'; in the first 'we saw how Christ judged all; now we are to see how he judges none; *I judge no man*'.[3] Another such complementary pair of sermons was preached not long afterwards: on Job 19: 26, with its affirmation 'yet in my flesh shall I see God', and on 1 Corinthians 15: 50, where Paul states that 'flesh and blood cannot inherit the kingdom of God'.[4] The first of these two sermons is the earliest in which Donne dwells on the decay of the body in the grave. This part of the sermon arises naturally out of the first part of the text, 'And though, after my skin, wormes destroy this body', yet it by no means gives the tone to the whole discourse; it is rather inserted to enhance the even more powerful climax in which Donne dwells at length on the resurrection. One more sermon belongs to the period immediately following his return from Germany. This is his earliest wedding sermon, and was preached at the beginning of February on the occasion of Sir Francis Nethersole's marriage, which could be celebrated now that the embassy was over. The bride was Sir Henry Goodyer's eldest daughter, and Donne's friendship with both bride and bridegroom made it natural that he should be the one to perform the ceremony and preach the sermon. An account of the marriage

---

[1] *Lives*, p. 54.
[3] Ibid. ii, no. 16, ll. 11–16, p. 325.

[2] *Sermons*, ii, nos. 15 and 16.
[4] Ibid. iii, nos. 3 and 4.

was given by Chamberlain in one of his letters to Sir Dudley Carleton: 'I forgat in my last [of 12 February] that Sir Fra[ncis] Nethersole was then newly maried to Mistris Goodyeare that served the Lady of Bedford who gave her 500^{li} or 700^{li}, besides 500^{li} she bestowed upon them in gloves, which brought in a great contribution of plate to make up a portion which her father Sir Henry could not geve.'[1] Lucy Goodyer was Lady Bedford's godchild but, even so, it is difficult to believe that the Countess could have been as generous as Chamberlain reports.

Donne, then, soon found himself immersed again in his regular employments, and there is little else to record of his life during 1620. He returned to find that good progress was being made towards the new chapel for Lincoln's Inn. The levy had been imposed on all the members of the Society; the earlier committees had been replaced by a group of three members (which included Christopher Brooke) with full power to act; and demolition to clear the site had begun. That Donne was at Keyston for a part of the summer is clear from a letter to Goodyer. At Bedford, on the way back, as he sat at dinner at the inn, he saw Goodyer and some other friends from the window, but thought it wisest not to call on them at Wrest Park, the Earl of Kent's estate, where they were staying. The one scrap of news he added was that he expected later to accompany Viscount Doncaster into the country; the close relations established during the embassy were being maintained.[2] On 20 August Donne was visiting Sir Thomas Grymes at Peckham, for Edward Alleyn wrote in his diary that on that day he 'Herd doc: done att Cambewell & after dynd *with* Sr Tho: grymes; theys & Mr. angell came to dull-[wich] in *th*e after noone'.[3]

The Black Books of Lincoln's Inn show that Donne's position in the Society was not merely that of preacher, but rather that of director of the Society's religious life. The House expected religious

---

[1] Chamberlain, *Letters*, ii. 291, dated 26 Feb.

[2] *Letters*, p. 202. The text reads 'my L. of *Dov*.' but '*Don*.' is almost certainly the right reading. That the letter belongs to 1620 is established almost beyond doubt by the following facts: Hay was made Viscount Doncaster on 5 July 1618 and was created Earl of Carlisle on 13 Sept. 1622; during the summers of 1619, 1621, and 1622 he was abroad, so that 1620 is the only possible year for this letter.

[3] W. Young, *The History of Dulwich College with a Life of the Founder* (1889), ii. 187; Alleyn's diary is MS. IX at the College.

conformity of its members, and refused to call to the bar any who were papists. On 14 November 1620 a certain Peter Clynton was 'respited untill he shall receave the Comunion in the Chappell, and uppon certificat thereof he shall be called'; but two months later, when he had still not taken communion, the minutes assert that 'Mr. Clynton, for that hee is a Popish recusant and will not conforme himselfe, is declared not to bee called to the Barre, and for the same cause is likewise expelled out of this Societie'.[1] Not long afterwards a second such case arose. Mr. Anthony Hunt was ordered to 'attend the Masters of the Benche . . . and to giue them satisfaccon touching his conformitie in Religion'; this he did not do, and on 23 April 1621 the Benchers felt that they could postpone his case no longer. They therefore resolved that

Whereas Mr Anthonie Hunt was by a former order suspended the house, and was to bring a Certificate from Mr Doctor Donne of his Conformitie in Religion and therevpon order was to be taken for his expulsion or continuance in the house, And whereas at this Counsell it appeared that the said Mr Hunt had notice of the said Order, and yet hath neither conferred with the said Mr Doctor Donne nor appeared & made any answeare, Hee is therefore nowe by order of this Counsell absolutelie expelled the house, And this order for his expulsion is to bee published & sett vpon the Skreene.[2]

In yet another case of a somewhat different sort, though there is no mention of Donne's name in the minutes, he must have been very closely concerned. He was, it will be recalled, assisted by a chaplain, Edward May, whose main duties consisted in reading morning prayers at 6 o'clock every morning during term time and in preaching on Sundays during vacations. May's appointment had given general satisfaction, and his salary had been raised. Nothing more is heard of him in the minutes for five years, though Donne's leave of absence to go to Germany must have added considerably to his duties. Then, on 16 October 1621 the Council suddenly took notice of him. Mr. Digges and Mr. Sherfield were 'intreated to read Mr Maye the Chaplens booke and the preambles of the same, and to consider of the scandalles and indiscreet passages therein, conceaved to be taxacious and imputacious to some of this House, and to

---

[1] *Black Books*, ii. 219, 220.   [2] Black Book no. 7, ff. 47, 48.

present and exhibit them at the next Counsell, that hee may bee questioned and examyned about the same'. May's book was a sermon he had preached on the last Sunday of the previous Hilary term, entitled *A Sermon of the Communion of Saints*. It had been entered in the Stationers' Register on 13 June, and thus had appeared early in the summer; hence, because of the intervening long vacation, it could not receive any official attention until Michaelmas term. May had a trick of blending literal and figurative language in a most undisciplined fashion, so that his meaning is often far from clear. But it was the preface more than the sermon itself that gave offence; this was in the form of a mock dedication to an unnamed bishop, and contained an attack on the more puritanically minded members of the Inn, who

grow old in affected-Ignorance, learned mis-interpretation, zealous-malice, and in an holy contempt of all Sacred and spirituall things, as sacred *deriuation of the holy Ghost*; sacred *imposition of hands*, sacred *succession of Bishops and Presbyters*; sacred *orders*; sacred *offices*; sacred *ceremonies*; the sacred *patrimony of the Crucified*; the *necessitie of* sacred *repentance*; th'*Authoritie of* the sacred *Church*: Yea, the sacred *Scepter of Christ himselfe*, and (for which let the world expect the heauy hand of Gods anger) *th'efficacie, necessitie, the life and fruits, the reuerence, and honour oȷ* Sacred *Sacraments* themselues, and of all those *holy-reall Donations*, (though spirituall) which Christ Iesus bequeath'd vnto his Church: O Lord *God of patience, and long-suffering*, what holy thing haue not their hearts prophaned, their tongues blasphem'd, their handes polluted and destroy'd? (Sig. A3).

In the sermon itself (pp. 8-9) he protests against the lot of the clergy:

I am sensible of contempt and persecution, and Greatnesse complaines shee is disgraced, if perchance once a yeare she bee seene in companie of a poore Priest, when as their Greatnes hath made vs poore: yea, now the world takes it selfe, little beholding vnto the Father of *Lights* for his *Starres*; they doubt not but to see the light of life well enough without them. . . .

Then is it a vsurpation of transcendent presumption, not onely to lay hand vpon our Benefices, but our holy Offices beside, as if wee were but Church-men for their ease, as some of them haue Chappels.

The attack is made in general terms, and even then does not seem very offensive, but it must have had a pertinence that can no longer be perceived, for a week after the earlier Council meeting it was resolved 'by the generall voice of all the Masters of the Benche, noe man contradictinge, [that] Mr Maye, who served the House as Chaplen there during pleasure, is amoved and absolutelie discharged of and from his said place'.[1] Donne must have at least acquiesced in May's dismissal and have been consulted by the Benchers, even if he did not take a more active part in securing it.

Donne seems to have returned from Germany not only assured of Doncaster's friendship but also confident that he now had sufficient influence at Court to justify a hope that he would soon achieve promotion to a higher office. Every time a bishop died there was a kind of general post among a segment of the higher dignitaries of the Church, and Donne, now cherishing expectations of a deanery, was eagerly on the watch. On 20 March 1619/20 Chamberlain wrote to Carleton that

Dr. Fotherbie bishop of Salisberie died some eight dayes since, and his bishopricke bestowed on the Dean of Westminster, to whom one Williams deane of Salisberie succeeds, and Dr. Bowles (who pretends a promise of Westminster) must content himself with the deanrie of Salisberie: in the mean time poore Dr. Dun is cast behind hand and fallen from his hopes.[2]

A year later another opportunity occurred with the death of Donne's old friend John King, Bishop of London.[3] Once again Chamberlain reported the current gossip: 'The bishop of London died on Goode Friday. . . . Yt was publikely geven out that Dr. Williams deane of Westminster, had (almost a yeare since) a promise of the place, but now the voyce runs with Dr. Mountain bishop of Lincoln, Dr. Williams to succeed him, Dr. Bolles deane of Salisberie to come to Westminster, and Dr. Dun to Salisberie.'[4] But events moved

---

[1] *Black Books*, ii. 224–5.   [2] Chamberlain, *Letters*, ii. 296.
[3] Gosse (ii. 139) says that Donne 'was selected to conduct the funeral in St. Paul's Cathedral of Dr. John King, Bishop of London, who died on the 30th of Mar. 1621'; but this is wrong. The officiating clergyman was Thomas Morton, Bishop of Coventry, assisted by the Bishop of Ely (see Henry King, *A Sermon preached at Pauls Crosse, the 25 of November. 1621.*, p. 72). One would expect that Donne attended the funeral of his friend and diocesan, but of this there is no evidence.
[4] Chamberlain, *Letters*, ii. 360.

slowly, and two months later Chamberlain was still reporting that 'The bishop of Lincoln is like to come to London, Dr. Williams to Lincoln, and [here a new name is introduced] Dr. Laud president of St. Johns in Oxford and Deane of Glocester to Westminster, and Dr. Dunne to Glocester.'[1] It is clear from Chamberlain's references that Donne was keeping himself prominently before those in authority, and that he was regarded as certain to secure a deanery when a suitable vacancy arose.

In some respects the rumours that Chamberlain retailed to Carleton proved true prophecies. George Mountain (or Montaigne) was in fact translated from Lincoln to London, and Williams became Bishop of Lincoln. But the see of Lincoln was not the next step in the meteoric rise of John Williams, for James had already decided to confer on him the Great Seal, which lacked a Keeper after the impeachment of Bacon, and the bishopric was added in order to provide him with sufficient dignity (and income) for so high a post. Bacon had fallen because he had accepted gifts from litigants, and his successor had to have sufficient wealth to be able to reject any such temptations. By insisting on his need for financial independence Williams not only won his see but secured a dispensation to retain the deanery of Westminster as well. Hence Bowles stayed on at Salisbury until he became Bishop of Rochester in 1630, and his deanery never became available for Donne. Yet at one stage Donne was apparently promised Salisbury by no less a person than Buckingham, whose power and influence were far greater than Somerset's had ever been. By 8 August Donne had heard of Williams's intention not to resign from Westminster, and wrote to Buckingham in the country. Buckingham had just been entertaining the King at Burley-on-the-Hill, which he had recently bought from Lady Bedford.

May it please your Lordship.

Ever since I had your Lordship's letter, I have esteemed myselfe in possession of Salisbury, and more then Salisbury, of a place in your service; for I tooke Salisbury as a seale of ytt. I hear that my Lord Keeper finds reason to continue in Westminster, and I know that neyther your Lordship nor he knowes how narrow and penurious a fortune I wrestle with in thys world. But I ame so far from dependinge upon the assistance of any but your Lordship, as that I do not assist myselfe so far as with a wishe that my Lord Keeper would have left a hole for so poore a worme as I ame to have crept in at. All that I meane in usinge thys boldnes, of puttinge myselfe into your Lordship's presence by thys ragge of paper, ys to tell your Lordship that I ly in a corner, as a clodd of clay, attendinge what kinde of vessell yt shall please you to make of

> Your Lordship's
>> humblest and thankfullest and devotedst servant,
>
> 8° August 1621.   J. Donne.[1]

This 'poore worme', this 'clodd of clay' awaiting the potter's hand, had no recourse in this moment of disappointment but to assert his utter dependence on his patron in the hope that he would not be forgotten next time.

There was another reason for the delay of the new ecclesiastical appointments. On 24 July Archbishop Abbot had gone to consecrate a chapel in Lord Zouch's house at Bramshill. Whilst there he was taken hunting in the park, and, missing a deer with the arrow which he aimed at it, accidentally killed a keeper. Though there was never any question of his innocence, the unprecedented situation arose in which the Primate of All England had been the direct instrument of the death of another human being. Williams refused to accept consecration from his hands, and Laud, who was now to become Bishop of St. David's, had similar scruples. The upshot was that the Archbishop of Canterbury was suspended from his ecclesiastical functions until a royal commission, after a full inquiry, cleared him of all guilt. The new bishops were consecrated in November by a committee of bishops while Abbot's case was still pending.

Donne remained in London during the summer of 1621, except for visits to friends who had retired to the country near by, and the one long letter that survives from these months produces a curious effect of content and placidity, which the events of the weeks immediately before and immediately after seem to belie. The letter is, of course, to Goodyer and is dated 30 August.[2] It is of a kind surprisingly rare

---

[1] *Fortescue Papers*, ed. S. R. Gardiner (Camden Society, N.S. vol. i, 1871), pp. 157–8.
[2] *Letters*, pp. 154–9. The year is given as 1611, but the events referred to place it without question in 1621.

in Donne's correspondence, full of news and gossip, with references to the progress of the war in Germany and kindly messages to Goodyer's daughters, who, we learn from this letter, were on warm terms of friendship with Constance Donne. Lady Bedford had been briefly in town; 'this afternoon', writes Donne, 'I presented my service to her, by M^{ris} *Withrington*: and so asked leave to have waited upon them at supper: but my messenger found them ready to go into their Coach.' There is a reference to Sir Edward Herbert's proposed return from Paris (where he was ambassador), and to a letter he had written to Sir Edward Sackville; another to the Lord Doncaster and another to the recently fallen Lord Chancellor (Bacon). Then Donne continues:

I have been some times with my L. of *Canterbury*, since [his] accident, to give you his own words. I see him retain his former cheer-fulnesse here and at *Croydon*, but I do not hear from Court, that he hath any ground for such a confidence, but that his case may need favour, and not have it. That place, and *Bedington*, and *Chelsey*, and *Highgate*, where that very good man my Lord *Hobard* is, and *Hackney*, with the *Master* of the Rolls, and my familiar *Peckham*, are my cir-cumference.

That Donne should visit his brothers-in-law at Beddington and Peckham, and Sir John and Lady Danvers at Chelsea, was natural enough, but nowhere else do we learn that he was on such friendly terms with Archbishop Abbot, Sir Henry Hobart (Lord Chief Justice of Common Pleas), and Sir Julius Caesar (Master of the Rolls). Then he mentions that Constance was for the time being at home to keep house for him; evidently she normally lived in the Grymes household, or even perhaps in the household of some greater lady on whom she attended:

she is my servant below stairs, and my companion above: she was at the table with me, when your Letter was brought. . . . But that she is gone to bed two hours before I writ this, she should have signed, with such a hand as your daughter *Mary* did to me, that which I testifie for her, that she is as affectionate a servant to them all, as their goodnesse hath created any where.

He had begun with an apology for not having written out a sermon for which Goodyer had asked, owing to a pain in his right wrist which had made writing impossible for three weeks: 'The writing of this Letter will implore a commentary for that, that I cannot write legibly; for that I cannot write much, this Letter will testifie against me.' If all Donne's letters were like this one, our picture of him would be much fuller and more intimate.

Though disappointed of the deanery of Salisbury, Donne did not have long to wait for another vacancy to occur. His letter to Buckingham was dated 8 August; on the 26th the Bishop of Exeter died. It was decided almost immediately that he was to be succeeded by Valentine Cary, Dean of St. Paul's, and that Donne was to succeed Cary. In a pleasant anecdote Walton relates how the King himself told the news of his promotion:

the King sent to Dr. *Donne*, and appointed him to attend him at Dinner the next day. When his Majesty was sate down, before he had eat any meat, he said after his pleasant manner, Dr. *Donne, I have invited you to Dinner; and, though you sit not down with me, yet I will carve to you of a dish that I know you love well; for knowing you love* London, *I do therefore make you Dean of* Pauls; *and when I have dined, then do you take your beloved dish home to your study; say grace there to your self, and much good may it do you.*[1]

But the story is suspect, for Aubrey tells a very similar anecdote about Bishop Andrewes and his promotion of poor but worthy clergy in the diocese of Winchester,[2] and it looks very much as if the same basic tale was told and retold of different participants. Nevertheless Donne must have known of his promotion, of which he was probably told by the King, by 13 September, for on that date he wrote to Buckingham an effusive and grateful letter of thanks:

---

[1] *Lives*, pp. 54–5.
[2] '. . . which Bishoprick he [Andrewes] ordered with great Prudence as to government of the Parsons, preferring of ingeniose persons that were staked to poore livings and did *delitescere*. He made it his Enquiry to find out such men. Amongst severall others (whose names have escaped my memorie) Nicholas Fuller (he wrote *Critica Sacra*), Minister of Allington, neer Amesbury in Wilts, was one. The Bishop sent for him, and the poor man was afrayd and knew not what hurt he had donne. Makes him sitt downe to Dinner and, after the Desert, was brought in, in a dish, his Institution and Induction, or the donation of a Prebend; which was his way' (Aubrey, *Brief Lives*, ed. O. L. Dick, 1949, p. 7).

My most honoured Lord,

I most humbly beseech your Lordship to afford this ragg of paper a room amongst your evidences. It is your evidence not for a Mannour, but for a man. As I am a Priest it is my sacrifice of prayer to God for your Lordship; and as I am a Priest, made able to subsist, and appear in Gods service by your Lordship, it is a sacrifice of my self to you. I deliver this paper as my Image; and I assist the power of any Conjuror, with this imprecation upon my self, that as he shall tear this paper, this picture of mine, so I may be torn in my fortune, and in my fame, if ever I have any corner in my heart, dispossessed of a zeal to your Lordships service. His Majestie hath given me a royal Key into your Chamber, leave to stand in your presence, and your Lordship hath already such a fortune, as that you shall not need to be afraid of a suitor, when I appear there. So that I protest to your Lordship, I know not what I want, since I cannot suspect, nor fear my self for ever doing, or leaving undone any thing by which I might forfeit that title, of being alwaies

Your Lordships, &c.

J. D.[1]

It is obvious that Donne regarded Buckingham as a principal, or at least an essential, agent in his promotion. In later years, however, Williams apparently claimed at least a share in his advancement as well:

The Bishopric of *Exon* being also then void, it came into the Lord-Keeper's head to gratifie a brace of worthy Divines, if he could attain it, his old Friends, who had been both bred in the House of Wisdom, with the Lord-Chancellor *Egerton*, Dr. *Carew* who had been his Chaplain, a man of great Reason and polish'd Eloquence, and Dr. *Dunn* who had been his Secretary, a Laureat Wit; neither was it possible that a vulgar Soul would dwell in such promising Features. The Success was quickly decided, for these two prevailed by the Lord-Keeper's Commendation against all Pretenders; the Bishopric of *Exeter* was conferred upon Dr. *Carew*, and Dr. *Dunn* succeeded him in his Deanery of St. *Paul's*.[2]

---

[1] *Cabala: sive Scrinia Sacra*, 1654, p. 314.

[2] J. Hacket, *Scrinia Reserata*, 1693, p. 63. Williams did not become chaplain to Lord Ellesmere until 1611 (op. cit., p. 19), so that he and Donne did not meet as fellow members of the Lord Keeper's household. On the other hand, both John Panton (p. 35) and Ellis Wynn (pp. 44–5; see above, pp. 333–7) were kinsmen of Williams as well as acquaintances of Donne, and it is quite likely that Williams and Donne had been well known to one another for some years before Donne's appointment to his deanery.

Williams's biographer speaks as if he had had the sole responsibility for Donne's advancement, but this cannot possibly be true. What is more likely is that Donne had sedulously enlisted the aid of everyone who was capable of influencing the King in his favour.

Donne, then, seems to have owed his deanery largely to the successful employment of the courtier's arts which he had cultivated, and persisted with in spite of heart-breaking disappointments, during the decade preceding his ordination. Another question which will arise almost automatically in the minds of those who are familiar with Christopher Hill's *Economic Problems of the Church* is whether Donne paid the Duke of Buckingham for his deanery. Buckingham, it is said, exacted a price for every bishopric and deanery during the period of his power. The ultimate source for such statements appears to be Sir Anthony Weldon, who does not mince words on the subject:

> Yet did not Buckingham doe things gratis, but what their purses could not stretch unto they paid in pensions out of their places, all which went to maintain his numerous beggerly kindred. Bacon paid a pension; Heath, atturney, paid a pension; Bargrave, dean, paid a pension, with many others. Nor was this any certain rule, for present portions must be raised, for the marriage of a poor kitchen-maid, to be made a great countesse; so Fotherby made bishop of Sarum, paid 3500*l.* and some also, worthy men, were preferred gratis, to blow up their fames, and trumpet forth their nobleness, (as Tolson, a worthy man, paid nothing, in fine, or pension; after him, Davenant, in the same bishoprick;) but these were but as musick before every sceane; . . . There were books of rates on all the offices, bishopricks, deanries in England, that could tell you what fines, what pensions, otherwise it had been impossible such a numerous kindred could have been maintained with the three kingdomes revenue.[1]

There were exceptions, he admits, but they only proved the rule. On the other hand, there is the evidence of Godfrey Goodman, who was appointed to a deanery just a few months before Donne received his. Goodman denies point-blank that Bargrave paid a pension, for his promotion, on Goodman's own personal knowledge,

---

[1] A. Weldon, *Court and Character of James I*, in Sir Walter Scott's *Secret History of the Court of James the First*, i (1811), 437–8. It scarcely need be added that Weldon is far from being an unbiased historian.

was due solely to the King, and not to Buckingham at all. As for himself, the King had told him of his intention to promote him when an opportunity arose, and made sure that he should be properly reminded of Goodman's claims.

Being a little known to King James, when I never used any means unto him, nor to my knowledge did ever any man speak one word in my behalf, then did King James in a morning send John Packer unto me, to tell me, that his majesty had a full resolution to prefer me, and to bring me to some good place in the Church; and lest his majesty should forget me, he had therefore commanded Buckingham to put him in mind of me; and lest Buckingham, having many suitors, might forget me, the King commanded John Packer to put him in mind of me; and lest John Packer should forget me, the King had sent unto me, to engage himself unto me that he would solicit my business. Hereupon I never came unto John Packer but I had instantly access: I never proposed anything but I had a true and real answer; no dilatory or complimental words.

When the appointment was made the King told him in so many words that he would not have to pay a farthing for it, and 'did seem to be more joyful in giving it than I could express joy at receiving it'. He admits that when he became a bishop there were some faults of transcription in the wording of his patent, so that the document had to be re-copied, and this made Goodman suspect that the clerks were seeking more than their fee. He also sent Buckingham a present of plate worth between £40 and £50, but this was not accepted; it was returned with thanks, and a reward for the bearer.[1] Later on Goodman learnt more of the ways of the world, for he came to covet the see of Hereford, and when a vacancy arose he laid out £3,000 to secure his translation. But news of what had happened reached the ears of Laud, who indignantly saw to it that Goodman never went to Hereford, and lost his £3,000 to boot. The later incident may be thought to render the account of the earlier one suspect, but this does not necessarily follow. Goodman's account is so circumstantial, and so much in character with the participants, that it is probably accurate.

It looks as if Donne's appointment followed a pattern not unlike

<hr />

[1] G. Goodman, *The Court of King James the First*, ed. J. S. Brewer (1839), i. 355–7.

Goodman's. The latter's story makes it clear that James was genuinely interested in promotions within the Church—probably more interested than his favourite. Whether James himself first thought of Donne in connection with the vacancy, or whether he was suggested to the King by Buckingham, cannot be known, but the suggestion seemed a good one. Donne's letter to Buckingham makes it clear that James had commended Donne and his affairs to him: 'His Majestie hath given me a royal Key into your Chamber, leave to stand in your presence.' John Packer's aid was also called upon, for on 19 September he added a postscript to a letter he had just been writing to Viscount Doncaster in France: 'It is by this tyme no newes to your Lordship that my Lord hath procured the Deanry of Paules for Dr. Donne: and because it should not be subiect to any vncertaintie, the letter is signed by his Majestie, which I haue in my custodie till it be tyme to passe it vnder seale.'[1] Donne could not, of course, enter upon the deanery until it was vacated by his predecessor, and Cary's consecration was being held up by the inquiry into Abbot's homicide. Packer was a Clerk of the Privy Seal, and all he had to do with the royal missive was to affix the seal when the right moment came, so that the letter might go forward with a minimum of delay. Finally, though there are probably apocryphal elements to Walton's story, it is quite likely that the King had himself told Donne of his promotion; and as Goodman felt that 'his majesty did seem to be more joyful in giving it than I could express joy at receiving it', so probably was it also in Donne's case.

Such, then, were the tone and the habits of Court and officeholders when Donne was made Dean. It is impossible at this day to say that he did, or did not, pay for his promotion, but, his probable lack of funds apart, there are some pieces of evidence in his favour. One is a tale of an encounter between Donne and Williams (who is presumably the Bishop Billie of the story) that by no means implies the friendship alleged by Hacket:

Bishop Billie falling in out termes with Doctor Done, said, None save some Popish fellowes as hee thought otherwayes; to which Done, I would not give so much to be Pope, as ye did to be Bishop. Hold your peace, said Billie. I know better how to hold my peace than yee

---

[1] MS. Egerton 2594, fo. 109.

how to speake. Yee are a foule. That, my Lord, said Done, is your owne; yee may give it to whom yee please.[1]

The story is almost certainly apocryphal, since there is, in fact, no evidence to suggest that the relations of Donne and Williams were ever anything but cordial. In the one surviving letter from Donne to Williams he addresses him with a certain degree of familiarity ('My very good Lord'), takes it for granted that Williams knows something of his early history and his connection with Sir George More, and acknowledges his indebtedness to Williams ('my humble thanks to your Lordship for your manifold fauors to me').[2] Nevertheless, the anecdote does show that, in the popular mind at least, Donne had clean hands, whereas Williams had not.

Stronger evidence is to be found in the comments in Donne's official sermons about questionable practices in the Church. At St. Paul's, commemorating the Powder Treason in 1622, he said: 'Alas, (to looke into no other profession but our owne) how often do we excuse *Dispensations*, and *pluralities*, and *non-residencies*, with an *Omnes faciunt*, I do, but as other men of my profession, do?'[3] These practices, he thought, needed excuse; and he at least confined his own indulgence in them to that strictly allowed by law, and, although his benefices in the country were specifically designed to admit of non-residence, he made efforts (unusual in that day) to visit them and preach in the churches of which he was rector. Even on a less formal occasion, at a christening, he spoke out—all the more forcefully because current practices in the Church are measured against the standards of its Head:

Here Christ bought a Church [with His blood], but I would there were no worse Simony then this. Christ received no profit from the Church, and yet he gave himselfe for it; and he stayes with it to the end of the world; Here is no such *Non-residency*, as that the Church is left unserved: other men give enough for their Church, but they withdraw themselves, and necessary provision. . . .[4]

Sevenoaks certainly, and presumably Keyston also, did not lack 'service'. There is a certain moral fastidiousness about Donne's

[1] *Archaeologia Scotica*, iv (1857), 81.
[2] Lincolnshire Archives, L. T. & D., 1626/11. Cf. p. 487 below.
[3] *Sermons*, iv, no. 9, ll. 470–3, p. 249.   [4] Ibid. v, no. 5, ll. 415–21, p. 124.

comments on these matters which one feels to be very much in character. His most forthright denunciation of the sin of simony, however, was made in a sermon to the Court itself, in February 1619; he was only too aware of the situation that would arise if he preached against such sins and were guilty of them himself: 'Who will believe me when I speak, if by my life they see I do not believe my self? how shall I be believed to speak heartily against Ambition and Bribery in temporall and civil places, if one in the Congregation be able to jogge him that sits next him, and tell him, That man offered me money for spirituall preferment?'[1] Would the man who preached in these words, and before such a company, be the one to fall? There is a strong probability on this ground alone that Donne's hands were clean.

As we have seen he knew of his promotion by 13 September 1621, when he wrote his letter of thanks to Buckingham but, having more than once had office within his grasp, he could not help being full of apprehensions, even though the King had already signed the order for his election. 'Truly all things that are upon the stage of the world now', he wrote to Goodyer on 11 October,

are full of such uncertainties, as may justly make any man loth to passe a conjecture upon them; not only because it is hard to see how they will end, but because it is misinterpretable and dangerous to conjecture otherwise, then some men would have the event to be. That which is especially in my contemplation, which is the issue of my L. of *Canterburies* businesse, (for thereupon depends the consecration of my predecessor, upon which the Deanery devolves to the King) is no farther proceeded in yet, then that some of the 10 Commissioners have met once; and upon Saterday next there will be a fuller meeting, and an entrance into the businesse, upon which, much, very much in consequence, depends.[2]

Nevertheless a few weeks later Donne's appointment was sufficiently widely known for Chamberlain to report it to Carleton,[3] and Donne

---

[1] *Sermons*, ii, no. 7, ll. 316–21, pp. 172–3.

[2] *Letters*, pp. 199–200. The letter is addressed to Sir Thomas Lucy, but is certainly to Goodyer. Donne sends him a sermon ('but it is not my copy, which I thought my L. of *South-hampton* would have sent me backe') and promises to write out another for him ('though in good faith, I have half forgot it'); he also asks Goodyer why he says nothing of '*my little book of Cases*'.

[3] Chamberlain, *Letters*, ii. 407–8 (17 Nov. 1621).

himself, in his next letter to Goodyer, could relate with some aston-
ishment that 'Though I be not Dean of *Pauls* yet, my L. of *Warwick*
hath gone so low, as to command of me the office of being Master of
my game, in our wood about him in *Essex*.'[1] He was already beginning to taste some of the sweets of office.

Valentine Cary was consecrated Bishop of Exeter on 18 November, and the way was now open for the election of his successor at
St. Paul's. The royal letter to the Chapter commanding Donne's
election was issued the following day, and the election took place
on Thursday 22 November.[2] The ceremonial was rigidly prescribed.
After the receipt of the King's letter the members of the Chapter
met and cast their votes. Meanwhile Donne was waiting in the
house of Dr. Mountfort, the senior residentiary and the president
of the Chapter in the absence of a Dean. There he was notified of his
election and was next presented to the Bishop, who had the responsibility of assuring himself that there was no canonical obstacle to
his institution. When the election had been confirmed, the Bishop
and the canons led the new Dean into the Cathedral and up to the
high altar, where a *Te Deum* was sung. Then the Dean prostrated
himself while the Bishop led the responses and prayed for him:
'Misere quaesumus Domine famulo Tuo N. et dirige eum secundum
Tuam clementiam in viam salutis aeternae, ut Te donante Tibi
placita cupiat; et quae Tibi placita sunt tota dilectione perficiat,
per Christum, &c.' The new Dean rose and kissed the altar, and next
the Bishop led him to his seat in the choir and installed him there.
After the service he was led to the Chapter House and placed in his
seat; then he swore a solemn oath to reside at the Cathedral, to
protect the rights and privileges of the Cathedral, to keep and
cause to be kept its ancient laws and customs, and to preserve its
possessions. Then came the turn of the canons who, both major and
minor, took the oaths of canonical obedience to the Dean. Finally
the Dean took a similar oath of obedience to the Bishop.[3] A

[1] *Letters*, p. 227 (25 Oct.).

[2] Donne's epitaph states that he became Dean on 27 Nov., but the copy of the
notary's certificate in Register Donne at St. Paul's quite clearly gives 'die Jovis
vicesimo secundo die mensis Novembris' as the day on which he took his oath and
was installed (fo. 3).

[3] W. Sparrow Simpson, ed., *Registrum Statutorum et Consuetudinum Ecclesiae Cathedralis Sancti Pauli Londinensis* (1873), pp. 14–15, 219–20.

transcript of the whole proceedings was entered in a new volume of
the Cathedral Register, and included a copy of the royal missive
authorizing the election and a notarized certificate that the election
had been held. (A new volume of the Register was begun with each
new Dean, and this one was known by the title 'Donne'.)

Donne now had his Deanery, but some of the other steps which
were the result of his promotion were taken with disconcerting
slowness. Not till 9 August 1622 did two patents pass the Great
Seal, one conferring on him a stall in the choir and a place in the
Chapter House, the other granting him a prebend.[1] He became
Prebendary of Chiswick, as his predecessor had been. When he was
able to move into the Deanery would have depended on how fast
Cary moved out; the Churchwardens' Accounts of the parish of St.
Clement Danes, as we have seen, show that 'The deane of powles'
(not 'Dockter Dun', as he had been in previous years) paid his usual
assessment for 1621–2, which suggests that he did not leave the
parish immediately, though, not unnaturally, his name does not
appear in any subsequent years. Not till 11 February 1621/2 do the
Black Books of Lincoln's Inn make any mention of Donne's resignation, though the subject of the minute is not primarily his resignation but his parting gift of the six-volume edition of the Vulgate
Bible with the *glossa ordinaria* and postils of Nicholas de Lyra, which
is still preserved in the Library of Lincoln's Inn and which contains
a lengthy inscription in Donne's own handwriting. He looked back
with some pride to his efforts as a preacher to the Society, and regretted that he had not seen the completion of the new chapel, the
foundation stone of which he had laid:

> Munere suo, frequenter et strenue hoc loco concionandi
> Per quinque annos functus,
> Novi Sacelli primis saxis sua manu positis
> & ultimis fere paratis.[2]

The minute of the Benchers which acknowledged Donne's resignation and the gift of the Bible was sincere and cordial, and, like all

---

[1] P.R.O., Patent Rolls, 20 James I, C66/2285, nos. 70 and 75; cf. S.P. 14 James I,
vol. 141, p. 353. Donne was inducted and installed in his prebend on 11 Aug.
(P.R.O., E331/ Dean and Chapter of London, 6; E331/ Diocese of London, 12, gives
the date of his admission and institution as 12 Aug.).

[2] *Black Books*, ii. 445.

their references to him from the time of his appointment as Reader, showed unusual warmth of feeling. It expressed regret at his departure and congratulated him on his promotion; the Benchers desired to keep him a member of the Society for as long as possible:

the Masters of the Bench Acknowledging this and many other the kind and loving respectes of the said Mr. Doctor Dvnne towardes them whereof they have had good experience Haue nowe entred into Consideracion of some fitting retribucion to expresse their thankfull Remembrance of him And to that purpose And to thend it may Appeare that though they are glad of his preferment yet being loath wholly to parte with him And that he may at his pleasure and convenient leisure repaire to this house being A worthy member thereof and be noe stranger here, Haue thought fitt and with one voice and assent haue soe ordered That the said Mr. Doctor Donne shall continue his Chamber in this house which he nowe hath, as a Bencher of this house with such priviledges touching the same as the Masters of the Bench nowe haue and ought to haue for their seuerall and respectiue chambers in this house.[1]

Donne was, in effect, made an honorary Bencher of Lincoln's Inn.

His successor, John Preston, was appointed at the Council meeting of 21 May 1622, but until he took up his duties Donne seems to have preached at the Inn when he could. The sermon preached on Candlemas Day (2 February) and assigned by Potter and Simpson to 1622[2] seems to be a Lincoln's Inn sermon, and that for Ascension Day (30 May) of the same year was, according to the specific statement in the heading, preached there.[3] This, though largely an anti-Roman Catholic sermon is in many ways the most familiar of Donne's discourses. It is the last of the regular Lincoln's Inn sermons, and illustrates perhaps best of all the relations between Donne and the society of lawyers he was now to leave.

There was, however, a special occasion later when he preached to them again. When the new chapel was at last finished and dedicated by George Mountain, the Bishop of London, on Ascension Day 1623, it was appropriate that Donne was invited to preach the first sermon in it. The sermon is a closely argued one, without any attempts at eloquence, yet it must have given considerable pleasure

---

[1] Ibid., p. 230; from Black Book no. 7, fo. 66.
[2] *Sermons*, iii, no. 18; on its date see pp. 42–3.   [3] Ibid. iv, no. 4.

to the members of the Inn. He reminded them that the decision to build a new chapel had given them a far more onerous task than they had been prepared for:

strangers shall not know, how ill we were provided for such a work, when we begun it, nor with what difficulties we have wrastled in the way; but strangers shall know to *Gods* glory, that you have perfected a work of full three times as much charge, as you proposed for it at beginning: so bountifully doth *God* blesse, and prosper intentions to his glory, with enlarging your hearts within, and opening the hearts of others, abroad.

He himself

by your favours was no stranger to the beginning of this work, and an often refresher of it to your memories, and a poore assistant in laying the first stone, the materiall stone, as I am now, a poore assistant again in this laying of this first formall Stone, the Word and Sacrament, and shall ever desire to be so in the service of this place.

Yet even on so festive an occasion he did not hesitate to chide his auditors, and urge on them the duty of more regular attendance at church, with as much directness and openness as he had always used towards them:

Now *it was Winter*, sayes the *Text*: *Christ* came *etsi Hyems*, though it were Winter; so small an inconvenience kept him not off. Beloved, it is not alway colder upon *Sunday*, then upon *Satterday*; nor at any time colder in the *Chappell*, then in *Westminster Hall*. A thrust keepes some off in *Summer*; and colde in *Winter*: and there are more of both these in other places, where for all that, they are more content to be. Remember that *Peter* was warming himselfe, and hee denyed *Christ*. They who love a warme bed, let it bee a warme Studie, let it bee a warme profit, better then this place, they deny CHRIST in his Institution. That therefore which CHRIST sayes, *Pray that your flight bee not in the Winter, nor upon the Sabboth*; we may apply thus, Pray that upon the *Sabboth* (I tolde you at first, what were *Sabboths*,) the Winter make you not flie, not abstaine from this place.[1]

This was, so far as we know, Donne's last sermon at Lincoln's Inn; and judging by Chamberlain's account it was certainly one of the best attended:

[1] *Sermons*, iv, no. 15, ll. 280–95, pp. 371–2, and ll. 471–84, pp. 376–7.

Lincolns Ynne new chappell was consecrated with more solemnitie by the bishop of London on Ascension Day, where there was great concourse of noblemen and gentlemen wherof two or three were indaungered and taken up dead for the time with the extreme presse and thronging. The Deane of Paules made an excellent sermon (they say) concerning dedications.[1]

This was not, however, the end of Donne's relations with the Society. His connection with the chapel is perpetuated in one of the stained-glass windows. The east window and the two side windows nearest it are filled with panes containing the arms of the Treasurers of the Inn; the next two windows on each side contain four panels and are glazed with four prophets and twelve apostles, each having below it the arms of a peer who was a member of the Inn. The second window on the north side has the arms of the Earls of Southampton, Pembroke, Bridgewater, and Carlisle, all of whom were friends of Donne. The Earl of Carlisle's arms are beneath the figure of St. John the Evangelist, and beside the coat of arms on two small pieces of glass is painted 'Io: Donne / Dec: S: Pauli'. This panel, presumably, was Donne's gift towards the decoration of the chapel and at the same time a tribute to his friend and patron. The press of other business, however, made it increasingly difficult for Donne to keep closely in touch with his old friends at the Inn. He resigned his chamber towards the close of 1624, and a minute of 23 November recorded that

Att this Counsell Mr. Doctor Donne Deane of Paules declared by his letter his free disposition to resigne his Chamber with an expression of his humble thankes and assurance of all readinesse to serue this Societie or any member therof with his best endevors, whose resignation was very kindly accepted by the Masters of the Bench and thervpon ordered that Mr. Andrewes one of the Masters of the Bench shall haue and be admitted into that intire Chamber.[2]

This is the last certain reference to him in connection with Lincoln's Inn. Probable evidence of the impact of his personality upon at least one of the youngest members is, however, provided by a poem in manuscript on the death of James I ('your gracious Master')

<hr />

[1] Chamberlain, *Letters*, ii. 500.   [2] *Black Books*, ii. 255.

dedicated to Donne ('this, which (as it is) I lay at your feete, with his hand, and hart whoe honours, and admires you') by James Barrye. This is presumably the man who eventually became Baron Santry and Chief Justice of Ireland, who entered Lincoln's Inn on 11 July 1621, and would have seen Donne there during the last ten months or so before the new Reader took up his duties.[1]

One final complication that arose out of Donne's promotion has yet to be considered. The letters patent appointing him to the rectory of Keyston (for the living, it will be remembered, was then in the gift of the Crown) passed under the Great Seal on 16 January 1615/16; on 8 March, however, a warrant was issued under the sign manual for the presentation of John Scott to Keyston.[2] Someone had blundered, for Donne had already entered into possession of the rectory, and the living was not, in fact, vacant. Naturally, Scott was a very disappointed man, and Donne seems to have entered into an understanding with him that if he ever resigned Keyston he would use all his endeavours to have Scott appointed his successor. In the meantime the King had granted the manor and advowson to Sir James Wingfield, who was now patron of the living and who, incidentally, had embarked on an extensive policy of enclosures within the parish. In a law suit of 1622 it was alleged that Scott had 'a promise from the said Dr. Dunne the then incumbent that he the said Dr. Dunne would resigne the said Rectorye vnto him the said Complaynante [Scott] vpon the said Dr. Dunnes better preferment'.[3] Donne carried out his promise, for he solemnly resigned from Keyston by an instrument executed before a public notary and in the presence of witnesses—the proper legal way in which to resign a benefice. This resignation took place while Donne, on the strength of Buckingham's assurance, 'esteemed himself in possession of Salisbury' and before 8 April, when he learned that Williams had no intention of relinquishing the deanery of Westminster and thus making way for him. But no resignation was valid until accepted by the proper ordinary, and when Donne realized that he was not going to be Dean of Salisbury he saw to it that the resigna-

[1] The poem is in Sloane MS. 1394 in the British Museum, and in MS. 652 at Trinity College, Dublin; cf. N&Q., cxcv, 2 Sept. 1950, p. 381.
[2] C.S.P. Dom., 1611–18, p. 353.
[3] Scott v. Bate, etc., P.R.O., C3/379/26.

tion was withheld. It was not, in fact, accepted until 20 October, when Donne felt quite sure of securing St. Paul's and when, perhaps, arrangements for Cary's consecration and his own installation were being made.

It had got about, however, that Donne had resigned, soon after the instrument of resignation had been executed, and it was the law that if a patron did not present within six months of the occurrence of a vacancy the patron's right of presentation lapsed, and devolved upon the bishop or the metropolitan. As Keyston was in the diocese of Lincoln, and the see of Lincoln was vacant (for Williams had not yet been consecrated), any right of presentation would be in the hands of the Archbishop of Canterbury, who in fact, on 18 October, presented a young clergyman fresh from Emmanuel College, Cambridge, named Henry Seyliard, 'iure ad eum rite devoluto, ratione lapsus temporis'.[1] Seyliard, apparently, attempted to take possession of the benefice; Donne, on his side, denied that his resignation was accepted when Seyliard's presentation was made. He had himself nothing to gain at this stage, but was determined to honour his promise to Scott to the letter. He acted promptly by bringing a suit against Seyliard in the Court of Delegates in order to quash his claim. In accordance with regular procedure, the Archbishop appointed a panel of five civilians (including Sir Henry Martin) of whom any two or more could hear and determine the case. The judges' commission was exhibited in court on 23 November, the day after Donne was elected Dean, and there were hearings on 23 January, 29 January, and 6 February.[2] The case, however, never got beyond the initial stages; by 6 February not only had Donne's resignation from Keyston been accepted but in addition the patron had appointed Scott. At any rate, the rival claimants were now Seyliard and Scott, and they proceeded to test their claims in the Court of Chancery. For a report on the ecclesiastical law as it affected the case the Lord Keeper referred the matter to Sir Henry Martin; this we learn from a letter which Donne wrote to Martin on 9 May 1622 just after returning from a visit to Blunham, where he had been instituted as rector:

[1] Lambeth Palace, Reg. Abbot, pt. 2, fo. 265.
[2] P.R.O., Del. 8/70, fo. 8ᵛ, and Del. 4/9, ff. 4, 10, 18.

Sir

I wayted upon you heretofore, when a Cause which concernd me, was brought before you and others, in another way, as Delegates: It ys for a pretended Resignation of the churche of Keiston, upon which pretence one Mr Silliard procurd a superinstitution. To My Lord Keeper I haue declard the direct truth of the whole proceedinge for matter of fact; and for matter of law, I haue told him, and them, that if any man learned in eyther law, of Mr Silliards own Counsayle, would say that the church upon such a Resignation was voyd, I would relinquish yt. And now, I ame enformed, that my Lord Keeper hath referrd that poynte to you If I had not come home from Bedford-shire, late and weary, I would haue wayted upon you, but it had been onely to salute you, not much to solicite you (for that I know needs not) that you wyll be pleasd to take that poynte into your good consideration: and so, Sir, I rest

Yours euer to be disp[o]sd
J: Donne

At my house at S: Pauls
9° Maij. 1622.

On the blank pages of Donne's letter Martin sketched out a draft of his report. It is from this document that we learn that Donne had formally resigned, but that the resignation had not been accepted until two days after Seyliard's collation to the benefice. It was Martin's opinion that the patron's 'tyme to present vpon payn of laps shall not beginn to runn before the Ordinarie have pronounced the church voyd & the same bee intimated vnto the Patron'.[1] Accordingly Seyliard's claim failed, and Scott was instituted as rector. He soon found himself embroiled with his patron and some of his other parishioners over the payment of tithes because of the enclosures in the parish,[2] so perhaps Donne was fortunate in resigning when he did. In later life Scott became Dean of York and was, according to Bishop Hacket, a notorious gambler. Seyliard, his opponent, had to wait three years longer for a benefice, when he became rector of Tostock in Suffolk.

[1] The manuscript of this letter and of Martin's report is now in the Houghton Library, Harvard University. For the text of Martin's draft, see Appendix D.

[2] The case of Scott v. Bate, etc., has already been cited (p. 386, n. 3); an apparently parallel case brought by Scott against his patron, Scott v. Wingfield, is said by the officers of the Public Record Office to be unfit for inspection.

XV

DEAN

THE Chapter of which Donne, as Dean of St. Paul's, now became head, was a complicated one. There were in all thirty prebendaries, and each had his prebendal stall in the choir, on which were inscribed the opening words of a psalm. Following an ancient French custom, which had been introduced into the Cathedral soon after the Norman Conquest, the Psalter was divided into thirty parts, and each prebendary had daily to recite his allotted verses, so that each day the whole Psalter would ascend from the Cathedral in praise and prayer. The prebends took their names from the various manors that endowed them, and Donne, as we saw, succeeded to the prebend of Chiswick, which his predecessor had held before him. As a rule the more important officers of the diocese and of the Cathedral also held prebends. There were five archdeacons (who divided among them the administration of the diocese under the Bishop), a precentor (who superintended the singing school and had the main responsibility for the conduct of the Cathedral services), a treasurer (who had oversight of the treasures of the Cathedral), and a chancellor (who kept the records).[1] Within the larger group was a smaller but much more privileged group, of whom the Dean was one, consisting of four residentiary canons (or stagiaries, as they were often called). The other prebendaries had their benefices, which were their primary concern, for technically (as far as the Cathedral was concerned) prebendaries were 'without cure of souls'; but the residentiaries, even though they might hold benefices, lived within the precincts of the Cathedral and made it the centre of their lives. Also in residence were the minor canons, twelve in number,

[1] The principal sources of information about St. Paul's, its history, and its constitution are: W. Sparrow Simpson, ed., *Registrum Statutorum et Consuetudinum Ecclesiae Sancti Pauli Londinensis*, 1873; Sir William Dugdale, *History of Saint Paul's*, 2nd ed., 1709; W. R. Mathews and W. M. Atkins, eds., *A History of St. Paul's Cathedral*, 1957; G. Hennessy, *Novum Repertorium Ecclesiasticum Parochiale Londinense*, 1898.

who constituted a separate college with an endowment of its own. At their head was the sub-dean; next in order of seniority were two other minor canons who bore the title of cardinal. The minor canons also occupied stalls in the choir, and on them the Cathedral depended for the regular succession of services every day at the prescribed hours. Next, there were six vicars choral, or singing men, who, with the boys from the choir school, sang the services and the anthems. Finally, the Dean had under his governance a number of secular officers, such as the bailiffs who administered the properties of the Cathedral, and the vergers, who were in attendance in the Cathedral itself.

The prebendaries were a various group of men. Probably a good half of them were of the type one would expect to find making up such a body today: active parish priests, usually in charge of large parishes, well known for the vigour with which they performed their pastoral duties or for their intellectual distinction. Such men often in due course became archdeacons, as did Richard Cluett, rector of St. Anne's, Aldersgate, and vicar of Fulham,[1] and William Paske, vicar of Hendon and rector of Ashdown, Essex. Thomas Westfield, rector of St. Bartholomew the Great and archdeacon of St. Alban's, later in life rose to become Bishop of Bristol. A second group of the prebendaries consisted of more obvious ecclesiastical careerists, of men who used their energies and influence to accumulate benefices and batten upon a system which condoned pluralities as a reward for the talented. Here one would include two men who were both Students and subsequently Deans of Christ Church, Oxford: William Piers, who later became Bishop of Bath and Wells, and Samuel Fell, father of the better-known John Fell. For both of these men the prebends which they held at St. Paul's can never have involved more than occasional visits to the Cathedral; their main interests lay elsewhere. There were others, however, who had prospered sufficiently to live in London and rely on the country benefices which they held as non-residents to support them in affluence. Such was John Barkham, who had been chaplain to two archbishops and had managed to amass four rectories as well as a rural deanery in

---

[1] Cluett had been bishop's chaplain under Bishop John King (see Henry King's sermon after his father's death, referred to in Chap. XIV, p. 370, n. 3 above).

Essex. Two of the stagiaries also had reputations as pluralists. Thomas Mountfort had as a young man been chaplain to the Earl of Warwick; he gradually acquired the vicarage of St. Martin-in-the-Fields and three country rectories; in addition, he became a canon of Westminster and was a residentiary of St. Paul's until his death in 1632. Thomas Whyte, still remembered as the founder of Sion College and of Whyte's Professorship of Moral Philosophy at Oxford, was rector of St. Gregory's for a time, then vicar of St. Dunstan-in-the-West; in addition to his London parish and his canonry at St. Paul's he was also canon of Christ Church, canon of Windsor, and Treasurer of Salisbury Cathedral. A final group of prebendaries owed their positions to nepotism. Isaac Singleton in 1614 succeeded his father in the prebend of Brondesbury; the father was Principal of Brasenose College and Vice-Chancellor of the University of Oxford; he had apparently surrendered his prebend to make provision for his son. Theophilus Aylmer, prebendary of Holywell and archdeacon of London, was the second son of John Aylmer, a former Bishop of London, and John Bancroft (afterwards Bishop of Oxford) was a nephew of the famous Richard Bancroft, Bishop of London and later Archbishop of Canterbury. Thomas Mountfort as a residentiary was able to secure a prebend for his son John. But Donne's old friend, Bishop John King, had in 1615 put two of his sons into prebendal stalls: Henry King, afterwards Bishop of Chichester, was already, when Donne became Dean, canon residentiary and archdeacon of Colchester; and the younger John King was prebendary of Kentish Town, but spent most of his life in and near Oxford, and came but rarely to London. One other important officer of the Cathedral never went beyond deacon's orders: Patrick Young, a Scot, who was keeper of the King's Library, and was appointed treasurer of the Cathedral at the same time as Donne was made Dean.

Inevitably Donne was thrown into closest relations with the three other residentiaries. Whyte died less than two years after Donne's appointment and was replaced by Thomas Winniff, who became Dean after Donne's death. Thomas Mountfort, Henry King, and Winniff all became his close friends. King, of course, was very much the youngest of the group; he had been appointed a prebendary at the age of twenty-four and archdeacon a year later, but he was a poet as well as a churchman and had many friends in the world of letters. King and Mountfort's son were appointed by Donne to be executors of his will, and Winniff received the bequest of a picture. It was well that Donne should have been on such close and friendly terms with the other residentiaries, for, as Newcourt remarks, 'they ought always to reside; for to them belongs the Care of the whole Church, where they may be Examples in the Choir; frequently transact the Business of the Church in the Chapter, and daily take Care of the Concerns of the Church'.[1] Harmonious relations among the residentiaries must have meant a great deal in the administration of the Cathedral and its affairs; as Newcourt suggests, the main burden of these tasks fell upon them.

The full Chapter of the Cathedral met normally only once a year, on St. Barnabas's Day (11 June). Extraordinary meetings were held for the election of a bishop or a dean. Otherwise, in the conduct of the day-to-day affairs of the Cathedral, everything was entrusted to the Dean and the three other residentiaries. Unfortunately there are no act-books of the Chapter for Donne's period as Dean, but the nature of at least some of the more important business transacted is known from other sources. The Dean and Chapter had a number of livings in their gift, and owned a good deal of property in the City and in the country. Though livings did not fall vacant every day, leases fell in, and new leases were granted; rents were collected and accounts were rendered by the bailiffs, and at the end of the year the profits (after all the expenses of the Cathedral had been paid) were shared among the residentiaries. There was thus sufficient business to warrant frequent meetings and unremitting care.

When livings in the nomination of the Dean and Chapter fell vacant, the residentiaries nominated in turn, and the nomination was automatically confirmed at the next meeting of the Chapter. The one such appointment Donne is known to have made was that of William Woodford as rector of St. Faith's. Donne had known Woodford for some years, for he had been chaplain to Viscount Doncaster when Donne went with him to Germany in 1619. Woodford, however, stayed at home with Lady Doncaster and the child-

---

[1] R. Newcourt, *Repertorium Ecclesiasticum Parochiale Londinense*, i. 116.

ren, and had been instructed to write to his master weekly reports
of their health.[1] Doncaster may, indeed, have used his influence
with Donne to secure St. Faith's for Woodford, to which he was
appointed by the Dean and Chapter on 26 March 1624. He held the
rectory, however, for less than a year. The Dean and Chapter
received a royal missive announcing that: 'We are moved by our
especial favour to William Woodford, now minister of St. Faith's, to
dispose of him in another place, which, for some consideration,
cannot well be effected without your consent and allowance of
Emmanuel Smith to succeed him in the Cure of St. Faith's.' Woodford had been granted the living of Upton-on-Severn in Worcester-
shire, and the Chapter obediently chose Emmanuel Smith to succeed
him, but in a letter to Sir Edward Conway (the Secretary of State)
in which Donne recounted the action that had been taken he
made it clear that the royal command had put them to some
inconvenience:

That churche ys, at thys auoydance, according to our courses, in
my particular gift; as allso yt fell out to be so, when Mr Woodford
receyud yt at my hands: And upon iust confidence in that title, I had
giuen the next presentation therof (before any intimation, or imagination of hys Ma*jes*ties pleasure) to a person that hath deserued a greater
seruice from me. So that, to make myselfe able, to do that w*h*ich ys
allways intirely my desire, to serue hys Ma*jes*tie, I was put, first to
worke the Chapter, and then to recall my graunt, and after to wayue
my course and turne of presentinge.[2]

Emmanuel Smith almost immediately received another and better
living, for a month after his appointment the Dean and Chapter
appointed John Lesley, a Scot who later became Bishop of Sodor and
Man. It would be interesting to know if Donne got his turn, but
the records are not explicit enough to show this.

Another appointee of Donne was almost certainly Matthew
Griffith. He is mentioned in more than one seventeenth-century
account as 'Dr. Donne's favourite'. Griffith was appointed to the

---

[1] Two of these letters survive in MS. Egerton 2592 (British Museum), ff. 97, 134.
[2] S.P. 14, James I, vol. 176, fo. 78 (7 Dec. 1624; the King returned thanks on
31 Dec.). The 'difficulty' James had caused, Donne adds, had given him many
occasions to testify his desire to serve the King 'from whom J haue, not onely (as
other men haue) receyud my lyuelyhood, but my preisthood'.

rectory of St. Mary Magdalen, Old Fish Street, by the Dean and
Chapter of St. Paul's in 1624, and one would guess that he owed the
benefice to Donne's nomination. He also became lecturer at St.
Dunstan-in-the-West, but this was on 31 October 1631, after
Donne's death. He was ejected by the Parliamentarians in 1642, but
lived through the years of the Commonwealth and was restored in
1660. He figures prominently in Walker's account of the ejected
clergy.

Thomas Adams was another holder of one of the livings in the
gift of the Dean and Chapter. He had begun his career in a country
parish, where he had written devotional works and made some small
name for himself, but in 1619, two years before Donne was made
Dean, he came to the church of St. Benet's, Paul's Wharf, close
beside the river on the south side of the Cathedral. He became a
preacher of considerable eminence, published a folio edition of his
sermons in 1629, and was later called by Southey 'the prose Shakespeare of Puritan theologians . . . scarcely inferior to Fuller in wit or
to Taylor in fancy'. In 1623 he dedicated *The Barren Tree. A Sermon
Preached at Pauls Crosse October 26. 1623.* to 'the Reverend and
learned, Doctor Donne, Deane of St. Pauls, together with the
Prebend-Residentiaries of the same Church, my very *good Patrons*'.
He addresses them with respect and cordiality, and clearly wishes
to maintain good relations with them.

Another dedication Donne received was from Elias Petley, who
addressed to him a sermon entitled *The Royall Receipt: or, Hezekiahs
Physicke* (1623). Petley was another country clergyman, rector of a
Lincolnshire parish, and his visit to London in 1622 to deliver this
Paul's Cross sermon (on Michaelmas Day) is almost the only known
event in his career. His dedication asserts a humble independence:
'being wholy destitute of any dependance on the Patronage and
Mecaenaship of Great ones, . . . I know not what strong confidence
resoluing on the goodnesse of your nature, so preuailed' on him to
dedicate his book to Donne. The present-day reader may well
wonder too, but the explanation is simple. Among the minor officers
and tenants of the Dean and Chapter was a certain Peter Petley, the
brother or perhaps the father of Elias. Petley's name would therefore
have been known to the Dean; he cherished hopes, probably, of a

City living which the Dean and Chapter could confer. But if so his
hopes did not come to fruition; he had to remain content with
his country cure. More success possibly attended the Revd. Daniel
Donne, who dedicated to the Dean of St. Paul's in 1623 a Paul's
Cross sermon published as *A Sub-poena from the Star-Chamber of
Heaven*. He is thought to have been the son of John Donne, rector
of St. Bennet's, Gracechurch Street, and to have succeeded there
after his father's death in 1636.[1]

Donne has left a clear statement of his attitude towards the dis-
pensing of Church patronage. During the last years of his life he met
a young protégé of his friend Mrs. Cockayne and her sister Lady
Aston named Nathaniel Hazard, and promised to help him. In due
course Hazard arrived in London armed with a letter from his two
patronesses in which they asked that he should be given the next
living of which Donne had the nomination. In reply Donne wrote
at some length to Mrs. Cockayne to explain why he was unable to
fulfil her request:

If my promise, which was, that I should be readie to assist him in
any thing I could, were translated by you, or your noble Sister, or
him, that I would give him the next Living in my gift, certainlie we
speak not one language, or understand one another, and I had thought
we had; . . . if a person of my place, . . . who hath otherwise a latitude
of importunate friends and verie many obligations, have a Living once
in five or six yeares fall in his gift, (for it is so long since I gave any)
and may not make a good choice with freedome then, it is hard; yet
it is not my fortune to doe so now: for, now there is a living fallen;
. . . I am not left to my choice. For my Lord⟨s⟩ *Carlile*, and *Percy* have
chosen for me: but trulie such a man as I would have chosen; and for
him, they laid an obligation on me three yeares since, for the next
that should fall. . . .[2]

---

[1] See Venn and Venn, *Alumni Cantabrigienses*; his Christian name suggests a
connection (which, however, cannot be proved) with the family of Sir Daniel Dun
the civilian.

[2] *Tobie Mathew Collection*, pp. 351–2. [Mr. I. A. Shapiro considers that this letter
cannot be later than 1628 and may be as early as 1625–6; see *John Donne—Selected
Prose*, chosen by Evelyn Simpson and ed. Helen Gardner and T. Healy, p. 162.]
Venn and Venn, *Alumni Cantabrigienses*, state that Hazard matriculated sizar from
Queens' in 1615, took his B.A. in 1619–20, his M.A. in 1623, was incorporated at
Oxford 1627, ordained deacon (London) 1624 and priest in March 1624/5. Sir Aston
Cokayne has a poem addressed 'To Mr. Nathaniel Hazard and his Wife, on their
Marriage', *Poems*, 1658, p. 152.

This letter shows that, inevitably, vacancies occurred very irregularly. If it could fall to Donne's turn to nominate twice for St. Faith's within a single year, five or six years could also elapse without his having any opportunity to nominate at all. On the other hand, livings were often promised years in advance of the time at which they fell vacant; indeed, Donne himself had been promised both Blunham and St. Dunstan's while the previous incumbents were still alive. The letter shows, too, that Donne was ready to discharge some obligation to important friends like Doncaster (created Earl of Carlisle in September 1622) and his brother-in-law Lord Percy by accepting their nominations—provided that they named 'such a man as I would have chosen'. Above all, the occupant of a London pulpit had to have some distinction as a preacher: 'You know the ticklishnesse of *London*-Pulpits', wrote Donne in the same letter, 'and how ill it would become me, to place a man in a *London*-Church that were not both a strong and a sound man.'

Even more interesting are Donne's remarks in the letter about his eldest son. The younger John Donne was apparently still on the brink of taking orders; he was long in making up his mind. Donne would not at this stage put pressure on him or grant him a cure, but would be prepared to make some provision for him by giving him a prebend, for which priest's orders were not necessary. Actually, the younger Donne was instituted in the vicarage of Tillingham in Essex, a living in the gift of the Dean and Chapter of St. Paul's, some months after his father's death. It looks as if, by this action, the Chapter was fulfilling a promise made to his father.

It is clear that, as Dean, Donne exercised such patronage as came his way with integrity. A London pulpit must be supplied with a man of some strength; such a man as Hazard, who had so far been no more than a tutor in a wealthy household, would not do until he had proved himself; and even Donne's own son eventually got, not a London rectory, but a country vicarage. And though Donne knew that there were 'many Prebends and other helps in the Church, which a man without taking Orders, may be capable of', he did not, in fact, secure such a prebend for his son, though he was surrounded by men who owed their position as prebendaries of St. Paul's to fathers and uncles who wished to provide for them.

Of Donne as an administrator of Church property it is less easy to write. In the reign of James the lands of the Church were not quite so easy an object of plunder as they had been in the previous century, and as Laud grew in power he took further steps to protect them. Register Donne in the archives of St. Paul's contains transcripts of all the Cathedral leases and other grants made during the period of Donne's deanship, and it suggests that relatively few changes of policy were made in his time. There was, for instance, no visible tightening up after Laud became Bishop of London, doubtless because none was needed. Certainly it would have been impossible for some of the things to happen that had happened in the previous century. An example may be given to illustrate.

There were two manors within the parish of Chiswick, both of which belonged to the Cathedral. The smaller one, the prebendal manor, constituted the endowment of the prebend which Donne held.[1] In 1570 the prebendary of Chiswick had been Gabriel Goodman, who was at the same time Dean of Westminster. He leased the prebendal manor of Chiswick to the Dean and Chapter of Westminster on a ninety-nine-year lease for use as an appendage to Westminster School, which apparently more than once moved out to Chiswick lock, stock, and barrel during plague times when London was unsafe. The lease was several times renewed, so that even at the end of the eighteenth century the reserved rent received by the prebendary was only £39. 2s. 6d. Yet when the manor was confiscated and sold during the Commonwealth it fetched £1,551. 5s. 3d. The value of the prebend was given in the King's Book (1535) as £17. 19s. 4d., and it is doubtful if Donne received much, or any, more from it; he and his successors up to the time of the Civil War were bound by Goodman's lease, although the capital value of the manor at the time of the sale under the Commonwealth shows that it should have been capable of bringing a much higher revenue. This is an authentic instance of robbing Paul to pay Peter, and illustrates the evils of long leases.

On the other hand, the rents of ecclesiastical properties were relatively stable. The other manor of Chiswick, the manor of Sutton Court with the parsonage attached, was bringing in an annual rent

[1] D. Lysons, *The Environs of London*, 1795, ii. 186.

of £43 in 1554 and was still being leased for the same amount in
1624. The manor was one of the peculiars of the Dean and, according
to a composition between the Dean and the residentiaries made
in 1544, though it was part of the *communa* of the Cathedral,
its revenues went wholly to the Dean.[1] This manor was almost
certainly the subject of an anecdote told by Walton of Donne's
illness at the end of 1623:

In this distemper of body, his dear friend Doctor *Henry King* . . .
visited him daily; and observing that his sickness rendred his recovery
doubtful, he chose a seasonable time to speak to him, to this purpose.

'Mr. *Dean*, I am by your favour no stranger to your temporal estate,
and you are no stranger to the Offer lately made us, for the renewing a
Lease of the best Prebends Corps belonging to our Church, and you
know, 'twas denied, for that our Tenant being very rich, offered to
fine at so low a rate as held not proportion with his advantages: but
I will either raise him to an higher sum, or procure that the other
Residenciaries shall join to accept of what was offered: one of these I
can and will by your favour do without delay, and without any trouble
either to your body or mind; I beseech you to accept of my offer, for
I know it will be a considerable addition to your present estate, which
I know needs it.'

To this, after a short pause, and raising himself upon his bed, he
made this reply.

'My most dear friend, I most humbly thank you for your many
favours, and this in particular: But, in my present condition, I shall
not accept of your proposal; for doubtless there is such a Sin as
Sacriledge; . . . Our times abound with men that are busie and litigious
about trifles and Church-Ceremonies; and yet so far from scrupling
Sacriledge, that they make not so much as a *quaere* what it is: But I
thank God I have; and dare not now upon my sick-bed, when
Almighty God hath made me useless to the service of the Church, make
any advantages out of it. But if he shall again restore me to such a
degree of health, as again to serve at his *Altar*; I shall then glady
take the reward which the bountiful Benefactors of this Church have
designed me; for God knows my Children and Relations will need it.'[2]

It is true that the manor of Sutton Court was not a prebendal corps,
though it could easily have been confused in King's recollection

---

[1] Simpson, *Registrum Statutorum &c.*, p. 267.   [2] *Lives*, pp. 57–9.

with the other Chiswick manor, which was. Sutton Court also fills the other requirements implicit in Walton's story; though the lease was granted by the Dean and Chapter, the profits, as we have noted, went solely to the Dean. Furthermore, a letter of Edward Alleyn during his quarrel with Donne in 1625 contains the information that Donne was expecting to profit by a lease to the extent of at least £500, which was to be given as the dowry of his daughter Constance; in fact, Alleyn alleges, Donne received £550. It is interesting also to learn that the Chapter was prepared to refuse to renew a lease if they regarded the fine offered as insufficient. Sutton Court was the only considerable manor leased by the Dean and the Chapter during the earlier years of Donne's deanship, and it is difficult to see how either Walton's story or Alleyn's allusions could have referred to any other property. The Cathedral register shows that Sutton Court was leased to Valentine Saunders the Six Clerk and William Smethe by an indenture of 30 April 1624 for a term of twenty-one years.[1] Thus the transaction was completed (perhaps only after some dickering) when Donne had recovered from his illness, and not with the imminence of death hanging over him.

By Donne's time there were no longer any ninety-nine-year leases of Cathedral lands. The usual terms were forty years for City properties, and for country properties twenty-one years or, less commonly, three lives (i.e. for the life of the longest liver of three men named in the lease).[2] The City properties were usually tenements or shops, and occasionally a larger building such as the mansion house of the vicars choral. The country properties were usually manors and parsonages, though sometimes only woods or even grazing rights. Occasionally a lease was granted by the Bishop subject to a rent reserved to the Dean and Chapter; the endowments of the prebends were leased by the individual prebendaries: both kinds of lease were subject to the approval of the Chapter, though

---

[1] These men had been granted a twenty-one-year lease on 28 Nov. 1614; they surrendered this earlier lease on securing the new one. This lease was in turn surrendered for a new one (again for twenty-one years at the same rent of £43) on 1 June 1630.

[2] A form of renewal of a 'lease for lives' may be found in Prideaux's *Precedents in Conveyancing*, 18th ed., ii. 164.

this seems to have been granted automatically. Prebendal leases, however, seem to have been subject to the gravest abuses. During the period of office of Donne's predecessor (Valentine Cary) a certain Thomas Sharman secured three prebendal leases for rent obviously far below their values: the prebends of Mora and Hoxton at 13*s*. 4*d*. per annum, and the prebend of Ealdstreet at 10*s*. per annum.[1] Sharman must have been prepared to pay very heavy fines. The only non-prebendal lease of Cary's time that one is inclined to question is the lease of the manor of Hawkesbury with Lambroke Marsh for a rent of £5. 7*s*. 8*d*. Otherwise one has the impression that rents were fairly stable; if the example of Sutton Court is at all typical (and I think it is), the Cathedral rents had, in the main, been unchanged since the Reformation. There had nevertheless been a phenomenal rise in prices during the previous eighty years, and this must have been reflected in the amount of the fine paid by the lessee at the time the lease was made or renewed. Occasionally a lease states that it was made 'in consideration of a certen some of lawfull money of England . . . in hand before th' ensealing hereof', but the amount is never specified. One, and only one, instance of Donne's dealing with Cathedral tenants has been recorded: his servants Thomas Roper and Robert Christmas testified that on 29 March 1625 Tobias Massey and John Foster paid Donne as Receiver General of the Cathedral the sum of £100, on receipt of which he clearly stated that 'hee receaued not the said 100^li to make good or approue or iustifie any newe lease whatsoeuer w*h*ich they pretended to haue of the Mannor and Rectorie of Tottenham . . . nor would hee doe any act or thing that might ought or should conclude or binde succession touchinge the said pretended lease'.[2] He was evidently at pains to avoid any suggestion of bribery or other action which could be construed as creating an obligation of the Cathedral authorities towards the two tenants.

The evidence, such as it is, suggests that Donne performed his administrative functions with integrity, and certainly the contrast between the haphazard records in the Bishop of London's Registers

[1] These prebends were valued in the King's Book at £19. 17*s*. 6*d*., £10. 5*s*., and £5. 15*s*. a year respectively. The leases are recorded in Reg. Carey, ff. 257–8.
[2] Reg. Donne, fo. 97^v.

(before Laud tightened up the administration) and the Registers and accounts of St. Paul's during Donne's term gives one great respect for his care and efficiency. He made, however, little attempt to change existing practice and hence cannot be looked upon as a reforming dean. Grants and leases to kinsmen still continued during his deanship. Theophilus Aylmer (archdeacon of London) granted the office of Registrar to the Archdeacon of London to John and Samuel Aylmer jointly, and Henry King (archdeacon of Colchester) granted the office of Registrar to the Archdeacon of Colchester to Philip King. Thomas Mountfort (prebendary of Harlesdon) granted a lease of the manor house at Harlesdon and another of the canonical houses at Harlesdon to John Mountfort. John Bancroft (prebendary of Mapesbury) leased the prebend of Mapesbury to Richard Bancroft. The Bishop (George Mountain) awarded the office of keeping the site of the manor of Hadham jointly to Isaac Mountain, Samuel Paske (William Paske was one of the prebendaries), and Thomas Stockton. And so it went on. Henry King secured a lease of part of the lodgings of the vicars choral and Thomas Winniff secured from Thomas Goad (the precentor) the chanter's mansion house. As residentiaries they may have wanted the houses to live in, but it is much more likely that they were speculating in Cathedral property.[1] On the other hand, there is no shred of evidence that Donne used his position to secure leases for himself or offices for his kinsmen. The principal appointments he made were of competent and hard-working officials who soon became his friends. Martin Pearson, who was appointed master of the choristers in 1626, was a distinguished musician and composer;[2] Thomas Roper was successively keeper of the Library, auditor to the Dean and Chapter, and Collector of rents and revenues first for the old and then for the new fabric; Robert Christmas was appointed Dean's verger soon after Donne took office, and succeeded Roper as keeper of the Library.[3] These last two Donne referred to in his will as his 'faithful servants',

---

[1] Ibid., ff. 16, 22, 68, 86, 89, 98, 107, 222.

[2] Pearson had been (for a time at least) a recusant. He, with Thomas Lodge and Ben Jonson and sixteen others, was indicted for non-attendance at church on 5 Oct. 1605; see J. George, 'Additional Materials on the Life of Thomas Lodge between 1604 and 1613', *Papers Mainly Shakespearian*, ed. G. I. Duthie, 1964, at p. 92.

[3] Reg. Donne, ff. 62, 63, 97, 176, 208, 233.

bequeathing to them legacies and copies of his seal ring engraved with his cross and anchor device.

Since the Cathedral was a medieval building, the fabric had crumbled and was in need of repair. There was among the Cathedral endowments a 'fabric fund' from which money for upkeep came, but this was quite inadequate for what was needed in the way of repair. James I was persuaded to make a state visit to the Cathedral on Sunday, 26 March 1620, where he heard matins and then attended a sermon at the Cross ('he *visited this Church*, and these wals, and meditated, and perswaded the reparation thereof').[1] Soon afterwards a Royal Commission was appointed to determine what needed to be done, to procure estimates and to collect contributions. But enthusiasm soon flagged; when Donne became Dean some money, but not enough, had been raised and some building supplies had been bought; but it was clear that the appeal had been a failure. Donne, who had successfully exhorted the members of Lincoln's Inn to rebuild their chapel, might have been expected to see a greater opportunity here to distinguish himself by raising funds for the repair of the Cathedral, but there is no hint that he made any effort to do so. At Lincoln's Inn he had had a keen and energetic committee behind him; at St. Paul's he may have felt that the initiative belonged to the Bishop, and that to try to seize it himself would only arouse antagonisms. At any rate, he did nothing, and a large quantity of Portland stone that the Bishop had purchased for the repairs was 'borrowed' by the Duke of Buckingham towards the rebuilding of the old York House, which was now the town residence of the favourite. The restoration of St. Paul's was not undertaken until shortly after Donne's death when Laud became aware of its urgency and took it in hand with his characteristic vigour.

In one respect Donne as Dean did not escape public censure, and that without wholly deserving it. The problem of making visitors behave in an orderly and reverent fashion inside the walls of the Cathedral was, then as now, a difficult one, and one which cannot be said ever to have been solved. Every student of the literature of Donne's period recalls the chapter in Dekker's *Gull's Hornbook* on

---

[1] *Sermons*, iv, no. 9, ll. 396–9, p. 247.

how the gallant should behave in Paul's walk, or recollects the character of the same place in Earle's *Microcosmographie*. The nave and transepts were one of the most popular meeting-places for Londoners; 'the noise in it', wrote Earle, 'is like that of bees, a strange humming and buzz mixed of walking tongues and feet; it is a kind of still roar or loud whisper. It is the great exchange of all discourse, and no business whatsoever but is here stirring and afoot.' Services went on in the choir behind the screen, but the noise from the other side was often intolerable. The transepts were a thoroughfare through which all kinds of porters carried goods from the wharves to warehouses in the northern part of the city; every kind of business was transacted in the nave. One simple man, haled before the authorities for urinating within the building, apologized and gave as his excuse that he did not know he was in a church. On Sundays and holidays the children from the neighbouring parishes of St. Gregory and St. Faith 'presently after dynner come into the Church, there they playe in such manner as children vse to doe till darke night, and hence cometh principally that inordinate noyse, which many tymes suffereth not the preacher to be heard in the Quyre'.[1] In 1631, shortly after Donne's death, a commission appointed to inquire into the profanation of the Cathedral issued its report, and placed the blame squarely upon the Dean and Chapter. The parishes of St. Gregory and St. Faith, the report said, were within their jurisdiction; therefore they could insist that parents and masters put a stop to the playing of games within the Cathedral. As for adults who created disturbances, 'it will well beseeme Mr. Deane and the Canons in their proper persons and habits in tyme of dyuine Service, to come into the bodie of the church some certayne tymes, and to requyre such as they shall fynde walkinge or talkinge there, either to come in the Quyre, there to heare divyne service, or to depart the church'. The vergers, too, should be instructed 'to warne such men, as they shall fynde there walkinge, either to come into the Quyre, or to depart the Church. And vppon such refusall to gyve in their names to his Maiesties Avocate. That prosecution maye be had against

---

[1] *Documents illustrating the History of St. Paul's Cathedral*, ed. W. Sparrow Simpson, Camden Society, N.S. xxvi (1880), 131.

them.'[1] Donne had not been entirely neglectful of order and decency at the Cathedral services, and a record exists which shows that he had been prepared to take measures very like those that the commissioners recommended. On 12 March 1629/30 the Court of Aldermen had before them

Christopher Ruddy one of the yeomen to Mr. Sheriff Smyth for sitting in the tyme of Divine Service in Paules and refusing to kneale notwithstanding he was thrice admonished by the virgers from the Deane then present, but in contempt did therevpon depart thence. [He] was by this court comitted to the gaole of Newgate there to remayne vntill other order bee taken for his enlargement.[2]

The reprimand to Ruddy was no accident, and was aimed at his master as much as himself. Humphrey Smith was evidently a stiff Puritan; he was a former Master of the Grocers' Company, who was chosen alderman in 1629 and was almost immediately afterwards elected sheriff.[3] The newly elected magistrates of the City went in procession to attend divine service at St. Paul's on Halloween, and on that occasion Donne must have noticed the behaviour of Sheriff Smith and his household, for he was prepared on the next occasion on which the Lord Mayor and the aldermen came in state to St. Paul's, which was Christmas Day.[4] In the Dean's Christmas sermon of 1629, there is a long passage, not particularly relevant to the festival being celebrated, on the necessity of kneeling in church,[5] prefaced by these pointed remarks:

Deus stetit, saies David, God standeth in the Congregation; does God stand there, and wilt thou sit? sit, and never kneele? I would speake so, as the congregation should not know whom I meane; but so, as that they whom it concernes, might know I meane them; I would speake: for, I must say, that there come some persons to this Church, and persons of example to many that come with them, of whom, (excepting some few, who must therefore have their praise from us, as, no doubt, they have their thanks and blessings from God) I never

---

[1] Documents . . ., Camden Society, N.S. xxvi (1880), pp. 131–2.

[2] Repertory, City of London Muniments, vol. 44, fo. 176ᵛ, quoted by B. W. Whitlock, 'The Dean and the Yeoman', N&Q, cxcix (1954), 374–5.

[3] A. B. Beaven, The Aldermen of the City of London (1908–13), ii. 61, 179.

[4] For a list of days when the Mayor and aldermen went to service at St. Paul's, see Stow's Survey of London, ed. C. L. Kingsford, ii. 190.

[5] Sermons, ix, no. 5, ll. 773–833, pp. 152–3.

saw Master nor servant kneele, at his comming into this Church, or at any part of divine service.

As subsequent events proved, Sheriff Smith was one, if not the principal, target of these remarks. But Donne could scarcely take any further measures against one of the sheriffs; he evidently waited until a member of Smith's household came to the Cathedral alone, warned him fairly, and finally under provocation had him arrested. It says much for Donne's prestige that the Court of Aldermen, already reputed to be puritanically inclined, supported his action rather than that of one of their own number. This incident shows clearly that Donne was at least on the watch to prevent certain kinds of profanation and disrespect, even though the problem of keeping any but worshippers out of the Cathedral at service time was too much for him or for any other Dean.

In the letter to Mrs. Cockayne referred to earlier in this chapter, Donne speaks of being 'under a necessitie of Preaching twelve or fourteen solemn Sermons every year, to great Auditories, at *Paules*, and to the Judges, and at Court'; and certainly his preaching duties at St. Paul's were neither irksome nor onerous. As Dean he was expected to preach in the Cathedral on Christmas Day, Easter Day, and Ascension Day; his only prescribed duty as prebendary of Chiswick was to preach on Whit Monday. Actually, he preached more often, as there have survived a number of sermons preached on the anniversary of the conversion of St. Paul (a major festival at the Cathedral, 25 January), on Candlemas Day (2 February), and on the penitential psalms. In addition, he imposed on himself the congenial task of preaching a series of sermons from the five psalms (62–6 inclusive) which it was his duty as prebendary of Chiswick to recite daily:

In this Church, by ancient Constitutions, it is ordained, That the whole booke of Psalmes should every day, day by day bee rehearsed by us, who make the Body of this Church, in the eares of Almighty God. And therefore every Prebendary of this Church, is by those Constitutions bound every day to praise God in those five Psalmes which are appointed for his Prebend. And of those five Psalmes which belong to mee, this, out of which I have read you this Text [62: 9], is the first. And, by Gods grace, (upon like occasions) I shall here handle some part of every one of the other foure Psalmes, for some testimony, that those my five Psalmes returne often into my meditation, which I also assure my selfe of the rest of my brethren, who are under the same obligation in this Church.[1]

And, though we may be absent from this Quire, yet wheresoever dispersed, we make up a Quire in this Service, of saying over all the Psalmes every day.[2]

None of the sermons preached to the judges seems to have survived, but at Court Donne preached regularly on the first Friday in Lent and was in attendance as royal chaplain during April, when he preached at least once and sometimes twice. He visited his country parishes during the summer and usually preached there; in addition, a number of the sermons preached at St. Dunstan's have been preserved. Donne, it is clear, thought of preaching as one of his talents and as one of the principal instruments of his ministry, which he must not fail to use. Walton describes him as preaching at least once a week, but while this was certainly true of his period at Lincoln's Inn during term-time, as Dean he was under no obligation to preach so frequently. No doubt he received frequent invitations to preach at special services, and he probably preached at St. Dunstan's more often than there is any record to show; but there is no reason to suppose that his duties as a preacher were unduly irksome or demanding.

It is evident, however, that he put a great deal into his preaching. Walton describes how Donne prepared his sermons:

The latter part of his life may be said to be a continued study; for as he usually preached once a week, if not oftner, so after his Sermon he never gave his eyes rest, till he had chosen out a new Text, and that night cast his Sermon into a form, and his Text into divisions; and the next day betook himself to consult the Fathers, and so commit his meditations to his memory, which was excellent. But upon Saturday he usually gave himself and his mind a rest from the weary burthen of his weeks meditations, and usually spent that day in visitation of friends, or some other diversions of his thoughts.[3]

---

[1] *Sermons*, vi, no. 15, ll. 45–57, pp. 293–4; cf. vii, no. 1, ll. 10–26, pp. 51–2. A list of prebends with their appropriate psalms and lessons is given by Newcourt, *Repertorium Ecclesiasticum &c.* i. 53–4; cf. Hennessy, *Novum Repertorium &c.*, p. 21.

[2] *Sermons*, vii, no. 9, ll. 10–12, p. 237.   [3] *Lives*, p. 67.

Such a passage, perhaps, deserves the Johnsonian comment that it depicts a regularity possible only in a college or a cloister (and Donne was a busy churchman in a great capital), but this criticism does not invalidate Walton's description of Donne's method. In accordance with the best practice of the time, he would have delivered his sermons either with no notes at all or with a minimum of notes; it was the preacher's aim to appear to speak directly to his hearers, without any suggestion of a script to which he was tied. But this seeming naturalness did not imply any lack of preparation —far from it, as Walton's account insists. Donne planned his sermons, collected and organized his materials, all with the greatest care; he made plentiful notes and may, on occasion, have written out the sermon in full before delivery—a kind of preparation which he must have undertaken for many of his Court sermons, including the last, *Deaths Duell*. Most often, however, he worked from notes and outlines, and it was from such materials as these that in 1625, while the plague raged in London, he beguiled his temporary exile by revising 'as many of my sermons as I had kept any note of, and I have written out a great many, and hope to do more'.[1] From such revised and expanded versions the majority of *LXXX Sermons* and *Fifty Sermons* were printed.

After he became Dean there was a change in the tone of Donne's preaching. Two characteristics distinguish the sermons delivered in St. Paul's: Donne seems now to speak with the authority of the Church behind him; and he strives to make sure that what he says will be intelligible to the simpler minds among his auditory. At Lincoln's Inn he had been addressing a highly trained audience, at Court a compact and civilized social group; he had been able to appeal to both congregations by addressing himself sometimes to their knowledge, whether of law, of politics, or of letters, and sometimes to their subtler intellectual capacities. At St. Paul's (far more than at St. Dunstan's, which must have drawn its congregations almost as much from the Inns of Court as from the citizens) he was addressing

[1] To Sir Thomas Roe, Gosse, ii. 225 (from S.P. Dom.). For a fuller discussion of this topic, see J. Hayward, 'A Note on Donne the Preacher', in *A Garland for John Donne*, ed. T. Spencer (1931), pp. 73–98; J. Sparrow, 'John Donne and Contemporary Preachers', *Essays and Studies by Members of the English Association*, xvi (1930), 144–78; [and *Lancelot Andrewes—Sermons*, ed. G. M. Story (Oxford, 1967), pp. xliv–xlvii.]

a real cross-section of Londoners, and he had to make his message clear to them all. The St. Paul's sermons are also the most elaborately wrought, and often among the longest, of the sermons, with a touch of formality (or 'distance') absent in the others.

It was at St. Paul's that Donne's reputation as a preacher was made, for till he became Dean he had never had to preach regularly to large and miscellaneous congregations such as gathered in the Cathedral on Sundays and holy days. The growth of his reputation is interestingly reflected in Chamberlain's letters to Carleton. On 17 November 1621, reporting that Donne is likely to become Dean any day now, he relates that 'a pleasant companion saide that yf Ben Johnson might be made deane of Westminster, that place, Paules, and Christchurche, shold be furnished with three very pleasant poeticall deanes',[1] but by July the following year he was reporting that 'our Deane made a very goode sermon in the church as he hath don divers of late with great concourse'.[2] Flippancy has given way to respect. There must have been a vital, even a histrionic, quality in Donne's preaching which attracted listeners. Walton says that he was

A Preacher in earnest; weeping sometimes for his Auditory, sometimes with them: always preaching to himself, like an Angel from a cloud, but in none; carrying some, as St. *Paul* was, to Heaven in holy raptures, and inticing others by a sacred Art and Courtship to amend their lives; here picturing a vice so as to make it ugly to those that practised it; and a vertue so, as to make it be beloved even by those that lov'd it not; and all this with a most particular grace and an unexpressible addition of comeliness.[3]

But the fullest description of Donne in the pulpit is to be found in the Latin elegy appended to the *Poems* and written by a young clergyman, Daniel Darnelly:

Vidi,
Audivi et stupui quoties orator in Aede
Paulina stetit, et mira gravitate levantes
Corda, oculosque viros tenuit: dum Nestoris ille

---

[1] Chamberlain, *Letters*, ii. 407–8. Richard Corbet had recently been appointed Dean of Christ Church, Oxford.
[2] Ibid., p. 443.   [3] *Lives*, p. 49.

Fudit verba (omni quanto mage dulcia melle?)
Nunc habet attonitos, pandit mysteria plebi
Non concessa prius nondum intellecta: revolvunt
Mirantes, tacitique arrectis auribus astant.
   Mutatis mox ille modo, formaque loquendi
Tristia pertractat: fatumque et flebile mortis
Tempus, et in cineres redeunt quod corpora primos.
Tunc gemitum cunctos dare, tunc lugere videres,
Forsitan a lachrymis aliquis non temperat, atque
Ex oculis largum stillat rorem; aetheris illo
Sic pater audito voluit succumbere turbam,
Affectusque ciere suos, et ponere notae
Vocis ad arbitrium, divinae oracula mentis
Dum narrat, rostrisque potens dominatur in altis.[1]

Other elegists also expressed their admiration, but none so fully as this. Yet Donne was not always received with unreserved approval, and another elegist, 'R. B.', reports some of the criticism of the Puritans, whom Donne so frequently attacked in his preaching:

> They humm'd against him; And with face most sowre
> Call'd him a strong lin'd man, a Macaroon,
> And no way fit to speake to clouted shoone,
> As fine words [truly] as you would desire,
> But [verily,] but a bad edifier.[2]

The issue, as the Puritans saw it, was between the plain and the ornate—plain moral instructions or a style of preaching that made use of all the resources of learning and of rhetoric.

All the sermons preached by Donne in St. Paul's on the solemn festivals at which he was required to preach have survived, with a fairly considerable number of others delivered in the Cathedral. As we have noted, none of the sermons he was accustomed to preach before the judges seems to have come down to us; presumably they were preached at the beginnings of law terms. These were occasions

---

[1] Grierson, i. 391.

[2] Ibid., pp. 386–7. Giles Oldisworth, in his copy of the 1639 edition of the poems, identifies R. B. as R. Busby, presumably the famous headmaster of Winchester; this is more likely than Gosse's suggestion of Richard Brathwaite or Grierson's of Ralph Brideoak. See J. Sampson, 'A Contemporary Light on John Donne', Essays and Studies by Members of the English Association, vii (1920), 82–107.

of some ceremony, since 'All the Aldermen do meet the Lord Maior and the Sheriffs at *Paul*'s, wearing their Scarlet Gowns either furred or lined, [according as the Time of the Year requireth] without Cloaks or Horses, when the Term beginneth'.[1] As for the many other invitations to preach which came to him, it is often difficult to distinguish those which he received as Dean from those which came to the successful Court preacher, or even from those which were extended to him by his highly placed friends. Sermons such as that in memory of Magdalen Herbert (Lady Danvers), or the sermon 'at Hanworth to my Lord of Carlisle and his company', or the sermon at the marriage of the Earl of Bridgewater's daughter to the son of Lord Herbert of Cherbury, were all preached at the request of friends or patrons. On the other hand, Donne occasionally acted as an official spokesman or apologist for the actions of the King and his ministers, as in his sermon at Paul's Cross on 15 September 1622 in support of James's directions for preachers. Another *ex officio* sermon, of a rather different sort, delivered soon after Donne's appointment as Dean, was that 'Preached at the Spittle, upon Easter Monday, 1622'. This was delivered at the Cross by St. Mary's Hospital in Bishopsgate, where there was an open-air pulpit like that at St. Paul's Cross. According to Stow, every year

on Good Friday, in the after noone, some especiall learned man, by appoyntment of the Prelats, hath preached a Sermon at *Paules* crosse, treating of Christs passion: and vpon the three next Easter Holy-dayes, Monday, Tuesday, and Wednesday, ... the like learned men ... haue vsed to preach on the forenoones at the sayde Spittle, to perswade the Article of Christs resurrection; and then on low Sunday, one other learned man at *Paules* Crosse, to make rehearsall of those foure former Sermons, either commending or reprouing them.[2]

The Lord Mayor and the Aldermen attended Donne's sermon in their scarlet robes, and in a separate stand the governors and children of Christ's Hospital were accustomed to sit. At the beginning of the sermon Donne refers to its place in the series: 'that which shall be said by me, and by my Brethren which come after, and were worthy to come before me, in this place, is to be said to you again,

---

[1] Strype's ed. of Stow's *Survey of London* (1720), ii, bk. v, p. 170a.
[2] *Survey of London*, ed. C. L. Kingsford, i. 167–8.

by another, who alone, takes as much pains, as all we, and all you too: Hears all, with as much patience as all you; and is to speak of all, with as much, and more labour, then all we.'[1] A little later there is a skilful allusion to the school children and the City magnates among his auditory:

> Hath God brought thee from an Exposititious Child laid out in the streets, of uncertain name, of unknown Parents, to become the first foundation-stone of a great family, and to enoble a posterity? . . . Hath God brought thee from one of these Blew-Coats, to one of those Scarlet Gowns? Attribute not this to thine own Industry, nor to thine own Frugality; (for, Industry is but Fortunes right hand, and Frugality her left;) but come to *Davids* Acclamation, *Dominus Fecit, It is the Lords doing*.[2]

The text (2 Cor. 4: 6) was suitable enough for the occasion, and Donne was, of course, conscious that his sermon was to be judged in the context of the three other Easter sermons; nevertheless he did not hesitate also to justify and defend in the City his sacred calling, and to insist that the City should pay it more honour: 'I may be bold to say, that this City hath the ablest preaching Clergy of any City in Christendom; must I be fain to say, that the Clergy of this City hath the poorest intertainment of any City that can come into comparison with it? it is so.'[3] This sermon is much the longest of Donne's which has survived, and his editors calculate that (unless it was subsequently expanded) it must have taken about two and a half hours to deliver.[4] Yet at the beginning Donne promised that 'farther then the custom, and solemnity of this day, and place, lays an Obligation upon me', he would not extend himself 'to an unnecessary length'.[5] The Spital sermons must therefore have been traditionally much longer than most sermons, but it can be said in Donne's favour that this one is capable of holding the attention of an adult auditory, even for so long a time; of the Christ's Hospital children it is less easy to speak. Easter week was an occasion not only of much sermonizing within the City, but of banqueting as well. Middleton wrote entertainments the previous year for banquets given both by the Lord

---

[1] *Sermons*, iv, no. 3, ll. 113–18, p. 92.
[2] Ibid., ll. 256–65, p. 96.
[3] Ibid., ll. 895–8, p. 113.
[4] Ibid., iv. 30.
[5] Ibid., no. 3, ll. 111–13, p. 92.

Mayor and by the sheriffs.[1] These too seem to have been a regular feature, and Donne was doubtless a guest at one of them when his sermon was over.

Many people besides Walton and the other writers of elegies on Donne's death must have remembered his sermons. In his *Discours Apologetical* Thomas Gataker (who had been Reader at Lincoln's Inn from April 1602 until February 1613) writes:

> And I remember, that being called over by the Lord Cheif Justice of the Common Pleas [Sir Henry Hobart], to whom, as before was said, I had some relation, lying then very sick, and requested to stay a Sabbath day with him, I heard at the publike Assemblie in the fore-part of the day, Dr. *Donne* one of my Successors at *Lincolns-Inn*, then lately preferred to the Deanrie of *Pauls*; When after my return from the Sermon, his Lordship having demanded of me whom I had heard? *you see*, said he; *how some of your Successors rise, and why do not you seek for some Prebend at least?*[2]

Yet such references are surprisingly few.[3] It is interesting, however, to see Hobart, a friend of Donne, pointing to him as an example of (no doubt well deserved) success.

Early in 1622 Donne learned that another benefice was soon to come his way. Though there is very little to suggest it, he had evidently been acquainted for some time with the Earl of Kent. The sole hint of any such friendship occurs in a letter of the summer of 1620 to Goodyer, in which, it will be recalled, Donne speaks of meditating a visit to Wrest Park after leaving Bedford on his way back to London from Keyston ('I went out of this Town, in a doubt whether I should turn in to *Wrest*; and you know the wisdome of

---

[1] Thomas Middleton, *Honourable Entertainments*, Malone Soc. Reprints, 1953, Entertainment no. 8.

[2] [*Discours Apologetical*, 1654, p. 52; noted by W. Gifford, 'A Donne Allusion', *NQ*, ccxi, Jan. 1966, p. 14. The sermon referred to must have been delivered between Christmas 1621 and Hobart's death on Christmas Day 1625.]

[3] On 1 June 1630 a Mr. Hinton told Crosfield of 'Dr. Donne deane of Pauls, his powerfull kinde of preaching by his gestur & Rhetoriquall expression' (*The Diary of Thomas Crosfield*, ed. F. S. Boas, 1935, p. 43). In a letter to Pepys, 15 Aug. 1671 (Bodleian Library, MS. Rawl. A174 fo. 372) Richard Gibson says he is put in mind 'of a Speech of Dr Donn's Deane of St Paules in a Sermon there, vizt, that ye Goodness of God was not soe much seene in our Creation as Redemption, nor soe much that wee are his, as that nothing can take vs out of his hands'; [Mr. Shapiro tells me that Gibson is referring to the same quotation in a letter (1616) of Somerset printed in *Cabala*, 1654, p. 3].

the Parliament is, to resolve ever in the Negative');[1] Wrest Park was the Earl of Kent's principal residence. Donne had apparently been promised for some time the rectory of Blunham in Bedfordshire, a living in the Earl's gift, when it next fell vacant. That a vacancy was imminent he learned on 26 February 1622; on that day he wrote to Goodyer, sending with an enclosure for Lady Bedford his humble services to Lady Ruthyn, wife of the Earl of Kent's son and heir. Only that day, he added, he had received

a letter from my *L.* of *Kent,* written yesterday at *Wrest:* in that his Lordship sends me word, that that favour which he hath formerly done me, in giving me *Blo[n]ham,* is now likely to fall upon me, because the Incumbent is dangerously ill: and because this is the season in which he removes from *Wrest* thither, he desires (for I give you his own word) that he may be accommodate there, (if it fall now) as heretofore. Out of my absolute and intire readiness to serve that family, I sent back his messenger with this answer, that I esteemed it a great part of my good fortune, that I should become worthy to be commanded by him.[2]

The Earl evidently spent part of each year at Blunham in the old manor-house ('a 17th-century building now used as a butcher's shop, [which] is opposite the church. It was once the residence of Charles Earl of Kent, who died here' [1624]),[3] for he had considerable estates there. The original parsonage must in the course of time have come to serve as the manor house, otherwise it is difficult to see why Donne's permission should have been so courteously asked. The living fell vacant shortly afterwards, and Donne was instituted in the rectory by 18 April.[4] Though a curate was in charge of the parish, Donne, as had been his custom in his other country benefices, paid an annual visit to Blunham and preached there for a few weeks; a recent rector found that some of the older people of the parish preserved the oral tradition that Dr. Donne 'stayed at the manor,

---

[1] *Letters,* p. 202.   [2] Ibid., pp. 176–7.

[3] *Victoria County History of Bedfordshire,* iii. 228. The new Earl and his wife, the Lady Ruthyn of Donne's letter, were close friends of John Selden, and it is said that after becoming a widow the Countess married Selden. The youthful Samuel Butler entered the service of the Earl at Wrest Park in 1628. He was certainly well acquainted with Selden, and it is more than possible that he also knew Donne.

[4] His first payments for Blunham appear on 18 Apr. 1622 in the Office of First Fruits and Tenths, Composition Books Ser. 3, vol. i, and Receiver's Accounts (E341/13), P.R.O.

and went back to London with a load of cucumbers in his carriage'.[1]
In 1626 he presented to the church a silver-gilt chalice,[2] and in his
will he remembered the poor of the parish of Blunham, as he did also
the poor of his parishes of Sevenoaks and St. Dunstan-in-the-West.

In his lines 'On Doctor Donne' Richard Corbet claimed that
anyone who would write a fit epitaph for Donne

> must have learning plenty; both the Lawes,
> Civill, and Common, to judge any cause;[3]

but it is not generally realized how much Donne himself needed the
legal knowledge that he possessed and how often, after he became
Dean, he had to act in a judicial capacity. In a list of Justices of the
Peace tentatively dated 1622 his name is interlined in the counties
of Kent and Bedford; in a later list of 1626–30 his name appears under
Bedford alone.[4] The commission of peace for each county usually
included two or three doctors of divinity, and Donne served in two
of the counties in which he held livings. Whether he ever sat on the
bench is not discoverable, but Corbet seems to imply that he did,
and that his early training in the common law was of value to him.

After he became Dean, Donne was appointed thirteen times in all
to hear appeals from the lower ecclesiastical courts and to sit in the
Court of Delegates. This court owed its existence to the provisions
made by statute (25 Henry VIII, c. 19) for appeals from the higher
ecclesiastical courts after the right of appeal to Rome had been
abolished. Appeals were now to be made by petition to the Crown
in Chancery, and a special commission of delegates was appointed
by letters patent for each case. The summary of one such commission which included Donne is to be found in the *Calendar of State
Papers, Domestic*:

July 13   Commission to Bishops Buckeridge of Ely, and Field
[1628]   of St. David's; Sir William Jones, one of the Justices
Westminster   of the King's Bench; Sir George Croke, one of the

---

[1] *Sermons*, v. 428.

[2] The chalice is hall-marked 1626, and is inscribed round its base 'From Dr Donne
Deane of Pauls, for Blunham Church'. The photograph in ibid., p. 427, of the
inscribed base is wrongly said to be of the paten, shown on the previous page. But
the *Victoria County History of Bedfordshire*, iii. 233, states that the paten was given
(1682) by a Dr. Archer, and is hall-marked 1681.

[3] Grierson, i. 374.   [4] P.R.O., C193/12/2, fo. 1, and 13/1, ff. 6 and 53.

Justices of Common Pleas; John Donne, Dean of St.
Paul's; Sir Charles Caesar, one of the Masters in Chan-
cery; Sir John Lambe, and Doctors John Pope, Edmund
Pope, Nathaniel Brent, and Thomas Gwynne, to re-
examine the proceedings in the Prerogative Court of
Canterbury, relative to the last will of Thomas
Payne, of Plymouth; issued on the petition of Thomas
Vaughan, on behalf of himself and others, the children
and grandchildren of Katherine Vaughan, daughter
of the said Thomas Payne.[1]

In this instance a panel of eleven was appointed: two bishops, two
judges, a dean, a Master in Chancery, and five civilians. The case
was a testamentary one, and it was well that both common and civil
law should be fully represented. Two of the eleven formed a quorum,
and some of the more formal business of the case was conducted by
only two judges, but a larger number was usually present when the
more important points of the case were argued and when sentence
was given. This particular case was opened on 19 July 1628, and
judgement was given on 1 February 1629/30. The actual sentence,
which survives, was signed by the Bishop of Ely, the two common
law judges, Donne, and four of the civilians.[2]

Most of the commissions of which Donne was a member were on
the model of this one: two or three bishops, two or more doctors
of divinity, a couple of judges, and a good strengthening of ecclesiastical lawyers. Donne sat with Lancelot Andrewes in two cases,
with Samuel Harsnet in two others, and with Thomas Morton in
one. Most of the common law judges he would have met at one time
or another, if he did not know them already from his earlier legal
associations, and he must eventually have come to know pretty well
all the members of Doctors' Commons. In one case, however (that
of Wagstaffe v. Cockayne), the panel was much larger and contained
three earls, a privy councillor, the Master of the Rolls, and the Dean
of the Arches, besides the usual selection of bishops, deans, judges,
and civilians—a tribute more perhaps to the social importance of

[1] C.S.P. (Dom.), 1628–9, p. 208; cf. 'Donne the Lawyer', TLS, 1 Aug. 1942. The
enrolment of the commission (P.R.O.) is at C66/2481/pt. 1. (Other enrolments
including Donne's name are at C66/2306/1 and 2352/4.)
[2] P.R.O., Del. 8/70, fo. 37ʳ, and Del. 5/7, no. 66.

the litigants than to the issues in dispute. In this case Donne was present at the early stages of the argument but not at the later ones. The Delegates most commonly sat on Saturday afternoons; there was no fixed place of sitting, which could vary from Doctors' Commons or the Consistory Court at St. Paul's to an upper chamber in the Bishop of London's palace. Indeed, in the more formal stages of the suit, when little more was required than an order signed by two members of the panel, one reads in the act books of the Court such notations as that a session was held 'in [a]edibus venerabilis viri Johannis Dun sacre theologie professoris decani ecclesiae Cathedralis diui Pauli London infra Cemiterium diui Pauli London'.[1]

Donne's attendances and no doubt his interest varied from case to case among those which he was called upon to judge. The size of the various panels meant that members of the commission need attend only when they were conveniently able, or wanted, to do so. Donne seems as a rule to have been interested in the cases to which he was appointed and attended fairly often—more often, on the whole, than any of the other judges except the professional civilians. He was also called on for some of the formal work of the Court because he was relatively accessible; the Deanery was but a short distance from Doctors' Commons, the Consistory Court, and the Bishop's Palace, whereas most of the other non-civilians had to be sought out at Westminster or at the Inns of Court. Donne's work with the Court of Delegates spans the period from June 1622 until his death.

He was also a member of the Court of High Commission during most of the time during which he was Dean. This Court owed its existence to commissions which were issued from time to time appointing a selected number of important men, lay and clerical, to inquire into and redress spiritual and ecclesiastical abuses. The number so appointed was considerable, and by the end of James I's reign had grown to over a hundred.

In 1620 it contained the Archbishop of Canterbury and fourteen southern bishops, sitting *ex officio*, the Lord Chancellor, the Lord Treasurer, the Lord Privy Seal, the Master of the Rolls, the Chief Justices and Chief Baron, the ecclesiastical judges, the Master of

[1] Del. 4/9, fo. 102ʳ

Requests and Master of Chancery, and several doctors of divinity and doctors of civil law—in all forty-five. In 1626 it included both archbishops, all the bishops sitting *ex officio*, the Deans of Canterbury and St. Paul's, also *ex officio*, and all the other members of the quorum of 1620—in all fifty-five.[1]

At least one of these members of the quorum had to be present at every sitting of the Court, and a minimum of five in all was necessary. The remaining members were drawn from a selection of the nobility and gentry. Sir George More, for instance, was a member, as were two of his sons-in-law, Sir Nicholas Carey and Sir Thomas Grymes. The other residentiaries of St. Paul's, Henry King, Thomas Winniff, and Thomas Mountfort, were also members. Donne was not likely to be among strangers when he sat on the bench of the High Commission. The formal sessions of the Court had by this time come to be held in London on Thursdays during term. The formal sittings took place at Lambeth Palace, St. Paul's Consistory, Doctors' Commons, and the Chapter House at Westminster, while the more informal sessions were usually held at St. Paul's, at Bow Church, or at Doctors' Commons.[2]

The Court of High Commission was a much-used Court; it not only had its own original jurisdiction but had also usurped a good deal of that which had formerly belonged to the Court of Delegates; hence the load of its business was heavy. The records of the Court were destroyed soon after its abolition by Parliament, and it is therefore impossible to determine how often Donne participated in its sittings. From other sources, however, it is possible to recover the particulars of three actions with which he was concerned. The first was one of those cases which explain why the Long Parliament abolished the High Commission. The rector of Stourmouth in Kent was a certain George Huntley, who was a man of some learning but who, despite his Oxford M.A., had never obtained a licence to preach. In 1624 Huntley received instructions from his archdeacon to preach at the forthcoming archidiaconal visitation, but this he refused to do. The archdeacon appealed to the Archbishop, who

---

[1] R. G. Usher, *The Rise and Fall of the High Commission*, 1913, pp. 252–3; see also p. 350.
[2] Ibid., pp. 258–9.

commanded Huntley to preach the sermon the following year. He still refused, and as a result was called before the High Commission, which ordered him not only to preach the sermon but also to acknowledge his fault before the assembled clergy. Since he still persisted in his refusal (for he maintained not only that being unlicensed he was incompetent to preach but also that according to the ancient canon law it was the duty of the archdeacon himself to preach on such occasions), he had to appear before the High Commission again on 19 April 1627. Donne had not been present at Huntley's first appearance, but was a member of the panel that passed judgement on the second occasion. Incidentally, both the Archbishop of Canterbury and the archdeacon (Dr. Kingsley) whom Huntley had disobeyed were also members of the panel, and he could justly complain that he had been tried by his accusers. For contempt of court Huntley was sentenced to a fine of £500 and was committed to prison until he had given sureties not only for the payment of his fine but also for the performance of his submission.

This was obviously exemplary punishment, but the High Commission was used to imposing such sentences, which it did not expect to be carried out because they would be mitigated when the offender had been reduced to the proper mood of penitence. Unfortunately for him, Huntley was impenitent, and became only the more convinced that he was being ill-used. After two years in prison he was deprived and degraded; then in 1630 he was committed again and excommunicated. In 1633 proceedings were brought against him in the Exchequer for the non-payment of his fine, and he spent two periods of imprisonment in the Fleet. In 1631 he had tried to retaliate by bringing a suit against the High Commissioners for false imprisonment; the case dragged on for some years without coming to trial because, apparently, no barrister could be persuaded to accept the brief. It was not till after the assembly of the Long Parliament that Huntley's chance came; he published an account of his ill-treatment in 1642, and in 1644 gave evidence for the prosecution at the trial of Archbishop Laud.[1]

---

[1] [George Huntley], *An argument upon a generall Demurrer*, 1642, sig. A3; John Johnson, *The Case of a Rector refusing to preach a Visitation Sermon*, 1721, p. 10; W. Laud, *The Troubles and Tryal*, pp. 270–1; R. G. Usher, *The Rise and Fall of the High Commission*, pp. 318–19; R. Phillimore, *Ecclesiastical Law*, ed. 1873, ii. 1348–9. Phillimore remarks:

Donne's second case before the High Commission involved William Prynne's earliest brush with the authorities. His first book *The Perpetuitie of a Regenerate Mans Estate*, was, as the title suggests, a Calvinistic work, and it attacked the 'purblinde, squint-eyed, ideall Arminian Novellists', of whom Richard Montague, the author of *Appello Caesarem*, was the chief. But Arminianism was in favour with the King and many of the bishops, led by Laud, and Prynne's attack was not allowed to pass unchallenged. On 11 October 1627 Prynne, William James the printer, and Michael Sparkes the publisher of his book were all summoned to appear before the High Commission. At this time Prynne had not yet been called to the bar and was living in chambers in Lincoln's Inn. But writs could not be served by officers of the courts within the Inns of Court, and so Prynne's summons was enclosed in a letter to the Benchers asking them to allow service, or to serve it themselves. The summons was signed by four bishops and three civilians (including Sir Henry Martin) but the letter was signed by three of the four bishops (Mountain, Laud, and Field of St. David's), Martin and two other civilians, and Donne. It is just possible that Donne was asked to sign the letter because his friendly relations with the Benchers were well known, but it is equally possible that he merely happened to be more accessible when the letter was signed than when the summons was signed.[1] Whether Donne was in court when the case came up for hearing a fortnight later is not known, but Prynne and his lawyer friends outwitted the efforts of the High Church party to silence him by producing a writ of stay of proceedings from the common law courts, and the case had to be dropped.[2]

The third High Commission case in which Donne is known to have taken part was a matrimonial suit, and was in many ways more typical than Huntley's or Prynne's of the kind of case usually before the Court. Yet the participants stood high in the social scale, and the case provided one of the major society scandals of the age, a fact which explains why there was such a large and distinguished panel to try it. Viscount Purbeck was Buckingham's elder brother,

'This is one instance, amongst others, in which that court [the High Commission] whilst it subsisted carried matters with a pretty high hand' (p. 1349).

[1] *The Black Books of Lincoln's Inn*, ii. 271–4.

[2] E. W. Kirby, *William Prynne, a Study in Puritanism*, 1931, pp. 12–13.

and in 1617, while still Sir John Villiers, he had married Frances
Coke, daughter of Sir Edward Coke. The match had been warmly
supported by the King, and the sixteen-year-old bride was used as
a mere pawn by her parents in their notorious quarrels and in their
attempts to recapture the royal favour. Villiers was subject to
periodical fits of insanity, and after four years of marriage his wife
left him for Sir Robert Howard, a younger son of the Earl of Suffolk,
by whom she had a child. Buckingham fiercely resented this slight
on his family's honour, and pursued his erring sister-in-law with
some ruthlessness.[1] She was before the High Commission early in
1625 and was excommunicated (as was Sir Robert); thereupon she
retired to the country with her lover, and lived with him on his
estate in Shropshire. In 1627 the pair were indiscreet enough to
come to London; they were arrested and brought before the High
Commission again. This time the penalty was more severe; Lady
Purbeck was sentenced to do public penance in a white sheet in the
Savoy Church. The record of the sentence survives in the words of
Archbishop Laud:

> Now, the Cause of Sir *Robert Howard* was this. He fell in League
> with the *Lady Viscountess Purbeck*. The *Lord Viscount Purbeck* being in
> some weakness and distemper, the Lady used him at her pleasure, and
> betook her self in a manner, wholly to Sir *Robert Howard*, and had a
> Son by him. She was delivered of this Child in a Clandestine way,
> under the Name of *Mistress Wright*. These things came to be known,
> and she was brought into the *High-Commission*; and there, after a Legal
> Proceeding, was found guilty of *Adultery*, and Sentenced to do *Pen-
> nance*; Many of the great Lords of the Kingdom being present in Court,
> and agreeing in the Sentence. Upon this Sentence she withdrew her
> self, to avoid the *Penance*. This Sentence passed at *London-House*, in
> Bishop *Mountain*'s time, *Novemb.* 19, *An. Dom.* 1627. I was then
> present, as Bishop of *Bath* and *Wells*.

A sidenote adds:[2]

> There were present, and concurring in the Sentence, Sir *Tho.
> Coventry*, Lord Keeper of the Great Seal, *Hen.* Earl of *Manchester*, Lord

[1] [T. Longueville], *The Strange Case of Lady Purbeck*, 1909, and G. E. C., *Complete
Peerage*, *sub* Purbeck.
[2] *The History of the Troubles and Tryal of . . . William Laud* (1695), p. 146. The note
is presumably by Henry Wharton, Laud's editor.

President of the Council, *W.* Earl of *Pembroke*, Lord Steward, *Philip* Earl of *Mountgomery*, Lord Chamberlain, *Edw.* Earl of *Dorset*, *Oliver* Lord Viscount *Grandison*, *George* Lord Bishop of *London*, *Rich.* Lord Bishop of *Duresme*, *Sam.* Lord Bishop of *Norwich*, *Jo.* Lord Bishop of *Rochester*, *William* Lord Bishop of *Bath* and *Wells*, Sir *Jo. Coke* Secretary, Sir *Hen. Martin*, *Jo. Donn*, Dean of St. *Paul's*, *Walt. Balcanquall*, Dean of *Rochester*, *Tho. Worrall*, Doctor of Divinity, *Edm. Pope*, and *Hugh Barker*, Doctors of Law, and Sir *Charles Caesar*, who only desired to be spared, and so gave no Sentence.

Lady Purbeck, as Laud intimates, refused to do penance and made her escape from London. The story of her escape, which provoked a diplomatic incident, is told by Sir John Finet:

In time of Christmas, the Viscountess of *Purbeck*, having for execution of a sentence against her in the high Commission Court, her house beset by a Serjeant at Armes, with other Officers of Justice; a Gentleman came in the morning from the Countess of *Buckingham* to the Ambassador of *Savoy*, demanding leave of him for the said Officers to pass through his house into his Garden (joyned to the Ladies) for her more easie apprehension, and arrest by that way, which though at first he somewhat stuck at (as wronging and lesning (he thought) the respect of his quality, to leave his house free of entrance to such persons, especially for the surprize and arrest of a fair Lady his Neighbour) he at last, notwithstanding, suffered the Constable to enter it, and with convenience to remain in it and in the Garden, watching his opportunity till dinner-time, when some of the Gentlemen attendants on him, contriving a way to be rid of that incumbrance, dressed the Ambassadors Page (a handsome fair Boy) in womans apparell, thrust him suddenly into the Lords Coach, (as if it had been the Lady making her escape) and drove fast with him down the Strand, followed by a multitude of people, and those Officers (not without danger to the Coach-man, from their violence) but with ease to the Ambassador, that had his house by this device cleared of the Constable, but himself after charged by the Duke, That all this was done of designe for the Ladies escape (which in that Hubbub she made) to his no small prejudice, and scorn in a business that so neerly, he said, concerned him (she being Wife to His Brother, and bringing him Children of anothers begetting, yet such as by the Law (because begotten and born while her Husband was in the Land) must be of his Fathering.)[1]

[1] *Finetti Philoxenis* (1656), pp. 239–40.

With this sequel Donne, of course, had nothing to do. The fact that
Lady Purbeck was brought into the High Commission was largely
due to Buckingham's rancour, but once the case was before the
Court it is difficult to see what other sentence they could have
promulgated, since the facts were apparently so open and well
known. It is worth adding that the child who was christened
Robert Wright in due course grew to manhood and became a
staunch republican. He married a daughter of Donne's old friend
Sir John Danvers, and obtained a licence from Cromwell to take the
name of Danvers. After the Restoration he was summoned to Parliament as Viscount Purbeck, but he renounced the name of Villiers
and the title, preferring a career as a member of the House of
Commons.[1]

One more record of Donne's judicial activities should be added to
those already produced. Here Donne appears in the company of the
Archbishop and four bishops; they are submitting a report on a
dispute between the Bishop and the Dean and Chapter of Salisbury:

May it please your most excellent Majesty.

According to your gracious Reference, wee whose names are vnder-
written have severall times mett and endeavoured to accomodate the
differences betweene the *Bishop* on the one side, and the Deane and
Chapter of *Salisbury* on the other side. But not being able to prevaile
with both parties as wee desired, wee have held it our duty to certify
your Majesty, that vpon the whole hearing of both sides, wee finde no
reason to thinke otherwise, then that *Giles Tomkins* was lawfully
elected into the places now in question, and that hee ought to bee
admitted into the possession of the same. Yet notwithstanding wee
submitt all vnto your Princely pleasure.

At Lambeth. June. 22. 1629.

      G. Cant:

                   R. Winton: Jo: Eliens:
                       Fra: Noruicen:
                       Guil: Landauen:
                       J. Donne[2]

---

[1] Howard was sent to the Fleet in 1625 and again in April 1635. The Long Parliament voted him £1,000 as compensation for false imprisonment; a fine of £500 was
imposed on Laud as president of the High Commission, and fines of £250 each on his
legal assistants, Sir Henry Martin and Sir Edward Lambe (*DNB*).

[2] P.R.O., S.P. 16, Chas. I/145, no. 24 (of which no. 25 is a certified copy). The four
bishops were Neile (Winchester), Buckeridge (Ely), White (Norwich), and Murray.

This is not the decision of a court but rather the report of a committee of conciliation and arbitration. The situation was evidently one which called for the exercise of knowledge of ecclesiastical law combined with tact and a spirit of compromise. The fact that in this instance Donne was the sole dean associated with the Archbishop and four of the bishops suggests that, though much of the legal work he undertook in the higher Church courts was *ex officio*, he nevertheless performed it with a distinction that earned Corbet's encomium. Many of his listeners would have appreciated the weight of experience behind such passages in his sermons as these:

Many times I have seene a suitor that comes *in forma pauperis*, more trouble a Court, and more importune a Judge, then greater causes, or greater persons. . . .

Thou maist have a *Commission* too; In that of the Peace, in that for Ecclesiasticall causes, thou maist have part. But be not hasty in the execution of these Commissions; Come to an Inquisition upon another man, so as thou wouldst wish God to enquire into thee. . . . Thou canst not assist in the execution of those *Commissions*, of which thou art, till thou have taken the oathes of *Supremacie*, and of *Allegeance* to thy *Soveraigne*. Do it not, till thou have sworne all that, to thy *Super-soveraigne*, to thy God. . . . The *holy Ghost* staid for his *Mission*; stay thou for thy *Commission*, till it be sealed over againe in thine owne bosome; sealed on one side, with a cleerenesse of understanding, and on the other, with a rectitude of conscience; that thou know what thou shouldst doe, and doe that.[1]

One imagines that various other public duties fell on Donne because of his position as Dean of St. Paul's, though it is not always easy to identify them. One such, however, was certainly his appointment as a governor of the Charterhouse (Sutton's Hospital) in 1626. Dean Overall had been one of the original governors appointed by Thomas Sutton when he established his foundation in 1611, and when Overall died in 1619 his place was taken by Valentine Cary (Bishop of Exeter after 1621) who died on 10 June 1626; and Donne was shortly afterwards chosen to fill the vacancy on the board. The foundation was still in its early, experimental, stages, and statutes for its administration were still in process of being formulated. They

---

[1] *Sermons*, vii, no. 6, ll. 393–6, p. 175 and no. 18, ll. 327–43, p. 443.

were adopted by the governors in 1627, soon after Donne joined the board, and remained in force until 1872.[1] The governors had the right of nominating in turn when vacancies occurred in the school, and it would be interesting to know if Donne had anything to do with the admission of Richard Crashaw, son of the Revd. William Crashaw, rector of Whitechapel, on 2 July 1629; he was certainly present at the meeting of governors on that day, but the lists of admissions before 1635 apparently do not mention the nominator, and no conclusions can be drawn.[2] Donne's old friend George Garrard eventually became Master of the Charterhouse, but this was not until 1637, after Donne's death, so that Donne had nothing to do with his appointment. The Assembly Books show, however, that Donne attended all the meetings of the governors held during his term of office, from 27 October 1626 (a meeting adjourned to 6 November for the completion of the business) until 26 February 1630/1; and he joined the other governors present in signing the minutes on each occasion, except for the Assembly of 7 December 1626 (when nobody signed) and that for 26 February 1630/1 (Donne having died before the minutes were signed at the following meeting). The business at all these Assemblies consisted of the routine administration of the Hospital's affairs, and the minutes are brief and, as to Donne's part in the proceedings, uninformative.[3] Nevertheless it seems clear that he brought to the service of the Charterhouse the conscientiousness which he displayed in everything he undertook.

One final topic in relation to Donne's status as Dean is worth discussing: his finances. The accounts of St. Paul's are complete for two of the years of his deanship, but there are serious difficulties in the way of using them to make an estimate of Donne's profits: it is impossible to tell how much he received from fines for leases, which

[1] G. S. Davies, *Charterhouse in London*, 1921, pp. 229, 352–3. In *Suttons Synagogue, or, The English Centurion . . . by Perci. Burrell, Preacher at King James his Hospitall in the Charterhouse . . .*, 1629, Donne's name appears (sig. E2) in a 'Catalogue' of the Governors of the Hospital.

[2] B. Marsh and F. A. Crisp, eds., *Alumni Carthusiani*, 1913, p. 9.

[3] [Professor Bald was unable to consult the muniments of the Charterhouse, which were in store in the country during the Second World War and the subsequent restoration of the buildings. I owe my information about the contents of the Assembly Books to the courtesy of the Master and of the Registrar, who very kindly supplied the facts recorded here and in Appendix A.]

are not shown in the accounts, and it is uncertain how some parts of the Cathedral income were divided.[1] Fortunately another approach is possible, though here again accuracy is scarcely attainable. For some of Donne's benefices the information is a little more precise. The living of Keyston, as is proved by a lawsuit over the tithes initiated by Donne's successor, must have been worth £250.[2] According to a manuscript at Sion College the tithes of St. Dunstan-in-the-West were worth £240. 4s. 9d. in Donne's time; the glebe was worth £53. 6s. 8d., and the parsonage house was divided and let out for £50.[3] So much is fairly definite; for the rest one has to guess. We have the values of benefices as they were recorded in the *Liber Ecclesiasticus* of 1535[4] and again, about three centuries later, in the Report of the Ecclesiastical Commission of 1831.[5] The values of the benefices held by Donne at these times were given as follows:

	1535	1831
Sevenoaks	£13 6s. 8d.	£629
Keyston	£30 1s. 6d.	£336 (and house unfit for habitation)
Blunham	£46 13s. 4d.	£731 (and house)
St. Dunstan's	£35 11s. 9d.	£490
Dean of St. Paul's	£210 12s. 1d.	£2,965
Prebend of Chiswick	£17 19s. 4d.	£16

From the contemporary estimates of the values of Keyston and

[1] For example, according to the composition between the Dean and the Residentiaries of 1554 (*Registrum Statutorum*, pp. 264–72) the Dean was to receive twice as much as the other Residentiaries; but in such parts of the accounts as show a division of income, the Dean and the other Residentiaries share alike.

[2] Scott *v.* Bate, etc., P.R.O., C3/379/26.

[3] 'Abstract of the yearely Values . . . belonging to the severall Parsonages and Vicarridges of the Parish Churches in London and the liberties thereof. Anno: 1636.' The valuation of St. Dunstan's is apparently based on that given in the agreement for payment of tithes made by Donne with the parishioners in May 1624, Guildhall MS. 2983, p. 154.

[4] *Valor Ecclesiasticus temp. Henr. VIII*, 1810. By statute 26 Hen. VIII, c. 3, tenths and first fruits were henceforward to be paid to the Crown, and a new survey of the Church's possessions was to be made. This record, often called 'The King's Book', was the basis of all subsequent interpretation of rights and restrictions under any statute in which the value of ecclesiastical property was involved, until the Commission reported in 1835.

[5] *Report of the Commissioners . . . to inquire into the Ecclesiastical Revenue of England and Wales*, Parliamentary Papers, 1835, xxii.

St. Dunstan's it will be seen that in Donne's time they were bringing in about eight times as much as in the reign of Henry VIII. It would obviously be rash to use this factor to estimate the values of the other livings held by Donne, since it has been shown earlier in this chapter how variable such increases in value were, and how they could affect the livings of the clergy. Yet over the centuries Keyston and St. Dunstan's, as the estimates of 1831 show, appreciated less rapidly than Donne's other livings, except, of course, for the prebend of Chiswick, which had virtually passed out of the hands of St. Paul's. As Christopher Hill remarks,[1] the poor were growing poorer and the rich were growing richer; Donne was obviously no longer one of the poor. Let us, however, be on the safe side, and use a factor of six for assessing the values of the livings for which fairly exact figures are unavailable. Here are the results of such estimating, hazardous as it may be. Before he became Dean, Donne had from Lincoln's Inn a stipend of £60, and in addition received £80 a year in lieu of his wife's dowry.[2] Sevenoaks brought him 6× £13. 6s. 8d. = £80, and Keyston, say, £200. This gives a total of £420 a year. On becoming Dean, Donne resigned Keyston as he had promised, and refused to accept any further financial assistance from his father-in-law,[3] but soon afterwards he received both Blunham (1622) and St. Dunstan's (1624). His income may then be estimated at £80 (Sevenoaks), plus £280 (Blunham, 6× £46. 13s. 4d.), plus £303 (St. Dunstan's), plus £1,264 (the deanery, 6× £210. 12s. 1d.), plus £18 (prebend of Chiswick), which gives a total of £1,945. If one adds to this various rectorial perquisites, and fees such as those received for services as an ecclesiastical judge and for sermons preached on special occasions, it may safely be conjectured that Donne's receipts were above £2,000 a year. There were, of course, expenses: Donne had to pay the salaries of the curates at Keyston, Blunham, and St. Dunstan's, and he was also responsible to the Earl of Dorset for the rent of the impropriation of the tithes of St. Dunstan's. As we shall see, he claimed, indeed, to have made no profit from the last-named benefice at all. Nevertheless, during the Lincoln's Inn years Donne was in comfortable circumstances,

[1] *Economic Problems of the Church*, 1956, p. 112.
[2] For the latter piece of information, see Walton, *Lives*, p. 35.   [3] Ibid., p. 55.

thanks mainly to his two additional benefices; as Dean of St. Paul's he was affluent.

From the end of 1621 he lived, of course, in the Deanery, 'a fayre old House', as Stow calls it, to the south-west of the Cathedral. In his will Donne mentions the hall, the little dining room, the parlour, his study, the chapel (all perhaps on the ground floor), the great chamber, his own chamber and the lobby leading to it, and 'that chamber which we call the flannel chamber and the inner chamber thereof' (all perhaps upstairs), and the garden. It was a large house, for there was a long tradition of generous hospitality attached to the principal offices of the Cathedral that was not entirely dead. Until the middle of the nineteenth century the canon in residence for the day was expected to provide a feast on Sunday for all those who had participated in divine service that morning. One of Donne's predecessors, Dean Overall, it will be remembered, had been able to put a set of rooms at the disposal of his friend Thomas Morton for some years, and had in addition given house room to Isaac Casaubon during the earlier part of his stay in England. Of such guests during Donne's term of office we know nothing, but his elderly mother seems to have come to stay at the Deanery (where, according to Walton,[1] she died), and there were also Donne's children and his servants to fill its rooms. Of other kinds of hospitality we catch only an occasional glimpse. There is an interesting note to Sir Robert Ker, dated 4 January 1626/7, in which Donne has to confess that his time is so taken up with Christmastide hospitality that he has been unable to see the Bishop in connection with some business of Ker's:

I have obeyed the formes of our Church of *Pauls* so much, as to have been a solemn Christmas man, and tryed conclusions upon my selfe, how I could sit out the siege of new faces, every dinner. So that I have not seen the B. in some weeks. And I know not whether he be in case, to afford that privacy, which you justly desire. This day, I am in my bondage of entertaining. Suppers I presume, are inconvenient to you. But this evening I will spie upon the B. and give you an account of his disposition. . . .[2]

This letter, incidentally, contains almost the only reference anywhere

---

[1] Ibid., p. 71.   [2] *Letters*, p. 315.

to Donne's relations with his bishop, though a further reference
to Mountain occurs in a letter which Donne sent to Ker the
following day as he had promised. Donne refers to the Bishop as 'my
great neighbour', and makes it clear that he too still had his burden
of Christmas entertaining: 'I perceive he is under an inundation of
uncertain commers, which he cannot devest, except I had your
leave, to speake plain to him. A second inconvenience is, that he is
so deafe, that we must speak to the whole house, if we will speake
to him.' He presses Ker to come in any case, and to dine with him
if not with the Bishop.[1] As Dean, therefore, Donne kept a large
household (his will left legacies to servants, but does not specify
them all), and dispensed frequent hospitality.

   He did not, however, achieve the prosperity of his later years at
one bound. He himself wrote towards the end of his first year as
Dean: 'I had locked my self, sealed and secured my self against all
possibilities of falling into new debts, and in good faith, this year
hath thrown me 400*l* lower then when I entred this house.'[2] This is
understandable if Donne, as Walton says,[3] immediately 'after he
came to his Deanry, . . . employed work-men to repair and beautifie
the Chapel; suffering, as holy *David* once vowed, *his eyes and temples
to take no rest, till he had first beautified the house of God*'. Furthermore,
he was still in his 'first residence', and not yet entitled to his full
share of the revenues of the Cathedral; besides, he had resigned
Keyston, had only just been appointed to Blunham, and was having
to compound for the first fruits of his new benefices. Just a year
later, at the time of the illness which is the theme of the *Devotions*,
his worldly estate was still small, for Walton tells of Henry King's
well-meant offer to help him to increase it, and thus to make better
provision for his children if he died. But from this point onwards
Donne's financial position steadily improved. Walton possessed the
private account book which Donne kept while he was Dean; there
are no quotations from the accounts themselves, but only from the
'thankful Prayer' with which he 'blest each years poor remainder'.
Casting up the accounts for the two years 1624 and 1625, he wrote:[4]

---

[1] *Letters*, pp. 312–13.   [2] Ibid., p. 135.   [3] *Lives*, p. 55.
[4] Ibid., pp. 71–3. The dates against the prayers are found only in the 1640 edition
of Walton's *Life*, from which the text of the first extract is taken; for further comment
see D. Novarr, *The Making of Walton's 'Lives'*, pp. 88–9.

So all is that remains of these two years
Deo Opt. Max. benigno
Largitori, a me, & ab iis quibus
haec a me reservantur, Gloria
& gratia in aeternum. Amen.

Year by year the prayers become progressively longer and more
fervent, so that by the end of 1629 he wrote:

Quid habeo quod non accepi a Domino?
Largitur etiam ut quae largitus est
Sua iterum fiant, bono eorum usu; ut
Quemadmodum nec officiis hujus mundi,
Nec loci in quo me posuit; dignitati, nec
Servis, nec egenis, in toto hujus anni
Curriculo mihi conscius sum me defuisse;
Ita & liberi, quibus quae supersunt,
Supersunt, grato animo ea accipiant,
Et beneficum authorem recognoscant.
                                    Amen.[1]

It is clear that he was able each year to save, and that his possessions grew steadily. Yet the increase in income also brought an
increase of charitable gifts. Walton tells how, on becoming Dean,
Donne refused to accept any more the £20 a quarter which Sir
George More paid him in lieu of a dowry for his daughter, and when
he was able he sent £100 'to an old Friend' (almost certainly Sir
Henry Goodyer) 'whom he had known live plentifully, and by a too
liberal heart and carelessness, become decayed in his Estate'. There
were also other constant acts of charity:

he was inquisitive after the wants of Prisoners, and redeemed many

---

[1] The arrangement of the lines and the capitalization are odd; did Walton think
that they were verse?

The two extracts quoted are thus translated by A. H. Bullen, in his edition of
Walton's *Lives* (1884), pp. 67–9:

'To God all Good, all Great, the benevolent Bestower, by me and by them, for
whom, by me, these sums are laid up, be glory and grace ascribed for ever. Amen.'

'What have I, which I have not received from the Lord? He bestows, also, to the
intent that what he hath bestowed may revert to him by the proper use of it: that,
as I have not consciously been wanting to myself during the whole course of the
past year, either in discharging my secular duties, in retaining the dignity of my
station, or in conduct towards my servants and the poor,—so my children for
whom remains whatever is remaining, may receive it with gratitude, and acknowledge the beneficent Giver. Amen.'

from thence that lay for their Fees or small Debts; he was a continual Giver to poor Scholars, both of this and forraign Nations. Besides what he gave with his own hand, he usually sent a Servant, or a discreet and trusty Friend, to distribute his Charity to all the Prisons in *London* at all the Festival times of the year, especially at the *Birth* and *Resurrection* of our Saviour.[1]

Walton's account of these kindnesses is substantiated in various ways. In one letter Donne admits that he supports a scholar in each of the universities;[2] in another he tells of relieving Sir Henry Goodyer's son (who had been arrested for debt) not in his own person, but by sending his servant to accommodate him.[3] The St. Dunstan's accounts record gifts from the vicar to the poor of the parish in time of plague, and towards apprenticing the orphaned daughters of the late curate.[4] Above all Walton stresses the thoughtfulness and sensitiveness with which Donne's gifts were made. In his prosperity, then, amid summonses to Court and the fulfilment of many other worldly duties, besides the calls on his time made by his preaching and the performance of his functions as Dean, Donne strove hard to lead a truly Christian life.

[1] *Lives*, p. 70.   [2] *Tobie Mathew Collection*, p. 352.
[3] *Letters*, pp. 229–30.
[4] B. W. Whitlock, 'Donne at St. Dunstan's I', *TLS*, 16 Sept. 1955.

XVI

PREACHER AND PARISH PRIEST

'IMMEDIATELY after he came to his Deanry' Donne 'employed work-men to repair and beautifie the Chapel.' The presence of workmen in the house may have delayed his removal to his new quarters, and it is possible that he stayed in his house in Drury Lane for a while longer. He was certainly settled in the Deanery, however, by 9 May 1622, when he dated his letter to Sir Henry Martin (about the dispute over the Keyston rectory) from 'my house at S: Pauls'. He had paid his first fees for Blunham on 18 April, and had just returned, he told Martin, from Bedfordshire, where he had been instituted as rector. Ten days later an old friend dispatched to him a pleasant gift. Viscount Doncaster was at this time ambassador in France, and had occasion to visit Bordeaux. This excursion to one of the great wine-growing districts evidently provided him with the opportunity of making some purchases on the spot not only for himself but for his friends also. He did not forget Donne, and the letter which accompanied the gift of a tun of claret well illustrates the warmth and affability of the man to whom Donne owed so much:

My dear Dean,

I must now live upon the crums of my German Devotions; which, if I had carefullie gathered up, had been an eternall Feast. Love me still, and reserve in the Ship which parts from hence, a Tun of excellent Wine, against your Michaelmas-Hospitalitie, where I mean to be. In haste, from *Bourdeux*, this 19th. May.   *Your domestick humble Servant.*[1]

Doncaster kept his word, and was back in England well before Michaelmas, for Donne, in a letter dated 2 August,[2] mentions having spoken to him.

[1] *Tobie Mathew Collection*, p. 323. The letter has no year in the date, but it is addressed to Donne as Dean and is therefore after 1621, and is signed 'Doncaster' and is therefore earlier than 1623; hence it must belong to 1622.

[2] *Letters*, p. 279 (to Ker).

Judging by the surviving sermons, Donne's first year as Dean was a very active one; he seems to have accepted preaching engagements whenever the invitations came. It is unlikely, moreover, that all the sermons he preached have come down to us. He preached in the Cathedral at Christmas and Easter, as he was bound to do, and again on Midsummer Day. It is to the last sermon that Chamberlain refers in his letter of 1 July 1622 ('a very goode sermon in the church'), at the same time alluding to 'divers' others preached 'of late' which had helped to establish Donne's reputation.[1] He also preached occasionally at Lincoln's Inn until the appointment of his successor in the Readership. During the summer Edward Alleyn heard Donne preach at Camberwell (on 14 July).[2] On 25 August, within a month of the conversation he had had with Doncaster, Donne preached for the Viscount at one of his splendid entertainments, given at Hanworth.

Hanworth was a royal manner bordering on Hampton Court which had been granted on a long lease to Donne's friend Sir William Killigrew,[3] but had evidently been recently sublet to Doncaster. Here Doncaster continued the lavish entertainments for which he was famous. According to one writer he was one of those

that brought in the vanity of ante-suppers, not heard of in our fore-fathers time, and, for ought I have read, or at least remember, unpractised by the most luxurious tyrants. The manner of which was, to have the board covered, at the first entrance of the ghests, with dishes, as high as a tall man could well reach, filled with the choycest and dearest viands sea or land could afford: And all this once seen, and having feasted the eyes of the invited, was in a manner throwne away, and fresh set on to the same height, having only this advantage of the other, that it was hot.[4]

The occasion to which Donne was invited was probably the first time Doncaster had been able to show hospitality to his father-in-law, the Earl of Northumberland, since his release from the Tower, and Northumberland's presence at this entertainment seems to

---

[1] Chamberlain, *Letters*, ii. 443.
[2] W. Young, *History of Dulwich College*, ii. 244.
[3] See A. Harbage, *Thomas Killigrew*, 1930, pp. 24–6.
[4] W. Scott, ed., *Secret History of the Court of James the First*, i. 270–1; see also pp. 331–4.

have marked his reconciliation with Doncaster and his acceptance of him as a son-in-law. The other distinguished guest was the Marquess of Buckingham. Donne's sermon was an eloquent one, notable for the unusual range of secular learning to which he referred. Only in the peroration did he mention his distinguished auditors, to whom God had given 'Titles and places of honour in this world'. Courts, he went on to say, were 'the place of *Honour*, and the place of *Crosses* too, the place of *rising* and the place of *falling* too'.[1] The host, however, was still rising, and the services he had performed on his embassies were very soon rewarded with an earldom (13 September), so that henceforth he was Earl of Carlisle.

Donne's next surviving sermon was preached at Paul's Cross, and in it he declared himself on a burning public issue for almost the only time since he had entered the Church. The month of September 1622 was a time when news both from home and abroad filled the average Englishman with gloom. The protracted negotiations with Spain to provide the Prince of Wales with a Spanish bride seemed to be coming to a conclusion, and James, to show his goodwill to the Spaniards, released large numbers of imprisoned Catholics. Not only this, but he showed such other favours to acknowledged Romanists that the Venetian ambassador reported that never before since England became Protestant had the Roman Catholic faith been so openly professed. Yet abroad the cause of Protestantism seemed in greater danger than ever; Heidelberg had fallen to the imperial armies and the Palatinate seemed lost. Murmurs of discontent arose everywhere; the negotiations with Spain were unpopular, and many demanded an active intervention in the struggle in Europe. James attempted to quell criticism and unrest by issuing the 'Directions to Preachers' on 4 August. In future preachers were to confine themselves to topics covered by the Thirty-Nine Articles and the Book of Homilies, and Sunday afternoons were to be devoted to catechizing instead of to preaching. No one under the degree of bishop or dean was to 'preach in any popular auditory the deep points of Predestination, Election, Reprobation, or of the universality, efficacy, resistibility or irresistibility of God's grace'; no preacher of any rank was to 'meddle with matters of state and the

[1] *Sermons*, iv, no. 6, ll. 518–23, p. 177.

differences between prince and people', and there was to be an end to 'railing against either papists or puritans'.[1] These orders stimulated public unrest still further, and Donne was instructed to explain the King's motives from the pulpit at Paul's Cross. He preached on 15 September to 'as great a Congregation as ever I saw together' (as he told Goodyer),[2] for the issue was one which stirred widespread popular interest.

Actually, Donne was already, at least in part, in sympathy with the King's directions; more than once in the Lincoln's Inn sermons he had complained against excess of freedom in preaching:

> It is not always a bold and vehement reprehension of great persons, that is argument enough of a good and a rectified zeale, for an intemperate use of the liberty of the Gospell, and sometimes the impotency of a satyricall humor, makes men preach freely, and over-freely, offensively, scandalously; and so exasperate the magistrate; God forbid that a man should build a reputation of zeale, for having been called in question for preaching of a Sermon.[3]

Most good Anglicans were disturbed by the vehemence of Puritan preaching, and those who supported the policy of the Government must have been irked by the criticism (often, no doubt, ill-informed) which poured from the pulpits. Yet Donne's defence of the King's directions scarcely touches the real issues. To wish to intervene in the struggle going on in Europe is, he maintains, to distrust the providence of God, Who directs all human affairs for His ends. When he turned to the specific defence of the 'Directions', Donne argued that catechizing was one of the principal methods of instruction used in the primitive Church; the Articles and the Homilies both took up the points of difference between the Anglicans on the one hand and papists and Puritans on the other, so that no cessation of controversial divinity was intended. The 'Directions' were therefore unexceptionable. There is no mention at all of the list of forbidden topics. Yet the Puritanically minded were passionately interested in 'Predestination, Election, Reprobation' and grace; furthermore,

---

▶ [1] The text of the 'Directions' is given by Arthur Wilson, *History of Great Britain*, p. 200, and by Fuller, *Church History of Britain*, 1655, bk. x, pp. 108–10. Cf. *Sermons*, iv, pp. 24–8, 33–4.

[2] *Letters*, p. 231.

[3] *Sermons*, iii, no. 16, ll. 168–75, pp. 336–7; cf. iii, no. 6, ll. 397–401, p. 167.

the pulpit had become a rallying point for public opinion, so that to forbid 'meddling' with matters of state was, in effect, to stifle opposition. Such issues, intentionally or not, Donne skirted completely. Chamberlain, writing to Carleton, reported that Donne had given his hearers 'no great satisfaction, or as some say spake as yf himself were not so well satisfied'.[1] Nevertheless it satisfied the King. James sent for a copy, read it, and returned it by the Earl of Carlisle, who wrote:

My dearest Dean,

By his Majestie's commandment, I return your Sermon with his own word, That it was a piece of such perfection, as could admit neither addition nor diminution. He longs to see it in Print, as concerning highly his service; and the sooner it be dispatcht, it will be the onely employment it needs. Your other businesse was moved by my noble Lord of *Buckingham*, in my hearing, which had a better answer than was desired or expected, whereof you shall have an account at our meeting. If you prefer an Epistle, in my opinion, it shall be fittest to my Lord of *Buckingham*. So I rest

Your faithfull humble servant.[2]

This was the first of Donne's sermons to see print, and it appeared shortly afterwards. Donne took the hint, and dedicated it as Carlisle had suggested; the opening words of the dedication seem, indeed, to allude to Buckingham's recent kindness in speaking to the King on Donne's behalf. 'When I would speake to the *King*, by your *Lordships* Meanes, I doe', Donne began; 'Now, when I would speake to the *Kingdom*, I would do that by your *Lordshippes* Meanes to[o].'

Having defended 'the godly designes of our religious *King*', Donne in a later sermon in 1622 took occasion to remind others of the godly part of their designs. On 22 May Donne had been made a member of the Virginia Company; this was purely an honour, since he had not invested any money in the venture, and his membership was presumably conferred upon him as Dean of St. Paul's. Many of his friends were, however, shareholders. The list included Sir George More, Sir Walter Chute, Sir Thomas Roe, Christopher Brooke, and William Hakewill, all of whom had invested various sums and were actively interested in the slowly growing colony; in addition, Sir

---

[1] Chamberlain, *Letters*, ii. 451. [2] *Tobie Mathew Collection*, pp. 303–4.

John Danvers was an important member of the Council. On 3 July Donne, together with six others (who included the Marquess Hamilton, the Lord Mayor, the Recorder of London, and Sir Edward Conway) was chosen an honorary member of the Council. Consequently, towards the end of October a delegation from the Company, consisting of Sir John Danvers, Nicholas Ferrar (it is pleasant to know of a definite contact between him and Donne), Sir Philip Cary, and a Mr. Byng, paid him a visit. They had come to ask him if he would preach their annual sermon at St. Michael's Cornhill on a Wednesday in Michaelmas term, for which an anonymous donor had promised 'forty shillings per annum for ever'. Donne readily agreed; 'the Deanes Answeare', Sir John Danvers reported at the next meeting of the Council, 'was verie fauourable and respectiue of the Companie, and that hauinge acknowledged with many thanks that courtesie they had donn him, by choosinge him to be of their Counsell, hee seemed glad they had occasion to vse him in that kinde wherein he was able to do them seruice'. In conjunction with the sermon a feast was to be held in Merchant Taylors' Hall at a cost of 3s. a head: 'And for that at such great feastes Venizon is esteemed to bee a most necessary Complement, the Court hath thought fitt that letters be addressed in the name of the Company vnto such Noblemen and Gentlemen as are of this Society to request this fauo^r at their handes and withall their presence at the said Supper.'

The sermon and the feast which followed it were held on 13 November; between three and four hundred were present, though, Chamberlain remarked, 'many of the nobilitie and counsaile were invited but few came'.[1] Donne's sermon on this occasion has been termed 'the first missionary sermon', but this is not altogether accurate, for Donne was not the first preacher to exhort the Company to take the gospel to the natives of the lands they were opening up for trade.[2] He did not speak, he said, 'to move a wheele that stood still, but to keepe the wheele in due motion; nor perswade you to begin, but to continue a good worke, nor propose forreigne, but

---

[1] *Records of the Virginia Company of London*, ed. Susan M. Kingsbury, 1906–35, iii. 65, 80–9; ii. 76, 89, 114, 119, 123; and Chamberlain, *Letters*, ii. 464. See also S. M. Johnson, 'John Donne and the Virginia Company', *ELH*, xiv (1947), 127–38.

[2] See Johnson, op. cit., pp. 136–7.

your own Examples, to do still, as you have done hitherto'. In spite of meagre returns, in spite, above all, of the serious setback the colony had recently received from the massacre by the Indians of a large proportion of the white settlers, Donne urged that, not increased trade or vengeance against the natives, but the spread of the gospel was their primary duty: 'act over the *Acts* of the *Apostles*; bee you a light to the *Gentiles*, that sit in darkenesse . . . [for] *God* taught us to make Ships, not to transport our selves, but to transport him.' Donne shows a fine sense of the far-reaching consequences of the plantation, and of the wider economic and human issues, especially in a passage in which he emphasizes the effects of colonization on the mother country itself:

the Plantation shall not discharge the Charges, not defray it selfe yet; but yet already, now at first, it shall conduce to great uses; It shall redeeme many a wretch from the Jawes of death, from the hands of the Executioner, upon whom, perchaunce a small fault, or perchance a first fault, or perchance a fault heartily and sincerely repented, perchance no fault, but malice, had otherwise cast a present, and ignominious death. It shall sweep your streets, and wash your dores, from idle persons, and the children of idle persons, and imploy them: and truely, if the whole Countrey were but such a *Bridewell*, to force idle persons to work, it had a good use. But it is already, not onely a *Spleene*, to draine the ill humors of the body, but a *Liver*, to breed good bloud; already the imployment breeds Marriners; already the place gives essayes, nay Fraytes of Marchantable commodities; already it is a marke for the Envy, and for the ambition of our Enemies; I speake but of our *Doctrinall*, not *Nationall* Enemies; as they are *Papists*, they are sory we have this Countrey; and surely, twenty Lectures in matter of Controversie, doe not so much vexe them, as one Ship that goes, and strengthens that Plantation. Neither can I recommend it to you, by any better *Rhetorique* then their malice. They would gladly have it, and therefore let us bee glad to hold it.

The Company was not to be dismayed by setbacks,

though you see not your money, though you see not your men, though a *Flood*, a *Flood* of *bloud* have broken in upon them, be not discouraged.

And then,

You shall have made this *Iland*, which is but as the *Suburbs* of the old world, a Bridge, a Gallery to the new; to joyne all to that world that shall never grow old, the Kingdome of heaven.[1]

This sermon, too, gave satisfaction, and the Company requested Donne to put it in print; it was published with a dedication to the Company. This was, however, the last of the annual sermons. Donne was at meetings of the Company on 4 and 5 February 1622/3, on 5 March, and on the following 7 and 14 May, though he did not participate in the debates. The anonymous donor sent the money for the sermon in November 1623, but agreed that the occasion should be postponed during the Company's troubles.[2] Six months later its charter was revoked, and after eighteen years of operation the Virginia Company went out of existence.

Donne's letters during the autumn of 1622 reflect some of the anxieties expressed in his Paul's Cross sermon. He was deeply concerned at the loss of the Palatinate, of which he immediately sent news to Goodyer; he was also following eagerly the course of the negotiations for the Spanish marriage, and referred to George Gage, Toby Mathew's friend, who had been sent to Rome to clarify the conditions on which the Pope would be prepared to grant a dispensation.[3] He was convinced, however, and had tried to convince the crowd that thronged about Paul's Cross, 'of his Ma*jest*ies constancy in Religion, and of his desire that all men should be bred in the knowledge of such things, as might preserve them from the superstition of *Rome*'. He wrote also of concerns closer to the everyday lives of himself and his correspondent. Goodyer's son, as we have seen, had been imprisoned for debt. Donne and John Selden had decided that the best thing to do for the young man would be to await instructions from his father.[4] In the meantime Donne, with his usual delicacy, took measures to relieve his immediate needs; he 'took order with the Keeper to accommodate him, and I bade my man *Martin*, as from himself, to serve his present want with some things'.

---

[1] *Sermons*, iv, no. 10, ll. 592–5, p. 281; ll. 7–28, pp. 265–6; ll. 264–84, pp. 272–3; ll. 233–5, p. 271; ll. 575–7, pp. 280–1.

[2] Kingsbury, *Records*, ii. 225, 231, 244, 300, 391, 422, 480–1.

[3] *Letters*, pp. 229–31.

[4] Ibid., pp. 229–30. This is the sole reference to Selden in Donne's correspondence, but it is clear from this letter that Selden was a friend of both Donne and Goodyer.

Both Donne and Goodyer had daughters of marriageable age, and neither was in a position to find the dowries necessary to provide them with suitable husbands. Gloomily reviewing his finances, Donne wrote in another letter (4 October): 'I think they will not murmure if heaven must be their Nunnery, and they associated to the B. virgins there: I know they would be content to passe their lives in a Prison, rather then I should macerate my self for them, much more to suffer the mediocrity of my house, and my means, though that cannot preferre them: yours are such too. . . .'[1] A fortnight later he told Goodyer of a marriage he had hoped to arrange for his eldest daughter, Constance:

Tell both your daughters a peece of a storie of my *Con.* which may accustome them to endure disappointments in this world: An honourable person (whose name I give you in a schedule to burn, lest this Letter should be mis-laid) had an intention to give her one of his sons, and had told it me, and would have been content to accept what I, by my friends, could have begged for her; but he intended that son to my Profession, and had provided him already 300[l] a year, of his own gift in Church livings, and hath estated 300[l] more of inheritance for their children: and now the youth, (who yet knows nothing of his fathers intention nor mine) flies from his resolutions for that Calling, and importunes his Father to let him travell. The girle knows not her losse, for I never told her of it: but truly, it is a great disappointment to me.[2]

Thus in the seventeenth century did the best-intentioned fathers try to manage their children's matrimonial affairs.

In the first of the letters just mentioned, Donne alludes to a dinner at Sion House, where he had been the guest of the Earl of Northumberland (who, it will be remembered, had broken the news of Donne's own marriage to Sir George More); perhaps the sermon at Hanworth had led to a renewal of their acquaintance. Shortly afterwards, too, he was the guest of the Archbishop, for Edward Alleyn noted in his diary for 21 September: 'I went to Croydon fayre dined with the Archbishop wher wase the Deane off pawls & Sʳ Ed: Sackvile.'[3] Sir Edward Sackville, the younger brother of the

---

[1] Ibid., p. 136.   [2] Ibid., pp. 185–6.
[3] W. Young, *History of Dulwich College*, ii. 249.

Earl of Dorset, succeeded to his title two years later. It must have been about this time also that Donne exchanged letters with Archbishop Abbot. A continental theologian (presumably German or Dutch) whom Donne had met abroad had sent Donne his most recent book and had enclosed a second copy for the Archbishop. Abbot's reply is little more than a bare acknowledgement of Donne's letter (for the book had not yet arrived), and little can be inferred from it about the feelings of the two men towards one another.[1]

The final surviving letter of 1622 is that addressed from the Deanery on 1 December to Sir Thomas Roe, now ambassador in Constantinople.[2] It was to be carried by Roe's chaplain, along with one from the Earl of Carlisle ('the directest man that ever I knew'), which Donne was to call for that day when the Earl returned from Court. Donne offers his friend spiritual comfort for certain slanders of which Roe had been the victim: 'Outward thorns of calumny, and mis-interpretation do us least harme; Innocency despises them; or friends and just examiners of the case blunt or breake them. Finde thorns within; a woundinge sense of sin; bringe you the thorns, and Christ will make it a Crown. . . .' He goes on to speak of the disquiet felt in many quarters about the proposed alliance of the Prince and the Infanta, and refers obliquely to the effect of the King's direction to preachers. He then mentions his three most recent sermons on great occasions, that defending James's 'Directions', that on 'The Anniversary Celebration of our Deliverance from the Powder Treason' (5 November),[3] and that preached to the Virginia Company. He seems to have awakened to the possibilities for his ministry of putting his sermons into print, and was obviously pleased with the requests he had already received to publish two of them:

One of these occurrences, gave the occasion to this sermon, which by commandement I preached and which I send your Lordship. Some few weekes after that, I preachd another at the same place: upon the Gun-powder day. Therin I was left more to mine owne liberty; and therfore I would I could also send your Lordship a Copy of

[1] *Tobie Mathew Collection*, pp. 309–10.
[2] S.P. 14, vol. 134, no. 59. I quote the text given in Hayward, pp. 475–8.
[3] *Sermons*, iv, no. 9; cf. pp. 35–6 of that volume.

that; but that one, which, also by commandement I did write after the preachinge, is as yet in his Majesties hand, and, I know not whether he will in it, as he did in the other, after his readinge thereof, command it to be printed; and, whilst it is in that suspence, I know your Lordship would call it Indiscretion, to send out any copy thereof; neither truly, ame I able to committ that fault; for I have no Copy. A few days after that, I preached, by invitation of the Virginian Company, to an honourable auditory, and they recompenced me with a new commandment, in their Service, to printe that: and that, I hope, comes with this: for, with papers of that kinde, I ame the apter to chardge your chapleyne in the Exercise of my Ministery.

The King did not, in fact, order the printing of the Gunpowder Plot sermon. The letter concludes with news of the loss of two friends, Lady Jacob, Christopher Brooke's wife, and Sir William Killigrew, father of Sir Robert. Donne had 'assisted in the tyme of sicknes, and now attended at the funeralls'.

It is in connection with the Killigrews that we are given a glimpse of Donne as he was at this time by a visiting foreigner. A Dutch embassy that was in London in 1622 and 1623 brought with it a young secretary, Constantijn Huygens. It was not his earliest visit, but the one on which he managed first to feel at home in certain English social groups. Many years afterwards, in 1678, Huygens wrote a poem about his early life, *De Vita Propria Sermones inter Liberos*.[1] In it he describes the circle he met at the house of Sir Robert Killigrew, who had many connections with Holland and was for a brief time ambassador to The Hague. The house was a hospitable one, and friends seem to have gathered there to listen to music, for Lady Killigrew and her children were accomplished performers:

> Tota domus concentus erat: pulcherrima Mater,
> Mater (adhuc stupeo) duodenae prolis, ab illo
> Gutture tam niveo, tam nil mortale sonanti
> Quam coeleste Melos Cytherae sociabat, et ipso
> Threicio (dicas) animatis pollice chordis!

---

[1] *De Gedichten van Constantijn Huygens*, ed. J. A. Worp, viii (1898), 205–9; bk. ii, ll. 65–144 contains an account of the embassy that brought him to London, and ll. 145–220 an account of the friends he met there. The periods which Huygens spent in England are fully discussed in A. G. H. Bachrach's D.Phil. thesis in the Bodleian Library, and in his *Sir Constantine Huygens and Britain*, of which vol. i (1596–1619) was published in 1962.

Among the guests were such men as Nicholas Lanier, musician and art connoisseur, and the French lutenist Jacques Gaultier, both of whom were in the service of the King. Huygens also mentions meeting the Dutch scientist Cornelis Drebbel and Sir Walter Raleigh's widow, a 'memorable matron' who delighted him with anecdotes of the times when the Duc d'Alençon came to England to sue for Elizabeth's hand. But of all those he met at the house he put Donne first, and saluted his memory in enthusiastic lines:

> Te, maxime *Donni*,
> Omnibus antefero, divine vir, optime Rhetor,
> Prime Poetarum: O, quoties sermonibus illis
> Aureolis, quos vel priuatos inter amicos
> Vel de suggestu, Praeco facunde, serebas,
> Intereram, quo me visus sum nectare pasci![1]

He had heard Donne preach, and he had enjoyed his familiar conversation; in both situations the effect was equally striking. Huygens confirms Walton's statement that Donne's company was 'one of the delights of Mankind'. There is plenty of other evidence that Donne was acquainted with the Killigrews, and it is obvious that he must have known Lady Raleigh, whose brother had married one of his wife's sisters, but nothing is known from any other source of his friendship with the other members of the circle; nor, indeed, could we otherwise have been certain that Donne would have taken pleasure in the musical gatherings to which Huygens seems to refer. Not much is known about Donne's interest in music. It had a large place in the lives of some of his friends, among whom George Herbert was one, and Herbert himself mentions that his mother possessed some musical talent.[2] But for Donne there is only this reference by Huygens, and an anecdote by Walton, who relates that Donne caused his 'Hymne to God the Father'

to be set to a most grave and solemn Tune, and to be often sung to the *Organ* by the *Choristers* of St. *Pauls* Church, in his own hearing; especially at the Evening Service, and at his return from his Customary Devotions in that place, did occasionally say to a friend, *The words of*

[1] ll. 170–5.
[2] See Edmund Blunden, 'George Herbert's Latin Poems', *Essays and Studies by Members of the English Association*, xix (1933), at p. 33.

this Hymn *have restored to me the same thoughts of joy that possest my Soul in my sickness when I composed it. And, O the power of Church-musick! that Harmony added to this Hymn has raised the Affections of my heart, and quickned my graces of zeal and gratitude*; and I observe, *that I always return from paying this publick duty of* Prayer *and* Praise *to God, with an unexpressible tranquillity of mind,* and a willingness *to leave the world.*[1]

Reference has already been made to the fact that, as Dean, Donne received various dedications, usually of sermons. The fact in itself is not so surprising as that the printed books with dedications to him all came from the years 1622 and 1623. Conceivably Donne did not respond as those who received dedications were expected to do, and so the dedications ceased. Certainly, they were mostly of a rather formal kind, and Donne is quite likely not to have been flattered by them. The one exception was the earliest dedication which he received; it was not prefixed to a sermon, and it came from a friend of his student days. The title of the work was *The Lawyers Philosophy: or, Law Brought to Light. Poetized in a Divine Rhapsodie or Contemplative Poem,* 1622, and its author was Roger Tisdale. He was possibly an older man than Donne, and not an exact contemporary, for he declares that he was now 'in the wayne-time of . . . life'; 'The very candles of my life burne dimme, which shewes it to bee bed-time. But I know not how, a friend, a deare and dearely respected friend, . . . knockt at the doore. . . . No sooner I heard who it was, but I had *Donne.*' He probably held some minor office at St. Paul's. 'You, deare Sir,' he writes, '. . . haue now lighted vpon a faire Tree, vnder whose branches it is my fortune to hold a poor cottage.' Donne, he knows, loves 'pure, and vndefiled *Poesie*', and their acquaintance goes back many years. 'To your friends I was heretofore bound in dutie, and (in our youthfull societie) to your selfe in loue. . . . I must ingenuously confesse, as an ancient obseruant of your worth, that your yong daies were to me of much admiration, as these dayes are now of deserued reuerence.' The poem itself was intended for the instruction of the author's young son Roger, 'the desire of my Youth, and hope of mine Age'. It has not been possible to discover much about Tisdale, or anything bearing on his relations with Donne. It appears from a lawsuit of 1600 that he then had a house

---

[1] *Lives,* p. 62.

adjoining Lincoln's Inn,[1] and from a privy seal of June 1619 that he and John Moyle gent. were appointed joint clerks and registrars to the Commissioners for the relief of the poor prisoners in the King's Bench and the Fleet.[2] Roger the son was admitted to Gray's Inn on 26 November 1617. The father died on 12 January 1630/1 and was buried the next day, 'an Anchient Man out of Grays Inn Lane', in the church of St. Andrew's Holborn.[3]

One would assume that by the end of 1622 Donne was well established at the Court. The King had a regard for him, and Donne's own loyalty was unquestioned. Buckingham, the favourite, was willing to exert himself on Donne's behalf, and Donne had many other warm friends, like the Earls of Carlisle, of Dorset, and of Pembroke, among the more influential courtiers. Yet, according to Walton, it was about this time that Donne, at least temporarily, fell out of favour with the King:

He was once, and but once, clouded with the Kings displeasure; ... which was occasioned by some malicious whisperer, who had told his Majesty that Dr. *Donne* had put on the general humor of the Pulpits, and was become busie in insinuating a fear of the Kings inclining to *Popery*, and a dislike of his Government: and particularly, for the Kings then turning the Evening Lectures into *Catechising*, and expounding the *Prayer* of our *Lord*, and of the *Belief*, and *Commandments*. His Majesty was the more inclineable to believe this, for that a Person of Nobility and great note, betwixt whom and Dr. *Donne*, there had been a great friendship, was at this very time discarded the Court (I shall forbear his name, unless I had a fairer occasion) and justly committed to prison; which begot many rumors in the common people, who in this Nation think they are not wise, unless they be busie about what they understand not: and especially about Religion.

The King received this news with so much discontent and restlesness, that he would not suffer the Sun to set and leave him under this doubt, but sent for Dr. *Donne*, and required his answer to the Accusation; which was so clear and satisfactory, that the King said *he was right glad he rested no longer under the suspicion.* When the King had said this, Dr. *Donne* kneeled down and thanked his Majesty, and protested his answer was faithful and free from all collusion, and therefore

---

[1] P.R.O., C3/292/47.   [2] Privy Seal Docket Book, Index 6744.
[3] Parish Register.

desired that he might not rise, till, as in like cases he always had from God,
so he might have from his Majesty, some assurance that he stood clear and fair
in his opinion. At which the King raised him from his knees with his
own *hands,* and *protested he believ'd him: and that he knew he was an honest*
man, and doubted not but that he loved him truly. And, having thus dismissed him, he called some Lords of his Council into his Chamber,
and said with much earnestness, *My Doctor is an honest man: and my*
Lords, I was never better satisfied with an answer then he hath now made me:
and I always rejoice when I think that by my means he became a Divine.[1]

The incident makes a pleasant story and is told very circum-
stantially, but it is suspect none the less. As we have seen, Donne
was in sympathy with the 'Directions concerning Preachers', and
his sermon defending them at Paul's Cross had met with the King's
warm approval; there is no surviving clue to anything else in his
behaviour at this time that could have been given an unfavourable
interpretation to the King. Nothing else is heard of this incident
from any other source, but there is a well-authenticated incident
which occurred in the next reign when Donne was suspect for a
brief period and successfully cleared himself after an interview with
Charles I. It seems likely that Walton had heard of a later incident,
had mistaken the occasion and the references to 'the King', and had
then dressed up the episode in the form in which we have it.

For the greater part of 1623 the issue which agitated the nation
was still the Spanish match, and popular concern was heightened by
the dramatic journey to Spain secretly made by Prince Charles and
Buckingham. They set out early in the year in the hope of being
able to bring the protracted negotiations to a conclusion; but, to
the intense joy of the English people, the Prince returned at the
beginning of the autumn without a bride. The nation, already
alarmed at the concessions James had made to conciliate the Catholics, was profoundly disturbed when reports arrived from Spain of
the efforts being made to convert the Prince, and greeted his return
with relief. The Prince and Buckingham had left England on
17 February, and at the end of March the Prince's entourage had
been sent to Spain so that he would be enabled to appear there
in sufficient state; on 5 October the Prince landed in England again.

[1] *Lives,* pp. 56–7.

Two of Donne's letters this year were written to Spain, the first to Buckingham himself and the second to Sir Robert Ker, who had been sent to Madrid with the Prince's household. The letter to Buckingham is often quoted from:

Most Honored Lord,

I can thus far make myselfe beleeve, that I ame where yor Lordship is, in Spaine, that in my poore Library, where indeed I ame, I can turne mine Ey towards no shelfe, in any profession, from the Mistresse of my youth, Poetry, to the wyfe of mine age, Divinity, but that I meet more Autors of that nation, than of any other. Their autors in Divinity, though they do not show us the best way to heaven, yet they thinke they doe: And so, though they say not true, yet they do not ly, because they speake their Conscience. And since in charity, I beleeve so of them, for their Divinity, In Civility I beleeve it too, for Civill matters, that therein also they meane as they say: and by this tyme yor Lordship knowes what they say. I take therfore this boldnes to congratulate thus with yor Lordship the great honor which you receyve, in beeinge so great an instrument of that worke, in which the peace of christendome so much consists. How to use a sword, when it is out, we know you know: Thinke you that commandement of our Savyours to be directed upon you, Put up the sword; study the ways of peace. The hardest Autors in the world, are Kings; And yor Lordship hath read over the hardest of them. Since you have passed from the Text of the King of Kings, the booke of God, by the Commentary of the wiesest Kinge amongst Men, the Counsayls of our Soveraigne, the knowledge of other states, and other kings is down-hill, and obvious to yor Lordship and you finde it in postinge. And for this blessed clearnesse in yor Lordship all mighty God receyves every day, not the prayers (their tyme [is] not when the thinge is given allready) but the thanks [of]

Yor Lordships
humblest and devotedst and

[Pa]uls   thankfullest Servant in Christ Jesus
[1]623   J. Donne.[1]

The interest aroused in modern times by what Donne says about his books and his Spanish studies has obscured the main purport of the letter, which is a curious, and an extreme, example of the kind

---

[1] Bodleian Library, Tanner MS. 73, as printed in Hayward, pp. 479–80.

of indirection which Donne sometimes found it advisable to cultivate. He is warning Buckingham against the Spaniards and urgently appealing to him not to be deceived by them. Yet he knew only too well the thick incense of flattery in which the favourite lived, and he knew the real danger of offending him by outspokenness. So he was forced to choose this devious means of expressing the concern which he and the majority of his fellow-countrymen felt. In his slightly later letter to Ker he is still devious, but his own opinions are more openly expressed. North and south can never meet, though (in the terms of one of Donne's favourite conceits) east and west may do so; England and Spain are north and south. 'They have hotter daies in *Spain* than we have here, but our daies are longer; and yet we are hotter in our businesse here, and they are longer about it there.'[1] The thought of midsummer days in Spain (and one guesses that the letter was written about midsummer) suggests the contrast between the two national temperaments, and allows Donne to express his impatience with Spanish prevarication.

Relatively few sermons have survived from 1623, and only one was specially commissioned. This was the sermon published soon afterwards as *Encaenia. The Feast of Dedication. Celebrated at Lincolnes Inne, in a Sermon there vpon Ascension day, 1623. At the Dedication of a new Chapell there, consecrated by the Right Reuerend Father in God, the Bishop of London.* It was printed at the request of the Masters of the Bench, and Donne dedicated it to them. He professed to be all the more ready to make his sermon public 'because, though in it I had no occasion to handle any matter of Controversie between us, and those of the *Romane Perswasion*, yet the whole body and frame of the *Sermon*, is opposed against one pestilent calumny of theirs, that wee have cast off all distinction of places, and of dayes, and all outward meanes of assisting the devotion of the Congregation.'[2] He seems to imply that the publication of a sermon is justified only if it contains something beyond mere homilectic instruction; it should either have a special application to the problems of the day, like his own defence of the 'Directions concerning Preaching', or it should, as here, have a controversial value in the unending conflict between Protestant and Catholic.

---

[1] *Tobie Mathew Collection*, p. 306.   [2] *Sermons*, iv. 362.

Of Donne's activities this summer little is known, except that in one letter[1] he speaks of going to Hanworth with Lord Carlisle. During the autumn there is the record of one sermon preached, but never published, by Donne. The occasion was the Law Sergeants' feast, given on 23 October in the hall of the Temple, in honour of the creation of fifteen new sergeants, among whom were Sir Heneage Finch, the Recorder of London, and Donne's friend John Hoskyns. 'In the forenoone they went dabling on foote and bareheaded save their beguins to Westminster in all the raine, and after dinner to Powles, where the Dean preacht, though yt were sixe a clocke before they came; and that all might be sutable, their feast (though otherwise plentifull and magnificent) was so disorderly performed, that yt was rather a confusion then a feast.'[2] From another source we learn that the text of Donne's sermon to the sergeants was from 1 Timothy 1: 8, 'We know that the law is good, if a man use it lawfully.'[3]

Two days before delivering this sermon, Donne had had as guests to dinner Sir Thomas Grymes and Edward Alleyn, and after dinner the three men settled down to discuss the financial arrangements for a marriage between Alleyn and Constance Donne. Alleyn's wife had died about four months previously, and the new match seems to have been suggested by Grymes. Sir Thomas and Lady Grymes showered kindness on the motherless Donne children, but Constance seems to have been their special favourite, and they had given her name to one of their own younger children. The Grymeses at Peckham and Alleyn at Dulwich both lived within the parish of Camberwell, and hence were neighbours. Alleyn was by now, in fact, an old friend of the family, and he reciprocated this friendship by making Sir Thomas Grymes one of the trustees of his new 'hospital' at Dulwich. Alleyn afterwards wrote an account to Donne of what happened on this 21 October:

After motions made by Sir Thomas Grymes on booth sides I wase envited to your Hows the 21 off October 1623 wher after dinner in your parlore you declard your intencon to bestow with your daughter

---

[1] *Letters*, p. 84.   [2] Chamberlain, *Letters*, ii. 518.
[3] See I. A. Shapiro, 'Walton and the Occasion of Donne's *Devotions*', *RES*, N.S. ix (1958), pp. 18–22, at p. 18.

Con: all the benefits off your pryme Leas which as you said you knew would shortly bee renewed and that you were assured iff I stayd till Michaelmass next to be worth 500 *l.* att the Least, and when so euer itt showld rise to more itt showld wholy bee Hirs. My offer was to doe as much for Her as your self, and add to that at my death 500 *l.* more and so Her estat showld be a 1000 *l./* This gaue not Content and Sir Thomas perswaded me to doe som what more, which I did, and promised to Leaue Her att my death 2000 markes. This was accepted and securyty demanded. I then towld you all my Landes weer stated on the College: 3 Leases I Had, one off Them wase giuen to the College, the other 2 being the manor and recktory off Lewsham worth 130 *l.* a year and diuers tenements in the Black Fryars worth 120 *l.* the year booth which cost me 2500 *l.*; iff nether my statute nor recognisanc would serv those 2 leases showld be past over to some persone in trust that after my death shee surviving should be least 2000 markes [£1,333. 6s. 8d.]. This wase accepted on all syds.[1]

Constance was not kept in ignorance of these discussions, for Alleyn recalled that 'I presently returnd to Peckham and coming then to Con towld Her what Had past and more to show my Loue to Her off my owne voluntary I towld Her before Sir Thomas I would make it vpp to 1500 *l.*' At the time Constance was staying, as she frequently did, with her aunt and uncle at Peckham; thus she was well acquainted with Alleyn, who in his diary specifically mentions her presence on one occasion when he dined there, so the match was not proposed without her consent. Perhaps, like the Goodyer girls, she was beginning to feel desperate, for she was now 21, and most of her contemporaries were already married. Certainly Donne's letters to Goodyer on a father's responsibilities towards his unmarried daughters suggest that the problem was one which had been much discussed in both households. At any rate, Constance accepted without any unwillingness on her part the arrangements that were being made on her behalf. Alleyn, on his side, seems to have been both ardent and generous.

---

[1] Dulwich College MS. III. 102, ff. 145–6. The letter has been printed several times, e.g. by W. Young, *History of Dulwich College*, ii. 36–8, and B. W. Whitlock, 'Ye Curioust Schooler in Cristendom', *RES*, N.S. vi (1955), 365–71. I have expanded contractions and normalized capitalization and punctuation. After 'black fryars' the words 'as the plaiehowse theare' are inserted, but this is one of Collier's forgeries (see G. F. Warner, *Catalogue of the MSS. at Dulwich College*, 1881, p. 115, and E. K. Chambers, *William Shakespeare, a Study of Facts and Problems*, 1930, ii. 390).

On the very day of the Law Sergeants' feast a certain Sir John Jackson, who was to have been one of the stewards there, died, as a newsletter reported, 'of the spotted fever (as is said), whereof many die in two or three days' space'.[1] An epidemic was sweeping the city, and before long Donne himself fell a victim. He must have been taken ill at the very end of November, but because of his illness and its possible fatal consequences he urged that his daughter's marriage should be celebrated as soon as possible. Accordingly, Constance was married to Alleyn at Camberwell on 3 December, and no doubt Sir Thomas Grymes gave away the bride. It was, in Chamberlain's opinion, 'the straungest match', and one calculated, he feared, to diminish Alleyn's 'charitie and devotion' towards his foundation.[2]

The illness from which Donne was suffering has been diagnosed in recent times as relapsing fever.[3] This illness is sudden in its onset, and reaches a crisis in from five to seven days. In spite of insomnia and prostration, the sufferer remains in full possession of his faculties, and, if he passes the crisis, is so weakened that convalescence is slow. The principal danger at this period is the possibility of a relapse, a fact which gives the fever its name.

Donne was apparently out of danger by 6 December.[4] His mind remained remarkably active throughout his illness; it was working literally at fever heat. He must even have made notes about the various stages of his sufferings and some of the thoughts that passed through his mind. He was too ill to be allowed to read; books, we are told, were forbidden him; yet his mental activity was unceasing and apparently he found some distraction in putting pen to paper. Even during his convalescence he was not permitted to read, but he systematically organized his notes into the little book that was soon afterwards published as *Devotions vpon Emergent Occasions and seuerall steps in my Sicknes*. In a letter to Sir Robert Ker he described the later stages of its composition:

> Though I have left my bed, I have not left my bed-side; I sit there still, and as a Prisoner discharged, sits at the Prison doore, to beg

---

[1] I. A. Shapiro, loc. cit.

[2] Chamberlain, *Letters*, ii. 534.

[3] I. A. Shapiro, op. cit., at pp. 20-1.   [4] Chamberlain, *Letters*, ii. 531.

Fees, so sit I here, to gather crummes. I have used this leisure, to put the meditations had in my sicknesse, into some such order, as may minister some holy delight. They arise to so many sheetes (perchance 20.) as that without staying for that furniture of an Epistle, That my Friends importun'd me to Print them, I importune my Friends to receive them Printed.[1]

The *Devotions* were entered in the Stationers' Register by Thomas Jones on 9 January 1623/4, 'vnder the hands of Master Doctor Wilson and Master Bill Warden'. By that date, in other words, the book had not merely been composed and been seen by friends (some of the residentiary canons of St. Paul's, one would guess) who had importuned Donne to publish it, but had also been read by Dr. Wilson, the official licencer. When Donne wrote to Ker (the letter, unfortunately, is undated) he may have already had the proofs, as Gosse suggested,[2] and was enclosing some of them for Ker to see, with a query whether there could be any objection to his dedicating the book to the Prince of Wales, of whose household Ker was a member. Yet he was still so weak that it was inadvisable for him to go out. Surely the *Devotions* are unique in the annals of literature. They were written within less than a month, being first jotted down during a fever which nearly cost the writer his life, and were then put into shape during a convalescence that left the patient so weak that the book was almost in print before he was able to leave his bedroom. By 1 February it was published,[3] yet even after publication Donne wrote in a letter that accompanied a presentation copy, 'since I am barred of my ordinarie diet, which is Reading, I make these my exercises, which is another part of Physick'.[4]

The book is divided into twenty-three sections, each corresponding to a stage of the illness, and each being made up of a meditation, an expostulation, and a prayer. The phases of the illness are the occasion rather than the subject of the *Devotions*; nevertheless the reader is able to trace its progress. The onset was sudden: 'this minute I was well, and am ill, this minute. I am surpriz'd with a sodaine change, and alteration to worse, and can impute it to no

---

[1] *Letters*, p. 249.   [2] Gosse, ii. 189.
[3] According to a letter written on that date by Donne to a lady at the court of the Queen of Bohemia, Gosse, ii. 206 (Anderdon MS.).
[4] *Tobie Mathew Collection*, pp. 302-3.

cause, nor call it by any name.' His body is soon out of control: 'Is this the honour which Man hath by being a *little world*, That he hath these *earthquakes* in him selfe, sodaine shakings; these *lightnings*, sodaine flashes; these *thunders*, sodaine noises; these *Eclypses*, sodain offuscations, and darknings of his senses; these *Blazing stars*, sodaine fiery exhalations; these *Rivers of blood*, sodaine red waters?' His state is made worse by his fears, his 'sad apprehensions'. His senses are all disturbed: 'In the twinckling of an eye, I can scarse see, instantly the tast is insipid, and fatuous; instantly the appetite is dull and desirelesse: instantly the knees are sinking and strength-lesse; and in an instant, sleepe, which is the *picture*, the *copie* of *death*, is taken away, that the *Originall*, *Death* it selfe may succeed, and that so I might have death to the life.' He is forced to take to bed and send for the doctor, 'that *Phisician* who is my faithfull *friend*'—presumably Dr. Fox, whom Walton mentions as attending Donne in his last illness. 'I observe the *Phisician*, with the same diligence, as hee the *disease*; I see hee *feares*, and I feare with him; I overtake him, I overrun him in his feare, and I go the faster, because he makes his pace slow; I feare the more, because he disguises his fear, and I see it with the more sharpnesse, because hee would not have me see it.' The physician wished for another opinion and the King, hearing of Donne's illness, sent his own doctor (doubtless Sir Theodore de Mayerne). The earlier symptoms had passed away:

The *pulse*, the *urine*, the *sweat*, all have sworn to say nothing, to give no *Indication*, of any dangerous *sicknesse*. My forces are not enfeebled, I find no decay in my strength; my provisions are not cut off, I find no abhorring in mine appetite; my counsels are not corrupted or infatu-ated, I find no false apprehensions, to work upon mine understanding; and yet they see, that invisibly, and I feele, that insensibly the *disease* prevailes.

Therefore the doctors prescribed, and used 'Cordials, to keep the venim and Malignitie of the disease from the Heart'. They also gave Donne the strange treatment of applying dead pigeons to his feet 'to draw the vapors from the Head'.[1] Then, as the critical days

---

[1] Cf. Pepys, *Diary*, 19 Oct. 1663: 'the Queene . . . was so ill as to be shaved, and pidgeons put to her feet' (noted in Simpson, *Prose Works*, p. 243 n.); and Webster, *The Duchess of Malfi*, II. i. 39–41: 'I would sooner eate a dead pidgeon, taken from the soles of the feete of one sicke of the plague, then kisse one of you fasting.'

approached, his body broke out in a rash of spots. He was racked by sleeplessness, and haunted by the incessant tolling of bells, especially from the nearby church of St. Gregory. The epidemic was at its height, and deaths in the neighbouring parishes were frequent. The three sections on the tolling of the bells mark the period of crisis: first, they remind him that he is mortal; then, more insistently, they say 'Thou must die'; and at last, as his weakness increases, they tell him that he is dead. From the second of these meditations (xvii) emerges the thought that

No man is an *Iland*, intire of it selfe; every man is a peece of the *Continent*, a part of the *maine*; if a *Clod* bee washed away by the *Sea*, *Europe* is the Lesse, as well as if a *Promontorie* were, as well as if a *Mannor* of thy *friends* or of *thine owne* were; any mans *death* diminishes *me*, because I am involved in *Mankinde*; And therefore never send to know for whom the *bell* tolls; It tolls for *thee*.

But the crisis passed, and Donne was not dead, and the seven days of the fever were accomplished: '*Seven dayes*, O my *God*, have we looked for this *cloud*, and now we have it.' The patient began to wish to recover, the physicians administered purges, and his convalescence began. He felt like Lazarus, called back from the tomb. At last he was allowed to get up, but he was weak and dizzy: 'I am *up*, and I seeme to *stand*, and I goe *round*; and I am a new *Argument* of the *new Philosophie*, That the *Earth* moves round; why may I not beleeve, that the *whole earth* moves in a *round motion*, though that seeme to mee to *stand*, when as I seeme to *stand* to my *Company*, and yet am carried, in a giddy, and *circular motion*, as I *stand*?'[1] But he could not think yet of his recovery as sure; there was still, and would be for some time, the danger of a relapse. Fortunately no such relapse occurred, and Donne slowly grew stronger, recovering his health as winter changed to spring.

During this same illness and convalescence, he also wrote his 'Hymne to God the Father', and most probably the 'Hymne to God my God, in my sicknesse'. Walton, in the second edition of his *Life* of Donne, added the date 'March 23. 1630' to the latter poem,

---

[1] For the passages quoted, see Sparrow, *Devotions*, pp. 1, 2, 6, 26, 28, 56, 60, 67, 96, 98, 118, 128. Chamberlain, *Letters*, ii. 545, reports the book as 'newly come abrode' (21 Feb. 1623/4).

whereas a transcript survives among Sir Julius Caesar's papers in the British Museum endorsed 'D. Dun Dene of Pauls / his verses in his greate / siknes. / in Decemb. 1623'. Though the phrase in the title as given by Walton, 'in my sicknesse', suggests that the words were added by Donne himself after his recovery (whereas Walton's date is only eight days before Donne's death), able arguments have been presented in favour of each of the two possible dates.[1] Yet Caesar seems in this matter a better witness than Walton. Caesar had been, since 1 October 1614, the Master of the Rolls[2] (succeeding Sir Edward Phelips) and presumably lived in quarters in the Rolls Office (in Chancery Lane) within the parish of St. Dunstan-in-the-West. The Churchwardens' Accounts of St. Dunstan's for 1628-9 contain an item for repairs to 'the Lady Cesars pew doore'. But Lady Drury was Lady Caesar's cousin, and stayed with her 'at the Rolls' in May 1621 or 1622,[3] two or three years before Donne became vicar of the parish. It seems very likely, therefore, that Sir Julius knew Donne before the illness described in the *Devotions*. In any case, he must almost certainly have had contacts with Donne as a member of the parish a few months after the date he gives for the composition of the 'Hymne'.[4] The probability of his being a reliable witness for the date is thus considerably increased.

During his illness Donne had been as carefully and conscientiously attended as the medical science of his age allowed. He clearly had confidence in his own doctor, and he had had the additional advantage of the advice of the King's physician. His own servants tended him carefully: 'Thou hast not suffered that, that my *servants* should

---

[1] The arguments are reviewed by Helen Gardner, *Divine Poems*, Appendix E. She leans to Caesar's date, and the further evidence now adduced adds support to her opinion.   [2] See above, p. 373.

[3] A letter among the Bacon papers (Redgrave Muniments, University of Chicago Library, item 4230) from Sir John Holles to Lady Drury, is addressed 'To Y^e Noble, and my mutch estemed worthye Ladye ye Ladye Drurye at the Roulles ... London' from Saxham, 6 May 1622 (it looks as if the figure 1 has been written over the last '2' of the year, and 1621 may be the correct date); cf. *Donne and the Drurys*, p. 165, and see above, p. 311. There is a postscript: 'I praye present my Seruise to ye M^rs of ye M^r of ye Roules and his worthye Ladye.'

[4] Caesar and Donne were in later years fellow members of the High Commission, and were twice appointed to commissions in the Court of Delegates in 1627 (Del. 8/70, ff. 32^r, 33^v); it is in no case certain that they actually sat on the bench together but it is likely that they did so, and almost certain that they were personally associated in some at least of these matters.

so much as *neglect* mee, or be *wearie* of mee, in my *sicknesse*.'[1] Nevertheless, he was not without contact with the outside world, and
he probably received more visitors than a present-day patient would
have been allowed. We have already seen that he was able to hasten
Constance's marriage from his sick bed, and Walton tells[2] how he
was visited daily by Henry King, who came on one of his visits with
a proposal which he hoped would ease Donne's fears of dying and
leaving his children unprovided for. But Donne refused to benefit by
the hasty renewal of a lease at too low a fine when, if he lived, far
better terms might be secured. Donne was also able to arrange for
the publication of the *Devotions*, though, it will be recalled, he had
not fully recovered his strength by 1 February 1623/4 when copies
started coming off the press. As he usually did, he began to send out
complimentary copies. Encouraged by Prince Charles's acceptance
of the dedication, he sent a copy to the Princess Elizabeth, now in
exile in Holland as Queen of Bohemia, enclosing it with another
to one of the ladies of her court. The Duke of Buckingham also
received a copy, and the letter accompanying one more such gift
has survived, though the name of the recipient is not known, since
the address is simply to 'My Lord'.[3]

Donne's health does not seem to have allowed him to preach his
usual sermon at Court at the beginning of Lent in 1624. Though
there are no surviving sermons preached at Whitehall in April this
year, he managed to deliver his Easter Day sermon in St. Paul's on
28 March, so that by then he had in large measure regained his
strength. With his return to health came a new responsibility. On
1 March 1624 Dr. Thomas Whyte, one of the prebendaries of St.
Paul's, died at an advanced age. He had also been vicar of the church
of St. Dunstan-in-the-West. The patron of this living was the Earl
of Dorset, who had some time previously promised it to Donne
when it should fall vacant. Donne was formally appointed by the
patron on 18 March. The Earl died ten days later and was succeeded
in the title and the estates by his brother Sir Edward Sackville, with
whom Donne had long been well acquainted. Whyte seems to have

[1] Sparrow, *Devotions*, p. 131.   [2] *Lives*, pp. 57–9.
[3] *Tobie Mathew Collection*, p. 302. Gosse (ii. 208) conjectured that he was the Earl of
Dorset.

had some difficulties with his patron and had been engaged in a lawsuit with him; but to Donne's credit it must be said that he maintained the warmest of relations with those who had tried to promote his interests.

Donne was now to hold, besides his deanery and its attendant prebend, the rectory of Sevenoaks, the rectory of Blunham, and the vicarage of St. Dunstan's. The prebend of Chiswick and the rectory of Sevenoaks were sinecures in the technical sense, that is to say, benefices without cure of souls, and could be held in conjunction with others. Donne's status as a royal chaplain gave him the right to hold two benefices with the cure of souls, and the act of Parliament which conferred this right (21 Hen. VIII, c. 13) also provided that such persons should acquire a licence or dispensation to hold livings in plurality in this fashion.[1] The requisite dispensation was granted to Donne on 9 March 1623/4, and consisted of

> your Maj^{ties} Graunt of Dispensation to Dr Donne Dean of Pauls, & one of your Maj^{ties} Chaplains in Ordinary enabling [him] to hold during his life, the Rectory of Blunham in the Diocese of Lincoln, & any one other Benefice, having Cure of Soules, wch he shall hereafter obteyne from your Maj^{tie} together with all those Ecclesiastical Dignities, & other Spirituall Promotions, wch he now holdeth, with a clause of premutacõn to alter & chaunge any of them for any other Ecclesiasticall Benefices.[2]

This is quoted from the summary at the foot of the actual document which was added for the King to read before he signed it, to save him the trouble of reading laboriously through the whole. Then, at the end of the summary, comes the notation, 'And is done by the order of the Lord Duke of Buckingham', followed by the signature of the Secretary of State, 'Fra: Windebanck'. Donne did not err when he wrote in an earlier dedication to Buckingham, 'When I would speake to the *King*, by your *Lordships* Meanes, I doe.' It is quite likely that Donne had sought this dispensation immediately on being appointed to Blunham, but that it had been held up by his illness. By the time it was actually signed Dr. Whyte was already

---

[1] See above, p. 307.
[2] From the transcript of the whole document, University Library, Cambridge, MS. Mm. I. 45, p. 199. Cf. Signet Office Dockets, vol. 7, Index 6806 (P.R.O.) and *C.S.P.* (*Dom.*), 1623–25, p. 727. The dispensation is also listed among the Privy Seals.

dead, and Donne must certainly have known that he was to be his successor at St. Dunstan's, but the fact that the dispensation does not refer to a second benefice by name shows clearly that it was originally drawn up before there was any thought that Donne would so soon acquire it. Donne was a pluralist in an age when all the higher dignitaries of the Church were pluralists, and when the practice lacked the stigma that has since attached to it, but his was not the flagrant pluralism of some of his contemporaries. He did not, for instance, seek prebendal stalls at Westminster and Windsor, or at two or three other cathedrals beside his own, and he accepted his two benefices with cure of souls because they were a privilege conferred on royal chaplains by act of Parliament.

Donne had in fact become involved in the affairs of St. Dunstan's even before he succeeded to the vicarage; apparently it was well known who was to take Whyte's place, for on 31 July 1623 (while Whyte was still alive) the vestry minutes record that the church-wardens were 'desired to attende the Deane of Paules and the Lo: Keeper to sue out a ne exeat regnum against Captaine Harvye for the more security of recouery of the twoo hundred poundes given by Mr Hares will to the vse of the poore of this parish'.[1] Nicholas Hare was Clerk of the Court of Wards, an office which he had inherited from his father and had accepted rather reluctantly after prolonged travels abroad. He died, while still a relatively young man, on 13 January 1622. By his will (which, incidentally, was witnessed by Izaak Walton) he left £200 for the poor of the parish of St. Dunstan's, the interest of which was to be distributed by the Dean of St. Paul's.[2] It is difficult not to believe that Hare was already acquainted with Donne and also knew of his expectations at St. Dunstan's when he made him the dispenser of his charity. But Hare's executor was a certain Captain John Harvey who, though he erected a handsome monument to the memory of his dead friend,[3] had not yet handed over the money that was to benefit the poor of the parish. Harvey had recently been appointed a member of a commission to investigate

[1] London Guildhall Library, MS. 3016/1, p. 100. Cf. B. W. Whitlock, 'Donne at St. Dunstan's', *TLS*, 16 and 23 Sept. 1955.
[2] J. Carey, 'The Poems of Nicholas Hare', *RES*, N.S. xi (1960), 365–83, especially pp. 370–2.
[3] J. Stow, *Survey of London*, 1633 ed., p. 880.

the affairs of the Virginia Company, and left England not long afterwards on a visit to the colony. The Lord Keeper (Williams) was presumably to be approached because he was both a judge and a clergyman who would sympathize with the predicament of the vestry, and Donne because of his interest in the charity under the testator's will; nor should it be forgotten that he was also a member of the Council of the Virginia Company. Harvey set out without meeting his obligations, but after he returned in 1627 the parish brought an action in Chancery against him. Before it was concluded he had been appointed Governor of Virginia and had returned (with a knighthood) to the New World. He came back in 1635 after he had been expelled by the colonists, and the vestry was able to force him to sign an agreement for the settlement of the debt.[1] He was, however, reinstated in his office by the King, but he finally returned to England in 1639, heavily in debt. It is very doubtful whether the parish ever received Hare's legacy.

On 4 March 1623/4, three days after Dr. Whyte's death, the churchwardens again called on Donne. The meeting was evidently cordial, for the parish accounts contain an item for 13d. 'paid for wine when wee went to visitt the Deane of St. Pauls church'.[2] No doubt the future of the parish was discussed. Donne was formally appointed a fortnight later and paid the first fruits of his living (March 18).[3] From the first he took the affairs of the parish much more seriously than his predecessor had done. St. Dunstan's was a City parish, inasmuch as it was within Temple Bar, but it was also close to the more fashionable areas just outside the City boundaries, and it was in the centre of the legal district of London. The Temple was immediately opposite the church, on the other side of Fleet Street; Clifford's Inn, which abutted it on the north side, used the church as its chapel; Sergeants' Inn was close by in Chancery Lane; and Lincoln's Inn and the Office of the Rolls were only a little further away. Regulations governing the apparel of judges made on 4 June 1635 allow the wearing of black or violet gowns in term, 'except on holy days, when they were to sit in scarlet . . . also when the judges

[1] Guildhall MS. 2983, p. 392. Cf. Appendix D, pp. 572–3 below.
[2] Guildhall MS. 2968, vol. 2, fo. 228; Whitlock, op. cit.
[3] First Fruits, Lib. Comp., vol. 17, fo. 7ᵛ (P.R.O.); Whitlock, op. cit.

went to Westminster Abbey to hear a sermon, and after sit in court; and when they went to St. Paul's, or any other public church in Term'. The judges seem to have frequented St. Dunstan's, since in 1614 the churchwardens ordered 'a dozen green cushions for the judges' pews in the church, and a seat for Edward Lile the warder'.[1] As we have seen, Lady Caesar, wife of the Master of the Rolls, had a pew in the church. When Donne preached at St. Dunstan's, as he often did, his congregation must usually have included not only the citizens and their families who lived in the parish, but also a large sprinkling of lawyers, and of fashionable folk from the neighbouring parish of St. Clement Danes, in which he had lived for many years.

The concentration of so many members of the legal profession in or alongside the parish brought to it an unusual number of printers and stationers, and to read the vestry minutes for this period is to encounter names famous in the annals of English printing and publishing. Most of the stationers had their shops in the churchyard of St. Dunstan's, which was second only to St. Paul's churchyard as the headquarters of the book trade. John Smethwick, William Jaggard and his brother John, John Marriot and his son Richard, and Matthew Lownes were among the better-known stationers who at one time or another lived in the parish. John Jaggard and Smethwick held various parish offices and Smethwick became a senior churchwarden while Donne was vicar. Other stationers, not quite so well known, who had their shops in the churchyard, were Thomas Dew, Anne Helm, Richard More, William Washington, and George Winder. More published the 1611 and 1626 editions of *Ignatius his Conclave* and Dew the 1621 and 1625 editions of the *Anniversaries*, so that the vicar must on more than one occasion have been reminded of these products of his secular life as he approached the church. The Marriots, of course, published his collected poems after his death. Izaak Walton, when Donne came to the parish, was still a relatively young man of thirty, and he did not attain his first parish office until after Donne's death. Another name with literary association that appears frequently in the parish records is Robert Gomersall, the father (apparently) of the Robert Gomersall who wrote *The Tragedy of Lodowick Sforza*. The son published four books with

---

[1] E. Foss, *The Judges of England*, vi (1857), pp. 227 and 34.

the Marriots, as would be natural if he came originally from the parish.[1]

Donne preached his first sermon at St. Dunstan's on 11 April and a second one two weeks later. It is difficult to believe that the congregation was not startled when the new vicar ascended the pulpit and announced his text from Deuteronomy 25: 5: 'If brethren dwell together, and one of them die, and have no child, the wife of the dead shall not marry without, unto a stranger; her husband's brother shall go in unto her, and take her to him to wife, and perform the duty of an husband's brother unto her.' He soon made it clear, however, that he was not concerned with the literal application of the words: 'wee lay hold onely upon the *Typique signification*, and appliablenesse of the law, as that *secular Mariage* there spoken of, may be appliable to this *spirituall Mariage*, the Mariage of the Minister to the Church.'[2] The sermon is a most elaborate and ingenious piece of textual interpretation on the 'typic' level, though the theme is the relatively simple one of the relations between the pastor and his flock. The second sermon continues the theme of the first. The text on this occasion was more obviously suitable: 'Come ye children, hearken unto me, I will teach you the fear of the Lord.' From the outset the emphasis is on the message, not the man; the text does not call 'such as wish *themselves away*, nor such as wish *another man here*; but such as value Gods ordinance of *Preaching*, though it be, as the Apostle says, but the *foolishnesse of Preaching*, and such, as consider the *office*, and not the *person*, how meane soever'.[3] One wonders as one reads the sermons whether there had not been some feeling in the parish against Donne and a reluctance to accept him. More probably, he was guarding himself against the discontent that had accumulated during the tenure of his predecessor, who does not seem to have given the parish much attention (judging by his default of attendance at vestry meetings), and giving notice that henceforth the relations of minister and people were to be on a cordial Christian footing. For whatever reason, the existence of a

---

[1] The author is said to have been born in London. The Robert Gomersall of St. Dunstan's parish is described in a document of 1640 as 'Citizen and Painter Stainer of London' (Guildhall MS. 2983, p. 216). Cf. R. C. Bald, 'Dr. Donne and the Booksellers', *Studies in Bibliography*, xviii (1965), 69–80.

[2] *Sermons*, vi, no. 3, ll. 44–7, p. 82.   [3] Ibid., no. 4, ll. 6–10, p. 95.

ticklish situation seems to be implied by such remarks as the following:

For where the Congregation loves the Pastor, hee will forbeare bitter reproofes, and wounding increpations, and where the Pastor loves his Congregation, his *Rebukes*, because they proceed out of *love*, will bee acceptable, and well interpreted by them. . . . Even in our spirituall mariages to widow Churches, we must have a care to preserve the *temporall rights* of all persons; That the Parish be not oppressed with heavy *extortions*, nor the *Pastor* defrauded with unjust *substraction*, nor the Patron damnified by *usurpations*, nor the *Ordinary* neglected by *disobediences*; but that people, and Pastor, and Patron, and Ordinary, continuing in possession of their severall rights, *love* being the *root* of all, the *fruit* of all may be peace. . . .[1]

The attention that Donne gave to the parish from the outset was so much more than Whyte had given it, for many years at least, that, if there was any initial dissatisfaction, he soon allayed it.

Another surviving sermon that was preached at St. Dunstan's this year is the sermon on Trinity Sunday (23 May), and the parish records show that on 29 June he preached a commemorative sermon which had been established by a former parishioner named Adams. Donne delivered this annual sermon again in 1626, 1627, and 1628. One of these sermons has survived, 'An Anniversary Sermon preached at St. Dunstan's, upon the commemoration of a Parishioner, a Benefactor to that Parish', but the year to which it belongs is not known.[2] Donne not only preached in the church; he also took an active interest in the affairs of the parish. The first indication of this interest is his signature affixed on 26 April 1624 to the churchwardens' accounts; Whyte had always left it to a deputy to act for him on these occasions. Soon afterwards he came to an agreement with the parish for the payment of the tithes. He granted a twenty-one-year lease to twelve of the leading parishioners by an agreement signed on 11 May, of which a copy is preserved in the parish archives.[3] From this we learn that the parishioners were rated at £240 for tithes, but that the vicar was now to be paid £200 a year by the lessees in equal quarterly instalments. Certain of the vicar's rights

---

[1] Ibid., no. 3, ll. 478–94, p. 94.   [2] Ibid. x, no. 8.
[3] Guildhall MS. 2983, p. 154.

were not affected by this agreement; he was still to receive the rents of the 'vicarage-house' and the two adjoining tenements in Fleet Street which had originally constituted the glebe. It was further provided that if any composition of tithes was made with the inhabitants of Whitefriars two-thirds of that sum was to go to the lessees, but that certain other perquisites of the vicar, such as Easter oblations, offerings made at marriages and burials, and fees from burials in the chancel, should be undisturbed. The agreement was confirmed and approved at a meeting of the whole parish on 25 June; and a committee of fifteen was appointed to consider how the rent of £200 was to be 'conveniently rated and gathered'.[1] In this way Donne was relieved of the trouble of collecting the tithes for himself.

The vicarage of St. Dunstan's was an impropriation; in other words, the tithes were the property of a layman, in this instance the Earl of Dorset. Provision for the care of the parish was made by means of the combined rents of the parsonage and the glebe, both of which fronted on Fleet Street. In 1636, as we have seen,[2] the parsonage was said to be worth £50 per annum and the glebe £53. 6s. 8d. When Donne wrote to Mrs. Cokayne that 'I make not a shilling profit of S. *Dunstans* as a Church man, but as my L. of *Dorset* gave me the lease of the Impropriation, for a certain rent, and a higher rent, the*n* my predecessor had it at',[3] he meant that the profits of the parsonage house and glebe all went towards the salary of the curate and various other expenses he incurred in connection with the parish. On the other hand, he received his £200 a year from the tithe collectors, and was entitled to keep what was left over after he had paid his rent to the Earl of Dorset; but this he regarded as little different from any other secular investment.

Donne next proceeded to persuade the vestry to undertake renovations in the interior of the church. In addition, a new pulpit was erected, and nine new pews were installed, for a total cost of £122. 2s. 8d.[4] Stow remarked of St. Dunstan's in 1633 that 'It is since this Church was repaired 20. yeeres, yet though so long, it

---

[1] Vestry Minutes, Guildhall MS. 3016/1, pp. 102–3.
[2] See above, p. 425.   [3] *Letters*, p. 318.
[4] The 'necessary reparac*i*ons' and other work were begun on 11 Aug. 1624 and finished on 24 Jan. 1624/5; cf. Whitlock, op. cit.

hath more of that beauty still, and still remaines fresher and fairer than many other Churches, that halfe so much time hath not wrought upon',[1] though he may have been referring to the exterior. It was, however, characteristic of Donne that he should show particular care for the beauty and orderliness of any place of worship for which he had the responsibility. He also helped to bring to an end a dispute which had been going on for some time between the parishioners and the members of Clifford's Inn. The latter used St. Catherine's Chapel within the church as their Inn chapel, but it was claimed that they were encroaching more and more on the body of the church, with the result that the parishioners wanted to evict them. The dispute was referred to Sir Henry Martin, who upheld the rights of the Inn. Naturally, the parishioners were still dissatisfied, and in 1624 the quarrel was submitted for settlement to a group of six, three from each side. Towards the end of the year agreement was finally reached: Clifford's Inn retained the use of its chapel, but agreed to rebuild its pews so as to provide more seating accommodation and in smaller space.[2] This is only one of several indications that St. Dunstan's was very well attended, and that the vestry was constantly concerning itself with the problem of seating all those who came to services. It can safely be said that Donne's reputation and the frequency with which he preached did nothing to alleviate the overcrowding.

Other records of Donne's activities in 1624 are scanty. On 13 June he preached 'to the Earl of Exeter, and his company, in his Chappell at Saint Johns'.[3] Lady Exeter was a sister of Sir Robert Drury, and this connection no doubt explains why Donne was invited to preach on this occasion. In July he was evidently host at some kind of feast, as can be inferred from a letter he wrote on the 23rd of the month to his brother-in-law Sir Nicholas Carey:

Sir,—I am forc'd at thys tyme to do a bolder thinge towards you then ever I shall againe. I was surprized with such a necessity of usinge a buck, as *that* I tooke one from Sr John Davers when he could hardly spare yt, and to repayre that I ame constrayned to beg one of *yours*

---

[1] *Survey of London*, 1633 ed., p. 879.
[2] Vestry Minutes, Guildhall MS. 3016/1, fo. 104^v, 25 Nov. 1624. The vestry was also concerned to retain space for burials.
[3] *Sermons*, vi, no. 7.

to pay that debt, which did me so seasonable a kyndnes. If it be very inconvenient to you I crave your pardon for asking yt; but if yt disorder no purpose of yours to give yt, you have your *Quietus est* from me for all my lyfe, and, howsoever, duringe all *that* tyme I shall recommend you and all your family to our B[lessed] Savyer in *the* best prayers of your poor brother-in-law & servant in Chr[ist] Jes[us].[1]

Another letter to Sir Nicholas Carey written on 1 September is mostly taken up with a message from the new Earl of Dorset. Carey had done him 'a curtesy . . . out of [his] parke', and he now planned to send a stag in return, if Carey would let him know when to send it.[2] Incidentally the letter reveals that Donne intended to accompany Dorset to Knole on the following Sunday, and while there he would almost certainly have preached at Sevenoaks. One other letter in quite a different key belongs to a somewhat later date. This is the letter Donne wrote to Lady Kingsmill, the former Bridget White, to console her for the death of her husband.[3] The theme of the letter is submission to the will of God, and in form it closely resembles one of the meditations from the *Devotions*. Donne preached at St. Dunstan's on New Year's Day 1625.

The next episode in his career is far less devout and distinctly unclerical. Early in 1625 a gradual coolness which had been growing up between Donne and his son-in-law burst out into a quarrel. The immediate cause of the explosion was Donne's refusal to lend Alleyn the fairly considerable sum of £500, which he had been encouraged to believe would be at his disposal if he needed it. During the last years of Alleyn's life his financial dealings were fairly complicated, and his obligations to his foundation at Dulwich were such that he was more than once in need of loans to tide him over.[4] He had felt sure that he could rely on Donne, and when the loan was refused he found himself in an awkward situation. He confronted Donne, and charged him with deliberately trying to disgrace him by withholding the loan at the last moment and esteeming £500 'beefor my honesty, your own reputacon or your daughters good'. To this Donne

[1] *The Collection of Autograph Letters and Historical Documents formed by Alfred Morrison* (Second Series), iii (1896), 128.
[2] British Museum Add. MS. 29598, fo. 13.
[3] *Letters*, pp. 7–10, dated from the Deanery 26 Oct. 1624.
[4] See W. Young, *History of Dulwich College*, ii. 38.

'presently being enflamd sayd twise itt wase fals and a lye'—words, added Alleyn, more 'fitting you 30 years ago when you might be question[ed] for them then now vnder so reverent a calling as you are'. On his return home Alleyn vented his feelings in an indignant letter to his father-in-law in which he reviewed all their dealings since the marriage with Constance had first been proposed. As he wrote, grievances came welling up into his mind. When the newly married couple came to see Donne during his convalescence he had promised Constance her mother's childbed linen as a New Year's gift, but had never sent it. (Constance had no children by Alleyn.) Constance had wanted 'a little nagg' of her father's which was scarcely used, and she persuaded her brother George to urge their father to give it to her; he had consented, but had then sent it away to Oxford (where their eldest brother John had been at Christ Church for the past two years). Donne had also obtained from Constance a diamond ring by promising to exchange it for a better one which he wore, but had not kept his side of the bargain. Donne had received £550 for his lease but had told Alleyn that it was worth £500 and had kept the extra £50 for himself. Alleyn had been offered the hospitality of the Deanery whenever he was in London, but when he sought to take advantage of the offer he was told it was not convenient.[1]

Of course, we have only Alleyn's side of the story, and one cannot help noticing that some of his statements are unconscious admissions, or will not bear the weight he puts on them. Was a loan of £500 really 'that comon curtesie afforded to a frend' which Alleyn calls it? He complained too that 'many tymes haue I moue[d] you for matters off endiffrence belongin to your plac, but they wear eather put by to Circumstance or flattly deni[e]d'. One can sense Donne's resentment at Alleyn for believing that he could rely on Donne's favour in dealings in cathedral offices or property. Alleyn ends his letter with a final stab by pointing out that Lucy Donne has been making a rather lengthy stay with her sister, and suggests that her father is 'better able to bear her Charg' than he.

[1] See p. 449 n. above. The letter is in Alleyn's original draft, much corrected and interlined. The fact that the draft was kept suggests that the letter was in fact sent (in fair copy). The state of the manuscript is such that none of the transcripts is wholly reliable.

In Alleyn's letter one glimpses a Donne quite different from the man portrayed in all other accounts of him. Both he and Alleyn were obviously quick-tempered men, and one recalls Walton's remark that Donne was 'highly passionate, but more apt to reluct at the excesses of it'. Even so, Alleyn's grievances, petty as some of them are, cannot be lightly dismissed. There was, one would guess, a conflict of temperaments that gradually developed, which Donne for a time tried to overcome but in the end was unable to resist. There seems to have been in Alleyn something of the extrovert's heartiness and expansiveness; he boasted in the letter that he was 'a playn man . . . for I thank God I never Could disguise in my lyfe' —a rather unexpected statement to come from one of the greatest actors of the day—and he reveals a strain of insensitiveness which probably offended Donne's more fastidious nature. Donne, too, was obviously resolute in refusing to let him have any influence in 'matters belonging to [his] place'. One senses also in Donne's behaviour the attitudes of a man who for years had had to struggle to make ends meet, and was still not fully used to affluence; hence his reluctance to part easily even with what he had promised to bestow. As for the loan, the truth is that Donne had probably come to believe that Alleyn was not a good risk; as his will shows, he was prepared to make such loans to friends like Sir John Danvers whom he felt that he could trust. It must also be added that Alleyn had not yet made his promised settlements on Constance. Evidently, however, Alleyn managed to obtain the money (or credit) he needed, for he stayed solvent and at his death his obligations to his wife, as we shall see, were more than fulfilled.

Soon after this episode Donne wrote what is almost certainly his last poem, 'An Hymne to the Saints, and to Marquesse Hamylton', on the death of this Scottish nobleman, 2 March 1624/5. It is still very much in the manner of the earlier memorial poems, though the title suggests that Donne was trying to give the verses a stronger religious tinge than his similar pieces had previously had. The poem was written at the urging of Sir Robert Ker, and with some reluctance on Donne's part. 'I thank you', he wrote in an accompanying letter, 'that you would command me that which I was loath to doe, for, even that hath given a tincture of merit to the obedience of

Your poore friend and servant in Christ Jesus.'[1] Nevertheless Donne did not escape charges of frivolity, and Chamberlain, in sending a copy of the verses to Carleton, commented: 'Though they be reasonable wittie and well don yet I could wish a man of his yeares and place to geve over versifieng.'[2]

Shortly afterwards another death occurred which affected Donne far more deeply, for on 27 March 1625 the King died, and for Donne, as for many of the courtiers, his death marked the end of an epoch. It was almost inevitable that the minds of such men should dwell with mingled apprehension and anticipation on the changes that the new regime would bring. Donne had learned to feel at ease in the presence of James and had become sufficiently familiar with Buckingham to have some confidence that his standing with both King and favourite was secure. But so far his contacts with the new King had been mostly formal ones, and he still had little notion what Charles's attitude to him would be. While he was human enough to be agitated by such uncertainties, he was also profoundly grieved by the death of the old King, to whom he always professed a deep sense of gratitude for having led him into the Church. In 1625 he had been assigned as usual the duty of being in attendance at Whitehall during the month of April, and it fell to his lot to preach the first sermon to the new King on the 3rd of the month. On hearing the news of his father's death Charles had remained for nearly a week in the strictest seclusion, but ordered a sermon to be preached before him on the Sunday after James had died. The sermon was commanded for St. James's Palace, where Charles was still residing. Donne, by now accustomed to the arrangements at Whitehall, was disturbed at the thought of the unfamiliar surroundings and wrote hurriedly to Ker, on 2 April, to ask if he might have the hospitality of his rooms in the palace, to compose himself and prepare himself for the service.[3] In a note sent the following day, he refused Ker's invitation to eat either before or after the sermon (which was fixed for the afternoon), and makes it clear that it was not his custom to eat before preaching, nor after it until he was quietly settled at home. He pleads weak health ('so much hath my this years debility

---

[1] Grierson, i. 288. [2] Chamberlain, *Letters*, ii. 613.
[3] *Letters*, pp. 313–14.

disabled me'),[1] but it is clear that the delivery of his more important sermons imposed a severe strain upon him.

A contemporary letter-writer relates that on 3 April Charles I left his private chambers for the first time since his accession, 'and then dined abroad, in the privy-chamber, being in a plain black cloth cloak to the ancle; and so went after dinner into the chapel, Dr. Donne preaching, Lord Davers carrying the sword before him, his majesty looking very pale, his visage being the true glass of his inward, as well as his accoutrements of external mourning'.[2] Normally, on special occasions and anniversaries, Donne left all reference to the occasion until the concluding part of the sermon, but this time he opened by referring to the grief which the whole nation felt:

> Wee are still in the season of *Mortification*; in *Lent*: But wee search no longer for *Texts* of *Mortification*; The Almightie hand of *God* hath shed and spred a *Text* of *Mortification* over all the land. The last *Sabboth* day, was his *Sabboth* who entred then into his everlasting *Rest*; Be this our *Sabboth*, to enter into a holy and thankfull acknowledgement of that *Rest*, which *God* affords us, in continuing to us our *Foundations*; for, *If foundations be destroyed, what can the righteous do?*[3]

Then, knowing that the new King was soon to marry a French princess, he went on, with great tact and moderation, to warn him against the dangers of Catholicism, and to remind him of his duty to the Church of England:

> as wee, at last, shall commend our Spirits, into the hands of *God*, *God* hath commended our Spirits, not onely our civill peace, but our Religion too, into the *hand* of the *Magistrate*. And therefore, when the *Apostle* sayes, *Studie to bee quiet*, it is not quiet in the blindnesse of the *Eye*, nor quiet in the *Deafenesse* of the *Eare*, nor quiet in the *Lamenesse* of the *Hand*; the just discharge of the dueties of our severall places, is no *disquieting* to any man.[4]

Donne probably realized that he had to take a risk of giving offence, but none was taken. The sermon was published soon afterwards, certainly with Charles's approval and probably by his command.

---

[1] *Letters*, p. 311.
[2] Sir William Neve, in *The Court and Times of Charles the First*, i (1848), 3–4.
[3] *Sermons*, vi, no. 12, ll. 1–8, p. 241.   [4] Ibid., ll. 147–54, p. 245.

Donne still had his final tributes to pay to the old King. James had died at Theobalds, but his body was brought to London and lay in state at Denmark House, the former residence of his Queen. Here Donne preached on 26 April to the Court. He chose a text from the Song of Solomon (3: 11), and to the modern reader much of the sermon seems strained and unnatural by reason of the figurative interpretation which the medieval tradition placed on the words of the ancient Hebrew love poems. But the last three pages, in which Donne spoke of the King whose body lay before him, constitute a passage of sustained and unequalled eloquence. Even as he drew to an end, he knew that for many of his hearers the death of James was also an end, an end which was the prelude to a new beginning—'a going forth in many severall wayes: some to the service of their *new Master*, and some to the enjoying of their Fortunes conferred by their old; some to the raising of new *Hopes*, some to the burying of old, and all; some to new, and busie endeavours in Court, some to contented retirings in the Countrey'.[1] For Donne himself it meant the transition to a new regime, and one which for a while still seemed to have for him opportunities as great as the old. A few days later, clad in mourning and attended by a servant, he walked solemnly with the other royal chaplains[2] in the slow procession that followed James to his last resting-place in Westminster Abbey, and with this last act the final vestiges of the old reign passed away.

[1] Ibid., no. 14, ll. 418–22, p. 291.
[2] The accounts for the funeral of James I (P.R.O., L.C. 2/6) list Donne as the 47th out of 70 of the King's Chaplains, and show that he received nine yards of mourning for himself and six for a servant. Sir Henry Goodyer received mourning for himself and a servant as a Gentleman of the Privy Chamber; and Edward Alleyn appears as Master of Bears and Bulls just below the King's Players.

XVII

ACTIVE YEARS

WHEN James I died Donne was 53 years old, and had six more years to live. In 1625 he was at the height of his powers, and though he suffered from periods of ill health his vitality was still unimpaired. He had won a place for himself at Court, so that he was on friendly terms with most of the important figures there, from Buckingham downwards. He was active in Church affairs, not merely as Dean of St. Paul's, and in all the supplementary activities which that office entailed; all the evidence shows that he was also unusually conscientious in giving attention to the other parishes of which he was nominally in charge. In addition to all this, he still bought books and read widely, as the list of surviving titles from his library shows; early in life he had formed the habits of a student, and they never left him. As Walton reports, 'his bed was not able to detain him beyond the hour of four in a morning: and it was no common business that drew him out of his chamber till past ten. All which time was employed in study.'[1] At every stage of his life one is conscious of the vigour and untiring activity of his mind.

Donne seems to have had a bout of illness not very long after the beginning of the new reign. It is true that on 8 May he preached one of those annual sermons which as prebendary of Chiswick he was bound to deliver.[2] Appropriately in these sermons he always chose his text from one of the five psalms associated with his prebend. A few days later, too, he must have been present at a parish meeting at St. Dunstan's to sign the annual accounts of the Senior Church-warden.[3] Thereafter there is no further record until two letters written during the second half of June.[4] Walton seems to have

---

[1] *Lives*, p. 67. [2] *Sermons*, vi, no. 15.
[3] 12 May. Cf. B. W. Whitlock, 'Donne at St. Dunstan's I', *TLS*, 16 Sept. 1955.
[4] Mrs. Simpson (*Sermons*, vi. 30–1) believed that Donne preached at St. Paul's on Whit Sunday (5 June), mainly because an undated Whitsun sermon would fit conveniently into this year, but she would have been the first to admit that the evidence is inconclusive.

known that Donne was ill in 1625, but he confused this illness with that in which the *Devotions* were written.[1] In one of the letters of late June, written while he was recovering, Donne says, 'I had bin long in my chamber, and practised how to put out breath, almost to my last gasp'; this sounds like the illness that 'ended in a Cough, that inclined him to a Consumption', of which Walton speaks.[2] Donne probably suffered from some form of bronchial affliction, with a great deal of coughing, that made him lose weight and troubled him for a long time.

The two letters to which reference has been made belong to the period of his recovery. What is perhaps the earlier is undated, and is addressed to Sir Robert Ker.[3] In it Donne describes his illness (in the passage already quoted) and says that he has just returned from a day's outing to Chelsea where he had obviously visited Sir John and Lady Danvers. A fine day had probably encouraged him to venture out, but his health would not allow him to accept Ker's invitation. He was all the more regretful because 'my Lord Chancellor' was to have been a fellow guest; 'I desired much to have been in my Lord Chancellor's sight'—'For, as when I sit still, and reckon all my old Master's Royall favours to me, I return evermore to that, that he first inclined me to be a Minister: So, when I reckon all the favours that I have received from my Lord Chancellor, I return to that, that he was the first man that ever presented my name to my Lord *Carlile*, and entred me into his service.'[4] He hopes, however, soon to

---

[1] The point is made by I. A. Shapiro, 'Walton and the Occasion of Donne's *Devotions*', *RES*, N.S. ix (1958), at pp. 21–2.

[2] In the first version of the *Life* prefixed to *LXXX Sermons* (1640).

[3] *Tobie Mathew Collection*, p. 307. This letter was misdated by Gosse, who placed it (ii. 190) between two letters of 1623. The reference to James I as 'my old master' seems to place it after James's death, and the reference to Bacon ('my Lord Chancellor') places it before Bacon's death on 9 Apr. 1626. Within this period of just over a year there are a number of months in which it is unlikely it could have been written, and it seems from its contents to belong to a date close to that of Donne's letter of 21 June 1625 to Sir Nicholas Carey.

[4] *Tobie Mathew Collection*, p. 308. It may perhaps be necessary to insist that this is a reference to Bacon, although he had lost the chancellorship several years previously: (1) The habit of addressing a man by the title of an office, or a woman by a rank no longer held, was even stronger in the seventeenth century than it is in England today. (2) Bacon's two successors were Lord Keepers not Lord Chancellors, so that after the death of old Lord Ellesmere in 1617 there was no one else to whom the title could apply. (3) Compare Howell, *Epistolae Ho-Elianae*, bk. 1, sec. iv, letter viii: 'My Lord Chancellor Bacon is lately dead. . . . They say he shall be the last Lord

see Ker at a 'house, where I have a prescription, and have not us'd
to be kept out' (perhaps another reference to the Danvers household
at Chelsea). He has learnt, too, that Ker's wife is nearing her time,
and promises his prayers on her behalf.

The other letter is addressed to Sir Nicholas Carey, and is dated
21 June. He had evidently made an excursion to Beddington similar
to the Chelsea one, but since then the weather had kept him indoors.
'I am glad I tooke so much good ayre with you', he begins, 'for since
I came from you, I have taken none at all; for I have been, by my
indisposition, a prisoner in my chamber, ever since.' He goes on to
announce his main item of news, that he has made arrangements to
go to Chelsea to complete his recovery:

> I thanke God, I have so far passd over thys fitt, as that I thinke of
> changinge my prison; to that purpose I have determined to remove
> myselfe and some few of my family, to Chelsey, where I shall have
> roome inough for so few, with conveniency, and so be near the busi-
> nesses of our churche, and not far removd from means of takinge the
> liberty you have allowd me, to visit you sometymes. I go to a family,
> to which I owe much, and therfore must intreat you to be my surety
> for one debt to them, which ys, some tyme, thys Summer to bestow
> a Bucke upon me. For Gods sake, Sir, teache me good manners, and
> deny me, if any way yt disorder your purposes. If yt do not, and that
> I hear not to the contrary from you, I wyll be bold to fetche yt, or
> send for yt, when yt may least trouble you, and best fitt us.[1]

Thus the request for a buck two years previously was not his last,
though Donne had promised that it would be.

The visit to Chelsea lasted much longer than Donne had anticipated. The first year of Charles I's reign, like that of his father's, was
marked by a serious visitation of the plague. It was already raging
in the City before Donne left and as the summer drew on the number of deaths increased greatly. 'The returns for July, August, and
September show that London was in the clutches of a plague more
deadly than any experienced since the days of the Black Death.'[2]

Chancellor, . . . hereafter they shall be only *Keepers of the Great Seal*, which for title
and office are disposable; but they say the Lord Chancellor's title is indelible.'

[1] The manuscript of this letter is at Harvard; it was printed with a note by
Theodore Spencer, *John Donne's Letter to Sir Nicholas Carey*, Cambridge, Mass., 1929.

[2] F. P. Wilson, *The Plague in Shakespeare's London*, p. 136.

The progress of the plague can be illustrated from Donne's own parish of St. Dunstan's, where normally the number of deaths was twenty or fewer a month. In June there were 23 burials, in July, 87; then in August they reached a peak of 337. In September the plague was still raging, with 210 burials, but in October it began to abate, with 52. Then the totals drop: November, 23; December, 20; and January 1626, 12. Not until December can there have been any real assurance that the visitation was over. A vivid description of London at this time has been left by the astrologer William Lilly, who was then a young man in service in Donne's old parish of St. Clement Danes:

The most able people of the whole city and suburbs were out of town; if any remained, it were such as were engaged by parish officers to remain; no habit of a gentleman or woman continued, people dying in the open fields and in open streets. At last, in August, the bills of mortality so encreased, that very few people had thoughts of surviving the contagion; the Sunday before the great bill came forth, which was of five thousand and odd hundreds, there was appointed a sacrament at Clement Danes; during the distributing whereof I do very well remember we sang thirteen parts of the one hundred and nineteenth psalm. One Jacob, one minister (for we had three that day, the communion was so great) fell sick as he was giving the sacrament, went home, and was buried of the plague the Thursday following. Mr. James, another of the ministers, fell sick ere he had quite finished, had the plague, and was thirteen weeks ere he recovered. Mr. Whitacre, the last of the three escaped not only then, but all the contagion following, without any sickness at all; though he officiated at every funeral, and buried all manner of people, whether they died of the plague or not.[1]

Donne too wrote some account of the plague in a letter to Sir Thomas Roe, now ambassador at Constantinople. He had learned from Roe that Constantinople was afflicted with the plague, and he replied:

your number of 2000 a day, was so far attempted by us, that in the city of London, and in a mile compas, I believe there dyed 1000 a day. But, by reason that these infections are not so frequent with us, the horror,

---

[1] William Lilly, *History of His Life and Times*, 1822, pp. 47-8.

I presume was greater here; for the Citezens fled away, as out of a house on fire, and stuffd theyr pockets with their best ware, and threw themselfs into the high-ways, and were not receyvd, so much as into barnes, and perishd so, some of them with more money about them, than would have bought the villadge where they died: A Justice of Peace, into whose Examination it fell, told me, of one that dyed so, with 1400 *l.* about him. I scattered my family; and, to be as near as I could, to the inspection of our churche, I removd for a tyme to Chelssey, where within a few weeks, the infection multiplyed so fast, as that it was no good Manners, to go to any other place, and so I have been in a secular monastery, and so far, in a conformity to your Lordship too.[1]

At first, during the months at Chelsea, before the infection had reached its height, there was visiting such as Donne had told Sir Nicholas Carey to expect. A letter of 12 July to Sir Henry Wotton is dated 'From Sir John Danvers house at Chelsey (of which house and my Lord of Carlils at Hanworth I make up my Tusculum)',[2] so it would seem that he had been at least once to Hanworth. But, as the plague deaths increased and as the flocks of fleeing citizens spread out over the countryside it became 'no good Manners, to go to any other place, and so I have been in a secular monastery'; and later in the same letter to Roe he remarked that 'the infection hath made this vylladge so infamous that I go not to Court, though it be at Hampton'.[3] Obviously Donne had fully recovered his health during the summer, and the confinement imposed on the whole household must have been irksome to them all.

Nevertheless the house was large and pleasantly situated, and it was surrounded by fairly considerable grounds. It lay near the river just to the west of Chelsea Church, and the present Danvers Street

---

[1] Gosse's text of this letter (ii. 222–5) is very faulty; that printed by Hayward (pp. 486–9) is far superior. I have followed Hayward's text with but one correction, 'the inspection' for 'your inspection'.

[2] Hayward, pp. 485–6 (Loseley MS.).

[3] The situation does not seem to have been quite as bad at Chelsea as Donne suggests. Daniel Lysons, *Environs of London*, ii. 117, has a note on the deaths in Chelsea in the plague years of the seventeenth century: 'The number of burials at Chelsea in 1603, was thirteen; in 1625, thirty-six; in 1665, seventy-eight; being at neither period [*sic*] quite double the average number. It appears that this village, and its opposite neighbour Battersea, suffered much less from that dreadful calamity the plague, than Putney and Mortlake, though situated, like Chelsea, by the waterside, and at a greater distance from London.'

cuts through what was once its site.[1] The garden was a notable one. To Aubrey, his kinsman, Sir John Danvers was 'an ingeniose person', and his house and garden declared the fact. Bacon took much delight in this 'curious' garden, and Lady Danvers loved and cared for it.[2] Later times have awarded Sir John Danvers the distinction of being the first to introduce the Italian mode of gardening into England; certainly it was adorned with statuary. Aubrey describes a 'figure of the gardener's wife in freestone, coloured, and the like of the gardener, both accoutred according to their callings', carved by Nicholas Stone, who had also executed a sundial for the garden. In addition, we hear of two seated figures of shepherds, and a group of Hercules and Antaeus, by Stone's assistant John Schoerman.[3] No doubt English yews replaced Italian cypresses as a background for the statues, but besides hedges and walks there were also flowers in the garden, as one of George Herbert's poems in memory of his mother testifies. Everything suggests that it was one of the most unusual and delightful gardens in England, and all through the summer it must have been a refuge for the members of the household and their guests.

During those months Donne would have come to know the Danvers household more intimately than he had been able to know it before. Lady Danvers's hospitality he had taken for granted for many years, and he was well aware of her lively mind and cheerful piety. But he probably had not realized with what regularity morning and evening prayers were read daily in the household, and that his hostess attended church not only on Sundays but when there were weekday services as well, hastening 'her *family*, and her *company* hither, with that cheerful provocation, *For God's sake let's go, For God's sake let's bee there at the Confession*'.[4] Her household was extremely well managed; it was carefully organized, and there was no idleness

---

[1] Lysons, *Environs of London*, ii. 123.

[2] John Aubrey, *Brief Lives*, ed. Clark, i. 75, 196, and Edmund Blunden, 'George Herbert's Latin Poems', *Essays and Studies by Members of the English Association*, xix (1934), 34. Aubrey refers to the garden also in his *Natural History of Wiltshire*, ed. J. Britton, 1847, p. 93; his full description of it is among the Aubrey MSS. in the Bodleian Library.

[3] *The Notebooks of Nicholas Stone*, ed. A. J. Fineberg, Walpole Society, vii (1918–19), 34, 50.

[4] *Sermons*, viii, no. 2, ll. 858–60, p. 86.

in it. To Donne it was 'a *Court*, in the conversation of the best, and an *Almeshouse*, in feeding the *poore*, so was it also an *Hospitall*, in ministring releefe to the *sicke*. . . . Of which, my selfe, who, at that time, had the favour to bee admitted into that *family*, can, and must testifie this, that when the late heavy *visitation* fell hotly upon this *Towne*, when every doore was shut up, and, lest *Death* should enter into the house, every house was made a *Sepulchre* of them that were in it, then, then, in that time of *infection*, divers persons visited with that *infection*, had their releefe, and releefe *appliable to that very infection*, from this house.'[1] Yet Donne began to notice signs of strain; Lady Danvers, for all her gaiety and activity, was beginning to fail; 'some sicknesses, in the declination of her yeeres, had opened her to an overflowing of *Melancholie*'.[2] Her more youthful husband, with his 'sober staidnesse', was a stabilizing influence, and Donne came to feel for him a friendship that is reflected in the complete trust in his honour that is expressed in his will. For part at least of Donne's stay, George Herbert also was at home; he was trying to make up his mind to resign his orator's post at Cambridge, and had already resolved to enter holy orders. Donne had probably known him since his boyhood, but he was now old enough for the difference between his age and Donne's to matter less than formerly, and the friendship between the two men inevitably ripened in the close contact in which they were placed. There is but one reference to him in all Donne's correspondence, the single sentence 'Mr *George Herbert* is here' in a letter written near the end of his stay at Chelsea; the only other record of their friendship is found in the poem which Donne addressed to Herbert on his cross and anchor seal, and the verses in which Herbert acknowledged Donne's gift to him of one of the seals.[3]

What little else there is to relate of Donne's activities during the second half of 1625 is to be gleaned from his letters. There was the

---

[1] *Sermons*, viii, no. 2, ll. 972–89, pp. 89–90.   [2] Ibid., ll. 872–4, pp. 86–7.
[3] *Letters*, p. 236. Helen Gardner has an important appendix to her edition of the *Divine Poems*, pp. 138–47, 'Donne's Latin Poem to Herbert and Herbert's Reply'; she argues that Donne's poem to Herbert concerning his new seal belongs to 1615 and refers to his adoption of the seal; it was not sent, as Walton states (*Lives*, p. 64) 'with one of my Seals'. Donne's gift of a seal in 1630 or 1631 inspired Herbert to write three Latin epigrams, two of which imply that Donne was dead when they were composed.

letter of 12 July to Sir Henry Wotton (now Provost of Eton) which
had as its object the securing of a place in the College for a son of
Sir Robert More, his brother-in-law.[1] The much longer letter to Sir
Thomas Roe, dated 25 November, was a reply to one written from
Constantinople on 16 August; this letter of Roe's is not extant, but
an earlier one from him, dated 4 May, which Donne must have
received while at Chelsea, has survived. Donne usually wrote at
greater length to Roe than to most of his correspondents (perhaps
because Roe was so far away), and tended to add a certain amount of
pious moralizing. Probably Donne was affected by the tone of Roe's
letters; Sir Thomas writes in a solemn and long-winded fashion,
with a spice of unction; he must have been a rather humourless
man. His letter of 4 May is much taken up with the prospects of
his return to England and the choice of his successor at the Porte,
but two passages are of wider interest. The opening shows how
acceptable Donne's spiritual advice was to Roe:

My most woorthy & reuerend frend,

I haue receiued your Benediction, and enioy therein more and more
assurance of Gods fauour that his Saincts on earth (which certeynly are
the ministers and Guides of his Church, and Priests and Prophetts, of
these wee haue Testimony of their doctrine, from dead Saincts none,)
doe remember and commend mee to his Grace, and protection in so
great an absence; and of this I find a singular Comfort, that therby I
am comprehended in a Church, though I liue where there is none.

---

[1] Loseley MSS., Folger Shakespeare Library; also among the Loseley MSS. is a
letter from Sir Robert More himself to Sir Henry Wotton about his son:

Sir,

Hauing obtained by the fauor of Mr. Deane of Paules at the last election at Eaton
a scholar's place in the Colledge there for a sonne of mine, which hath not happened
to fall within the yeare, I am occasioned at this time to presume, though vnknowne to
you, through the same fauour and mediation to become your humble suitor for some
such place at the next election for my sonne as out of your noble worth you may be
pleased to giue him for which I shall euer remaine

Your seruant readie to be commaunded

Loseley   Robert More
29 of June 1625

Sir Robert More died early in the following year. The boy who was the subject of the
letters to Wotton was presumably his fourth son Nicholas, who was admitted to
King's College, Cambridge, as a King's scholar from Eton in 1633. He became a
Fellow of the College in 1636 but was expelled by the Parliamentary visitors in 1644.
He entered the Church, and a few months before his death in 1684 succeeded to the
Loseley estates.

The second passage is part of a postscript, and it names some of their common friends:

My seruice, as you encounter them, to *Doctor Chapman*, *Doctor Foxe*, *Doctor Brooke*, and my friend his brother, And though his name come out of order, I will not for that cause omit my humble and entire affection to my *Lo[rd]* of *Cou[entrie]* and *Lichfield Doctor Morton.*[1]

Roe and Donne seem to have been members of the same circles to a greater degree than has previously been suspected.

In his letter of 25 November Donne spoke of rumours which for a time had prophesied Roe's promotion to a secretaryship of state and attempted to console him because he had missed the office; then, in an interesting passage, he alludes to his own experiences as an office-seeker:

My Lord, in the poore low way that I have gone, in which I have not made many, nor wide stepps, since my first leape, which was my very entrance into this callinge, I have found, that missinge and faylinge of some places, have advancd my fortune, and that, though I were no great pretender, nor thruster myselfe yet the promises in which some great persons had enlarged themselfs towards me, and even the voyce and rumor, which sometymes had invested me, in some vacant places, conduced to my future settlinge.[2]

Roe's reply to Donne's letter is extant. He is still much concerned about securing leave to return home and is hopeful of it, although in fact he had to stay in Constantinople for more than another year. He thanked Donne for his religious consolations, and went on to comment on the rumours of his promotion of which, apparently, he had heard for the first time:

I haue receiued and enioyed your benediction; Vpon *the* wings of Gods fauorites I am borne vpp, and by them I hope to recouer my beloued Cuntry; The strange newes you send mee (I know for my Comfort) filleth mee rather with wonder, then hope of any such preferrment; I confess they are good presages, where myne owne Ambition hath not blowne them, and therefore I am enforced to an

---

[1] S.P. 97/10/257. It is worth adding that Roe cultivated the favour of a number of the same people as Donne. Besides Buckingham (who was almost the sole avenue to promotion) he looked to Carlisle as his patron, did errands abroad for Lady Bedford, and wrote flattering letters to the Countess of Huntingdon.

[2] Hayward, pp. 487–8.

Apology, that I haue bene so farr from a Pretender, that I neuer vsed any meanes, nor had *t*he vanity in my thoughts, of being capable of such an honor. . . .

One piece of news about his own activities at Constantinople he sends because he believes it will be of special interest to Donne as a churchman and an ex-controversialist against the Romanists; for other news of the Grand Seigneur's empire he refers Donne to a letter he had recently written to the Earl of Carlisle:

> My present Imployment is to furnish England with *Arabicque* and *Greek Manuscripts,* either incorrupt, or not extant; what my success willbee, I will not disaduantage with boasting: but my proiect is very faire; Allready I haue in my possession, but not myne owne as yet, *t*he Jewell of *t*he East, a Copy of antient Councells, with their history, and Acts; A Book sought by *t*he *Popes.* It will resolue many doubts, and discouer many falshoods; you may please to conferr with his *Grace,* and *Doctor Goad,* for my ease in this matter, to whom I haue made larger Relations, and haue sent one *Canon, t*he 37th of *t*he *Nicene* Councell, purposely omitted. I hope to imprime 3 more, that are missing in Bynny; I speake of *t*he 80 *Canons,* which are 84 not of *t*he 20 agreed vpon, for *t*he vniversall *Church*; I haue no help and doe but guess at things out of my profession; but I doubt not to minister worthy matter to great witts and learned men, and so to bee a builder by carrying stones from *t*he Quarr[y], for others hewing.[1]

Roe had been appointed in order to further mercantile relations rather than to conduct negotiations affecting high matters of state, but he made use of his opportunities in the East (and had sufficient learning) to further the cause of Protestant controversy, and was able to inspect the ancient manuscripts he acquired with the eye of a scholar. The manuscript of which he tells Donne is still in the Bodleian,[2] where are also a number of others he purchased.

When Donne was concluding his letter of 25 November to Roe he added a postscript telling him of his principal occupation during the summer and autumn he had spent at Chelsea: 'I have reviewd as many of my Sermons, as I had kept any notes of; and I have wrtten out, a great many, and hope to do more. I ame allready come to the number of 80: of which my sonne who, I hope, will take the same

---

[1] S.P. 97/11/257 (8 April 1626).   [2] MS. Roe 2.

profession, or some other in the world of middle understandinge, may hereafter make some use.'[1] This passage is of some value, since it clearly states that Donne normally preached from notes and that only on a few special occasions was the sermon written out in full as it was to be, or had just been, preached. The majority of the sermons as they are read today have come down in a form imposed on them, in many instances, years after they were originally delivered. The energy and industry of Donne's achievement must also be noticed; eighty sermons in five months is an average of about one every two days.[2] The sheer physical effort of so much transcription was no light one, but Donne did more. As he wrote he cast into literary form the notes from which he had preached.

Donne had gone to Chelsea 'to be as near as I could, to the inspection of our churche'. There are no records to show the extent to which he kept in touch with St. Paul's and its affairs, but the accounts of St. Dunstan's record the receipt of 20*s.* for the poor from 'Mr. Deane' on 29 August and 40*s.* more on 23 December.[3] At the time of the second gift Donne had just returned to London, for he wrote to Sir Henry Goodyer from Chelsea on 21 December, sending mostly general news and contradicting a rumour of his own death: 'the report of my death, hath thus much of truth in it, that though I be not dead, yet I am buried.'[4] But Donne returned in time to preach his annual Christmas sermon, which is extant. Three weeks later he preached at St. Dunstan's his 'First Sermon after Our Disperson, by the Sickness'. Unlike his recent Christmas sermon, this one is full of references to the ordeal through which the City had so recently passed. The text, 'For there was not a house where there was not one dead', drew attention to the empty pews and the missing faces and all the changes in the life of the parish since Donne had last preached there. He embarked on a fourfold interpretation of his text which at every stage must have reminded his hearers of those they had lost, but not until near the end did he turn to apply what he had been saying to the inhabitants of the City and the parish itself. He reminded them of the horrors of the plague, and told them of

[1] Hayward, p. 489.
[2] It took Donne about eight hours to copy out a sermon in full; cf. *Letters*, p. 154.
[3] Whitlock, loc. cit.   [4] *Letters*, pp. 233–4.

Men whose lust carried them into the jaws of infection in lewd houses, and seeking one sore perished with another; men whose rapine and covetousness broke into houses, and seeking the Wardrobes of others, found their own winding-sheet, in the infection of that house where they stole their own death; men who sought no other way to divert sadness, but strong drink in riotous houses, and there drank up *Davids* cup of Malediction, the cup of Condemned men, of death, in the infection of that place.

Next, he reminded them more poignantly of their own dead:

Every grain of dust that flies here, is a piece of a Christian; you need not distinguish your Pews by figures; you need not say, I sit within so many of such a neighbour, but I sit within so many inches of my husbands, or wives, or childes, or friends grave.[1]

Then, turning from such sharp reminders with the sentence, 'But there was a part in every one of them, that could not die', he passed on to his peroration by holding out the hope of reunion and immortality. Few of Donne's sermons can have moved the hearts of his congregation as this one must have done.

On 2 February 1626 the coronation of Charles I took place, and Donne was probably present among the attendant clergy, although no definite record of the fact has survived. A few days later Charles's second Parliament assembled, and at the same time the Convocation of the province of Canterbury met in Westminster Abbey. Convocation, although it had certain powers to legislate for the Church, normally met when Parliament did because of the ancient claim of the Church to tax itself. There were two houses: the House of Bishops, presided over by the Archbishop, and the lower house, consisting of deans and various elected clergy, presided over by a prolocutor whose election had to be confirmed by the upper house. Very little is known of the activities of the Convocation of 1626 except that Donne was chosen prolocutor.[2] Apparently pains were taken to

---

[1] *Sermons*, vi, no. 18, ll. 386–93 and 493–7, pp. 359 and 362.

[2] The record of this convocation as given by David Wilkins in his *Concilia Magnae Britanniae et Hiberniae* (1737), iv, 469–71, are as follows:

Archiepisc. Cant.	Anno Christi	Reg. Angliae
Geo. Abbott 15.	1625	Carol. I. 1.

. . . .

Alia hujus anni convocatio die septimo mensis Februarii [1625/6] in ecclesia B. Petri Westm. congregata nihil scitu dignum nobis reliquit, praeterquam quod D.

keep the meetings of Convocation from imitating the turbulence characteristic of the parliaments of this time. Jeremy Collier, for instance, points out that Montague's *Appello Caesarem*, with its strong appeal for a modification of the prevailing Calvinist temper of the Church of England, became a burning issue in Parliament, but was never discussed in Convocation, to which it should properly have been referred. Bishop Andrewes, it is said, advised against any discussion of the book in Convocation, because 'They knew the Archbishop, and many of the Bishops and Clergy, were rather of the *Calvinian* side'.[1] Donne's sermons show that in many respects he was sympathetic towards Montague's views, and no doubt he acquiesced in this decision, but the fact that the issue never arose in Convocation shows that the clergy were far more amenable to manipulation than the Commons. One controversial issue was, however, brought before Convocation; this was a sermon recently preached before the King by Godfrey Goodman, Bishop of Gloucester, in which he had asserted rather too strongly the doctrine of the Real Presence. 'The *Convocation* examin'd the exceptionable Passages, but came to no Decision',[2] so the King appointed a committee of three bishops (Abbot, Andrewes, and Laud) to report to him.

As prolocutor Donne delivered a Latin oration to the full Convocation, which was first printed in the 1650 edition of his *Poems* and appeared in all subsequent editions until 1719.[3] Instead of the terser Latin of the *Conclave Ignati* or the *Catalogus Librorum* this speech is extravagantly Ciceronian in style. It is to be feared that Donne was showing off. It may be doubted if, even in that age, many of his audience fully understood what he was saying, so long are the periods and so prolonged are some of the suspensions of the sense.

Donne prolocutor electus fuerit et confirmatus ibidem: ea per varias continuationes prorogata fuit. . . .

In decima octava sessione convocationis praelatorum et cleri provinciae Cantuar. quae 16. die Junii contigit, episcopus Sarum virtute brevis regii et commissionis archiepiscopi convocationem dissolvit.

I have preferred to follow Wilkins as the more reliable authority; Fuller, however, in his *Church History of Britain*, 1655, bk. x, p. 112, writes under the year 1623: 'As for the *Convocation* contemporary with this *Parliament*, large subsidies were granted by the *Clergie*, otherwise no great matter of moment passed therein. I am informed Doctor *Joseph Hall* preached the *Latine Sermon*, and *Doctor Donne* was the Prolocutor.'

[1] *Ecclesiastical History of Great Britain*, ii (1714), 737–8.

[2] Collier, op. cit. ii. 738.   [3] It is reprinted in Appendix D.

Compliments, too, that would not have seemed much more than common courtesies in English sound hyperbolically extravagant in Latin, and, *tour de force* though the piece may be, it is doubtful if it could have achieved much effect, other than to impress the simple-minded.

The business of Convocation did not cause Donne to neglect St. Dunstan's-in-the-West. On 4 February 'M^r: Deane receaved the xxix^{li} out of the Chests'. From 13 April 1626 the vestry minutes begin regularly to list the names of those present, and Donne's attendances can now be checked. He attended on 13 April, and again in the next month. At the second of these meetings the vicar proposed that the pulpit should be moved from the south side of the church to the north side, 'where now the new pulpitt is placed', in order to make room for a number of new pews in the chancel, six in all and each apparently capable of accommodating three subscribers. One of these six pews was to belong to the vicar, as was another new one to be built 'on that side of the Chancell at the end of the new pewes on the South side'. Those who occupied the vicar's pews were to pay him pew-rent at the rate of 6s. 8d. per occupant.[1]

Not long after the opening of Convocation Donne preached his annual Lent sermon at Court. It won the approval of the King, who was present and recommended to Donne that he should print it. Donne presented a copy to the Earl of Bridgewater on 10 March, and sent another to the Queen of Bohemia, which was duly acknowledged.[2] The sermon was dedicated to the King and the dedication contains a reminiscence of King James:

Amongst the many comforts of my *Ministery*, to the embracing wherof, *Almightie God* was pleased, to moove the heart of *your Majesties blessed Father, of holy memory*, to moove mine, this is a great one, That your *Majesty* is pleasd some times, not only to *receive* into your selfe, but to *returne*, unto others, my poore *Meditations*, and so by your gracious commandement of *publishing* them, to make your selfe as a *Glasse*, (when the *Sun* it selfe is the *Gospell of Christ Jesus*) to reflect, and cast them upon your *Subjects*. It was a *Metaphor* in which, your *Majesties Blessed Father* seemd to delight; for in the name of a *Mirroir*,

---

[1] Whitlock, loc. cit.; Vestry Minutes, p. 113.
[2] Keynes, p. 116; *Tobie Mathew Collection*, pp. 298-9.

a *Looking Glasse*, he sometimes presented *Himselfe*, in his publique declarations and speeches to his *People*.[1]

It is evident that Charles wished, by conviction as well as by custom, to preserve his father's practices in respect of worship at the Court. Twice in later years Donne draws a spiritual lesson from the King's presence in the royal chapel:

> But for prayer there is no difference, one humiliation is required of all. As when the King comes in here, howsoever they sate diversly before, all returne to one manner of expressing their acknowledgement of his presence: so at the *Oremus*, Let us pray, let us all fall down, and worship, and kneel before the Lord our maker.
>
> And yet this . . . coyn of *Constantines* [showing him kneeling at prayer], was not so convincing, nor so irrefragable a testimony of his piety, (for *Constantine* might be coyned praying, and yet never pray) as when we see as great a Prince as he, actually, really, personally, daily, duly at prayer with us.[2]

In the parish churches, however, those who were too poor to pay for pews suffered no such temptation as the courtiers, to remain comfortably seated instead of kneeling at prayer, for the poor had to stand, and consequently afforded a different kind of moral lesson: 'They cannot maintain Chaplains in their houses; They cannot forbear the necessary labours of their calling, to hear extraordinary Sermons; They cannot have seats in Churches, whensoever they come; They must *stay*, they must *stand*, they must *thrust*, . . . They must take pains to hear.'[3]

The year 1626 was an unusually busy one for Donne in the pulpit, and more of his sermons survive for this year than for any other. The fine second Prebend Sermon delivered at St. Paul's on 29 January 1625/6 set the tone of his preaching throughout the year. Most other preachers dilated on harsh texts to point to the visitation of the plague as a sign of the wrath of God; but Donne's emphasis is upon the comfort and joy of the Christian message, and upon the need for a positive and undespairing spiritual life. He preached to the King 'in my Ordinary wayting' in April, and a few days later 'to

¹ *Sermons*, vii. 72.
² Ibid. ix, no. 1, ll. 476–81, p. 60, and no. 9, ll. 268–72, p. 220.
³ Ibid., no. 4, ll. 514–21, p. 123.

the Houshold at White-hall' (30 April), the King apparently not
being present. In the latter sermon he defends hospitality and the
enjoyment of cheerful company, Christ Himself, 'though a Churchman, and an Exemplar-man', being 'not depriv'd of a plentiful use
of Gods creatures, nor of the chearfulness of conversation'.[1] Donne
preached at St. Paul's on the evening of Easter Day the first of a
series of three sermons on 1 Cor. 15: 29, the others being delivered
on 21 May and 21 June. He gave his third Prebend Sermon on Gunpowder Plot day, 5 November, in the evening. All these sermons
testify to the vigour with which he resumed his duties after his
enforced retirement during the plague months, and the one cloud
upon his own practice of cheerful piety was also lifted this year.

His quarrel with Edward Alleyn is, apart from the initial anger of
Sir George More, the only recorded breach (and this again not with
a close friend) between Donne and any of his numerous and varied
acquaintances. In the early summer Alleyn finally made a settlement
on his wife Constance. A much mutilated letter from Donne has
survived, addressed to Sir Nicholas Carey, in which Donne asks his
brother-in-law to be present, when he comes to town, at the signing
of the deeds and to act as co-trustee of the settlement along with
Sir Thomas Grymes: 'Beinge now to [receyue tha]t which may be
had for my poor daughter Constance [I ame] bold to ioyne you, with
Sir Thomas Grymes in re[ceyuing] assurance from her husband.
Those writings will be ready within 2 or 3 days.'[2] The letter was
sent on 26 June, and the documents were signed on the 29th.[3]
Alleyn assigned two leases, one of the Unicorn Inn in Southwark,
and the other of a messuage on the Bankside known as the Barge,
Bell, and Cock, to Carey and Grymes and also gave them a statute
staple for £2,000 as security that on his death Constance should
receive the £1,500 he had promised to settle on her. In so doing
Alleyn kept his word and probably brought to an end the period of
strained relations between himself and his father-in-law. These two
leases, it will be noticed, were not the ones he had originally planned

[1] Ibid. vii, no. 5, ll. 78–83, p. 143; cf. pp. 1–11.
[2] Huntington Library, MS. 7281; Gosse, ii. 233, wrongly dates the letter 26
January.
[3] The date is correctly given in Alleyn's will, Young, *History of Dulwich College*, i.
93; but Young gives the year as 1625, ii. 39.

to settle on his wife; he had probably been forced to part with these in the interim because of financial stress. Ironically enough, the Barge, Bell, and Cock was a well-known brothel.[1] Alleyn had only a few months longer to live; he died on 25 November, and by his will, made less than a fortnight earlier, he confirmed the settlements of 29 June, and added a gift of £100 in cash, to be paid immediately after his death to his widow. Incongruous as his second marriage may have seemed, it does not appear to have been unsuccessful.[2]

Donne was in London for the greater part of the summer of 1626, and spent less time than usual in the country. On the same day as Alleyn's assurances were signed he preached at St. Dunstan's a commemorative sermon under the bequest of Mr. Adams, for which the accounts show that he received the customary sum of 10s. Adams's will also provided for a dinner, which this year was held at the Horn Tavern and was attended by Donne and the vestrymen. He also attended vestry meetings on 4 and 12 July; the second meeting was followed by a 'greater [quarterly] Vestry Dinner for Mr Deane of Paules and the rest of the Vestrymen' at St. Dunstan's Tavern. On 20 July the Warden paid Donne 6s. 8d. apiece for the placing of two parishioners in the 'new pewes in St Dunstans Quire'; John Smethwick joined them on the 29th. Shortly afterwards Mr. Gray, the curate of the parish, died, leaving two unmarried daughters, and the parish busied itself to apprentice them and find good homes for them. Donne sent a contribution to help them; 'the guifte of M^r: Deane of Paules towarde the placing of 2 daughters of M^r: Gray our late Curate . . . xx^s' is noted in the accounts.[3] It is not often that any record remains of such small acts of kindness and charity. A fortnight later, on 22 August, Donne

---

[1] *Henslowe's Diary*, ed. W. W. Greg, pt. ii—Commentary, pp. 3, 25.

[2] This may have been due, in some small part, to the relationship of Alleyn with Grymes, which was much more intimate than that of Alleyn with Donne. A letter survives in answer to a request by Alleyn in February 1624/5 (Young, op. cit. ii. 38) that Sir Thomas should be bound for a loan of £200 to tide Alleyn over a period of financial difficulty. Grymes offers in the letter to let Alleyn have £200 'at a quarter of an howres warning', and in addition all the plate not in use in the Grymes household which Alleyn might pawn to obtain further funds. He commends his love to his niece and to Alleyn. It is obvious that Grymes trusted Alleyn implicitly, and the letter is proof of his warm and affectionate nature.

[3] Whitlock, loc. cit. Some of the sermons 'preached at St. Dunstan's' possibly belong to this period; cf. *Sermons*, vii. 17.

wrote to Bishop Williams on behalf of the son of Mr. Holney, Sir George More's chaplain:

My very good L:

Thys poore Man, Mr Holney, was, in the quality of a chapleyne, in Sr George Mores house, then when I marryed into that family. By that occasion I knew him first, and haue since receyud him to haue been honest and painfull: and, out of hys smalle meanes, to haue brought up hys sonne, to some ability of seruinge God, in the Ministery. In wch sonns behalfe, the father desires my testimony of him to yor Lp: To wch I do also willingly add my humble suite, that yor Lp: would be pleasd to admitt that resignation in hys behalfe, w^{ch}, (as he informes me) the present incumbent ys wyllinge to make if yt dis-appoint no other purpose of yor Lps therin. And so w^t my humble thanks to yor Lp: for yor manifold fauors to me, and my humble prayers for all kinds of happinesses to yor Lp: I rest

yor Lps

humblest and thankfullest

At my poore house at pauls
22. Aug: 1626.

servant

J. Donne.[1]

Some of the friends for whom Donne felt most warmly in the last five years of his life have already been mentioned in this chapter; others were no doubt included in the list of those to whom Walton says[2] he sent copies of his seal of the Cross upon an anchor or were among those to whom he left bequests in his will. Sir Henry Wotton was given a seal, and copies were also given to Joseph Hall, Henry King, George Herbert, and Bryan Duppa. Duppa was some sixteen years younger than Donne, and had been led to take holy orders in 1625, when he became chaplain to the Earl of Dorset. It was probably through the Earl that Donne made his acquaintance. In 1628 Duppa became Dean of Christ Church, and after Donne's death became successively Bishop of Chichester, Salisbury, and Winchester; he lived on until after the Restoration. Walton suggests that the gifts of the seal were made in 1630 or 1631, and that this was the reason why Goodyer, Sir Robert Drury and Lady Danvers were not among the recipients, being already dead; the gift to

[1] Lincolnshire Archives, L. T. & D. 1626/11 (J. Donne), discovered by Miss D. Williamson (Gardner, *Divine Poems*, p. 138). See plate facing p. 567 below.

[2] *Lives*, p. 63.

George Herbert was also made towards the end of Donne's life.[1] In his will Donne made bequests to Henry King and John Mountfort, his executors, and to another of his close associates at St. Paul's, Thomas Winniff, his successor as Dean. Further bequests were also made to the Earl of Kent as patron of Blunham, to the Earl of Carlisle and Sir Robert Ker, to Sir John Danvers and to Donne's older friends Samuel Brooke and George Garrard. Donne also left a picture of his own choosing to Jean l'Oiseau de Tourval, whose letter telling of the death of Ann Donne has already been quoted[2] and who seems by 1617 to have been well acquainted with her husband. His name is first encountered (in the State Papers) on 2 June 1610, when, writing to Salisbury from France claiming some payment for his services, he says that he has executed six works for the King and has now been given a seventh; he has travelled from city to city to find a printer for the King's book, and has then stayed three months hidden in Paris to superintend its printing there and keep it concealed from the Jesuits. On 4 July 1611 Francis Windebank wrote from Drury Lane, probably to Tourval, apologizing for tardy thanks for his entertainment at Oxford. On 3 August 1616 de Tourval wrote to Windebank in Spanish, and in another letter of 21 August he told Windebank that he had to go to France; Windebank replied in Italian. On 28 September of the same year he speaks in a further letter to Windebank of a hasty journey to Cambridge and Colchester. On 23 July 1619 a grant of denization (or naturalization) was made to John l'Oiseau, alias de Tourval, born in France.[3] Donne's acquaintance with him might have arisen from a common interest in covert diplomatic work concerning church affairs on the Continent, which was recognized, as we have seen, in Donne's being given a cipher on two occasions for use in secret correspondence. At any rate, another bond of sympathy was probably forged by de Tourval's ordination into the English Church. He was presented to the parish of St. Martin Orgar on 28 May 1625; the date of his successor's appointment was 1 October 1628, and it is not known what duties de Tourval then undertook.[4] When Donne made his will,

---

[1] See above, p. 476.   [2] See above, p. 324.
[3] *C.S.P. (Dom.)*, *1603–10*, p. 4; *1611–18*, p. 54; *1619–23*, p. 66.
[4] See the list of presentations to livings in Hennessy, *Novum Repertorium*.

however, de Tourval was still alive and 'a Frenche Minister but by the ordination of the Englishe Churche'. One would like to know more of his friendship with Donne.

A friend about whom we know a great deal more was Izaak Walton, though he was neither among those whom Donne remembered in his will nor, apparently, among those to whom he gave a copy of his seal. Walton had been made free of the Ironmongers' Company in 1618, and had taken a linen-draper's shop in Fleet Street, near Chancery Lane, in 1624. He was thus of Donne's congregation at St. Dunstan's, but it seems to have been some time before an acquaintance developed between the two men. It was not Donne who officiated at Walton's marriage to Rachel Floud in 1626. Indeed, Walton's account of the composition of the *Devotions* suggests that he did not know that Donne had been ill in 1623, or that the book was in print before he again fell ill in 1625. Walton's confusion about the occasion of its writing makes it very probable that he had no very intimate knowledge of Donne until late 1625 or afterwards.[1] Nevertheless Donne became an object of Walton's close and admiring study—so close that he has left us an unrivalled account of Donne's preaching and of his personal characteristics.

On 10 October 1626 Donne was present at a vestry meeting at St. Dunstan's at which it was decided that sureties for any churchwardens' account or for repayment of any loans from the parish funds must be persons resident in or near the City but not within the parish itself.

It is alsoe ordered That Mr Clarke the Schoole master shall have tyme vntill the Feast of the Birth of our Lord God next to provide himselfe of another Schoolehouse where he shall thincke fitt out of this parish, and that he departe and leave the possession of the Questhouse where he now teacheth against the said Feast.

Att the same Vestry it is further ordered That M^r: Valentyne the Lecturer shall continue the readinge of the lectures according to doctor White's will and that he shall have the xviij^li per Annum paid him given by the same will duringe the tyme that he shall performe the same lectures.[2]

[1] See I. A. Shapiro, 'Walton and the Occasion of Donne's *Devotions*', *RES*, N.S. ix (1958), at pp. 21–2.

[2] Minutes, p. 116.

Other business concerned bonds and accounts, and Donne signed three of the accounts of the wardens. A vestry dinner followed (costing £3. 5s.) at the Kingshead Tavern.[1] There is nothing more to relate of Donne's activities before Christmas, save that on 27 October, 6 November, and 7 December he attended meetings of the governors of the Charterhouse;[2] and on 12 December he preached the sermon 'at the funerals of Sir William Cokayne Knight, Alderman of London'. This was one of Donne's richest discourses, which brings in only towards the end a finely wrought eulogy of the dead magnate, a view of whose character less flattering than that given by Donne has been formed by a study of Cokayne's business dealings. In this sermon Donne begins a practice, to be noted increasingly in the sermons of the ensuing year, of defending the Church of England not so much now against the Roman Church as against the attacks of Puritans, to whom the High Church policy of Laud, obviously favoured by the King, was a growing provocation.[3] The sermon is more memorable nowadays, however, for such passages as the following:

But when we consider with a religious seriousnesse the manifold weaknesses of the strongest devotions in time of Prayer, it is a sad consideration. I throw my selfe downe in my Chamber, and I call in, and invite God, and his Angels thither, and when they are there, I neglect God and his Angels, for the noise of a Flie, for the ratling of a Coach, for the whining of a doore; I talke on, in the same posture of praying; Eyes lifted up; knees bowed downe; as though I prayed to God; and, if God, or his Angels should aske me, when I thought last of God in that prayer, I cannot tell: Sometimes I finde that I had forgot what I was about, but when I began to forget it, I cannot tell. A memory of yesterdays pleasures, a feare of to morrows dangers, a straw under my knee, a noise in mine eare, a light in mine eye, an any thing, a nothing, a fancy, a Chimera in my braine, troubles me in my prayer. So certainely is there nothing, nothing in spirituall things, perfect in this world.[4]

Donne preached his usual Christmas sermon at St. Paul's, but before the Christmas season was over his second daughter Lucy

[1] Whitlock, loc. cit.   [2] See Chap. XV, p. 424, n. 3.
[3] See Sermons, vii. 19–22.
[4] Ibid., no. 10, ll. 271–86, pp. 264–5.

died, shortly before she reached the age of 18. Her death must have come suddenly and unexpectedly, for on 4 January, when Donne wrote a letter to Sir Robert Ker,[1] he was still in the midst of a round of Christmas entertaining and seemed to have little thought for much beyond the pressure of his social engagements. Lucy was buried at Camberwell on 9 January 1626/7.[2] She must have been staying either with Constance (if the newly widowed Constance was still at Dulwich) or with the Grymeses at Peckham. That Donne felt her death keenly and found consolation in the hope of reunion in another world is clear from a passage in his Easter sermon of this year; the dramatic 'I' of the sermons has an added poignancy when one recalls the loss he had himself suffered so recently:

> . . . If I had fixt a Son in Court, or married a daughter into a plenti-full Fortune, I were satisfied for that son and that daughter. Shall I not be so, when the King of Heaven hath taken that son to himselfe, and maried himselfe to that daughter, for ever? I spend none of my Faith, I exercise none of my Hope, in this, that I shall have my dead raised to life againe.
>
> This is the faith that sustaines me, when I lose by the death of others, or when I suffer by living in misery my selfe, That the dead, and we, are now all in one Church, and at the resurrection, shall be all in one Quire.[3]

It is possible that this loss to the family was shortly afterwards offset by the addition of a new member to it, for the Camberwell parish register records the marriage on 27 March of John Donne and Mary Staples. It is difficult to see who the bridegroom could have been other than Donne's eldest son, though nothing is ever heard other-wise of his wife, and it is usually assumed that he lived and died a bachelor. If he married in 1627 it is probable that his wife lived but a short time, though the record of her death has still to be discovered.

This year Donne preached his fourth Prebend Sermon on 28 January and his usual Lent sermon at Court, and was in attendance on the King during April. The King was present at his sermon in the

---

[1] *Letters*, p. 315.   [2] W. H. Blanch, *Ye Parish of Camerwell*, p. 177.
[3] *Sermons*, vii, no. 15, ll. 498–516, pp. 383–4. See also Mrs. Simpson's introduction to this volume of the *Sermons*, pp. 25–6, and her article, 'The Biographical Value of Donne's Sermons', *RES*, N.S. ii (1951), 339–57, especially at p. 345.

Chapel Royal on 1 April, and almost immediately afterwards Donne learned, to his alarm, that he had unintentionally given offence. The next morning there came, first, a warning from Sir Robert Ker, and then a letter from Laud demanding in the King's name a copy of his sermon. Donne went at once to see Laud: 'I waited upon his Lordship, and laid up in him this truth, that of the B. of *Canterburies* Sermon, to this hour, I never heard syllable, nor what way, nor upon what points he went: And for mine, it was put into that very order, in which I delivered it, more then two moneths since.'[1] At this time Archbishop Abbot was out of favour with the King, who was more and more dominated by Laud's ecclesiastical policies. Abbot had not only incurred disfavour by his refusals to licence, first, Montague's *Appello Caesarem*, with its advocacy of High Church doctrines, and, more recently, a sermon preached by Robert Sibthorpe, which 'carried the Prerogative to an unwarrantable length';[2] but in addition he had preached a sermon that had given offence to the King. Accordingly authority was suspicious, and from some remarks of Donne it had looked as if he were deliberately following Abbot's lead and taking sides against the policies of Laud. Donne's sermon was, in fact, more politically oriented than usual with him. At one point he spoke of the duty of subjects towards the King, and began somewhat coyly:

And into this part I enter with such a protestation, as perchance may not become me: That this is the first time in all my life, (*I date my life from my Ministery*; for *I received mercy*, as I received the ministery, as the *Apostle* speaks) this is the first time, that in the exercise of my Ministery, I wished the King away; That ever I had any kinde of loathnesse that the King should hear all that I sayd. Here, for a little while, it will be a little otherwise; because in this branch, I am led, to speak of some particular duties of subjects; and in my poor way, I have thought it somewhat an Eccentrique motion, and off of the naturall Poles, to speake of the Duties of subjects before the King, or of the duties of Kings, in publike and popular Congregations.[3]

---

[1] *Letters*, p. 305.

[2] Collier, *Ecclesiastical History*, ii. 740. Collier adds, concerning Sibthorpe's sermon: 'To argue from *Palestine* to *England*, and make the Jewish Constitution a Standard for all other Governments, is slender reasoning, . . . [and] would make *Magna Charta*, and other Laws for securing Property, signify little.'

[3] *Sermons*, vii, no. 16, ll. 374–85, p. 403.

Nevertheless he went on to argue that subjects were in duty bound to contribute to their sovereign's necessities, especially in time of war. Obviously this was not uncomfortable doctrine to the King. On the other hand, as the editors of Donne's sermons have pointed out, there were certain passages that could have been held to reflect on the Queen, such as the following:

The Church is the spouse of Christ: Noble husbands do not easily admit defamations of their wives. Very religious Kings may have had wives, that may have retained some tincture, some impressions of errour, which they may have sucked in their infancy, from another Church, and yet would be loth, those wives should be publikely traduced to be Heretiques, or passionately proclaimed to be Idolaters for all that. A Church may lacke something of exact perfection, and yet that Church should not be said to be a supporter of Antichrist, or a limme of the beast, or a thirster after the cup of *Babylon*, for all that.[1]

The parallel was not a tactful one, and the King may well have felt irritated. On the other hand, Donne was most conscious of his exhortation to the subject to fulfil his duties towards the King, and could not help feeling that he had deserved well of his sovereign: 'I hoped for the Kings approbation heretofore in many of my Sermons; and I have had it. But yesterday I came very near looking for thanks; for, in my life, I was never in any one peece, so studious of his service.'[2] The sermon was at once copied out in full and handed to Bishop Laud, as Donne informed Ker on the following day. He had also taken the precaution of enlisting the aid of his powerful friends: 'I writ yesterday to my L. Duke, by my L. *Carlile*, who assured me of a gracious acceptation of my putting my self in his protection.' Yet he was still puzzled as to what could have given offence:

For, as Card. *Cusanus* writ a Book *Cribratio Alchorani*, I have cribrated, and re-cribrated, and post-cribrated the Sermon, and must necessarily say, the King, who hath let fall his eye upon some of my Poems, never saw, of mine, a hand, or an eye, or an affection, set down with so much study, and diligence, and labour of syllables, as in this Sermon I expressed those two points, which I take so much to conduce to his service, the imprinting of persuasibility and obedience in the subject.

---

[1] Ibid., ll. 582–90, p. 409.   [2] *Letters*, p. 305. Cf. *Sermons*, vii, pp. 35–43.

He had sent to ask Laud if he might appear at Court, and had been told that he might come. He concluded by asking Ker to let him know if he heard anything of the fate of the sermon, 'because the B[ishop] is likely to speake to the King of it, perchance, this night', and to warn him if the King should be so much further offended as to make it inadvisable for him to present himself at Court on the following day.[1]

The next day brought the matter to an end. Laud had evidently read the sermon and reported on it to the King, and Donne was admitted to a special audience. Laud's diary contains a brief note of the occasion: '*Apr. 4. Wednesday*, When his Majesty King *Charles* forgave to Doctor *Donne* certain slips in a Sermon Preached on *Sunday, Apr.* 1. what he then most graciously said unto me, I have wrote in my Heart with indelible Characters, and great thankfulness to God and the King.'[2] Donne did not clear himself of guilt, but, Laud states, the King forgave him, so there is no doubt that Donne had to show penitence and ask for forgiveness. Then, after granting it, the King presumably turned to Laud and thanked him warmly for his zeal in checking anything that might be thought to reflect on himself or his family. Donne does not seem to have preached at Court a second time during April this year, but the incident was forgotten by the time his turn came round again in the succeeding year. This surely was the 'once, and but once' when he was 'clouded with the Kings displeasure', and not the incident which Walton relates and sets in the later part of the reign of James I.

As Donne grew older he had to face the sadness of seeing old friends, whose lives had for so long seemed almost a part of his own, drop away one by one as death overtook them. Sir Henry Goodyer died on 18 March 1627.[3] For years he had been staving off his creditors by securing a royal protection, which he was able periodically to renew. As long ago as 1618 his estate at Polesworth had been settled on trustees for the payment of his debts,[4] and he had

---

[1] *Letters*, pp. 308–10. The King was evidently interested in Donne's poetry. His copy of the 1635 edition of the *Poems* is in the British Museum.

[2] *The History of the Troubles and Tryal of . . . William Laud*, p. 41.

[3] Not 1628, as Gosse says (ii. 248).

[4] P.R.O., C. 66/2197, no. 8. Michael Drayton was one of the trustees. Nos. 54 and 72 are related documents.

gradually sold as much as he could of his other possessions. The letters of his later years, of which a number have survived among the State Papers, are pathetic appeals, on the grounds of his and his family's services to the Crown, for some alleviation of his lot. Towards the end of his life he was forced to live at Polesworth in conditions not far short of penury. There is little doubt that he was the subject of an incident related by Walton:

He [Donne] gave an hundred pounds at one time to an old Friend, whom he had known live plentifully, and by a too liberal heart and carelessness, become decayed in his Estate: and, when the receiving of it was denied, by the Gentlemans saying, *He wanted not*; for the Reader may note, that as there be some spirits so generous as to labour to conceal, and endure a sad poverty, rather than expose themselves to those blushes that attend the confession of it; so there be others to whom Nature and Grace have afforded such sweet and compassionate souls, as to pity and prevent the Distresses of Mankind; which I have mentioned because of Dr. *Donne*'s Reply, whose Answer was, *I know you want not what will sustain nature, for a little will do that; but my desire is, that you who in the days of your plenty have cheared and raised the hearts of so many of your dejected friends, would now receive this from me, and use it as a cordial for the chearing of your own*: and upon these terms it was received.[1]

Goodyer's only son had died in 1624. Besides Lucy, his eldest daughter who had married Sir Francis Nethersole, he left three other daughters, all unmarried because of their father's inability to provide them with dowries. After their father's death the daughters obtained a renewal of the protection against his creditors, and Nethersole received a grant of £1,000 in recognition of his and his father-in-law's services with which to pay off some of the more pressing debts.[2]

The two patronesses to whom Donne had addressed so many letters and poems and whose friendship he had enjoyed for over twenty years, died within a few days of each other, Lady Bedford on 31 May and Lady Danvers early in June.[3] Since his ordination he had seen much less than formerly of Lady Bedford, although there

---

[1] *Lives*, pp. 70–1. [2] *C.S.P. (Dom.), 1627–28*, p. 432.
[3] Lady Danvers was buried in Chelsea parish church on 8 June.

had never been any real breach and Donne had accepted an invitation to preach before her on at least one occasion. On the other hand, the friendship with Lady Danvers and her family had grown and deepened with the years. The house at Chelsea, Donne knew, was one in which he was always welcome, and he had not hesitated to spend a full six months there while the plague raged in London in 1625. It was inevitable that Donne should be asked to preach at her funeral, but because of other engagements he was unable to preach at Chelsea until Sunday 1 July: 'which office, as I ought, [he said in apology] so I should have performed sooner, but that this sad occasion surprized me under other *Pre-obligations* and *Pre-contracts*, in the services of mine own Profession, which could not be excused, nor avoided.'[1] The congregation at the service was composed not only of family and friends, and the villagers who had known Lady Danvers well, but of strangers too, among whom was Izaak Walton, who had walked out from London to hear Donne preach. This was the sole occasion on which Walton saw George Herbert, whose biography, like Donne's he was to write, and in that Life he relates that he had seen and heard Donne 'weep, and preach' the funeral sermon upon Herbert's mother.[2] As usual on such occasions, Donne first devoted himself to an analysis and interpretation of his text before he applied it to the present circumstances, but the portrait of his dead friend is far fuller and more intimate than any to be found in his other funeral sermons. He dwells on her lineage, her fortune, her comeliness, and her attire; he describes her management of her household and her charities to the sick. He had been told, too, of her last hours, how 'not two houres before she died' prayers were read to her, and 'with a *cleere understanding*, with a *constant memory*, with a *distinct voyce*' she joined in the responses. At the very end 'Shee shew'd no feare of [Death's] face, in any change of her owne; but died without any change of *countenance*, or *posture*; without any *strugling*, any *disorder*; but her *Death-bed* was as quiet, as her *Grave*'. And so Donne passed on to console the bereaved with the assurances of immortality, and proclaimed:

That *body* upon which you tread now, That *body* which now, whilst I speake, is mouldring, and crumbling into lesse, and lesse dust, and

---

[1] *Sermons*, viii, no. 2, ll. 4–7, p. 63. [2] *Lives*, p. 267.

so hath some *motion*, though no *life*, That *body*, which was the *Taber-nacle* of a *holy Soule*, and a *Temple* of the *holy Ghost*, That *body* that was eyes to the blinde, and hands, and feet to the lame, whilst it liv'd, and being dead, is so still, by having beene so *lively* an example, to teach others, to be so, That *body* at last shall have her last expectation satis-fied, and dwell *bodily*, with that *Righteousnesse*, in these *new Heavens*, and *new Earth*, for *ever*, and *ever*, and *ever*, and *infinite*, and *super-infinite* *evers*.[1]

The sermon was soon afterwards printed, probably in a small edition and more for private distribution than for general sale, for relatively few copies have survived,[2] and it was not reprinted by Donne's son in any of the folios. Appended was a collection of poems in Latin and Greek, 'Memoriae Matris Sacrum', by George Herbert, and it seems likely that publication was arranged by Lady Danvers's family rather than by Donne.

Throughout this period, when Donne was perturbed by the danger of falling out of favour at Court and distressed by the loss of old and dear friends, his customary busy life continued. He preached at St. Dunstan's on 20 May and was regular in attendance at vestry meetings (on 30 January,[3] 29 March, 10 October), where the church-wardens were actively concerning themselves with their abortive Chancery suit against Captain Harvey, and with other lesser matters, such as Mr. Clarke's occupancy of the Guesthouse, a negligent churchwarden, elections, and the placing of some father-less children at Christ's Hospital; he signed the accounts on 10 May. Four days earlier Donne preached at Paul's Cross. This sermon is not as long as the discourses usually delivered from that open-air pulpit, nor does it seem to deal with political issues, for it avoids controversy more than once where it might have plunged right into

---

[1] *Sermons*, viii, no. 2, ll. 1022–6, 1046–8, 1067–77, pp. 91–3. These passages made a powerful appeal to Izaak Walton, who not only heard them delivered, but also bought a copy of the sermon when it was published. He echoed Donne's words in both the *Life* of George Herbert ('where she now rests in her quiet Grave') and in the *Life* of Donne ('that body, which once was a *Temple of the Holy Ghost*, and is now become a small quantity of *Christian dust*: But I shall see it reanimated'); *Lives*, pp. 267, 84. For further comments on the relation of this sermon to the *Life* of Donne, see E. M. Simpson, 'The Biographical Value of Donne's Sermons', *RES*, N.S. ii (1951), at pp. 349–51, and D. Novarr, *The Making of Walton's 'Lives'*, pp. 65–7.

[2] The most interesting of these is Walton's copy, now in the library of Mr. Robert H. Taylor, of Princeton, N.J.   [3] Cf. Appendix D, pp. 572–3.

it. Nevertheless, it is an important sermon, and shows that Donne was fully conversant with the religious issues of the day. We have seen how Parliament was agitated over the High Church doctrines promulgated in Montague's *Appello Caesarem*, and how Convocation turned its attention to Bishop Goodman's preaching of the Real Presence. The lines were being sharply drawn between the Puritan party, headed by Abbot and strongly entrenched in the City of London, and the High Church party, led by Laud and warmly supported by the King. In this sermon Donne took sides on these issues, and perhaps for the first time clearly and firmly stated his sympathy for the High Church position. He defends vestments and ritual and pictures in the churches. 'Rituall, and Ceremoniall things move not God,' he declared, 'but they exalt that Devotion, and they conserve that Order, which does move him.' Nor need sacred pictures be stigmatized as idolatry:

since, by being taught the right use of these pictures, in our preaching, no man amongst us, is any more enclined, or endangered to worship a picture in a Wall or Window of the Church, then if he saw it in a Gallery, were it onely for a reverent adorning of the place, they may bee retained here, as they are in the greatest part of the *Reformed* Church, and in all that, that is *properly Protestant*.

Further, he did not hesitate to touch on the doctrine of the sacrament and to criticize sharply the Puritan distaste for the old words and the old concepts; 'The *Communion Table* is an *Altar*; and in the *Sacrament* there is a *Sacrifice*', he insisted, but at the same time he sharply distinguished the doctrine of his Church from that of Rome:

We doe not, (as at *Rome*) first invest the power of God, and make our selves able to *make* a Christ, and then invest the malice of the Jews, and *kill that Christ*, whom we have made; for, *Sacrifice*, Immolation, (taken so properly, and literally as they take it) is a *killing*; But the *whole body* of *Christs actions* and *passions*, we sacrifice, wee represent, wee offer to God. *Calvin* alone, hath said enough, *Non possumus*, except we be assisted with outward things, wee cannot fixe our selves upon God.

Donne also protests against unmitigated abuse of the Roman Church, for it is far more serious to be an atheist than a papist, and he ends his sermon with a prayer to God to 'bring our Adversaries to such a moderation as becomes them, who doe truly desire, that the Church may bee truly *Catholique, one flock, in one fold, under one Shepherd,* though *not all of one colour,* of one practise in all outward and disciplinarian points'.[1] This is the most emphatic statement he made on his concept of the Church of England as the *via media* and of the exact position he conceived it should take on the ground between Puritanism and Romanism.

Of Donne's activities during the rest of 1627 there is little to tell. He was present at an Assembly of the governors of the Charterhouse on 21 June;[2] but how he otherwise occupied himself during the summer is not known; presumably he visited friends, besides paying his annual visits to Sevenoaks and Blunham. It was about this time that he presented a chalice to Blunham church.[3] The oak screen and the pulpit at Blunham are both typical pieces of early seventeenth-century workmanship,[4] and there is a strong probability that Donne, who set a high value on the decent furnishing of all places of worship, was responsible for their erection. When he visited Blunham, as we have seen, he usually stayed at the manor house, where the Earl of Kent was accustomed to spend part of every year. However he spent this summer of 1627, he was certainly back in London by the beginning of Michaelmas term, preaching (on 30 September) one of the sermons in St. Dunstan's provided for by 'the guift of Mr. Adams'; and on 19 November he preached at the wedding of Lady Mary Egerton, daughter of the Earl of Bridgewater and elder sister of the Lady in Milton's *Comus,* to the son and heir of Lord Herbert of Cherbury.[5] The parents of both bride and bridegroom were friends of long standing, and Donne's presence in the pulpit on such an occasion was almost inevitable. About this time he probably preached the last of his Prebend Sermons at St. Paul's. Another sermon at St. Dunstan's on 2 December was provided for by 'the guift of Mr. Robert Jenkinson', but this sermon, like the earlier one at the end of September, does not seem to have

[1] *Sermons,* no. vii, ll. 565–7, 626–32, 523–4, 533–40, 676–9, pp. 429–33.
[2] See Chap. XV, p. 424, n. 3.   [3] See above, p. 414.
[4] For a photograph of the pulpit see *Sermons,* v. 21.
[5] Ibid. viii, no. 3. [An indenture relating to the marriage contract, signed 'John Done', was offered for sale by Hofman and Freeman, Cat. no. 24, May 1968.]

survived; both are known of only from the parish accounts. Donne was paid the usual fee of 10*s.* for both sermons, and probably shared the memorial dinner after the second at the Horn Tavern. Mr. Pryor, who followed Mr. Gray as curate, did most of the memorial preaching, and we do not know why Donne preached on some of these occasions. His activities at St. Dunstan's were evidently very much appreciated by the parishioners, for at Christmas they sent him a gift of six gallons of sack and two sugar loaves. The gift, 'by the appointment of Mr. Kemp', was with the consent of the churchwardens and vestrymen, and cost the parish the sum of £3. 4*s.* 6*d.*[1]

As was to be expected, Donne preached his Christmas sermon at St. Paul's and, in the early months of 1628 his usual round of sermons: the first Friday in Lent before the King, his Easter sermon at St. Paul's, and two sermons at the Court during April. He had also preached at the Cathedral on 27 January. But Mrs. Simpson finds in these sermons a certain spiritual aridity; there is no loss in them of intellectual power, but there is a lack of poetic insight, and far less of that sense of Christian joy which inspires a message of hope and comfort.[2] This mood lasted, she argues, until Easter 1628, when Donne seems to have recaptured some of his power and elevation. It is true that in this group of sermons there are no great oratorical flights nor any of those passages in which Donne struggles to describe the joys of heaven. The preacher seems to be concentrating on the interpretation of his texts and their application to the more practical details of the Christian life. He has unquestionably lost some of his desire to sway the emotions of his listeners. How far such a mood can be described as spiritual drought is uncertain; Mrs. Simpson attributes it in part to the loss of his daughter and of some of his most valued friends. If so, his sense of loss must have been intensified by the illness and death of Christopher Brooke early in February 1628. It must not be forgotten, too, that this was a period of national humiliation because of a succession of failures in the war with France. First, in 1627, there was the unfortunate expedition

---

[1] Whitlock, 'Donne at St. Dunstan's', *TLS*, 16 and 23 Sept. 1955.
[2] 'The Biographical Value of Donne's Sermons', *RES*, N.S. ii (1951), 339–57 and *Sermons*, viii. 10–15.

against the Isle of Rhé (in which George Donne took part); then, in 1628, there was the failure to relieve Rochelle. Donne seems to have shaken off his melancholy mood before the assassination of Buckingham on 23 August; but all these events must have brought anxiety and gloom to Donne as well as many thousands of his countrymen. How far all these causes combined to depress his spirits, whether he was in addition overworked and fatigued, one can only guess, nor am I sure that the mood of his sermons must be diagnosed as spiritual aridity. Even so, that there was a change of tone in Donne's preaching is undeniable, and it is not until the sermon preached on Easter Day, 1628, that one again comes to what can be reckoned as one of Donne's greater sermons.

Christopher Brooke had evidently been in failing health at the beginning of December 1627, when he made his will. He died at the beginning of February, and was buried in St. Andrew's, Holborn.[1] His will is interesting, for it reveals that he possessed a considerable number of pictures and was evidently somewhat of a connoisseur. To his cousin Sir John Brooke he left his portraits of the Earl of Southampton and of his old friend Richard Martin; 'my picture of Mary Magdaline, and my night shadowed picture, and peece of Appollo and the Muses being an originall of an Italian Masters hand (as I haue bin made beleeue) I giue vnto my deere ancient and worthie freind doctor Dunn the deane of Pawles'.[2] These three pictures must have joined what was already quite an impressive small collection at the Deanery.[3] Donne, in his turn, bequeathed the picture of Mary Magdalen to George Garrard.

There were, however, some newer friends who, while they probably never took the place of the friends whom he had lost, warmly engaged Donne's affections. The one who figures most often in the later correspondence is Mrs. Cokayne, the mother of the minor poet Sir Aston Cokayne. She was Ann, the daughter of Sir John Stanhope of Elvastone, and after her marriage to Thomas Cokayne of Ashbourne in Derbyshire she bore him seven children, of whom Sir Aston was the eldest. The task of bringing up the children fell on Mrs. Cokayne, for her husband suddenly left her and went up to

---

[1] He was buried on 8 Feb. (*DNB*).   [2] 112 Barrington.
[3] See W. Milgate, *NQ*, cxciv (July, 1949), 318–19 [and Gardner, *Elegies etc.*, p. 269].

London, where he lived obscurely under the name of Browne and devoted the rest of his life to the compilation of a Greek lexicon. Pooley Hall in northern Warwickshire, which adjoined Sir Henry Goodyer's Polesworth estates, was also a Cokayne manor, so Donne almost certainly met the family through Goodyer. Ashbourne was the principal residence of the Cokaynes, however, and a room in the house was for many years known as 'Dr. Donne's chamber',[1] so it can be presumed that he stayed there on more than one occasion. Ashbourne also took pride in its garden, which Mrs. Cokayne oversaw; but it was more utilitarian than elegant, if one is to believe a poem addressed by Sir Aston to his mother in praise of the garden's produce:

> Let none our *Ashbourn* discommend henceforth;
> Your Gardens shew it is a place of worth.
> What delicate Sparagus you have growing there,
> And in how great abundance every year?
> What gallant Apricocks, and Peaches brave,
> And what delicious Nectorins you have?
> What Mellons that grow ripe without those Glasses
> That are laid over them in other Places?
> What Grapes you have there growing? and what wine
> (Pleasant to tast) you made last vintage time?
> Plant Vines; & (when of Grapes you have got store)
> Make Wine enough, and I will ask no more:
> Then Mr. *Bancroft* (in high lines) shall tell
> The world, your cellar's *Aganippe*'s well.[2]

Thomas Bancroft, referred to in the concluding lines, was a neighbour and cousin, and poet too; he addressed a couplet to Donne, anticipating a pun on the Dean's name that Coleridge in later days was also to use:

> To Doctor *Donne*
> Thy Muses gallantry doth farre exceed
> All ours; to whom thou art a *Don* indeed.[3]

---

[1] E. F. Rimbault, 'Mrs. Cokayne of Ashbourne', *NQ*, 3rd Ser. iv, 415; A. Gray, *A Chapter in the Early Life of Shakespeare*, 1926, pp. 91–3. Donne seems to have known the family before his ordination; see p. 509 below.

[2] *Poems*, 1658, p. 147 (*for* 247).

[3] *Two Bookes of Epigrammes and Epitaphs*, 1639, bk. i, no. 136.

Mrs. Cokayne valued her friendship with Donne so much that she bequeathed as special legacies to members of her family her copies of his *Sermons* and *Devotions*, and Sir Aston, in listing the poets of his day with whom he was personally acquainted names Donne first:

> *Donne, Suckling, Randolph, Drayton, Massinger,*
> *Habbington, Sandys, May,* my Acquaintance were:
> *Johnson, Chapman,* and *Holland,* I have seen.[1]

One of Mrs. Cokayne's sisters was Cordelia, wife of Sir Roger Aston; she is presumably the sister referred to in one of Donne's letters. Another sister was Olive, who had married Charles Cotton, one of the most elegant gentlemen and amateurs of letters in his day, who was the father of the younger Charles Cotton, the poet and friend of Izaak Walton. In a poem addressed to Walton the younger Cotton recalled his father's friendship with some of the subjects of the Lives:

> How happy was my Father then! to see
> Those men he lov'd, by him he lov'd, to be
> Rescu'd from frailties, and mortality.
>
> *Wotton* and *Donne,* to whom his soul was knit:
> Those twins of Vertue, Eloquence, and Wit,
> He saw, in Fames eternal Annals writ.[2]

On a different social level, no doubt, but certainly by now among Donne's younger friends, was Izaak Walton himself, still a rising linen draper with a shop in Fleet Street two doors west of Chancery Lane. Walton, who described himself as Donne's 'convert', was clearly something of a hero-worshipper, but he had an unusual charm of manner as well as a gift for friendship that earned for him the fellowship of men like Donne and Wotton, Bishop King and Bishop Morley, and the Cottons, father and son, as well as antiquaries like Aubrey and Wood. Clearly Walton had qualities which set him off from the majority of his fellow-parishioners of St. Dunstan's. Walton's acquaintance with Donne can, however, scarcely have begun before 1625, and the only hint of its development before the last days of Donne's life is his statement that he went to Chelsea to hear Donne's sermon at the memorial service for Lady Danvers.

---

[1] *Poems,* 1658, p. 234.   [2] Walton, *Lives,* p. 9; first included in 1670.

During 1628 Donne continued his interest in the affairs of St. Dunstan's. Three of the parishioners paid for pews in the chancel, the money being handed over to Donne by the Warden on 20 January. Donne missed the vestry meeting three days later, but he attended on Saturday, 19 April, and no doubt joined his colleagues at dinner in St. Dunstan's Tavern. Another vestryman paid for a seat in the chancel that day, but the Senior Warden did not give the money to Donne until the 22nd. On Sunday, 4 May, he preached at the church a sermon 'on the First Sonday of Easter terme of the guift of Mr Henry Adams' and was paid the usual 10s.; and ten days later he signed the two Churchwardens' accounts. Another memorial sermon was delivered by Donne on 29 June, 'beinge Mr Adams his funerall day'. He attended the next vestry meeting, on 16 July, when an agreement was received from a George Sparke, who was erecting a building adjoining the churchyard, to pay 4d. per annum for his infringement of ancient lights, not to have any windows in his wall looking on to the churchyard, and to replace a shed in it which had been taken down during his building operations.

At the same Vestry it is agreed and ordered that the Churchwardens shall place in the Galleries of the said Church soe many of the auncientest and better sort of the parrishioners which have not borne office as conveniently may be there well placed and that the Churchwardens shall appoint some fitt person at each of the doores of the said Galleries to attend on the Sabbath dayes and other Sermon dayes to let in the Parrishioners there seated and to keepe out Servingmen apprentices and other servauntes and boyes.

The vestry discussed the loan of some charity money, granted pensions to two widows, and then adjourned for dinner to the Horn Tavern.

But greater matters occupied Donne's attention at St. Paul's; for there was to be a new Bishop of London. For some time the King had been concerned over the laxness of the administration of the diocese, where the Puritans were gaining an increasing hold over the popular pulpits, and where restiveness against the royal policies for the Church was always stirring. A firmer disciplinarian was needed, and William Laud had known for some time that the King intended to make him Bishop of London as soon as there was a vacancy. The problem was how to create the vacancy. Mountain, the Bishop, was an elegant and courtly man, famous for his lavish entertainments, but too indecisive and easy-going. His worldliness evidently became legendary, for thirteen years after his death Milton, after describing the episcopacy of the primitive Church, ironically remarked: 'What a rich bootie it would be, what a plump endowment to the many-benefice-gaping mouth of a Prelate, what a relish it would give to his canary-sucking, and swan-eating palat, let old Bishop *Mountain* judge for me.'[1] The story of his translation is told by Peter Heylin in his life of Laud:

It was thought expedient to translate *Neile* (whose accommodations *Laud* much studied) to the See of *Winchester*, then vacant by the death of *Andrews*, and to remove *Mountain* unto *Durham* in the place of *Neile*: But the putting of this design into execution did require some time. . . . In *Mountains* hands the business did receive a stop: He had spent a great part of his Life in the air of the Court, as Chaplain to *Robert* Earl of Salisbury, Dean of *Westminster*, and Bishop *Almoner*; and had lived for many years last past in the warm City of *London*. To remove him from the Court, and send him into those cold Regions of the *North*, he looked on as the worst kind of Banishment, next neighbour to a Civil death; But having a long while strived in vain, and understanding that his Majesty was not well pleased with his delays, he began to set forward on that Journey, with this *Proviso* notwithstanding, That the utmost term of his Removal should be but from *London*-House in the City, to *Durham*-House in the Strand. And yet to beget more delays toward *Laud's* Advancement, before he actually was confirmed in the See of *Durham*, the *Metropolitan* See of *York* fell void by the death of the most Reverend Prelate Dr. *Toby Matthews*: This Dignity he affected with as much ambition, as he had earnestly endeavoured to decline the other; and he obtained what he desired: But so much time was taken up in passing the Election, facilitating the Royal Assent, and the Formalities of his Confirmation, that the next Session of Parliament was ended, and the middle of *July* well near passed, before *Laud* could be actually Translated to the *See* of *London*.[2]

Mountain, it is said, owed his archbishopric to a happy pun: 'Your Majesty can cast this Mountain into the see of York.'

---

[1] *Of Reformation Touching Church-Discipline in England,* 1641, *The Columbia Milton,* iii, pt. 1, p. 19.

[2] *Cyprianus Anglicus* (1668), pp. 174-5.

With the bishopric of London at last vacant, the Archbishop of Canterbury issued a commission (dated 4 July) to the Dean and stagiaries of St. Paul's to administer the see during the vacancy; four days later Donne took an oath (of which a notarized copy was sent to the Archbishop) to fulfil certain episcopal functions according to the laws of the Church while the vacancy lasted.[1] The vacancy, however, was of brief duration, for the King had no uncertainties about Mountain's successor, and Laud became Bishop of London on 25 July.

There is almost no evidence as to Donne's day-to-day relations with his bishops, which must inevitably have been close. The only references to Mountain in Donne's correspondence are in two letters of 4 and 5 January 1627 to Sir Robert Ker, which have already been commented on.[2] We are not even sure that Donne was present at the Bishop's visitation to St. Dunstan's on 20 October 1624 and the dinner that followed at the Horn Tavern, or when Mountain, his chaplain, and others, on 29 June 1625 during the plague, consecrated 'the West parte of the new Churchyard in Fewter Lane'—the occasion being celebrated by two dinners, one at the Kingshead Tavern and one at St. Dunstan's Tavern; but it is probable that Donne attended these functions.[3] Of Laud Donne had already had some experience in the incident of the questioned sermon, but this does not seem to have been held against him. A few months after Laud's translation the public outcry against his attempts to enforce his policies in his new diocese grew stronger, and threats were made against his life. He noted in his diary under the date of Sunday, 29 March 1629:

Two Papers were found in the Dean of *Paul*'s his Yard before his House. The one was to this effect concerning my self: *Laud*, look to thy self: be assured thy Life is sought. As thou art the Fountain of all Wickedness, Repent thee of thy monstrous Sins, before thou be taken out of the World, *&c.* And assure thy self, neither God nor the World can endure such a vile Councellor to live, or such a Whisperer; or to this effect. The other was as bad as this, against the Lord Treasurer. Mr. Dean delivered both Papers to the King that Night.

---

[1] Lambeth Palace Library, Reg. Abbot, pt. ii, ff. 303ᵛ and 304ʳ.
[2] See above, pp. 427–8.   [3] Whitlock, loc. cit.

Lord, I am a grievous Sinner; but, I beseech thee, deliver my Soul·
from them that hate me without a Cause.[1]

The murder of the Duke of Buckingham by Felton had taught the
people that the only way to remove a hated counsellor was by death
and, though assassination did not become a political weapon consistently used, the death of the oppressor, whether Laud, or Wentworth, or the King himself, seemed to this century the only means
of putting an end to his tyranny. One wonders if, when Donne
handed these threats to the King, he had any inkling of the clouds
that were gathering, and of the storm that was to break within a
decade of his death.

[1] Laud, *History of the Troubles and Tryal*, p. 44.

XVIII

LAST DAYS

BY 1628 Donne was 56 years old. It is difficult to know whether he yet felt any consciousness of ageing, any lack of vigour, and any need to husband his energies. He was close to the age when many men begin to feel that their physical powers are showing signs of diminishing, and that they will soon have to curtail their activities. On the other hand, many men are still at the height of their powers. Certainly there is no sign that Donne's health had been seriously impaired by his illnesses in 1623 and 1625, and he seems until quite near the end of his life to have been able to cope with the many activities which his position in the Church imposed on him. Perhaps he tired more easily, perhaps he found some tasks more of a burden than they had formerly been, but familiarity made some kinds of effort less of a strain, and he was still the busy Church dignitary, immersed in his office and capable of energy and decision. Until his final illness there are few signs that his strength was failing.

To 1628 belongs a letter to Mrs. Cokayne. Its date is fixed by a reference to the news that Sir John Brooke had married Sir William Bamfylde's third daughter, an event which, according to Gosse, occurred on 16 May 1628.[1] Mrs. Cokayne had written from Bath, and Donne replied briefly, apologizing by saying that he was pressed for time as he had not yet 'got through my preparation for my *Paul*'s service upon *Sunday*'. There is among the sermons one 'preached at St. Paul's upon Whitsunday, 1628', and this is probably the one to which he refers.[2] If he could have postponed his letter until the next day he would have written at greater length, 'for

---

[1] *Tobie Mathew Collection*, pp. 340–1. Sir William Banfield, or Bampfylde, had been tenant of Christopher Brooke's house in Drury Lane after the death of Brooke's wife; Sir John Brooke was a cousin of Christopher. Donne, therefore, was probably acquainted with both participants in the wedding. Cf. Gosse, ii. 256, and Christopher Brooke's will (112 Barrington).

[2] The letter was written on the Friday before Whit Sunday, which in 1628 fell on 1 June. The date of the letter is therefore 30 May.

Saturday is my day of conversation and liberty'. Walton observed that

upon Saturday he usually gave himself and his mind a rest from the weary burthen of his weeks meditations, and usually spent that day in visitation of friends, or some other diversions of his thoughts; and would say, that *he gave both his body and mind that refreshment, that he might be enabled to do the work of the day following, not faintly, but with courage and chearfulness.*[1]

This was a settled habit, and one that was well known to his friends.

Another (undated) letter to Mrs. Cokayne probably belongs to 1628; in it he attempts to console her on the death of Thomas, the younger of her two sons, who had died at Bath 'about the *18th* year of his age, and lies there Buried'.[2] Besides the comfort and encouragement which Donne tried to give the bereaved mother, the letter contains some information about his own life. It becomes clear that he had known Mrs. Cokayne (and therefore also her husband, who did not leave her until after 1616, and when their youngest child was born) since before his ordination, for he begins: 'If I had had such an occasion as this to have written to you, in the first year of our acquaintance, I had been likelie to have presented you with an Essay of Morall Comfort. Now my Letter may be well excused, if it amount to an Homilie.'[3] Donne certainly knew of the situation between Mrs. Cokayne and her husband, and he adds one detail not usually mentioned in this connection. Evidently she had been afraid that her husband would seize the children and take them away from her so that she would have no redress; accordingly, she scattered them in various places where he would not be likely to find them.

The perversnesse of the father [Donne wrote] put you to such a

---

[1] *Lives*, p. 67. Donne was, however, engaged on a good many Saturdays upon work connected with the High Commission and the Court of Delegates; his colleagues in these courts evidently capitalized on the fact that he was at 'liberty' that day.

[2] From the title of Sir Aston Cokayne's 'Epitaph on my younger Brother Mr. *Thomas Cokaine', Poems of Several Sorts*, 1669, p. 140. Gosse (ii. 260) refers to the parish register of Ashbourne as showing that Thomas was born on 1 Jan. 1611/12; cf. *Cokayne Memoranda* (1873), p. 10. An earlier edition of the latter work, 1869, includes the information that he 'died in Bath in 1628 at the age of 18' (pp. 40–1). In view of Sir Aston's 'about', however, I think it safe to accept 1628 as the year of Thomas's death.

[3] *Tobie Mathew Collection*, p. 344.

necessity of hiding your sons, as that this son is scarce more out of your sight, by being laid under ground, than he was before.

Cold comfort, no doubt; but Donne goes on to argue that 'we do but borrow Children of God, to lend them to the world', and

when I lend the world a daughter in marriage, or lend the world a son in a profession, the world does not alwaies pay me well again; my hopes are not alwaies answered in that daughter or that son. But, of all that I lend to, the Grave is my best pay-Master. The Grave shall restore me my child. . . .[1]

This is one of the passages in which, though Donne uses the first person, one cannot be sure whether he is dramatizing the situation by thinking of himself as the typical Christian, or whether he is speaking in his own voice—whether, in this case, he is confessing to a sense of disappointment at the outcome of Constance's marriage, or at his son John's hesitation to leave the University and take priest's orders. He does, however, go on to say 'I am well content to send one sonne to the Church, the other to the Warrs.' George Donne, by this date, had already served against the French at the Isle of Rhé, but John was still at Oxford on the point of taking his M.A., unwilling as yet to commit himself to the career that his father had marked out for him.

Donne managed to make his usual summer visits to his country parishes, going first to Sevenoaks. On his return home he found that his youngest daughter Margaret was ill with smallpox. Rather than risk infection he went immediately to Sir Thomas Grymes's at Peckham and stayed there until he was sure that his daughter was out of danger before setting out for Blunham. But there, he wrote to Mrs. Cokayne at the end of August,

upon my third *Sunday*, I was seized with a Feavour, which grew so upon me, as forced me to a resolution, of seeking my Physitian at *London*. Thither I came in a day, and a little piece; and within four miles of home, I was surprised with an accident in the Coach, which never befell me before, nor had been much in my contemplation, and therefore affected me much. It was a violent falling of the *Uvula*. Which when Doctor *Fox* (whom I found at *London*, and who had not been

---

[1] *Tobie Mathew Collection*, pp. 345–6.

there in ten daies before) considered well, and perceived the feavour complicated with a Squinancie; by way of prevention of both, he presentlie took blood; and so with ten-daies-starving in a close prison, that is, my bed, I am (blessed be God) returned to a convenient temper, and pulse, and appetite, and learn to eat.[1]

A squinancy, or quinsy, was an aggravated form of tonsilitis, and this infection of the throat hindered Donne from preaching for some time; mention of it recurs more than once in succeeding letters.

It was soon after this that he received a letter from Sir Robert Ker inviting him to spend some days at his country house at Kew. Ker's letter is dated 7 October, and is endorsed 'The coppy of an ansure I wrote to this lettre of doctor Donnes', but Donne's letter has long since been detached and lost. As it is interesting to see how some of Donne's friends expressed themselves towards him, Ker's letter is given in full:

Sir,

I uas never better pleasd then uhen I mett with your letter at this house when I came to it from Court, for by it as more by my wyffe and childrens being in it, I had cause to lyke it better then the Court, for I longed to heare from yow, and to fynde yow so much maister of these encombrances which assail your invincible spirit through the mudd of your bodye. I would the Rochell could hold out as wele. Whatever your contemplation be of angells, I am so much conversant with creatures of another nature, that I would be glade to meet with yow who, I am sure, are of a midle temper at least between them and me, besyde the infection of my dayly conversation, that by your help I myght be maide fit not to be vnworthy of your company, or at least I myght knaw how to be usefull to yow or my self, or any bodye els in this new spheare of courtship ue are enterd by the Duke's death. For this cause, or any other reason, iff yow will remember that uhersoever yow have lost your self all the rest of this soumer, none of it uas cast away on me, and therefore in this fayre weather, which God, I think, hath bestowed on our navye onlye to make it so much the less excusable iff it cum back *sans coup frapper*, iff yow will (and I pray you will it) come and spend some pairt of your lyffe more with me, bringing with yow what men or bookes yow please, and wee shall talk of all that is past freely, and it may be take some not impertinent

[1] Ibid., pp. 342-3.

resolutions for the rest of this yeir and of our lyffe to cum iff God have
allowed vs any; and iff eyther of vs dye quickly it will mitigat our
separation so farr that we have taken so freshe goodnyght. Iff I be the
first that pairts, I will think my familye the happyer that yow were so
lately in it; and iff yow goe before me, there be none now living on the
earth whom I will so implicitly trust to chalk me a way that I may
follow, or with whom I will more contentedly converse so long as wee
lyve heir, so hath your extraordinary worth made happy by your
friendship your faithful friend and servand,

Kew, 7 October, 1628   Sr Rob. Karr[1]

Though Donne probably passed some pleasant days with Ker at Kew
he was still much concerned with his health when he wrote to Lionel
Cranfield, Earl of Middlesex, on 18 November. 'I should be sorry,
if thys should make me a silenc'd Minister', he sardonically
remarked, but continued: 'I have tryed once, at S. Dunstans, since
thys distemper overtooke me, and, I thanke God, not been the
worse for yt.'[2] He seems to have taken care for a while to avoid
over-straining his throat, and eventually recovered. His next sermon
was at St. Paul's on 23 November, and he preached there again, of
course, on Christmas Day. His health had not allowed him to attend
any vestry meetings at St. Dunstan's during the autumn, but the
vestry this year repeated the previous year's gift of sack, and also
added a further gift of 4s. 3d.: 'Item the first of January given to the
porter Butler and Cooke at Mr Dr Dunns house';[3] perhaps they were
acknowledging hospitality of Donne's own.

There is very little to relate of Donne's life during the year 1629.
In the first half of the year he preached in the Cathedral three times,
and at Court three times. He is not known to have preached at St.
Dunstan's, or to have attended a vestry meeting, throughout the
whole year, although he signed the Churchwardens' accounts on 20
May. One item from the minutes of the parish meeting of 11 July, however, deserves notice for its testimonial to the belief of the London

<hr>

[1] *Correspondence of Sir Robert Kerr, first Earl of Ancram and his son William, third Earl of Lothian*, ed. D. Laing, Roxburghe Club, 1875, i. 46. Buckingham was murdered on 28 Aug.; the fleet sailed on 7 Sept. to relieve La Rochelle, which was surrendered on 18 Oct.

[2] *Sermons*, viii. 24–5.

[3] Churchwardens' Accounts, Guildhall MS. 2968/3, 1628–9.

townsfolk at this period in dinner meetings of all sorts, whether to expedite business or encourage good fellowship:

> Whereas aunciently for many yeres there was alowed iiij^{li} yerely for a meetinge of all the Inhabitant*es* and parrishion*ers* of this parish w*h*ich had borne office at the givinge vp of the Churchwardens accompts which good order hath of late yeres bene forborne out of the private respect[es] of some particular parsons And whereas the Readers of the Inner and Middle Temple have yerely accustomed in the time of theire S*u*mmer reading*es* to send vnto the parrishion*ers* two Buck*es* for a neighbourly meetinge the Charges in bakinge & spendinge of w*h*ich Buck*es* of late yeres hath grown to soe high a rate in respect of the price of Victualls as neighbours could not meete thereat vnder iiij^s vj^d or v^s the husband and wife In respect whereof many refused and forbeard to come to those meeting*es*. Vpon Consideraci*on* whereof And for the mainteininge and increase of neighbourly love & freindshipp occasioned by those meeting*es* It was at the aforesaid generall meetinge by all the persons before named fully assented vnto and agreed that from henceforth yerely at the meetinge of the neighbours for the spendinge and eatinge of the said Buck*es* there shalbe alowed by the Parrish xl^s at the spendinge of ech Bucke. . . .[1]

This passage is particularly interesting because it emphasizes the close relations existing between the parish of St. Dunstan's and the senior members of the Temple.

This year Donne sat on a commission with the Archbishop and several of the bishops to resolve a dispute that had broken out within the chapter at Salisbury, and immediately after the commission had rendered its report he wrote to Sir George More:

S^r

The busines of thys Churche and all other busines which concerne me in thys town determine thys weeke: so that I might be at my liberty to go to do the duty to my Churche in the Cuntry, next weeke, but for the expectation of that 100^l, which you are to pay some days after that. If therefore yt stand not with your conveniency to pay yt before, because I presume you wyll be gone out of town, before that 10th of July, I ame bold to intreat you to let me know, by whose hands yt shall be payd me then, for besides that yt were a

---

[1] Vestry Minutes, 1588–1663, p. 129. Cf. Whitlock, loc. cit.

great disappointment of my necessary service in the Cuntry, to be
stayed any longer in thys town, so not to receyue yt at that day, wyll
put me to so great a trouble as to make my poore wyll anew, and to
substract from my other children, theyr part of thys 100 *l*. Therfore
I humbly intreat you, that I may hear from you, befor your goinge
out of town, and rest

your poore sonne in law
and humble servant in Christ Jesus
J. Donne[1]

At Pauls house
22 Jun: 1629

One learns from this letter that Donne's plans for the summer were
the usual ones, but it is more interesting to learn that he, who for so
many years had been dependent on his father-in-law, was now able
to lend him money. If he had hesitated to help Alleyn with a loan,
he did not fail to trust Sir George More. Walton reports him as
saying in the last days of his life: 'I have liv'd to be useful and
comfortable to my good Father-in-law Sir *George Moore*, whose
patience God hath been pleased to exercise with many temporal
Crosses.'[2]

Donne attended meetings of the governors of the Charterhouse
on 2 July and 8 December, and on 22 November preached his last
sermon at St. Paul's Cross. We know no more about his life in 1629;
and for 1630 there is even sparser information. For the latter year
only three dated sermons survive, a sermon on the anniversary of
the conversion of St. Paul and an Easter Day sermon, both preached
in St. Paul's Cathedral, and a sermon preached to the King, probably
at the beginning of Lent. In addition, however, there is a Whitsun
sermon which Mrs. Simpson plausibly assigns to this year. Donne
also attended meetings and dinners at St. Dunstan's on 20 January
and 21 April.[3] During this winter, too, he was active in the business
of the Court of Delegates; his attendance is recorded at a number of
hearings and between 3 December 1629 and 1 February 1629/30 he
joined in passing sentence in three important cases. He was present

---

[1] Loseley MS., Folger Shakespeare Library; cf. M. de Haviland, *London Mercury*,
xiii (1925), 159–62.   [2] *Lives*, p. 76.
   [3] Whitlock, loc. cit.; at the second meeting the vestry decided to care for an Irish
waif about five years old who had 'longe since layne in the streets of this parish'.

at an Assembly of the governors of the Charterhouse on 12 May 1630.[1] Even if he was conscious of a gradual loss of vigour, there were still many demands on him, and he was fulfilling them. The surviving sermons show no loss of power; indeed, as Mrs. Simpson points out, they continue the recovery from the aridity she finds in the preaching in the winter of 1627–8 and maintain the energy of the sermons delivered since the spring of 1628.[2] Though there are no letters until late in the year to give any clues as to the day-to-day events of his life, his state of health, or the thoughts he shared with his friends, there are no signs of weakness or failing.

Donne seems to have consolidated his position at Court after his temporary check, and to have been well regarded. Charles I thought highly of him and admired his poetry, and the closer relation of Bishop and Dean at St. Paul's had caused Laud to know him better and to trust him. This, at least, seems to be inferable from a document among the State Papers[3] headed: 'If any of these whose Names are underwritten shall be advaunced to a Bishoppricke, some of the Benefices annexed to them will fall into his Majesties donation.' The three whose names follow are the Master of the Savoy (Dr. Balconqual), Donne, and William Piers, Dean of Peterborough, and each name has against it one or more benefices. Piers was consecrated Bishop of Peterborough on 24 October 1630, so the document is likely to be at least a month or two earlier, before Piers's promotion had been decided on. Incidentally, Donne is credited with the livings of St. Dunstan's and 'Pancridge neare London'; the last-named he never held. The vicar there at this time was one John Elborow who had been appointed in 1625 in the normal way by the patrons, the Dean and Chapter of St. Paul's.[4] There seems to be no doubt, however, that by the summer of 1630 Donne was being seriously considered for promotion to a bishopric, and, if he had lived, would almost certainly have been appointed when a suitable vacancy occurred.

On 24 June Constance remarried. Her second husband was a man nearer her own age, Samuel Harvey, grandson of a former alderman

---

[1] See Chap. XV, p. 424, n. 3.
[2] *Sermons*, ix. 25.   [3] P.R.O., S.P. 16, Charles I/172, no. 114.
[4] See G. Hennessy, *Novum Repertorium Ecclesiasticum Parochiale Londinense*, p. 358.

of London, Sir James Harvey, who had an estate at Abury, or Aldborough, Hatch in Essex. The marriage took place at Camberwell,
once again from the Grymes's house. After it had occurred Donne,
one would guess, spent the early part of the summer in his usual
manner, visiting and preaching at Sevenoaks and Blunham, and
then in August paid a visit to the newly married couple. He was
accompanied by at least one of his other daughters and by his
mother, who had been living in the Deanery for several years and
who must by now have been in her late eighties; with her came a
poor relation, Jane Kent, who acted as her servant. What had been
intended as a happy family reunion soon lost its gaiety, and the
household became a tense and anxious one. Donne fell ill; in
Walton's words,

he there fell into a Fever, which with the help of his constant infirmity
(vapours from the spleen) hastened him into so visible a Consumption,
that his beholders might say, as St. *Paul* of himself, *He dyes daily*;
and he might say with *Job*, *My welfare passeth away as a cloud, the
days of my affliction have taken hold of me, and weary nights are appointed
for me.*[1]

His sickness was probably an intensification of a recurrent ailment
to which he refers in an earlier letter to Mrs. Cokayne:[2]

I am come now, not onely to pay a Feavour every half year, as a
Rent for my life; but I am called upon before the day, and they come
sooner in the year than heretofore. This Feavour that I had now, I
hoped, for divers daies, to have been but an exaltation of my damps

---

[1] *Lives*, p. 60.

[2] See above, pp. 395–6. [Professor Bald was inclined to place the letter about
Aug. 1630, but Mr. Shapiro thinks it cannot be later than 1628, and may be two
or three years earlier still; there are indications that Professor Bald would have come
to agree with him.] The date of this letter is particularly difficult to determine. It
would be odd if Donne had two medical friends visiting him at Aldborough Hatch.
But immediately after the passage quoted in the text Donne says: 'At the same time,
little *Betty* had a Feavour too; and, for her, we used Doctor *Wright*, who, by occasion,
lies within two miles of us; and he was able to ease my sicknesse, with his report of
your good health. . . .' Donne would not have been likely to say that Dr. Wright 'lies
within two miles of us' if they were both in the city. Yet when Donne speaks of
having Dr. Fox and Dr. Clement with him, one thinks of his being in London and
calling them in. [I have not attempted to resolve these difficulties.] The letter
contains the only reference in Donne's correspondence to his youngest daughter,
Elizabeth.

and flashings, such as exercise me sometimes four or five daies, and passe away, without whining or complaint. But, I neglected this somewhat too long, which makes me (though, after I took it into consideration, the Feavour it self declined quickly) much weaker, than, perchance, otherwise I should have been. I had Doctor *Fox* and Doctor *Clement* with me, but, I thank God, was not much trouble to them. Ordinary means set me soon upon my leggs. And I have broke my close prison, and walk'd into the Garden; and (but that the weather hath continued so spitefully foul) make no doubt, but I might safely have done more. I eat, and digest well enough. And it is no strange thing, that I do not sleep well; for, in my best health, I am not much used to do so.[1]

This is the same letter in which Donne describes the visit of Nathaniel Hazard, the former tutor of the Cokayne children. He had not been impressed by Hazard, thinking him unduly persistent, ill-mannered, and conceited. When Donne told him that his 'often sicknesses' compelled him sometimes to find substitutes for his more important preaching engagements, 'And surely, said I, I will offer them no man in those cases which shall not be at least equall to my self; and, Mr. *Hazard*, I do not know your faculties. He gave me this answer, I will not make comparisons, but I do not doubt but I should give them satisfaction in that kind.' Nevertheless Donne promised to do whatever he reasonably could for the young man, but whether he lived long enough to do anything for him is uncertain; there is no record to show that Hazard ever obtained more than a curacy. Donne had, he told Mrs. Cokayne, fulfilled an obligation of this kind to the Lords Carlisle and Percy, and he was one 'from whom, one Scholler in each Universitie sucks something, and must be weaned by me'. This confirms a statement by Walton that Donne was 'a continual Giver to poor Scholars, both of this and forraign Nations'.[2] Evidently he not merely contributed to the expenses of one student at Oxford and another at Cambridge but also took sufficient interest in them to see that after ordination they were suitably placed in a curacy or perhaps in a household where they would act as chaplains and tutors. In another letter he wrote that 'in these times of necessity, and multitudes of poor there is no

---

[1] *Tobie Mathew Collection*, pp. 349–50.   [2] *Lives*, p. 70.

possibility of saving to him that hath any tendernesse in him'.[1]
Donne's charitable feelings were easily stirred, and there is no
reason to suppose that his regular gifts were disturbed by his
illnesses. The only case of his causing personal disappointment to
anyone in this sickness in 1630 is found in the vestry minutes of St.
Dunstan's for 23 June. A Ralph Foster came to the meeting hoping
to get a new lease of his dwelling but was 'putt ofe by reason of M[r]
Deane of Paules absence and ys apponted to attend M[r] Deane
against the next vestrie' when, the vestrymen hoped, the matter
could be concluded. The marriage of Constance the following day,
Donne's visits to the country, and then the onset of illness, all
probably kept Donne from hearing of Mr. Foster, who had, in the
event, to wait for the next vicar, Dr. James Marsh, to arrange the
lease.[2]

A succession of four letters to George Garrard, of which the
second was dated 2 November when it was printed with the *Poems*
in 1635, indicate the progress of Donne's illness. Garrard, now in
the service of the Percy family, was in close touch with Lord Percy
and his brother-in-law the Earl of Carlisle. Donne was less inclined
to enter into details of his health with Garrard than with Mrs.
Cokayne because, he said, 'it is not for my gravity, to write of
feathers, and strawes'.[3] In the first letter he expressed a belief that
he would make a better recovery in London than in the country,
'but the very going would indanger me', and accordingly he had
had to decline an invitation from the Lord Chamberlain to preach
the annual 5 November sermon before the King.[4] In the letter of
2 November his health is ever variable:

whensoever I tell you how I doe, by a Letter, before that Letter comes
to you, I shall be otherwise, then when it left me. At this time, I
humbly thank God, I am only not worse; for, I should as soon look for
Roses at this time of the year, as look for increase of strength. And if
I be no worse all spring, then now, I am much better, for, I make
account that those Church services, which I would be very loth to
decline, will spend somewhat; and, if I can gather so much as will
bear my charges, recover so much strength at *London*, as I shall spend

[1] *Letters*, p. 242.   [2] Whitlock, loc. cit.   [3] *Letters*, p. 240.
[4] Ibid., pp. 281–2.

at *London*, I shall not be loth to be left in that state wherein I am now, after that's done; But I do but discourse, I do not wish; life, or health, or strength, (I thank God) enter not into my prayers for my self.[1]

In spite of the last sentence, one cannot think that Donne yet felt that death was imminent; rather, his attitude was one of resignation to ill health and all its attendant disabilities. Like all those suffering from continued illness, however, he was perforce becoming more self-centred, for there is nothing in this set of letters about his daughter and her husband, or about his mother and her health, or about news from London and abroad; he himself and his affairs occupy the centre of the stage. Two or three weeks after the letter of 2 November he wrote to Garrard again, of a new bout of illness: 'I was possessed with a Fever, so late in the year, that I am afraid I shall not recover confidence to come to *London* till the spring be a little advanced.'[2] Finally, in the fourth letter he relates that he has further postponed his return and has arranged for a substitute to preach the Christmas sermon in St. Paul's, but that he intends to preach at Candlemas and expects to be back in good time for that festival.[3]

Another topic that runs through all these letters is Donne's anxiety over the plight of his son George. Garrard is besought to 'intreat my Lord *Percy* in my behalfe, that he will be pleased to name *George* to my L. *Carlile*, and to wonder, if not to inquire, where he is'. Later he asks 'Because you did our poor family the favour, to mention our *George* in your Letters to *Spain*, with some earnest-nesse, I should wonder if you never had any thing from thence concerning him; he having been now, divers moneths, in *Spaine*'; and in the last letter to Garrard he thanks him for 'keeping our *George* in your memory', though it is clear that he has not yet had any real news of him.[4] In 1627 the Earl of Carlisle had been granted a patent which made him Lord Proprietor of all the colonies in the West Indies, and (doubtless through his father's influence) George Donne, after his service in the French war, had been sent out to

---

[1] Ibid., pp. 240–1.   [2] Ibid., p. 286.
[3] Ibid., p. 243. Gosse (ii. 269) dates this letter 7 Jan. 1630/1 on the authority of *Poems*, 1635, where it was first published; but this date cannot be right, for the letter was clearly written before Christmas, and perhaps as early as about 10 Dec.
[4] *Letters*, pp. 282, 286, 243.

St. Kitt's by the new Lord Proprietor as 'cheife commaunder of all forces in the Isle of St. Christopher' (as his father's funeral certificate states). In the autumn of 1629 a Spanish 'armada' consisting of twenty-four warships and fifteen frigates was sent out against the Dutch colonies in Brazil; on its way there it appeared off the islands of St. Kitts and Nevis, where the colonists returned what fire they could, but were soon overcome. George Donne 'Commaunded the defence, [and] Articled the Conditions of Surrender';[1] the English colonists (who had as their sole alternative entering the service of the King of Spain) engaged themselves to return to England, and the Spaniards took five hostages who were to be responsible for the performance of the conditions of surrender. Among these were George Donne and a Lieutenant Hay, who was clearly a young kinsman of Carlisle's.[2] The hostages were sent to Spain; on 7 March 1629/30 a Captain Richard Plumleigh reported to Carlisle that he had met at Cadiz George Donne, Lieutenant Hay, and the others, and had promised to hasten their delivery; they were in great want, and he had relieved them with advice and with money.[3] George Donne was, in fact, a Spanish captive when his father died, and had to endure over four years of imprisonment in Spain before he was able to return home, a fact which 'iustified my duty to the Lord of Carlisle then livinge whose Memory I euer honoᵣ and will professe nobly deseruing'; he was forced 'to purchase [his] liberty at last wᵗʰ hazard of a greater danger'.[4]

A third topic running through these letters involves an unknown person referred to as the Diamond Lady, or the Lady of the Jewel. She had evidently left with Donne a jewel as security for a sum of money; one gets the impression that the security was far greater in value than the loan, and that Donne was eager to see the debt discharged so as to be rid of the responsibility of the safe-keeping of the diamond. 'For the rest,' he wrote to Garrard, 'let them be but remembred how long it hath been in my hands, and then leave it

[1] British Museum, Harl. MS. 7021, ff. 289–318, 'Virginia Reviewed' (in the form of a letter to Charles I signed 'George Donne') at fo. 306 (fo. 18 of the letter).

[2] He is also referred to as Captain George Hay and had been sent out as governor by Carlisle. See J. A. Williamson, *The Caribbee Islands under the Proprietary Patents*, 1926, pp. 77, 81.

[3] *C.S.P. (Col.), 1594–1660*, v. 59.   [4] 'Virginia Reviewed', loc. cit.

to their discretion. If they incline to any thing, I should chuse shirt *Hollond*, rather under then above 4*s*.'[1] In interpreting such cryptic sentences, one can only resort to conjecture. Since Donne had held the security for so long, he evidently felt that something was due to him either for his forbearance or by way of interest, but how much extra should be paid he would leave to the debtor. Anything he received would be by way of commodity and not cash, so he suggested shirt holland of a suitable quality; possibly he had been dealing with a draper or a draper's wife. In the third letter he came back to the topic: 'If you be in *London* and the Lady of the Jewell there too, at your conveniency informe me, what is looked for at my hands, in that businesse; for, I would be loath to leave any thing in my house, when I die, that were not absolutely mine own. I have a servant, *Roper*, at *Pauls* house, who will receive your commandments, at all times.'[2] Apparently Garrard made the necessary arrangements, for Donne finally wrote: 'For the Diamond Lady, you may safely deliver *Roper*, whatsoever belongs to me, and he will give you a discharge for the money.'[3] It would seem that Garrard had received what was due, had restored the pledge, and was instructed to pay what he now held on Donne's behalf to Roper.

The last letter to Garrard comments on a rumour that was current to the effect that Donne was dead. Even now Donne's sense of humour had not deserted him, for he wrote:

A man would almost be content to dye, (if there were no other benefit in death) to hear of so much sorrow, and so much good testimony from good men, as I, (God be blessed for it) did upon the report of my death.[4]

He also told Mrs. Cokayne that

the hour of my death, and the day of my buriall, were related in the highest place of this Kingdom. I had at that time no kind of sicknesse, nor was otherwise, than I had been ever since my feavour, and am yet; that is, too weak at this time of the year to go forth, especiallie to *London*, where the sicknesse is near my house, and where I must necessarilie open my self to more businesse, than my present state would bear.[5]

---

[1] *Letters*, pp. 282–3.   [2] Ibid., p. 287.   [3] Ibid., p. 243.   [4] Ibid., p. 242.
[5] *Tobie Mathew Collection*, p. 339. Gosse (ii. 259) dates this letter Nov. 1628, but

But another rumour suggested that he had secluded himself in the country in order to avoid preaching, and to save expense; this drew his indignation, for it was his desire, he declared,

that I might die in the Pulpit; if not that, yet that I might take my death in the Pulpit, that is, die the sooner by occasion of my former labours.[1]

Donne's last surviving letter was written to Mrs. Cokayne on 15 January 1630/1. He proposed to be in London within a fortnight, for he still intended to preach as he had arranged on Candlemas day (2 February); he expected, too, to be called on for his Court sermon on the first Friday in Lent, and he hoped to preach at St. Dunstan's as well. Nevertheless he was by this time feeling the weight of his illness, and his tone is one of resignation to a kind of half-life which he must endure:

I have never good temper, nor good pulse, nor good appetite, nor good sleep. Yet, I have so much leasure to recollect myself, as that I can thinke I have been long thus, or often thus. I am not alive, because I have not had enough upon me to kill me, but because it pleases God to passe me through many infirmities before he take me either by those particular remembrances, to bring me to particular repentances, or by them to give me hope of his particular mercies in heaven. Therefore have I been more affected with Coughs in vehemence, more with deafenesse, more with toothach, more with the [uvula], then heretofore.[2]

He was not so weakened, however, as to be unable to return to London as he had planned.

Ill health had never before curbed the actitivy of Donne's mind, nor did it now, and even if the wintry weather kept him indoors for long stretches of time he was not as a rule too ill to sit up and read or write. While at Aldborough Hatch he occupied himself as he had done during that summer when he was confined to the house and grounds of Sir John Danvers's house at Chelsea, by going over his

---

this is wrong, as it must refer to the same rumour of his death which he mentions in his letter to Garrard. [Mr. Shapiro dates the letter confidently in Dec. 1625.]

[1] *Letters*, p. 243.

[2] Ibid., pp. 316–17. The letter reads 'vurbah', emended to 'uvula' in Hayward, p. 499.

old sermon notes and writing them out in full. Sermon 71 of the *LXXX Sermons* bears the heading: 'At the Haghe Decemb. 19. 1619. I Preached upon this Text. Since in my sicknesse at Abrey-hatche in Essex, 1630, revising my short notes of that Sermon, I digested them into these two.'[1] It is fairly certain that the greater part of the contents of the folio volumes of Donne's sermons owe their survival to the two prolonged periods of inactivity in the country in 1625 and 1630, when they were put into permanent form from the notes on which the spoken words were based.

On 13 December 1630 Donne made his will. It was written throughout in his own hand, and its clarity shows that his early legal training made it unnecessary for him to consult a lawyer.[2] It is symptomatic of the gradual progress of his illness that though he had been at Aldborough Hatch since August it was not until mid December that he was finally convinced of the need to put his affairs in order though, even then, he still had more than three months to live. Henry King and John Mountfort were to be the executors and Sir Thomas Grymes the overseer. Since he had already sent replicas of his cross and anchor seal to many friends, the usual gifts of mourning rings, so common in the wills of the period, are omitted, although Robert Christmas and Thomas Roper, the two Cathedral officials and Donne's 'faithfull Servant*es*', were to have £5 apiece for such rings. The mementoes which Donne left to his closest friends were pictures. To the Earl of Carlisle he left a picture of the Virgin which subsequently passed into the royal collection; to the Earl of Dorset a picture of Adam and Eve; to the Earl of Kent a picture of the Entombment. Sir Robert Ker received 'that Picture of myne w*hi*ch is taken in Shaddowes' (and has only recently emerged into the light);[3] Sir Thomas Grymes was to have,

[1] *Sermons*, ii, no. 13, p. 269.

[2] The transcript of the will is to be found at Somerset House (see Appendix D, 11). The will was proved at the Consistory Court of Canterbury. The 'original' of the transcript which is also preserved is not the original, but a copy closely following some of the scribal characteristics of the original; the signature, for instance, is a careful imitation of Donne's. Apparently the executors were allowed to keep the original if they wished—even for sentimental reasons—and to deposit a copy. It is fairly clear from Walton's remarks that he had seen the original of Donne's will, which had probably been shown to him by Henry King.

[3] See J. Bryson, in *The Times*, 13 Oct. 1959 [and Gardner, *Elegies, etc.*, Appendix E, pp. 266–70]. The portrait is reproduced in Plate II.

besides 'that Strykinge clock which I ordinarilye weare', a portrait
of King James. To Henry King went portraits of Padre Paolo and
Padre Fulgenzio,[1] besides the gold medal struck to commemorate
the Synod of Dort. Other friends who received pictures were Sir
John Danvers, Dr. Winniff, George Garrard, Samuel Brooke, and
'Mr Tourvall a Frenche Minister'.[2] Legacies of varying amounts
went to all the servants, so that for the first time one glimpses the
extent of Donne's household. It included one manservant besides
the coachman and a boy; a maid who attended Donne's daughters,
another who looked after his mother, besides kitchen and parlour
maids. All were remembered in one way or another. There were
also gifts to the poor of the parish in which he lived and the parishes
of which he was incumbent;[3] and others to the petty canons, vicars
choral, and vergers of the Cathedral. The special furnishings,
including a number of pictures within the Deanery, were to remain
there for the enjoyment of his successors. The rest of the estate was
to go to his family. After provision was made for his mother, the
residue was to be divided between the six surviving children. How
much they would each receive Donne did not know, but it is clear
that he expected them to get between £500 and £750 apiece; his
estate was therefore between £3,000 and £4,000.

The provision Donne made in his will for his mother was not
needed, for she died before January was out.[4] The parish register
of the church at Barking records the burial on 28 January 1630/1
of 'Widdow Ranford D. Donnes mother'. It must not be forgotten

---

[1] For an account of Sarpi and Fulgenzio, see L. Pearsall Smith, *Life and Letters of
Sir Henry Wotton*, ii. 478–9; cf. above, pp. 150–1.

[2] See pp. 488–9 above.

[3] The records of St. Dunstan's note the receipt of Donne's bequest from his
executors on 13 July 1631. The charities of the parish included (at a meeting which
Donne attended, Minutes, p. 125) the grant of a pension to two widows and (in
entries not connected directly with him) help to needy sailors of all countries and to
unmarried mothers, and the sending of children to what was doubtless hoped would
be a better life in Virginia. Incidentally, the parish records show the close relationship of the parishes of St. Dunstan's and Sevenoaks, and business dealings with St.
Dunstan's by Donne's friends Sir Robert Rich, Sir Julius Caesar, and Izaak Walton
(see B. W. Whitlock, 'Donne at St. Dunstan's II', *TLS*, 23 Sept. 1955).

[4] Walton specifically states that she died 'in his house but three Moneths before him'
(*Lives*, p. 71), which is not quite accurate as she died in fact at his son-in-law's house
and two, not three, months before her son. Nevertheless, even so careful a writer as
Jessopp (p. 195), and Gosse (ii. 295) following him, state that Donne's mother survived
him by nearly a year.

that the death of his mother, as well as his own approaching end, hangs over Donne's last sermon.

It is possible that his mother's illness and funeral delayed Donne's departure for London. There is no evidence that he fulfilled his intention of preaching in St. Paul's on Candlemas day; Walton merely says that he had received notice to preach at Whitehall on the first Friday in Lent, which in 1631 fell on 12 February, and came to London 'some few days before his appointed day of preaching'. Those who had not seen him since his illness were horrified at the change in his appearance, for his ailment had wasted him away, and, believing his strength too small for the task, attempted to dissuade him from appearing at Whitehall. But he 'passionately denied their requests'. His sermon had already been prepared to the last detail, and it must have been written out in full, since it is unlikely that it would have been subsequently prepared for publication.[1]

It would be impossible to improve on Walton's account of Donne's last days,[2] and of its authenticity there can be no question. While it is unlikely that he heard Donne's last sermon, he must have been able to speak to some who did, and for other details, where his own first-hand knowledge could not be drawn upon, he would have had the word of men like Henry King and Thomas Mountfort, who probably saw Donne almost daily during the last weeks of his life. More than thirty years later King wrote to Walton recalling that Donne 'but three days before his death delivered into my hands those excellent Sermons of his now made publick; professing before Dr. *Winniff*, Dr. *Monford*, and, I think, your self then present at his bed side, that it was by my restless importunity, that he had prepared them for the Press'.[3] Here then, is King's testimony to Walton's presence at an episode of some importance that took place in Donne's bedroom during his last illness.

Donne seems to have consulted his doctor as soon as he returned to London. This was his friend Dr. Simeon Fox, youngest son of John Fox, author of the *Boke of Martyrs*, who had probably not seen

---

[1] It may have become his habit, especially after he had been in trouble over one of them in 1627, to write out his Court sermons in full; or it may be that on this last occasion he mistrusted his strength and felt that he might need his manuscript.

[2] *Lives*, pp. 74–83.   [3] Ibid., pp. 14–15.

him since the beginning of his illness. Fox seems to have felt that the most urgent thing was to try to build up his strength and put some flesh on his bones, and said 'That by Cordials, and drinking milk twenty days together, there was a probability of his restauration to health'. This Donne, who disliked milk, 'passionately' refused to do, though Fox, 'who loved him most intirely', persisted in his request, and eventually persuaded his patient to drink milk for ten days. At the end of that period he refused to take any more, and told Dr. Fox 'that he would not drink it ten days longer upon the best moral assurance of having twenty years added to his life'.

On Friday, 25 February Donne duly came to the chapel at Whitehall to preach:

when to the amazement of some beholders he appeared in the Pulpit, many of them thought he presented himself not to preach mortification by a living voice: but, mortality by a decayed body and a dying face . . . after some faint pauses in his zealous prayer, his strong desires enabled his weak body to discharge his memory of his preconceived meditations, which were of dying: the Text being, *To God the Lord belong the issues from death*. Many that then saw his tears, and heard his faint and hollow voice, professing they thought the Text prophetically chosen, and that Dr. Donne *had preach't his own Funeral Sermon*.

The effort of preaching left Donne exhausted, and after returning home he rested quietly for a day or so. Walton tells of a friend who saw him on the day after his sermon, and asked him why he was sad. Donne denied that he was, and went on to describe the thoughts that occupied his mind:

at this present time, I was in a serious contemplation of the providence and goodness of God to me: to me *who am less than the least of his mercies*; and looking back upon my life past, I now plainly see it was his hand that prevented me from all temporal employment; and that it was his Will I should never settle nor thrive till I entred into the Ministry; in which, I have now liv'd almost twenty years (I hope to his glory) and by which I most humbly thank him, I have been enabled to requite most of those friends which shewed me kindness when my fortune was very low, as God knows it was: and (as it hath occasioned the expression of my gratitude) I thank God most of them have stood in need of my requital. I have liv'd to be useful and comfortable to my good Father-in-law Sir *George Moore*, whose patience God hath been pleased to exercise with many temporal Crosses; I have maintained my own Mother, whom it hath pleased God after a plentiful fortune in her younger days, to bring to a great decay in her very old age. I have quieted the Consciences of many that have groaned under the burthen of a wounded spirit, whose prayers I hope are available for me: I cannot plead innocency of life, especially of my youth: But I am to be judged by a merciful God, *who is not willing to see what I have done amiss*. And, though of my self I have nothing to present to him but sins and misery; yet, I know he looks not upon me now as I am of my self, but as I am in my Saviour, and hath given me even at this present time some testimonies by his Holy Spirit, that I am of the number of his Elect: *I am therefore full of unexpressible joy, and shall dye in peace.*

Two things emerge here. First, Donne was able to look back over his past life and see it as a whole; he discerned a divine purpose directing it. He felt that God had used him as an instrument of his power and grace, and had brought him to a safe haven. Secondly, there had also come to him a sense of illumination, which brought with it the assurance of salvation. At last he had achieved the certain knowledge of God's favour to him, of which he had been so doubtful in that period of spiritual crisis during which he wrote the 'Holy Sonnets', and of which doubts came back to haunt him even in the illness of which he wrote in the *Devotions*. It was characteristic of his complex and divided mind that even after his ordination uncertainties should sometimes press upon him, but now at last they were all banished by the 'testimonies of the Holy Spirit' which had been vouchsafed to him.

In considering the final weeks of Donne's life the reader must remember that the seventeenth century, unlike the twentieth, made no attempt to turn away its face from the facts of death and to remove from everyday life all the constant reminders of its omnipresence. Earlier ages faced death more realistically, and the Londoner who had lived through a plague year knew far more about its horrors than a large proportion of those who live in the western world today. Life, men thought then, was a preparation for death, and it behoved each one to be ready to meet it. The surest way to meet such a moment was to have been through it often in the mind, to have endured it all in anticipation, and so to be able to meet it with the confidence becoming a Christian who trusted in the saving grace of Christ's sacrifice. There were many manuals instructing men how to die; the scholar kept a skull on his desk or carried some other *memento mori* on his person; the great man who fell from high place was judged by the propriety of his behaviour on the scaffold.

> Of death and judgment, heaven and hell
> Who oft does think, must needs die well,

wrote Sir Walter Raleigh,[1] and events were to put him to the test.[2]

Walton's account of Donne's last days, then, may seem extravagant, even macabre, to the twentieth century, but it was in the tradition of his own age and evoked much admiration. Donne's lifelong talent for the dramatic gesture and the still vital force of his own personality enabled him to make of his own death a kind of new ritual expressing the doctrines of his religion. He had contemplated death for many years and had passed beyond its horrors so that he could welcome it as the gateway to eternal life.

Though weakened by illness and conscious that his earthly life was approaching its end, Donne was present at an Assembly of the governors of the Charterhouse on 26 February 1630/1;[3] and this was probably the last engagement away from home that he was able to keep. His will makes it clear that some time previously the residentiaries had at his request assigned him a place of burial in the Cathedral, in the south aisle behind the choir, not far from the monument of Dean Colet. Dr. Fox, who by this time had evidently given over trying to persuade his patient that careful dieting could restore his health, raised with Donne the question of a monument to be erected over his grave. Donne consented to a monument, and it was left to him to determine the design. Walton then tells how Donne, with a fixed plan already in his mind, first caused a wooden urn to be carved and then procured a plank the size of his body.

---

[1] This couplet appears at the end of some texts of 'The Pilgrimage', but is not found in all, and editors have tended to look on it as spurious.

[2] Cf. B. Langeston, 'Essex and the Art of Dying', *HLQ*, xiii (1950), especially pp. 112–18.

[3] See Chap. XV, p. 424, n. 3.

Then, when charcoal fires had been lighted in his study, he took off his clothes, and had his shroud put on him, with knots tied at head and foot. With the shroud turned back to show his face, and his face towards the east, he stood on the urn with closed eyes while an artist sketched his figure life-size on the wooden plank. This drawing Donne kept at his bedside to remind him of what he was soon to be, and it provided the sculptor of the monument with a design from which to work. Droeshout, the engraver of the frontis-piece to *Deaths Duell*,[1] must also have copied this drawing, and the engraving gives a far truer portrayal than the monument of the sunken and emaciated flesh of the dying man.

A few days after the picture had been drawn Donne left his study for the last time and thereafter remained in his bedroom; he was conscious of growing weakness. Then, from time to time he sum-moned various friends to his bedside and took a last leave of them; it was probably on such an occasion that Walton was present with the three residentiaries when Donne handed over the manuscripts of his sermons to Henry King. After all these farewells had been taken 'he appointed his servants, that if there were any business yet undone that concerned him or themselves, it should be prepared against *Saturday* next; for after that day he would not mix his thoughts with any thing that concerned the world'. These instruc-tions are confirmed by the Cathedral registers in which are enrolled a lease, two bonds, and two grants of offices, all dated 21 March

---

[1] Donne's last sermon was entered in the Stationers' Register, under the hands of the two Wardens and the Revd. Thomas Buckner, chaplain to the Archbishop of Canterbury, on 30 Sept. 1631, though not with the title (beginning *Deaths Duell*) under which it appeared in print (with the date 1632 on the title-page). On the previous 13 June there is an entry of a 'booke called *Deaths Duell* by W.C.', i.e. Walter Colman, which appeared, presumably after Donne's sermon, as *La Dance Machabre, or Death's Duell*. After his poem, Colman added on the final page 'The Authours Apologie for the title of his Booke iniuriously conferd by *Roger Muchill*, vpon a Sermon of Doctor *Donnes*', beginning

> Death in a furie hath the Fellon tooke
> That stole my Title, *Donne*, to grace thy booke . . .
> I am but too much honord to be stil'd
> Th'vnwilling Gossip to thy vnknowne child.

He added an unflattering Epitaph on Roger Michell, the publisher of Donne's sermon. See G. L. Keynes, *TLS*, 24 Sept. 1938, p. 620, and Rosemary Freeman, *English Emblem Books*, 1948, p. 239; and for Colman, *DNB*. Donne's sermon has often been reprinted (cf. *Sermons*, x. 33), [most recently in *John Donne—Selected Prose*, chosen by Evelyn Simpson, ed. Helen Gardner and T. Healy, 1967].

1630/1. Donne granted the office of Auditor of the Cathedral to James Singleton, and the office of Collector of the New Works to his servant and friend Thomas Roper. These are the last entries in the volume of the register that bears Donne's name.[1]

'And now he was so happy as to have nothing to do but to dye.' Walton says that he lay quietly for fifteen days awaiting his end, though actually it was ten days after his last transacting of Cathedral business that his end came:

in the last hour of his last day, as his body melted away and vapoured into spirit, his soul having, I verily believe, some Revelation of the Beatifical Vision, he said, *I were miserable if I might not dye*; and after those words, closed many periods of his faint breath, by saying often, *Thy Kingdom come, Thy Will be done*. His speech, which had long been his ready and faithful servant, left him not till the last minute of his life, and then forsook him not to serve another Master (for who speaks like him) but dyed before him, for that it was then become useless to him that now conversed with God on earth, as Angels are said to do in heaven, *only by thoughts and looks*. Being speechless, and seeing heaven by that illumination by which he saw it; he did, as St. *Stephen, look stedfastly into it, till he saw the Son of man, standing at the right hand of God his Father*; and being satisfied with this blessed sight, as his soul ascended, and his last breath departed from him, he closed his own eyes; and then disposed his hands and body into such a posture as required not the least alteration by those that came to shroud him.

Donne died on 31 March; his funeral took place on 3 April.[2] In his will he had asked to be buried 'in the moste private manner that maye be', but his wish was not granted, for (to quote Walton once more) 'beside an unnumbred number of others, many persons of Nobility, and of eminency for Learning, who did love and honour him in his life, did shew it at his death, by a voluntary and sad

---

[1] Only two later entries in the St. Dunstan's records mention Donne by name, but in connection with matters that were the responsibility of the vestry. On 19 Apr. 1631 the Junior Warden paid a bill for bread 'lefte vnpaid by Mr Doctor Dunne wch by his appoyntemt was deliuered in the firste 3 yeres of his being Viccar here', but this was bread which the vestry distributed regularly to the poor (cf. Minutes, p. 121, of a meeting in 1627 at which in Donne's presence the vestry ordered the payment of the baker's account). On 20 Oct. 1631 the 'Farmers to Dr Dunne of the tythes of this parish' paid in the money collected. Cf. Whitlock, loc. cit.

[2] The date of his death is given in his epitaph, that of his funeral in the funeral certificate at the College of Heralds.

attendance of his body to the grave, where nothing was so remark-able as a publick sorrow'. It has been said[1] that Laud preached Donne's funeral sermon; this is possible, but doubtful. The state-ment is based on Sir Lucius Cary's 'Elegy on Dr. Donne', in which Cary exclaims:

> Let Lawd his funerall Sermon preach, and shew
> Those vertues, dull eyes were not apt to know.[2]

But Cary is merely enumerating the things that ought to happen on so sad an occasion, not the things that have happened. In the lines immediately preceding he envisages Jonson paying a poetical tribute to Donne:

> Whil'st Johnson forceth with his Elegie
> Teares from a griefe-unknowing Scythians eye,

but Jonson is not known to have written anything on the occasion of Donne's death. If Laud had preached at Donne's funeral we should probably have heard of the fact from other sources as well. Nevertheless Donne received all the tributes of admiration and grief that the age lavished on those whom it cherished. An anony-mous versifier inscribed an epitaph in charcoal on the wall above the grave:

> Reader! I am to let thee know,
> *Donne*'s Body only, lyes below:
> For, could the grave his Soul comprize,
> Earth would be richer then the skies,

and until the paving stones were replaced that had had to be removed for his grave, the earth that covered his body was heaped with a succession 'of curious and costly Flowers'.[3]

The executors secured probate of Donne's will two days after the funeral and proceeded to carry out his instructions for the dis-position of his property. There was probably a schedule attached to the will that has not survived, for in directing that his plate and books should be sold, Donne qualified this by adding, 'such bookes only beinge excepted as by a Scedule signde with my hand I shall

---

[1] By Gosse, ii. 285 and W. H. Hutton, *History of the English Church from the Accession of Charles I to the Death of Anne*, 1903, p. 112.

[2] Grierson, i. 380.   [3] Walton, *Lives*, p. 82.

give awaye'. Henry King in his will bequeathed to his sister his
'great French Bible with prints, which once belonged to my
honored Friend Doctor Donne'; Donne's copy of the *Chirurgia Magna*
of Paracelsus bears the notation in a later owner's hand, 'bought in
Duck Lane 13. 10^ber. 1633 preciũ 7s. 6d.'. The first book was almost
certainly listed in the schedule of gifts, the second was bought from
the bookseller who disposed of Donne's books. A copy of St.
Gregory's *Pastoral Care* with both Donne's and Walton's signatures
on the title-page could have come to Walton in either way, but was
probably given to him by Donne.[1]

Donne made no provision in his will concerning his literary
property, nor was it to be expected that in that age he should. His
poems had passed into manuscript circulation, and it was beyond
his power to recall them, but while alive he had doubtless been able
to stop their publication. After his death they soon appeared, and
even Donne's clerical friends made no attempt to suppress them.
But Donne's unpublished manuscripts, which were very considerable in bulk, were a different matter. As King recalled, Donne had on
his death-bed handed over the manuscripts of his sermons, telling
King that because of his importunity they had been written out
and prepared for the press. At the same time, King says, Donne
gave him 'all his Sermon-Notes, and his other Papers, containing
an Extract of near Fifteen hundred Authors'.[2] There is no need to
doubt King's good faith, and the fact that Walton published King's
statement makes it clear that it tallied with his own recollection;
nevertheless, Donne had declared earlier that he had transcribed
the sermons for his son's use, and that he hoped that his labours
would be of profit to his son if the latter entered the ministry.
Accordingly, the younger Donne seems to have thought that he
had a claim to his father's papers and a duty laid upon him to give
them to the world.[3] John Donne Jr. made use of Walton to secure
these papers, and apparently refused to return them. 'How these
were got out of my hands,' King wrote to Walton, 'you, who were

---

[1] Keynes, p. 207, and items L 135 and L 89. [Donne gave Walton a copy of Richard
Montague's 'A Gagg for The New Gospel, No: A New Gagg For An Old Goose',
1624; see R. S. Pirie, *TLS*, 23 Dec. 1965, p. 204.]

[2] Walton, *Lives*, p. 15.

[3] See the statement of the younger Donne in Appendix D.

the Messenger for them, and how lost both to me and your self, is not now seasonable to complain.' It is probably unnecessary to deplore the younger Donne's efforts to profit himself by means of his father's unpublished remains, since if they had stayed in King's hands the likelihood of their publication would have been less, and there is a strong probability that they would have perished when the soldiers of the Parliamentary army overran the Bishop's palace at Chichester in 1643.

Not long after Donne's death the executors received the gift of 100 marks (£66. 13s. 4d.) towards the erection of a monument. The gift was anonymous, and it was not known until after the death of Dr. Fox some years later that he was the donor. Nicholas Stone's account book records the arrangement made with the executors under the date 18 July 1631: 'Agreed with the Right Wor*ship*full Doctor Monford and Doctor King Ex*e*cetors of the Will and testament of Doctor Done for on monement of whit and Blak marbell for and in memorell of Doctor Done for the wich I am to have on hundred and twenty ponds and I received in part thar of in plat the som of fifty sixe pond 8 shillens and 6d.' Then follows a list of the plate, which was credited at the rate of 5s. 1d. an ounce.[1] One wonders if the plate had been Donne's (for he had given directions in his will that his plate, like his library, was to be sold), and if the balance was paid for by Dr. Fox's gift. Stone gave some of the work on the monument to carvers who worked for him; for instance, on 27 February 1631/2 he agreed with Humphrey Mayer 'for the finesheri of Doctor doons pictor for the which he is to have 8 poond', and on 14 May following he came to an agreement with Robert Flower 'for the nech [niche] of Doctor done and the under stone and the tabell [tablet]' for £6. Not until 30 November 1632 was the monument completed, when Stone paid Mr. Babbe 10s. 'for Doctor Dones tabell of inscription and blaking the wall'.[2]

From the first the monument attracted a great deal of attention. Engravings of it appeared in the second edition of Henry Holland's *Ecclesia Sancti Pauli Illustrata*, 1633,[3] and in Sir William Dugdale's

[1] *The Note Book and Account Book of Nicholas Stone*, ed. A. J. Fineberg, Walpole Society Publications, vii (1919), 85; see also p. 63.
[2] Op. cit., pp. 90–1.   [3] Sigs. E2v–E3.

History of St. Paul's Cathedral, 1658; the epitaph is transcribed in the
1633 edition of Stow's *Survey of London*. Within a short time it was
copied in other monuments, and during the next thirty years a
shrouded figure, whether full length or half length, was carved
over a number of tombs in various parts of England.[1] But in 1666
the Great Fire of London overwhelmed the Cathedral. Miraculously
Donne's monument suffered less damage than any other, and survived almost intact. When Wren's new Cathedral was built it was
stored with other fragments of old sculpture from the ruins in the
crypt, and an engraving in John Peller Malcolm's *Londinia Rediviva*
shows the shrouded replica of Donne propped against a wall. There
it remained throughout the eighteenth century and well into the
nineteenth until it was re-erected in its present position, as near to
its original site as possible.

The niche in which the statue stands is topped by an entablature
containing the epitaph, surmounted in its turn by a coat of arms in
which that of Donne impales the Cathedral's. The Latin epitaph
must have been of Donne's own composition; he had composed
other epitaphs, and this one, especially in its concluding lines, is
characteristic of his thought and expression.

JOHANNES DONNE,
Sac. Theol. Profess.
Post varia studia quibus ab annis
Tenerrimis fideliter, nec infeliciter
incubuit;
Instinctu et impulsu Sp. Sancti, monitu
et hortatu
Regis Jacobi, ordines sacros amplexus
Anno sui Jesu MDCXIV. et suae aetatis XLII.
Decanatu hujus ecclesiae indutus
XXVII. Novembris, MDCXXI
Exutus morte ultimo die Martii MDCXXXI.
Hic licet in occiduo cinere aspicit eum
Cujus nomen est Oriens.[2]

---

[1] Katharine A. Esdaile's *English Church Monuments, 1510–1840* (1946) illustrates two
of them in figs. 107 and 110, and in *TLS*, 23 Aug. 1947, p. 427, Mrs. Esdaile enlarged
her list of such monuments.

[2] Gosse (ii. 282) quotes the translation of Francis Wrangham:

Gosse mentions that the back of the effigy, which faces the niche, is flat, and adds that the sculptor Hamo Thornycroft had pointed out that the direction of the folds of the drapery is that of a recumbent figure. It is probable that Stone's assistant could not conceive of a shrouded figure in any position except a recumbent one. The face, which has lost much of the cadaverousness of the drawing, is almost certainly the work of Stone himself, and it must not be forgotten that in the treatment of the features he had, besides the sketch, his own memories of Donne to draw upon; Donne had come to him to commission the tablet that was put over his wife's grave, and Stone is further likely to have seen Donne in the pulpit from time to time. The statue was felt by Donne's contemporaries to be 'as lively a representation . . . as Marble can express; a Statue indeed so like Dr. *Donne*, that (as his Friend Sir *Henry Wotton* hath expressed himself) *it seems to breath faintly; and, Posterity shall look upon it as a kind of artificial Miracle*'.[1]

We have been so fascinated by the frail figure standing before the painter on the wooden urn among the glowing braziers that we have forgotten to inquire into the meaning of the role he was trying to enact. It seems to have been Donne's intention to represent the resurrection of the body; the shrouded figure is rising from the funeral urn, and what seems at first glance to be a crouching attitude suggests rather that he is still emerging, and has not yet drawn himself erect. That the resurrection was in Donne's mind is clear from Walton's statement that he faced the east while the

JOHN DONNE,
Doctor of Divinity,
after various studies, pursued by him from his earliest years
with assiduity and not without success,
entered into Holy Orders,
under the influence and impulse of the Divine Spirit
and by the advice and exhortation of King James,
in the year of his Saviour 1614, and of his own age 42.
Having been invested with the Deanery of this Church,
November 27, 1621,
he was stripped of it by Death on the last day of March 1631:
and here, though set in dust, he beholdeth Him
Whose name is the Rising.

The epitaphs of Donne and his wife are transcribed in some brief 'Memoirs' of Donne in Lansdowne MS. 984, ff. 156–7, British Museum.

    [1] Walton, *Lives*, p. 83.

drawing was being made, and the last lines of the epitaph speak of him as watching for the coming of him 'Cujus nomen est Oriens'. The monument was originally placed 'within the choir in the south aisle, against the south east pier of the central tower of St. Paul's'. If, therefore, the niche in which it stood was in the pier (as is shown in Dugdale's plan), and not in the southern wall of the aisle behind the choir (where it stands at present), it must have faced the altar and have looked towards the east, not towards the north as it does today. But why then the closed eyes? One can only suggest that he is but half aroused, and that he dare not yet open his eyes to the glory of the Lord.

But let us leave him in his quiet grave.

APPENDICES

A. CHRONOLOGY OF DONNE'S LIFE

1572   Born at his father's house in Bread Street, London, between 24 January and 19 June.

1576   Father dies (will proved 8 February); mother marries (by July) Dr. John Syminges of Le Priors House, Trinity Lane.

1577?   Sister Elizabeth dies.

1581   Sisters Mary and Katherine die (buried 25 November).

1583   Dr. Syminges and his family move to St. Bartholomew's Close.

1584   Matriculates with his brother Henry from Hart Hall, Oxford, 23 October.

1585   Sister Anne marries Avery Copley (who died in 1591).

1588   Dr. Syminges dies (7 July); mother moves to Southwark (?).

1588–9   ?Donne at Cambridge.

1590   (?; certainly by 7 February 1591) mother marries Richard Rainsford.

1589–91   ?Donne travels abroad.

1591   Enters Thavies Inn (?May).

1592   Admitted to Lincoln's Inn (6 May); keeps Autumn vacation.

1593   Made (6 February) Master of the Revels at Lincoln's Inn; does not keep Easter vacation.

      Signs acknowledgement of receipt of part of his inheritance at the Guildhall (19 June); brother Henry dies in Newgate prison; sister Anne by now married to William Lyly.

1594   Receives further payment of inheritance (11 April). Keeps Easter and Autumn vacations at Lincoln's Inn; is chosen Steward of Christmas (26 November) but declines the office.

1595   Takes Thomas Danby into his service.

1596   Sails on the expedition to Cadiz (June), Faro, Corunna, Ferrol (July); ships return to Plymouth (August).

1597   Sails on the 'Islands' expedition (July); ships return to Plymouth owing to a storm, and sail again (15 August) to the Azores (September); ships return to England (October). Enters service of the Lord Keeper, Sir Thomas Egerton, at York House (?November, or in 1598).

1598 Bill against Christopher Danby (10 May; see Appendix D, III); receives judgement in his favour (29 May).

1599 Bears the sword at the funeral of Egerton's son, Sir Thomas, in Chester (26 September). ?Meets Magdalen Herbert.

1600 (Lady Egerton dies 20 January; Egerton marries Alice, Countess of Derby, ?November.) ?D. takes lodgings beside the Savoy.

1601 (Fall of Essex.) Enters Parliament as member for Brackley (October–December).
Given lease of lands belonging to John Heywood (July) until 1605.
Ann More returns from Loseley with her father; D. marries her secretly (December).

1602 Reveals his marriage to Sir George More (2 February); is imprisoned in the Fleet; is dismissed by Egerton; the Court of Audience upholds the validity of the marriage (27 April).
Moves to Pyrford, home of Francis Wolley.

1603 ? Daughter Constance born.
James I visits Pyrford (10 August) and Loseley (11–12 August).
Death of William Lyly (by 16 August).

1604 Son John born (Spring).

1605 Licence to D. and Sir Walter Chute to travel (16 February). ?Travels to France, and perhaps Italy.
Son George baptized 9 May.

1606 Returns to England (April); moves to Mitcham.

1607 Son Francis baptized 8 January.
Takes lodgings in the Strand (until 1611); unsuccessfully seeks employment in the Queen's household (June).
Latin verses on *Volpone* published (Keynes, no. 69).

1608 Daughter Lucy baptized 8 August, the Countess of Bedford standing as her godmother.
Seeks secretaryship in Ireland (November) through Lord Hay, without success.

1609 Vain attempt to secure secretaryship with the Virginia Company (February).
'The Expiration' published in Ferrabosco's *Ayres* (Keynes, no. 69a).
Daughter Bridget baptized 12 December.

1610 Publishes *Pseudo-Martyr* (January); receives honorary M.A. from Oxford (17 April).

1611 Daughter Mary baptized 31 January.
Ignatius his Conclave published in Latin and in English (Keynes, nos. 1–6).

Attends convivial gathering at the Mitre Tavern; contributes to Coryate's *Crudities* and *The Odcombian Banquet* (Keynes, nos. 70, 70a). Goes with Sir Robert Drury to the Continent (November) leaving wife and children with Ann's brother-in-law, John Oglander, in the Isle of Wight; stay at Amiens.

An Anatomy of the World published (Keynes, no. 74).

1612 *The First and Second Anniversaries* published (Keynes, no. 75).

D. and the Drurys go to Paris; D. ill, learns that his wife had been brought to bed of a still-born child (buried 24 January).

Accompanies the Drurys to Frankfurt (late April), Heidelberg, Spa (July), Maastricht, Louvain, Brussels (August), and back to England (September).

Moves with his family into a house at Drury House.

'Breake of Day' published in Corkine's *Second Booke of Ayres* (Keynes, no. 71).

1613 Pays pew-rent at St. Clement Danes (until 1621).

Visits Sir Henry Goodyer at Polesworth and Sir Edward Herbert at Montgomery Castle (April).

Son Nicholas baptized 3 August (died in infancy).

Elegy on Prince Henry published in 3rd ed. of *Lachrymae Lachrymarum* (Keynes, no. 72).

Illness of D. and his family.

1614 Sits in 'Addled' Parliament as member for Taunton (5 April–7 June) and serves on four select committees.

Daughter Mary buried 18 May.

Last attempt at obtaining state employment.

'Newes from the Very Countrey' published in Overbury's *Wife* (Keynes, no. 73).

Son Francis buried 10 November.

1615 Ordained deacon and priest at St. Paul's Cathedral, 23 January, by Bishop John King.

Appointed a royal Chaplain; attends James I to Cambridge; is made an honorary D.D. (March).

Daughter Margaret baptized 20 April.

Preaches at Greenwich (30 April), at Camberwell and at the Inner Temple (June).

A cipher entrusted to D. for diplomatic correspondence, ?about religious developments abroad (see Appendix D, IV).

1616 Granted rectory of Keyston, Hunts., 16 January.

Preaches at Court (Whitehall) 21 April.

Daughter Elizabeth born 14 June.

Presented with rectory of Sevenoaks 7 July.

Chosen Divinity Reader at Lincoln's Inn 24 October.

1617 Preaches at Paul's Cross 24 March. Witnesses indentures of leases to Christopher Brooke by Lady Drury of property near Drury House. Visits Knole and preaches at Sevenoaks (July).

Wife Ann gives birth to a still-born child (10 August) and dies 15 August.

Preaches at St. Clement Danes, at Whitehall (2 November), and at Denmark House before the Queen (14 December).

1618 Preaches at Court 20 February, 12 and 19 April; and at Lincoln's Inn 'preparing them to build their Chappell'.

Deposes in the suit Leigh *v.* Bridgewater.

1619 Preaches at Court (12 February), to the Countess of Montgomery at the Cockpit (21 February), to the Lords during the King's illness at Newmarket (28 March), and a sermon of valediction at Lincoln's Inn (18 April).

Leaves (12 May) as chaplain with Viscount Doncaster's embassy to Germany.

Preaches at Heidelberg to the Prince and Princess Palatine (16 June and 18 July); at The Hague is presented with a gold medal struck as a memento of the Synod of Dort, and preaches (19 December).

1620 Returns to London with Doncaster's embassy 1 January.

Preaches at Lincoln's Inn (30 January); at the marriage of Sir Francis Nethersole to Lucy Goodyer (February); and at Court (3 March, 2 and 30 April).

Preaches at Lincoln's Inn (Trinity Sunday) and at Camberwell (20 August).

1621 Preaches to the Countess of Bedford at Harrington House (7 January), at Court (16 February, 8 April), and at the wedding of Margaret Washington and Robert Sands (30 May).

The *Anniversaries* republished (Keynes, no. 76).

Resignation from Keyston accepted 20 October.

Elected and installed as Dean of St. Paul's 22 November.

Brings case against Henry Seyliard over his claim to Keyston rectory; judges' commission exhibited in the Court of Delegates 23 November. Preaches in the Cathedral on Christmas Day.

1622 Hearings in Donne *v.* Seyliard in the Court of Delegates 23 and 29

January, 6 February; dispute Seyliard *v.* Scott settled by Sir Henry Martin (see Appendix D, v).

Preaches at (?) Lincoln's Inn on Candlemas Day (2 February).

Resigns his Readership at Lincoln's Inn 11 February.

Preaches at Court 8 March.

Instituted as rector of Blunham, Bedfordshire, 18 April.

Justice of the Peace for Kent and Bedford.

Preaches at St. Paul's (21 April) and at the Spital Cross (22 April).

Made honorary member of the Virginia Company 22 May, and of its Council 3 July.

Preaches at Lincoln's Inn (30 May) and at St. Paul's (24 June).

Appointed as judge in the Court of Delegates 28 June, in Piggott *v.* Corbett (P.R.O., Del. 8/70, ff. 10ᵛ, 13ʳ).

Preaches at Camberwell 14 July.

Patents conferring on D. a stall in the Choir of St. Paul's, a place in the Chapter House, and the prebend of Chiswick (9 August).

Preaches at Hanworth to the Earl of Carlisle and his guests (25 August). Preaches at Paul's Cross 15 September; sermon published as *A Sermon upon the xv. Verse of the xx. Chapter of the Book of Judges* . . . (Keynes, nos. 12, 13, 14).

'The True Character of a Dunce', 'An Essay of Valour', and 'Newes from the Very Countrey' published in Overbury's *Wife* (Keynes, no. 73a).

Preaches at St. Paul's 13 October, 5 November, 25 December.

Hearing of Piggott *v.* Corbett at the Deanery of St. Paul's 21 October (Del. 4/9, fo. 102ʳ).

Preaches to the Virginia Company 13 November; sermon published as *A Sermon upon the viii Verse of the I Chapter of the Acts of the Apostles* . . . (Keynes, no. 15).

1623   Wotton sends D. a cipher from Venice (January).

Appointed to case Coniers *v.* Sunderland in Court of Delegates 29 January (Del. 8/70, ff. 12ʳ, 14ᵛ; cf. C66/2306/1).

Preaches at Court (28 February) and at St. Paul's (?2 February, 28 March).

Attends Council meetings of Virginia Company on 4 and 5 February, 5 March, 7 and 14 May.

Preaches at the dedication of the new chapel at Lincoln's Inn; sermon published as *Encaenia* . . . (Keynes, no. 16).

Approached by the Churchwardens of St. Dunstan's-in-the-West for help in recovering Nicholas Hare's bequest 31 July.

Three Sermons upon Speciall Occasions published (Keynes, no. 17).

Arranges daughter Constance's marriage to Edward Alleyn 21 October (celebrated 3 December).

Preaches for the Law Sergeants' Feast at St. Paul's 23 October.

Present at hearings of Piggott *v.* Corbett on Saturdays 15 and 22 November (Del. 4/9, fo. 239).

Seriously ill with relapsing fever (end of November).

1624   *Devotions upon Emergent Occasions* published (Keynes, nos. 34, 35, 36). Churchwardens of St. Dunstan's call on D. 4 March.

Appointed vicar of St. Dunstan's 18 March.

Preaches at St. Paul's 28 March.

A Sermon upon the Eighth Verse of the First Chapter of the Acts of the Apostles . . . republished (Keynes, no. 18).

Three Sermons upon Speciall Occasions republished (Keynes, no. 17a).

Preaches at St. Dunstan's 11 and 25 April.

At St. Dunstan's, signs Churchwardens' accounts 26 April; makes agreement with parish for payment of tithes 11 May (confirmed 25 June); work begins 11 August on new pulpit and pews.

Commemorative sermons at St. Dunstan's 23 May, 29 June.

Preaches to the Earl of Exeter at St. John's 13 June.

Christmas sermon at St. Paul's.

1625   Preaches at St. Dunstan's (1 January), St. Paul's (30 January), and at Court (4 March).

Death of James I 27 March; D. preaches at Court 3 April a sermon published as *The First Sermon Preached to King Charles* . . . (Keynes, no. 19).

Quarrel with Alleyn.

Preaches at St. Paul's on Easter Day and 8 May; and at Denmark House 26 April.

Signs Senior Churchwarden's accounts at St. Dunstan's 12 May.

D. ill (June).

Foure Sermons upon Speciall Occasions published (Keynes, no. 20).

The *Anniversaries* republished (Keynes, no. 77).

Retires to Chelsea during plague months (by 12 July).

Sends gifts to the poor of St. Dunstan's parish 29 August and 23 December.

Preaches Christmas sermon at St. Paul's.

1626   Preaches at St. Dunstan's (15 January) and St. Paul's (30 January).

Chosen Prolocutor of Convocation (February).

Coronation of Charles I 2 February; D. preaches at Court 24 February a sermon published as *A Sermon, Preached to the Kings M^{tie}* . . . (Keynes, no. 21).

Preaches at Court 18 and 30 April, and at St. Paul's on Easter Day, 21 May and 21 June.

At St. Dunstan's attends vestry meetings 13 April and 8 May; preaches commemorative sermon 29 June.

Alleyn's settlement on D.'s daughter Constance signed 29 June (Alleyn dies 25 November).

Attends vestry meetings at St. Dunstan's 4 July (signs accounts) and 12 July.

Appointed to judge case Williamson *v.* Hilles in the Court of Delegates 9 July (Del. 8/70, fo. 26^r).

Appointed governor of the Charterhouse (after 10 June).

Presents chalice to Blunham Church.

Appointed J.P. of Bedford.

Ignatius his Conclave republished (Keynes, no. 7).

Five Sermons upon Speciall Occasions published (Keynes, no. 22).

Appointed judge in Arnold *v.* Morgan in the Court of Delegates 9 October (Del. 8/70, ff. 26^v, 31^r).

Attends vestry meeting at St. Dunstan's and signs accounts 10 October.

Attends meeting of governors of the Charterhouse 27 October and adjourned meeting 6 November.

Preaches at St. Paul's 5 November.

Attends meeting of governors of the Charterhouse 7 December.

Preaches at funeral of Sir William Cokayne 12 December.

Christmas sermon at St. Paul's.

1627 Daughter Lucy dies (buried 9 January).

Preaches at St. Paul's 28 January and (?) 2 February; and at Court ? 11 February and 1 April.

Attends vestry meeting at St. Dunstan's 30 January (see Appendix D, VI).

Hearing of Arnold *v.* Morgan at the Deanery of St. Paul's 10 February (Del. 4/11, fo. 20^v).

Hearing by D. at his house in case Drewett *v.* Tomes 10 March;

commission of judges exhibited in Court of Delegates on 13 March (Del. 4/11, fo. 29ᵛ; 8/70, fo. 30ʳ).

(Sir Henry Goodyer dies 18 March; the Countess of Bedford dies 31 May.)

Preaches at St. Paul's 25 March and 13 May; and at Paul's Cross 6 May. Attends vestry meeting at St. Dunstan's 29 March and signs accounts 10 May.

Sits on Court of High Commission at sentence of George Huntley 19 April.

Preaches commemorative sermon at St. Dunstan's 20 May.

Attends meeting of governors of the Charterhouse 21 June.

Magdalen Lady Danvers buried 8 June; D. preaches memorial sermon at Chelsea 1 July, published as *A Sermon of Commemoration of the Lady Dāvers* . . . (Keynes, no. 23).

Devotions upon Emergent Occasions republished (Keynes, nos. 37, 38).

Preaches at St. Dunstan's 20 September and 2 December.

Attends vestry meeting at St. Dunstan's 10 October.

Signs letter accompanying summons (11 October) served on William Prynne to appear before the High Commission.

Appointed as judge in Thorrold *v.* Havers in the Court of Delegates 31 October (Del. 8/70, fo. 33ʳ).

Appointed as judge in Wagstaffe *v.* Cockayne in the Court of Delegates 10 November (Del. 8/70, fo. 33ᵛ).

Preaches at the Earl of Bridgewater's house for the marriage of his daughter 19 November.

Present on High Commission at sentence of Viscountess Purbeck 19 November.

Attends hearing in Wagstaffe *v.* Cockayne in Consistory Court within St. Paul's 22 November (Del. 4/11, fo. 121ᵛ).

Preaches Christmas sermon at St. Pauls.

1628   Preaches at St. Paul's 27 January.

Attends hearings in Wagstaffe *v.* Cockayne at Doctors' Commons 30 January and on 7 February (Del. 4/11, ff. 148ᵛ, 156ʳ).

Attends meetings of governors of the Charterhouse 25 February and 19 March.

Preaches at court 29 February, 5 and 15 April; and at St. Paul's 13 April.

Attends vestry meeting at St. Dunstan's 19 April; preaches commemorative sermon there 4 May; and signs accounts on 14 May.

Appointed judge in case Chaundler *v.* Weston in the Court of Delegates 8 May (Del. 8/70, fo. 35ᵛ).

Preaches at St. Paul's 1 June; at St. Dunstan's 29 June.

Commission to Dean and Stagiaries of St. Paul's to administer see of London 4 July; oath administered to D. to fulfil some episcopal functions 8 July (until appointment of Laud 25 July).

Present at hearing of Drewett *v.* Tomes at the Bishop's Palace, London, 8 July (Del. 4/11, fo. 213ᵛ).

Attends vestry meeting at St. Dunstan's 16 July.

Commission 13 July, and appointment 19 July, as judge in the case Vaughan *v.* Colmer.

Acts at his house in the case Aunger *v.* Lisley, Saturday, 27 August; judges' commission for the case exhibited in the Court of Delegates 27 September (Del. 4/11, fo. 219ʳ; 8/70, fo. 38ʳ).

D. ill August–October.

Attends meeting of governors of the Charterhouse 31 October and 8 December.

Preaches at St. Paul's 23 November and Christmas Day.

1629   Preaches at St. Paul's 25 January and (?) Easter Day.

Preaches at Court 20 February and twice in April.

Present at sentence in case Drewett *v.* Tomes at the Bishop's Palace, London, 1 May, and signs sentence (Del. 4/12, fo. 55ʳ; 5/7, no. 34).

Preaches at St. Paul's on Whitsunday.

Signs Churchwardens' accounts at St. Dunstan's 20 May.

Present at hearings in Wagstaffe *v.* Cockayne 9 and 26 June (Del. 4/12, ff. 91ʳ, 99ʳ).

Member of judicial committee considering a dispute of the Bishop with the Dean and Chapter of Salisbury; signs report to the King 22 June.

Attends meeting of governors of the Charterhouse 2 July.

Preaches at Paul's Cross 22 November.

Present at sentence in Chaundler *v.* Weston at Sergeants' Inn, Thursday, 3 December, and signs sentence (Del. 4/12, fo. 153ʳ; 5/7, no. 60).

Attends meeting of governors of the Charterhouse 7 December.

?Christmas sermon at St. Paul's.

1630   Attends vestry meeting at St. Dunstan's 20 January.

Preaches at St. Paul's 25 January.

Present at hearing at Doctors' Commons 26 January, and at sentence in the Hall of Sergeants' Inn, Saturday, 30 January, in Arnold *v*. Morgan (Del. 4/12, ff. 162ʳ, 169ʳ), and signs sentence (Del. 5/7, no. 65).

Present at hearing in Wagstaffe *v*. Cockayne, 29 January (Del. 4/12, fo. 167ᵛ).

Present at sentence in Vaughan *v*. Colmer and signs sentence 1 February (Del. 5/7, no. 66).

Appointed judge in case Denne *v*. Sparkes in the Court of Delegates 9 February (Del. 8/70, fo. 44ᵛ).

Preaches at Court 12 February.

Reprimands Christopher Ruddy in St. Paul's 12 March.

Preaches at St. Paul's on Easter Day and ?Whit Sunday (16 May).

Attends vestry meeting at St. Dunstan's 21 April.

Appointed judge in cases in the Court of Delegates, Cowpland *v*. Senhouse 4 May, and Bridgman *v*. Gregorie 7 May (Del. 8/70, part ii, ff. 1ᵛ, 5ᵛ).

Attends meeting of governors of the Charterhouse 12 May.

Daughter Constance marries Samuel Harvey of Aldborough Hatch 24 June.

'The Broken Heart' and part of 'Goe, and catche a falling starre' printed in *A Helpe to Memory and Discourse* (Keynes, no. 73b).

Beginning of D.'s last illness (Autumn) at Aldborough Hatch.

Makes his will 13 December (see Appendix D, 11).

1631   D.'s mother dies (buried 28 January).

Last sermon at Court 25 February (published posthumously as *Deaths Duell*).

Attends meeting of governors of the Charterhouse 26 February.

Attends to last Cathedral business 21 March.

Dies 31 March (buried in St. Paul's 3 April).

B. DONNE'S CHILDREN

1. CONSTANCE, Donne's first child, was born at Pyrford about the beginning of 1603. During her girlhood, and especially after her mother's death in 1617, she had at times considerable responsibility as a companion and housekeeper for her father. She was a close friend of the daughters of Sir Henry Goodyer, and was warmly welcome at the house of her uncle and aunt, Sir Thomas and Lady Grymes. It was probably through the Grymeses that, after an unsuccessful attempt by Donne to arrange a marriage for her in October 1622, she met Edward Alleyn, whom she married at Camberwell on 3 December 1623. The wedding settlement agreed upon on 21 October 1623 was a point at issue in Alleyn's quarrel with Donne in 1625; a revised settlement was concluded on 29 June 1626, five months before Alleyn's death. On 24 June 1630, at Camberwell, Constance married Samuel Harvey of Aldborough Hatch, near Barking in Essex, and on a visit which Donne made to the couple there in the following August he contracted what turned out to be his last illness. Samuel Harvey was one of the witnesses of Donne's will, made on 13 December 1630. A pedigree of Harvey's grandfather, Sir James, formerly Lord Mayor of London (*Visitation of Essex, 1634*, Harleian Soc., p. 416) shows that Constance had three children by the date of the visitation, John, James, and Thomas; of only one of these has any record survived—the baptism of Thomas at Aldborough Hatch on 13 September 1632 (Barking Parish Register).

2. JOHN, Donne's eldest son, was born at Pyrford (before the middle of May) in 1604. When the family moved to Drury House in 1612 he was sent to Westminster School, of which he became a King's Scholar in 1619. He was elected Student of Christ Church, Oxford, in 1622 (*DNB*; Wood, *Fasti Oxonienses*, ed. Bliss, i, col. 503; cf. Appendix D, no. VIII), and contributed Latin verses to *Carolus Redux* (1623), *Camdeni Insignia* (1624), and *Oxoniensis Academiae Parentalia* (1625) (Keynes, nos. 152–4). His father was hopeful that he would enter the Church, but this decision was delayed, perhaps until shortly before the poet's death. He may have been the John Donne who married Mary Staples at Camberwell on 27 March 1627 (*DNB*), but there is no record that he had any children. He took his M.A.; and by 30 June

1631 he must have been in orders, for on that day he was instituted in the parish of Tillingham, Essex, a living in the gift of the Dean and Chapter of St. Paul's (P.R.O., Index of Institutions, Ser. A, 1556–1660; First Fruits Composition Book. But E331, Dean and Chapter of London, 7, gives the date as 2 July). He seems never to have resided in any of his country parishes, and he was still in Oxford in 1633–4, presumably (as he claims, Appendix D, VIII) awaiting the fulfilment of the King's promise to make him a canon of Christ Church. Laud relates (in his *History of his Chancellorship of Oxford*, *Works*, Oxford, 1853, v. 99) that John Donne Junior, M.A. of Christ Church, was tried on 26 August 1634 for the alleged killing of a boy named Humphry Dunt. From the official University archives it appears that Donne was riding with another Christ Church man along St. Aldate's when the eight-year-old boy startled the horse of Donne's companion; whereupon in a fit of temper Donne struck Dunt four or five times about the head. The boy afterwards complained of pain but went about for eight days, after which he fell ill, and died a fortnight later. Two surgeons and a physician testified that they could not assign the cause of his death, since there was no appearance of hurt, and Donne was acquitted.

He was in Rome in February 1635 (Hist. MSS. Com., 6th Rep., App. p. 279b), and spent two years at Padua, taking the degree of D.C.L. He returned to England in 1637, and was incorporated D.C.L. at Oxford on 30 June 1638. A letter written probably in 1637 shows him travelling with Jerome, Lord Portland, and a Mr. (?Edmund) Waller (M. A. Beese, 'John Donne the Younger . . .', *MLR*, xxxiii (1938), 356–9). He was presented by the King to the living of High Roding, Essex, on 10 July 1638, and also received that of Ufford, Northants., late in the same year. Ufford was apparently in exchange for Tillingham, but the arrangement had not worked smoothly. In April 1639 Donne brought a suit against Richard Titley (Titlor, Tilley), vicar of Bourne, Lincs., who had taken up residence in the parsonage at Ufford and disputed Donne's claim. Titley was ordered to give possession to Donne on 22 May (*C.S.P.* (*Dom.*), *1639*, pp. 33–4, 204), but on 29 November he again appears as rector of Ufford, being replaced on 9 December 1639 by John Palmer (Beese, loc. cit.). Apparently Donne recovered his living, as a document discovered by Professor Leslie Hotson shows (P.R.O., C 2, Chas. I, W/39/19): Alice Wells, widow and executrix of John Wells, gent., on 20 November 1641 brought a suit against John Donne, Doctor of Laws and Rector of Ufford, claiming that in August 1640 John Wells leased the parsonage house of Ufford, etc., from Donne for one year at a rent of £136. 13*s.*; Wells was also to take the tithes by agreement 'as the said John Donne not beinge residente upon his rectorye or parsonage, it could not be beneficiall' to him to keep them in his possession. Afterwards 'the said John Donne did repaire vnto the said John Wells and acquaintinge him with great and vrgente occasions that he the said John Donne had to use seuerall summes of mony by reason of a tryall which he the said John Donne was to haue in his Ma*j*esties Court of common pleas for or concerning his rectory or parsonage of Ufford did earnestly sollicit and importune him the said John Wells to lend and accomidate him with the summe of thirtie pounds' which was to be taken out of the rent. Shortly after the loan John Wells died, and Donne took the tithes and said he had never had a loan; he also said that the tithes were not included in the lease. The outcome of this case is unknown. The Revd. Titley is said to have been presented to Ufford on 29 November '1641' (J. Bridges, *History of Northants.* ii. 603), but this seems to be an error for '1639'. At any rate, in 1643 Titley was still fighting his case; he petitioned the House of Commons for the living, claiming that he had lost it through Laud, who 'admitted Dr. Donne upon a pretended title for the King' (*C.S.P. (Dom.)*, *1641–3*, p. 526). In a letter to Sir Edward Hyde (14 January 1640/1) Donne complained that he was 'cozened' out of the living of Tillingham, by means of a pretended exchange for Ufford, by Thomas Nicholson, his predecessor at Ufford, and by the Revd. Michael Hudson. (Nicholson was rector of Tillingham, as the First Fruits Composition Book shows, on 17 October 1639; Beese, loc. cit.)

Meantime Donne had also acquired the livings of Polebrooke, Northants., in 1639, and of Fulbeck, Lincs., on 10 June of the same year. Earlier, on 14 June 1638, the Lords considered a petition from Donne against his arrest contrary to the privilege of Parliament (*DNB*). In 1643 he is reported as being under restraint (*C.S.P. (Dom.)*, *1625–49*, p. 650). From 1640 until his death he seems to have lived in Covent Garden, and may have been in charge of a church in the area; his burlesque petition on behalf of the inhabitants of Covent Garden to the Lord Chancellor (1661) for the removal of Sir John Baber (q.v., *DNB*) was published as a broadside (Keynes, no. 155). In 1645 Sir George Grymes, Donne's kindly and gullible cousin, filed the complaint printed in Appendix D, IX, with what ultimate success we do not know. In 1648 Donne became chaplain to Basil Fielding, second

Earl of Denbigh (cf. Appendix D, VIII), whom he had probably met in Padua in 1635, and who had become Speaker of the House of Lords on 14 December 1638. It was to Denbigh that he dedicated his father's *Fifty Sermons* in 1649 (Keynes, no. 30).

Donne had got hold of the manuscripts of his father's sermons, sermon notes, and 'an extract of near Fifteen hundred Authors' from Bishop Henry King, apparently using Walton as an intermediary (Walton, *Lives*, p. 15). He tells us (Appendix D, VIII) that Charles I commanded him to print the sermons, and the first volume, *LXXX Sermons*, was published in 1640 with a dedication to the King (Keynes, no. 29). The printing of this book and of *Fifty Sermons* was in 1648 the subject of a law-suit between Donne and the printer Francis Bowman (J. M. French, 'Bowman *v.* Donne', *TLS*, 12 December 1936; R. Krueger, 'The Publication of John Donne's Sermons', *RES*, xv (1964), 131–60). Donne had petitioned Archbishop Laud in 1637 (cf. Grierson, ii, lxvi–lxvii) to help him gain control of others of his father's works that had been published without authority—the *Juvenilia* (for allowing the pirated edition of which in 1632 Sir Henry Herbert was called in question by the Star Chamber; cf. Keynes, p. 72), *Ignatius his Conclave* (Keynes, nos. 8, 9), and the first two editions of the *Poems*. Though Laud supported him, it was not until 1650 that Donne secured the rights of his father's poems and published an edition of them with additional matter (Keynes, nos. 81–3), and with a dedication to William, first Lord Craven. In 1646 he published *Biathanatos*, copies of which, with inscriptions or accompanied by letters, he gave not only to the Earl of Denbigh but also to Lady Kingsmill, 'Mr. Lee at the Cockpitt', Edward Carter (using the same phrasing as in the document in Appendix D, VIII: 'I did not only preach to the present adge, but to our childrens children'), Sir Constantijn Huygens, the Marquess of Newcastle, J. Marckham, and the Earl of Oxford (Keynes, pp. 88–91 and nos. 47, 48). In the same year he apparently edited Corbet's *Poems*, with a dedication to Lady Teynham.

Donne had had the second volume of his father's sermons ready and entered at Stationers' Hall in 1644, but delayed publication for fear of persecution from the Commonwealth government; he complained in that year to Philip Herbert that his study had been often searched and his books sequestered for the use of the Committee. Nevertheless, the book appeared as *Fifty Sermons* in 1649. In 1650, we learn, he offered to give (or sell) all his birds, with one exception, to Lord Conway (he bequeathed his doves to the dramatist Thomas Killigrew);

and Conway was also to receive some books, including books of prints which he had proposed to bequeath to the Earl of Pembroke; Conway was to supply Donne with some venison (*C.S.P.* (*Dom.*), *1650*, pp. 329, 347, 358). The document printed below as Appendix D, VIII, seems to have been preparatory to an address to the Lords Commissioners in similar terms. In July 1651 Donne was again arrested, by a warrant from the Council of State (*C.S.P.* (*Dom.*), *1651*, p. 280). Nevertheless in that year he was able to publish his father's *Letters to Severall Persons of Honour*, and to prepare the *Essayes in Divinity*, which he included, with a reprint of *Ignatius his Conclave*, in the volume of *Juvenilia* (1652), dedicated to Francis Lord Newport (Keynes, nos. 45, 46). In 1658 Donne wrote from Covent Garden to the Earl of Dorset, saying that the Earl of Thanet had given him leave to get a presentation from the State of the rectory of Hartfield, Sussex, from which Dr. Morley had been ejected in 1648; but the Protector had put another man in the living; he therefore proposed to bring a suit before the courts about the matter, and warned Dorset not to give the Protector's nominee any further assistance without consulting counsel (Hist. MSS. Com., 4th Rep., App. p. 310a).[1] In 1660 he published at his own expense the third collection of his father's sermons (as *XXVI Sermons*) with a dedication to Charles II, and edited Sir Toby Mathew's *Collection of Letters*, and *Poems* by the Earl of Pembroke and Sir Benjamin Rudyer. Though other minor pieces have been doubtfully attributed to Donne, he seems certainly to have been the author of a 'Satire on Sir W. Davenant', of which a manuscript survives, and which was published in *Certain Verses . . . to be Reprinted with the Second Edition of Gondibert*, 1653, and in *Merry Drollery*, 1661; his authorship is established in a volume replying to the first of these, *The Incomparable Poem Gondibert Vindicated . . .*, where there is reference to his haunts in Bloomsbury, Finsbury, and Covent Garden.

The younger John Donne seems not to have been notable for distinction of mind, for honesty, or moral sensitiveness. Anthony Wood's description of him (loc. cit.) as 'an atheistical buffoon, a banterer, and

[1] [My colleague, Professor C. M. Williams, has drawn my attention to a letter from John Donne Junior to Henry Martin the regicide, son of the poet's friend Sir Henry Martin, in the Brotherton Collection, Leeds; it is calendared under 'Denne' in 'Henry Marten Papers, Political & Miscellaneous', vol. ii, fo. 55, at the Brotherton Library. Donne thanks Martin for securing the Broad Seal from Lord Commissioner Lisle upon his suit for the living of Hartfield and asks him to influence Colonel Henry Morley in favour of it; it is clear that he is interested only in the tithes and does not mind if the Committee's nominee attends to the actual duties of the parish. The letter is dated from Covent Garden 'Dec: 2[o]', and cannot be later than 1653. W. M.]

a person of over free thoughts: yet valued by K. Ch[arles] II' is well known. He never got his canonry at Christ Church, but he certainly found plenty of opportunity for the exercise of his training as a civilian. He died at the end of January 1662/3, aged 58, and his will was published (Keynes, no. 157) as a broadside in the following month. The will was witnessed by the Earl of Marlborough and William Glasscocke on 2 November 1661, and the Earl of Portland was named as executor. Donne bequeathed all his father's manuscripts to Walton, and returned to Henry King the 'Cabinet' that belonged to his father and the abstracts of authors originally given into King's possession; he left 'Sir Thomas More's head' to his friend Sir Christopher Guise.

3. GEORGE, the poet's second son, was born at Peckham and baptized on 9 May 1605 in the parish church at Camberwell. When the family moved to London in 1611 he presumably accompanied his brother John to Westminster School; he may have been the George Donne (p. 267 above) who entered Broadgates Hall, Oxford, in 1615 at the age of 10. Little is heard of his early manhood, and it is doubtful when he became a soldier. In his letter of 1625 Edward Alleyn mentions that when Constance wished to have a 'little nagg' of her father's she 'Causd Her brother georg to moue [him] for itt in Her be Half'; he was therefore still in England and able to go home at some time between December 1623 and early 1625. In 1627 he took part in Buckingham's unfortunate expedition to the Isle of Rhé, and his father's funeral certificate describes him as Captain and Sergeant-Major on that occasion; evidently at the age of 22 he was an able and fairly promising soldier. He may have been the Lieutenant 'George Don' whose promotion as Captain in 1626 caused Ensign Nathaniel Otby to petition Buckingham 'that he may have the place of lieutenant' (C.S.P. (Dom.), 1625–6, xxiv, no. 66, p. 308; 11 April 1626). Fairly soon after his return to England in 1627, George Donne was sent out to the Island of St. Christopher, or St. Kitt's, as 'cheife commaunder of all the forces' there.

During the autumn of 1629 a Spanish fleet overcame the colonists on the island. In his 'Virginia Reviewed' in the form of a letter to King Charles I (B.M. Harl. MS. 7021, ff. 289–318) George Donne wrote that he had 'Commaunded the defence, [and] Articled the Conditions of Surrender'; the English colonists undertook to return to England, but the Spaniards took five hostages who were to guarantee the return of the 'Men and Shippinge' supplied by the Spaniards to take the colonists home. The hostages were sent to Spain; on 7 March 1629/30 Captain Richard Plumleigh told the Earl of Carlisle (Lord Proprietor of the colonies in the West Indies since 1627) that he had met the hostages, including George Donne and Lieutenant Hay (Carlisle's kinsman) at Cadiz (*C.S.P. (Col.), 1574–1660*, p. 108). The last year of the poet's life was clouded by anxiety about his son's fate. In 'Virginia Reviewed' George claimed that his imprisonment lasted for 'more then five years' (fo. 306^r); but this seems to have been a slight exaggeration, since on 6 December 1633 George Garrard wrote to Strafford that '*George Donne* hath broken Prison at *Cales*, and is come into *England*, my Lord of *Carlile* was so slow in getting him off, that he was constrained to take this Course, to corrupt his Keepers and get away' (*The Earl of Strafforde's Letters and Dispatches*, 1739, i. 167).

'Virginia Reviewed' was written after the Earl of Carlisle's death (which took place on 25 April 1636); it was 'my firste Presumption, very likely, my last' (fo. 316^v); it acknowledged the King's 'serenity and grace, which was pleased to vouchsafe I dare not more acknowledge a motion, then a treaty for my enlargement' (fo. 306^v), and spoke of 'The memory of yor gracious Excellent singular favours to my father in his life and vnto his end', which 'requires the best of my Services; If I deserue the hono^r of being acknowledged his sonne; or the greater, of liveinge vnder yor scepter. The bounty of your Grace to my selfe, during my Imprisonment in Spaine, freely granted, formerly mentioned Comaunds and ever shall Comaund the All, what I am . . . / Yo^r Maiesties / Most humble Subiect / George Donne.' The purpose of the document is not made clear; perhaps Donne was merely hoping for some preferment. In the course of the letter he twice refers to the military preparedness of Virginia; he complains of the lack of firearms there for purposes of instruction, and later explains why St. Kitt's was easily taken and why, by contrast, Virginia could be easily defended and held. He mentions the Governor of Virginia, Sir John Harvey, and 'delinquent' planters. (His comments on the people of New England are more severe—'in A manner desperate *Enthusiasticks*'); and, as the document given in Appendix D, IX, shows, he was in fact on his way to Virginia when he died. Nevertheless he does not actually say that he had ever been in Virginia, and chronology seems to forbid our identifying him positively with the Sergeant-Major George Donne who became Muster-Master-General and Marshal of Virginia.

A petition of this George Donne to the King (*C.S.P. (Col.)*,

1574–1660, vi, no. 25) in August 1631(?) states that 'he was appointed and filled' these positions 'from the time of his going over with Sir John Harvey [1628?] until employed by Gov. Harvey as agent for the colony, to prosecute those persons that were lately seditious and disturbed the peaceable government, but is now returning to his charge. Prays for a confirmation . . . of the office which he has filled these two years past [i.e. apparently since 1629]'; confirmation was quickly given. Sergeant-Major Donne was associated with other business in the colony on 20 February and 30 March 1637 (op. cit., pp. 245–6, 250). In 1639 he petitioned on behalf of Harvey that, since the five planters who were sent as prisoners to England and were proceeded against in the Star Chamber for deposing Harvey from the governorship had taken advantage of Donne's illness and Harvey's 'present want' to petition the Lord Keeper and the Attorney-General to report on their case, Harvey should be heard by counsel with all speed 'that they may be punished as they deserve' (op. cit., p. 314). The petition of the planters is referred to in *Acts of the Privy Council* (*Col. Ser.*), *1613–80* (p. 262): on 2 August 1639 it was represented that they had been in England for about three years and their case had not been decided, and were now petitioning to be allowed to return to attend to their estates in Virginia, on bond of their wives and children that they would attend for judgement at convenient notice. 'Their Lordshipps vppon consideration had thereof alsoe for that John Donne [*sic*] the prosecutor on behalfe of Sir John Harvey is lately dead. Sir John Harvey himselfe remaineing yet by occasion of sicknesse in Virginia' (see H. L. Osgood, *The American Colonies in the Seventeenth Century*, iii (1926), p. 101). In 1641 (?August) John West was appointed Muster-Master-General 'vice George Dunn deceased' (cf. *C.S.P.* (*Col. Ser.*), *1574–1660*). This evidence seems to show that the Muster-Master-General had been at work in Virginia during years in which the poet's son was a prisoner at Cadiz and that he was not likely to have been on his way back to the colony at the time of his death. The statement of Sir George Grymes (Appendix D, IX) suggests that the poet's son was rather a man making a desperate bid to recover his fortunes by trying a new venture in Virginia than the Marshal of the colony returning there after executing an important duty on the Governor's behalf. Further, if the poet's son were the Marshal we should expect to find in 'Virginia Reviewed' more specific reference to the turbulent career of Harvey in the colony; and he would have been unlikely to refer to the document as his 'first presumption' on the King's notice. Yet the dating of the documents cited on p. 554 is dubious; and it would be too improbable a coincidence that there should have been two Sergeant-Major George Donnes interested in Virginia who died in the same year.

If the poet's son was not the Muster-Master-General, we are at a loss to know how he was occupied after his escape from Cadiz at the beginning of December 1633. His letter to the King, and Grymes's report that he lacked £5 in cash to pay a debt before leaving the country, suggest that he was not prospering. In 'Virginia Reviewed' he mounts a gauche display of erudition (citing Boethius, Plutarch, Cicero, Lactantius, Tacitus, Bodin, Cardan, Montaigne, Scaliger, etc.), but the letter shows a complete lack of literary competence. Hence there is little to support the suggestion (by Hunter, *Chorus Vatum*, B.M. Add. MS. 24,491, p. 171), that he was the George Donne who has poems before the works of Ford and Massinger and in *Jonsonus Virbius* (1638), or the G. D. who has Latin verses before Sir Thomas Hawkins's translation of Horace's *Odes*. He was married, since his daughter Margaret was baptized on 22 March 1638 at Camberwell (W. H. Blanch, *Yᵉ Parish of Caṁerwell*, p. 172; Gosse, ii. 297), and Sir George Grymes stated (Appendix D, IX) that about 23 December 1638 George Donne had told him that he was without means to support his wife and child. Grymes's statement also informs us that Donne died on his way to Virginia apparently early in 1639.

4. FRANCIS, baptized on 8 January 1607, at Mitcham (Sir Francis Wolley being perhaps his godfather), was buried on 10 November 1614 at St. Clement Danes.

5. LUCY Donne was baptized at Mitcham on 8 August 1608, the Countess of Bedford standing her godmother. We hear in Alleyn's letter that she was making a lengthy stay with her sister Constance early in 1625; and she was staying either with Constance or with Sir Thomas and Lady Grymes at Peckham when she died unexpectedly. She was buried at Camberwell on 9 January 1627.

6. BRIDGET, baptized on 12 December 1609 at Mitcham, married at Peckham about 1633, Thomas Gardiner, son of Sir Thomas Gardiner of Camberwell. She settled at Camberwell with her husband, and a child was born to them on 7 March 1634 (Gosse, ii. 297; D. Lysons, *The Environs of London*, 1795, i. 89). Thomas Gardiner was buried at Camberwell on 5 November 1641 (see *The Gentleman's Magazine*, 1835, i. 610–11 and ii. 150).

7. MARY, baptized on 31 January 1611 at Mitcham, was buried on 18 May 1614 at St. Clement Danes.

8. Stillborn child buried at Brading in the Isle of Wight on 24 January 1612, while Donne was abroad.

9. NICHOLAS was baptized on 3 August 1613 at St. Clement Danes; he died in infancy, since he was apparently not alive when Donne composed his wife's epitaph in 1617.

10. MARGARET was baptized on 20 April 1615 at St. Clement Danes, Sir Robert Ker standing her godfather. We hear nothing of her girlhood, save that she was ill with smallpox in the summer of 1628. In 1633 she married Sir William Bowles, second son of Robert Bowles, Groom and Yeoman of the Tents to all the sovereigns from Elizabeth I to Charles II. Her eldest daughter was baptized at Chislehurst parish church, but during the Civil War the family left the parish. Lady Bowles and her husband are next heard of after the Restoration, when they lived at Clewer, near Windsor; they had a town house on Clerkenwell Green. Sir William was appointed Gentleman of the Privy Chamber in 1661, J.P. in 1662, Master of the Tents in 1663, and was knighted in 1666. (He applied for a baronetcy, and could have had this honour, but it was changed to a knighthood at his desire, because his extravagant eldest son would have wasted his estates.) Lady Margaret Bowles died on 3 October 1679 at Chislehurst and was buried there, as was her husband in 1681. The couple had three sons: William (died 1697), Charles (born 23 July 1652; died in 1700), and Duodecimus (who died before 1681); and five daughters: Margaret, wife of Peter Scott, Rector of Sunning-Hill and Canon of Windsor (Lysons, *Environs of London*, i. 77, notes a monument in Camberwell church to Canon Scott, who died in 1689, and his wife Margaret, who died in 1682); Emma, wife of James Spelman; Elizabeth, wife of James Tempest; Cornelia, wife of John Wight of Katharine Hall, Windsor; and Frances, wife of Thomas Bispham of Lancashire (see Gosse, ii. 375–7).

11. ELIZABETH, who was baptized on 14 June 1616, married on 18 May 1637 Cornelius Laurence, Doctor of Physic, at All Hallows, Barking (Gosse, ii. 297).

12. Stillborn child, buried with Ann Donne on 16 August 1617.

C. DONNE'S LIBRARY

TO the 197 books from Donne's library listed by Sir Geoffrey Keynes in the third edition of his *Bibliography of John Donne* (1958), Appendix iv, some additions have been made, of which the following is a summary.

Professor Bald noted that the book by Serarius, *Rabbini, et Herodes . . .* (Keynes, L166), is bound with a smaller work by the same author, *Lutherus Theosdotos*, issued with separate signatures and pagination by the same publisher, dated 1607 on the title-page, but with a colophon dated 1605. The two books are bound together in original limp vellum, and there are small pencil markings throughout. While at least some copies of the two books were probably issued together, *Lutherus Theosdotos* seems to be a separate work (cf. Maggs Bros., *Mercurius Britannicus*, no. 98, July 1946, item 30).

Mr. Clifford Dobb reported (*TLS*, 30 December 1965) the discovery by Miss H. M. Black, in the Library of the University of Glasgow, of Donne's copy of Giovanni Francesco Bordoni's *De rebus praeclare gestis a Sixto V. Pon. Max. . . . . Carminum liber primus*, Rome, Jacobus Tornerius, 1588, 4°. It has the poet's signature in the bottom right-hand corner of the title-page and his motto 'Per Rachel ho servito, & non per Lea' in the right-hand side of the upper margin; the binding is limp vellum, but the ties are missing.

Sir Geoffrey Keynes has noted Mr. Paul Morgan's discovery of two books at Oxford which once belonged to Donne: (*a*) Paolo Beni, *Qua tandem ratione dirimi possit controversia quae in praesens de efficaci Dei auxilio et libero arbitrio inter nonnullos Catholicos agitatur*, Padua, 1603, 4°. The book has Donne's motto and signature on the title-page, and was bequeathed to Corpus Christi College in 1684 by John Rosewell, a master at Eton; (*b*) Sir Philip Sidney, *Peplus. Illustrissimi viri D. Philippi Sidnaei supremis honoribus dicatus*, Oxford, 1587, 4° (STC 22552). The title-page has the inscription 'Donum cognati mei Johannis Donne', but there are traces of what was probably Donne's motto at the top, the rest having been trimmed off; the book was therefore probably part of the poet's own collection. The copy is in the Library of Balliol College (see *TLS*, 13 January 1966).

In addition, Mr. Morgan discovered two others of Donne's books:

(*a*) Antonius Clarus Sylvius, *Commentarius ad leges . . . Romani iuris antiqui*, Paris, 1603, 4°, with Donne's motto and signature on the title-page, and pencil marks and annotations in the margins. The volume is bound in eighteenth-century calf and bears the signature of George Royse, Provost of Oriel 1691–1708, on a fly-leaf; it is in Oriel College Library; (*b*) Iacobus Pamelius, *Missale SS. Patrum Latinorum*, 2 vols., Cologne, 1609, 4°. The volumes are bound in original calf; each has Donne's motto and signature on the title-page, and each bears the book-plate of John Hall, Master of Pembroke 1664–1710, in the Library of whose college the books are now included (see J. Sparrow, *TLS*, 25 November 1965).

Mr. John Sparrow acquired two parts of a work by Girolamo Menghi, *Compendio dell'Arte Essorcistica*, Venice, Paolo Ugolino, 1599, 8°, and *Parte Seconda Dell'Arte Essorcistica*, Venice, Georgio Varisco, 1601, 8°. The two parts are bound together in limp vellum, and Donne's motto and signature appear on the title-page of the first part (J. Sparrow, *TLS*, 28 February 1958, 6 January 1966).

In the Chapter Library at Windsor Castle Mr. J. Callard discovered Donne's copy of Conrad Schluesselburg's *Haereticorum catalogus*, vol. xiii, Frankfurt, 1599, 8°. The title-page bears his motto and signature, and the book has his characteristic pencil-marks in the margins (J. Callard, *TLS*, 23 December 1965).

The existence of the title-page of another of Donne's books (unspecified) is reported by R. S. Pirie (*TLS*, 23 December 1965).

Of the books which Donne gave away, Sir Geoffrey Keynes, with justice, included as part of Donne's library Gregory the Great's *Pastoral Care* (L89) since the volume bears Donne's signature and was not bought in the first place to be passed on to Izaak Walton (who may, indeed, have bought it after Donne's death); and the same may be said of the *Corpus* of Latin authors (L12) perhaps given by Donne himself to the library of Sidney Sussex College. For a similar reason the Sidney volume mentioned above should be counted as part of Donne's library. But this cannot be said of two further books recently described. Mr. R. S. Pirie also owns a copy of Bishop Richard Montague's *A Gagg for The New Gospel, No: A New Gagg for An Old Goose*, London, 1624 (STC 18038); within the ornament at the top of sig. [π] 2ʳ is written 'Isaak Walton given me by Doc Don 1625' (*TLS*, 23 December 1965). The other gift volume, discovered by Mr. E. J. S. Parsons in the Bodleian Library, is a copy (in German) of Sebastian Munster's *Cosmographia*, Basel, 1578, f°, with the inscription on the fly-leaf,

'Liber Ed: Parvyshe ex dono J. Donne'; for the possible occasion of its presentation, cf. p. 52 n. above. The book is bound in continental blind-stamped pigskin, and the initials 'E P' are stamped in black in a panel on the front cover. It was given by Parvish, with another book, to the Bodleian in 1603; it was first described by Mr. John Sparrow (*TLS*, 25 November 1965; correspondence ensued in *TLS*, 9 December 1965, 6, 13, 20, and 27 January 1966, from L. Forster, J. Sparrow, G. Keynes, and I. A. Shapiro).

Counting the two volumes by Pamelius and the two parts of Menghi's book as single works, the number of books now known to have been in Donne's library may reasonably be said to be 206.

D. APPENDIX OF DOCUMENTS

1. *The Will of Donne's Father*

In the name of God Amen   The Sixtenth Daie of Januarie 1575 And In the Eightenth yere of the Raigne of o^r Sov*e*raigne Ladie Quene Elizabeth—I John Donne Citizen and yremonger of London being sick in bodie but of good and perfitt mynde & remembraunce Doe make this my present testament in forme following. That is to saie. First and principallie I geve and Comend my soule into the hands of Allmightie God my maker saviour and Redeamer in whome and by the merrit*es* of the second person Jesus Christ I trust and beleve assuredlie to be saved and to haue full and clere remission and forgevenes of my synnes. And I com*m*ytt my bodie to the earth to be buried in the p*a*rishe of Saint Nicholas Olive in Bredstreat in London where I am nowe a parrisheon*er* in suche convenyent place there as shalbe apointed by my executrix herunder named. And after that done Then I will that all my goods and Chattells, plate, househoulde stuffe, Redie money and debt*es* and all other my moveable goods and Chattells whatsoeuer shalbe devided into three equall and indifferent partes and Por*t*ions accordinge to the laudable vse and custome of the Cittie of London Wherof one equall parte therof I geve and bequeath vnto Elizabeth my wief to her owne propper vse. And one other equall parte therof I geve and bequeath to and amongest all my children aswell nowe livinge as to the childe which my wief nowe goeth withall equallie amongest all my said children to be devided porcion and porcion like. And to be paid to my said children equallie porcion and porcion like That is to saie when my said sonnes shall come to their ages of Twentie and one yeres And my said Daughters shall accomplishe their seuerall lawfull ag*es* of Twentie and one yeres or mariage. And the other parte therof I Reserve to my selfe and to my executrix hervnder named to paie my debt*es* and performe my legacies hervnder expressed. And the Remainder of my said parte my debt*es* and legacies paid and performed I whollie geve and bequeath vnto my said executrix and my children equallie amongest them to be devided por*t*ion and por*t*ion like & everie of my said children to be heire to other yf death shall happen vnto anye of them in the meane tyme.

Item I geve and bequeath vnto Mr Frauncis Sandbache one hundreth pounds in money to be emploied in deedes of Charitie and Relief of poore people at his discretion within six monethes after my decease. Item I geve and bequeath vnto Mr Edmond Adamson gent one hundred poundes in money to be likewise emploied and bestowed by him in workes of Charitie and of releving of poore and nedie persons at his discretion within the like space of Six monethes next after my decease. Item I geve and bequeath vnto Christofer Rust gent one hundreth pounds in money to be by him employed and bestowed in workes of charitie and releving of poore and impotent people within the space of three monethes after my decease at his discretion. Item I geve and bequeath vnto the worshipfull companie of the Iremongers in London wherof I my selfe am a member the some of Tenne pounds in money. Item I geve and bequeath to my lovinge Frends Robert Est and William Skydmore Tenne pounds a pece in money to make them and their wyeves Rynges with deaths heddes. Item I geve and bequeath vnto John Ewstace Iremonger Tenne Pounds in money to make him and his wief ringes with deaths heddes. Item I geve and bequeath vnto Robert Harryson salter my best gowne welted wth veluett and faced wth Budge. Item I geve and bequeath vnto the beadle of the said Companye of Iremongers my best gowne faced with Damaske and not garded with veluett. Item I geve and bequeath vnto xii poore men whiche shall attend vpon my bodie to buriall xii gownes. Item I geve and bequeath vnto the prisons in london and the suburbes therof that is to saie Newgate, Ludgate, the Flete, the twoe Compters, in the Poultrie and Woodstrete and to bedlem, and to the Relief of the poore prisoners in the Kinges benche the marshalsey the White Lyon and the Compter in Southwarke Twentie shillinges a pece. Item I geue and bequeth vnto and amongest the poore people harboured in the hospitalls of Christe Churche, S^t bartholomews Bridwell and Saint Thomas in Southwark Twentie pounds. That is to saie, To everie of the same hospitalls five pounds. Item I geve and bequeath vnto my brother Dawson of the Cittie of Oxford One hundreth Markes in money. Item I geve and bequeath vnto my Syster Marven a gowne of blacke clothe. Item I geve and bequeath vnto my said brother Dawson & my syster his wief & to their twoe children and to everie of them gownes of blacke clothe. Item I geve & bequeth vnto my cozen Alice Donne nowe dwelling with me Twentie pounds in money to be paid vnto the said Alice at her age of Twentie and one yeres (yf she so longe shall live). Item I geve and bequeath vnto John Dawlsoll my kynnesman the some of Tenne pound*es* in money to be paid to the said John within three monethes next after my decease. Item I geve & bequeath to and amongest the poore people dwelling in the p*a*rishe of Saint Nicholas Olave aforesaid to be delt & distributed By the person and Chirchewardens of the said parrishe chirche where most nede shall apear w*th*in one weeke next after my decease the some of three pounds in money. Item I geve and bequeath vnto John Sayward parson of the said parrishe chirche Twentie Shilling*es*. Item I geve and bequeath vnto my servaunt John White Six pounds thirten shillings and fouer pence in money. Item I geve & bequeath vnto Agnes Cow-p*er* and Agnes Dawson my maiden Aunt*es* and to eche of them fyftie shillings apece. Item I geve and bequeath vnto Christofer Rust gent three pounds in goulde to make him a Ringe to be engraved with a deathes hedd. Item I giue and bequeath vnto my cozen John Heywood three pound*es* in golde to make him a ringe w*th* a deathes hedd. The Resydue of my third parte of all & singuler my goods Chattells plate, househoulde stuffe redie money and debts and all other my moveables whatsoever my debt*es* paid my legacies and this my will perfourmed accordinglie I whollie geve and bequeath vnto and amongest Eliza-beth my wief and my children porcion and porcion like. And I make and ordaine the said Elizabeth my wief sole executrix of this my Testa-ment and last will And overseers of my said Testament to see the same trulie performed accordinglie, I ordaine and make M*r* Franc*is* Sandbache Esquier and Edmond Dauison gent. And I geve and bequeath vnto either of them for their paines to be taken in that behalfe five pounds in goulde apece to make either of them a Ringe with a deathes hedd Requiring them to be ayding and assisting to my said Executrix in the dew execu*t*ion of this my present testament as my trust is in them. Item I geve and bequeath vnto Mr*es* Plankney Twentie shillinges. And I doe by this my present Testament revoke & adnithilat [*sic*] all other wills and Testament*es* by me hertofore made, and I will that none of them shall stand or abide in force or effect but onlie this my present Testament in suche manner and forme as I haue afore willed and devised. In witnes wherof to this my present Testament and last will I the said John Donne haue sett my seale the daie and yere abouewritten. By me John Donne witnesses herunto, Robert Harrison salter Will*ia*m Brodbanke scrivener, and John White.

[*Somerset House, P.C.C. 56 Pyckering, proved 8 February 1575/6*]

II. *Donne's Will*

In the name of the holy blessed and glorious Trinitie Amen: I *John Donne* by the mercye of Christe Jesus and by the callinge of the Churche of Englande *Preist* beinge at this tyme in good & perfect vnderstandinge praysed be God therfore doe hereby make my last Will and Testament in manner and forme following Firste I giue my good & gracious God an intire Sacrifice of Body & Soule wth my most humble thank*es* for that assurance wch his blessed Spiritt ymprint*es* in me nowe of the Salvation of the one & the Resurrection of the other And for that constant & cheerfull resolu*ti*on wch the same Spiritte establishes in me to live & dye in the Religion nowe professed in the Churche of England In expectation of that Resurrection I desyre that my body maye be buryed in the moste private manner that maye be in that place of St Paules Churche London wch the nowe Residentiaries of that Church have bene pleased at my request to assigne for that purpose Item I make my welbeloved Frend*es* Henrye Kinge Doctor of Divinitie & John Montfort Doctor of Divinitie bothe Residentiaries of the Churche of St Paules London Executors of this my Will And my will & desyre is that my verie worthie Friend and kynde Brother in lawe Sr *Thomas Grymes* of Peckham in the Countye of Surrye knighte be Overseer of this my Will To whome I give hereby that Strykinge clocke wch I ordinarilye weare and alsoe the Picture of *Kinge James* To *Doct*or Kinge my Executor I giue that Medall of gold of the Synod of Dort which the States presented me w^thall at the *Hague* as alsoe the twoe Pictures of *Padre Paolo* and *Fulgentio* wch hange in the Parlour at my howse at Pauls And to Doctor Montfort my other Executor I giue Forty ounces of white Plate and the twoe Pictures that hange on the same syde of the Parlo*u*r Item I giue to the Righte hono*u*rable the Earle of Carlile the Picture of the blessed Virgin Marye wch hang*es* in the little Dynynge Chamber And to the Righte hono*u*rable the Earle of Dorsett the Picture of Adam and Eve wch hang*es* in the greate Chamber Item I give to Doctor Winniffe Deane of Gloces*te*r & Residentiarie of St Pauls the Picture call'de the Sceleton wch hang*es* in the Hall And to my kynde Frend Mr George Garrard the Picture of Marie Magdalene in my Chamber And to my ancient frend *Doct*or Brooke Master of Trinitie Colledge in Cambridge the Picture of the B: Virgin and Joseph wch hang*es* in my Studdy And to Mr Tourvall a Frenche Minister but by the ordination of the Englishe Churche I giue any

Picture wch he will chuse of those wch hange in the little Dynynge Rowme & are not formerly bequeathed   Item I give to my twoe faithfull Servant*es* Robert Christmast & Thomas Roper officers of the Churche of St Paule to eache of them Five poundes to make them Seale ringes engrav'd wth that Figure wch I vsuallye sealle w^thall Of wch sorte they knowe I haue given many to my particuler Frendes Item I giue to my Goddaughter Constance Grymes Tenn poundes to be bestowed in Plate for her   Item I giue to that Mayde whoe hathe many yeares attended my Daughters whose name is Elizabeth Twenty poundes if shee shalbe in my service at the tyme of my deathe   And to the other Maydeservant*es* wch shalbe in my service at that tyme I give a yeares wages over and besydes that wch shall at that tyme be due to them   Item I give to Vincent my Coachman and to my servant John Christmast to eache of them Tenn pound*es* if they be at the tyme of my deathe in my service   Item I giue to Thomas Moore a younge boye whome I tooke latelie Five pound*es* if he shalbe in my service then   And if any of these Servant*es* shalbe departed from me before I give to everie Manservant that shall at that tyme be in my service a yeares wages over & above that wch shalbe then due to them Item I giue to eache of the Petty Canons & Vicars chorall wch shalbe in the Churche of St Paule at the tyme of my deathe To eache of them Fourtye shilling*es* and Forty shill*ings* to the M*aste*r of the Choristers and Forty shilling*es* to be equally distributed amongste the then Choristers Item I giue Thirtye shilling*es* to eache of the Vergers And to eache of the Bellringers Twenty shilling*es* Item I will & bequeathe to my Cosyn Jane Kent whoe hathe heretofore bene servant to my Mother Twelve poundes And to my cosyn Edward Dawson beinge decayd' Twelve poundes And to his Sister Grace Dawson Six poundes. W^ch propor*t*ion they beinge aged persons I make accounte dothe aunswere those pen*s*ions wch I haue yearlie heretofore given vnto them & meant to haue contynewed for theire lives if it had pleasd to God to haue contynued myne   Item my will is that the fower large Pictures of the fower greate Prophett*es* wch hange in the Hall and that large Picture of auncient Churcheworke wch hang*es* in the Lobby leadinge to my Chamber And whatsoeu*er* I haue placd in the Chappell (excepted that wheele of Deskes wch at this tyme stand*es* there) shall remayne still in those plac*es* As also the Marble Table Sonne Dyall and Pictures wch I haue placd'e in the Garden   Of all wch I desyre an Inventorie maye be made by oure Register and the thing*es* to contynewe alwayes in the Howse as they are   Item I giue to my daughter Harvy all the Furniture wch is vsuallye in that Chamber wch wee call the Flannell Chamber and in the ynner Chamber thereof Item I give to the Poore of the parishe of St Gregories where I dwell Five poundes And to the Poore of eache of the Parrishes of St Dunstans in the West London & of Seavenoake in Kent & of Blunham in Bedfordshire To eache parishe Twentye poundes Item I giue to the Right honourable the Earle of Kent patron of that Churche of Blunham the Picture of layinge Christe in his Toombe wch hanges in my Study Item my will is that all theis former legacies given in monye be payde within six weekes after my deathe All which Legacies beinge soe payde and all charges that can any waye fall vppon my Executors beinge discharged my will is That my Plate & Bookes (such bookes only beinge excepted as by a Scedule signde wth my hand I shall give awaye) and all my other goodes beinge praysde & soulde all my poore estate of monye left & monye soe raysde & monye lent maye be distributed in manner and forme followinge Firste I will that for the mayntenaunce of my dearely beloved Mother whome it hathe pleased God after a plentifull fortune in hir former tymes to bringe in decaye in her very olde age there be ymployde Five hundred poundes Of wch my meaninge is not that the propretye but only the proffitte shoulde accrue to her during hir naturall lyfe and after hir deathe the sayd Five hundred poundes to be devided amongste those my Children wch shalbe then alive And because there maye be some tyme before any proffitt of that monye will come to her handes My will is that Twenty poundes be payde vnto her over & besydes the benefitte of the Five hundred poundes at the breakinge vp of my Familye & her removinge from thence Item my will is that my Childrens portions shoulde be equall yf they be vnmarried at my deathe But if they be marryed before they are to content themselfes wth that wch they shall haue received from me at theire marriage Excepte I make some other declaration of my will by a Codicill hereafter to be annexed My will neverthelesse is that my eldeste daughter *Constance Harvye* whoe receyved from me at hir firste marriadge but Fyve hundred poundes for portion shalbe equall wth the rest whoe at my deathe are to receive portions thoughe theire portions amounte to noe more then Five hundred poundes And therfore whereas there is at this tyme in my handes a Conveighance of a certaine Farme calld'e the Tannhowse from hir husband Mr Samuell Harvye in consideration of Twoe hundred and fiftye poundes payde by me for his vse in wch there is a Provisoe for redemption for a certaine tyme My will is that if that

Twoe hundred & fiftie poundes be accordinglie payde it be then added to the whole Stocke wch is to be devided amongste the Children If for defaulte of payment it become absolutelie myne my will is that that Land be reassured vnto him & his heires wth this Condition & not otherwise that it be added to her Joyncture for hir lief if shee survive him And if it fall oute that this Land be thus given backe whereby my daughter receives Twoe hundred and fiftie poundes above hir former Five hundred My will is that shee make noe clayme to any parte of my state by any thinge formerly sayd in this my will till all the rest of my Children haue received Seaven hundred & fiftie poundes because vppon the whole matter shee hathe receyved soe muche yf I give backe that Land   But if by Godes goodnes theire portions come to more Then shee is alsoe to enter for an equall parte of the Surplusage as well in that wch returnes to the Children after my mothers deathe as any other waye   In all wch accrues wch maye come to my daughter Harvye my will is that vppon receipt thereof her husband make a proportionable addition to her Joyncture in land or els that that monye wch shall soe accrue vnto them maye come to the Longer liver of them   Item I giue to my sonne George that Annuytye of Fortye poundes yearelie for the payment of wch my honourable frend Sr John Davers of Chelsey knighte hathe some yeares since accepted from me   Firste Twoe hundred poundes and after one hundred marckes. Of wch Annuytye thoughe there be as yett noe assurance made yett there remayne wth me Bandes for those seuerall sommes And Sr John Davers will vppon request made either make suche assurance or repaye the monye as he hath alwayes promisde me   And my will is that whatsoeuer aryses to my other Children my sonne George be made equall to them that Twoe hundred poundes & one hundred marckes beinge accounted as part of the Somme   Item my will is that the portions wch shall become due to my twoe Sonnes John and George & to my eldest daughter Brigett yett vnmarryed be payde to them assoone after my deathe as maye be because they are of yeares to governe theire portions   But for my twoe younger daughters Margarett and Elizabeth my will is that theire portions be payde at the dayes of theire severall marriages or at their age of Twoe & twenty yeares theire portions to be ymployed in the meane tyme for theire mayntenance and for the encrease of their portions if it will beare it And if they or either of them dye before that tyme of marriage or of twoe and twentye yeares that then the portions of them or either of them soe dyenge shalbe equallye devided amongste my other Children wch shalbe alyve at theire deathe And because there maye be some tyme before they receave any thinge for theire mayntenance oute of the ymployment of theire por*t*ions my will is that to eache of my Children John, George, Brigid, Margarett & Elizabeth there be Twenty poundes payde at the same tyme as I have formerlie appoynted the like somme to be payde to my mother. Item I giue to my hono*u*rable & faithfull freindes [*sic*] Mr Robert Karr of his Ma*jesties* Bedchamb*er* that Picture of myne wch is taken in Shaddowes and was made very many yeares before I was of this profession And to my hono*u*rable Frend Sr John Davers I give what Picture he shall accept of those that remayne vnbequeathed And this my last Will and testament made in the feare of God whose mercy I humbly begge & constantlye relye vppon in Christe Jesus & in perfect love & charitie wth all the worlde whose pardon I aske from the lowest of my Ser-vant*es* to the highest of my Superiors I writt all wth myne owne hand & subscribed my name to everie Page thereof of wch there are five & sealled the same & published & declared it to be my last Will the thirtenth daye of December. 1630. *J. Donne* in the presenc*e* of *Samuell Harvye Edw: Pickerell* John Harrington John Stibes Robert Christmast. [*Somerset House, P.C.C. 46 St. John, proved 5 April 1631*]

III. *Donne's Complaint against Christopher Danby*

x° die Maii
1598

To the right honorable Sr Thomas Egerton Knighte
Lord keeper of the greate Seale of England

In most humble wise complayninge sheweth vnto your good Lord-shipp*e* your poore and dayly Orator John Donne of Lincolnes Inn in the County of Middlesex gent That whereas one Christopher danbye of the Countie of yorke gent did heretofore that is to saye about the twent*i*eth daye of Julye in the year of the Queenes Mat^{ies} raigne that nowe is the seaven and thirtethe [*sic*] in considera*c*on and for that your Orato^r did at the speciall request and earnest intreatie of the sayde Christopher take into his service to instructe and bringe vpp one Thomas Danbye of the age of fifteene yeres or there about*es* naturall brother of the sayde Christopher Danbye Assure and pmise vnto your Orator that he the sayde Christopher woulde be at and paye the one halfe of all such Charge as should arise and growe vnto your Orator by the apparellinge and diettinge with meate and drinke of the sayd Thomas Danby his brother, and likewise would save and keepe harmelesse your sayd Orato^r of and from all losses and hindrances which any wayes by the sayd Thomas his indirect and vnhonest dealinge vnto your Orato^r during all the tyme that the sayde Thomas shoulde soe serve him should be done, wherevppon your Orator did take the sayde Thomas Danbye into his service and did bringe him vpp by the space of eighteene monethes or more, during wch tyme the meate and drinke of the sayde Thomas, allowinge him necessarylie fower shillinges by weake at the least, and the apparrell wch the sayd Thomas did weare came and amounted in the whole (makeinge a verie reasonable and easie recconinge and account) vnto the so$\~m$e of twentie poundes, The moytie whereof namely tenn poundes was and is to be answered by the sayde Christopher Danbye vnto your Orato^r— during wch tyme allsoe of the sayde Thomas his service, the sayd Thomas did dishonestly and indirectly take from yor Orato^r as to this honorable Cou^{r}te shalbe $p$ved one blacke Cloake of the valewe of xx^{tie} ^{s} one laced satten suite of y^e valewe of iij^{li} one payer of blacke velvet laced hose of y^e valewe of iiij^{li}x^s & as much gold lace as came to y^e valewe of v^{li} amountinge in all vnto the valewe of xiij^{li} x^s wch severall somes of ten poundes for diet and apparell and xiij^{li}x^s for losses by the dishonest dealinge of the sayde Thomas sustayned your sayde Orato^r hath often tymes heretofore of the sayd Christopher Danbye demanded and required, yet them or any $p$te of them to paye, [the] sayde Christopher hath refused and still doth refuse agaynst all righte and equetie and contrarie to his fayt⟨h⟩full $p$mise and to the losse and d$\~m$age of yor Orator of thirtie poundes In tender consideraco̅n whereof, and for that the wittnesses wch were by at the tyme when the sayd Christopher did make the sayde $p$mise in maner aboue sayde are dead, and soe yor sayd orator remedilesse by the stricte Course of the common lawe, and that the sayd Christopher happylie will not soe vtterly hazard and endanger his conscience, but that he will confesse the truthe by his answere vppon his oath May it please your good Lordshippe to grant vnto your sayde Orato^r her Maties most gratious writt of Subpoena to be directed vnto the sayde Christopher Danbye, commandinge him thereby at a certayne daye, and vnder a certayne payne, therin by your Lordshippe to be limited, to be and $p$sonally to appeare before yor good Lordshippe in her Maties highe Courte of Chancerie, then and there aswell to answere to the p^rmisses, as allso to stand to and abide suche further order and direc̅c̅on therein, as to yor Lordshippe shalbe thought to stand with equetye, and good conscience, and your sayde Orator, accordinge to his bounden dutye, shall daylye pray to god for your Lordshippes Longe lyfe wth all increase of honoure./

Chr: Brooke

(*Donne v. Danby, bill; P.R.O., C3/266/93*)

IV. *A Cipher Entrusted to Donne*

1 William Parckhurst.
2 William Wise.
3 The Arche Bishop.
4 Mr Secretarie Winwood.
5 Mr Hackwel.
6 Nicolas Paye.
7 Dr Donne.
8 Sr Biondi.
9 Fitzwilliams.
10 Mr Trumbal.
11 Isaake Wake (*added*)

A	E	I	O	V
4	9	14	19	24
5	10	15	20	25
6	11	16	21	26
7	12	17	22	27
8	13	18	23	28

Memoranda
All shalbe written with interpunctions.
Any number with a stroake over it is numerus numerans.

Nulla 1. 2. 3.

B	C	D	F	G	H	K	L	M	N	P	Q	R	S	T	W	X	Y	Z
29	31	33	35	37	39	41	43	45	47	49	51	53	55	57	59	61	63	65
30	32	34	36	38	40	42	44	46	48	50	52	54	56	58	60	62	64	66

Owre King	67	The Duke of Vrbin	96
The Queene	68	The Frenche King	97
The Prince	69	The Frenche Queene	98
The Ladie Elizabeth	70	The Queene Mother	99
The Counte Palatine	71	The Prince of Spayne	100
The Protestant Vnion	72	His Wife	101
The States	73	The Jesuites	102
The Protestant Cantons	74	The General of the Jesuites	103
The Grisons	75	The Turke	104
The French Protestants	76	The Persian	105
The Italian Protestants	77	The Howse of Austria	106
The Greeke Churche	78	The Vsiocchi	107
The King of Danimarck	79	Shipps	108
The King of Sweden	80	Monnye	109
The Emperour	81	Munition	110
The Pope	82	Warre	111
The Signorie of Venice	83	Peace	112
The Duke of Savoie	84	Truce	113
The Prince of Piedmont	85	Marriadge	114
The Infanta Maria of Savoie	86	The note of Certaintie	115
The Infanta Catharina	87	The Writer	116
The Cardinal of Savoie	88	England	117
The King of Spayne	89	Scotland	118
The Gouvernor of Milan	90	Ireland	119

The Duke of Mantoua	91	The Earle of Somersett		120
The Duke of Modona [*sic*]	92	His Wife		121
The Duke of Florence	93	Sr Thomas Muntson		122
Genoua	94	Sr William Muntson	Added to	123
Lucca	95	Secretarie Winwood	the Zypher	124
		Secretarie Lake	of Will.	125
		The Venetian Am-	Wise and	
		bassador	Doc^r Donne	126
		My Lo: Threasurer		127
		Sr George Villiers		128
		Dr Donne		129

The addition to Mr Bargraues—Sr Robert Na*u*nton—130
                  copy[?]   Mr William Lake—131

(*On extreme right, opposite no. 119:*)   —120 Donato
                                 122 Marini
                                 Claudio

                                               And Isaac
                           Piscina   Wake
                              123
                      the King of
                        Bohemia
                         124

(*P.R.O., S.P. 106/4, no. 44; assigned in index to 'Italy'. There is a pencil note with dates '1614–17' after Winwood's name.*)

v. Draft of Sir Henry Martin's Judgement on Henry Seyliard's Claim to Keyston Rectory

my very good Lord: That I might the better deliver my opinion to yor Lo^p according to yor Lo^{ps} direction
I have at the request of both parties heard there Councell learned on both sides concerning the pñt controverted between Mr Henry Sylliard Clark—collated to [the L. Archb of Cant] the Rectorie of Keyston in Lincoln dioce*s* as devolved p*er* lapsū temporis and m^r John Scott clark p^{r}sented by the patron [to the same] to the same rectorie whereof hee desireth institution wherein though there were many poynte*s* of law incidentlie argued yet to my vnderstanding the substance of the case will necessarilie relye only vpon two poynte*s*
i: Whether a benefice resigned by the Incumbent before a publique Notarie & Witnesses, and the same knowen to the patron maketh the same benefice voyd so farr as that before admittance thereof to the Ordinarie the Patron may present yf hee will [& the Bishop may admitt this clark] especially yf such a resigned benefice were held by grace & dispensation & not by coñon right?

2 Whether a benefice so resigned maketh the same benefice voyd in such sort as before admittance thereof by the Ordinarie [& the church the Patron] a laps can runn ag^t the patron? [& voyd of collation] for not p^{r}senting.

To the former: I am of opinion that yf the resigned benefice were held Jure com̃uni, then notwthstanding such resignation the title & propertie of the benefice continued in the resigner vntill the Ordinarie had accepted the resignacion: and therefore it was [not] in the power of the patron to have presented before such acceptacion yf hee would, & his p̃rntacion made before the Ordinaries acceptacion of the Resignation had been voyd notwthstanding the Ordinarie showld afterwards have accepted the resignacion

But yf such a resigned benefice were held only for grace & dispensation I think (salvo meliore iudicio) it were sufficient of it selfe to work a present voydance vpon such a benefice wthout the allowance from the ordinarie, and in that case the patron might present yf hee pleased

To the 2. I am of opinion that whether such resigned benefice were held by com̃on right or by dispensation & knowen to the patron, yet his tyme to present vpon payn of laps shall not beginn to runn before the Ordinarie have pronounced the church voyd & the same bee intimated vnto the Patron.

Upon thes premisses it will necessarilie follow that Mr Sylliardes collation being obtayned as is confessed wthin 2 daies afore the acceptance of that resignacion came too soon: & that the Patrons p^{r}sentacion being made long wthin his 6 months after that acceptance & before any intimacion: was right, & his clark accordinglie to bee instituted into Keyston. All wch things I submitt to yor lo^{pps} better iudgement

13 Maij 1622
Henry Marten.

A coppie of my m^r his report
vnto my lo: Keeper about a
Presentac̄on & Instituc̄on, vnto
the Parsonage of Keyston in
Huntington sheire

(*Houghton Library, Harvard University, MS. Eng. 930*)

VI. *Minutes of a Vestry Meeting at St. Dunstan's-in-the-West*

Att a Vestry holden the xxx^th day of January 1626[7]
Anno RR*is* Caroli secundo then beinge pr*e*sent

Mr Deane of Paules Vicar		John Hallywell	John Smith
Mr Andrew ffeild		Thomas Benyon	Henry Coke
ffr. Kemp } Cōen Councell		William Hide	Nicholas Halle
Ro: Morgan } men		Richard Wotton	John Hoath
Thomas Hide } Churchwardens		John Smethwicke	Thomas Bell
John Stutevile }		Henry Parkinson	Toby Berry
Thomas Chesheir			

At this Vestry it is ordered by the most voices That Cuthbert Clarke the Schole master shalbe admitted agayne to teach his Schollers in the Questhouse at the will and pleasure of the parishioners and to departe and leave the same house and to give over his teaching there vppon reasonable warninge hereafter to be given him by the Churchwardens of this parish, soe as the said Cuthbert Clarke before his said admittance doe become bound to the Com̄on Councell men and Churchwardens of this parish in the some of ffifty pound*es* with two sufficient sureties inhabitinge within the Citty of London or the Suburbes thereof (and yett not within this parish of St Dunstan) safelie to maynteyne preserue and keepe the Armor munition and other good*es* belonginge to the said parish and now remayninge in the said Questhouse from tyme to tyme to the vse of the parishioners duringe the tyme of his teaching there, and likewise to discharge and save harmelesse the parishioners and inhabitant*es* of the said parish from all manner of charge hereafter to ensue touchinge or concerninge any [of] the Children of the said Cuthbert Clarke or his wife wch they now have or wch hereafter shalbe borne within the said parish.

That ffrancis Kemp and the Churchwardens shall take considerac̄on of Alice Browne's demand of vj^li xiiij^s x^d by her alledged to be disbursed by her late husband John Browne by the appoyntment of Robert Wade in the tyme of his Churchwardenshipp.

Att the same Vestry it is ordered, that after Mr Deane of Paules shall have conferred with Stephen Brogden concerninge the CCxx^li due from Captayne Harvey as a legacy give by Mr Hare to the poore of this parish, if Mr Deane shall not receaue a satisfactory answere, That then a Bill in Chancery shalbe brought against the said Brogden for the said CCxx^li, and ffrancis Kemp is requested to sollicite the cause, and the Churchwardens appoynted to disburse the charges of the suite to be allowed the[m] vppon their accompt*es*.

Att this Vestry it is likewise ordered That Thomas Taylor Shoomaker Thomas Taylo[r] Cutler and Stephen Parkinson late Constables shalbe paid by the elder Churchwarden the severall somes of money by them disbursed in the tyme of their Constableshipp for passinge and conveyinge of vagran*tes* accordinge to their severall Billes.

Att the same Vestry it is alsoe ordered That if William Allen the Sexton att or before the ffeast of Easter next doe not pay vnto the elder Churchwarden ffive pound*es* remaynder of the Ten pound*es* formerly lent him vppon Bond, Then the same ffive pound*es* by his owne agreement is to be deducted out of his wages hereafter to be due, and noe wages to be paid him vntill that ffive pound*es* be satisfied as aforesaid.

(*Vestry Minutes, 1588–1663, Guildhall MS. 3016, i, pp. 118–19*)

VII. *Donne's Address to Convocation, 1626*

Ut primum per literas, eo quo solent Ordine, a vobis, Amplissime, eaque Amplitudine Dignissime Antistes, Reverendissimique Patres, ad nos dimanantes, nobis innotuit; Potentissimum, simul & consultissimum Regem, etsi a Spiritu sancto, spiritu consilii, in semet abunde repletum, suorum tamen consilio, in solenni Ordinum Conventu uti non dedignatum esse; habui & ego, etsi in antro delitescens, nec in fulgore omnino, parum in aprico versatus, hujus tamen roris guttulas meas, & Gomerulum meum, (si ita diminuere liceat) hujus Mannae; sensum partemque meam, ejus qua universum regnum perfusum est, laetitiae. Vere enim mihi videre visus sum exemplar ipsum, quod vidit Patriarcha Jacob, Deum innixum scalae & Angelos ascendentes, & descendentes, cum videam eum, qui inter eos summus est, de quibus Deus dixit, Vos Dii estis, non ita sui contentum esse, nec ita in semet acquiescere, (quo tamen uno conteni, & in quo solo acquiescimus libenter omnes) quin & in hanc scalam innitatur, in qua, illa quae a vobis, Ecclesiae proceribus, in nos descendit, influentia, & is qui a nobis, ad vos ascendit, Odor quietis, Descensum Ascensumque Angelorum possit imitari. Quid enim non licet nobis, nobis jam spondere, tam foeliciter auspicatis ut non ex aliis, quam

ipsa coelesti Columba, avibus, divinationem statuamus, omnia har-
monice, summaque cum concordia transigenda, cum videamus Deum
coelestem, terrestremque Deum, ita in unum coalescere, ut quemadmodum nec Deus ipse ita Unus esse voluerit, ut non etiam sit Trinus,
ita nec Rex summus sibi ita voluit inniti, ut non & tres Ordines bona
sua cum venia, accersituque convenirent? Vidit Deus opt. Max. in
principio Lucem bonum, & bonam terram, solem bonum, & bonum
Mare, singula bona, sed cum uno intuitu omnia complexus est, vidit
omnia valde bona. Vidit & ille, qui ejus apud nos vices gerit, quae in
Corde suo diffusa est, lucem bonam, quae ab iis, qui ei a Consiliis
sunt, & qui a Concionibus, inseruntur, singula bona; Et cum jam
per eum coadunata sint omnia, cum jam, sicut de exercitibus Israel-
iticis saepe usurpatum, Omnes sicut unus vir exiverunt, ita & nos
sicut os unum, una anima convenimus, viderit, (precamur) videbit,
(ominamur) omnia valde bona. Hujus cum ego benigni roris guttulas
meas, & almae hujus Mannae Gomerulum meum mihimet pollicerer, ut
aut in umbra familiari, ea quae hoc in loco transigenda essent, precibus
promovere, aut quae acta erant, praesentia mea, suffragioque testari
possem, nec amplius memet ingerere, ingenua ista spe, & pollicita-
tione non injusta, dejectum me video, Oneri, viribus meis impari, &
importuno, repente supposito, & a litore, ubi omnibus adprecando,
& sanioribus annuendo, satis officio meo fecisse putari possem, 'in
arenam, in aestum maris jam protrusum, proloquendi & praeloquendi,
Conciliandi & Consulendi, Colligendi & Referendi, Argumentandi &
Arguendi, aliaque peragendi, tot & tanta, ut sepositis, penitusque
neglectis, quae a corpore imbecilli, fractis viribus, & valetudine per-
quam incommoda, enim in oculos vestros, catervatim se injiciunt,
excusationibus & argumentis, (libens enim ea praetereo, cum misera
sit eloquentia, quae, non ex aliis Topicis, quam miseria ipsa hauriatur)
cum mihi ad eos qui in animi dotibus positi sunt, defectus, propa-
landos necessario deveniendum sit, in congerendis quae in excusa-
tionem conferri possent, non longius discurrendum, non amplius
disquirendum sit, quam candide profiteri, me ab hoc munere rite
praestando tam longe abesse, ut quantum abfuerim, ipse nesciam:
Tam non valere, hoc in munere, aliis satisfacere, ut nec mihimet
dicere ipse valeam, in quibus versetur, praestarive posset haec satis-
factio: Tam non spondere, facturum me quod exigat, ut & ignorem
plane, penitus, quid exigat. Canos istos non dicent istae excusationes?
Sed & ipse Moses, dierum jam plenus, totoque, quod ipse in psalmo
statuit humanae vitae stadio, eoque longissimo, octoginta annorum,

jam decurso, incircumcisa labia professus est, & ursit; nec infantilis aetatis erat, cum se puerum & infantem profiteretur Jeremias. Ideo autem eorum excusationes non admisit Deus, quia qui potis erat solus, omnia se resarturum, in se sumpsit. Si nec meas admitti fas sit, nec patiatur mos, & consuetudinis improba tyrannis, ut id fiat, quod fecit erga Mosen, & Jeremiam Deus, faciatis, Oro, quo valetis, modo, erga nos, RR. RR. ut id operetur in vobis patientia vestra, quod in illis operata est potentia Dei, ut benignitate vestra freti, ad omne opus quantumvis arduum, sancta fortitudine, & alacritate pia nos accingamus. Etsi enim non egeant Davide tempora nostra, cum in nos nullus exurgat Goliah, (nec enim haereses a nobis debellandae, nec schismata occurrunt resarcienda, quod vigilantiae vestrae, solicitudinique unice debet Ecclesia) & quamvis in hoc me soler, Deum qui numerosum Gedeonis exercitum, domum remisit, ut in paucioribus Victoriam reportaret, posse etiam & in me, homine inexercito, exercitatis tot Athletis, strenuisque viris relictis, opus suum perficere: Tamen cum satis sciam, sicut & libri a captu lectorum, ita & opera ab animis recipientium, sua fata habere, rogandae sunt Reverendissimae Paternitates vestrae, ut meminisse dignentur, imbecilliores stellas, a benigno fortiorum aspectu, reddi fortiores, molitionesque nostras, a radiis vestris vegetari, & in sinu vestro animari Embryones nostros. Et si intempestivum sit jam orare, ut a me hoc eximatur Onus, oremus Patrem in filio Jesu, ut per Spiritum sanctum, Onus commune leve faciat ut singulis nostrum panem suum quotidianum impertiatur, ita ut, nec officiose nimis maturando, nec nimis scrupulose retardando, ad gloriam Dei, ad Ecclesiae bonum, ad utilitatem Reip. ad solamen pientissimi principis, opus diei semper in die suo peragatur. Amen.

(*Poems, 1650, pp. 380–4*)

VIII. *Statement by John Donne the Younger*

Beeinge chosen from Westminster to X[t] church in Oxford by Election, I continued ther, a Student for manie yeares, encouradged by the Kings promisse to bee made one of the Cannons of that Place Vppon the death of my Father, I was called awaie, beeinge commaunded by the Kinge, and encouradged by most of the cheefe men in the Kingdome, to recollect and printe my Fathers Sermons, beeinge often told, how well I should deserue both from Kinge and People, by such an Act; for, by that meanes, I should not only preach to the present adge, but to their childrens children as longe as the Christian Religion should last: and, the Kings promisse was then refresht to mee, of mackinge mee Cannon of X^t church, againe

I had in my proceedings with the Bysshop of Canterburies Chaplaines, (who were to licence them), manie disputes, thay offeringe to expunge manie things, which hee openly preached, and, in the Bysshops hearinge, withoute anie dispute, all his lyfetime: by which meanes, I soe farr incurred the Bysshops displeasure, that hee thrice put mee by the Cannonry, which was my promissed rewarde, both by the Kinge and himselfe./

In the beginninge of this Parliament I published fower-score Sermons in one Volume, and the Cannonry then fallinge voyde, and the Achbysshop [sic] beeinge then in the Tower, the Kinge beeinge put in minde of his promisse, he was pleased to beestow it vpon mee, but vpon suggestion to the Kinge, that I was deeply engadged in the seruice of the Parliament, hee withdrew his Graunt, and gaue it to another, which act, when hee had well considered, and what a condition hee had leaft mee in, after soe longe an expectation, hee was pleased to renew his fauor, soe much, as to send mee a Warrant for a Reuersion, vpon the same place, with this addition, that it was more then euer hee did since hee came to his Croune./

Presently after this, the Kinge leaft the Par^{nt}; the warrs succeeded; I remained personally in their seruice, beeinge Chaplaine to the Earle of Denby, when hee was one of their Generalls, and euer since in attendance vpon him

Wherevpon this reuersion fallinge when the Kinge was at Oxforde by the death of one of the Cannons, and I beeinge in the seruice of the Parliament, it was giuen awaie to another that had neyther right to the place, nor was euer of the foundation.

Quaere
These things beeinge considered, whether I may not reasonaby [sic] petition the Parliament, to bee restored to that condition, I was first thrust oute of, and afterwards, twice put by, by beeinge only in their seruice

Sr

There is a Place in the College now voyde by the death of D[r] Morrice,[1] if by your fauor I can get the Broade Seale to bee put into that I will giue him that brings mee the Seal 100[l]. If it come soe farr as to bee moued and anie bodie obiect that D[r] Morrice his place as [sic] annext to the Ebrew Professor, tis easily answered I am as fitt for the one as the other, beesides noe annexion in [sic] goode in Lawe. A great manie of the house, haue seene my Case, and apprehend it very reasonable   if you doe soe toe, pray keepe this Paper, if not pray send it back to your humble Seruant I Donne/

S[r] next to the efficacie of your power
my great hope is that the house will easily
giue awaie that, that, thay meane nobodie
shall enoy [sic].

(*Folger Shakespeare Library*, MS. *V.b.* 201; *the addressee and precise date are unknown*)

IX. *Pleadings in the Suit of Sir George Grymes against John Donne the Younger*

(*a*) SIR GEORGE GRYMES

27° die Octobri[s], 1645
        Smythe

To the Right ho[ble] the Lords and others Commissioners for the great Seale of England.

Humbly complayning sheweth to yo[r] good Lordshipps S[r] George Crimes [sic] of Peckham in the County of Surrey kn[t]. That Whereas one George Donne kinsman of yo[r] Orator having severall times vppon play wth him att Cards by false dealing vnto himself the said George Donne more Cards then did belong vnto that Game whereat yo[r] said Orato[r] plaid w[th] him and by vseing other false and fowle play and advantages did fraudently and deceitfully winn of yo[r] said Orato[r] vppon Tickett or creditt the some of Two hundred pounds as hee p[r]tended or neere thereabouts but yo[r] said Orato[r] takeing the said

---

[1] Dr. John Morris, Canon of Christ Church from 1632; he died on 21 Mar 1647/8.

George Donne in the manner of fact of vseing the said false and
deceitfull play the said George Donne not being able to deny the same
yor said Orato^r therevpon did refuse and declare to the said George
that hee would never pay any part of the said mony being deceit-
fully and fraudulently gott as aforesaid And the said George Donne
knowing himself conscious and guilty thereof did never require or
demaund any one penny of yor said orato^r for the same but afterwards the said George Donne being to goe vnto Virginia into the
parts beyond the Seas and being vtterly destitute of frends and meanes
to furnish him for his said voyage or to gaine creditt or trust being in
such streights the said George Donne in or about the three and twentieth of December one thowsand six hundred thirty eight repaired to
yor said Orato^r and requested him to doe so much for him being a
distressed kinsman having a wief and child to provide for as to make
him a bond for the paym^t of the said some of two hundred pounds as
aforesaid and to move and draw yor said Orato^r herevnto he promised
and protested wth solemne oathes vnto yor said Orato^r that the
said bond should never therafter by himself or any his Executo^{rs}
adm^{rs} or assignes be made vse of against yor said Orato^r or yet be
made over to any other in trust for him or otherwise further declaring
vpon like oathes and protestacons that his only aime and intent in
this was in regard of his present and pressing necessity and poverty
by shewing thereof to obtaine some creditt vpon the Exchange and
obteine some Merchants to adventure wth them to Virginia aforesaid
wch creditt he should be able to satisfie by retornes from thence by
Tobacco and other comodities as soone as hee came from Virginia or
any sooner retorne made by any Merchants from thence further pro-
testing and promising to yor said Orato^r that if it should please god
that hee should not safely arrive att his iourneys end that the said
bond should be buried wth him vpon wch promises agreem^{ts} and
protestacons of the said George Donne yor said Orato^r was induced
to make vnto the said George Donne [his kinsman then necessitated
yet welbeloved by him] the said bond and therevpon about the time
abovemenconed yor said Orato^r did become bound vnto the said
George Donne in a bond of fower hundred pounds condiconed for the
paym^t of the some of Two hundred pounds att the full expiracon of
two yeares after wthout any interest wch time was so given in and by
the said George Donne for that as hee then said hee should be able
by his place and plantacon in Virginia by that time to pay and satisfie
all his Credito^{rs} and would then retorne and redeliuer the said bond

vpp againe to yor said Orato^r And yor said Orato^r further sheweth
that the said George Donne then going to the [said] shipp wch was
to proceed in the voyage to Virginia then rideing in the Downes in
his way thither was arrested att Grauesend in the Countie of Kent
by Nicholas Hunt for the some of fiue pounds or thereabouts wch the
said George Donne being nowaies able to pay was inforced to send
and intreat his brother John Donne Docto^r of the civill law to furnish
and lend him so much in a case of such pressing necessity that wthout
the p^{r}sent supply thereof the said George Donne was in great danger
to loose his voyage and be left behind by the speedy departure of the
shipp wherevpon the said docto^r Donne did as hee p^{r}tends lend and
furnish the said five pounds or thereabouts to the said George for
paym^t of the said debt and freeing him of the said arrest And therevpon
the said George to satisfie the mony then lent only and vpon noe
other reall consideracon paid or given did by letters of Attorney assigne and sett over his said bond vnto the said docto^r Donne and
shortly after the said George Donne dying in his passage to Virginia
the said John Donne begann now to devise and contriue wth himself
how to make his private benifitt and gaine of the said bond and gett
the same made good and applyed to his own vse And seeking all
occasions to effect the same came to heare that yor said Orato^r had
very pressing and important occasions to vse mony and therevpon
the said docto^r Donne invited yor orato^r to his Lodgeings and finding
his p^{r}sent occasion for ready money hee offered to lend yor said
Orato^r the some of ffifty pounds but wthall pressed yor said Orato^r
that the same might be added to the other p^{r}tended debt of Two
hundred pounds for wch yor said Orato^r had given the said George
Donne bond as aforesaid and to gett him to condescend herevnto
the said docto^r Donne promised and protested vnto yor said Orato^r
that hee intended not to take any advantage of the said bond made
over vnto him by his said brother but the same should as to the Two
hundred pounds be vnder the same tearmes as the former bond And
made the like protestacon^s and promises as his said brother George
had formerly done or to such effect wherevpon and vpon the promises
and protestacons aforesaid of the said docto^r Donne being his neere
kinsman yor said Orato^r not then knowing of the death of the said
George Donne nor that the said Lres of Attorney was thereby avoided
and become void and of none effect in or about the moneth of August
in the yeare of our Lord God one thousand six hundred thirty and
nine became bound to the said docto^r Donne in a bond of five hundred

pounds or some such great penall [?] some condiçoned for the paym^t
of two hundred and fifty pounds and odd mony to be paid on or about
the three and twentieth day of May one thousand six hundred and
forty being Nine monethes next ensewing wth vse and interest not
only for the fifty pounds wch yor said Orato^r then receaued of the said
Doctor Donne but also for the other two hundred pounds for wch yor
said Orato^r by the bond made to the said George Donne as abouesaid
was not to pay any vse att all And yor Orato^r further sheweth that
not long after yor said Orato^r paid vnto the said John Donne seu^{r}all
somes of mony amounting to the some of threescore pounds or thereabouts and afterwards yor said Orato^r borrowed of the said John
Donne the some of fifty pounds more and then yor said Orato^r together wth one William fferrers of Barne Elmes became bound vnto the
said John Donne for the paym^t of the some of three hundred pounds
being aswell for the said fifty pounds as two hundred and fifty pounds
for wch the said former bond was given as aforesaid wth such interest
as should be due for the same and shortly after yor said Orato^r being
inforced to make a iourney into Yorkshire and the said last mençoned
bond being att this time become due or then shortly after becomming
due and payable the said John Donne coming to yor said Orato^r
pressed him in respect of his said iourney and his danger thereby to
giue vnto him a Judgem^t for the further security of the monies then
due or to become due vpon the said bond and that otherwise as soone as
the same became due hee would arrest and proceed against the said
William fferrers the surety for the same whereby yor said Orato^r was
likewise inforced to acknowledge to the said Donne a Judgem^t of six
hundred pounds according to his obligaçon by bond wch was agreed
to be defeazanced for paym^t of three hundred pounds and twelue
pounds the Twelue pounds being the interest for six monethes in his
Maties Court of Kings bench And yor orato^r further sheweth that
since the retorne of yor said Orato^r the said John Donne often repairing
to and pressing vpon him for satisfacçon and interest of monies then
thus owing and finding that hee had noe p^{r}sent meanes to satisfie him
by reason of a Sequestraçon from the Parliam^t vppon his land and
intending to make a further advantage and benifitt of yor said Orato^r
offered to lend vnto yor said Orato^r one hundred pounds more wth
condiçon to pay the interest wch hee the said Donne p^{r}tended to be
due vpon the former Judgem^t if one Henry Grove of Southwark
Grocer would become bound for the same wch Condiçon yor said
Orato^r having great vse for monyes being constreyned to accept of hee

together wth the said Henry Grove on or about the three and twentieth day of August in the yeare of our Lord God one thousand six
hundred forty and fower became bounden vnto the said John Donne
in an obligacōn of the some of two hundred pounds condicōned for the
paym^t of one hundred and fower pounds wch said bond yor said Orato^r
and the said Grove having sealed and deliu^red your said Orato^r did
then expect to haue receaued the said one hundred pounds promised
to be lent as aforesaid but the said John did then pay vnto yor said
Orato^r the some of Two and fortie pounds only part of the said
hundred pounds p^rtending that as hee had offered Tenn pounds for
Broakage of one hundred pounds hee expected the like otherwise hee
would not lend that one hundred pounds vnto him although the bond
was made in his owne name and consequently prooving the mony to
be his owne prop*er* monies and that hee spent noe labour or travaile
or was att any costs or charges in procuring or obteyning thereof and
abated and deducted forty eight pounds vnder p^rtence of being due
to him for vse money for the money [*sic*] formerly lent as aforesaid
And now so it is may it please yor good Lo^rpp that the said John
Donne hauinge by the waies and meanes aboue mencōned and divers
other indirect courses gained and circumvented yor said Orato^r to
make vnto him the said seu^rall bonds and to acknowledge the Judgem^t
aboue mencōned doth publish and giue out in speeches that yor
Orato^r is indebted to him in seu^rall great somes of mony and that the
said Judgem^t and seu^rall bonds aboue mencōned were made vnto him
for seu^rall and distinct debts really owing vnto him for monies lent and
other good and reall consideracōns and p^rtendeth that yor Orato^r and
himself came to accompt and that on such accompt the said monies
were due to him whereas there was noe other accompt but only the
computeing of the mony to be furnished anew by the said John w and
adding it to ye former said debt or p^rtended debt due to the said
George and if any accompt were the ground of it was the former debt
aforesaid due or p^rtended to be due to George Donne and there was
not otherwise due to the said John Donne any monies other then
herein is exp^rssed and yet the said John Donne refuseth to shew how or
for what or when hee lent yor orato^r any monies or that yor orato^r
became indebted to him and doth threaten and giue out in speeches
that hee will take out execucōn vpon his said Judgem^t against yor
orato^r his lands and goods and putt ye said bonds in suit against him
and recou^r the seu^rall penalties thereof and now likewise p^rtends that
hee lent & paid vnto yor said Orato^r seu^rall somes of mony amounting

to the seu^rall somes of mony mencõned and conteyned in the said Judgem^t & condicõns of the se^ruall bonds abouemencõned and p^rtends likewise hee made noe such promises or protestacons to yor said Orato^r aboue sett forth although the truth is and the said John Donne well knowes that yor orato^r nor any for him either had or recd of the said John Donne or any for him other somes of mony then the said seu^rall somes of fifty pounds & ffiftie pounds & forty and two pounds aboue mencõned and that yor said Orato^r hath seu^rall times since the lending thereof and before ye borrowing of ye last one hundred pounds paid to the said John for interest seu^rall somes amounting to the some of two hundred pounds or thereabouts and yet the said Donne doth giue out that hee will recouer as aforesaid to the great wrong & damage and lessening of the estate of yor said Orato^r contrary to equity & good conscience. Now to the end the said John Donne may vpon his corporall oath sett forth & declare what was the true & reall consideracõn the said John Donne did truly lend and deliuer vnto yor said Orato^r vpon the same and when and what monies for vse and otherwise hee hath receaued from him or any other by couler of ye said bonds or Judgem^{ts} and when and may sett forth what debt or somes of mony hee doth demaund of yor said Orato^r and why and vppon what consideracõn and that yor said Orato^r may be aided & releiued in the p^rmises and may be protected in & by this ho^{ble} Court so farr as to equity & iustice shall apperteine May it therefore please yor Lo^rpps to grant vnto yor said Orato^r his Maties most gratious writt of Subp^a. to be directed to the said John Donne thereby comanding him att a certen day and vnder a certen paine therein to be limitted personally to be and appeare before yor Lo^rps in his Maties high Court of Chancery then & there vppon his corporall oath to answere ye p^rmises and to stand to & abide such further order & direccõn as to yor Lo^rps shall seeme to stand wth right equity & good conscience And yor Orato^r shall pray &c   Ed Johnson

(*P.R.O.*, *C2*/*Chas. I*/*C2*/*46*)

(*b*) JOHN DONNE

Jurat 3? die Novembr: 1645
   Robt Aylett
   Maydwell

   The Plea and demurrer of John Donn docto^r of the Civill Law def^t to the Bill of Comp^{lt} of Sr George Crymes alis Grymes K^{nt} Comp^{lt}.

The said def[t] not confessing or acknowledging any the matters materiall in the said Bill of Comp[lt] to be true in such manner as in the said Bill of Comp[lt] they are alleadged. ffor plea saith that the said Complayn[t] did exibit an Information in his Ma[ties] Atturneyes name of the Court of Wards and Liveryes into the sayd Court against the def[t] to the same effect and purpose as is now sett forth in the said Complayn[ts] Bill To w[ch] Information this def[t] answered and the same cause is still dependinge in the said Court, ffor w[ch] Cause the said defend[t] doth Plead and Demurr in Law. And demandeth Judgm[t] of this hono[rble] Court Whether he shalbe dublely vexed and compelled to Answer one and the same Cause in both Courts And humbly prayeth to be from hence discharged. W[th] his Costs and Charges in this behalfe most wrongfully sustayned.

W. Baber

(Ibid.)

INDEX

Abbot, George, Archbp., 293–4, 314–15, 317 n., 322, 372–3, 378, 380, 387, 417–18, 422, 439–40, 479, 481–2, 492, 498, 506, 513, 529 n., 569, 570.
Act of Supremacy, 42, 45, 46, 66, 423.
Adams, Henry, commemorative sermons at St. Dunstan's, 461, 486, 499, 504, 543, 544.
Adams, Revd. Thomas, *The Barren Tree*, 394.
Adamson, Edmund, 37, 561.
Addington, Kent, 23.
Addison, Joseph, 2.
'Addled' Parliament, *see* Parliament—of 1614.
Adlington, 105.
Admiral's Men, The, 107.
Aix-la-Chapelle, 261–2, 322, 358.
Alabaster, Revd. William, *Roxana*, 282.
Albert, Archduke, 340, 345, 347–9.
Aldborough Hatch, Essex, 306 n., 364, 516, 522–3, 524 n., 546, 547.
Aldwych, 265.
Alençon, Duc d', 442.
Alford, Henry, Dean, 15–16, 241 n.
Allegiance, Oath of, 212–13, 215, 222, 224, 267, 423.
  controversy concerning, 203–4, 207–8, 212–18, 222–6.
All Hallows, Barking, 556.
Allen, D. C., 40 n.
Allen, William, 573.
Alleyn, Edward, 74, 367, 399, 432, 439, 448–50, 464–6, 469 n., 485–6, 514, 542–3, 547, 552, 555.
Allington, Wilts., 374 n.
Althorpe, 110.
Amadis de Gaul, 187.
Amazon, River, 86.
Ambassadors, English, *see* Carew, Sir George; Carleton, Sir Dudley; Cornwallis, Sir Charles; Cottington, Francis; Edmundes, Sir Thomas; Eure, Ralph, Lord; Hay, James; Herbert, Sir Edward; Howard, Lord Charles; Killigrew, Sir Robert; Nevill, Sir Henry; Roe, Sir Thomas; Seymour,

Edward, Earl of Hertford; Strafford, Sir Edward; Wotton, Sir Henry.
Ambrose, Saint, 302.
Amesbury, Wilts., 374 n.
Amiens, 86, 143 n., 244, 245, 246, 247, 248, 250, 256, 261, 309, 539.
Anabaptists, 261–2, 322.
Anderton, Lawrence ('John Brerely'), S.J., 204, 207, 209–10.
  Apologie of the Romane Church, The, 204, 209, 211, 212 n.
  Protestants Apologie, A, 209–10.
Andrewes, Lancelot, Bp., 40 n., 213, 226 n., 247, 284, 307, 312, 374, 407 n., 415, 482, 505.
  Tortura Torti, 213.
Andrews, Dr. Richard, 250–1.
Andrews, Mr., of Lincoln's Inn, 385.
Angel, Mr., 367.
Angra (Azores), 91.
Anker, River, 270 n.
Anne of Austria, Queen of France, 253.
Anne, Queen, consort of James I, 141, 160, 171–2, 177, 198, 241 n., 312, 329, 469, 540, 569.
  D seeks post in her household, 160, 538.
  death of, 341, 343.
Anne, Queen of Spain, 569.
Antwerp, 10, 26, 35, 115, 260, 261.
  Jesuit college at, 25.
Appleby Castle, 324.
Aquaviva, Claude, S.J., 56–7 n.
Arber, E., 122 n.
Archduke, The, *see* Albert.
Archer, Dr., 414 n.
Arches, Court of, 227, 246, 415.
Archpriest controversy, 66–7.
Aretino, Pietro, 121.
Ariosto, 124.
Aristotle, 48.
Arley, 105.
Arminianism, 284, 419.
Arnhem, 364.
Arthur, King, 20.
Arundel, Earl of, *see* Howard, Thomas.
Arundel House, 176.

Hay, James, Lord; Viscount Doncaster; Earl of Carlisle, 4, 7, 100 n., 142, 160–2, 240 n., 262, 272–3, 289, 307, 322, 331–2, 432–3, 435, 478 n., 479, 518, 520, 563.
career of, 143–4, 160–1, 314, 367 n., 393, 396, 519–20, 553.
embassy to France, 332 n., 343, 378, 431.
embassy to Germany, 7, 143 n., 262, 321, 338–65, 367, 392–3, 431, 540.
patronage of D, 100 n., 142, 160–2, 272–3, 289, 292–3, 304, 308–9 n., 314, 367, 370, 373, 385, 395–6, 410, 431, 444, 448, 471, 474, 488, 493, 517, 523, 538, 541.
character of, 160–1, 272, 347–8, 350, 431–3, 440.
Hayward, J., 407 n., 474 n.
Hayward, Sir John, *History of Henry IV*, 121.
Hazard, Revd. Nathaniel, 395–6, 517.
Healy, T., S.J., 211 n., 299 n., 395 n., 529 n.
Heath, Sir Robert, 376.
Heidelberg, 257–8, 347, 349–52, 357, 358, 364, 433, 539.
Heilbronn, 350–1, 352.
Helm, Anne, 459.
Helpe to Memory and Discourse, A (1630), 546.
Helvicus, Christopherus, 281.
Hendon, 390.
Hennessy, G., 327 n., 389 n., 406 n., 488 n., 515 n.
Henri II, King of France, 254.
Henri, III, King of France, 60, 61.
Henri IV, King of France, 60, 147 n., 149, 237, 253, 255, 363 n.
Henrietta Maria, Queen, 468, 493.
Henry IV, King, 20, 121.
Henry VII, King, 21, 237.
Henry VIII, King, 27, 103, 425–6.
Henry, Prince of Wales, 141, 191, 192, 198, 222 n., 240 n., 245, 257, 268–9, 276, 539.
Heralds, College of, 21 n., 530 n.
Herbert, Sir Edward, Lord H. of Cherbury, 114, 118–19, 141, 183, 187 n., 192 n., 284, 285, 305, 312, 410, 499.
ambassador to France, 344, 373.
friendship with D, 114, 119, 184–5, 270, 285, 304–6, 499, 539.

literary relations with D, 183, 184, 269.
a letter of, 184.
Autobiography, 183 n., 185, 187 n.
Elegy on Prince Henry, 185, 269.
'Epitaph' on Cecilia Bulstrode, 178 n.
Satires, 185.
Herbert, Revd. George, 118, 305–6, 442, 476, 487, 488, 496–7.
poems 'Memoriae Matris Sacrum', 475, 497.
Herbert, Sir Henry, 550.
Herbert, Magdalen (Newport), Lady Danvers, 9, 181, 184, 442, 544.
meeting and friendship with D, 118–19, 180–4, 373, 471–2, 487, 495–6, 538.
D's sermon commemorating, 410, 475–6, 496–7, 503, 544.
Herbert, Philip, 1st Earl of Montgomery, 4th Earl of Pembroke, 143–4, 183 n., 341 n., 421, 550–1.
Herbert, Richard, 2nd Baron Cherbury, 410, 499.
Herbert, William, Earl of Pembroke (d. 1469), 20.
Herbert, William, 3rd Earl of Pembroke, 21, 294, 351, 385, 421, 444.
his poems, 21, 351, 551.
Herbert, William, 118, 119 n.
Hereford, see of, 377.
Hertford, Earl of, *see* Seymour, Edward.
Hertfordshire, 26, 32, 282.
Heylin, Peter, *Cyprianus Anglicus*, 505.
Heywood, Christopher, 24.
Heywood, Elizabeth, *see* Donne, Elizabeth; Marvin, Elizabeth.
Heywood, Ellis (Elizaeus), S.J., 25–6, 32, 39.
Heywood, Jasper, S.J., 25, 39–42, 44–5, 52, 57 n., 64.
Heywood, Joan, *see* Stubbes.
Heywood, John (son of Richard; friend of D), 24, 36, 53, 116–17, 538, 562.
Heywood, John, 22, 23, 25, 31–5, 36 n. 37, 40, 53.
interludes of, 22, 40.
Heywood, Richard, 24, 33, 37, 53, 116 n.
Heywood, Thomas, 24.
Hicks, L., 40 n.
Hide, Thomas, 572.
Hide, William, 572.
High Church party, 419, 482, 490, 492, 498, 506.